BOYHOOD IN AMERICA

An Encyclopedia

THE AMERICAN FAMILY

The six titles that make up **The American Family** offer a revitalizing new take on U.S. history, surveying current culture from the perspective of the family and incorporating insights from psychology, sociology, and medicine. Each two-volume, A-to-Z encyclopedia features its own advisory board, editorial slant, and apparatus, including illustrations, bibliography, and index.

Parenthood in America

EDITED BY Lawrence Balter, New York University

Adolescence in America

EDITED BY Jacqueline V. Lerner, Boston College,
and Richard M. Lerner, Tufts University;
Jordan W. Finkelstein, Pennsylvania State University,
Advisory Editor

Girlhood in America

EDITED BY Miriam Forman-Brunell,
University of Missouri, Kansas City

Boyhood in America

EDITED BY Priscilla Ferguson Clement, Pennsylvania State
University, Delaware County, and Jacqueline S. Reinier,
California State University, Sacramento

Infancy in America

EDITED BY Alice Sterling Honig, Emerita, Syracuse University;
Hiram E. Fitzgerald, Michigan State University;
and Holly Brophy-Herb, Michigan State University

The Family in America

EDITED BY Joseph M. Hawes, University of Memphis,
and Elizabeth F. Shores, Little Rock, Arkansas

BOYHOOD IN AMERICA

An Encyclopedia

Volume 2
L–Z

Priscilla Ferguson Clement, EDITOR
Professor of History
Pennsylvania State University–Delaware County
Media, Pennsylvania

Jacqueline S. Reinier, EDITOR
Professor Emerita
California State University–Sacramento
Sacramento, California

FOREWORD BY **Elliott West**
University of Arkansas
Fayetteville, Arkansas

A B C ⬤ C L I O

Santa Barbara, California
Denver, Colorado
Oxford, England

Library of Congress Cataloging-in-Publication Data

Boyhood in America : an encyclopedia / edited by Priscilla Ferguson Clement, Jacqueline S. Reinier ; foreword by Elliott West.
    p. cm. — (The American family)
Includes bibliographical references and index.
   ISBN 1-57607-215-0 (hardcover : alk. paper) 1-57607-540-0 (e-book)
   1. Boys—United States—Encyclopedias.   I. Clement, Priscilla Ferguson, 1942–   II. Reinier, Jacqueline S.   III. American family (Santa Barbara, Calif.)
HQ775 .B635 2001
305.23—dc21

07 06 05 04 03 02 01   10 9 8 7 6 5 4 3 2 1 (cloth)

ABC-CLIO, Inc.
130 Cremona Drive, P.O. Box 1911
Santa Barbara, California 93116-1911

This book is also available on the World Wide Web as an e-book.
Visit www.abc-clio.com for details.

This book is printed on acid-free paper ∞
Manufactured in the United States of America

CONTENTS

A-to-Z List of Entries

L

Learning Disabilities

Learning disabilities (LD) currently consumes the largest amount of study in the field of special education. The very vagueness of the term *learning disabilities* and the imprecision with which the label has been applied have led to concerns about etiology, diagnosis, and remediation. According to federal law 94-142, a learning disability is "a disability in one or more of the following basic psychological processes involved in using language, spoken or written, which may manifest itself in an imperfect ability to listen, think, speak, read, write, spell, or to do mathematical calculations." LD is also a field in which three different professions—medical, educational, and psychological—are attempting to stake their claim to identifying and solving the problems associated with this spectrum of disorders. Definitional imprecision has led to a wide interpretation of the very meaning of learning disabilities. Because of the lack of a definitive labeling procedure, gender becomes an important variable in the process of identification of those labeled as having LD. Increasingly identified with the labels of attention deficit disorder (ADD) and attention deficit hyperactivity disorder (ADHD), LD is often viewed as a problem of squirmy little boys who can't learn to read because they can't sit still. The prevalence of boys labeled as having LD is both a manifestation and a reflection of larger gender trends in twentieth-century America.

The label *learning disabilities* is of relatively recent origin. Its initial usage came in 1963, when Samuel Kirk of the University of Illinois used it to identify children of normal intelligence who had trouble learning, particularly learning to read. However, this was not the first attempt at labeling this diverse group of problem learners. In the late 1930s, Alfred Strauss and Heinz Werner, German refugees then working at the Wayne County Training School in Northville, Michigan, identified a group of students who had trouble learning. They categorized these children as brain-injured. By 1947, Strauss and a new collaborator, Laura Lehtinen, published their seminal *Psychopathology and Education of the Brain-Injured Child*, which not only identified these individuals but also recommended strategies for remediation. The research emanating from Northville, led by such followers of Strauss as William Cruickshank and Newell Kephart, continued to categorize these children as brain-injured. Simultaneously, Samuel Orton, a University of Pennsylvania–trained neurologist, was examining children with reading difficulties in a variety of settings. Funded by grants from the Rockefeller Foundation, Orton hypothesized that these students suffered from developmental alexia, or dyslexia—an inability to read words due to problems in the different hemispheres of the brain. This medical model of the disorder held prominence in the field until the 1960s when Kirk "de-medicalized" the problem.

Although Strauss and Orton set about to medically define a group of individuals with specific learning problems, they did not do so without regard to social factors. The social issues impinging on midcentury America helped shape the emerging category of learning disabilities and tie it to gender. The general development of special education and the specific development of learning disabilities are tied to trends within the larger field of general education. By the late 1930s, educators had developed a system of tracking, whereby students were placed in a rank-ordered curriculum designed to put students in appropriate vocational or educational settings upon high school completion. Usually, tracking verified existing race and class structures within American society. Twenty years later, education achieved paramount importance as the Cold War and the "space race" pointed to the need to train a highly literate population in order to fight off the encroachments of communism. With both tracking and the reforms initiated in the face of Soviet scientific achievement, those students who had problems in reading remained problematic, especially if they showed no overt signs of intellectual disability. Unable to classify them as retarded—the nomenclature was slowly changing from the earlier term *feebleminded*—psychologists and educators searched for both a label and a rationale for failure. Latching on to Strauss's medical model, they embraced the idea of "exogenous brain-injury" and shaped it into the category of "learning disabilities." The variables of class and race were important factors in

the emerging definition of learning disabilities. Though not overtly established to provide remediation for white middle-class children, the category of learning disabilities did just that. By 1973, according to published journal article samples, over 96 percent of students with LD were white and over 90 percent were middle-class or above. Poor and minority students with similar educational problems were labeled as culturally deprived or educably mentally retarded, with the etiology assumed to be cultural or environmental. Presently, the medical model of LD has seen a revival with the conflation of ADD, ADHD, and the term *learning disabilities* itself. Increasingly, medical intervention—usually pharmacological in nature—has been seen as a major part of the answer to learning problems.

The very conception of "learning disabilities" is therefore related to this struggle between proponents of organic etiology and those emphasizing its societal components. Intertwined with this debate is the issue of gender LD; more specifically, why significantly larger numbers of boys are labeled, categorized, and remediated as "learning disabled." This has been assumed as a given since the initiation of the label, yet relatively little substantive research has been done on the subject, especially compared to that compiled on race and class and their relationship to learning disabilities. Two closely related questions can be generated from this analysis. First, why is there a gender discrepancy? Second, why is this gap considered unimportant or—to use a more interesting word—natural? The answers to these questions go far beyond a simple analysis of learning disabilities to shed light on broad issues of the meaning of education in twenty-first-century America.

The number of males enrolled in programs designed for those labeled as having LD has consistently ranged from 65 percent to 90 percent. These numbers have changed relatively little since Kirk applied the name to this range of educational disorders. There have been many reasons for the gender discrepancy, and they relate to both the imprecision of the term's definition and the social context of education in America. Most of the public discourse on this issue—especially from right-wing pundits such as John Rosemond—point to the referral process in which students are labeled and categorized as having LD as the cause for discrepancies. Boys are often referred because their inappropriate classroom conduct and hyperactive out-of-seat behavior inhibit their ability to learn, especially their ability in learning to read. Teachers, the primary agents of the referral process, tend to refer students with overt behaviors that not only inhibit learning but also disrupt the class environment itself. Boys make up the preponderant majority of this population. Behavior problems and learning problems often go hand in hand in referrals of male students. Conversely, girls labeled as having LD usually only exhibit learning difficulties with few concomitant behavioral problems. Because they do not act out in a disruptive manner, girls are often overlooked in the referral process. This conflation of learning problems with behavioral disorders has been exacerbated by the recent trend to equate LD with ADD and ADHD. Learning disorders are manifested in inappropriate classroom behaviors—for example, the classic "hyperactive boy."

This explanation for the large numbers of males labeled as having LD speaks to the broader issues of gender roles in American education and society. But is this preponderance of males simply a social phenomenon? Is the skewing caused by teacher referrals based on classroom behavior problems? Many researchers have made this conclusion, based particularly on the relationship among LD, ADD, and ADHD. But others, particularly Robert Nass, who use a more physiological approach, have come to different conclusions. They hypothesize that hormonal sex differences, differing maturation rates, and genetic factors place males at a higher risk for learning disorders. Nass also believes that girls may have a sex-based advantage in the acquisition of language. Still, more tentative research points to differences in brain physiology based on sexual difference as a causal factor in male reading difficulty. Finally, researchers are examining the possibility that there is a gene that puts individuals at risk for reading difficulties and that this characteristic may be sex-linked.

Are males therefore more "at risk" for learning disabilities? Or is the large number of males classified as having LD a function of referral bias and the conflation of behavioral disorders and learning problems? Answers are not easily available, especially to questions about such a vague and ill-defined disorder as learning disabilities. What is readily apparent, however, is that males as well as females suffer from an education "gender gap." When tied to the increasing medicalization of educational difficulties, the gap causes serious educational consequences for male students. The social implications of male LD have yet to be determined, but they are bound to have implications for educational policy in twenty-first-century America.

Steven Noll

References and further reading
Anderson, Kristen. 1997. "Gender Bias and Special Education Referrals." *Annals of Dyslexia* 47: 151–162.
Carrier, James. 1986. *Learning Disability: Social Class and the Construction of Inequality in American Education.* Westport, CT: Greenwood Press.
Franklin, Barry. 1987. *Learning Disabilities: Dissenting Essays.* New York: Falmer Press.
Nass, Robert. 1993. "Sex Differences in Learning Abilities and Disabilities." *Annals of Dyslexia* 43: 61–77.
Riordan, Cornelius. 1999. "The Silent Gender Gap: Reading, Writing and Other Problems for Boys." *Education Week* 19 (November): 46–49.
Sleeter, Christine. 1986. "Learning Disabilities: The Social Construction of a Special Education Category." *Exceptional Children* 53: 46–54.

Left-Wing Education

By the early twentieth century, boys were not only experiencing mainstream education, either public or private, but also were enrolled in schools and summer camps and read publications sponsored by left-wing political groups and individuals. First the Socialist Party and then the Communist Party and other radical groups established various forms of weekday as well as Sunday schools in order to educate boys as well as girls to oppose capitalism; discern their particular political, social, and cultural views; or just avoid the authoritarian structures of public schools. Such left-wing schools and publications began to disappear following World War II with the coming of the anticommunist red scare, although the summer camps continued in some form. While in existence, however, they offered an alternative educational exposure and experience for thousands of boys with varying degrees of success. Left-wing educational endeavors were not

specifically organized for boys, since girls were equally welcomed, but boys were considered to be somewhat more politically oriented and active, particularly in leadership positions.

The Socialist Party of America was founded in 1901 and within the following two decades established about 100 English-speaking Sunday schools throughout the country, designed to supplement the public schooling of working-class boys and girls. Socialists had organized various schools before 1900, but it took the Socialist Party to launch more organized Sunday schools, starting in San Jose, California, in 1902, quickly followed by Chicago, Cincinnati, Newark, Los Angeles, New York City, Cleveland, and scattered smaller towns. The schools were written about in the *Young Socialists' Magazine*, published by the Young People's Socialist League (YPSL), the party's youth wing, particularly in 1918, when schools reached their peak. But splits within the party, combined with government repression, soon led to their rapid decline, although some survived through the 1920s. The most active schools, in Rochester, New York, Milwaukee, and New York City, concentrated on criticizing capitalism, establishing a sense of community, and spreading an understanding of socialist principles and positions. Ranging in age from five to fourteen, the "little comrades" and "kiddie socialists" who attended were exposed to organized lessons dealing with economic subjects and socialist tenets as well as games, songs, plays, and festivals. There were texts specifically written for the schools, for example, Nicholas Klein's *The Socialist Primer* and John Spargo's *Socialist Readings for Children*. They also had songbooks, such as Josephine Cole's *Socialist Songs, Dialogues, and*

Recitations, with tunes like "My Money Lies over the Ocean" and "Kid Comrade." Paralleling the socialist Sunday schools were Workmen's Circle Sunday schools, which started in 1906. Schools started by the Workmen's Circle, a Jewish fraternal society, initially used English and emphasized the teaching of socialism but within ten years had basically switched their focus to Yiddish-language instruction and Jewish culture, with socialism still part of the curriculum.

Somewhat similar to the socialist Sunday schools in appeal and outreach were the libertarian-/anarchist-influenced modern schools based on the educational principles of Francisco Ferrer y Guardina. Executed by the Spanish government in 1909 for radical activities, Ferrer had promoted rational schools based on self-learning and limited adult authority. The Radical Library of Philadelphia, an anarchist branch of the Workmen's Circle, opened the first Modern Sunday School in 1910. Soon there were Sunday and even weekday schools in New York, Portland, Oregon, and throughout the country, most of them short-lived. *The Modern School* magazine, founded in 1912, promoted Ferrer's ideas and criticized the tyranny of public schooling. A summer camp was opened in 1927 in Lincoln Park, New Jersey, that charged $3 a week and had pictures of Karl Marx and Friedrich Engels hanging in the dining room. In 1915 the weekday Modern School moved from New York City to Stelton, New Jersey, teaching eighty-odd pupils during the first year in New Jersey. The most famous of the Ferrer full-time schools, it survived until 1953 under the auspices of the Modern School Association of North America.

As the socialist and Ferrer schools limped along or began to fade, the newly emerging Communist Party, formed in 1919 out of the chaos of World War I and the destruction of the Socialist Party and spurred into existence by the emergence of the Soviet Union, developed a strategy for educating and influencing the young. Like the socialists and anarchists, communists desired to counter the conservative thrust of public schools while inculcating boys (and girls) with radical political ideas and countering restrictive bourgeois family values. Communists early established sundry children's and youth organizations and camps, rather than formal schools, that served to supplement the public schools. The party founded the Young Workers League in 1922, which became the Young Pioneers of America (1926–1934), mostly comprising the younger children of party members. Affiliated publications, starting with the *Young Comrade*, helped to spread the word. There was also the *Young Worker* (1922–1936), written by and aimed at the party's youth wing. Articles covered the country and included poems such as "Song of Youth." In the late 1920s and throughout the 1930s, the Young Pioneers helped workers on strike and worked with other radical youth organizations, such as the International Workers Order (IWO) Juniors, the Worker's International Relief Scouts, and the Junior Liberators, all aspects of the Communist Children's Movement. Such organizations were designed to foster a revolutionary identity and mentality, initially separating both boys and girls from conservative family values and any particular ethnic identity.

The Young Pioneers organized summer camps during the 1920s, open from two to six weeks a year, including the Workers' Children's Camp near Los Angeles in 1929—also supported by the Non-Partisan Jewish Workers' School, the Miners' Relief Scouts, Friends of Culture, and the

Finnish, Ukrainian, and Czech Labor Schools—and others in Chicago; Grand Rapids, Michigan; Boston; Philadelphia; and around New York state. Starting with an early-morning salute to the Red Flag, in addition to their outdoor activities campers studied the class struggle, listening to stories from Herminia zur Muhlen's *Fairy Tales for Worker's Children* and William Montgomery Brown's *Science and History for Boys and Girls*. Indeed, perhaps forty books of children's literature were published by the party between 1925 and 1950.

After being dissolved in 1934, the Young Pioneers was replaced in boys' lives by the junior section of the IWO, first organized in 1930. The communist-dominated IWO was a federation of ethnic fraternal benefit societies. The IWO organized after-school programs (art classes, music lessons, dance classes), the IWO Juniors, summer camps (such as Camp Robin Hood near Cleveland), and even drum-and-bugle corps and marching bands, emphasizing a radical cultural milieu with a sensitivity to ethnic family identities and values. Moreover, by December 1938 there were fifty-three IWO Jewish schools in New York City, including a kindergarten and three high schools, attended by more than 4,000 students, and others in Detroit, Los Angeles, Chicago, and Philadelphia, with an emphasis on Yiddish-language instruction and discussions of social issues. During World War II the IWO Juniors organized paper drives, raised money for the United Services Organization (USO), and knitted socks for soldiers before being dissolved in 1944. Within the IWO, the Jewish sections conducted after-school programs and summer camps, and the Russian Mutual Aid Society had a nationwide system of after-school programs.

When communist boys reached sixteen, they were eligible to join the Young Communist League (YCL), organized in 1922 and designed to educate and socialize youth through the semimonthly *Young Worker* and diverse political activities. Members supported labor strikes and civil rights, sold the *Daily Worker* and *Sunday Worker*, in the 1930s became active in antifascist demonstrations, and established clubhouses, with perhaps 12,000 members in New York City alone. In 1943 the YCL became American Youth for Democracy (AYD), then the Labor Youth League (1949–1957), and finally the Du Bois Clubs (1965–1971). Membership in the YCL often served as a bridge into the Communist Party, for many members had developed valuable skills as political pamphleteers, speakers, and strike organizers.

Left-wing summer camps, which were established early in the twentieth century and were scattered around the country, proved to be the most memorable and influential of radical activities for boys and girls. Assorted left-wing organizations established adult colonies and children's camps, such as the Workmen's Circle Kinder Ring in upstate New York, Highlander Folk School's Junior Union camp in the South, and the Sholom Aleichem Folk Institute's Camp Boiberik. One of the most active was Camp Kinderland, founded by communists in 1925 on Sylvan Lake in Dutchess County, New York, and finally sponsored by the Jewish People's Fraternal Order of the IWO. Campers engaged in rural sports and political and cultural activities, and Yiddish classes were mandatory through the 1930s. Visiting dignitaries were greeted with dramatic presentations, dances, and songs. Some, such as Camp Unity in upstate New York, originated as adult colonies but eventually became exclusively children's camps by the late 1930s.

Camp Wo-Chi-Ca (Workers Children's Camp), founded in 1936 in Port Murray, New Jersey, by both communists and others on the left, was less ethnically oriented than Camp Kinderland. Interracial (staff and campers) and initially heavily Jewish, Wo-Chi-Ca also attracted Puerto Rican, Italian, and other boys and girls by the late 1940s. Boys studied black culture and the labor movement while exercising and breathing fresh air. Political pressure closed the camp in the mid-1950s, when it merged with Camp Wyandot, another left-oriented camp. Camp Woodland (1939–1961) in the Catskill Mountains was less politically oriented and more attuned to local rural culture than Wo-Chi-Ca and Kinderland. It was organized by Norman Studer, a teacher at the Little Red School House in Greenwich Village and later director of the Downtown Community School. Having studied with John Dewey, Studer was more influenced by the Progressive education movement than the Communist Party. The interracial camp attracted the children of the Old Left as well as liberals and for a while featured folk musician Pete Seeger as a music teacher. Boys experienced democratic, rural living and were heavily exposed to local craftspeople, storytellers, and musicians, with folk dancing and singing a vital part of camp life.

Left-wing summer camps allowed boys to experience different cultures in a rural setting while being exposed to radical cultural and political influences, at least into the 1950s. Many of the left-wing schools, camps, and organizations had folded by the 1960s, generally due to the demise of the Old Left, which had been battered during the anticommunist movement of the 1950s. Camp Kinderland continued to operate, however, as did the Little Red School House and adjoining Elizabeth Irwin High School in Greenwich Village, keeping alive the flame of left-wing education into a new era. Throughout the century boys who had been exposed to left-wing schools and camps experienced a variety of educational experiences that politically and culturally countered mainstream influences. Whether or not such influences left a permanent mark, boys nonetheless learned folk songs and dances, studied radical political and cultural ideas, and in other ways practiced alternatives to the dominant value system.

Ronald D. Cohen

See also Camping

References and further reading
Avrich, Paul. 1980. *The Modern School Movement: Anarchism and Education in the United States.* Princeton: Princeton University Press.
Buhle, Mari Jo, Paul Buhle, and Dan Georgakas, eds. 1998. *Encyclopedia of the American Left.* 2d ed. New York: Oxford University Press.
Kaplan, Judy, and Linn Shapiro, eds. 1998. *Red Diapers: Growing Up in the Communist Left.* Urbana: University of Illinois Press.
Mishler, Paul C. 1999. *Raising Reds: The Young Pioneers, Radical Summer Camps, and Communist Political Culture in the United States.* New York: Columbia University Press.
Schrank, Robert. 1998. *Wasn't That a Time! Growing Up Radical and Red in America.* Cambridge: MIT Press.
Teitelbaum, Kenneth. 1993. *Schooling for "Good Rebels": Socialist Education for Children in the United States, 1900–1920.* Philadelphia: Temple University Press.

Little League
See Baseball

M

Manners and Gentility

Boys learned manners and correct behavior in the eighteenth and nineteenth centuries by consulting time-honored manuals of advice. The behavioral ideals they contained can be traced back to the Italian Renaissance and such manuals as Baldassare Castiglione's *Book of the Courtier*, delineating personal and social behavior that was emulated in England by the 1620s at the court of Charles I. Aristocratic courtly behavior was repudiated during the English Civil War in the 1640s, and revived with the Restoration of the monarchy in 1660. Yet the court, especially after the Glorious Revolution of 1688, became less central in English culture than it previously had been. In the increasingly commercial nation, cultural activity came to focus on the town—the lively taverns, coffeehouses, clubs, and drawing rooms of London's newly fashionable West End. By the early eighteenth century, this coffeehouse culture of the urban bourgeoisie was idealized and diffused to provincial centers and the colonies through such periodicals as *Tatler* and *Spectator*. Joseph Addison, who wrote for both of them, hoped to create a culture of "politeness," convinced that the art of sociable, urbane, and pleasing conversation would generate a new moral authority and taste. As England's commercial economy prospered, this civility of manners was linked to the refinement of architectural style and material culture available to larger numbers of people through their purchase of consumer items. Tea tables, ceramic teapots, silver spoons, and looking glasses, as well as books of advice, inundated the American market by the 1760s, as the demand for items that indicated social merit spread to farmers, artisans, and even laborers and the poor. These behavioral ideals, however, also have been linked to the emergence of the public sphere, as private individuals engaged in rational and critical discourse in this forum of coffeehouses, clubs, and drawing rooms located between the intimacies of family life and the official state. As civil society expanded through commercial consumerism and voluntary association, a public opinion developed that led to political activity and debate, extending the boundaries of political participation.

Manuals advising boys on correct behavior for participation in the world dated to the beginning of printing in the English language in the fifteenth century. William Caxton printed the first *Book of Curtsye of Lytyll John* in 1477 in beautiful manuscript type. Following continental manuals of courtly manners, he provided maxims and instructions for young boys in the service of the "great." As the genre of these advice manuals developed, it took the form of letters from a father to his son, as in

John Singleton Copley portrays Daniel Commelin Verplanck in 1771 according to the behavioral ideals of gentility. (Metropolitan Museum)

Peter Idley's Instructions to His Son, also published in the fifteenth century. A popular eighteenth-century manual was *Letters Written by the Late Right Honorable Philip Dormer Stanhope, Earl of Chesterfield, to His Son, Philip Stanhope,* which was published in London in 1774, reprinted in Boston by 1779, and reissued as a revised version entitled *Principles of Politeness* in Philadelphia two years later. Chesterfield was the quintessential eighteenth-century aristocrat. Polished at the court of Louis XIV, seasoned as a statesman and adviser to kings, and friend of Addison, Alexander Pope, and Jonathan Swift as well as Montesquieu and Voltaire, he represented a worldly and pleasure-oriented yet shrewd and rational notion of good breeding. His letters originally were very private ones written to his illegitimate and only son and reveal an absent father's anxious wish to feel himself effective. For twenty-seven years, Chesterfield instructed Philip by letter, teaching him not only the ancient languages, history, and geography but also how to behave in public with civility, affability, and an easy manner.

Especially during the years of the American Revolution, citizens of the emerging republic objected to Chesterfield's racy, aristocratic tone. Mercy Otis Warren of Massachusetts admired his elegance of writing and code of politeness. In a letter to her own son, however, she argued that refinement need not exclude principle. When Chesterfield sacrificed truth to convenience and virtue to momentary gratification, she found him deeply reprehensible. She also objected to his attitude toward women because he connived in their seduction and did not recognize a feminine capacity for education, reflection, and rational conversation. When the Presbyterian printer

Robert Aitken published the Chesterfield letters in Philadelphia, he took a similar view. In his volume, the racy pleasure-oriented instructions are eliminated, and what remains could provide the kind of polish to finish the education of an American boy. The boy is given tips on achieving a genteel carriage, on maintaining cleanliness of person and dress, and on conversing with elegance and wit. He is taught how to do honors at table, how to propose a toast, and how to behave with grace toward those of lower social status. Yet the Aitken volume also includes Chesterfield's wary and shrewd advice. A boy should learn to observe others, studying their foibles and susceptibility to flattery. Keeping his own impulsive behavior under strict control with good breeding, he could then gently flatter and play on the weaknesses of others to advance his own reputation in the world.

No American colonial boy worked harder to train himself in the code of politeness than George Washington. In 1746, when he was fourteen, Washington copied 110 such "Rules of Civility & Decent Behavior in Company and Conversation" in his commonplace book, acquiring self-consciously the disciplined self-restraint he later exemplified in his revolutionary leadership. The commands Washington copied focused on respect for others and correct behavior in a social hierarchy. "Let thy ceremonies in courtesy be proper to the dignity of his place with who thou converses," he wrote, "for it is absurd to act the same with a clown and a prince." Other rules taught bodily restraint; for example, "Shift not yourself in the sight of others nor gnaw your nails," and "Shake not the head, feet, or legs; roll not the eyes; lift not one eyebrow higher than the other; wry not the mouth; and bedew no man's face with your spittle by approaching too near him when you speak" (Reinier 1996). Although these particular rules were based on French maxims of courtly behavior, Washington also learned self-restraint and genteel taste from reading Joseph Addison's *Spectator*. Addison was a monarchist, but Americans tended to identify him with the Roman concept of citizenship expressed in his 1713 tragedy *Cato*, which the young Washington read in the company of Sally Fairfax, a neighbor he admired. "Turn up thy eyes to Cato!" Addison wrote:

> There mayst thou see to what a godlike
> height
> The Roman virtues lift up mortal man,
> While good, and just, and anxious for
> his friends,
> He's still severely bent against himself.
> (Fischer 1989)

Washington was so taken with the stoic virtue in public life exemplified by *Cato* that he ordered the play performed for his officers at Valley Forge during the American Revolution. Still later he included quotations from Addison's tragedy in his presidential papers.

Although the code of politeness, as adapted by Americans, weathered their revolutionary shift in consciousness, by the end of the eighteenth century it was increasingly out-of-date. Expressed in a proliferation of novels that inundated the American market, British cosmopolitan culture began to shift from the rational self-discipline Washington admired to an emphasis on feeling. Cutting a figure in the town became less important than retreat from artificial convention and achievement of transparency in human relationships. The new model of refinement placed human affection as the basis of moral life and regarded those of great

sensitivity as morally virtuous. In *The Man of Feeling* (1771), Henry Mackenzie distinguished between sentiments of the heart and rational discourse of the head, and Samuel Richardson's *Sir Charles Grandison* (1753) created a new model of male virtue that was greatly admired by female readers. In the American context of republican citizenship and emerging democracy, however, such sentimental fiction seemed dangerously effeminate. Yet the emphasis on feeling would be retained for boys in a proliferation of manuals written by evangelical authors. Religious tracts and evangelical children's literature in the nineteenth century sought to instill in boys self-restrained behavior appropriate for a capitalist economy—cleanliness, industry, record keeping, and self-improvement. Feeling was channeled into spiritual experience and the effort to achieve "a new heart" through religious conversion. Children's literature, such as Anna Reed's *Life of George Washington*, written for the American Sunday School Union in 1829, admired the first president's regular habits and ability to hold great passion under restraint but attributed his hard-won virtue to the influence of his pious mother. It was she who had tamed the "manly superiority" of the young Washington to a "self-denying tenderness." Such nineteenth-century books on behavior, however, did not abandon the older emphasis on politeness. Gentility blended with evangelical religion would define respectability for the new middle class, forming the basis for Victorian culture.

Jacqueline S. Reinier

References and further reading
Brewer, John. 1997. *The Pleasures of the Imagination: English Culture in the*

Eighteenth Century. New York: Farrar, Straus and Giroux.

Bushman, Richard. 1992. *The Refinement of America: Persons, Houses, Cities.* New York: Alfred A. Knopf.

Carson, Cary, Ronald Hoffman, and Peter J. Albert, eds. 1994. *Of Consuming Interests: The Style of Life in the Eighteenth Century.* Charlottesville: University Press of Virginia.

Fischer, David Hackett. 1989. *Albion's Seed: Four British Folkways in America.* New York: Oxford University Press.

Reinier, Jacqueline. 1996. *From Virtue to Character: American Childhood, 1775–1850.* New York: Twayne Publishers.

Richards, Jeffrey H. 1995. *Mercy Otis Warren.* New York: Twayne Publishers.

Masculinities

The term *masculinities* refers to the social roles, behaviors, and meanings prescribed for men in any given society at any one time. As such, the term emphasizes gender, not biological sex, and the diversity of identities among different groups of men. Although people experience gender as an internal facet of identity, masculinities are produced within the institutions of society and through daily interactions (Kimmel 2000).

Much popular discourse assumes that biological sex determines one's gender identity, the experience and expression of masculinity and femininity. Instead of focusing on biological universals, social and behavioral scientists are concerned with the different ways in which biological sex comes to mean different things in different contexts. *Sex* refers to the biological apparatus, the male and the female—the chromosomal, chemical, anatomical organization. *Gender* refers to the meanings that are attached to those differences within a culture—to what it means to be a man or a woman. Although biological sex varies very little, gender varies enormously. Gender takes shape only within specific social and cultural contexts.

The use of the plural—masculinities—recognizes the dramatic variation in how different groups define masculinity, even in the same society at the same time, as well as individual differences. Although social forces operate to create systematic differences between men and women, on average on some dimensions, even these differences *between* women and men are not as great as the differences *among* men or *among* women.

The meanings of masculinity vary over four different dimensions, and thus four different disciplines are involved in understanding gender. First, masculinity varies across cultures. Anthropologists have documented the ways that gender varies cross-culturally. Some cultures encourage men to be stoic and to prove masculinity, especially by sexual conquest. Other cultures prescribe a more relaxed definition of masculinity, based on civic participation, emotional responsiveness, and collective provision for the community's needs. The different definitions of being a man in France or among aboriginal peoples in the Australian outback are so far apart that they belie any notion that gender identity is determined mostly by biological sex differences. The differences between two cultures' version of masculinity is often greater than the differences between the two genders.

Second, definitions of masculinity vary considerably in any one country over time. Historians have explored how these definitions have shifted in response to changes in levels of industrialization and urbanization, position in the larger worldwide geopolitical and economic context, and development of new technologies. What it meant to be a man in colonial America is quite different from what it meant in 1900 or what it might mean to be a man in the United States today.

Third, definitions of masculinity change over the course of a person's life. Developmental psychologists have examined how a set of developmental milestones leads to differences in experience and expression of gender identity. Both chronological age and life stage require different enactments of gender. In the West, the issues confronting a man about proving himself and feeling successful will change as he ages, as will the social institutions in which he will attempt to enact those experiences. A young single man defines masculinity differently than a middle-aged father and an elderly grandfather.

Finally, the meanings of masculinity vary considerably within any given society at any one time. At any given moment, several meanings of masculinity coexist. Simply put, not all American or Brazilian or Senegalese men are the same. Sociologists have explored the ways in which class, race, ethnicity, age, sexuality, and region all shape gender identity. Each of these axes modifies the others. Imagine, for example, two "American" men, one an older, black, gay man in Chicago, the other a young, white, heterosexual farm boy in Iowa. Would they not have different definitions of masculinity? Each is deeply affected by the gender norms and power arrangements of their society.

If gender varies so significantly—across cultures, over historical time, among men and women within any one culture, and over the life course—then masculinity cannot be addressed as though it were a constant, universal essence common to all men. Thus, gender must be seen as an ever-changing fluid assemblage of meanings and behaviors, and the term *masculinities* must be used. Pluralizing the term acknowledges that masculinity means different things to different groups of people at different times.

Recognizing diversity ought not obscure the ways in which gender definitions are constructed in a field of power. Simply put, all masculinities are not created equal. In every culture, men contend with a definition that is held up as the model against which all are expected to measure themselves. This "hegemonic" definition of masculinity is "constructed in relation to various subordinated masculinities as well as in relation to women," R. W. Connell writes (1987, 183). Erving Goffman (1963, 128) once described the process this way:

> In an important sense there is only one complete unblushing male in America: a young, married, white, urban, northern, heterosexual, Protestant, father, of college education, fully employed, of good complexion, weight, and height, and a recent record in sports. . . . Any male who fails to qualify in any one of these ways is likely to view himself—during moments at least—as unworthy, incomplete, and inferior.

Definitions of masculinity are not simply constructed in relation to the hegemonic ideals of that gender but also in constant reference to each other. Gender is not only plural but also relational. Surveys in Western countries indicate that men construct their ideas of what it means to be men *in constant reference* to definitions of femininity. What it means to be a man is to be unlike a woman; indeed, social psychologists have emphasized that although different groups of men may disagree about other traits and their significance in gender definitions, the "antifemininity" component of masculinity is perhaps the single dominant and universal characteristic.

Gender difference and gender inequality are both produced through human relationships. Nancy Chodorow (1979) argues that the structural arrangements by which women are primarily responsible for raising children create unconscious, internalized desires in both boys and girls that reproduce male dominance and female mothering. For boys, gender identity requires emotional detachment from mother, a process of individuation through separation. The boy comes to define himself as a boy by rejecting whatever he sees as female, by devaluing the feminine in himself (separation) and in others (male superiority). Girls, by contrast, are bound to a pre-Oedipal experience of connection to the same-sex parent; they develop a sense of themselves through their ability to connect, which leads to a desire to become mothers themselves. This cycle of men defining themselves through their distance from and devaluation of femininity can end, Chodorow argues, only when parents participate equally in childrearing.

It is possible to recognize gender diversity and still conceive masculinities as attributes of identity only. For example, gendered individuals bring all the attributes and behavioral characteristics of their gendered identity into gender-neutral institutional arenas. But because gender is plural and relational, it is also situational. What it means to be a man or a woman varies in different institutional contexts. Those different institutional contexts demand and produce different forms of masculinity. "Boys may be boys," Deborah Rhode comments cleverly, "but they express that identity dif-

ferently in fraternity parties than in job interviews with a female manager" (1997, 142). Gender is thus not only a property of individuals, some "thing" one has, but a specific set of behaviors that are produced in specific social situations. And so gender changes as the situation changes.

Institutions are themselves gendered. Institutions create gendered normative standards, express a gendered institutional logic, and are major factors in the reproduction of gender inequality. The gendered identity of individuals shapes those gendered institutions, and the gendered institutions express and reproduce the inequalities that compose gender identity. Institutions themselves express a logic—a dynamic—that reproduces gender relations between women and men and the gender order of hierarchy and power. Not only do gendered individuals negotiate their identities within gendered institutions, but also those institutions produce the very differences assumed to be the properties of individuals. Thus, "the extent to which women and men do different tasks, play widely disparate concrete social roles, strongly influences the extent to which the two sexes develop and/or are expected to manifest widely disparate personal behaviors and characteristics." Different structured experiences produce the gender differences often attributed to people (Chafetz 1980).

For example, take the workplace. In her now-classic work, *Men and Women of the Corporation* (1977), Rosabeth Moss Kanter argued that the differences in men's and women's behaviors in organizations had far less to do with their characteristics as individuals than they had to do with the structure of the organization and the different jobs men and women held. Organizational positions "carry characteristic images of the kinds of people that should occupy them," she argued, and those who do occupy them, whether women or men, exhibited those necessary behaviors. Though the criteria for evaluation of job performance, promotion, and effectiveness seem to be gender-neutral, they are, in fact, deeply gendered. "While organizations were being defined as sex-neutral machines," she writes, "masculine principles were dominating their authority structures." Once again, masculinity—the norm—was invisible. For example, secretaries seemed to stress personal loyalty to their bosses more than did other workers, which led some observers to attribute this to women's greater level of personalism. But Kanter pointed out that the best way for a secretary—of either sex—to get promoted was for the boss to decide to take the secretary with him to the higher job. Thus the structure of the women's jobs, not the gender of the job-holder, dictated their responses.

Joan Acker has expanded on Kanter's early insights and specified the interplay of structure and gender. It is through people's experiences in the workplace, Acker maintains, that the differences between women and men are reproduced and the inequality between women and men is legitimated. Institutions are like factories, and one of the things that they produce is gender difference. The overall effect is the reproduction of the gender order as a whole (see Acker 1987, 1988, 1989, 1990).

Institutions accomplish the creation of gender difference and the reproduction of the gender order through several gendered processes. Thus, "advantage and disadvantage, exploitation and control, action and emotion, meaning and identity, are patterned through and in terms of a distinction between male and female, masculine and feminine" (Acker 1990, 274). It is erroneous to assume that gendered individuals enter gender-neutral sites, thus maintaining the invisibility of gender-as-hierarchy and specifically the invisible masculine organizational logic. However, it is just as incorrect to assume that genderless "people" occupy those gender-neutral sites. The problem is that such genderless people are assumed to be able to devote themselves single-mindedly to their jobs, have no children or family responsibilities, and may even have familial supports for such single-minded workplace devotion. Thus, the genderless jobholder turns out to be gendered as a man.

Take, for example, the field of education. The differences assumed to be the properties of boys and girls are often subtly—or not so subtly—produced by the educational institutions in which they find themselves. This process takes place in the structure of the institution itself—by having boys and girls form separate lines to enter the school through different entrances, separating boys and girls during recess and encouraging them to play at different activities, and tracking boys into shop and girls into home economics (as if boys would naturally want to repair cars and girls would naturally want to learn how to cook). It also takes place in the informal social interactions with teachers who allow boys to disrupt or interrupt classes more easily than girls or who discourage girls from excelling in science and math classes. And it takes place in the dynamics of the interactions among boys and girls as well, both in the classroom and outside (see Thorne 1983).

Embedded in organizational structures that are gendered, subject to gendered organizational processes, and evaluated by gendered criteria, then, the differences between women and men appear to be the differences solely between gendered individuals. When gender boundaries seem permeable, other dynamics and processes can reproduce the gender order. When women do not meet the criteria (or, perhaps more accurately, when the criteria do not meet women's specific needs), we see a gender-segregated workforce and wage, hiring, and promotional disparities as the "natural" outcomes of already-present differences between women and men. In this way, differences are generated, and the inequalities between women and men are legitimated and reproduced.

There remains one more element in this exploration of masculinities. Some psychologists and sociologists believe that early childhood gender socialization leads to gender identities that become fixed, permanent, and inherent in our personalities. However, many sociologists disagree with this notion today. As they see it, gender is less a component of identity—fixed, static—that people take with them into their interactions than the product *of* those interactions. In an important article, Candace West and Don Zimmerman argue that "a person's gender is not simply an aspect of what one is, but, more fundamentally, it is something that one *does*, and does recurrently, in interaction with others" (1987, 140). People are constantly "doing" gender, performing the activities and exhibiting the traits that are prescribed for them.

Doing gender is a lifelong process of performances. As people interact, they are held accountable for displaying behavior that is consistent with gender norms, at least for that situation. Thus consistent gender behavior is less a response to deeply internalized norms or personality characteristics and more a negotiated response to the consistency with which others demand that they act in a recognizable masculine or feminine

way. Gender is less an emanation of identity that bubbles up from below in concrete expression than an emergent property of interactions, coerced from people by those around them.

Understanding how people "do" masculinities, then, requires that they make visible the performative elements of identity and also the audience for those performances. It also opens up unimaginable possibilities for social change; as Suzanne Kessler points out in her study of "intersexed people" (hermaphrodites, those born with anatomical characteristics of both sexes, or with ambiguous genitalia):

> If authenticity for gender rests not in a discoverable nature but in someone else's proclamation, then the power to proclaim something else is available. If physicians recognized that implicit in their management of gender is the notion that finally, and always, people construct gender as well as the social systems that are grounded in gender-based concepts, the possibilities for real societal transformations would be unlimited. (Kessler 1990, 25)

Kessler's gender utopianism raises an important issue. If people "do" gender, then gender is not only something that is done to them. They create and re-create gendered identities within the contexts of their interactions with others and within the institutions they inhabit.

Michael Kimmel

References and further reading
Acker, Joan. 1987. "Sex Bias in Job Evaluation: A Comparable Worth Issue." In *Ingredients for Women's Employment Policy*. Edited by C. Bose and G. Spitze. Albany: SUNY Press.

―――. 1988. "Class, Gender and the Relations of Distribution." *Signs: Journal of Women in Culture and Society* 13.

―――. 1989. *Doing Comparable Worth: Gender, Class and Pay Equity.* Philadelphia: Temple University Press.

―――. 1990. "Hierarchies, Jobs, Bodies: A Theory of Gendered Organizations." *Gender and Society* 4, no. 2.

Acker, Joan, and Donald R. Van Houten. 1974. "Differential Recruitment and Control: The Sex Structuring of Organizations." *Administrative Science Quarterly* 19, no. 2.

Chafetz, Janet. 1980. "Toward a Macro-Level Theory of Sexual Stratification." *Current Perspectives in Social Theory* 1.

Chodorow, Nancy. 1979. *The Reproduction of Mothering.* Berkeley: University of California Press.

Connell, R. W. 1987. *Gender and Power.* Stanford: Stanford University Press.

Goffman, Erving. 1963. *Stigma.* Englewood Cliffs, NJ: Prentice-Hall.

Kanter, Rosabeth Moss. 1975. "Women and the Structure of Organizations: Explorations in Theory and Behavior." In *Another Voice: Feminist Perspectives on Social Life and Social Science.* Edited by M. Millman and R. M. Kanter. New York: Anchor Books.

―――. 1977. *Men and Women of the Corporation.* New York: Basic Books.

Kessler, Suzanne J. 1990. "The Medical Construction of Gender: Case Management of Intersexed Infants." *Signs* 16, no. 1.

Kimmel, Michael. 2000. *The Gendered Society.* New York: Oxford University Press.

Rhode, Deborah. 1997. *Speaking of Sex.* Cambridge: Harvard University Press.

Risman, Barbara. 1999. *Gender Vertigo.* New Haven: Yale University Press.

Thorne, Barrie. 1983. *Gender Play.* New Brunswick, NJ: Rutgers University Press.

West, Candace, and Don Zimmerman. 1987. "Doing Gender." *Gender and Society* 1, no. 2.

Masturbation

Masturbation, the erotic stimulation of one's own genitals, is a persistent human practice, especially among boys and young men. Although common in Western culture, masturbation has historically been discouraged by parents, religious leaders, physicians, and other child care professionals. Recently, some researchers and therapists have asserted that masturbation is part of normal development and may have positive benefits for children, youth, and adults alike (Christensen 1995). Yet masturbation remains a controversial practice that produces anxiety among many parents and generates intense debate among scholars, therapists, and policymakers.

Because masturbation is usually a private, solitary act, it is difficult, if not impossible, to be certain about the precise extent of this behavior now or in the past. Surveys of sexual practice, which are widely used today, may not be representative and depend on individuals to be honest about a behavior that is typically ridiculed or censured by others (Okami and Pendleton 1994). Furthermore, there are virtually no survey data about masturbation before the twentieth century, so evidence about the practice in the past is usually anecdotal and inferential. According to Vern Bullough's (1976) comprehensive review of sexual variance in history, masturbation was noted in many ancient cultures. Contrary to common opinion, however, masturbation is not addressed directly in the Bible. The passage usually associated with masturbation is Genesis 38:7–10, which describes the fate of Onan, who failed to meet his levirate obligations to inseminate his dead brother's wife, engaging instead in coitus interruptus, thus spilling his semen on the ground. Another passage sometimes used to condemn masturbation is Leviticus 15:16–18, which declares as unclean anything touched by semen and describes the process for ritual cleansing, but this passage refers to semen produced during intercourse and makes no direct reference to masturbation. Even so, masturbation was proscribed in medieval Jewish law, which forbade males even from holding their penises when they urinated, warning masturbators that their hands were "full of blood" (Phipps 1977, 184).

Leaders of the early Christian church roundly condemned masturbation as a sinful, despicable act. Writing in the fifth century, St. Augustine rejected masturbation as an unnatural sexual act because it did not lead to procreation. Thomas Aquinas, preeminent medieval theologian, concluded that masturbation was a mortal sin justifying damnation, although his view was not universally accepted (Phipps 1977; Bullough 1976). Masturbation appeared regularly in early church penitentials, but the penalties assigned for this transgression were usually not as severe as those for bestiality or sodomy. Early Protestant leaders such as Martin Luther and John Calvin found masturbation equally objectionable and warned against it in their sermons and writings.

Thus, before the eighteenth century, commentators in the West generally objected to masturbation on religious grounds and rarely if ever claimed that it was physically harmful to those who practiced it. This changed with the publication of an anonymous pamphlet authored by a British physician or cleric. *Onania; or the Heinous Sin of Self-Pollution, and All Its Frightful Consequences, in Both Sexes, Considered* (1724) defined masturbation as "that unnatural practice, by which persons of either sex may defile their own bodies, without the assistance of others, whilst yielding to filthy imaginations, they endeavour to imitate and

procure to themselves that sensation, which God has ordered to attend the carnal commerce of the two sexes for the continuance of our Species" (Anonymous 1724, 1). This description of masturbation was consistent with earlier ones, but the author of *Onania* went well beyond earlier statements when he identified an astonishing array of physical maladies that could be caused by this self-polluting act: stunted growth, "consumptions," "fainting fits," "epilepsies," "phymosis," "paraphymosis," "stranguries,""preiapisms" "and other disorders of the penis and testes, but especially gonorrheas," "premature ejaculation," "loss of erection," "infertile seed," and weak, sickly offspring with "meager jaws and pale looks, with feeble hams, and legs without calves" were just some of the many ills males could suffer if they masturbated (Anonymous 1724, 14–17). Readers of *Onania* who wished to prevent or eliminate this dangerous habit were warned, among other things, to avoid butter and not to sleep on their backs or spend too much time in bed. To avoid nocturnal emissions, males were instructed "to tie a string, when you go to bed, about your neck and the other end about the necks of your penis, which when an erection happens, will timely awaken you, and put an effectual stop to the seminal emission" (Anonymous 1724, 44).

Onania proved to be very popular. By 1730, *Onania* was in its sixteenth edition and had grown from the original 60 pages to 194 pages, plus a 142-page supplement of personal letters and testimony on the topic (MacDonald 1967; Hare 1962). By 1750, *Onania* had appeared in nineteen editions and sold 38,000 copies (Bennett and Rosario 1995), partly because it had little competition. Cotton Mather, a leading New England minister, published

The Pure Nazarite: Advice to a Young Man, Concerning an Impiety and Impurity (Not Easily to Be Spoken of) Which Many Young Men Are to Their Perpetual Sorrow, Too Easily Drawn Into (1723), the first publication on masturbation in North America. Mather's work, though more moderate and empathetic in tone than *Onania*, remained relatively unknown outside New England. In 1724 an edition of *Onania* was published in Boston.

Onania continued to dominate the field until 1758, when a second *Onania* appeared, this one by Samuel Tissot, a highly respected Swiss physician, devoutly Catholic, and adviser to the Vatican on epidemics (Phipps 1977). Perhaps in part because of his excellent reputation, Tissot's *Onania* sold very well and was translated into several languages. Although Tissot criticized the first *Onania* as disorganized and unsystematic, he actually expanded its long list of physical maladies attributed to masturbation. Moreover, he stressed masturbation's potential harmful effects on mental health, warning that it could lead to insanity. He cited one case in which a masturbator "dried out his brain so prodigiously that it could be heard rattling in his skull" (Spitz 1952, 495). Tissot's *Onania* was read well into the nineteenth century, and his insanity hypothesis influenced several writers, including Benjamin Rush, who identified masturbation as one of the causes of madness in his important work, *Medical Inquiries and Observations upon the Diseases of the Mind* (1812).

Several explanations are possible for the growing secular concern about masturbation during the eighteenth century: the earlier onset of puberty and later age of marriage; fear of venereal disease; de-

clining authority of the church and increasing individualism; emergence of print culture, which encouraged private fantasies; and the need to regulate sex "through useful and public discourses," in a rapidly changing social and cultural environment (Foucault 1980, 25). Whatever its sources, the public, secular discussion of masturbation that began in the eighteenth century intensified in the nineteenth and led to a remarkable anti-masturbation campaign that persisted into the twentieth century.

At first, those who spoke against masturbation in the nineteenth century, like Benjamin Rush, warned against both the physical and mental consequences of masturbation. Gradually, however, concern for the masturbator's mental health became more important in the discussion (MacDonald 1967; Hare 1962). Sylvester Graham (1794–1851), a noted American nutritionist, believed all forms of excessive sexual desire led to insanity, which in turn contributed to sexual excess, clearly a dangerous trap for masturbators who seemed to lack self-control (Bullough 1976, 543). Victorians pursued their campaign against masturbation with an amazing and revealing enthusiasm. The more they exposed this vice, the more threatening it seemed and the more severe the remedies they considered to prevent or eliminate it. By the 1870s, American children who masturbated risked being subjected to a horrific array of "treatments," including infibulation and clitoridectomy for girls, circumcision and even castration for boys, and physical restraints and genital cages for both (Phipps 1977). Even though these extreme measures were not commonly used, the fact that they were discussed indicates the intensity of the antimasturbation campaign and the deep anxiety of those who supported it. As Rene Spitz notes, "in the eighteenth century physicians endeavored to *cure* masturbation," and "in the nineteenth century they were trying to *suppress* it" (Spitz 1952, 499).

The campaign against masturbation may have reached its peak between 1880 and 1914 when social reformers, educators, physicians, religious leaders, and psychologists joined in the social purity movement to promote "the idea of salvation through renunciation" (Hunt 1998, 579). This movement drew much of its remarkable energy from an invigorated evangelical Christianity and the powerful antisexual feminism that emerged in the nineteenth century. However, the belief that masturbation caused insanity and serious physical maladies became increasingly difficult to sustain as the results of systematic investigations became more widely known. Havelock Ellis questioned the scientific basis for these claims in his *Auto-Eroticism* (1900), the first volume in his *Studies in the Psychology of Sex*. Furthermore, the social purity crusade soon dissipated in the aftermath of World War I, and opposition to masturbation reverted to more informal, less visible forms.

Since 1920, attitudes toward masturbation have remained profoundly ambivalent, but they have reflected a growing awareness that masturbation is very common and that it does not, in fact, cause serious physical or mental harm. Although the masturbatory hypothesis continues to have some currency as folk knowledge, scholars and therapists have generally rejected it. After 1920, masturbation was more likely to be seen as an undesirable but normal behavior, especially among boys, and at worst a symptom of illness or weak moral character rather than their cause (Hunt 1998). Surveys of sexual attitudes and behavior played an important role in shaping these perceptions of masturbation. Beginning with the post–World War II surveys by Leslie Hohman and Bertram Schaffner (1947) and by Alfred Kinsey, Wardell Pomeroy, and Clyde Martin (1948), virtually all (85–93 percent) males surveyed under the age of twenty-one reported they had masturbated, and the rates reported by females ranged from 33 to 64 percent (Leitenberg, Detzer, and Srebnik 1993). One illustration of how much attitudes about masturbation have changed during the twentieth century is the fact that masturbation has been used for some time as a technique in sex therapy to treat a range of sexual problems in both males and females (Christensen 1995). Indeed, some therapists have argued that masturbation is in some respects preferable to intercourse. The legitimate fear of acquired immunodeficiency syndrome (AIDS) and other venereal diseases has no doubt made this argument more convincing.

Masturbation is now viewed more positively than it was in the past, and few would wish to return to the antimasturbation hysteria of the nineteenth century. Yet some scholars and commentators object strenuously to using masturbation as a therapy technique or promoting it among youth. They often point to the narcissism inherent in masturbation and question whether it promotes or inhibits the capacity for mature sexual intimacy, which necessarily requires mutuality and sharing. Clark Christensen argues that recommending a program of masturbation for someone in a troubled relationship "may be similar to telling alcoholics to find time by themselves and indulge in drinking." The fact that masturbation "occurs with great frequency in the adult and adolescent population," he concludes, "does not mean that it need be prescribed *carte blanche* by professionals as therapeutic" (1995, 95). Robert C. Solomon has raised a related but different objection. He sees masturbation as symptomatic of the modern tendency to focus on sexuality as private enjoyment. He observes that although we "enjoy being sexually satisfied; we are not satisfied by our enjoyment." Why, he asks, would any human activity so "intensely promoted and obsessively pursued" as sex is today not produce greater "gratification"? (Solomon 1974, 341).

N. Ray Hiner

See also Bodies; Sexuality

References and further reading
Anonymous. 1724. *Onania; or the Heinous Sin of Pollution, and All Its Frightful Consequences, in Both Sexes, Considered.* 10th ed. Boston: John Phillips.
Bennett, Paula, and Vernon A. Rosario II, eds. 1995. *Solitary Pleasures: The Historical, Literary, and Artistic Discourses of Autoeroticism.* New York: Routledge.
Bullough, Vern L. 1976. *Sexual Variance in Society and History.* Chicago: University of Chicago Press.
Christensen, Clark. 1995. "Prescribed Masturbation in Sex Therapy: A Critique." *Journal of Sex and Marital Therapy* 21 (Summer): 87–99.
Ellis, Havelock. 1900. *The Evolution of Modesty; the Phenomena of Sexual Periodicity; Auto-Eroticism.* Philadelphia: E. A. Davis.
Foucault, Michel. 1980. *The History of Sexuality.* Vol. 1: *An Introduction.* New York: Vintage.
Hare, E. H. 1962. "Masturbatory Insanity: The History of an Idea." *The Journal of Mental Science* 108 (January): 2–25.
Hohman, Leslie B., and Bertram Schaffner. 1947. "The Sex Lives of Unmarried Men." *American Journal of Sociology* 52 (May): 501–507.
Hunt, Alan. 1998. "The Great Masturbation Panic and the Discourses of Moral Regulation in Nineteenth- and Early Twentieth-Century Britain." *Journal of the History of Sexuality* 8 (April): 575–615.
Kinsey, Alfred C., Wardell B. Pomeroy, and Clyde E. Martin. 1948. *Sexual Behavior in the Human Male.* Philadelphia: W. B. Saunders.
Leitenberg, Harold, Mark J. Detzer, and Debra Srebnik. 1993. "Gender Differences in Masturbation and the Relation of Masturbation Experience in Preadolescence and/or Early Adolescence to Sexual Behavior and Sexual Adjustment in Young Adulthood." *Archives of Sexual Behavior* 22 (April): 87–98.
MacDonald, Robert H. 1967. "The Frightful Consequences of Onanism: Notes on the History of a Delusion." *Journal of the History of Ideas* 28 (1967): 423–431.
Mather, Cotton. 1723. *The Pure Nazarite: Advice to a Young Man.* Boston: T. Fleet for John Phillips.
Okami, Paul, and Laura Pendleton. 1994. "Theorizing Sexuality: Seeds of a Transdisciplinary Paradigm Shift." *Current Anthropology* 35 (February): 85–91.
Phipps, William E. 1977. "Masturbation: Vice or Virtue?" *Journal of Religion and Health* 16: 183–195.
Porter, Roy. 1995. "Forbidden Pleasures: Enlightenment Literature of Sexual Advice." Pp. 75–98 in *Solitary Pleasures: The Historical, Literary, and Artistic Discourses of Autoeroticism.* Edited by Paula Bennett and Vernon A. Rosario II. New York: Routledge.
Solomon, Robert C. 1974. "Sexual Paradigms." *The Journal of Philosophy* 71 (June): 336–345.
Spitz, Rene A. 1952. "Authority and Masturbation: Some Remarks on a Bibliographical Investigation." *The Psychoanalytic Quarterly* 21 (October): 490–527.

Melodrama

In turn-of-the-twentieth-century New York City, the most popular form of theater was melodrama. Boys who worked during the day flocked to the theaters at night to see their favorite hero defeat the

A poster for the melodrama The Two Orphans, *ca. 1879 (Library of Congress)*

villain and save the heroine. For anywhere between 10 and 30 cents they could escape from their dreary lives and enter a world of excitement, suspense, tears, and laughter. In contrast to today's older theatrical audiences, in those days young men fought to enter the doors of the melodrama houses.

In the first half of the nineteenth century, French and English melodramas had been adapted and imported, but beginning in midcentury, American playwrights put their own stamp on the form with local characters and settings. By the end of the century, fed by the enormous waves of immigrants, American audiences were growing by leaps and bounds. Between 1890 and 1990, the population of New York City skyrocketed 126.8 percent (Rosen 1982). As urbanization and industrialization changed the face of society, men and women, young and old, worked outside the home earning enough money to afford inexpensive amusements. Producers, ever poised to exploit a new market, lowered the price of theater tickets considerably in order to attract these working-class audiences.

In this way the ten-twenty-thirty movement, known more familiarly as the "ten, twent', thirt'," was born. Originally a reference to ticket prices, the term came to encompass resident stock companies, various types of touring companies, and hundreds of plays, mostly melodramas, written expressly for this type of theater. Producers hired playwrights to churn out melodramas by the dozens, which were often performed in New York before being packaged, promoted, and sent on tour to cities throughout the country. These nationwide theaters formed a large "circuit" or "wheel," yielding fortunes for the producers despite the cheap admission.

New York theaters exhibited a "Broadway-Bowery polarity" separating middle-class entertainments, which often boasted European plays and stars, from the lower-class, homegrown melodrama theaters (Sante 1991). The term "Broadway" referred to the theaters farther uptown, whereas "Bowery" implied downtown or Lower East Side theaters in the immigrant neighborhoods (and several in Brooklyn as well). The higher-class theaters charged up to $2 per ticket, as opposed to the "popular-priced" theaters, some of which included the Grand Street Theater, the Academy of Music and the Fourteenth Street Theater (both on Fourteenth Street), the Star Theater (Thirteenth Street), and the Grand Opera House (Twenty-third Street).

These theaters catered to the needs of their public, who demanded cheap, thrilling, escapist entertainment. As Daniel Gerould explains in *American Melodrama* (1983), this genre is well suited to the American mentality because of its adherence to poetic justice. In melodrama ordinary people become heroes, defeating evil in every form. There are no limits to what the individual can do—nothing is impossible. Despite poverty and all manner of handicaps, the pure and the innocent triumph in the end. For the immigrant population, many of whom lived in squalor and worked under unbearable conditions, the melodrama theater offered the hope and optimism that did not exist in their own lives.

Owen Davis, one of the most popular and successful of the ten, twent', thirt' playwrights, explained that since much of his audience did not speak English, his plays had to appeal to the eye rather than the ear. They did so by making use of stock characters and spectacle. The characters were distinct types, clearly recognizable by every audience member because of their physical appearance, gestures, and behavior. These included the hero and heroine, the comic sidekicks, and the villain (who could be male or female; some plays had two villains—one male and one female). Davis and Theodore Kremer, another prolific playwright of the time, attest to the fact that they always wrote with their audience in mind. Davis, a Harvard graduate, would sit up in the cheapest gallery seats of the melodrama theaters, studying audience reactions. Kremer would read his plays to his barber, butcher, and bootblack to get their responses before submitting the play to his producer. They dared not change the melodrama formula for fear of upsetting their audiences, who were more dogmatic than religious fanatics. This formula mandated trouble in the first act, a heroine at the mercy of the villain in the second, a courageous rescue in the third, and a reunion of the lovers and punishment for the villain in the fourth.

One of the reasons for the popularity of these plays was that the audiences recognized themselves in the characters onstage. In its heyday during the first decade of the century, the ten, twent', thirt' theater featured the Irish, Jews, Italians, and Asians, as well as types like the "Bowery B'hoy" and "G'hal" speaking in the familiar dialects heard on the streets. In Scott Marble's play *The Sidewalks of New York*, we find an example of the latter couple—Tacks and his girlfriend Jane, who eventually end up together after alternating between verbal battles and attempts to save the hero and heroine. Tacks, who sells newspapers, hopes to earn enough money to convince Jane to marry him, but she is determined to assert her independence. In a short interchange in the third act he asks her:

Tacks: Ain't I engaged?

Jane: You're altogether too inferior to grasp the duties of the engager.

Tacks: Den you won't be me wife?

Jane: How dare you sir: Asking me to be your wife. That is my place now, when I'm ready. I may ask you to be my husband. I am the new woman. [She exits]

Tacks: Hully gee: What's to become of us men; suppose some old dame gets mashed on me and says I want you for my husband. Den I refuse an get arrested.

Love scenes alternated with comedy and suspense to keep the spectators off-balance and hungry for more. Unfortunately, the majority of plays written for the ten, twent', thirt' theater have never been published.

Characters like Tacks appealed to the newsboys who lived and worked in the Bowery area around the turn of the twentieth century. They were among the chief occupants of the gallery seats. With the expansion of cities, there was a need for "newsies" to sell papers to homebound commuters. Hundreds of thousands of these boys, mostly between the ages of eleven and fifteen, hawked their papers in U.S. cities (Nasaw 1985). Sometimes as an incentive they were given theater tickets by circulation managers who found themselves competing to fill an ever-increasing need for newsboys. These young men were independent wage earners who quickly learned to capitalize on the headlines of the day.

Often the galleries of the theaters were so crowded and noisy that a policeman was hired to keep order. These boys were demanding and difficult to please, and the success of the production depended on their response, which was vocal. They were the ones who hissed at the villain and cheered for the hero. Newspaper clippings of the time assert that actors were painfully aware of the importance of pleasing these "gallery gods," who could shout them off the stage if they were unsuccessful. Charles T. Aldrich claimed that instead of finding his stage reality from the lines, he first had to convince the gallery and ended by believing in himself. Actress Lottie Williams was praised as a favorite with the gallery, who reduced more eminent players to "fear and trembling." The famous producer A. H. Woods felt that if his productions did not please the gallery, they were "no go." Although these audiences were often criticized for their lack of taste and discernment, they kept the melodrama alive. Called the "Peter Pans of stage-land" by Porter Emerson Browne (1909) in *Everybody's Magazine*, they got more value for the few cents they paid than any higher-class audience.

Some local boys even found their way into the plays as "supers," or supernumeraries (extras). As an actor in the Metropolis Theater in the Bronx, Frank J. Beckman (1962) and several other neighborhood youths appeared in the plays in a variety of nonspeaking roles, including cowboys, newsboys, soldiers, sailors, convicts, bootblacks, messengers, and even cannibals. For Owen Davis's prison melodrama, *Convict 999*, Beckman and his friends dressed in convicts' stripes and chains and walked along the streets of their neighborhood, wearing placards advertising the play.

The other element of melodrama that attracted its large, uncultured audience was its use of spectacle. The stage not only mirrored its patrons but also reflected violent news events and disasters that befell them. It is here that the job of the stage carpenter became essential to the success of the production. Because this was a theater based on visual attractions, special effects and frequent scene changes were expected by every member of the audience. It was one of the most important selling points of melodrama. Posters in various sizes and colors advertising the "sensation scene" (the most dramatic event of the play: an escape, a murder, or a daring rescue) were made up even before the script was written and pasted on every available billboard. Newspaper advertisements listed the new scenic effects in each production.

Ben Singer (1992) points out that the dangers of everyday life, recounted in the headlines of the day, became the subject of melodrama: terrible injury and deaths caused by electric trolleys and railroads, factory machinery, the hazards of tenement life, and falls from buildings and bridges. The thrills of melodrama aped the violence of everyday life, presented onstage in as realistic a setting as possible. Actors were often injured in these productions because they had to perform their own stunts. The son of Laurette Taylor, whose husband Charles A. Taylor starred her in his melodramas early in her career, speaks of her brush with death in attempting to enact some of the perils of the heroine.

Thus in melodrama the young men of the time saw themselves and their lives represented onstage, spiced with comedy skits and songs (between acts as "olios" or even during the plays), and were assured of a happy ending with justice for all. Yet despite the popularity of these plays, the ten, twent', thirt' movement declined and disappeared by the end of the first decade of the twentieth century. Among the several explanations, the most weighty is competition with a new medium: film. Beginning in 1905, film exhibitors took over converted storefronts, dance halls, and restaurants, where for the admission price of 5 cents, they showed a program of short films, many of which borrowed their subjects from melodrama. By 1910 these "nickelodeons" numbered more than 10,000 nationwide, taking over the very theaters to which melodrama audiences had flocked several years earlier. Their patrons were primarily children and young people. David Nasaw (1985) points out that youngsters accounted for one-quarter to one-half of the audience of this "creation of the child." Each day they were offered a different program, which often, like melodrama, reflected their lives—the earliest ones were documentaries of everyday events. Although theatrical presentations took hours, programs shown at nickelodeons were so short (half an hour) that newsies could see them during the day or right after work. Films were more immediate and more realistic, and the audience did not have to wait for scene changes. In addition, because they were silent, there was no need to understand English. These "nickel dumps" went out of their way to attract young audiences by offering incentives like gum or two admissions for a nickel on Saturdays. Before long, the gallery gods deserted the melodramas for the movies, where they remain to this day.

Barbara M. Waldinger

See also Films; Newsboys; Performers and Actors; Theatre; Vaudeville

References and further reading
Beckman, Frank J. 1962. "The Vanished Villains: An Exercise in Nostalgia." Unpublished manuscript, Billy Rose Theater Collection, New York Public Library at Lincoln Center.
Browne, Porter Emerson. 1909. "The Mellowdrammer." *Everybody's Magazine* (September): 347–354.
Davis, Owen. 1914. "Why I Quit Writing Melodrama." *American Magazine* (September): 28–31.
———. 1931. *I'd Like to Do It Again.* New York: Farrar and Rinehart.
Gerould, Daniel. 1983. *American Melodrama.* New York: Performing Arts Journal.
Goodman, Jules Eckert. 1908. "The Lure of Melodrama." *Bohemian Magazine* (February): 180–191.
Marble, Scott. 189-. "Daughters of the Poor." Unpublished manuscript, Billy Rose Theater Collection, New York Public Library at Lincoln Center.
Nasaw, David. 1985. *Children of the City: At Work and at Play.* New York: Oxford University Press.
Rosen, Ruth. 1982. *The Lost Sisterhood: Prostitution in America, 1900–1918.* Baltimore: Johns Hopkins University Press.
Sante, Luc. 1991. *Low Life: Lures and Snares of Old New York.* New York: Farrar, Straus and Giroux.
Singer, Ben. 1992. "A New and Urgent Need for Stimuli: Sensational Melodrama and Urban Modernity." Paper presented at the Melodrama Conference, British Film Institute, London.
Taylor, Dwight. 1962. *Blood-and-Thunder.* New York: Atheneum.

Mexican American Boys

Mexican boys in the United States in the 1920s and 1930s existed in a cultural crucible. Whether they were the children of immigrants who journeyed north in the great migration of the 1920s to the agricultural fields or the city of Los Angeles, California, the descendants of New Mexican families dating back to the Spanish and Mexican eras, or the sons of once-independent cattle ranchers whose lands and status had been alienated to Anglos, Mexican boys were being exposed to the American popular culture, education, and system of wage labor. While their

A Mexican American boy, Chamisal, New Mexico, late 1930s (Library of Congress)

parents strained to maintain their and their children's Mexican ways, the modern modes of the Southwest proved attractive. At the same time, however, poverty and discrimination allowed for only paltry participation in consumer culture or educational advancement. In addition, adults in these very diverse Mexican communities of the Southwest sought not to assimilate to American culture or identity but rather to fortify their regional variety of Mexican culture in New Mexico or Texas or to rebuild what they understood to be the traditional ways of the interior of Mexico from which they had migrated to California. Mexican boys living in the United States in the interwar decades thus experienced contrary messages and prescrip-

tions about what they could, would, and should be like.

No other phrase is more central to the ideal form of Mexican family practice than *respeto y honor*. This refers to the respect a father should give his wife and children in return for their honoring him and submitting to his authority, will, and protectiveness. Children are to respect all elders, and the eldest brother must be obeyed and respected to the point that he becomes like a second father. The various Mexican regional cultures all evolved elaborate customs by which that deference was shown. Children, for example, always addressed their elders with the formal *usted*, never the informal *tú*. Although the realities of family life diverged in various degrees from the ideal, the good child was one who conformed to the prescribed social role. The Mexican boy was to learn dutifulness first to father and mother and then to wife and children, the latter accompanied by sovereignty over them. At the same time, he was to learn submission to the church and, if he was landless, to lord or patron. Traditional education, understood as the learning of these norms and conducted under the purview of family and church, provided the socialization of boys.

The 1920s, however, witnessed profound change in the matter of education on both sides of the border. As the postrevolutionary regimes of Mexico sought to replace church schools with secular ones sponsored by the federal government (a policy that sparked the bloody Cristero Revolt of 1927), Mexican children in the United States also encountered the complexities of state-sponsored education. In the north, however, their experience varied from place to place because school districts in the United States exercised local control over education. Consistent in intent but varying in intensity and success, the public schools sought to purge Mexican boys of their putatively inappropriate cultural traits, although not necessarily to replace them with values of American democracy and citizenship.

For example, Stanford professor Lewis M. Terman (1877–1956) argued that the intelligence quotient (IQ) test he promulgated and popularized "told the truth. These boys," he said, "are uneducable beyond the merest rudiments of training. . . . They represent the level of intelligence which is very, very common among Spanish-Indian and Mexican families of the Southwest and also among Negroes. Their dullness seems to be racial, or at least inherent in the family stocks from which they came" (quoted in Gould 1981). Such notions dominated the policies of school districts entrusted with the education of Mexican American children and circumscribed their experiences in American schools. Boys' education was overwhelmingly limited to vocational instruction and the rudiments of arithmetic and the English language.

Certainly, though, the educational experiences of Mexican boys varied widely. In the agricultural *colonias* of California, schooling was at best irregular as families moved from place to place. In settled rural communities and in the urban schools of El Paso, Texas, children found themselves segregated into "Mexican schools," which were underfunded and understaffed. In other urban centers, such as Los Angeles, Mexican boys could find themselves in classrooms in which they were a strong majority or ones in which they mixed with Anglo, Jewish, Japanese, and other immigrant children. School-sponsored programs in Los Angeles did provide inexpensive lunches, which included pasteurized milk, and instructions for parents in hygiene, both of which enhanced children's health. In New Mexico, where descendants of eighteenth- and nineteenth-century settlers were the majority in many counties, Latino boys, usually monolingual in Spanish, attended underfunded schools only for a very few years. In Texas, where insistence on Americanization waxed in the years after World War I, schooling in Mexican-majority counties centered more on instruction in the English language than on substantive subject matter. Ultimately, educators' negative assumptions about Mexican boys' intelligence, tests that were culturally biased against them, and the boys' need to work conspired to produce very high dropout rates, especially in the rural schools. Although some Mexican boys did complete school and learn to read in English, most achieved only a modicum of literacy.

In the agricultural regions of Texas and California, a boy's life in an immigrant Mexican family typically revolved around picking farm crops and travel. As young as five years of age, he learned his skills at his parents' side in the fields, and what he picked contributed to the family's total earnings. This was a boy's life rather unlike the images middle-class Americans associate with childhood, which is ideally a time of play, innocence, and freedom from the drudgery of work. His formal schooling was at best spotty, but his education had to do with learning the requisite skills for officially joining a picking crew at age sixteen.

However, if either or both parents had steady jobs in the city, boys could attend school and from such odd jobs as selling newspapers could earn enough money for their two favorite pastimes, movies and sports. Social work surveys done in the

1920s and 1930s reveal that Mexican children went to the movies once or twice per week. In the early years of the "talkies," Mexican boys liked such actors as James Cagney (the "tough guy"), Tom Mix (the "cowboy"), and Joe E. Brown (the "wise-cracking comedian") and such movies as the famous gangster epic *Scarface* (1932). Although the public schools often had limited success in the Americanization of Mexican boys, such movies introduced them to new modes of appearance and behavior in the urban north as interpreted by Hollywood.

No sport excited the passions of Mexican boys (and men) more than boxing. "Two or three Mexicans have become famous boxers and gotten rich, like Colima, Fuente, and the like," a Los Angeles playground director noted with only slight exaggeration in 1926. "Nearly every Mexican boy has the ambition to be a great boxer. This is the main thing that he thinks about until he gets married and has to go to work digging ditches or working for the railroad" (quoted in Monroy 1999). This affinity for boxing, like the sport itself, is much more complicated than is immediately apparent. Although the winner of the match can celebrate his might, many youthful fighters proved their fortitude in a losing cause by being able to take a punch and by enduring beatings. Boxing taught Mexican boys certain lessons about what it meant to be a man: to associate physical prowess and fortitude (in victory or defeat) with male virtue and character.

Few stories are more interesting than that of baseball and Latin American boys. U.S. mining companies and Marines, sent by the U.S. government to intervene in various Latin American countries, spread the sport to the Dominican Republic, Cuba, Nicaragua, Venezuela, and Mexico. In the late nineteenth century, the Latin American upper middle class saw playing baseball as a way to emulate the cricket-playing English gentry, but by the early twentieth century baseball had become popular among all classes of Mexican boys in the mining camps of southern Arizona and New Mexico and in Los Angeles. Informally, in their schools and in clubs that local businesses sponsored, Mexican boys in the United States rounded the bases and shouted encouragement to one another in Spanish.

It is of no little significance that at the same time Mexican boys became active in such pursuits, the police in urban centers such as Los Angeles began to connect them with criminality. The professionalization of police departments racialized crime. In Los Angeles, for example, police targeted many of the undertakings of Mexican boys for arrest. "Juvenile delinquency" increasingly concerned police and school authorities, though the activities of Mexican male youths differed little from those of other groups. Behaving with general rambunctiousness, drinking alcohol, and loitering caused most of the trouble. Here police presuppositions about Mexican boys that persist to this day and police actions toward the boys created an adversarial relationship that was in large part responsible for the creation of Mexican youth gangs.

The experiences of rural, northern New Mexican boys were very different. Children of "forgotten people," as George I. Sanchez called them in his path-breaking book (1940) of the same name, they lived in depressed communities where the land base continually shrank, public education was dull and unresponsive to boys' needs, and traditional artisanal skills deteriorated. New Deal programs in concert with the Spanish colonial arts movement and inspired by the exciting innovations in postrevolutionary Mexican education associated with the great philosopher and Minister of Education José Vasconcelos (1882–1959) sought to reinvigorate Latino New Mexican life by expanding education and stimulating the production of traditional crafts. The Federal Emergency Relief Administration (May 1933), along with the Civilian Conservation Corps and the Works Progress Administration (WPA), built schools and recreational facilities for Latino youth. By 1939 the WPA had instituted a hot lunch program that delivered one nourishing meal per day to kids who otherwise might have gone hungry. The WPA also initiated other programs to instruct parents in hygiene and nutrition. The National Youth Administration (NYA) gave boys jobs on highway and street improvement projects and instructed them in handicrafts. NYA residence camps took youths out of rural villages to Albuquerque and Las Vegas, New Mexico, where they worked in construction, and Latino NYA workers built hundreds of recreational facilities throughout New Mexico. Boys were exposed to 4-H club work and sports, as well as to folk music, dance, and dramas, and were taught such ancestral arts and crafts as furniture and religious figurine production. Such federal efforts assumed, rightly or wrongly, that boys in New Mexico needed outside intervention to keep them and their families from despondency. Such an attitude inevitably kindled resentment on the part of local adults. The patronizing nature of these programs, their relative effectiveness, and their degree of success are subjects of debate. Nonetheless, these New Deal programs (terminated in 1943) brought relief for many from the poverty, isolation, and monotony of boyhood in rural New Mexico.

One is tempted to position the history of Mexican boys in the United States within the older paradigm of assimilation. But it would be a mistake to conceptualize such a history simply as the process by which Mexican Americans were created. Rather we see here the process of cultural syncretization (*mestizaje* in Spanish) by which a regional or transborder culture was created. In some ways integrated into American culture and politics via Hollywood and the New Deal, in some ways rebuffed by the police who associated being Mexican with criminality, sometimes encouraged to maintain traditional ways in the service of arts and crafts but at other times pressured to deny Mexican ways in favor of Americanization, Mexican boys forged in their barrios and schools, car and sports clubs, pachuco groups and Texas *palomillas* (cliques) a new Mexican way of being on the landscape of the American Southwest.

Douglas Monroy

See also California Missions

References and further reading
Escobar, Edward J. 1999. *Race, Police, and the Making of a Political Identity: Relations between Chicanos and the Los Angeles Police Department, 1900–1945.* Berkeley: University of California Press.
Forrest, Suzanne. 1998. *The Preservation of the Village: New Mexico's Hispanics and the New Deal.* Albuquerque: University of New Mexico Press.
Galarza, Ernesto. 1971. *Barrio Boy.* Notre Dame: University of Notre Dame Press.
Gonzalez, Gilbert G. 1990. *Chicano Education in the Era of Segregation.* Philadelphia: Balch Institute Press.
Gould, Steven J. 1981. *The Mismeasure of Man.* New York: W. W. Norton.
Monroy, Douglas. 1999. *Rebirth: Mexican Los Angeles from the Great Migration to the Great Depression.* Berkeley: University of California Press.

Sanchez, George I. 1940. *Forgotten People: A Study of New Mexicans.* Albuquerque: University of New Mexico Press.

Military Schools

Many military schools were founded in the nineteenth century, usually at the secondary level but also as elementary schools and colleges. In the twentieth century some military schools opened their doors to girls, but the idea persists that military schooling is better suited for educating boys. Today military schools generally fall into two broad categories: private, single-sex and coeducational institutions (both boarding and day) focusing on college preparation and secondary, coeducational public day schools aimed at inner-city children with behavioral problems.

The origin of the military school movement begins with the foundation of the U.S. Military Academy in 1802. Many Americans in the late eighteenth and early nineteenth centuries were impressed by arguments urging the establishment of academies to train engineers and artillerists. Following the establishment of the U.S. Military Academy, a movement to found other military schools spread slowly across the country. This took various forms, causing the foundation of military, state, private, and denominational schools and colleges. After 1825, however, those promoting new military schools shifted the basis of their case. They no longer stressed the need to prepare military men to defend the southern and western states against the Spanish, the British, or the Indians, or the pressing need for more trained engineers. They argued instead that military schooling provided young men with a unique training, preparing them to become citizen-soldiers, not professional soldiers.

The chief advocate of military schooling was Captain Alden Partridge, founder of the American Literary, Scientific and Military Academy at Norwich, Vermont. Partridge's notions concerning the educational value of military training became the basis for the American military school movement of the nineteenth century. From 1860 to 1900, some sixty-five military schools or military departments were established throughout the United States in already existing schools. Partridge assumed, as did his followers, that youth educated in the military fashion would become leaders of the country. At the core of Partridge's thinking was the notion of the citizen-soldier who could perform military service in time of national need. The rationale for promoting military education was increasingly the idea that military training brought out "manly, noble and independent sentiments" of young men (Webb 1958, 186–187). The passage of the Morrill Act of 1866 and the subsequent establishment of military studies in many schools and colleges were a significant victory for Alden Partridge's ideas. His notion of encouraging young men to learn the "arts of war" in order to serve as citizen-soldiers was accepted by the mid-nineteenth century.

Toward the end of that century, however, proponents of military schooling once again shifted rationale. They based their case not merely on the argument that such education provided the nation with potential citizen-soldiers but also on the claim that military schooling ought to play a unique role in shaping the character of the adolescent. This view was a further transformation of perceptions about military schooling, appealing as it did to an age increasingly concerned about the

Four young boys play games in the dormitory during their spare time at the Black Foxe Military academy in Hollywood, California, 1933. (Bettmann/Corbis)

peculiar needs of the adolescent. This movement gained strength when some states and territories actively encouraged military training programs in their common school programs. The most notable of these flourished in California, New Mexico, Massachusetts, and Arizona. Throughout the nineteenth century, military schools and colleges flourished in the South; some were state institutions, such as the Virginia Military Institute and The Citadel in South Carolina.

During the latter part of the nineteenth century the military school movement expanded further with the foundation of private and denominational military schools throughout the country. A number of such institutions developed in the South before and after the Civil War; some thirty military schools were established in Virginia alone between 1840 and 1860. Following the Civil War, Virginia again led the field with twenty military schools. Other southern states accounted for an additional 111 military schools: thirteen in Alabama; twelve in Georgia; nine in Kentucky; eighteen in North Carolina; five in South Carolina;

fourteen in Tennessee and Texas; and from one to three each in Mississippi, Florida, and Arkansas.

This movement also grew in other parts of the United States, with 106 schools founded in New York, New Jersey, Ohio, Pennsylvania, California, Connecticut, Illinois, Massachusetts, New Hampshire, Wisconsin, Utah, Washington, Delaware, Vermont, Indiana, and West Virginia. The Morrill Act of 1866 aided these schools because the bill authorized the War Department to detail active or retired army officers as professors of military science and tactics to secondary schools.

The movement received added support when many religious denominations established schools on the military model. During the second half of the century, the Episcopal Church founded fifteen such schools; the Methodists and Baptists, thirteen schools each; the Roman Catholics, fourteen; the Presbyterians, seven; and various other denominations, including the Quakers, eight. Significantly, the rationale for using military training in these schools was not to prepare students to become soldiers or even to serve as citizen soldiers in case of war. Military education in these schools was essentially tied to character formation. Ancillary to that idea were notions linking military training to the physical health and well-being of adolescent boys.

The link between military schooling and character formation received added impetus from other powerful cultural and social forces in late-nineteenth-century and early-twentieth-century America. During those years many Americans expressed concern over what they perceived as growing softness and lack of discipline among the young, particularly among adolescent boys. Leaders of such

movements as the Boy Scouts and the Young Men's Christian Association (YMCA), for instance, focused on the adolescent boy, concerned that boys might not develop into manly men. There was a growing concern among many educators that modern life somehow threatened the morals, masculinity, and potential adult success of boys. Underlying all this, paradoxically, was fear that adults might also lose control of adolescent boys. Military schools saw themselves as playing a key role in developing the character of American boys. Boys were viewed on the one hand as being potentially wild and unruly, but on the other hand there was growing concern that boys would grow up soft and untested, surrounded by too much female influence. Military schools could remedy that problem; the military would develop a boy's character, curb his wild impulses, and channel them into more constructive lines. Throughout the rest of the twentieth century, military schools would address the problem of character education, but the understanding of that role would change dramatically as the century unfolded.

A decade later, in the midst of the Progressive era, intellectual fashions had changed: no longer was there concern to curb the potential wildness of the boy. Rather, many educators were concerned with the notion of social efficiency—the idea that individuals should "perform all of their functions efficiently and in a manner that would serve the state" (Church and Sedlack 1976, 310). Many military school leaders argued for a basic compatibility between military education and progressive values, specifically by cultivating in boys the spirit of democracy and the ideal of service to the community. Military school publicists also tried to distance themselves from militarism by making the paradoxical claim that the boys' experience of military life might give them "some small conception of what the horrors of war might be" (Gignilliat 1916, 81–82).

In the 1930s intellectual fashions had once again changed: parents and teachers grew concerned with developing the individuality of each child while not neglecting the cultivation of his social responsibility to the larger group. Many military schools offered their patrons an amalgam of the military, educational psychology, and the testing movement popular in that period as a means to develop a boy's individuality. The latest techniques of educational psychology were, in effect, wedded with drill to form the character of the adolescent. For example, upon entering Culver Military Academy, "boys were given elaborate tests covering every facet of their character and intelligence. They were rated in scholastic aptitude, I.Q., and personality traits, such as self-sufficiency, dominance and introspection. This data was interpreted by counselors trained in the latest techniques of educational psychology who used the military framework to develop the individuality of the cadet to its fullest" (Davies 1983, 281).

In the mid-1940s, following the war, the military came to be valued for its ability to produce leaders in business and the professions. Stress was placed in many military schools upon developing the skills necessary in becoming a business or professional leader. Military schools prided themselves in teaching boys the skills of leadership, namely, "the process of taking control in various types of situations" (McKinney n.d., 7). Leadership was viewed, somehow, as being cultivated independently from the other moral qualities that schools sought to instill in boys, such as courage, independence, trustworthiness, a sense of honor, fair play, and school spirit.

In the 1950s and intensifying in the 1960s and the 1970s, public perceptions of both the military and military schooling changed. Protests against the Vietnam War combined with the antiestablishment feeling of the late 1960s and early 1970s to put advocates of military schools on the defensive. Doubts about the value of the military arose even in military schools. What had once been regarded as a key in the development of maturity in the adolescent—the military—was often viewed as retarding it, taking time away from more valuable pursuits that developed the mind and spirit of the boy.

The military increasingly came to be viewed by the general public as too inhibiting and too rigid to produce the bright, innovative leaders society needed. In the late twentieth century, it was believed, access to the new elite status depended upon knowledge and expertise. It was the classroom, not the drill field, that held the key to both individual success and the social good.

Military schools went into a period of decline in the 1970s. In 1926 the *Handbook of Private Schools* listed eighty military schools. By 1966 only thirty remained. By 1976 the number of military schools remained at the same level, but enrollment in many of these schools had dropped alarmingly. The ferocious antimilitary feeling on the part of the public and especially the young slowly faded. Public perception of the military became more positive in the 1980s and 1990s, especially following the Gulf War, but this rise in the fortunes of the military was not accompanied by a similar change in public attitudes toward military schooling. Military schools continued to be perceived as on the fringes of American education. Many schools either closed their doors, like Staunton Military Academy in Virginia, or rebuilt themselves as civilian institutions, like the Harvard School in California, formerly known as the Harvard Military School. In 2000 there were thirty-two boarding military prep schools, five military day schools, and two elementary schools with "a military component."

More recently, some urban public school systems have turned to military schools as the organizing theme of new schools. The Chicago Public Schools recently opened a junior reserve officer training corps (JROTC) school, the Chicago Military Academy, Bronzeville. The school is located in an armory in a historic African American community in the city. Although this was Chicago's first public military high school, it was not the first such school in the nation. Franklin Military Academy had previously opened its doors in 1980 in Richmond, Virginia. A Naval ROTC High School in St. Louis also predates Bronzeville. The opening of schools like these may indicate that military schooling is still viewed by some educators as filling a vital need in the education of young people. A common theme among teachers at schools like Bronzeville is this sentiment: "Students want structure and discipline. We give them that" ("Special Report" 2000, 2). If this movement continues it will be yet another reformulation of the special ability of military schools to address the character formation of American youth.

One of the most common, if problematic, icons in American popular culture is the idea that military schools are places that deal successfully with unruly boys. Writers and filmmakers have often used military schools to illustrate the best and the worst aspects of the human psyche. Films in this genre run from the dark look at military schooling in *Taps* (1981) to the irreverent but oddly positive portrayal of the military in *Major Payne* (1995). An old cliché further illustrates the problematic character of military schooling: a local judge hectors a defiant and unrepentant boy standing before his bench: "Son, you have a choice—go to Nonesuch Military Academy or go to reform school." These stereotypical ideas linking military schools with troubled boys continue to plague such institutions to the present day. A less favorable image of military schools developed as strict military-type boot camps were established for drug rehabilitation. Such programs were touted as successful in the 1990s but have waned in popularity because their results have not been shown to last.

In the twenty-first century, most military schools see themselves as institutions that first and foremost prepare their students for college. The military is viewed as playing a separate but significant role in developing leadership skills and in shaping the character of the students. There is evidence of a revival of interest in what was once the central mission of military schools—forming the character of moral citizens and leaders of a democracy, not addressing the behavioral needs of troubled adolescents. Some institutions like Culver Military Academy and its sister institution, Culver Girls Academy, have placed character education and the cultivation of character back again at the center of their mission. The two schools share common academic and athletic facilities while maintaining separate leadership programs for young men and women. The school's mission statement boldly proclaims that the institution "educates its students for leadership and responsible citizenship in society by developing and nurturing the whole individual—mind, spirit and body—through an integrated curriculum that emphasizes the cultivation of character" ("School Goals" 2000). Central to the development of character is education "in the classical virtues of wisdom, courage, moderation and justice" ("School Goals" 2000). If Culver and other military schools are successful in placing leadership development and character formation on a par with college preparation, this may breathe new life into the military school movement.

It remains to be seen whether military schools will survive this century. Military schooling has its avid proponents, but the movement remains on the fringe of education in this country. Paradoxically, the success of the military in regaining its positive image with the public may not be helpful for military schools. The military is viewed in America as a professional and specialized force—not as a system to be used to develop the character of mainstream Americans. Ironically, the opening of schools in inner-city urban areas may reinforce a double stereotype: that military schooling is for those adolescents with behavioral needs—not ordinary children with ordinary needs—and that inner-city children are different from ordinary children with ordinary needs. To survive and thrive in the twenty-first century, military schools will have to market themselves as institutions that prepare any young person to be a moral citizen and active leader.

Richard G. Davies

References and further reading
Avery, Gillian. 1975. *Childhood's Pattern: A Study of Heroes and Heroines of Children's Fiction, 1750–1950.* London: Hodder and Stoughton.

Baird, Leonard L. 1977. *The Schools: A Profile of Prestigious Independent Schools.* Lexington, MA: D. C. Heath.
Church, Robert, and Michael W. Sedlack. 1976. *Education in the United States: An Interpretive History.* New York: Free Press.
Cunliffe, Marcus. 1968. *Soldiers and Civilians: The Martial Spirit in America, 1775–1865.* Boston: Little, Brown.
Davies, Richard G. 1983. "Of Arms and the Boy: A History of Culver Military Academy, 1894–1945." Ph.D. diss., School of Education, Indiana University.
Ekrich, Arthur A. 1956. *The Civilian and the Military.* New York: Oxford University Press.
Gignilliat, Leigh R. 1916. *Arms and the Boy: Military Training in Schools.* Indianapolis: Bobbs-Merrill.
Handbook of Private Schools, The. 1926. 17th ed. Boston: Porter Sargent.
Kett, Joseph. 1977. *Rites of Passage: Adolescence in America 1790 to the Present.* New York: Basic Books.
Kraushaar, Otto. 1972. *American Nonpublic Schools: Patterns of Diversity.* Baltimore: Johns Hopkins University.
Macleod, David I. 1983. *Building Character in the American Boy: The Boy Scouts, YMCA and Their Forerunners.* Madison: University of Wisconsin Press.
McKinney, C. F. N.d. "A Discussion of Leadership." Culver Military Academy, 7.
Napier, John Hawkins III, ed. 1989. "Military Schools." In *Encyclopedia of Southern Culture.* Vol. 1, *Agriculture—Environment.* New York: Anchor Books/Doubleday.
"School Goals: Draft." 2000. Culver Academies, October 27.
"Special Report." 2000. Available online at http://www.ausa.org/ausnews/items/chicagojan00.htm (accessed October 20).
Webb, Lester Austin. 1958. "The Origins of Military Schools in the United States Founded in the Nineteenth Century." Ph.D. diss., School of Education, University of North Carolina.

Money
See Allowances

Mothers

Throughout American history, a boy's relationship with his mother has been central to his physical, social, and emotional development. However, what it means to mother a boy has changed significantly over time. In the seventeenth and eighteenth centuries, mothers cared for boys when young, but preparing a boy for manhood was considered the father's responsibility. In the nineteenth century, as a result of political and economic changes, good mothering became key to preparing a boy to succeed; in turn, a boy was the key to his mother's future happiness. In the twentieth century, the mother-son relationship took on new, often negative overtones as developments in psychology and sociology increasingly blamed the mother for whatever might trouble the son.

During the American colonial era (1607–1776), the family home was also the location of the family business, and both parents engaged in hands-on child-rearing. However, this society was patriarchal, believing that men, who were assumed to be stronger morally as well as physically, should be dominant. A colonial mother's control over her children, especially her boys, was thus limited. A mother was responsible for caring for the children from their birth through the first five years. Busy colonial mothers integrated child care into their daily work routines. Mothers were also expected to teach their children the fundamentals of reading and writing, assuming they were themselves literate. After about age five, however, girls and boys followed different paths to adulthood. Girls usually remained under the tutelage of their mothers so that they might master the often complicated skills of housewifery and child care essential to successful woman-

hood. Boys, however, would be expected to assume more varied responsibilities as adult men. They were thus more likely than their sisters to receive an education if the family could afford it. But like their sisters, boys learned to be adults mainly by following the example of their appropriate parental role model. To learn to be a man in colonial America, boys looked to their fathers. A farmer's son learned to farm by working alongside his father in the fields and barns; a merchant's son learned the business by clerking in his father's store. Since manhood often demanded public service, boys also learned about politics by listening to and observing older men. Thus, in colonial America, it was the father, not the mother, who played the more prominent role in preparing boys for adulthood. Although colonial American mothers were often well loved and respected by their children, they were not expected to be able to provide much guidance to their adult sons.

By the end of the eighteenth century, as Americans fought for and gained independence, they sought to ensure that the citizens of the new United States would prove worthy of the unprecedented degree of political participation expected of most adult white men. To sustain their democratic revolution, American men would have to be not just citizens but *virtuous* citizens, who put the interests of the nation ahead of their own, private concerns. With so much at stake, it was vital that boys, as future U.S. citizens, be brought up to understand their moral duty. At the same time, a new theory of epistemology—a way of understanding how humans learn—associated with British philosopher John Locke (1632–1704) became popular. Rejecting religious arguments that humans were born with their moral characters already formed, Locke compared the human mind instead to a tabula rasa (Latin for "blank slate"). All of life's experiences, but especially the lessons learned in early childhood, wrote upon the blank slate to create an individual's character. And because mothers spent the most time with the very young, their role acquired new status. By the late eighteenth and early nineteenth centuries, Americans increasingly insisted that a boy's mother, rather than his father, held the key to his character and thus, ultimately, to the character of the new nation. Through a good mother's efforts, the future of the United States as a republic of virtuous citizens might be secured.

Further supporting this new appreciation of mothers were far-reaching economic changes. By the early nineteenth century, the American economy was rapidly moving away from a focus upon producing for subsistence or local trade in favor of producing for regional, national, and international markets. In addition, westward migration dramatically expanded the size of the country, and the growth of trade and the beginnings of industrialization spurred the rise of cities. Known collectively as the "market revolution," these changes generated unprecedented economic opportunities. But the market revolution also affected relations within the family with the development of a new, urban middle class. This group differed from earlier generations because home and work no longer overlapped. Instead, middle-class men left the house to go to work during the day, while middle-class women remained at home with the children.

American mothers replaced fathers as the parent in charge of a middle-class boy's development at a time when preparing for adulthood became more de-

A Native American mother with her baby boy, Winnebago, Wisconsin, early twentieth century (Library of Congress)

manding than ever. The opportunities unleashed by the market revolution held out the promise of significant upward mobility, but only to those who were equipped to take advantage of them. Anxious to prepare their sons to compete in the new market economy, middle-class families employed a number of strategies to benefit their children. Husbands and wives increasingly used birth control in order to concentrate the family's resources on fewer children. With their energies now focused on being good mothers, middle-class women formed maternal associations to learn effective parenting techniques from more experienced mothers

An African American mother picks up her son at a day care center. (Shirley Zeiberg)

and sought expert advice from books, such as *The Mother at Home*, which was a best-seller in the 1830s. These mothers also insisted that their daughters be well educated, leading to a surge in schools for middle-class girls and young women. Mothers also tried to steel their sons to resist the inevitable temptations of adulthood by overseeing their moral education at home and in church. Indeed, where colonial Americans had assumed that men had greater moral strength than women, nineteenth-century Americans reversed this: a good mother was now the family's conscience and the exemplar of morality. Thus trained by his mother, a middle-class boy might take advantage of the opportunities newly available to him. American newspapers, magazines, ser-

mons, political speeches, and even jokes all sent the same message: a boy's best friend and his best hope for a promising future was his mother.

But if boys had good reason to befriend their mothers, mothers also became increasingly dependent upon their sons. The developing market economy had strained traditional social welfare practices to the breaking point. This was especially problematic for women, who were assumed to be legally and economically dependent upon others, usually a husband. A woman whose husband did not or could not support her faced a future of extreme poverty. A good mother, however, was more fortunate, for she had invested in her son. A boy whose mother had sacrificed for his benefit was expected to provide for her comfort in old age. Thus in the nineteenth century the nature of the mother-son relationship changed greatly. Mothers now played a starring role in their sons' lives by preparing them to seize the opportunities of manhood. In return, boys who had benefited from a lifetime of maternal care were expected to support their aging mothers.

To be sure, not all boys and their mothers experienced these new roles and expectations. Most Americans were still farmers, where home and work space were one and the same; here, traditional patterns continued. Social class also influenced family practice. Among elite families it was fashionable to send boys to boarding school during their formative years. In many poor families the struggle to survive was paramount, and boys were expected to contribute to the family economy from an early age. Race was also a critical factor. Mothers held in slavery faced perhaps the greatest challenges in preparing their sons for adulthood. When slave mothers were forcibly separated from their children, other women stepped in to act as surrogates, expanding the definition of mother beyond a blood tie. Others sought to teach their children how to survive in an abusive system, even while encouraging their growth as individuals. For these groups, the middle-class ideal did not describe their reality. Nevertheless, the notion of the at-home mother who focused on her children was widely embraced. For example, where the law had once dictated that fathers were the proper guardians of children, judges increasingly ruled in favor of mothers, particularly when young children were involved. By the end of the century, the good mother had become a cultural ideal.

But if the nineteenth century at least paid lip service to honoring mothers, the twentieth century proved more suspicious. Emerging from the shadow of the good mother was her evil twin, the bad mother. Always implicit in the celebration of mothers—after all, if a good mother is responsible for her son's success, a bad mother must be held responsible for her son's failure—the bad mother began to move toward center stage. Indeed, what previous generations of Americans had seen as self-sacrificing maternal devotion, a new, more psychologically oriented generation viewed as "overprotective" and "stifling." Especially after World War II, psychologists, sociologists, social workers, and guidance counselors asserted their professional authority in the field of childrearing. Often antagonistic toward the traditional authority of mothers, these groups singled out mothers as the source of family troubles. The danger was particularly acute for boys, whose masculinity seemed to be at stake. Daughters

would become women by modeling their behavior after their mothers, but sons must separate psychologically from the mother in order to achieve manhood. If a mother impeded this separation by being overly involved in her son's life, psychologists argued, she endangered his masculinity and might even "make" him homosexual. However, if a mother was too detached from her son, psychologists accused her of endangering his emotional development as well. Mothers even took the blame for bad fathers: whether he was too authoritarian or too passive, a man's failure as a parent was usually traced back to his wife.

By the late twentieth century, American attitudes toward mothers constituted a series of no-win situations. If a mother worked outside the home, some considered her to be a bad mother who was insufficiently invested in her children. If a mother did not work outside the home, others considered her to be a bad mother who was overly invested in her children. The twentieth-century suspicion cast on mothers, especially the mothers of sons, hit a low point in the 1980s and 1990s. Demands for welfare reform blamed poor single mothers, particularly if they were women of color, for causing urban crime by failing to provide positive male role models for their sons. Female-headed families, which had once been poor but respectable, were now considered inherently pathological and the mothers incapable of guiding their sons into manhood.

Carolyn J. Lawes

See also Fathers; Siblings

References and further reading
Coontz, Stephanie. 1988. *The Social Origins of Private Life: A History of American Families, 1600–1900.* New York: Verso.

Grossberg, Michael. 1985. *Governing the Hearth: Law and the Family in Nineteenth-Century America*. Chapel Hill: University of North Carolina Press.

Kerber, Linda K. 1980. *Women of the Republic: Intellect and Ideology in Revolutionary America*. Chapel Hill: University of North Carolina Press.

Ladd-Taylor, Molly, and Lauri Umanski, eds. 1998. *"Bad" Mothers: The Politics of Blame in Twentieth-Century America*. New York: New York University Press.

Lawes, Carolyn J. "Capitalizing on Mother: John S. C. Abbott and Self-Interested Motherhood." *Proceedings of the American Antiquarian Society* 108, pt. 2: 343–395.

Ryan, Mary P. 1981. *Cradle of the Middle Class: The Family in Oneida County, New York, 1790–1865*. New York: Cambridge University Press.

———. 1982. *The Empire of the Mother: Americans Writing about Domesticity, 1830 to 1860*. New York: Institute for Research in History and Naworth Press.

Movies
See Films

Muscular Christianity

As a response to perceptions of both immorality and escalating effeminacy among American boys, late-nineteenth- and early-twentieth-century American Protestants embarked on an ambitious project to enhance the masculine tenor of Christianity. Drawing on British literary and organizational precedents, the movement for muscular Christianity represented an attempt to articulate and demonstrate the essential compatibility between Christian faith and virile, masculine expression. Advocates of this mission were convinced that American churches, dominated by female presence, were equally dominated by a feminine ethos incommensurate with boys' na-

ture. In such a religious milieu, they reasoned, boys would either reject religious influence, thus creating an opening for immorality, or embrace religion and risk an enfeebled transition from boyhood to manhood. Only a muscular Christianity could attract boys to the religious life, prepare them for manly service, and channel boys' instincts in positive ways. Rejecting the cultural identification of religion with the feminine private sphere and ideals of passive piety and self-restraint, self-proclaimed muscular Christians constructed a subculture that emphasized the athletic, militant, and businesslike components of Christianity to reflect the needs and interests of men and boys. The development of such a faith, rooted in the overarching model of the "masculine Christ," was far more than a simple attempt to redress gender imbalances in the institutional church. Through such organizations as the Young Men's Christian Association (YMCA), United Boys' Brigades of America, Men and Religion Forward bands, and a host of medieval clubs, proponents of muscular Christianity sought to provide for the efficient masculine socialization of American boys within the safe confines of the Christian faith.

Although the predominance of females in Protestant churches had been a consistent demographic pattern since the 1660s, there was a growing sense of urgency regarding these trends by the turn of the twentieth century. Between 1880 and 1920, religious leaders, educators, and social critics spoke of a pervasive "boy problem" in American society. On the one hand, many were troubled by the perceived delinquency of the American boy. Anchored by recapitulation theories of boy development suggesting that young males repeated in their own biological maturation process the history of the human race, many of those who worked with boys were convinced that the male instincts of savagery, wanderlust, and gang spirit might lead boys to inevitable immorality. If natural social processes and institutions were unable to channel inherited impulses in socially fruitful ways, they argued, boys would continually be perched on the edge of a biologically engendered moral precipice. Coupled with statistics delineating the growing number of male adolescents (particularly working-class and immigrant youth) committed to reform schools and juvenile detention centers, public concern was piqued. The *Reader's Guide to Periodical Literature*, which listed only thirteen articles on boyhood juvenile delinquency in the last decade of the nineteenth century, included more than 200 such citations in this field between 1900 and 1910. Although boys' instincts could be directed for both good and evil, the writers of these articles contended, the failure of educational and religious institutions to provide a necessary outlet for boys' nature meant that these dangerous proclivities would be exercised on the "school of the street."

On the other hand, social critics also used alarmist rhetoric to complain about the improper masculine socialization of American boys. If many were concerned with the inappropriate expression of boyhood instincts, many others were equally disturbed by the apparent blunting of these instincts altogether. Whether couched in the language of "degeneracy," "effeminacy," "overcivilization," or "overrefinement," the burden of this critique was unchanging. Because of pervasive social changes and institutional failures, boys were failing to develop the robust, masculine, self-assertive forms of faith and moral goodness that characterized true manhood. Directed chiefly at the urban middle and upper classes, the condemnation of boyhood flaccidity was rooted in a sense that the natural cultural dynamics reinforcing masculine development were experiencing comprehensive decline. The oft-cited closing of the American frontier had supposedly blunted the self-assertive wanderlust impulse, diminishing the need for bodily strength and courage while generating a sense of enervating confinement. More important, shifting economic realities in the fin-de-siècle United States complicated the development of masculine independence while also positioning boys within increasingly feminine settings.

This concern certainly included the lack of physical exertion awaiting boys in sedentary, white-collar professions, but the critique was more inclusive. In a broader sense, men were losing the masculine initiative and independence that had blossomed under the rubric of entrepreneurial capitalism. Corporate capitalism, by contrast, seemed to constrain manly self-assertion within webs of corporate bureaucratic norms. This new economic paradigm valued not the innovative entrepreneur but rather the other-directed team player who would fulfill his proper role in the larger corporate structure. With fewer men either owning their own farms and small businesses or possessing firsthand contact with the products of their labor, the necessary perception of individual potency was greatly curtailed. When combined with the rise of the "new woman," a highly educated competitor in the white-collar world, and the growing presence of muscular immigrants, these economic trends presaged a general demise of the male middle class. For boys, these trends meant that proper masculine development would require formal and purposeful activity in other domains.

In the midst of this economic transition, the home, the locus of the boys' upbringing, was increasingly separated from the world of manly exertion. Fathers were physically absent from the home, leaving mothers with the dubious task of promoting masculine socialization. In addition, as public and private spheres were progressively separated, the private, feminine, and consumption-oriented values of the home were contrasted with the public, assertive, and production-oriented values of the work world. Boys growing up within the home were therefore trained within an environment increasingly defined as "feminine" in nature. Many were hopeful that the public school could bridge the gap between the home and the world of work for the boy. It soon became clear, however, that the school was itself a primary component of the problem. Schools were dominated by feminine influence, both in personnel and in the style and content of teaching and learning. Female teachers constituted 59 percent of all teachers in 1870, but that number had escalated to 86 percent by 1920. Male teachers were typically described as weak and effeminate as well, members of a profession that allowed them to avoid the more demanding exigencies of the public sphere. In addition, the "bookish" curriculum and passive learning styles characteristic of schools were deemed incommensurate with the active, assertive nature of boys. As a variety of economic factors began to direct more and more boys into the high schools, social critics were clear in asserting that the youth were moving from the masculine to the feminine sphere during the most critical phase of male socialization—adolescence.

Yet despite these varied laments, it was the church that received unequivocal criticism with regard to the problem. A number of experts on boys and religious leaders remarked that the church was losing boys because of its inability to appeal to boyhood proclivities. Effeminate clergy, linked to women by virtue of their profession, were deemed unworthy to serve as heroic examples for growing boys. Like the public school, Sunday schools suffered from the feminine influence of teachers and passive book learning. In light of these factors, it was not surprising to educators and youth leaders that male Sunday school attendance dropped precipitously as boys moved into their adolescent years. Yet because adolescence was increasingly designated as the ideal incubation period for boyhood conversion experiences, these statistics were of major import. Blame was placed squarely on the program of the Sunday school itself. Although boys were "naturally religious," the religion of boyhood, characterized by practical, businesslike, and heroic fervor, was wholly absent from these gatherings. Whether the perception was correct or not, many boys seemed to feel that the development of Christian faith was a threat to masculine development. It was this perception that muscular Christians were out to disprove.

Of course, sponsors of muscular Christianity boldly proclaimed that institutional commitment to masculine forms of Christian expression would solve both aspects of the problem simultaneously, protecting boys from vice by channeling virile instincts and preparing boys for masculine service to society. Muscular Christians noted repeatedly that their recommendations were linked closely to the rediscovery of the "manly Christ," a worthy exemplar for boys to follow. Following the lead of G. Stanley Hall, who spoke vehemently against typical written and pictorial representations of Christ, muscular Christians rejected the emphasis on the passive, peaceful, and otherworldly Jesus of Sunday school lore. By contrast, they pointed out that the Jesus described in the Bible was a muscular carpenter with a strong physique, honed through his rugged and nomadic lifestyle. Far from a monolithic "prince of peace," Jesus fought courageously for personal and social righteousness against the forces of evil. Muscular Christians frequently suggested that Jesus possessed a strong business mind, training men to carry out a successful mission through his powerful leadership skills and personal magnetism. By 1925, it was therefore not unusual to see Bruce Barton, in *The Man Nobody Knows*, speak of Jesus as a burly carpenter who was alluring to women and a popular dinner guest, possessing a keen business and organizational acumen. A near-perfect embodiment of the Rooseveltian "strenuous life," Jesus was a model boys could emulate.

Following this example, muscular Christians urged church leaders to adopt a "Boy Scout model" for the Sunday school, providing virile male leaders, a more practical orientation, and regimented appeals to commitment through gang loyalty and oaths of allegiance to Christian ideals. Yet even though the attempt was made to transform the church and Sunday school along these lines, the ideals of muscular Christianity were perhaps most efficiently diffused through a proliferation of Christian youth organizations for boys. In their own unique ways, each of these club-based associations sought to encourage the formation of a masculine Christianity among growing boys. The YMCA, which by the late nineteenth century was growing increasingly interested in the urban middle classes, concentrated on the athletic elements of muscular faith, championing the manly character-building force of competitive sports. Paramilitary organizations like the United Boys' Brigades of America, imported to the United States in 1894, attempted to utilize the military proclivities of boys for the development of a muscular Christianity. In addition, the recrudescence of medieval boys' clubs revealed the vigilant antimodernism characteristic of these boys' organizations. Anchored in the belief that boys were recapitulating the medieval spirit of hero worship and chivalry, the stated goals of the Knights of King Arthur and other similar clubs reflected a desire for manly expression, the emulation of masculine heroes, and a return to chivalry and noblesse oblige. The Men and Religion Forward movement of 1911–1912, though brief in duration, maintained a youth division that emphasized boys' future role in recapturing vigorous male leadership in organized Christianity.

Yet despite these differences in the focus of manly exertion, many common features characterized all the groups influenced by muscular Christian ideals. All were committed to character development as a central theme, anchored in practical deeds rather than pious discussion. The emphasis on service was pervasive, enlisting boys in campaigns for purposeful change in society. Reacting to urban overrefinement and "spectatoritis," participatory outdoor activities were commonplace, and camping became a significant staple of club life. Lusty hymn singing remained a critical component of religious expression, and yet the hymn books changed dramatically to reflect muscular themes. Both in the revised YMCA hymnbooks and in other popular alternatives such as *Manly Songs for Christian Men* (1910), tunes that emphasized active and heroic service for the "manly man of Galilee" were the norm. Focused less on heaven and more on practical and martial ideals of kingdom building, popular hymns served as an important means of reinforcing muscular Christian ideals for "manly men." Perceiving their clubs as healthy and morally invigorating expressions of the gang impulse, such agencies provided an important means of Christian socialization for American boys at this time. Here was a means of ensuring that boys' instincts would be expressed in positive ways under direct adult supervision. In this way, leaders could guarantee for the future that Christianity would be manly and that manliness would be expressed in Christian ways.

Interestingly, many educators and youth workers argued that muscular Christianity was ultimately a means to save both the boy and the worker who focused on him. For men in the white-collar world, working with boys in the YMCA or serving as scoutmaster or brigade leader was a pathway to the masculine expression that was no longer provided by the world of work. For pastors and religious leaders, boys' work was a means of combating the crippling effeminacy of their profession. Cramped within a lifestyle that sponsored enfeebled passivity and female companionship, this work would therapeutically restore a sense of the heroic potency of the Christian life. Even though the purpose of the movement for boys was always linked to the salvation and masculine socialization of the boy, experts also hoped

that boys would be the salvation of "softened" men.

By the early 1920s, both the perceived urgency of the boy problem and the plea for a masculine Christianity for boys had begun to wane. Although between 1880 and 1920 many leaders spoke of the importance of boys' instincts in shaping their behavioral proclivities, books and articles printed after 1920 paid surprisingly little attention, even in retrospect, to this previously dominant paradigm. Replacing this early-twentieth-century consensus was a proportionately greater emphasis on cultural influence over and above natural instinct, of nurture over inherited nature. In addition, the 1920s introduced a whole new array of "youth" issues, many of which revealed equal concern for girls and young women. By this time, the fear that female students were becoming "male" in both appearance and attitude seemed to quell the cries for heightened masculinity among American boys. Yet between 1880 and 1920, muscular Christianity represented a significant attempt to help boys become both men and Christians in a society where such a combination seemed increasingly tenuous.

David Setran

See also Boy Scouts; Camping; Parachurch Ministry; Sunday Schools; Young Men's Christian Association

References and further reading

Barton, Bruce. 1925. *The Man Nobody Knows: A Discovery of the Real Jesus.* Indianapolis: Bobbs-Merrill.
Bederman, Gail. 1989. "'The Women Have Had Charge of the Church Work Long Enough': The Men and Religion Forward Movement of 1911–1912 and the Masculinization of Middle-Class Protestantism." *American Quarterly* 41, no. 3 (September): 432–465.

Bendroth, Margaret Lamberts. 1997. "Men, Masculinity, and Urban Revivalism: J. Wilbur Chapman's Boston Crusade." *Journal of Presbyterian History* 75, no. 4 (Winter): 235–246.

Case, Carl. 1906. *The Masculine in Religion.* Philadelphia: American Baptist Publishing Society.

Fiske, George W. 1912. *Boy Life and Self-Government.* New York: Association Press.

Forbush, William B. 1907. *The Boy Problem.* 3d ed. Boston: Pilgrim Press.

Hall, Donald E., ed. 1994. *Muscular Christianity: Embodying the Victorian Age.* Cambridge, UK: Cambridge University Press.

Hoben, Allan. 1913. *The Minister and the Boy: A Handbook for Churchmen Engaged in Boys' Work.* Chicago: University of Chicago Press.

Kett, Joseph. 1977. *Rites of Passage: Adolescence in America, 1790 to the Present.* New York: Basic Books.

Lears, T. J. Jackson. 1981. *No Place of Grace: Anti-Modernism and the Transformation of American Culture, 1880–1920.* New York: Pantheon Books.

Macleod, David I. 1983. *Building Character in the American Boy: The Boy Scouts, YMCA, and Their Forerunners.* Madison: University of Wisconsin Press.

Mangan, J. A., and James Walvin, eds. 1987. *Manliness and Morality: Middle Class Masculinity in Britain and America, 1800–1940.* New York: St. Martin's Press.

Merrill, Liliburn. 1908. *Winning the Boy.* New York: Fleming H. Revell.

Putney, Clifford W. 1995. "Muscular Christianity: The Strenuous Mood in American Protestantism, 1880–1920." Ph.D. diss., Brandeis University.

Music

For many Americans, the standard image of the musical boy is that of the sissified dandy, the kind of boy who trundles his violin to school, fastidiously protects his hands from work or dirt, and is beaten and robbed of his lunch money by his rougher fellows. Music, particularly the highbrow music of piano instructors and dancing masters, is not frequently associated with a healthy boyhood. Popular music is another story. From the first European settlements to the present, popular music has surrounded the American boy. It has served a dual role in his life, simultaneously functional and idiosyncratic, providing him with his first introduction to official culture along with a way of expressing unofficial yearnings. For every generation of American boys, popular music may be seen as a socializing agent and a vehicle for rebellion, a mode of expression that rigidifies lines of class, race, and gender while allowing for their temporary erasure.

Despite the tendency for many historians to address them as "puritanical" in values, Anglo-Americans of the early colonial period were surrounded by popular music. The dominant context for the European conquest of America was Elizabethan England, its models for boyhood and manhood more aligned with Shakespeare's Falstaff and Sir Toby Belch than with the comparatively dour Winthrops, Bradfords, and Mathers. For these Elizabethan types who settled in colonial British America, singing and dancing were common practices, introduced to young boys as traditional, albeit morally troublesome, holiday and leisure pursuits. Thus, although colonial Americans made few or no distinctions between songs for adults and music for children, their music included much youthful and boyish energy, from Scots-Irish fiddle tunes to springtime revels, alehouse "merriments," and sea chanteys picked up by young sailors from various regions of the Atlantic world.

Even the early religious dissidents and separatists who may rightly be called

A clarinet lesson (Shirley Zeiberg)

Puritans had their share of desires expressed through music. Officially sanctioned Puritan music was both popular and functional, centering on the communal singing of psalms and hymns frequently set to popular tunes. These soon spread throughout the colonies. As with Spanish mission hymns found in locales to the south and west, the purpose of these songs was to introduce neophytes—children as well as Native Americans and African Americans—to the tenets of Christian faith. Young boys would repeat lined-out psalms from the *Bay Psalm Book* (1640) in the seventeenth century, and a host of hymns like "Northfield," "Amazing Grace," and "Lamentation over Boston" written by Isaac Watts, John Newton, and William Billings during the revolutionary period. At the same time, younger Americans continued to have easy access to secular songs and dances.

For Puritans and non-Puritans alike, much of this music raised problems. Some early Americans felt that all secular music provided young people with an "incitement to adultery," whereas others held that some examples—particularly country dances "for as many as will" as opposed to "mixed" or couple dances—were harmless amusements. Along with the *Bay Psalm Book,* John Playford's *The English Dancing-Master* (1650) remained one of the most popular books in the United States well into the nineteenth century. Despite the ubiquity of these songs, many Americans agreed that the singing of "corrupt songs" or music arising from "gross disorderly carriage" was out-of-bounds for younger boys. Still, the records of even the most staunchly Puritan regions are filled with young people—the preponderance of whom seem to have been adolescent boys and young men—who were charged with "unseasonable night meetings." A typical case involved a youthful apprentice brought before the New Haven Colony Court in 1662. Accused of repeatedly sneaking away from his master, the boy confessed, as the court recorder put it, "'that his maine ground of goeing away was, that he might goe where he might have more liberty, for one from Connecticut told him if he lived there he might live merrily & sing & daunce &c'" (Dexter 1919, 23–25).

By the time of the American Revolution, this quest for liberty and its resultant conflict with social strictures would become a characteristic of Americans. Through this period and into the era of the early republic, admonitions against popular music as a corridor for desires remained but were increasingly muted with the rise of a more liberal and market-oriented society. As the three young brothers who later formed the wildly popular Hutchinson Family Singers recalled, even in the 1830s their father, once a renowned fiddler in their New Hampshire village, would smash his instrument as the devil's tool during a Baptist revival. Thus the brothers were forced to buy violins on the sly, practicing their chords and fingering while hiding behind a large rock on the family farm. Elsewhere, ministers and pamphleteers railed against popular tunes and defended hymnody, one typical example from 1833 declaring: "Many a young man has commenced his downward course by yielding to the influence of festive songs and sportive glees" (Lucas 1833).

Still, the number of these warnings, combined with their shrillness, suggests that they were fighting a lost cause. The turning of the nineteenth century witnessed the development of a truly popular American music, along with increasingly clear distinctions between adult and children's songs. Disconnected from their original meanings and some with frequently bawdy lyrics cleaned up or rewritten entirely, traditional English popular tunes such as "Three Blind Mice," "John Barleycorn," and "A Frog He Would a-Wooing Go" became children's songs. Others originated as broadside ballads yet quickly became integrated into the widening education system of the Jacksonian and antebellum period, where they were included as didactic exercises in early public school readers. Many of these seem to have been expressly designed to initiate young boys into official ideals of patriotism and national or regional identity. Thus boys of the period learned and sang endless classroom versions of "Yankee Doodle," "America, Commerce, and Freedom," "The Jolly Tar," and "The Indian's Lament," learning that Yankees were more liberal and entrepreneurial in values than their stiffly aristocratic English ancestors, that hard work was ennobling and healthful, and that the new nation's many Native American peoples were noble but doomed to an apparently "natural" extinction. If these songs were ardently didactic in content, by the 1830s and 1840s another more rebellious music had captured the attention of many American boys. It was blackface minstrelsy.

Blackface minstrelsy may be defined as white singers and actors, almost always young men, performing what they and their audiences perceived as authentic yet comical and exaggerated versions of African American song, dance, and speech. Although its origins may be traced to the eighteenth century, blackface received its modern form during the democratic ferment of the Jacksonian era. During this period, a growing host of young men began performing in the genre's standard trappings: donning striped frock coat and white gloves, applying burnt cork or black greasepaint to darken their faces, and speaking or singing in spurious versions of African American dialect.

Many historians and musicologists have identified this music as racist. Certainly, its imagery is filled with stereotypes: malapropisms, tortured diction, happy slaves longing for the old plantation, and northern black dandies whose efforts at gentility are exposed as "putting on airs." At the same time, these same scholars have linked blackface with "genuine" African American music or with the authentic folk expressions of an early American working class. Thus they have muted their own charges, making the very stereotypes their critique has identified seem natural and real. In actual fact, it takes practically no musical training to discern that the standard music of blackface was primarily a collection of Irish jigs, Scottish reels, and English sentimental songs. In addition, if the origins of blackface were working-class, it quickly passed into the middle classes with the rise of more commercial songwriters and promoters such as Stephen Foster and Edwin Christy. As early as the 1840s, one finds blackface tunes with new lyrics in the service of middle-class reform, providing sing-alongs for the meetings of widows' and orphans' associations, temperance unions, and even abolitionist societies.

In addition, if the music of blackface was racist, it reveals that racism itself has a history. For this was a racism composed of attraction, not revulsion, one of white yearnings and desires projected onto black bodies. At the minstrel show, young white males witnessed a stylized version of "blackness" as a rebellion against mothers, fathers, and etiquette guides and as a democratic release from authority, from proscriptions for proper manhood, and even from whiteness itself. Pioneered by a rapidly proliferating number of troupes from the Virginia Minstrels of the 1840s to the New Orleans Serenaders and Christy's Minstrels, minstrel songs like "Jump Jim Crow" (1831), "Old Dan Tucker" (1843), "Oh Suzanna!" (1848), "My Old Kentucky Home" (1851), and "Dixie" (1859) soon spread throughout the nation. What these and countless other songs expressed was predictable enough, for it fell well within the contemporary boundaries of liberation. At the minstrel show, male audiences could revel in stylized versions of erotic dances, fistfights, boundless appetites, and gender and racial transgressions.

With the rise of blackface minstrelsy, the American music that would characterize boys' rebellion reached its modern form. Aside from the slow disappearance of greasepaint, its basic dynamic would remain unchanged into and throughout the twentieth century. From Stephen Foster to Elvis Presley, from the burnt cork of the mid-nineteenth-century stage to the hip-hop affectations of the present, Anglo-American boys have enacted rebellion through a musical mask of exaggerated African American styles. Over time, this music would become the stuff of consumer society, as the producers of sheet music and later radio programs, records, and boy groups would strive to make rebellion a necessity of boyhood and a key foundation for corporate profits. Its idiosyncratic origins would also be blended with more didactic elements. Through this music of rebellion, American boys learned a variety of lessons that would keep hierarchies of class, race, and gender alive even as they apparently transgressed their boundaries: boys are rebellious, but girls are not (even though girls like rebellious boys); the characteristics of whiteness (possessive materialism, repression, and culture) are the opposite of African American characteristics (soulfulness, self-expression, and nature); and white boys are free to "slum" or "get down" with their more expressive ethnic and class opposites, while their "opposites" are locked into strict categories composed of stereotypes. And finally, through this music of standardized rebellion, generations of American boys learned that the violin-carrying schoolboy, the daring conformist, the rebel against rebellion is little more than a sissified dandy and thus deserving of a good beating.

Brian Roberts

See also African American Boys; Rock Bands

References and further reading

Anti-Slavery Melodies: For the Friends of Freedom; Prepared by the Hingham Anti-Slavery Society. 1843. Hingham: Elijah B. Gill.

Boston Temperance Songster: A Collection of Songs and Hymns for Temperance Societies, Original and Selected. 1844. Boston: William White.

Cassuto, Leonard. 1997. *The Inhuman Race: The Racial Grotesque in American Literature and Culture.* New York: Columbia University Press.

Cockrell, Dale, ed. 1989. *Excelsior: Journals of the Hutchinson Family Singers, 1842–1846.* New York: Pendragon Press.

Dexter, Franklin Bowditch. 1919. *Ancient Town Records.* Vol. 2: *New Haven Town Records, 1662–1684.* New Haven: New Haven Colony Historical Society.

Hamm, Charles. 1979. *Yesterdays: Popular Song in America.* New York: W. W. Norton.

Hutchinson Family's Book of Words. 1851. New York: Baker, Godwin and Co., Steam Printers.

Lambert, Barbara, ed. 1980. *Music in Colonial Massachusetts 1630–1820: Music in Public Places.* Boston: Colonial Society of Massachusetts.

Levine, Lawrence. 1988. *Highbrow/ Lowbrow: The Emergence of Cultural Hierarchy in America.* Cambridge: Harvard University Press.

Lhamon, W. T., Jr. 1998. *Raising Cain: Blackface Performance from Jim Crow to Hip Hop.* Cambridge: Harvard University Press.

Lott, Eric. 1993. *Love and Theft: Blackface Minstrelsy and the American Working Class.* New York: Oxford University Press.

Roediger, David R. 1991. *The Wages of Whiteness: Race and the Making of the American Working Class.* New York: Verso.

Rogin, Michael. 1992. "Blackface, White Noise: The Jewish Jazz Singer Finds His Voice." *Critical Inquiry* 18 (Spring): 417–453.

Saxton, Alexander. 1990. *The Rise and Fall of the White Republic: Class Politics and Mass Culture in Nineteenth-Century America.* New York: Verso.

Silverman, Kenneth. 1976. *A Cultural History of the American Revolution: Painting, Music, Literature, and the Theatre.* New York: Thomas Y. Crowell.

Southern, Eileen. 1971. *The Music of Black Americans.* New York: W. W. Norton.

Tawa, Nicholas E. 2000. *High Minded and Low Down: Music in the Lives of Americans, 1800–1861.* Northeastern University Press.

Toll, Robert C. 1974. *Blacking Up: The Minstrel Show in Nineteenth-Century America.* New York: Oxford University Press.

White, Shane, and Graham J. White. 1999. *Stylin: African American Expressive Culture, from Its Beginnings to the Zoot Suit.* Ithaca: Cornell University Press.

Discography

Brave Boys: New England Traditions in Folk Music. 1995. New World Records.

Don't Give the Name a Bad Place: Types and Stereotypes in American Musical Theater, 1870–1900. 1978. New World Records.

The Early Minstrel Show. 1998. New World Records.

English Country Dances: From Playford's Dancing Master, 1651–1703. 1991. Saydisc.

His Majestie's Clerks. 1996. *Goostly Psalmes: Anglo American Psalmody, 1550–1800.* Harmonia Mundi.

Music of the American Revolution: The Birth of Liberty. 1976. New World Records.

Penny Merriment: English Songs from the Time of the Pilgrims. 1986. Plimoth Plantation.

N

Nationalism and Boyhood: The "Young America" Movement

During the middle third of the nineteenth century, the idea of boyhood became a metaphor for the growth of and pride in the young American nation. Based on the American romantic nationalist trend at the time and inspired in part by similar romantic nationalist movements in Europe, the term *Young America* was adopted by both art and literary critics who called for an American- rather than a European-style art and literature and by young Democratic partisans who sought to create a new vision of westward expansion and an end of sectionalism for the political party of Andrew Jackson. In the aftermath of the Civil War, the term became a humorous or sentimental symbol exploited for advertising and entertainment.

The most recent scholarship argues that there were two phases of Young America. The first developed in the late 1830s and 1840s and was characterized by a romantic national political agenda of economic reform intertwined with cultural nationalism. The second emerged in the 1850s when a highly partisan Democratic factionalism focused on territorial expansion and foreign policy, turning a blind eye on slavery issues in an attempt to defuse sectional threats to the party (Widmer 1998). Ralph Waldo Emerson was responsible for coining and popularizing the name "Young America," which was the title he chose for an address to the Boston Mercantile Association in February 1844. He was probably influenced by the contemporary rise of similar romantic nationalist groups in Europe—such as "Young Italy," "Young Germany," and "Young Ireland"—whose members provided the intellectual leadership for the explosive European democratic revolutionary movements of 1848. In the United States, Emerson's call for a twofold nationalist agenda of an American rather than a European art and literature and westward expansion driven by an innovative American railroad and communication technology became the central issues for the rise of the Young America movement. In the next two decades, these ideas had a deep resonance in American culture (Kerrigan 1997).

The label was quickly adopted by a circle of nationalist literary figures led by the critic John O'Sullivan, who regularly called for American cultural independence in his reviews in the New York–based *U.S. Magazine and Democratic Review* from 1841 to 1848. Literary nationalism was further promoted by the publisher Evert Duyckinck, whose Library of American Books provided an outlet for the work of such members of the Young America group as Nathaniel Hawthorne, Herman Melville, and Walt Whitman. In the arts,

Young America became the title attached to a group of genre artists, such as William Sidney Mount and Francis Edmunds, who worked through the American Art Union to promote ordinary Americans as suitable subjects for an American painting tradition.

For the Young Americans, art and literature were inextricably tied to reform in American politics, which was at the time based on three things: a Jacksonian Democratic agenda of national westward expansion and land reform; the development of a simpler American jurisprudence through codification of state laws; and support for the development of railroads and other technologies enabling improved systems of distribution and mass marketing, which would tie the nation together and override sectionalism. George Henry Evans, who had been promoting land reform through his newspaper, the *Workingman's Advocate*, became a key figure in the political side of the movement, retitling his Democratic paper supporting Martin Van Buren with the name *Young America!* shortly after Emerson's speech.

From its beginning, Young America involved a generational challenge. Young politicians from the newer states in the Midwest—men like Stephen A. Douglas of Illinois and George Sanders of Kentucky—criticized the old fogey ideas of the leaders of the Democratic Party in the 1850s, supported intervention on the side of foreign republican movements, and enthusiastically endorsed O'Sullivan's coining of the phrase "Manifest Destiny" to argue for U.S. acquisition of lands reaching to the Pacific Ocean. Douglas's failure to win the presidential nomination in 1852 and the younger politicians' blindness to the importance of the slavery issue led to their downfall as a major political force by the end of the 1860s.

By then, however, the phrase *Young America* had entered into general cultural use, and its users often gave the symbolism of youth a concrete visual reality. An 1865 engraving titled *Young America Crushing Rebellion and Sedition* used an infant Hercules as the symbolic vision of the North's defeat of the Confederacy. Creative promoters adopted the imagery as well. The currency of the phrase is reflected in the titles of several publications, such as a *Bird's Eye View of Young America: Warren County, Illinois*, published by A. Ruger in Chicago in 1869, and a set of educational lantern slides illustrating the development of an American architectural tradition before 1840, titled *Young America Admires the Ancients*. A series of advertising promotions seized on the pictorial possibilities of Young America, such as the 1858 logo for Young America Denims. A Young America advertising card for Lilienthal's tobacco showed a young boy holding an American flag, and a post-1860 colorgraph promoted "Young America Hams and Breakfast Bacon." In 1871, the manufacturer of entertaining stereographic view cards, M. M. Griswold of Lancaster, Ohio, featured in his sentimental series of images of children, "Griswold Compositions," such titles as "Young America Bathing," "Young America in the Nursery," and "Young America Asleep."

Constance B. Schulz

References and further reading
Danbom, David B. 1974. "The Young America Movement." *Journal of the Illinois State Historical Society* 67: 294–306.
Kerrigan, William Thomas. 1997. "'Young America!': Romantic Nationalism in Literature and Politics, 1843–1861." Ph.D. diss., University of Michigan.
Reagan, Daniel Ware. 1984. "The Making of an American Author: Melville and

the Idea of a National Literature." Ph.D.
diss., University of New Hampshire.

Spiller, Robert E. 1971. "Emerson's 'The
Young American.'" *Clio* 1: 37–41.

Widmer, Edward L. 1998. *Young America:
The Flowering of Democracy in New
York City.* New York: Oxford University
Press.

Contemporary sources:

Advertising. Library of Congress Prints
and Photographs Division:

1858. "Young America Denims."

1860. "Young America" box label for NY
tobacco distributor C. H. Lilienthal.

1865. "Young America Hams and
Breakfast Bacon."

1866. Emerson, Ralph Waldo. 1844. "The
Young American." *The Dial* (April).

1867. Ruger, A. 1869. *Bird's Eye View of
Young America: Warren County,
Illinois.* Map: Warren County, IL.
Library of Congress Map Division.

1868. Sartain, William. 1864. "Young
America Crushing Rebellion and
Sedition." Engraving in Library of
Congress Prints and Photographs
Division.

1869. *Young America!: The Organ of the
National Reform Association.* Formerly
the *Workingman's Advocate.*
1844–1845. Periodical, New York City,
George H. Evans, publisher. Library of
Congress Newspapers and Periodical
Division. During the 1850s and 1860s,
several other newspapers and
periodicals also adopted this name.

1870. *Young America Admires the
Ancients.* 1783–1840. Set of 80 lantern
slides on American architecture. Library
of Congress Prints and Photographs
Division.

Native American Boys

The more than 550 American Indian nations in North America make generalizing about Native American boyhood a high-risk venture. It can at least be said that, in all cultures, Indian boys in the past spent their childhoods in training for their adult roles as men. Family, age, and gender were crucial to each individual's relationship to the larger society and determined each person's economic and political roles, responsibilities and obligations, and social status and authority. Most of what we know about Indian boyhood in the past comes from Indian men who in the early twentieth century wrote or otherwise recorded their experiences growing up in the late nineteenth century. European travelers, missionaries, and bureaucrats provided some information on Indian family life in the seventeenth and eighteenth centuries.

Indian societies were age-graded, some more rigidly than others, in which case transitions to a new age category were made explicit through a ceremony. Boys spent their infancy, like girls, under the immediate care of their mothers; in addition, fathers liked to play with their children, and aunts and grandmothers often stepped in as primary caregivers. Luther Standing Bear, a Lakota (Sioux) man who was a child in the late nineteenth century, remembered how all the women in the *tiyospaye,* or extended family, took care of him. In many Indian societies, babies commonly spent their first years in a cradleboard designed not only to ease the mother's tasks of carrying and watching over the baby but also to produce straight, sturdy spines.

Around the age of five, boys and girls began to live separate lives in terms of playmates and adult role models. Fathers and uncles taught boys the skills they would need as adults. Early in his life, every boy seems to have learned how to make and use bows and arrows. Other skills varied by region and economy. Navajo boys in the nineteenth century began herding sheep and learned how to care for livestock. On the plains, boys learned to ride and care for horses and to detect the patterns of buffalo and other prey. Among the Iroquois, famous for their oratory, boys learned the principles of a

Navajo boy, ca. 1906 (Library of Congress)

good speech. Boys practiced adult skills in the games they played with other boys. They hunted for rabbits and birds. Cherokee boys competed at shooting arrows at cornstalks. Lakota boys practiced stalking Crow or Pawnee enemies and looked out for the well-being of their sisters.

Most important in boys' education was learning what behavior led to respect for adult men: generosity, reserve, deliberation, and clearheadedness. Physical endurance, agility, and the courage to withstand pain or hardship were also highly valued. Looking back at their childhoods, Indian men remembered having to rise early and running to learn agility and endurance, and instead of learning under threats of physical punishment or coercion or through bribery, they saw that politeness was the best way to treat others.

In many Indian communities, public ceremonies marked transitions to new life-course stages. One of the earliest accounts of an Indian initiation ceremony is John Smith's description of the *huskenaw,* or *busk,* as practiced by Algonquian Indians in early-seventeenth-century Virginia. To be eligible to be councilors or shamans later in life, boys between the ages of ten and fifteen went through this arduous ceremony. After a day during which the entire village sang and danced, young men beat the boys with sticks as they ran a gauntlet. The boys then spent months in the woods, while their families and friends regarded them as dead. When they returned to the community, they were men.

Among the Lakota, boys passed through a series of ceremonies from the naming ceremony in their infancy to the vision quest undertaken in their early teens as they approached manhood. The vision quest was critical, for it determined a boy's future. After purifying in a sweat lodge for several days with his male relatives and friends, the boy left for a secluded spot, where alone and without food he waited many days for a vision. If graced, his vision would point out a spirit helper and indicate his future achievements, especially whether he would excel at war, hunting, or medicine. Only a rare few received visions powerful enough to start them on the path toward being a medicine man.

The Pueblo Indians in the Southwest had perhaps the largest number of ceremonies to mark children's progress toward adulthood. Zuni and Hopi boys went through frequent ceremonies; at each stage, they learned more of the community's religious knowledge and the secrets of the kachina society into which they would eventually be initiated. Like the *huskenaw* in the Southeast, at one point boys were publicly whipped in the plaza; however, most of their religious education took place in kivas, which were the religious centers located underground that symbolized the Pueblo peoples' origins and their emergence from the earth's womb.

By twentieth-century standards, Indian boys in earlier times, whether in seventeenth-century Virginia or on the nineteenth-century plains, became men at a young age. Boys faced formal coming-of-age ceremonies at around puberty, but even without such ceremonies, they began taking on the tasks of men in their early to midteens. Luther Standing Bear recalled accompanying his father on a war party at age ten. It would be several more years before boys accompanying war parties were considered more than camp helpers and ready to engage the enemy in battle. Among the Great Lakes tribes and in the Southeast, boys became literally known as "young men" in their late teens. If they had demonstrated their capability, they could then lead war parties and marry, two signs of the transition to adulthood. For Hopi and Zuni boys, donning a kachina mask carried a similar significance and also occurred at about age twenty.

The most direct challenge to native childrearing customs came with the U.S. government boarding school system. The first Indian Industrial School opened in Carlisle, Pennsylvania, in 1879. Several dozen others, located around the country, quickly followed. Christian missionaries had operated many Indian boarding schools throughout the United States in the nineteenth century, but Carlisle and its imitators were part of a larger federal initiative to assimilate Indians into the general population as individuals stripped of any tribal allegiance or ethnic customs. Carlisle, Haskell (Kansas), Chilocco (Oklahoma), Tomah (Wisconsin), and other Indian Industrial Schools took Indian children away from their families and communities, sometimes by force or coercion and usually for several years. Dressed in military-style uniforms, Indian children led a regimented life of drills, grammar school lessons, and work intended as on-the-job training for future occupations. Girls learned homemaking, and boys learned skills such as farming, carpentry, and metalworking. Despite the rigid, sometimes violent, discipline of boarding school life, children formed a subculture in which they exercised their own social code and regulated the behavior of younger members. Boys distributed themselves into gangs in which fistfights were the primary means to show who was outside the gang, and intense loyalties prevailed within the gang.

At the turn of the twentieth century, just as efforts to turn Native American children away from their own cultures peaked, American writers and educators began to glamorize Indian boyhood as a model for the middle classes. Back-to-nature enthusiasts such as Ernest Thompson Seton, Theodore Roosevelt, and especially the American Boy Scout movement appropriated Indian motifs and lore to promote the values of self-reliance, hard work, honesty, and simplicity. Concurrent with the historian Frederick Jackson Turner's theory that a unique American character had developed out of the frontier experience, American boys were encouraged to pass through a rugged and heroic stage of personal development by mimicking a romanticized Indian past. Several Indian writers contributed children's books to feed the growing interest in how Indians lived. Charles Alexander

Two young Hualapai boys stand on the rim of the Grand Canyon, 1991. (Tom Bean/Corbis)

Eastman's *Indian Boyhood* (1902), Luther Standing Bear's *My Indian Boyhood* (1931), and Arthur C. Parker's *The Indian How Book* (1927) tell about such experiences in growing up as surviving in the woods and hunting birds and rabbits, as well as the importance of their relatives in teaching them the values and social mores they would need as adults.

At the turn of the twenty-first century, Indian boyhood does not seem too different from American boyhood in general. Still the most rural minority group in the United States, more than half of the Indian population lives in cities. Most of the Indian children living on Indian reservations attend state public schools, especially at the high school level. Although many communities and families still mark children's transitions to new re-sponsibilities with a traditional ceremony, for most Indian families high school graduation has become the sign of arriving at adulthood.

Nancy Shoemaker

See also California Missions; Fathers

References and further reading
Axtell, James, ed. 1981. *The Indian Peoples of Eastern America: A Documentary History of the Sexes.* New York: Oxford University Press.
Dyk, Walter. 1938. *Son of Old Man Hat: A Navaho Autobiography.* Lincoln: University of Nebraska Press.
Eastman, Charles A. 1971. *Indian Boyhood.* 1902. Reprint, New York: Dover.
Hilger, M. Inez. 1992. *Chippewa Child Life and Its Cultural Background.* 1951. Reprint, St. Paul: Minnesota Historical Society Press.

La Flesche, Francis. 1963. *The Middle Five: Indian Schoolboys of the Omaha Tribe.* 1900. Reprint, Madison: University of Wisconsin Press.

Lomawaima, K. Tsianina. 1994. *They Called It Prairie Light: The Story of Chilocco Indian School.* Lincoln: University of Nebraska Press.

Penney, David. 1993. "Indians and Children: A Critique of Educational Objectives." *Akwe:kon* [*Native Americas*] 10 (Winter): 12–18.

Roscoe, Will. 1991. *The Zuni Man-Woman.* Albuquerque: University of New Mexico Press.

Simmons, Leo W. 1942. *Sun Chief: The Autobiography of a Hopi Indian.* New Haven, CT: Yale University Press.

Standing Bear, Luther. 1978. *Land of the Spotted Eagle.* 1933. Reprint, Lincoln: University of Nebraska Press.

Szasz, Margaret Connell. 1985. "Native American Children." Pp. 311–332 in *American Childhood: A Research Guide and Historical Handbook.* Edited by Joseph M. Hawes and N. Ray Hiner. Westport, CT: Greenwood Press.

Newsboys

Cold mornings. Cranky customers. Fearsome canines. Historic headlines. Cherished earnings. These are some of the common recollections of the millions of Americans who have hawked or delivered newspapers from colonial times to the present. Whether they grew up in small towns or big cities, many children's first and most formative job has been peddling papers. It is how generations of youths have learned the meaning of work, the value of a dollar, and the sometimes narrow difference between opportunity and exploitation.

Newsboys are real workers, but they are also mythic figures. Juvenile novels, genre paintings, and documentary photographs have made newsboys into enduring symbols of American democracy and the spirit of capitalism. Writers, artists, and reformers have alternately praised news selling as a public service and decried it as a social evil. What we find if we retrace newsboys' steps across time and listen to their words is that children's labor was integral to the rise of the newspaper industry, which, for better or worse, has been one of the most influential child welfare institutions in the United States.

The title of "first American newsboy" usually goes to Benjamin Franklin, who in 1721, at the age of fifteen, helped deliver his brother's paper, the *New England Courant*, through the streets of Boston. Newspapers were rarely cried on the streets in the colonial period or early republic. Most were picked up at the newspaper offices; sent by post; or delivered to subscribers, coffeehouses, and taverns by printers' apprentices or low-paid carriers. On New Year's Day they distributed carriers' addresses—poetical broadsides that always ended with an appeal for a tip.

Franklin notwithstanding, newsboys can better trace their professional ancestry to Bernard Flaherty and Samuel Messenger. These were two of the first boys recruited by Benjamin Day in 1833 to peddle the *New York Sun*, the first successful penny newspaper. Most New York papers were huge "blanket sheets" that cost 6 cents and specialized in financial news. Day's dream was a cheap, feisty tabloid for workingmen. He ran an ad addressed "To the UNEMPLOYED—A number of steady men can find employment by vending this paper. A liberal discount is allowed to those who buy and sell again." Profits looked to be so low that no men came forward, so Day hired Flaherty, Messenger, and a half-dozen other boys at $2 a week. He assigned them districts but otherwise gave them complete control of their areas; they could either peddle on

A newsboy selling newspapers announcing the beginning of World War II (Archive Photos)

"Young America," archetypal young men on the make, poised to profit from new markets linked by an expanding network of roads, rails, canals, and, of course, newspapers.

In the 1850s newsboys became feared members of what philanthropist Charles Loring Brace called the "dangerous classes" (Brace 1872). The decade saw two economic depressions that left an estimated 10,000 children to fend for themselves on the streets of New York. They "slept rough" under stairs, in alleyways, and on steam grates, particularly around newspaper offices where they could get papers on credit. The word *newsboy* became synonymous with street waif. Cold and hunger were well known to them. In his 1860 memoir, New York newsboy Johnny Morrow called hunger "the tyrant of animal life" and the most compelling force behind his trade (Morrow 1860, 131).

In 1853, Brace founded the Children's Aid Society and began shipping street children out west on "orphan trains" to live and work on farms. In 1854 he opened the Newsboys' Lodging House in the *Sun* building. For 6 cents it provided beds, baths, meals, and entertainment. Over the years dozens of similar institutions sprang up across the country, including several operated by the Catholic Church.

The Civil War raised the number and stature of newsboys. In Detroit they became "a noticeable feature of the town" with the first battle of Bull Run, and in New York they soon numbered "many thousands" and spanned "all the seven ages of man" ("Then and Now" 1896, 70; "New York Newsboys" 1869, 717). Many big-city dailies regularly sold 10,000 copies per day and began to issue multiple editions rather than extras. Some established separate "evening" papers,

the streets or build subscription routes. Many did both. The most active boys earned $5 a week, almost as much as a journeyman printer (Lee 1937, 261).

Realizing there was money to be made, adults began organizing routes and hiring their own boys. Penny dailies soon spread to other cities, giving rise to two systems of circulation: the London plan, which emphasized street sales and the use of middlemen; and the Philadelphia plan, which stressed home delivery and direct control of operations. Newsboys worked under both systems and were celebrated in song and story as symbols of

Lewis Hine photograph of newsboys on the steps of the White House (Library of Congress)

most of which were sold on the street rather than by subscription. Englishman Edward Dicey observed in 1863 that this "chance circulation" influenced the style of American journalism because it encouraged "the sensation system of newspaper headings and paragraphs, which offends our taste so constantly" (Dicey 1863, 30–31). Although offensive to some, newsboys were valorized in the press as war orphans who had a special claim on the public weal. Many became soldiers themselves, drilling in squads at newsboy homes and joining up when they were old enough.

Newsboys took in from 50 cents to $3 a day in the 1860s, but they made much more when the news was hot. Two fifteen-year-old newsboys reportedly "sold 2,000 papers between them when the telegraph announced the capture of Jefferson Davis; and on the evening that Mr. Lincoln was assassinated, they sold the enormous number of 3,400" ("New York Newsboys" 1869, 717). Among those who profited from war news was Thomas Edison, a train boy on the Grand Trunk Railroad. When word came of the carnage at Shiloh, Edison had wires sent to all the stations along the line. He ordered 1,000 copies of the *Detroit Free Press*—ten times his usual number—and retailed them at inflated prices to the crowds he knew would be waiting at every stop.

In the frenzy of industrialization that followed the Civil War, the U.S. urban population more than tripled, and newsboys emerged as unwitting advocates of laissez-faire capitalism. Horatio Alger portrayed them in his many novels as ragged individualists whose essential good character made success inevitable. Likewise, John George Brown, the most prolific and popular genre painter of his generation, pictured newsboys and boot-blacks as rosy-cheeked cherubs who thrived on the street. Alger's and Brown's works implicitly assured the middle class that poor city children could rise if they truly wanted to succeed.

Despite these idealized images, child peddlers reemerged as a pressing problem during the depression years of the 1870s and early 1880s. In 1874, concerned citizens in New York founded the Society for the Prevention of Cruelty to Children (SPCC) and renewed efforts to sweep them off the streets. Peddling papers was not a crime per se, but to officers of "the Cruelty" it was prima facie evidence of parental neglect.

Boston started licensing newsboys and bootblacks in 1868. It issued them leather badges and limited the number to 400. The city also established a special newsboys school that held two two-hour sessions a day. Detroit instituted a badge system in 1877 that was partly a response to the children's labor militancy. Newsboys struck the *Detroit Evening News* over its pricing policy, and their "generally unruly character" led to the passage of an ordinance requiring each newsboy to obtain a yearly license and badge for 10 cents. An amendment stipulated that the badges were to be issued "only on satisfactory assurance of good conduct" ("Newsboys' Riot" 1877, 4; Farmer 1889, 963). Nationally, the number of newsboys climbed as newspaper circulation shot up from 2.4 million in 1879 to 24 million in 1909 (West 1996, 37). Estimates of the newsboy population ranged from 800 in Philadelphia to 1,600 in Detroit and 5,000 in New York City. Turnover was constant; boys worked anywhere from a few weeks to a few years (Beach 1888, 202; Wager-Fisher 1880, 693; Ward 1875, 949).

Contrary to popular belief, relatively few newsboys were orphans. Most lived with one or both parents and worked the streets as part of a family business, often accompanied by siblings and monitored by relatives. Newsboys typically started to peddle between the ages of five and ten. Their earnings accounted for up to 20 percent of a household's income, which gave them greater autonomy and status within the family. Few newsboys continued in the trade after fifteen, the age at which working-class males typically entered the adult labor force. Some boys, particularly blacks, stayed on longer simply because there were no better jobs for them. The ethnicity of newsboys usually reflected the ethnic composition of a city's working class, with the newest and poorest arrivals tending to dominate. Thus most newsboys up to the 1880s were from Irish stock. They were followed primarily by the children of southern and eastern European immigrants.

Not all newsboys were boys. Girls also sold papers, but they rarely exceeded 2 percent of the workforce. Parents were less likely to let their daughters approach strangers for commercial purposes. As New York police captain Edward Tynan said in 1881, "Girls who begin with selling newspapers usually end with selling themselves" ("Miseries of News-Girls" 1881, 12). Such prejudices were inscribed in law in the early 1900s, when many municipalities required girls to be sixteen, eighteen, or twenty-one years old to obtain street trading licenses but allowed boys to trade as young as ten.

Most observers considered street hawking unskilled labor, but it required physical ability and mental acuity. Chief among the prerequisites was a big voice and an ability to assess the news. In crying their wares newsboys staked out their turf with their voices. Volume was not enough, though. They had to predict how many papers they could sell on a given day and which stories to shout. Newsboys sometimes developed little tricks, such as embellishing headlines, selling day-old papers, or short-changing customers. At times they were arrested for crying false news, violating the Sabbath, and peddling proscribed papers. They also needed street smarts to avoid being run down in traffic, molested by customers, cheated by suppliers, robbed by their peers, and caught in the crossfire of bloody circulation wars.

As in all retailing, newsboys' profits depended greatly upon location. The more heavily trafficked areas commanded the highest sales. Such sites were at a premium and had to be defended against all interlopers. "It was a case of survival of the fittest," recalled Joe "Awful Coffee" Rutkofsky, a professional boxer who started selling papers in 1917 at the age of twelve in Pueblo, Colorado. "In those days, everybody was tough. You had to fight for your corner. You had to fight for everything" (Leppek 1995, 46).

Newsboys competed fiercely with each other, but they also collaborated. They knew each other by a roster of colorful nicknames ("Carrots," "Squinty," "Dutchy"), and when one of their number died they took up collections for flowers, passed resolutions of condolence, and marched through the street in funeral trains. They developed elaborate proprietary rights to specific routes, corners, buildings, and streetcar lines. In ef-fect, they established shadow real estate markets in which they bought, sold, raffled, bartered, and bequeathed public space for private commercial purposes.

Newsboys also formed unions and mounted strikes. Documented newsboy strikes occurred in Detroit, St. Louis, and Chicago in the 1870s; Milwaukee, Lynn, Massachusetts, and Nyack, New Jersey, in the 1880s; and Cleveland, Toledo, New Orleans, and Lexington, Kentucky, in the 1890s. In 1899, New York newsies struck the nation's two largest newspapers to protest a price hike imposed during the Spanish-American War. For two weeks they sabotaged the distribution of William Randolph Hearst's *Evening Journal* and Joseph Pulitzer's *Evening World*. The walkout sparked a children's general strike in which newsboys, bootblacks, and messenger boys in scores of cities stopped work to demand better pay and working conditions. The strikers failed to reinstate the old price but won the right to return unsold copies for a full refund (Nasaw 1985). Other newsboy strikes followed in the twentieth century, prompting the industry to emphasize newsstand sales and experiment with "mechanical newsboys," or coin racks.

News selling required bursts of activity bracketed by periods of idleness. During their idle moments newsboys wrestled, played stickball, shot craps, and pitched pennies. With their ready cash, newsboys were among the most avid consumers of popular entertainment. They patronized cheap theaters, pool halls, penny arcades, movie houses, and brothels. To counter such vices, philanthropists and publishers opened newsboy reading rooms and night schools and hosted newsboy banquets and excursions. Circulation managers went on to establish newsboy clubs, bands, buildings, and sports teams to win the loyalty of the boys and keep them "gingered up." Such programs also helped deflect charges of exploitation and stave off child labor legislation.

In 1890, journalist Jacob Riis shamed the nation with *How the Other Half Lives,* a vivid portrait of New York tenement life. His impassioned reportage and now iconic photographs of "street Arabs" huddled in alleys exposed the dark underside of industrial capitalism. Riis praised newsboys for their "sturdy independence, love of freedom and absolute self-reliance," yet touched off a protracted campaign to rescue them from the slums (Riis 1890, 147). Reformers, many of them women working together in settlement houses, temperance unions, and trade unions, made elimination of child labor a priority. In Chicago, Hull House resident Florence Kelley likened street trading to "white child slavery" and lobbied for compulsory education laws to eradicate it. "There is no body of self-supporting children more in need of effective care than these newsboys and bootblacks," she wrote in 1895. "They are ill-fed, ill-housed, ill-clothed, illiterate, and wholly untrained and unfitted for any occupation" (Kelley and Stevens 1895, 54–55). Kelley, like most Progressive-era reformers, downplayed the economic and emotional importance of children's earnings.

In 1904, activists formed the National Child Labor Committee to coordinate their efforts. They produced reams of sociological and statistical studies that portrayed juvenile street trading as part of the problem of, not the solution to, youth homelessness, poverty, and delinquency. "The professional newsboy is the embryo criminal," declared economist Scott Nearing in 1907 (Nearing 1907, 784). To underscore the point, the committee polled prison wardens and reform school superintendents who reported that between 50 and 75 percent of their inmates were newsboys (Lovejoy 1910). The prototypical newsboy of this period was epitomized in the documentary photographs of committee investigator Lewis Hine, who portrayed them as both casualties and survivors of capitalism.

Between 1890 and 1918, every state in the union passed compulsory education laws (Postol 1997, 340). During the next decade, thirty-nine cities and twenty states regulated juvenile street trading (Shulman 1932, 13). Newspaper publishers at first resisted government interference and denounced reformers as meddling do-gooders and socialists infringing on the freedom of the press, but ultimately they came to embrace licensing schemes as a way to oversee their young workers. Newsstand operators and some newsboy unions also supported these measures because they limited competition. Yet enforcement was weak, and thousands of underage youths left school for work. Ironically, most child labor laws tended to push boys out of shops and factories where enforcement was relatively effective and into street trades where they could work more freely.

To encourage self-regulation and instill principles of citizenship, several cities instituted newsboy courts in which teen judges heard cases and imposed fines for misconduct. In Boston, Milwaukee, and Birmingham, Alabama, these courts grew into full-fledged newsboy "republics" with constitutions and elected representatives from various "states" or neighborhoods. Members of the International Circulation Managers Association, formed in 1898, sponsored similar self-government schemes for newsboys. In 1915, it established a Newsboy Welfare Committee to help recruit and retain boy labor and fight further government regulation.

World War I created havoc and opportunity in the newspaper industry. Newspapers were hit hard by the accompanying business decline of 1914. Advertising revenues dropped as operating expenses rose. Papers took drastic measures. Some arbitrarily limited circulation and banned returns. Most penny papers doubled in price, and that of many Sunday papers jumped from 5 cents to 10 cents. Sales dipped, but by war's end circulation and revenue climbed to new heights. The number and profile of news sellers changed during the war. In Buffalo, their ranks shrank by 25 percent between 1917 and 1919 (Juvenile Protective Department 1935, 13–14). One explanation is that as older boys entered the military, younger ones took their better-paying jobs in industry. Labor was in such short supply that circulation managers welcomed girls into the news trade. As with previous conflicts, the war presented new opportunities to honor newsboys. Fictional newsboys-turned-soldiers were the protagonists of several wartime talkies, and a hit song in 1919 was "I'd Rather Be a Newsboy in the U.S.A. Than a Ruler in a Foreign Land."

Despite the spread of a middle-class ethos that prized children for their sentimental rather than economic value and an overall decline in child labor, the number of newsboys rose in the 1920s (Mangold 1936, 303). In 1924, the U.S. Children's Bureau backed a constitutional amendment to regulate all forms of child labor. Congress approved the measure, but only four states ratified it. Reformers' efforts to characterize news selling as a corrupting occupation were undermined by positive portrayals of newsboys in advertisements and political campaigns. One of the most popular politicians of the day was former newsboy Al Smith. He outpolled publisher Hearst to become governor of New York in 1922 and won the Democratic nomination for president in 1928.

The stock market crash of 1929 negated whatever gains child labor reformers had made in persuading the public that news peddling was detrimental to the welfare of American youth. If anything, people now felt that the work was too valuable to relegate to children when nearly one-third of all wage earners—15 million adults—were unemployed. The hard times of the 1930s sent more men into the news trade and compelled youths to stay in the business longer than they normally would have done. Hawkers and carriers totaled 500,000 in the 1930s, with carriers comprising 70 percent of the workforce. The average age of newsboys climbed from eleven to fourteen, while their annual earnings declined along with everyone else's (Linder 1990, 836).

Publishers instituted sales training programs for their carriers; held subscription contests; and offered bikes, trips, and scholarships as prizes. Still, revenues declined; 400 newspapers failed during the 1930s, leaving 80 percent of communities one-newspaper towns. Meanwhile, the newsboy emerged as a proletarian hero on stage and screen. He was the star of the radical repertory piece "Newsboy," which became a standard with workers' theater groups nationwide. Adapted from a poem by a Communist Party cultural official, it blended dance, chants, and dialogue to expose the real class struggle behind the day's sensational headlines. At the same time Hollywood churned out reels of newsboy and gangster films; actors James Cagney, Humphrey Bogart, and John Garfield specialized in roles as street toughs who learned early in life to take capitalism to its limit, suspending all rules of morality.

In 1933, President Franklin D. Roosevelt pushed through the National Industrial Recovery Act, which created a system of codes regulating competition in every branch of the economy. The Newspaper Code set minimum age requirements for hawkers and carriers and prohibited night work. Publishers lobbied against it, insisting that the nation's newsboys were "little merchants" and not employees whose hours and conditions they could regulate. Besides, they said, news selling was more play than work and to deny carriers their routes "would constitute a national menace and drive them into the Devil's Workshop" (Trattner 1970, 194). The debate became moot when the Supreme Court invalidated the entire act in 1935. In 1938, the Fair Labor Standards Act raised the working age to sixteen and again tried to ban the interstate commerce of goods made by children, but newsboys, ruled independent contractors, were exempt.

In the early 1940s, World War II dominated the headlines, and labor shortages again led to a relaxation of child labor and school attendance laws. Selling and recycling newspapers were part of the war effort. Newsprint was rationed; hawkers sold out their allotments in half the normal time, and carriers could not accept new customers. Circulation managers now rejected the terms *newsboy* and *newsie* as suggestive of ragged urchins. They declared October 4 National Newspaperboy Day and estimated that there were 350,000 newsboys in the United States, 90 percent of whom were carriers (McDaniel 1941, 43). The U.S. Treasury authorized them to sell war savings stamps, and when victory came they had sold $1.7 billion in 10-cent stamps (Postol 1997, 340). The newsboy now morphed into a comic book superhero: Billie Batson had only to shout "SHAZAM!" to become Captain Marvel, "the world's mightiest man—powerful champion of justice—relentless enemy of evil." His nemesis was none other than Captain Nazi. In 1942, DC Comics introduced "The Newsboy Legion," a series featuring four crime-fighting slum kids.

Carriers with paper routes all but displaced newsboys on street corners in the 1950s and 1960s. These two decades brought full employment and increased incomes. More families could afford automobiles and houses in the suburbs. Children worked less than ever; only 2 percent of youths aged ten to fifteen were gainfully employed, whereas between 78 and 88 percent stayed in school up to age nineteen (West 1996, 207, 217). More people got their news via radio and television, which contributed to a long-term per capita decline in newspaper circulation. Newsboys nevertheless received a new kind of tribute. In 1952, after lobbying by circulation managers, the U.S. Postal Service issued a 3-cent stamp showing a newspaper carrier as a symbol of free enterprise. His shoulder bag bore the legend "Busy Boys . . . Better Boys."

Newspapers started to recruit more girls as carriers in the 1960s, although some states still barred them from the trade. In 1974, thirteen-year-old Lynn Warshafsky cited Title VII of the 1964 Civil Rights Act to challenge such a statute in Wisconsin, but the state supreme court held that Title VII did not apply to minors and that the state had a right to protect girl carriers, who would be more prone to sexual assaults than boy carriers. The threat of violence was real, but boys were no less vulnerable than girls. At least seven young carriers were kidnapped, raped, or murdered on their routes in the early 1980s (Stein 1987, 30–31). Eleven newsboys died "in the line of duty" in the mid-1990s (Linder 1997, 76–77). They were abducted, shot as burglars, or struck by vehicles. Aware of such dangers, insurance companies charge almost double what they charge workers in retail and other industries to cover newspaper deliverers. Yet most states do not require newspapers to provide independent carriers of any age with workers' compensation coverage, unemployment insurance, Social Security benefits, or the minimum wage. This exemption represented a $172 million savings in payroll taxes for the industry ("Are Newspapers Taking Advantage?" 1988, 8–10).

Safety concerns were just one factor in the decline of youth carriers. Falling birthrates shrank the pool of potential paperboys. The expanding fast food industry gave them other job options. Beginning in 1980, the number of carriers under eighteen declined at a rate of 10,000 a year. They were replaced by senior citizens who needed to supplement fixed incomes and new immigrants who saw the work as an alternative to welfare. Publishers realized that a corps of grownup, nonunion, independent carriers with their own cars and insurance was cheaper and more efficient than an army of adolescents on bikes. In some cities this realization led to the wholesale dismissal of youth carriers. In 1999, the Newspaper Association of America declared newsboys and newsgirls "an endangered species" ("Newsboys and Newsgirls" 2000, 5).

Vincent DiGirolamo

See also Jobs in the Nineteenth Century; Jobs in the Twentieth Century; Melodrama

References and further reading
"Are Newspapers Taking Advantage of Child Labor?" 1988. *Stark Metropolitan Magazine* (April): 8–10.
Beach, E. P. 1888. "A Day in the Life of a Newsboy." *Harper's Young People* 9 (January 17): 202.
Brace, Charles Loring. 1872. *The Dangerous Classes of New York and Twenty Years' Work among Them.* New York: Wynkoop and Hallenbeck.
Dicey, Edward. 1863. *Six Months in the Federal States.* London: Macmillan. Reprint, Herbert Mitgang, ed., 1971. *Spectator of America.* Chicago: Quadrangle Books.
Farmer, Silas. 1889. *The History of Detroit and Michigan.* Detroit: Silas Farmer.
Juvenile Protective Department. 1935. "Street Traders of Buffalo, New York," pp. 13–14. Buffalo: Juvenile Protective Department.
Kelley, Florence, and Alzina P. Stevens. 1895. *Hull-House Maps and Papers.* New York: Crowell.
Lee, Alfred McClung. 1937. *The Daily Newspaper in America: Evolution of a Social Instrument.* New York: Macmillan.
Leppek, Chris. 1995. "The Life and Times of Denver's Joe 'Awful' Coffee." *Western States Jewish History* 27, no. 1 (October): 43–61.
Linder, Marc. 1990. "From Street Urchins to Little Merchants: The Juridical Transvaluation of Child Newspaper Carriers." *Temple Law Review* (Winter): 829–864.
———. 1997. "What's Black and White and Red All Over? The Blood Tax on Newspapers." *Loyola Poverty Law Review* 3: 57–111.
Lovejoy, Owen. 1910. "Newsboy Life: What Superintendents of Reformatories and Others Think about Its Effects." National Child Labor Committee, pamphlet no. 32 (June).
Mangold, George B. 1936. *Problems of Child Welfare.* 3d ed. New York: Macmillan.
McDaniel, Henry Bonner. 1941. *The American Newspaperboy: A Comparative Study of His Work and School Activities.* Los Angeles: Wetzel.

"Miseries of News-Girls." 1881. *New York Tribune,* February 20, 12.

Morrow, Johnny. 1860. *A Voice from the Newsboys.* New York: A. S. Barnes and Burr.

Nasaw, David. 1985. *Children of the City: At Work and at Play.* New York: Oxford University Press.

Nearing, Scott. 1907. "The Newsboys at Night in Philadelphia." *The Survey* 17 (February 2): 778–784.

"New York Newsboys, The." 1869. *The Leisure Hours* (November 1): 717.

"Newsboys and Newsgirls Constitute an Endangered Species." 2000. *Editor and Publisher* (January 31): 5.

"Newsboys' Riot, A." 1877. *Detroit Evening News,* July 21, 4.

Postol, Todd Alexander. 1997. "Creating the American Newspaper Boy: Middle-Class Route Service and Juvenile Salesmanship in the Great Depression." *Journal of Social History* (Winter): 327–345.

Riis, Jacob. 1890. *How the Other Half Lives,* p. 147. Reprint, New York: Penguin, 1997.

Shulman, Harry M. 1932. "Newsboys of New York: A Study of the Legal and Illegal Work Activities During 1931," p. 13. New York: Child Labor Committee.

Stein, Mark A. 1987. "Carriers—The Young Are Fading." *Los Angeles Times,* April 10, 1, 30–31.

"Then and Now: Newspaper Distributing in Detroit in the '50s." 1896. *Friend Palmer Scrapbook* (Detroit Public Library) 13 (May 26): 70.

Trattner, Walter. 1970. *Crusade for the Children: A History of the National Child Labor Committee and Child Labor Reform in America.* Chicago: Quadrangle Books.

Wager-Fisher, Mary. 1880. "The Philadelphia Newsboys." *Wide Awake* 11, no. 1 (July): 16, 18.

Ward, Paul. 1875. "Street Arabs: Bootblacks and Newsboys." *Oliver Optic's Magazine* 18 (December): 949.

West, Elliott. 1996. *Growing Up in Twentieth Century America: A History and Reference Guide.* Westport, CT: Greenwood Press.

Nintendo

See Video Games

O

Orphanages

Orphanages were live-in asylums, common from the eighteenth century to the 1930s, that aided impoverished boys and girls (aged four to twelve) missing one or both parents. Most orphanages cared for children of both genders in separate sections of their buildings, but approximately 9 percent (in 1890) admitted boys only. Middle-class women, and to a lesser extent middle-class men, founded most orphanages to care for impoverished working-class children of immigrants, many of whom had lost a parent due to death. Orphanages were primarily local, privately run institutions with a religious orientation. Most operated on a shoestring. Many were founded by ethnic groups, especially recent immigrants, but few admitted African American boys and girls. Most boys remained in orphanages for a year or two and then were discharged to work for farmers or return to their families.

By the late nineteenth century, reformers criticized orphanages for separating children from families and raising them in an artificial environment. Nonetheless, orphan asylums continued in existence until the 1930s, when federal legislation in the Social Security Act created Aid to Dependent Children, making it possible for mothers to afford to keep their children at home rather than place them in orphanages. In the 1980s and 1990s, there was some public discussion about resurrecting orphanages, but little came of this discussion.

Changes in the economy, demography, and gender roles help to account for the growth of orphanages for impoverished boys and girls in the nineteenth century (only a few orphan asylums were founded in the eighteenth century). The economy changed from agrarian to industrial in the course of the century. As manufacturing plants expanded, largely in cities, demographic change occurred as laborers from the surrounding farms and immigrants from other countries flocked to urban areas seeking work. These immigrant men were very likely to be unskilled. They earned little, worked long hours in dangerous surroundings, and lived with their families in small apartments. Disease was rampant in crowded cities, and industrial accidents were all too common. It was not unusual for a boy to lose a father to death or sometimes desertion. His widowed or deserted mother had few jobs open to her, and those that were, as a seamstress or a servant, paid little. There was very little public welfare available either, so desperate, poor mothers often turned to orphanages to care for their children until the mothers were better off or the children were old enough to work.

Although industrialization worsened the lives of unskilled workers and their families, it had the opposite effect on the

Jacob Riis's photograph "Prayer Time, Five Points House of Industry," ca. 1889, shows small boys in a New York City orphanage. (Bettmann/Corbis)

middle class. Educated men found new jobs in industry as managers, accountants, and lawyers. They earned good wages and could afford to support their wives and children in large, comfortable homes staffed by many servants. For middle-class women, a change in gender roles occurred. No longer did they have to spend long hours at housekeeping and child tending. They could turn these tasks over to servants and spend their spare time in volunteer work outside the home. For them a natural area of interest was children, particularly those boys and girls who lacked fathers to support them and whose mothers were too poor to care for them adequately. It was primarily these middle-class women who founded and maintained orphanages.

Most orphanages were established in cities with large numbers of poor boys and girls. The founders of most orphanages were strongly religious Protestants who taught their orphan charges accordingly. Catholics and Jews feared the conversion of their children to Protestantism, and so they too founded orphanages to spread their respective faiths to their young inmates. Ethnic groups such as Poles and Italians often formed orphanages to care for poor children of the same background. Most asylum founders were whites, and very few admitted African American boys and girls. After the Civil War, African Americans in the South founded some orphanages, but most freed slaves did not have the money to build and support asylums for children.

The typical privately run orphanage held fewer than 100 children, although in the late nineteenth and early twentieth centuries some larger public orphanages were founded in the Midwest. Orphanages customarily housed boys and girls in separate wings of a large building, but by the late nineteenth century some orphanages housed groups of 30 to 50 boys or girls in large cottages. Founders believed that girls needed to be protected from the wild, loud antics of boys and from any sexual contact with them.

The regimen of orphanages was fairly strict. Founders believed that impoverished boys who had grown up without a parent in dangerous cities needed to be retrained in orphanages to more disciplined habits so they could mature into responsible adults. Boys presumably learned the value of regularity when bells rang to awaken them and send them to the washroom, dining room, playroom, and school. After the Civil War, many asylums introduced military drill to teach boys the value of disciplined action. Boys also learned that they had responsibilities when they were assigned to do yard work or heavy chores. Because orphan asylum founders feared that the impoverished parents of boys might interfere with their reform, asylum managers often limited parental visits to once a month in the afternoon. Some orphanage officials also censored the mail of boys and their families.

Inside asylums, orphanage officials also expected boys to learn to live a Spartan life. Presumably they would leave orphanages to return to a working-class existence, so there was no reason for them to get used to lives of luxury. Boys wore simple uniforms, bathed in cold water, and played in large rooms with very few toys.

Any boys who violated asylum rules were slapped, kicked, or hit on the palm with a switch.

Orphanage food was adequate but not plentiful. Older boys often left the table hungry. Sometimes boys found their way into asylum kitchens at night and stole food. Other times they sneaked out of asylums and purchased or stole candy and fruit from neighborhood stores. Despite their best efforts, orphan asylum officials could not completely control the lives of their young charges. Older boys in orphanages bullied younger ones or offered younger ones "protection" from teasing and violence in bathrooms and playrooms in return for favors such as giving over desserts or doing servile tasks like shining shoes. In some cases, younger boys were forced by older ones to provide sexual favors. Such activity was probably rare, however, given the young age of most orphans: few were older than twelve, and their average age was ten in the 1920s.

Because they were so young, orphan boys were likely to contract childhood diseases like scarlet fever and measles. Since antibiotics to treat scarlet fever and inoculations against diseases like the measles were not developed until the 1930s and after, contagious diseases were a very serious matter in nineteenth-century and early-twentieth-century orphan asylums. Often diseases spread quickly, and it was not uncommon for many children to die from them. By the late nineteenth and early twentieth centuries, orphanages tried to limit child deaths by having doctors examine new inmates carefully to prevent ailing youngsters from entering and spreading disease. Also, when despite doctors' best efforts boys did become sick, orphanages isolated them in special hospital wards until they recovered or died.

Even with all the disadvantages of asylum life, boys benefited from the schooling they received in orphanages. Before the end of the nineteenth century, schools were overcrowded and understaffed in most cities. Many poor boys did not attend them at all. However, all nineteenth-century orphanages maintained schools where female teachers taught their young charges to read and write and do elementary arithmetic. Many orphanages also tried to prepare boys for work by teaching them how to use tools and make simple objects out of wood. By the twentieth century, orphanages frequently closed their schools and sent their young charges to neighborhood public or, in the case of Catholic orphanages, parochial schools. Here orphans came in contact with a wider range of acquaintances and probably obtained a more well-rounded education than they did in asylums.

Orphan asylums grew in number throughout the nineteenth century, but they also had critics. One of the most influential was Charles Loring Brace, who founded the New York Children's Aid Society in 1853. He argued that orphanages were bad for boys and girls because they removed youngsters from families and raised them in artificial, overly regimented environments where they failed to learn independence or develop their own individuality. In 1909 President Theodore Roosevelt convened the first White House Conference on Dependent Children, which concluded that the best place for a boy to live was within a family, either his own or, if necessary, a foster family. Orphanages should be a last resort for the care of poor children. Nonetheless, despite criticism, orphanages continued to provide large numbers of boys and girls with temporary homes until the 1930s.

Orphan asylums were never intended to be permanent residences for boys and girls. Most remained for one to four years, although a few stayed five years or more. A boy's length of stay often depended on the condition of his natural family and his age when he entered the orphanage. If a child's family fell on hard times temporarily, he might be able to return to his mother or father in a short time. Conversely, if families broke up due to death or illness, boys might never return to them. Age mattered, for very young boys would probably stay longer than older ones provided their families were too poor to reclaim them. In the nineteenth and early twentieth centuries, boys of ten years, twelve years, and above were old enough to work. Sometimes poor mothers reclaimed their boys at this age so they could come home to work and help support their families. In other cases, orphan asylums signed indenture contracts with farmers and tradesmen who took older boys into their family homes to live and work while providing the boys with room, board, and sometimes schooling. By the twentieth century, indenture contracts were rare, but orphan asylums still placed out boys in foster family homes. Often the boys worked for their keep, but sometimes asylums paid families to take the children in.

The end of orphanages came after 1935 with the passage of the Social Security Act. One part of the act created Aid to Dependent Children (later renamed Aid to Families with Dependent Children, or AFDC), which provided federal government payments to needy mothers to allow them to keep and care for their children. Since the 1910s, some needy mothers had received pensions from state governments to enable them to afford to raise their own children. Yet because mothers' pensions provided minimal benefits to a few women, thousands of other impoverished mothers often had no choice but to place their children in orphanages to protect them from homelessness and even starvation. In the Great Depression, which began in 1929, most states did not have the tax dollars to pay mothers' pensions, and the population of children in orphanages skyrocketed. Removing boys and girls from their families purely because of poverty had been frowned upon since the 1909 White House Conference on Dependent Children. To prevent such family breakups, the federal government created AFDC. Now that they had the opportunity to choose, needy mothers elected to keep their children at home with the help of AFDC payments. Foster care programs also grew in number and accommodated more children. Orphanages either went out of existence or were transformed into homes for emotionally troubled or abused youngsters.

However, in the 1980s and 1990s, there was some talk of reviving orphanages to help care for the large number of children who were victims of abuse in their biological or foster family homes or whose parents were drug users. Some conservatives also favored orphanages as methods of discouraging illegitimacy by denying unwed mothers welfare and forcing them to give up their children to orphanages instead. The most thoughtful and articulate proponents of reviving orphanages regard them as one alternative for children in need and not a final solution to all problems of child welfare.

Priscilla Ferguson Clement

See also Foster Care; Placing Out

References and further reading
Ashby, LeRoy. 1997. *Endangered Children: Dependency, Neglect, and Abuse in American History.* New York: Twayne Publishers.
Clement, Priscilla Ferguson. 1997. *Growing Pains: Children in the Industrial Age, 1850–1890.* New York: Twayne Publishers.
Hacsi, Timothy A. 1997. *Second Home: Orphan Asylums and Poor Families in America.* Cambridge, MA: Harvard University Press.
McKenzie, Richard B., ed. 1998. *Rethinking Orphanages for the 21st Century.* Thousand Oaks, CA: Sage.

Orthodontics

Orthodontics is a branch of dentistry concerned with the development and growth of facial form. Orthodontic treatment focuses on the correction of irregularities of tooth alignment and malocclusion. It is a skilled and complex specialty, with its own techniques and procedures, and successful orthodontic treatment can bring about improvements in facial appearance and function. For many American boys, orthodontics is synonymous with *braces,* a broad lay term covering a wide variety of corrective appliances that have become an everyday experience of boyhood.

The earliest examples of orthodontic treatments have been found in Greek and Etruscan remains from pre-Christian times. In American history, there is no indication of anything more than sporadic attempts at the regulation of tooth development until the second half of the nineteenth century. Norman Kingsley was one of the first Americans to develop orthodontic techniques, which he outlined in his 1880 "Treatise on Oral Deformities as a Branch of Mechanical Surgery." Kingsley and others developed

A teenage boy with braces gives a big smile. (Bob Rowan; Progressive Image/Corbis)

methods for realigning teeth and correcting protrusions. By the 1890s, the failure of the upper and lower teeth to meet properly when the jaws are closed, or malocclusion, was also viewed as a problem and one that could be treated using orthodontic methods. Edward H. Angle developed the Angle classification of malocclusion around 1900, and it remains in use 100 years later.

By the early 1900s orthodontics had developed into a recognizably modern form, establishing its twin concerns of poor tooth alignment and malocclusion. The best ways to treat these problems have been the subject of ongoing debate, and the nature and extent of treatments have also changed, with the impact of these debates and changes being felt by generations of American children. In many ways, orthodontic treatment affects boys and girls in the same way, but some differences are apparent.

Angle and his colleagues at first developed techniques using extra-oral force and opposed the use of dental extractions as part of their treatment strategy. Good occlusion was their primary aim, often at the expense of proper facial proportions. The earliest orthodontic appliances were cumbersome and clumsy, and their degree of effectiveness was limited. In the early 1900s George Crocat developed appliances using gold wires and springs that were more effective and somewhat easier to wear, but their high cost meant that they were not available to the vast majority of boys.

In 1929 the American Board of Orthodontics was established as the first specialty board in dentistry. During the 1930s extraction came to be seen as a legitimate orthodontic strategy, helping to improve a boy's appearance and also stabilizing the improved occlusion produced by the use of appliances. For the next few decades, American orthodontists favored a combination of dental extractions and fixed appliances. These appliances, as the name suggests, were fixed into the boy's mouth using special wiring techniques and could not be removed by the wearer. In contrast, European orthodontists favored removable appliances that could be removed and reinserted by the wearer for cleaning or readjustment. From the 1960s, treatment developed further with the introduction of "functional" appliances that acted on the position of the mandible as a way of altering tooth position. Orthodontic appliances remained cumbersome, and boys were less likely to cooperate with treatment than were girls (Clemmer and Hayes 1979). After 1980, American and European orthodontists moved closer together with regard to treatment. Removable appliances are now common for early treatments, with fixed appliances being used for later or more complex treatment.

Studies using Angle's classification have found that only a minority of American children have normal occlusion according to Angle's strict definition. Estimates of the extent of malocclusion have ranged from 35 percent to 95 percent, depending upon the degree of deviation from normal that is considered to be acceptable. Research in the 1960s found that in six- to eleven-year-olds, only 22.9 percent of white children and 33.1 percent of black children had acceptable occlusion, with 13.7 percent and 16.9 percent, respectively, being assessed as having severe malocclusion.

Demand for orthodontic treatments rose markedly in the late twentieth century, but this increase does not necessarily indicate a worsening of American boys' dental occlusion or tooth alignment. More effective techniques, more comfortable appliances, and increased availability of orthodontic treatment may all have played their part. Indeed, as general health improved, perhaps parents could turn their attention away from other, life-threatening health problems toward a greater concern for dental comfort and facial appearance for their boys. However, although the *need* for orthodontic treatment is higher in boys than in girls, the *demand* for it is lower (Wheeler et al. 1994).

About 4 million people in the United States are being treated with braces at any one time, and almost one-quarter are adults (American Association of Orthodontists 2001). In the case of adult patients, 70 percent are female. In children, 60 percent of patients are girls, and 40 percent are boys. These percentages suggest that around 1.25 million boys in the United States receive orthodontic treatment at any one time. This gender difference in orthodontic treatment may well be because American society puts greater stress on facial appearance for women than for men, although many boys also undergo orthodontic treatment for aesthetic reasons.

Modern orthodontics offers a range of treatments. Fixed and removable appliances can be active, aimed at achieving tooth movement, or passive, designed to maintain tooth position. Retainers are an example of the latter and are used to maintain new tooth positions in the period immediately following active treatment. Since the 1980s new bonding techniques have enabled fixed appliances to be fitted without the need for metal bands. In the late 1990s, braces and retainers became available with a choice of colored wires or with logos on them. Boys were able to customize their braces to give them a distinct, stylish, and perhaps more masculine appearance. Orthodontics can still be a costly therapy—the average cost of comprehensive orthodontic treatment in the late 1990s was more than $2,000—but it is nonetheless increasingly common. Demand for orthodontic treatment tends to be higher in boys from urban settings than from rural ones and in boys from higher-income families.

The American Association of Orthodontists recommends that all children undergo an orthodontic assessment by seven years of age. Boys typically start treatment at eleven or twelve years old, slightly later than girls. Despite the greater need for treatment in boys, much of the promotion of orthodontics is aimed at girls. When "celebrities with braces" are identified as "role models," the vast majority are female and are targeted at girls, although some, such as athlete Carl Lewis and football players Terrell Davis and Brett Favre, are role models for boys ("Yo, It's Time for

Braces" 2001). Treatments that once stigmatized those boys who underwent them are now seen as a normal experience. "Braces" in their many forms are part of growing up. Indeed, in some parts of the United States, orthodontic treatment is so common that those boys who do not need it may feel left out.

Bruce Lindsay

References and further reading
American Association of Orthodontists. 2001. "Orthodontics Online," http://www.aaortho.org/ (accessed March, 2001).

Clemmer, E. J., and E. W. Hayes. 1979. "Patient Cooperation in Wearing Orthodontic Headgear." *American Journal of Orthodontics* 75, no. 5: 517–524.

Proffit, William R. 1993. *Contemporary Orthodontics.* 2d ed. St. Louis: Mosby Year Book.

Wheeler, T. T., S. P. McGorray, L. Yorkiewicz, S. D. Keeling, and C. J. King. 1994. "Orthodontic Treatment Demand and Need in Third- and Fourth-Grade Schoolchildren." *American Journal of Orthodontics and Dentofacial Orthopedics* 106, no. 1: 22–33.

"Yo, It's Time for Braces." 2001. http://tqjunior.thinkquest.org/5029/ (accessed March, 2001).

P

Parachurch Ministry

The term *parachurch* refers to "any spiritual ministry whose organization is not under the control or authority of a local congregation" (White 1983, 19). The phenomena of parachurch ministries and organizations, although not unique to the United States, has been and continues to be a central defining aspect of the American religious experience, particularly among evangelical Protestants. Parachurch organizations have played an important role in the religious and moral formation of boys for most of this country's history. These groups often work alongside churches and local congregations to gain support and funding but maintain independent structures and set their own doctrinal standards. Michael Anthony observes that "historically parachurch organizations have been on the cutting edge of ministry. They are more susceptible to change and do not have the same degree of bureaucracy associated with many church denominational structures" (Anthony 2000, 326). By design, parachurch ministries form to do specialized work that is often mission-oriented and geared toward specific subgroups. A conservative estimate puts the number of these groups at more than 10,000 in the United States alone (310).

From the colonial period until the Civil War, religious instruction of boys was primarily the role of the local parish and the family. When a boy in the Plymouth Colony was sent out of the home for service or apprenticeship, the host committed to provide the youth not only with training, a stipend, and room and board but also with religious instruction (Browning 1997, 56). In colonial America, a boy like the young Thomas Jefferson, who could afford a more formal education, was sent to live with educated clergy for tutoring and religious instruction.

In the southern colonies, the family was chiefly responsible for training boys and girls in religion. There the ideal was to "pray thrice daily, read scriptures at dawn and dusk or consult family members about the state of their souls." Samuel Davies (1723–1761), a Presbyterian pastor and hymn writer, commanded his flock in a sermon to "either set up the worship of God immediately in your families or sin willfully against the knowledge of the truth" (both quotes by Davies are cited in Heimert and Miller 1967, 199). Among the southern clergy, Davis was also one of those who strongly advocated targeting young African American slaves and freed persons in his preaching.

Children were not a primary focus of the colonial religious revivals of the eighteenth century, yet nonetheless male youths were some of the persons most affected by these spiritual renewals. George Whitefield (1714–1770) embarked on his first preaching tour in Georgia in 1738 to assist in the founding of an orphanage. Jonathan Edwards's (1703–1758) ministry in New England included attempts to educate and evangelize Native American youth. And Jonathan Parsons related the continuing effects on young people of Gilbert Tennent's three-month preaching tour in 1744:

> By the latter end of April our young people were generally sick of that vain Mirth and those foolish amusements that had been their delight and were form'd into several religious societies for prayer and reading books of piety under my direction. Many were in my study for advice and the bent of their soul was evidently towards things of another world. (Heimert and Miller 1967, 199)

The religious revivals in the period following the American Revolution came to be called the "Second Great Awakening." One of the lasting legacies from this movement was the proliferation of voluntary societies. These groups had a variety of agendas that included social reform and the evangelization of the frontier and world. The American Sunday School Union was founded in Philadelphia in 1824. These "Sabbath schools," as they were called, were formed to convert children outside the church and spiritually strengthen Christian young people. Prior to the emergence of public schools, the Sunday school movement provided a rudimentary education for many lower-class children. There were 70,000 Sunday school associations founded in the nineteenth century alone.

Secular historical studies of the Civil War have often failed to account for the deeply religious nature of the conflict both in the North and South. Religious impulses could inspire boys and men to enlist, fight, and die. Northern ministers and abolitionists consistently presented the northern cause as God's will for the nation. Southern clergy equally spoke of preserving God's preordained ways. Boys and men killed in combat in both armies were spoken of as martyrs for the cause. Religious revivals were a constant part of camp life and were particularly popular among Confederate troops. It has been estimated that between 100,000 and 200,000 boys and young men converted in the revival "camp" meetings during the war (Moorhead 1978, 70).

The spiritual, educational, and physical plight of the urban poor in general and wayward boys in particular became a mission focus for American churches and independent ministries in the industrial boom following the Civil War. One of the most influential voluntary groups, the Young Men's Christian Association (YMCA), founded in England in the 1840s, had its greatest success in the United States. Perhaps no other figure in the nineteenth century reflects the move from denominational ministries to a parachurch model better than the mass evangelist D. L. Moody (1837–1899). The greatest revivalist of his time, he worked across ecclesiastical boundaries and had a keen interest in children and youth. D. L. Moody began his evangelistic work with the YMCA, promoted the Sunday school movement, and founded the Herman School for Boys. With the help of Presbyterian and Baptist leaders, Moody founded the Student Volunteer Movement in 1876, which over the years recruited thousands of college-age men and women to overseas missions.

In 1881, a Congregationalist minister founded the Christian Endeavor Movement, a nondenominational organization formed explicitly for ministry to youth. Christian Endeavor became the prototype of youth ministry for both independent and denominational groups. Another famous group, the Boy Scouts, was founded in England in 1907 by Robert Baden-Powell and incorporated in the United States in 1910. Though not primarily a religious group, the Boy Scouts impressed upon boys the need for devotion to God, country, and church. Local church congregations often encouraged among their members the formation of independently functioning Christian Endeavor and Boy Scout groups. The Boys' Brigade, which was founded much later, was an explicitly Christian version of the Boy Scouts, which included Bible instruction and Christian training alongside recreational and outdoor skills training.

Perhaps the most famous parachurch ministry founded in the early part of the twentieth century was Roman Catholic. In 1917 Father Edward Flanagan began the work that would become Boys Town. From humble beginnings with a few boys rescued from the streets of Omaha, Nebraska, Boys Town became a national and then an international movement for rescue of orphaned and troubled boys. Spencer Tracy's Academy Award–winning portrayal of Father Flanagan in the 1938 movie helped Boys Town establish itself as a national institution. Today, Girls and Boys Town continues as an international advocacy group for children and families.

One of the bridges between the revivalism of the late nineteenth century and the fundamentalist modernist debates of the post–World War I period was the Bible Conferences and Holiness Camp Meetings. These conferences combined Bible study, moral exhortation, and recreation. They also served as models for an explosion of Christian-oriented camping for children and youth throughout the twentieth century.

Even as average attendance at church grew steadily after World War II, there was an increasing sense of the organized church's failure to reach many young people, especially boys. In Texas, Jim Rayburn, a young Presbyterian minister, began Young Life in 1940. It was designed to be a Christian meeting for non-Christian high school students. The Young Life approach is characteristic of that of many parachurch ministries. It emphasizes adult staff and volunteers building nonjudgmental, caring relationships with high school students, particularly the unchurched. It presents an evangelical message emphasizing the need for a personal commitment to and relationship with Christ. Held in private homes, Young Life meetings are informal and fun, and their leaders present the Christian faith in terms adolescents can understand. Carried out with sensitivity to the culture and context of contemporary youth, Young Life meetings include music, humor, activities, and a Christian message. The organization's commitment to excellence and Rayburn's adage, "It's a sin to bore a kid with the Gospel," is exemplified in its camping program, which is one of the best in the country, religious or secular. Young Life's relational, dynamic philosophy has proven especially appealing to many adolescent boys who were otherwise disinterested in formal religious involvement. It currently has branches in more than 550 communities and took more than 30,000 high school youth to camp in 1999 ("Where Is Young Life?" 2001).

Other parachurch organizations sprang up in the 1940s to bring more young people to religion. In 1941, the U.S. chapter of Inter-Varsity Christian Fellowship was formed and currently has a membership of more than 34,000 college and university students nationwide. Youth for Christ was founded in 1944. Its methodology was based on the traditional revival format and geared toward youth, and its first full-time staff person was a young Baptist preacher named Billy Graham. One of the largest parachurch organizations in the world is Campus Crusade for Christ, founded in 1951 by Bill Bright. It began as an evangelical ministry to college students and has since expanded to high school, adult, and family ministries.

In the spirit of "muscular Christianity," in 1954 a group of Pittsburgh businessmen began the Fellowship of Christian Athletes (FCA), which initially targeted male high school and college athletes. FCA sought to combine higher ideals of sportsmanship, team, and physical accomplishment with Christian spirituality. In its early years it attempted particularly to counter the cultural notion that Christianity was inherently a feminine activity. FCA has since added ministry to females and has more than 6,500 chapters nationally.

The turbulence of the 1960s and 1970s and the rise of the youth culture shaped the direction of parachurch activity. African American children and youth often led the way in the marches and boycotts of the civil rights movement. Beginning in the late 1960s, the rise of Christian rock and Woodstock-type religious festivals engaged thousands of youth. The counterculture "Jesus people" and the neo-Pentecostal movement directly addressed alienated youth and victims of the drug culture. Some existing parachurch ministries as well as new ones began to grapple with the complex issues of race and justice surrounding the

needs of boys and youth in the poor urban areas of the United States. The resurgent conservatism of the 1980s led to youth events and ministries geared around themes of sexual restraint outside marriage, the return to traditional values, and abstinence from drugs and alcohol. In the 1990s, the emerging Internet culture included innumerable points of contact for youth interested in spirituality outside the confines of traditional religious institutions.

There is a growing appreciation for the role parachurch ministries can play among urban youth in general and boys in particular in addressing the crisis of violent youth crime. John DiIulio, one of the nation's leading political scientists who was appointed in 2001 to lead the Bush administration's faith-based initiative, believes religion is the single most important strategy in countering predominantly male violent youth offenders whom he calls "super-predators" (DiIulio 1995, 27). Foundations like Public-Private Ventures and organizations like Boston's Ten Point Coalition and DiIulio's own Partnership for Research on Religion and At Risk Youth are leading the call for both private and governmental support for faith-based social initiatives targeting urban youth. The first decade of the twenty-first century will witness unprecedented opportunities for parachurch ministries to partner with public institutions in addressing the needs of urban and impoverished boys at risk.

Parachurch groups have served an important role in educating the religious community about the unique spiritual, emotional, and social needs of boys. One of the most important legacies of youth parachurch ministries at the beginning of the twenty-first century is the resurgence of children and youth as a priority in both

Protestant and Catholic parishes. The exponential increase in staffing and programming specifically for youth and children at the congregational level since 1970 is a direct result of parachurch influences. As Ellen Charry of Princeton Theological Seminary observes, parachurch groups may be the best hope of creating from childhood through youth a Protestant center in the postmodern and postdenominational United States (2001, 453).

William L. Borror

See also Boy Scouts; Boys Town; Muscular Christianity; Sunday Schools; Young Men's Christian Association

References and further reading
Anthony, Michael J. 2000. *Foundations of Ministry: An Introduction to Christian Education for a New Generation.* Grand Rapids, MI: Baker Books.
Browning, Don, ed. 1997. *From Culture Wars to Common Ground: Religion and the American Family Debate.* Louisville. Westminister/John Knox.
Charry, Ellen T. 2001. "Will There Be a Protestant Center?" *Theology Today* (January): 453–458.
DiIulio, John J., Jr. 1995. "The Coming of the Super-Predators." *The Weekly Standard* (November 27): 23–27.
Heimert, Alan, and Perry Miller. 1967. *The Great Awakening.* Indianapolis: Bobbs-Merrill.
Marty, Martin E. 1984. *Pilgrims in Their Own Land: 500 Years of Religion in America.* New York: Penguin.
Moorhead, James. 1978. *American Apocalypse: Yankee Protestants and the Civil War: 1860–1869.* Louisville: Westminster/John Knox Press.
Noll, Mark. 1992. *A History of Christianity in the United States and Canada.* Grand Rapids, MI: Eerdmans.
Rayburn, Jim III. 1984. *Dance Children Dance: The Story of Jim Rayburn, Founder of Young Life.* Wheaton, IL: Tyndale.
Walker, Williston, Richard A. Norris, David W. Lotz, and Robert T. Handy. 1985. *A History of the Christian Church.* 4th ed. New York: Charles Scribner's Sons.
"Where Is Young Life?" 2001. http://www.younglife.org.
White, Jerry. 1983. *The Church and the Parachurch: An Uneasy Marriage.* Portland: Multnomah Press.

Performers and Actors

Since colonial days, boys have acted in a variety of American public performance venues, including legitimate theater, minstrel shows, circuses, saloons, vaudeville, movies, and television. During the mid-nineteenth century, reformers began to investigate the effects of professional performing on children and to regulate it. Today, the entertainment industry employs thousands of boys who are governed by a complex—but not always effective—patchwork of health, education, and labor codes.

The United States inherited its theater practices from England, where the tradition of using boys as actors was long established. The Hallam troupe, arriving in 1752, was the first professional theater company to establish itself in America. Actor-manager Lewis Hallam employed three of his own children, Lewis, Jr., Isabella, and John, as working members of the troupe. Lewis Hallam, Jr., later reported that he was twelve years old and too frightened to say his one line when he made his debut as a servant in *The Merchant of Venice* during the group's first colonial performance. Although recent scholarship has discovered inconsistencies concerning his age, it is certain that Lewis continued to play small roles until the death of his father brought the company under new management. In 1758, Lewis Hallam, Jr., assumed the roles intended for a young, romantic male lead, playing opposite his mother, who re-

Gary Coleman and Conrad Bain in Diff'rent Strokes, *1981 (Kobol Collection/NBC TV)*

(1802–1804), he had made a lasting impression, and the public was eager to welcome a successor. Audiences praised Payne for his performances in the roles of Romeo and Hamlet. However, since Payne was nearly eighteen when he began his career, he was certainly not an "infant" and may scarcely be considered a boy actor. In addition to acting, as an adult Payne wrote plays and composed the lyrics to "Home, Sweet Home!"

Young boys were popular performers in all forms of nineteenth-century entertainment, especially the circus. Some worked with their families; others were loaned out to or adopted by professional performers. The possible exploitation or abuse of these children became a matter of concern to many reformers, including Elbridge T. Gerry, who founded the Society for the Prevention of Cruelty to Children (SPCC) in 1874. For the next forty years, the SPCC was the primary protector of juvenile performers. Gerry uncovered many instances of severe abuses of performing children. For example, a small boy billed as "Prince Leo" had been purchased from his parents by a circus acrobat who beat the boy continually to force him to walk the tightrope and perform dangerous tricks. Another professional acrobat who had adopted a sister and brother, aged seven and eight, burned them with hot irons and locked them in a closet when they failed to perform satisfactorily. There are documented cases of children abducted from Europe and Japan, forcibly trained as acrobats, and then sold to circus acts. "Families" of acrobats in the circus often comprised several unrelated boys who had been acquired—by sale, rental, or adoption—to supplement their "father's" act.

Because of such practices, Gerry was able to persuade legislators to establish

mained the troupe's leading lady. Lewis Hallam, Jr., is typical of many boys who performed as children; his historical fame is the result of his adult career rather than the juvenile work that formed its foundation. Until his death in 1808, Lewis Hallam, Jr.—actor, manager, and theater owner—was an important figure in American theater for more than fifty years.

John Howard Payne (1791–1852) has been hailed as the first infant prodigy of the American stage. When Payne made his debut in New York in 1809, critics favorably compared him to William Betty. Betty was the same age as Payne and had made a sensation as London's first child star. Although his career had been short the nation's first law protecting performing children. New York's Act to Prevent and Punish Wrongs to Children was passed in 1876 and forbade the exhibition of children as singers, musicians, acrobats, gymnasts, riders, or participants in any dangerous acts.

The provision against singers and musicians was most likely aimed specifically at the large numbers of Italian street performers. In the late nineteenth century, hundreds of Italian men and boys came to this country as little more than indentured servants under "padrones." Padrones provided room, board, and employment but were often unscrupulous. They sent small sums back to Italy in payment for the children's services but provided the boys with barely livable conditions and forced them to perform harsh labor. A great many of the boys were street musicians, forced to roam the city for eighteen or more hours a day in all weather and beg for money before returning to a small apartment to sleep on a small piece of floor with ten or twelve others. One of the first triumphs of Gerry and the SPCC was the conviction of a notorious padrone named Ancarola. At the time of his arrest, he had just "imported" seven boys between the ages of nine and thirteen. One testified that he was under contract to play the violin for Ancarola for four years.

Although the public applauded the SPCC in its work against circuses and street musicians, there was a different reaction when the nonexhibition law was enforced on more genteel entertainments. Juvenile casts of Gilbert and Sullivan operettas were quite popular in the 1880s and 1890s. Gerry maintained that these performances were not only against the law but also harmful to the long-term health of children. The SPCC did strive to protect children from all types of abuse, but Gerry seems to have had a particular focus on—some have called it an obsession—with performers. Both modern and contemporaneous critics have questioned the validity of his extreme position. Members of the press often ridiculed Gerry and attacked him for interfering in the lives of performers in operetta and legitimate theater. The general public believed that these performers led pampered, protected lives and received training for future careers. In a period when most poor children worked to support their families, performance was seen as a less harmful alternative to labor in factories or mines. Compulsory education for all was a new idea just beginning to gain acceptance. Many people believed that some vocational training was all that most children needed, and boy actors presumably received vocational training.

Beginning in 1888, a dramatic version of *Little Lord Fauntleroy* provided work for dozens of boy actors on the legitimate stage. "Fauntleroyism" swept the country. Major cities had their own productions, and road companies toured the show into the mid-1890s. Wallie Eddinger, Jr., age seven, starred in the West Coast production. In New York, a boy and a girl, Tommie Russell and Elsie Leslie, alternated in the title role. Russell began acting professionally at age two. According to a Pennsylvania newspaper report, the "mentally overworked" Russell had a breakdown in 1892. He later quietly pursued a career in real estate. Like Russell, the vast majority of boy actors do not maintain acting careers in their adult lives (New York SPCC, archives).

During the early twentieth century, Progressive reformers raised an outcry against child labor of all types. State after state passed laws restricting child labor and requiring education. A national debate developed concerning whether performance should be regulated under the child labor laws. The SPCC, the National Child Labor Committee, and reformers such as Jane Addams lobbied against children acting. The theater industry mobilized against them, using as spokesmen such popular performers as Francis Wilson and Joseph Jefferson, both former boy actors. Wilson, who began his career in minstrelsy and theater, was a particularly eloquent crusader for the right of boys to perform on stage. He later became the first president of the Actors Equity Association (AEA, formed in 1913) and was partly responsible for its solidarity. Professional actors, whose own income could easily depend on the presence of a child star, argued for a child's right to work.

The two sides squared off in test cases in Massachusetts, Illinois, and Louisiana during 1910, 1911, and 1912 respectively. Former boy performers of the time, including George M. Cohan, Buster Keaton, Milton Berle, and Fred Astaire, testified that they thought of the SPCC not as a protector but as an enemy trying to take the food out of their mouths. The results of the court cases were mixed. New York state ceded the regulation of child acting to the AEA, which fought for safe and sanitary conditions and better pay. It did not establish any safeguards specifically for children.

During the Great Depression in 1938, the federal government finally passed the Fair Labor Standards Act, in part to restrict child labor. However, because many officials thought that acting resembled play more than labor, the Fair Labor Standards Act exempted child performers from its provisions. When the National Child Labor Committee undertook a brief study of child actors in 1941, it reported an extreme variation among state laws at that time. There was and is today no consensus on what constitutes fair labor for performing children.

With the advent of film and later television came increased opportunities for work, fame, profit, and exploitation. The enormously popular *Our Gang* comedies of the 1920s relied on the permanent youth of their characters. As soon as an actor outgrew his part, he was replaced with a younger child. Over a span of seventeen years, 176 children belonged to *Our Gang*.

One of the first boys to achieve national stardom was Jackie Coogan, who began work at age three and starred with Charlie Chaplin in *The Kid* in 1921. Coogan worked steadily and earned more than $4 million, only to discover upon reaching adulthood that his parents had spent most of the money. He sued them for his earnings and received a settlement of $126,000—one-half of all that remained of his vast fortune. Another notorious case involved Freddie Bartholomew, whose aunt brought him to Hollywood from England. After he achieved stardom in *David Copperfield* (1935) and other Metro-Goldwyn-Mayer (MGM) films, his parents, grandparents, and sisters filed twenty-seven lawsuits against him for a share of his earnings. Bartholomew spent so much time in court that his employer fired him for nonperformance and legal fees consumed his savings.

As a result of the attention drawn to these cases, California passed the Coogan Law (1939), which required 50 percent of a child's earnings to be held in trust for him or her. California also instituted the position of "studio teacher," a combination of educator and health and safety

Macaulay Culkin in Home Alone, *1990 (Kobol Collection/Smetzer, Don/20th Century Fox)*

custodian who theoretically has the power to stop production if a child's welfare is endangered. In practice, the law provided protection only to those under long-term studio contracts, which soon ceased to exist. In addition, parents and teachers frequently cooperated with producers in evading the education and safety regulations. Since many states have few restrictions on child labor, some production companies still seek out locations specifically so that their child performers can be unregulated.

During the post–World War II baby boom, television idealized the American family, providing enormous earnings and exposure for many boy actors. During the 1950s and 1960s, Jon Provost spent seven years starring on *Lassie*, while Jerry

Mathers, Tony Dow, and Ken Osmond appeared in *Leave It to Beaver*. As in vaudeville, some adult performers incorporated their own children into their acts. Lucie Arnaz and Desi Arnaz, Jr., appeared on *The Lucy Show*. Ricky and David Nelson joined the cast of their parents' show, *The Adventures of Ozzie and Harriet*. Today, hundreds of children work in the television industry performing in shows, movies, and commercials. As in previous eras, the playlike quality of the work of acting disguises the fact that it is essentially labor.

The continued existence of economic exploitation was dramatized by the experiences of Macaulay Culkin and Gary Coleman. Culkin began work at age four, making several films before starring in the enormously popular 1990 film *Home Alone* and its sequel two years later. Culkin was aggressively marketed by his father, a former child and adult actor, who was able to obtain multimillion-dollar contracts for his son. Culkin's tremendous popularity revitalized the market for child actors and raised their income levels. After Culkin earned $23 million in two years, *Forbes* included him in its 1993 list of richest entertainers. Although Culkin's parents received management fees of 15 percent on his income and that of his four working siblings, by 1995 they were bankrupt. Culkin petitioned the court to authorize the release of money from his trust fund to pay their rent. Following his parents' subsequent separation, a bitter, two-year custody battle ensued, with each parent claiming a stake in Culkin's fortune. His mother was awarded sole custody in 1997.

As a boy, Gary Coleman starred in the television series *Diff'rent Strokes*, but found his fortune gone when he reached adulthood. In 1994 he sued his parents in an effort to recover it.

In 1991 former child actor Paul Petersen founded the nonprofit organization A Minor Consideration to support and assist former and current young performers. Based in California, A Minor Consideration has uncovered and publicized numerous abuses of the health, safety, and education statutes and has lobbied for better enforcement. Petersen has drawn attention to the physical exploitation of premature babies who are sometimes used on hospital shows to simulate newborns in order to evade minimum age limits. According to A Minor Consideration, prior to its involvement, officials routinely ignored abuses, and no film production company had ever lost its "Certificate of Eligibility to Employ Minors." Nor had any child ever been denied a work permit.

Petersen, who was an original Mouseketeer and cast member of *The Donna Reed Show*, joined the Young Performers Committee of the Screen Actors Guild (SAG). In 1998, at Petersen's instigation and under the direction of Lisa Rapport of Wayne State University, SAG sponsored the first scientific study of the psychological effects of celebrity on children. SAG also recently helped secure the passage of the first revision of the Coogan Law since 1939. The California statute is designed to provide economic protection to young performers. Effective January 1, 2000, the earnings of a child actor, musician, or athlete are, for the first time, solely his or her own.

Shauna Vey

See also Films; Jobs in the Nineteenth Century; Melodrama; Television: Domestic Comedy and Family Drama; Vaudeville

References and further reading
Brooks, Tim, and Earle Marsh. 1979. *The Complete Directory to Prime Time Network TV Shows 1946–Present*. New York: Ballantine.
Cary, Diana Serra. 1979. *Hollywood's Children: An Inside Account of the Child Star Era*. Boston: Houghton Mifflin.
Hewitt, Barnard. 1959. *Theatre U.S.A.: 1665–1957*. New York: McGraw-Hill.
Myers, Robert J., and Joyce Brodowski. 2000. "Rewriting the Hallams: Research in 18th Century British and American Theatre." *Theatre Survey* 41, no. 1: 1–22.
New York SPCC (New York Society for the Prevention of Cruelty to Children). Scrapbook collections in the archives contain the following clippings: On Wallie Eddinger, Jr., see *New York Herald*, November 1, 1892; Peoria, Illinois, *Transcript*, February 10, 1892; and *Everybody's Magazine*, September 1, 1903. On Tommie Russell, see Tyrone, Pennsylvania, *Daily Herald*, January 25, 1892; *New York Recorder*, May 1, 1892; and *New York Herald*,

December 29, 1897. On Elsie Leslie, see *Everybody's Magazine,* September 1, 1903; and *New York World,* April 10, 1910.

Petersen, Paul. 2001. "A Minor Consideration." Gardena, CA. www.aminorcon.org (accessed March 1, 2001).

Vey, Shauna. 1998. "Protecting Childhood: The Campaign to Bar Children from Performing Professionally in New York City, 1874–1919." Ph.D. diss., City University of New York.

Wilmeth, Don, with Tice L. Miller. 1996. *Cambridge Guide to American Theatre.* Cambridge: Cambridge University Press.

Zelizer, Viviana A. 1985. *Pricing the Priceless Child: The Changing Social Value of Children.* New York: Basic Books.

Pets

One of a boy's closest and most significant companions may be his pet. Pet keeping is of relatively recent origin in American culture and is strongly associated with the emergence of the middle class. Today it is very common in families with children. Psychological attachment characterizes many child-pet relationships and is built on the reciprocity of interactions with the animal. Pet keeping benefits boys' social development, mental health, and self-esteem. The costs of pet keeping include distress caused by what happens to the pet, financial costs, duties, and health risks. Abuse of animals is a societal concern, but there is potential for pets to contribute to humane attitudes. Pets offer boys in particular an outlet for nurturing behaviors.

Boys and their pets must be placed in historical perspective. Today having pets is socially acceptable—a $20-billion-per-year business in the United States—but pet keeping in the form we know it today is a relatively recent development. Two hundred years ago animals were kept, but the relationship was not one of special affection and virtual family member status. Dogs and cats were kept in sixteenth-century England for their usefulness in shepherding, ratting, hunting, and so forth. The then-extant breeds were called by names indicating their function, such as "fynder" (or water spaniel); only later were modern pedigreed breeds developed. It is easy for us to assume dogs and cats must always have been regarded with the same esteem in which we hold them, but diaries and memoirs from the 1700s do not discuss the relationship between pets and owners. William Shakespeare's references to dogs highlight distasteful connotations such as vulgarity, subversion, and bestiality. Someone showing affection or interest in an animal was subject to ostracism and satire. Individuals who did keep pets were those protected by both wealth and rank from the economic costs and the social derision. For example, King Charles II was notorious for doting on his lapdogs (Ritvo 1987).

By the eighteenth century, however, companion animals were increasing in England and, with some lag time, in America too. Books and periodicals appeared featuring dogs, especially sporting dogs. But not until well into the Victorian period did the institutions of dog fancying appear. The first formal dog show was held in 1859; the Kennel Club for owners or registered breeds of dogs was founded in 1873, and a year later came the first canine stud book to track breeding. Analogous organizations for cats appeared in a few decades. This infrastructure was accompanied by a vast Victorian literature expressing sentimental love for pets. Consistent with its origins, pet keeping by the lower classes was criticized as an indulgence at the expense of the family's children.

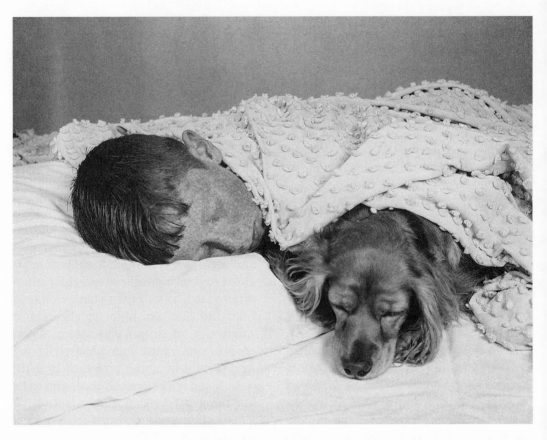

A boy asleep with his dog under the covers (Bettmann/Corbis)

Two explanations of the late-eighteenth- to early-nineteenth-century increase in the acceptability of middle-class pet keeping have been offered. First, it may be linked to industrialization. Industrial technologies made it economically possible for many people to support pets. But the practices of breeders who would manipulate strains of dog by selecting for purposeless or exaggerated features reveal how pet keeping expressed industrial society's dominance over nature. In Harriet Ritvo's view, animals symbolically represent nature, and people cannot form affectionate ties to nature until they dominate it (see also Tuan 1984).

Second, pet keeping may have reflected the concern for character formation in the early-nineteenth-century United States (Grier 1999). An emerging middle class was charting a new ideal of family life that can be called "domesticity." The home stood in contrast to the commercial domain and its rough pursuit of self-interest. The special mission of the domestic realm was to cultivate the countervailing virtue of gentility, which combined self-control and softened feelings. The potential for such kindness was extolled by parenting advisers in the antebellum United States as something "natural." As agents of a sea change in American attitudes toward parenting, they followed thinkers such as Jean-Jacques Rousseau in the view that children are innocent, good-hearted beings. Kindness to animals, in this perspective, was regarded as a foundation of virtue.

In this context, masculine violence stood out as especially problematic. Public and private corporal punishment, wife beating, child abuse, and beating of animals were targets of reformers. If children were naturally good, the special proneness to transgression of boys (later to be men) needed explanation. Expressing an older idea, reformers believed that childhood cruelty had a "hardening effect." Parents should be vigilant about any sign of boyhood cruelty to animals. Harming an insect could be a step down the slope to domestic violence. Voluminous literatures provided cautionary tales and exemplars for children; for parents, advice focused on the importance of instilling self-consciousness of the effects of one's actions and of dealing gently with young sentiments even when correcting them. These matters affected not only the family but the moral progress of society as a whole (Grier 1999).

For boys especially, pet keeping was thought to be critical for socialization in two ways. A pet in the house provided practice material for children learning to act kindly and gave mothers the "small world" where they could intervene and instruct at critical moments, such as when a child might be inclined to strike or hurt an animal. In addition, animals themselves were regarded as exemplars that could teach such virtues as gratitude, fidelity, and enduring love. Middle-class parents were encouraged to keep many different animals for their children. By the early twentieth century, these practices were rationalized by the influential psychologist G. Stanley Hall, who founded the "child study" movement that captured the attention of many middle-class mothers. He was also inspired by Charles Darwin's theory of evolution. In Hall's theory of psychological development, just as the embryo repeated the earlier stages of human evolution, so too did the course of childhood represent the stages of human cultural evolution. Pets played important roles in this repetition, culminating in an interest in horses, the last step before the industrial stage. A boy without pets was, in his view, deprived of his evolutionary inheritance. Outside the home, an active dog complemented boys' relatively greater mobility (in comparison to girls'). Boyhood adventures with dogs (including hunting) have been romanticized in American culture.

Boys and Pets Today
Knowledge of children and pets today still bears on questions of values and ethics, but it also draws on a growing body of empirical evidence. Not all of the work done has addressed or detected important differences for boys versus girls, so much of what follows applies to both sexes. According to the American Veterinary Medical Association, in 1996, 58.2 million U.S. households (58.9 percent) owned one or more pets; about half of these households owned dogs, cats, or both. The animals included 59 million cats, 52.3 million dogs, 12.6 million birds, 5.7 million rabbits, 4.8 million rodents, 3.5 million reptiles, 56 million fish, and 4 million horses. In surveys, dogs are consistently the favorite pet of about 50 percent of children, as are cats for about 30 percent. Another 20 percent favor some other group listed above (Statistics Research Group 1997).

Pets are common in families with school-age children and adolescents. A majority of parents believe pet keeping is good for children. In households with children aged eight to twelve, 75 to 90 percent have pets (Bryant 1990). The number of pets is not influenced by socioeconomic status, although rural families have more pets than urban or suburban ones. More children in the family predicts fewer pets. Most children want pets regardless of the reasons for a family not having them, and only 3 percent of children in non-pet-owning homes have no interest in pets (Kidd and Kidd 1990). Boys and girls are equally likely to own or spend time with pets, and childhood pet ownership is a good predictor of adult ownership.

Psychological Dimensions

The concept of psychological attachment describes a quality of child-pet relationship beyond ownership. Attachment is an emotional tie that bonds one person to another or, in this case, to an animal. It endures over space and time and is expressed by such actions as spending time with the pet; showing interest in it; having positive ideas about it; holding the pet and cleaning up after it; sleeping near the pet; giving gifts; and feeling that the pet knows what the child is feeling, is a family member, and likes the child. Older children express their attachment in emotion words and in thoughts of the pet. A child that becomes attached to a pet at an early age is more likely to hold positive attitudes toward pets in adulthood (an effect that is weaker for boys than girls). In addition, loss of a pet (through death or through the pet's being given away, abandoned, or lost) is like the loss of any other close partner. Children need the opportunity to grieve and mourn a lost pet.

Important roots of attachment lie in the degree and kind of interactions that transpire between child and pet. Human children are remarkable in the degree to which they can extend their developing social abilities flexibly across the species boundary (Myers 1998). From early infancy, boys and girls differentiate animals from both inanimates and other people. Analyses of dog-child pairs show that the child takes the most initiative in interactions but also that the dog acts as a responsive partner. Observations of children interacting with various species show them adjusting their interactive moves to accommodate the animal. Children also incorporate animals into their verbal world, talking to them, especially in times of stress. Most eleven-year-olds believe animals are capable of linguistic communication and moral responsibility. Animals' salience is suggested by their frequent appearance in the dreams of children, up to about age eight.

The patterns of interactiveness described above are analogous to other findings that show how a child's sense of self comes about through comparisons with others and through others' reflected appraisals of the child. The give-and-take of enduring relationships offers a child the opportunity to clarify his or her sense of self. Arguably, given the responsiveness of many pets, the child's self is defined within a more-than-human community of others. Pets (and other animals) help deepen the sense of what it means to be human by allowing comparisons and a sense of commonality not otherwise available.

Benefits and Costs

The psychological dimensions of the child-pet relationship underlie some of its effects. Benefits include companionship, involvement in play, and feelings of closeness and warmth. Pets may affect health positively, for example, by decreasing blood pressure. Several factors influence the social, emotional, and psychological benefits of pets, including age, gender, and especially the type of bond felt with the animal. A close bond with a pet has been found to correlate with a child's empathy, cooperativeness, social competence; a pet lowers anxiety, reassures, and reduces problem behaviors and withdrawal from society. Boys (but not girls) with high pet attachment are reported by teachers to do better at school. Species of animal and family structure do not appear to directly affect these benefits (Melson 2001). The use of pets in mental health treatment was pioneered in the 1960s and today includes using animals to treat special conditions, such as autism, severe learning disabilities (such as Down's syndrome), emotional illness, and multiple disorders. Part of the success of highly interactive animals such as dogs in such therapy may be due to the animal's ability to stimulate more interaction and initiation on the part of the child.

Benefits and costs have also been studied from the child's point of view. Four areas of benefit include mutuality (helping each other), enduring affection, self-enhancing affection (the pet makes the child feel good about him- or herself), and exclusivity (sharing private feelings). Costs children perceive include feeling distress over the pet's death, having it given away, caring for it when it is sick or hurt, doing pet chores, being blamed for something it did wrong or for not caring for it, and worrying for its safety (Bryant 1990).

Other, more objective costs include dog bites (2.8 million children were bitten in 1995); pet-related human health concerns (allergies, intestinal parasites, psittacosis or "parrot fever," rabies, etc.) and the dirt and messiness caused by pets; financial and time burdens; and building and space restrictions. Children also express fears of animals, though fewer boys (51 percent) than girls (73 percent) do so. The most frequently feared animals across sexes are snakes, lions, spiders, tigers, dogs, crocodiles, and bears.

Humane Attitudes and Nurturance
The connections between being abused as a child, abusing animals as a child, and developing sociopathology later have received much attention in recent years (Ascione and Arkow 1998). Sporadic, nonsevere, or infrequent tormenting of an animal, however, is not uncommon and may represent things other than profound emotional disturbance, such as experimentation, lack of understanding, imitation of a role model's behavior, cultural differences, and short-term stress. It should, however, always be taken seriously. In general, many children are disposed to show humane attitudes, that is, compassion and a positive attitude toward care and treatment of animals. Boys tend to score lower on tests of these attitudes than girls. Parental attitudes strongly affect them, but studies have inconsistently found pet ownership to do so. Humane education programs, such as those provided by the North American Association for Humane Education, have shown that it is possible for children to improve on measures of positive attitudes toward animals. Intensive programs, especially those that enhance empathy by role-playing, have the greatest effect.

Of particular interest concerning boys is nurturing behavior. Until about age five, both sexes show similar degrees of interest in nurturing babies. But after that age, girls increase and boys decrease this behavior. However, boys, but not girls, gain more over the next few years in their knowledge of the care of puppies and kittens. Baby care is associated with gender differently than is pet care, so that by the elementary years pet care is an especially important avenue for the expression of nurturance for some boys (Melson 2001).

Gene Myers

References and further reading

Ascione, Frank, and Phil Arkow, eds. 1998. *Child Abuse, Domestic Violence and Animal Abuse*. West Lafayette, IA: Purdue University Press.

Bryant, Brenda. 1990. "The Richness of the Child-Pet Relationship." *Anthrozoös* 3, no. 4: 253–261.

Grier, Katherine C. 1999. "Childhood Socialization and Companion Animals: United States, 1820–1870." *Society and Animals* 7, no. 2: 95–120.

Kidd, A., and R. Kidd. 1990. "Social and Environmental Influences on Children's Attitudes toward Pets." *Psychological Reports* 67: 807–818.

Melson, G. 2001. *Why the Wild Things Are*. Cambridge, MA: Harvard University Press.

Myers, Gene. 1998. *Children and Animals*. Boulder, CO: Westview Press.

Podbersek, A., Elizabeth Paul, and James Serpell, eds. 2000. *Companion Animals and Us*. Cambridge: Cambridge University Press.

Ritvo, Harriet. 1987. *The Animal Estate*. Cambridge, MA: Harvard University Press.

Serpell, James. 1986. *In the Company of Animals*. Oxford: Basil Blackwell.

Statistics Research Group. 1997. *U.S. Pet Ownership and Demographics Sourcebook*. Schaumburg, IL: American Veterinary Medical Association.

Tuan, Yi Fu. 1984. *Dominance and Affection: The Making of Pets*. New Haven: Yale University Press.

Photographs by Lewis Hine

Lewis Wickes Hine (1874–1940), a Progressive-era social reformer, photographed children at work for the National Child Labor Committee (NCLC) between 1906 and 1918. His documentary photography was part of a larger effort of the NCLC to educate the public about the dangerous and immoral conditions under which American children worked in mills, agriculture, canneries, mines, glass factories, tenement sweatshops, and a variety of street trades. The NCLC and Hine had as their ultimate goal passage of a national child labor bill, although they also worked for the passage and enforcement of state child labor legislation, especially in the South. Hine had a particular interest in the conditions faced by immigrant children and paid special attention to recording the ages of working children to document widespread abuse of existing state laws. His photographs thus provide images of working-class and rural boys of specific ages. They document not only the boys' clothing, general appearance, and physical surroundings but also the often dangerous jobs that comprised the working lives of a less-than-carefree boyhood—the normal experience of many boys at the beginning of the twentieth century.

Born the son of an owner of a coffee shop in Oshkosh, Wisconsin, Hine came to New York City in 1901, after studying briefly at the University of Chicago. He took classes in sociology at Columbia University and eventually earned a master's degree in education at New York University. From 1901 until 1908, he taught botany and nature studies at the Ethical Culture School in New York. At some point during his teaching, he taught himself to use a camera. In 1905, while studying the social conditions of the poor, he was hired to photograph immigrants arriving at Ellis Island. His photographs graphically illustrated the poverty of the new arrivals, as well as their fears, their hopes, and the dignity with which they withstood the roughshod bureaucratic treatment to which men and women and boys and girls were subjected. Shortly thereafter he completed the "Pittsburgh Survey," a photographic investigation of the working and living conditions of men and boys employed in the steel industry of that city. From 1906 onward, images from both the Ellis Island and Pittsburgh photographic projects were published in *Charities and the Commons* (later renamed *The Survey*), a weekly magazine published in New York by social reformers. Eventually such other Progressive-era magazines as *McClure's* also bought and published Hine's photographs.

Widespread publication of his dramatic images brought Hine to the attention of the National Child Labor Committee, which hired him on a part-time basis in 1906 and 1907 to photograph families with children doing piecework in the tenements of New York. The NCLC had been formed in 1904 to gather information, publish reports, and mobilize public opinion in order to pressure individual states and the federal government to pass child labor legislation. In 1908 Hine's job became a full-time one; for $100 a month and expenses he traveled to Ohio, Indiana, and West Virginia to photograph conditions under which children worked in coal mines and glass factories. The next year he carried out photographic investigative assignments in textile mills in New England and Georgia and photographed immigrant children at work in the shrimp- and oyster-packing industry of the Gulf states. By the time he left the NCLC in 1918 in a dispute over salary, Hine had traveled thousands of miles throughout the southern, midwestern, mid-Atlantic, and New England states, producing thousands of photographs that

"Day Scene. Wheaton Glass Works. Boy is Howard Lee. His mother showed me the family record in Bible, which gave birth July 15, 1894. 15 years old now but has been in glass works two years and some nights. Started at 13 years old. Millvill, N.J. Nov. 1909." (Library of Congress, Hine caption)

the NCLC used extensively in its posters and reports and as the basis for exhibitions at its annual meetings while also making them available to newspapers and other publications.

In his captions Hine made it clear that he was concerned about the impact of work before the legally permitted age of fourteen on all aspects of the lives and development of boys (and of girls as well). The kind of jobs most boys did paid them little and did almost nothing to teach

"Manuel the young shrimp picker, 5 years old and a mountain of child labor, oyster shells can be seen behind him. He worked last year & understands not a word of English. Biloxi, Miss. Feb. 20, 1911."
(Library of Congress, Hine caption)

them the value of work while surrounding them with unhealthy and inappropriate conditions that limited their physical, educational, intellectual, and moral development. In poster after poster Hine charged that child labor was making boys "human junk" (Hine 1915; Guimond 1991, 82; Kemp 1986, 10).

Using crude flash photography in underground coal mines, Hine captured the grimy faces and stunted physical devel-

opment of the young boys who worked as "greasers," "breakers," and "couplers" 500 or more feet below the surface. He wrote in outrage of the unhealthy conditions in the mine faced by a boy named Willie:

Waiting all alone in the dark for a trip to come through. It was so damp that Willie said he had to be doctoring all the time for his cough. A short distance from there the gas was pouring in so rapidly that it made a great torch when the foreman lit it. Willie has been working here for 4 months. . . . Jan. 16 I found Willie at home sick. His mother admitted he is only 13 years old. (Caption for National Archives and Records Administration photograph, negative 1920, S. Pittston, PA, January 7, 1911)

Although Hine believed that the worst offenders against child labor laws were textile mills, he objected most strongly to the moral risks of urban youngsters serving as "newsies," messengers, and delivery boys. Moving in and out of the worst districts of the cities, according to Hine, these boys carried messages to drug dealers and prostitutes, hung out in pool halls, gambled and smoked in alleyways and streets, and sometimes experimented with drugs and sex at a young age.

Yet the strength of Hine's work lies in his respect for the children he photographed. He usually avoided taking candid (unposed) shots of boys (and girls) and instead encouraged them to look straight into the camera lens. Thus Hine allowed the boys in his photographs to construct their own identities, and they often smile. Hine's photographs reveal that boys who labored were determined and fighting to

"View of the Ewen Breaker of the Pa. Coal co. The dust was so dense at times as to obscure the view. This dust penetrated the utmost recesses of the boys' lungs. A kind of slave-driver sometimes stands over the boys, prodding or kicking them into obedience. S. Pittston, Pa. Jan. 10, 1911." (Library of Congress, Hine caption)

retain their dignity in the face of exploitive working conditions. They were not simply victims. They were actors in their own right.

Constance B. Schulz

See also Jobs in the Twentieth Century; Newsboys

References and further reading
Major collections of Lewis Hine photographs are located at the Library of Congress; the National Archives and Records Administration (NARA); the George Eastman House in Rochester, New York; and the University of Maryland Baltimore County Library.
Guimond, James. 1991. *American Photography and the American Dream.* Chapel Hill: University of North Carolina Press.
Gutman, Judith Mara. 1967. *Lewis W. Hine and the American Social Conscience.* New York: Walker.
———. 1974. *Lewis Hine 1874–1940: Two Perspectives.* New York: Grossman.
Hine, Lewis. 1915. "The High Cost of Child Labor." Brochure. Washington, DC: Library of Congress.
Kemp, John R., ed. 1986. *Lewis Hine Photographs of Child Labor in the New South.* Jackson: University Press of Mississippi.
Rosenblum, Walter, Naomi Rosenblum, and Alan Trachtenberg. 1977. *America and Lewis Hine: Photographs 1904–1940.* Millerton, NY: Aperture.
Trattner, Walter I. 1970. *Crusade for the Children: A History of the National Child Labor Committee and Child*

Labor Reform in America. Chicago: Quadrangle Books.

Westbrook, Robert. 1987. "Lewis Hine and the Two Faces of Progressive Photography." *Tikkun* 2 (April–May): 24–29. Reprinted in Leon Fink, ed. 2001. *Major Problems in the Gilded Age and Progressive Era.* 2d ed. Boston: Houghton Mifflin.

Placing Out

Although placing out (a method of placing boys and girls in families other than their biological ones) had antecedents in the colonial era, it became especially important in the nineteenth century as a method of removing impoverished children from their urban family homes and placing them in farm family homes. The method was first widely employed by Charles Loring Brace's New York Children's Aid Society (CAS), and later child welfare agencies in New York and other cities placed out as well. Placing out meant removing needy city children from their natural families and sending them by train to farm communities in the East and Midwest, where they were usually expected to work for the families with whom they lived. The children were often from immigrant families, and virtually all of them were white. Some boys and girls profited from this exchange, but others suffered from it. Gradually, in the early twentieth century, placing out was replaced by foster care.

In colonial America, children were placed by their parents or local authorities in a family other than their own for a variety of reasons. Boys were placed under indenture to master craftsmen to learn the skills of a trade, but many parents also hired out their boys for wages, usually to farmers as agricultural labor. In cases of illness, even very young children were sent to live with families recommended for their ability to achieve a cure. Sometimes unruly boys were sent to live under the governance of another family. And during times of family crisis, such as extreme poverty or the illness, imprisonment, or death of a parent, relatives or local authorities would send a child to live temporarily in another family or to be informally adopted. Although historians long have speculated about the reasons for placing out children, Helena Wall (1990) has argued that economic considerations usually underlay this widespread practice. Families taking in children were expected to provide parental care for them, but they also received compensation, sometimes from local authorities but especially from the labor of boys during their childhood years.

Placing out practices changed in the nineteenth century with the growth of immigration, industrialization, and urban poverty. In the 1830s, 1840s, and 1850s, New York and other East Coast cities attracted large numbers of immigrants, mostly from Ireland and Germany. Many arrived in the city penniless and ended up living in overcrowded apartments with relatives. Immigrant fathers found it difficult to find jobs that paid enough to support their families. Mothers worked full-time keeping apartments clean, finding enough for everyone to eat, and caring for young children. By the time their sons were old enough to work, sometime between the ages of six and twelve, depending on the mental and physical maturity of the boy, needy parents sent them into city streets to earn money doing errands and odd jobs and selling newspapers. Parents expected that sons would repay their families for child care in infancy and early childhood by going to work and turning most of what they earned over to their mothers and fathers. Such working boys spent much of each day without parental supervision. Some even slept out in city streets.

At the same time, middle-class fathers who earned good money in business or the professions could afford to support their families in large city or suburban homes. Middle-class mothers had servants to help them with housekeeping and child care. Such prosperous families could afford to keep their children in school and never let their sons (or daughters) run about city streets or seek employment before their late teens. To the middle class, the influx of poor immigrant families to U.S. cities was alarming. They worried especially about needy children who, if they grew up unsupervised and uneducated, might never emerge from poverty and eventually turn to crime.

Middle-class men and women found a partial solution to the problem of urban child poverty in the placing-out program of the CAS, the agency founded by Charles Loring Brace in 1853. Brace came from a middle-class New England family and was educated as a minister. As a young man he traveled in England, where he observed how poor children were placed out in Canada and Australia to help populate the British Empire. He also visited Germany, where the "Friends in Need" program placed vagrant city children with rural families. When Brace began his ministry in New York, he was alarmed by the large number of boys who worked and seemingly lived in the city's streets. He and other ministers tried to preach to the boys about Christian values, but the boys were unruly, often threw stones and yelled at the pastors, or ran and fought among the benches set out for the meetings. This experience led Brace to seek another method of reform-

ing needy urban youths. With the formation of the CAS, he sought financial support from other concerned members of the middle class to "save" the city's impoverished children.

In 1854, Brace began his placing-out program of removing children of working age from their city families and placing such children in farm families. Brace admired enterprising city boys who were street-smart and hardworking. However, he believed there was little future for them in cities, which were both unhealthy places in which to live and areas where there was so much social stratification that poor boys might never rise above the working class and obtain well-paying jobs. Brace, like other members of the middle class of his day, believed that living on a farm was healthier than living in a city and that the countryside was a place where it was easier for boys to overcome class barriers and rise up the social scale. And although Brace admired the boys and hoped to provide them with a better future, he was critical of their families, who were usually immigrant and poor. He felt separating enterprising, needy boys from such families was beneficial to the boys.

Of course, placing out was not an entirely original program. In addition to its European antecedents, there was in the United States the system long employed by public welfare authorities of indenturing impoverished orphaned children to families that would provide them room and board and some education in return for their labor. Orphanages and reformatories also indentured children to work after they had spent a year or more in institutional care. However, Brace's placing-out program was unique in that it did not involve formal indenture agreements between the CAS and farm families willing to take in children. Brace had enormous confidence in the goodwill of farm families and believed the protection afforded by a formal indenture contract, promising room and board and education for children placed on farms, was unnecessary. He also believed that indenturing made it difficult for the CAS to remove children from poor homes and that it prevented enterprising boys from leaving homes they did not like and moving on to better ones.

Agents of the CAS walked through the poorer neighborhoods in New York City, recruiting children to be placed out on farms either in eastern states or in the Midwest. Parents were most likely to relinquish boys in their early teens who were old enough to work but who had not yet found well-paying jobs. Sixty percent of the children placed out by the CAS in its early years were male. Single mothers who could not support their families adequately on the low wages then paid women workers were especially willing to let their nonworking sons be placed out. Many boys were themselves eager to leave the city and seek employment and possibly adventure in the West. The agency recruited white boys and girls almost exclusively. It refused African American children, even though most were poor. The agency argued that in the rural Midwest, where few blacks lived, it was difficult to find farm families willing to take in nonwhite children. The construction of railroads between the East and Midwest made it possible for the CAS to take children some distance from the city to rural areas where laborers were scarce. Sometimes the railroads provided the CAS with discounted tickets for children on their way to being placed out.

Groups of twenty to thirty children, supervised by an agent of the CAS, embarked on an "orphan train" from New York City. When the CAS first began placing out, once the train reached what the agent believed to be a likely rural town, he ordered the children to disembark. The agent then contacted the mayor or other town officials and told them he had a group of city children in need of good farm homes. Town officials then called a meeting of families living in the area and lined the children up in front of them. The families then were invited to choose a child to take home with them. Sometimes farmers examined the children's teeth or felt their muscles. Later the CAS sent agents out in advance to towns to line up farm families for children, and in some communities committees formed to prepare for the children's arrival. The chief requirement the CAS had of prospective parents was that they be Christian. The agency placed children in both two-parent and single-parent families. If not all the children were chosen by families in a particular town, the agent set off on the train with the remaining youngsters and stopped at another town to find them homes.

The CAS was so confident that all would go well with youngsters placed out in farm families that at first it had no method of checking up on boys and girls, except to have the children write the agency periodically. Eventually, the CAS sent agents to visit boys and girls placed out, but because the children lived on scattered farms, it was difficult for an agent to visit most youngsters more than once a year. Many children were probably treated well, but others may have been punished harshly or abused. Older boys had the best chance of leaving abusive families. Boys usually worked in the fields, often without much supervision, so escape was fairly easy. When there was little work to do on farms in the winter months, boys were free to attend school, where they might meet other local youths who could tell them of better families in which to live or of paying jobs for which they might be qualified.

Children who were placed out were not always permanently separated from their natural families. The CAS informed parents where their youngsters were placed, and although the agency did not publicize it, of the 69 percent of boys and girls who lived with their families before placement in 1853 and 1854, 63 percent returned to those families after living on farms for a year or two. For many needy families, placing out was a temporary expedient: a method of providing for children when the parent or parents were unable to do so because of unemployment, illness, or some other family emergency.

Brace's Children's Aid Society placed out an enormous number of children: 60,000 between 1854 and 1884. It was also widely imitated: by 1867 there were fifty similar agencies placing out children in cities across the United States. Such a large and unique child welfare program inevitably attracted criticism. Roman Catholics opposed placing out by the CAS because its founder, Brace, and most of its financial supporters were Protestant. Catholics argued that the agency deliberately removed poor Catholic youngsters from their natural family homes and placed them in rural, Protestant homes where the children might very well forget Catholicism and be converted to a different faith. Catholics were not so much opposed to placing out as they were against placing out by an aggres-

sively Protestant child welfare agency. Eventually, Catholics formed their own placing-out societies, such as the New York Foundling Hospital and the Boston Home for Destitute Catholic Children.

Orphan asylum managers were also very critical of the CAS. They argued that it was a mistake to take children directly from city streets and place them in farm family homes. Boys and girls from desperately poor urban families needed some education and some disciplinary training before they were ready to live with respectable, more prosperous families than their own. Again, orphanage officials did not so much object to placing out as they did to placing out youngsters without first retraining them in institutions.

Finally, as the number of poor children who left eastern cities on orphan trains grew, states in the Midwest began to object. They argued that easterners were emptying cities of juvenile delinquents and paupers and dumping them in rural areas, where they might very well turn to lives of crime or become dependent on rural communities for public assistance. Ironically, even as some midwestern states objected to children from the East being placed within their borders, these same states were placing poor children even farther west. Thus, in the late nineteenth century, the New York Children's Aid Society still placed some children in rural Ohio, while agencies in Cleveland and Cincinnati were sending youngsters west to Indiana. By the 1890s, Indiana agencies were placing youngsters farther afield in Nebraska.

The CAS responded to its critics in various ways. The agency tried to be more careful about placing sons and daughters of Catholic parents in Catholic rural homes. However, the CAS never accepted the idea that children needed to be reeducated in orphanages before being placed out. Brace believed that any length of stay in an orphan asylum disadvantaged youngsters by isolating them from the real world of human feeling and familial emotion. He believed orphanage life turned boys and girls into automatons who knew only how to march about in lockstep. As for his midwestern critics, Brace responded to them by placing fewer children in states where there was strong objection to such placement.

Placing out continued into the twentieth century, and the New York Children's Aid Society did not end the practice until 1929. However, as professional social workers entered the field of child welfare, they became concerned about haphazard methods of selecting families in which to place needy children and about families willing to take in youngsters mainly for the labor they provided. Eventually, placing out was transformed into foster care.

Priscilla Ferguson Clement

See also Apprenticeship; Foster Care; Indentured Servants; Orphanages

References and further reading
Ashby, LeRoy. 1997. *Endangered Children: Dependency, Neglect, and Abuse in American History*. New York: Twayne Publishers.
Bellingham, Bruce. 1984. "'Little Wanderers': A Socio-Historical Study of the Nineteenth Century Origins of Child Fostering and Adoption Reform, Based on Early Records of the New York Children's Aid Society." Ph.D. diss., University of Pennsylvania.
Brace, Charles Loring. 1872. *The Dangerous Classes of New York and Twenty Years' Work among Them*. New York: Wynkoop and Hallenbeck.
Hollaran, Peter. 1989. *Boston's Wayward Children: Social Services for Homeless Children, 1830–1930*. Rutherford, NJ: Fairleigh Dickinson University Press.
Holt, Marilyn. 1992. *The Orphan Trains: Placing Out in America*. Lincoln: University of Nebraska Press.
Wall, Helena. 1990. *Fierce Communion: Family and Community in Early America*. Cambridge, MA: Harvard University Press.

Plantations

From the colonial period through the Civil War, boys in the American rural South grew up on plantations that differed in size from farms to vast estates. As Virginia was settled after 1607 and Maryland after 1632, family formation was impeded by high mortality. Surviving sons of planters labored with British indentured servants in tobacco fields surrounding the Chesapeake Bay and its tributaries. Not until the 1680s did African slaves significantly begin to replace indentured servants as the region's primary labor force. By the 1740s in both the Chesapeake area and Carolina (settled after 1663), wealth accumulated through ownership of land and slaves produced a small class of well-to-do families, whose sons enjoyed privileges of education and a genteel lifestyle. After the American Revolution, residents of Virginia and Maryland carried this plantation system based on slave labor into Kentucky and Tennessee, and cotton production spread rapidly into the backcountry of South Carolina and Georgia. Sons of slave owners and enslaved boys experienced this early-nineteenth-century westward movement, as families rushed into Alabama, Mississippi, Louisiana, and Texas in search of profit from the cotton boom. Privileged white boys on large plantations enjoyed the freedom of country life, often chafing at their parents' efforts to curtail and educate them, whereas sons of yeomen on

A white boy plays with slave children on a southern plantation. (Library of Congress)

smaller farms worked the fields under the direction of a patriarchal father. Yet all of them grew up living in close proximity to enslaved boys, with whom they played in plantation yards, roamed the woods and streams, and labored in tobacco and cotton fields.

In the mid-seventeenth century, when yeoman farmers constituted about half the population in Maryland and Virginia, a plantation was essentially a farm of 200–300 acres, of which no land was fully cleared and no more than 50 acres would be cultivated with corn and tobacco, planted in small hills among stumps of girdled trees. Because of the prevalence of malaria, dysentery, and typhoid fever, boys grew up in severely disrupted families in which infant and child mortality was high and a majority of children could expect to lose one or both parents. The result was often blended families, as spouses remarried and children of one partner encountered new siblings in the children of the other. Because planters invested scarce resources in land and imported servants, these families lived in one- or two-room impermanent wooden structures, built directly on the swampy ground without brick or stone foundations. Family members cooked, ate, worked, and slept in the hall, or one room with a large hearth, and older boys and servants slept in a loft that was also used for storage. Boys were raised on dried Indian corn made into bread or boiled and supplemented with pork, beef, wild game, dairy products, poultry, eggs, and fruit from a planted orchard. Although boys received some education and were taught to read and perhaps to write and keep accounts, all family members engaged in fieldwork. While younger boys pounded corn, fetched wood and water, and rounded up livestock, older boys participated in the endless round of activity—setting out plants, hoeing weeds, picking leaves and hanging them up to dry, and packing dried leaves in hogsheads—that tobacco cultivation required.

Frequently these boys worked with native-born or British indentured servants who were no more than boys themselves, purchased as half hands at the age of twelve or full hands at age sixteen. Servants were under the direction of masters for their four- to seven-year terms but eventually would be free to profit from the skills they had acquired. Because fathers often died when their sons were young, some boys became masters themselves. If the plantation lacked sufficient income to support them, orphans were bound out to other families by the county court, but many fathers provided in their wills for guardians to manage property until sons reached age eighteen and could receive the inheritance they began to manage by themselves.

Although most seventeenth-century yeomen were British immigrants, many of whom had arrived as indentured servants, an occasional African, such as Anthony Johnson on Virginia's Eastern Shore, owned a plantation. In the early years the status of Africans was rather fluid: some may have been indentured servants, and a man like Johnson, who had been a slave, could work to buy his freedom. His son Richard would marry a white woman, sire four children, and inherit property (Breen and Innes 1980). The status of Africans deteriorated, however, by the 1680s as the price of tobacco plummeted, indentured servants became more difficult to obtain, and planters with capital began to purchase slaves. Over 50,000 slaves were brought to the Chesapeake area in the first forty years of the eighteenth century (Kulikoff 1986, 320); because merchants preferred cargoes that were "Boys & Girls of about 15 or 16 years of Age, of which 2/3 Boys & 1/3 Girls," many of them must have been male teenagers. When the price of tobacco revived in the 1710s, planters with an adequate labor force were able to profit and to buy more land and slaves. The result was the growth of a class-conscious native-born gentry, able to import British consumer goods and to live a leisured, genteel lifestyle. Although yeoman and tenant families still worked the fields much as they had in the seventeenth century, boys on plantations could be sons of wealthy planters, born to privilege and expected to assume social and political leadership.

By 1732 Robert "King" Carter owned 333,000 acres of land, divided on his death among five surviving sons, four of whom he had sent to England to be educated. His grandson, Robert III, whose father had died when he was four years old, grew up in the large household assembled when his mother remarried a widower with several children. But his uncles held his inherited lands in trust and managed them until he reached the age of twenty-one. Five years later Robert Carter married sixteen-year-old Frances Anne Tasker of a wealthy Baltimore family and settled down at Nomini Hall and Williamsburg to manage his 70,000 acres of land and 500 slaves. Of seventeen children born to the Carters, twelve survived infancy, four sons and eight daughters who grew up in a Georgian brick house covered with white lime, surrounded by thirty-two dependent buildings. In 1773, when Benjamin was eighteen, Robert, sixteen, and John, four, Carter hired a Princeton graduate, Philip Fithian, to be their tutor and live in the schoolhouse with the older boys. Fithian found the boys "in perfect subjection to their parents," and "kind and complaisant to the servants who constantly attend them" (Farish 1957, 26). Like other children of the Virginia gentry, they were trained by a dancing master who gathered neighboring children for two-day lessons at a different plantation each time he visited. Parents often joined these occasions, and after watching minuets precisely executed by the children, the entire group delighted in high-spirited reels and country dances. But the Carter boys reveled in the freedom of plantation life, bursting forth when freed from studying Latin,

Greek, and math to engage in their favorite pursuits—Ben to ride his horse, Bob to hunt or fish by the river, and their cousin Harry, who joined them in school, to hang around skilled slaves at the blacksmith and carpenter shops. Fithian was somewhat surprised at the pleasure Bob found in the company of slaves and sons of yeomen, "persons much below his Family and Estate" (Farish 1957, 48). And both Bob and Ben, who could quake in the presence of their patriarchal father, were quick to respond with fisticuffs. Ben told his tutor that two persons in a dispute should fight it out manfully in order to be friends again, whereas Bob was "volatile & unsettled in his temper" and often in trouble for coming to blows, even with his sister Nancy (Farish 1957, 48). Neither boy, in fact, fulfilled his father's hopes for them. Ben died, perhaps from tuberculosis, at the age of twenty-two, and Bob, on a sojourn to England, was killed in a brawl outside a London coffeehouse.

Thomas Jefferson, of the same generation as Ben and Bob Carter, grew up to exemplify the genteel sensibility and political leadership expected of sons on Virginia plantations. Mindful of John Locke's belief that personality was formed by environmental influences, he came to fear that boys in a slave society would not acquire the self-discipline he so admired. "There must doubtless be an unhappy influence on the manners of our people produced by the existence of slavery among us," he wrote in *Notes on Virginia* in 1781.

The whole commerce between master and slave is a perpetual exercise of the most boisterous passions, the most unremitting despotism on the one part, and degrading submissions on the other. Our children see this, and learn to imitate it; for man is an imitative animal. This quality is the germ of all education in him. From his cradle to his grave he is learning to do what he sees others do. . . . The parent storms, the child looks on, catches the lineaments of wrath, puts on the same airs in the circle of smaller slaves, gives a loose to the worst of passions, and thus nursed, educated, and daily exercised in tyranny, cannot but be stamped by it with odious peculiarities. The man must be a prodigy who can retain his manners and morals undepraved by such circumstances. (Jefferson 1944, 278)

Robert Carter III was renowned as a humane master and was wealthy enough to free his 509 slaves. But other parents of the Virginia gentry, including Jefferson himself, would be trapped by debt and the institution of slavery, as their efforts to instill genteel restraint in their children were undermined not only by their own indulgence but also by plantation life.

After the American Revolution, cotton joined rice as the staple crop on plantations in the Low Country of South Carolina and Georgia. In an area where slaves could outnumber whites by 9 to 1 and a labor force number 100 to 1,000 slaves, plantation boys grew up deeply influenced by the Creole language and culture known as Gullah. It was said of young Benjamin Allston of All Saints Parish, between the Waccamaw River and the sea, that he spoke like a slave, "not only in pronunciation, but even in tone" (Joyner 1984, 208). White and black families shared the deeply rural rhythms of plantation life in cycles of birth, growth, sickness, and death. Boys on Low Country plantations suffered not only from the childhood diseases—measles, mumps, whooping cough, scarlet fever, croup, and colds—but also from the fevers that prevailed in late summer and early fall—malaria and sometimes yellow fever. Families who could afford it fled to Charleston, Savannah, or smaller towns or to encampments of rustic log or clapboard houses in the pine barrens.

A planter such as Thomas Chaplin, who owned 376 acres and about thirty slaves on St. Helena Island in the 1840s, struggled to raise the needed funds to house his four surviving children in St. Helena Village for the summer. Public education did not take hold in the rural South, and he also found it staggering to send his sons, Ernest, Daniel, and Eugene, to private boarding schools. The Chaplin boys lived in a two-story, six-room clapboard house, and grew up riding horseback, hunting, boating, and fishing with young slaves as their companions. Ernest was not sent to school until he was eleven and a year later still could not write. When Daniel, Eugene, and their sister Virginia also went off to school, their father was hard-pressed for cash, which he and other planters tried to raise by occasionally selling off a valuable slave child (Rosengarten 1986).

By the 1820s and boom years of the 1830s, South Carolina planters looked to fertile western lands to improve their fortunes, and the state joined the Chesapeake region in exporting slaves. After Indian lands were surrendered through conquest or treaty, white families moved into Alabama, Mississippi, Louisiana, and Texas. Migration removed boys from grandparents and the thick web of uncles, aunts, and cousins who had contributed to their socialization on the eastern seaboard. Members of nuclear families became more isolated and dependent on each other. Men embraced individualistic, competitive, and risk-taking behavior, and boys lacked the social graces, deference to authority, and perhaps emotional stability they may have gained in the East. Even a privileged boy like twelve-year-old Nicholas (Azby) Destrehan, who grew up on a sugar plantation near New Orleans in 1845, persisted in his own pursuits and resisted his father's authority. Azby spent his days hanging around the sugar house, fascinated by the machinery. He also cultivated his garden and enjoyed his horse, dog, gun, ducks and geese, and fishing tackle and little boat. When his father tried to instruct him "in reading and figuring," he admitted later, "I felt miserable at being called from my little amusements, I would sometimes get right mad and often damned my father . . . but this fit of madness only lasted during the time I was occupied at study; for as soon as I left the room I was as happy as ever" (Destrehan 1850). Although in the 1850s the plantation economy boomed from the Low Country to Texas, many of these southern boys would soon find themselves serving in the Confederate Army, an event that would destroy their unique boyhood forever.

Jacqueline S. Reinier

See also Indentured Servants; Slave Trade; Slavery

References and further reading
Breen, T. H., and Stephen Innes. 1980. *"Myne Owne Ground": Race and Freedom on Virginia's Eastern Shore, 1640–1676*. New York: Oxford University Press.
Carr, Lois Green, Russell R. Menard, and Lorena S. Walsh. 1991. *Robert Cole's World: Agriculture and Society in Early Maryland*. Chapel Hill: University of North Carolina Press.
Cashin, Joan E. 1991. *A Family Venture: Men and Women on the Southern Frontier*. New York: Oxford University Press.
Destrehan, Nicholas A. 1850. "Memoirs" in "Letter Book." Historic New Orleans Collection, New Orleans, LA.
Farish, Hunter Dickinson, ed. 1957. *Journal and Letters of Philip Vickers Fithian, 1773–1774: A Plantation Tutor of the Old Dominion*. Williamsburg, VA: Colonial Williamsburg.
Jefferson, Thomas. 1944. *Notes on Virginia*. First published in 1784. In *The Life and Selected Writings of Thomas Jefferson*. Edited by Adrienne Koch and William Peden. New York: Modern Library.
Joyner, Charles. 1984. *Down by the Riverside: A South Carolina Slave Community*. Urbana: University of Illinois Press.
Kulikoff, Allan. 1986. *Tobacco and Slaves: The Development of Southern Cultures in the Chesapeake, 1680–1800*. Chapel Hill: University of North Carolina Press.
Reinier, Jacqueline. 1996. *From Virtue to Character: American Childhood, 1775–1850*. New York: Twayne Publishers.
Rosengarten, Theodore, ed. 1986. *Tombee: Portrait of a Cotton Planter*. New York: Quill Press.

Play
See Games; Toys

Pokémon
See Gambling; Toys

Poliomyelitis

Poliomyelitis (usually referred to as polio) is a disease of the central nervous system caused by the poliomyelitis virus. It results in inflammation of the gray matter of the spinal cord, which in turn may lead to paralysis or wasting of muscles. Until the appearance of the first polio vaccine in the mid-1950s, polio was a serious health problem. Although it

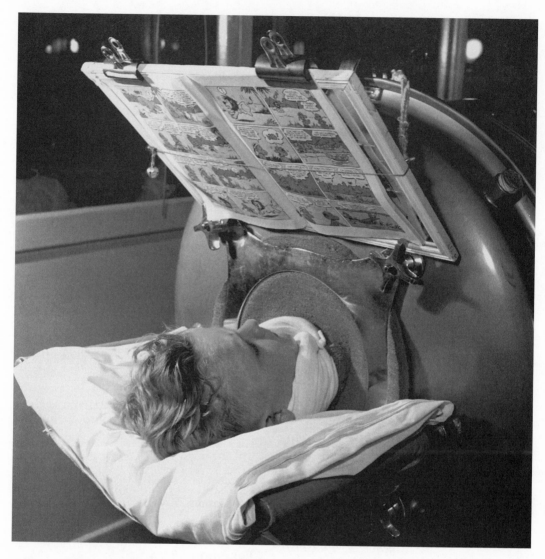

A young polio victim reads a comic book attached to the rim of his iron lung, ca. 1955. (Hulton Deutsch Collection/Corbis)

was not one of the major killers, treatments had only limited effect, and those who survived the acute phase of illness could be left with serious lifelong disability. For American boys, polio once represented a threat not only to life but also to ambition and livelihood. However, it is also a disease that can be prevented by vaccination. In the United States, the na-

tionwide vaccination program has been so successful that polio has been completely eliminated.

Polio has been known for thousands of years. Hippocrates and Galen both described the effects of a disease that was probably polio, and the first modern description of polio was given by an Italian surgeon, Monteggia, in 1813. Polio was endemic in pre–Industrial Revolution societies, a common infection of childhood but one that was rarely serious and that infrequently resulted in paralysis. Poor sanitation and hygiene meant that children were exposed to the poliovirus in infancy by the oral-fecal route, developed mild and often asymptomatic infection, and acquired immunity as a result. By the late nineteenth century, improved sanitation meant that this early exposure and immunity were lost. The age at which people became infected rose, and the effects of the disease worsened. In addition, polio changed from an endemic infection to an epidemic disease, often occurring in the summer months.

In the United States statistical evidence about the national incidence of polio, or "infantile paralysis" as it was also known, was not collected separately from evidence about other diseases until 1909. In that year polio was responsible for 2 deaths per 100,000 of the population. In comparison, pertussis (whooping cough) killed 22 per 100,000, and tuberculosis killed around 190 per 100,000. Despite its relatively low death rate, polio was much feared during the first half of the twentieth century. This fear may have been due in part to the outward signs of polio evident in many children and adults, such as leg braces or calipers, which served as reminders of polio's lifelong disabling effects and severely restricted boys' activities. It may also have resulted from an awareness that polio was a disease of the affluent as well as the poor. Physical disabilities prevented boys from entering active adult jobs in agricultural or industrial settings, and boys with ambitions to enter professions such as law could find that long periods of hospitalization and rehabilitation would prevent them from gaining the education necessary to enter such professions.

The early decades of the twentieth century saw regular and frequent polio epidemics, including the major epidemic of 1916 centered in New York and the northeastern United States, which led to a sharp increase in polio mortality. Although mortality from many other infectious diseases fell markedly during the first half of the twentieth century, that for polio fell only marginally, and indeed the death rate began to rise again from the early 1940s. In the years from 1951 to 1954 (immediately prior to the first polio vaccine), an average of 16,316 cases of polio were reported annually in the United States, with an average of 1,879 deaths. By contrast, more than 500,000 cases of measles were reported annually in the years from 1958 to 1962 (immediately prior to the introduction of the measles vaccine), but the average number of deaths was only 432.

Before the development of an effective polio vaccine, other forms of prevention were tried. Summer epidemics meant that public facilities such as swimming pools were closed during the summer months, and schools would stay shut until the epidemic had passed. Boys did not have to become infected to find their lives affected by polio: its presence in a locality was sufficient to threaten their sports and education opportunities. Some towns excluded travelers from epidemic areas. Parents were advised to keep children at home, with doors and windows tightly shut, even though this in itself created unhealthy conditions.

Future president Franklin Delano Roosevelt was affected by polio in the 1921 epidemic. In 1926 he bought a hotel in Warm Springs, Georgia, where he had benefited from water therapy, and established a charitable foundation there with his colleague Basil O'Connor. In 1938

O'Connor became president of the National Foundation for Infantile Paralysis, which began the fund-raising campaign "March of Dimes" and became central to the American attempt to overcome polio.

Many forms of treatment were introduced in an attempt to limit the long-term effects of polio and to reduce the numbers of deaths. Those people who suffered respiratory failure because of the virus had no effective treatment available to them until the invention of the Drinker Collins respirator, commonly known as the "iron lung," in the early 1930s. Treatment for most people with serious limb problems centered on immobilizing affected limbs with splints and calipers. Such treatments limited boys' opportunities for sports and their prospects for manual work in adulthood. They could also have a negative impact on self-image, especially in boys who saw themselves as active, athletic individuals.

Controversy about treatment was common, and alternative methods were often proposed with varying degrees of success. Sister Elizabeth Kenny, an Australian nurse who came to the United States in 1940, developed one alternative therapy. Kenny's therapy, based on heat treatment and exercise, ran counter to the prevailing ideas about treatment. Her work was controversial, but she established her own clinics and foundation and gained great public support.

In 1955 the first successful vaccine, produced by Jonas Salk, was introduced on a large scale. This vaccine, given by injection, used a killed form of the poliovirus to confer immunity. Its immediate success led to federal funding of vaccination programs. The oral vaccine, using the attenuated virus, was developed in the 1950s by Albert Sabin and used in mass vaccination from 1962, the year when the number of reported cases fell below 1,000 for the first time. In 1979 the last known case of indigenous transmission of the wild poliovirus occurred in the United States. From 1980 to 1997 a total of 142 cases of polio were reported in the United States: 140 of these were linked to vaccine transmission, with 2 being recorded as "indeterminate." In 1993 the wild poliovirus was declared to be eradicated from the Western Hemisphere. In 1998, with full vaccine coverage extending to 90 percent of three-year-olds, no cases of polio were reported in the United States.

Bruce Lindsay

See also Disease and Death

References and further reading
Daniel, Thomas M., and Frederick C. Robins, eds. 1997. *Polio*. Rochester: University of Rochester Press.
Rogers, Naomi. 1992. *Dirt and Disease: Polio before FDR*. New Brunswick, NJ: Rutgers University Press.

Pornography

Pornography, or porn, involves the written or visual depiction of sexual organs and practices with the aim of causing sexual arousal. It has served several purposes throughout its modern history—as a vehicle to criticize religious and political authorities, as a category to be censored for its alleged immorality, and as a means to provide soldiers and working men with tantalizing images of nude women. Much pornography targets a heterosexual male audience, and it often provides male youth with sex education.

The word *pornography* derives from the ancient Greek word *pornographos*, which the Greeks used to refer to writing about prostitutes. The sixteenth-century

Italian writer Pietro Aretino (1492–1556) is considered the father of modern Western pornography because of his sonnets and prose depicting explicit dialogues and scenes between lovers. He thus broadened the meaning of pornography to include realistic genital or sexual behavior, which deliberately violates widely accepted moral and social taboos.

In the seventeenth and eighteenth centuries in Europe, pornography was restricted to an educated elite male audience that was largely urban, aristocratic, and libertine. While providing titillation, it also served as a forum for criticizing religious and political authorities. For example, from 1740 to 1790 in France, pornography became increasingly political in its criticism of the monarchy, attacking the clergy, the court, and King Louis XV himself through depictions of their orgies.

In England, the word *pornography* first appeared in the *Oxford English Dictionary* in 1857, and most of its variations, such as *pornographer* and *pornographic*, date from the middle to the end of the nineteenth century. The entry of the term into popular jargon coincides with its increasing availability to the masses. John Cleland's *Fanny Hill, or the Memoirs of a Woman of Pleasure*, the first adult novel, was published in England in 1748. Arguably the most popular pornographic novel of all time, it was translated into numerous European languages during the nineteenth century.

Pornography has had a shorter but more explosive history in the United States. Although little such writing was available in the colonial period, no less a citizen than Benjamin Franklin wrote pieces such as "Advice to a Young Man on Choosing a Mistress," which remained unpublished in North America until decades after his death. Almost 100 years after *Fanny Hill* was first published in England, three publishers in Massachusetts were fined or jailed or both for publishing that novel in 1820 and 1821.

In the early nineteenth century, as the American public became more literate, decreased family size, and focused on health (including sexual health), the demand increased for literature providing advice. Such works included Charles Knowlton's *The Fruits of Philosophy; or the Private Companion of Young Married People* (1832), which contained contraceptive information, and William Alcott's *Young Man's Guide* (1833), addressed to male youth. As Catholic immigration increased, Protestants read works such as Maria Monk's detailed exposure of sexual activities in a Montreal convent. Before the publication of Harriet Beecher Stowe's *Uncle Tom's Cabin* (1851–1852), Monk's *Awful Disclosures of the Hotel Dieu Nunnery* (1836) was the best-selling novel in the United States (Gardella 1985, 25). The consumption of pornography, however, was limited to the elite, who could afford expensive imported books and prints (Kendrick 1996, 77).

Pornography began to be more affordable in 1846 when an Irish immigrant, William Haynes, published a version of *Fanny Hill* in New York, followed by 300 other titles over the next thirty years. During the Civil War, both commercial sex and publication of explicit literature expanded. After the war, cheaply produced pulp novels—dime novels for adults and half-dime or story papers for boys—could be mailed at new second-class postal rates. Single men who lived away from home in the expanding cities, as well as married men, became consumers of commercial sex, and sexually explicit literature began to be known as pornography.

The relatively sudden rise in publishing pornography caught many American civic leaders by surprise, especially because many states, including New York, did not have laws specifically forbidding the publication and sale of explicit sexual materials. Concerned by the potential impact on society in general and on male youth in particular, the Young Men's Christian Association (YMCA) of New York launched an antiobscenity campaign and successfully lobbied for the passage of a state statute barring the sale of explicit materials. When the state made little effort to enforce the law, however, the YMCA realized that an incentive was needed to prosecute the publishers and producers of pornography.

In 1871, Anthony Comstock, who became one of the most powerful moral censors in the history of the United States, contacted the YMCA, which gave him financial support and backed him as secretary of the New York Society for the Suppression of Vice. Comstock also was able to influence Congress to broaden and strengthen an 1865 law banning the use of the postal services to ship pornographic books and pictures and was appointed a special agent of the U.S. Post Office.

But the spread of pornography was difficult to control. Transportation improvements provided a network for distribution of materials. Population growth from roughly 100 million to more than 152 million people between 1915 and 1953 increased the potential size of the pornography market by 50 percent (Lane 2000, 19). Young people settled in cities and could partake in such leisure activities as attending dance halls, amusement parks, and movie theaters. Sexual mores loosened in the 1920s. Movies became more titillating, including flashes of nu-

dity. Provocative books, such as *Mademoiselle de Maupin* (1835) by Théophile Gautier and *The Well of Loneliness* (1928) by Radclyffe Hall, were legalized. During World War II sexual mores were further liberalized, as *Life* magazine introduced pinups for "the boys at the front," and Hollywood sent sexy performers to entertain the troops. Pornographers took advantage of this captive male audience, introducing "girlie" magazines for the troops and also providing them for sale at the nation's newsstands.

As these social changes liberalized sex in American society, Hugh Hefner, the founder of *Playboy*, helped to establish the pornography industry. In 1953, he offered a men's magazine featuring full-color photos of nude women and portraying a sophisticated, urban lifestyle. Hefner's first issue, with Marilyn Monroe on the cover, sold more than 50,000 copies in a little over a month; within two years he was selling more than 600,000 copies per month (Lane 2000, xvi). His success illustrated the demand for sexually explicit material, and competing magazines began to portray even more explicit photographs. *Penthouse* was the first men's magazine to show pubic hair and to portray its models more realistically than the stylized portraits of *Playboy*, and *Hustler* strove to appeal to the average working-class man.

After World War II, concern for the family and about male youth caused pornography to be associated with juvenile delinquency. In the 1960s, however, Supreme Court decisions in various obscenity cases further liberalized American sexual culture, establishing that sex and obscenity (defined as anything offensive to public morals) are not synonymous and that only materials with no redeeming social value whatsoever can be proscribed. These decisions effectively laid to rest moral objections to pornography, and as pornographic films, books, and magazines proliferated, mainstream media became more sexually explicit.

Today, pornography is a very profitable industry in the United States, which over the last quarter century has grown from $2 billion to at least $10 billion in annual revenue, about the amount Americans pay for sporting events and live music performances combined. Pornography also flourishes on the Internet, contributing an estimated $1 billion to $2 billion per year to the industry total, or 5 to 10 percent of money spent online in 1998 (Lane 2000, xiv). Americans buy millions of copies of *Playboy*, *Penthouse*, and *Hustler* each month, and more than 400 million X-rated videos are rented every year (Chancer 1998, 64). Not only is pornography produced and distributed for the purpose of making profits, but also appealing to sexual interest has become a marketing strategy for selling almost any product.

Pornography is easily accessible to youth and is very popular among boys in the United States. In testimony to the Attorney General's Commission on Pornography in 1985, Jennings Bryant reported that 100 percent of high school–age males surveyed had read or looked at *Playboy* or a similar men's adult magazine. The average age for first viewing was eleven, and boys in high school saw an average of 16.1 issues (Bryant 1985, 128–157). A study of high school adolescents in Canada found that one-third of the boys but only 2 percent of the girls watched pornography at least once a month. Further, although girls use other sources of information to learn about sex, including teachers, parents, peers, books, and magazines, 29 percent of the boys surveyed indicated that pornography was their most significant source for sex information (Check 1995, 90).

Feminists argue that rather than presenting sexual relations based on intimacy and equality, such magazines as *Playboy* cater to the objectification of women and the exclusive genital satisfaction of men. The Canadian study found that 43 percent of boys and 16 percent of girls surveyed either thought holding a girl down and forcing her to have intercourse if a boy was sexually excited was okay, or they were not sure if it was okay. Boys who answered in the affirmative overwhelmingly were those who read and watched pornography (Check 1995, 90–91).

Many adult magazines eroticize the vulnerability and innocence of youth. *Playboy* glamorizes the adolescent student as a sexual target, and the genre of Catholic schoolgirls is standard fare in both criminal child pornography and pseudo-child adult bookstore porn. Following the pattern of adult magazines, mainstream child pornography features young girls. But boys also are targets in child pornography, a situation that is valorized by organizations such as the North American Man-Boy Love Association (NAMBLA).

Child pornography, or kiddie porn, not only appeals to pedophiles (persons who desire prepubescent youth) but to any person who looks at magazines and films that eroticize youth. In the United States any sexual depiction of a person under eighteen is considered child pornography, and any distribution of such material is a federal crime. Child pornography is the most actively prosecuted form of sexually explicit material, but it is increasingly difficult to monitor the age of objects of pornography on the Internet, which allows considerable anonymity for those running sites.

Current debate on censorship of pornography focuses on three aspects. Political and religious conservatives consider pornography a moral issue. Feminists view it as a political problem of power and lack of power. Both groups contest the objectification of women and children for male pleasure and believe that women and children have the right to be agents in their own sexual lives.

Mia M. Spangenberg

See also Prostitution; Sexuality; Young Men's Christian Association

References and further reading
Bryant, Jennings. 1985. Testimony to the Attorney General's Commission on Pornography Hearings. Houston, Texas.
Chancer, Lynn. 1998. *Reconcilable Differences: Confronting Beauty, Pornography, and the Future of Feminism*. Berkeley: University of California Press.
Check, James. 1995. "Teenage Training: The Effects of Pornography on Adolescent Males." Pp. 89–91 in *The Price We Pay: The Case against Racist Speech, Hate Propaganda, and Pornography*. Edited by Laura J. Lederer and Richard Delgado. New York: Hill and Wang.
D'Emilio, John, and Estelle B. Freedman. 1988. *Intimate Matters: A History of Sexuality in America*. New York: Harper and Row.
Gardella, Peter. 1985. *Innocent Ecstasy: How Christianity Gave America an Ethic of Sexual Pleasure*. New York: Oxford University Press.
Hunt, Lynn, ed. 1993. *The Invention of Pornography: Obscenity and the Origins of Modernity, 1500–1800*. New York: Zone Books.
Kendrick, Walter. 1996. *The Secret Museum: Pornography in Modern Culture*. 2d ed. Los Angeles: University of California Press.
Lane, Frederick S. III. 2000. *Obscene Profits: The Entrepreneurs of Pornography in the Cyber Age*. New York: Routledge.

Portraiture

From the early colonial period until the invention and popularization of photography in the nineteenth century, the primary means of recording and remembering a young son's, brother's, or nephew's appearance was a painted portrait. During this period, Americans commissioned portraits depicting boys in a variety of formats and compositional arrangements from painters of varying artistic accomplishment. Despite their heterogeneity, portraits of male children executed at certain historical moments nevertheless share conventions of dress, pose, accouterments, and setting. These pictorial codes were gender- and age-specific and enabled contemporary viewers, who were more familiar with portrait conventions than are people today, to position the portrait subject within family and social hierarchies. Moreover, these conventions were meaningful because patrons, artists, and society held similar assumptions about the status of young boys. Thus, portrait paintings provide valuable insight into the historical construction of boyhood. Furthermore, when studied in chronological order, portraits provide evidence of changes in the status of boys within the family and society. Artists working in different centuries portrayed the male child, his dress, his pose, the objects he holds, and his environment according to different conceptions of boyhood. And although some of the patterns and changes represented in portrait painting often parallel themes articulated in textual sources, portraits also convey information about the experience of male children not described in texts, such as how clothing, material culture, and artistic representation reinforce gender roles and gender relations.

Seven-year-old David Mason is dressed and poses as an adult man in this portrait with his sisters. Attributed to the Freake-Gibbs Painter, The Mason Children: David, Joanna and Abigail, 1670. *(Museum of Fine Arts, San Francisco)*

It should be noted that American portrait painting presents a biased image of American boyhood. First, it was the father who most often commissioned and paid for a portrait depicting a young son, which when finished would hang in the semipublic spaces of the family home, where it declared parental values toward children, family refinement, and social position. Thus the painted portrait typically conveys a positive image of childhood, one designed to meet the approval of other family members and visitors to the home. Second, the father-patron expected the artist not only to paint a faithful record of his son's unique features but also to artistically arrange his clothing, his comportment, and the setting. The finished portrait is therefore neither an image of a sitter exactly as he appeared before the artist nor an idiosyncratic interpretation by the painter. Finally, the portraitist's skill came at a price, often a substantial one, and thus only financially secure parents could afford to commission a portrait of a junior family member. As a result, the experience of boyhood represented by American portrait painting is skewed toward young male children from elite and middle-class families. Commissioned portrait paintings of impoverished immigrant, African American, or Native American boys or others who lived beyond the routes of itinerant painters are rare in the history of American art. Despite these significant limitations, however, American portrait painting provides insight into the status of children from families who were in the mainstream and at times in the vanguard of social attitudes toward young boys.

Few portraits of children were painted in the early colonial period, but those that have survived portray male children between infancy and manhood in one of two ways. A boy no longer considered an infant but younger than seven is typically dressed in long, floor-length petticoats, a pinafore or apron, and hanging sleeves (e.g., Anonymous, *Robert Gibbs*, 1670, Worcester Museum of Art, illustrated in Calvert 1992). These same articles of clothing were also worn by girls and women and can be seen in contemporary female portraiture. However, a boy older than seven but not yet considered an adult appears dressed in the breeches and hose worn by adult men (e.g., David Mason in Attributed to the Freake-Gibbs Painter, *The Mason Children: David, Joanna and Abigail*, 1670, Museum of Fine Arts, San Francisco, illustrated in Simpson 1994). In both cases, conventions borrowed from

adult male portraiture explicitly convey the young subject's gender. Each holds objects associated with men, most significantly gloves and, in the case of the older child, a walking stick. More noticeably, both stand head square on the shoulders, one arm akimbo with the hand on the hip, commanding the surrounding space in emulation of conventions seen in contemporary portraits of elite men intended to express the subject's masculinity. Even though both of these young children are marked as male, the social position of each is very different. Male children under the age of seven appear more like women and therefore subordinate to those older males who wear breeches. A boy recently breeched, however, has made his initial entry into manhood and now shares with other men a personal mobility—facilitated by breeches—and the corresponding independence, authority, and domination that accompany unrestricted movement. He does not, however, hold objects affiliated with adult authority, such as a baton of command, underscoring the point that he has not yet fully entered into manhood. Regardless of differences in their ages, each will grow to be a man, but by portraying each with the material culture and conventions also used to represent adult women and men, the artist reveals boyhood—defined as a period in a male child's development that is distinct from adult men's and women's positions in the social hierarchy—to be nonexistent. Indeed, colonial society understood childhood not as a unique stage of development in a person's life but as something one passed through quickly in order to enjoy the privileges of manhood and old age.

Portraits painted during the first three-quarters of the eighteenth century continue earlier conventions, albeit with modifications in clothing and iconography. From the 1730s to the 1760s, young males, no longer considered infants but who had not yet been breeched, appear dressed in a long robe (e.g., Samuel Gore in John Singleton Copley, *The Gore Children*, ca. 1755, Henry Francis du Pont Winterthur Museum, Winterthur, Delaware, illustrated in Rebora et al. 1995). Like the petticoats and pinafores worn in the previous century, these long skirtlike garments signify a lack of mobility and, subsequently, a subordination to those who wear breeches. Painters also continued to portray these young males standing in characteristically male poses, with one hand on the hip and the other pointing into the distance. Finally, a boy's future dominant position in society is often encoded by the inclusion of a pet bird, squirrel, or dog he has trained and learned to control. Male children over seven years old are again portrayed breeched and posed like adult men (e.g., John Gore in John Singleton Copley, *The Gore Children*, ca. 1755). At the same time, details such as natural hair coifed in emulation of a wig or a black ribbon worn around the neck in place of a neckcloth signal they have not yet entered full manhood. Their relative immaturity is further underscored by the continued presence of small animals and the absence of items associated with professional pursuits, such as a telescope or a quill. As in the previous century, boys still appear as either subordinate like women or dominant like men, depending on whether they wear breeches, and in neither case are they portrayed according to conventions entirely unique to their age and sex.

During the last quarter of the eighteenth century, a dramatic shift in the portrayal of boys between the ages of four and twelve occurs in American portrait painting. First, male children are dressed in trousers, a shirt open at the neck with a ruffled collar, and a short jacket, an outfit eventually called a skeleton suit. Their natural hair is cut short with bangs. This clothing and hairstyle is age- and gender-specific and separates them from breeched males who wear wigs and from women and girls dressed in petticoats. Second, gender-specific toys are included for the first time in portraits, for instance, the toy drum. Third, books begin to appear in the hands of young boys and on nearby tables. Fourth, boys sit and stand in more relaxed poses. Thus, masculinity is no longer exclusively conveyed by male-oriented accouterments or the rigid rules of comportment reserved for adult men. Indeed, the introduction of informal poses for boys enabled artists to convey bonds of intimacy by picturing male children touching and leaning on siblings or parents (e.g., Daniel and Noah, Jr., in Ralph Earl, *Mrs. Noah Smith and Her Children*, 1798, Metropolitan Museum of Art, New York, illustrated in Kornhauser 1991). Taken together, these pictorial codes serve to identify young male children as now occupying a separate stage in life between infancy and manhood, one apart from the social position of adults.

These changes parallel, reflect, and confirm parental interest in Enlightenment theories of childhood development. The influential ideas of John Locke and Jean-Jacques Rousseau led parents to seek ways to stimulate the natural development of male children by promoting physical and mental activity. The skeleton suit facilitates greater mobility than both petticoats and breeches, and the relaxed and artful pose of boys in portraits often expresses a potential for movement less evident in earlier portraiture. The inclusion

By the mid-nineteenth century, portraits reveal children viewed androgynously. This boy and girl are dressed alike but masculinity is depicted by riding on the hobby horse. Unknown, The Hobby Horse, ca. 1850. (National Gallery of Art, Washington, DC)

of toys and books conveys the belief that physical development should complement intellectual growth. Although boys remain subordinate to adult men, boyhood now appears a distinct period of time in a male child's life, no longer represented according to the conventions of adult portraiture.

Beginning in the 1830s, American portrait painting features yet another conception of boyhood. At this time both boys and girls dress in similarly styled pantaloons and petticoats with their hair cut alike (e.g., Unknown, *The Hobby Horse*, ca. 1850, National Gallery of Art, Washington, DC, illustrated in Chotner

1992). Boys, however, are portrayed with an increasing variety of toys, including drums, whips, pull-toys, rocking horses, and small pets that distinguish them from girls, who most often hold dolls. Children of both sexes stand or sit calmly in domestic or nondescript interiors or out of doors, their young bodies filling the entire frame of the portrait. Unlike portraits of their fathers or grandfathers as children, young boys of this period appear androgynous and consciously separated from the world of adults.

Once again the change in portrait conventions parallels a shift in how parents understood the experience of their sons. In the nineteenth century, adults subscribed to romantic notions of boyhood as a period of innocence to be cherished and preserved. Many parents believed a child was born sinless, closer to angels than men, and when he entered into manhood he experienced the Fall. Portrait paintings from this time express the adult desire to represent a child as unaware of sexual difference by depicting boys and girls in similar clothing and hairstyles. But even when a male child appears unsexed, the depiction of gender-specific toys nearby indicates he is developing a natural masculinity that will blossom into manhood. Furthermore, artists conveyed a boy's separation from the outside world by portraying young subjects in settings where adult activities are absent and by filling the space of the composition with a boy's body. This focus on a child's body encodes the parents' desire to instill in their sons a sense of self-restraint and control, especially when in the company of other adults. Indeed, boys are portrayed in comparatively static poses, unlike the artfully relaxed positions that conveyed the potential for movement found in earlier portraits. By the mid-nineteenth century, the representation of boyhood in American portraits indicates it is a distinct period in a boy's life, one cut off from the world of adults and very much unlike the experience of his colonial ancestors.

Kevin Muller

See also Clothing

References and further reading
Calvert, Karin. 1992. *Children in the House: The Material Culture of Early Childhood, 1600–1900.* Boston: Northeastern University Press.
Catalogue of American Portraits, National Portrait Gallery, Smithsonian Institution. 2001. http://www.npg.si.edu/inf/ceros.htm (accessed March 24, 2001).
Chotner, Deborah. 1992. *American Naive Paintings.* Washington, DC: National Gallery of Art.
Kornhauser, Elizabeth Mankin. 1991. *Ralph Earl: The Face of the Young Republic.* Hartford, CT: Wadsworth Atheneum.
Lovell, Margaretta. 1988. "Reading Eighteenth-Century American Family Portraits: Social Images and Self Images." *Winterthur Portfolio* 22, no. 4 (Winter): 243–264.
Rebora, Carrie, Paul Staiti, Erica E. Hirshler, Theodore E. Stebbins Jr., and Carol Troyen. 1995. *John Singleton Copley in America.* New York: Metropolitan Museum of Art.
Simpson, Marc. 1994. *The Rockefeller Collection of American Art at the Fine Arts Museums of San Francisco.* San Francisco: Fine Arts Museums of San Francisco.

Poverty

Poverty is an economic condition experienced by boys whose families are unable to provide them with adequate food, shelter, clothing, and education. Impoverished boys are especially likely to suffer health problems, live in physically dangerous areas, work outside the home at a young age, and leave school at an early age. Over

Impoverished boy and his family living in Elm Grove, Oklahoma, 1936 (Library of Congress)

time, the methods of assisting boys from poor families have changed considerably. Nonetheless, no method has served to eradicate poverty among children, and by the late twentieth century, the largest group of persons living in poverty was boys and girls under the age of eighteen.

In the seventeenth and eighteenth centuries when America was first settled, most persons made their living by farming. If both his parents died or if his father died, a boy was very likely to become poor. Mothers of young children found it difficult to maintain a farm on their own. If a boy were old enough to help his widowed mother farm, he would soon find himself working long hours in the fields and barn and would be unable to attend school regularly, if at all. If a boy and his siblings were too young to help their mother on the farm, local poor relief officials would probably remove the children and place them with other farm families. Boys who were indentured or apprenticed to other local farmers were expected to work for them in return for some education and preparation for future employment. In some cases, boys received what they were promised, but many times they were denied schooling, sometimes physically abused, and often required to perform menial chores that did not prepare them adequately for self-sufficiency as adults.

By the nineteenth century, with the growth of cities and immigration, poverty among boys became a more serious social problem. First, large numbers of Irish and German immigrants came to the United States in the 1830s, 1840s, and 1850s, and later, after the Civil War, millions of persons from eastern and southern Europe flocked to the United States in search of opportunity. Families often arrived with little savings and had to take up residence in crowded and unsanitary housing. Many people shared the same toilets, garbage disposal was erratic, and illnesses spread rapidly. Boys were very likely to contract diseases such as measles, diphtheria, and tuberculosis. If they remained healthy, fathers and sons and daughters of recent immigrants or migrants to the city had to find work immediately to avoid destitution. Most immigrants had few skills, and consequently, the jobs they obtained were usually low-paying. Textile mills in New England and in the South welcomed whole families, and mill owners put all members, including children, to work. However, wages were very low, and boys and girls rarely received much education while employed in textile

mills. Factories other than textile mills employed mostly adult men, and their sons then sought work in street trades, selling newspapers or other small items or collecting junk and selling it to junk dealers. Boys from poor families who had to spend much of their days earning money in the streets lacked close parental supervision. Many attended school only sporadically between the ages of eight and twelve, when they quit to find full-time employment. Some slept out in city streets to avoid crowded and sometimes troubled homes; some engaged in illegal activities such as stealing; others joined gangs; and many frequented pool halls, theaters, movie houses, and gambling parlors. Impoverished parents who felt their sons were not providing their families with enough financial support or who were getting in trouble with the law too much sometimes placed the boys in juvenile reformatories.

In the nineteenth century, as in earlier centuries, boys were especially likely to be poor if their fathers died or deserted their families. Mothers with young children had a difficult time finding work to support them. Domestic service and sewing jobs were almost the only jobs available to urban women at the time, and neither paid enough to support a family adequately. Sometimes impoverished mothers could get by with a little food and clothing supplied by local welfare officials, but often such aid was insufficient, and mothers had to take their children with them to the local almshouse. There poor families received shelter, food, and clothing temporarily. Local officials also separated families and indentured boys in almshouses to local farmers or other citizens who put the youngsters to work. Contracts for this type of boy labor usually lasted until the youth was twenty-one years old. As with indenturing and apprenticeship in earlier times, sometimes boys were treated well and got the education and training promised them, but at other times they were physically and emotionally abused and poorly prepared to support themselves in later life.

By the late nineteenth century, many citizens had come to suspect that placing children in almshouses alongside adult poor persons for any length of time was doing the youngsters more harm than good. As a result, most states passed laws requiring that children be removed from almshouses and placed in other institutions such as orphanages or placed out with families. In the absence of a welfare system that provided much aid for impoverished mothers or an economic system that provided them adequate income, they continued to seek places to put their sons and daughters, either temporarily or permanently. White boys might remain in an orphanage for a year or so and then be returned to their mothers if the women were able to support the children, or if the boys themselves were old enough to work and help support their mothers. Younger boys whose mothers could not support them might leave an orphanage after a year or so to be indentured out to work for other families. In either case, family poverty usually led to family separation for boys and girls.

The experience of poverty among African American boys in the eighteenth and nineteenth centuries was somewhat different from that of white youngsters. Boys who grew up in slavery lived in poverty. Their masters usually provided them minimal food and clothing and, by the 1830s, most southern states forbade them from receiving any formal educa-tion. Older slaves cared for young slave boys, while their parents worked in the fields or plantation house. As soon as they were physically able, slave boys were expected to work—either around the slave cabins and plantation house or in the fields. After the Civil War, most freed slaves continued to farm in the South. Few were able to accumulate much money, and most labored as share-croppers, farming the land of a white owner and sharing the crop they har-vested with him. Boys on sharecropping farms worked alongside their fathers in the fields. In the off-seasons they accom-panied their fathers to find day-labor jobs in cities to help support their families. Some were able to attend school, but be-cause their labor was so necessary on the farm, few African American farm boys in the South attended school regularly.

African American families that moved north in the late nineteenth and early twentieth centuries often lived on the edge of poverty, although they were very likely to keep their sons and daughters in school, often through high school. Black parents had great faith in education, and mothers labored at domestic service jobs and fathers at day-labor jobs in order to earn enough to keep their sons and daughters in school. However, despite their education, boys and girls rarely found well-paying jobs after graduation. Racist employment policies kept boys out of higher-paying factory jobs before World War I. African American fathers, even if they had fairly good jobs, were usually not able to secure comparable employment for their sons.

When African American boys were or-phaned, there were few welfare programs to assist them. Most orphanages did not accept black children, and even though African Americans themselves founded a few orphan asylums after the Civil War, they were small and could not accommodate many youngsters. Consequently, African American boys whose parents were dead or unable to care for them were usually taken in by other relatives or friends.

Native American boys in the nineteenth century experienced poverty in still different ways than did other groups of boys. The U.S. government became determined to remove Native Americans from areas of the country where whites wanted to settle. As a consequence, Indians from the Southeast and the Great Lakes area were forced out of their ancestral homes and made to travel long distances, in what came to be called the "Trail of Tears," to lands in Oklahoma. On the way, boys and their families experienced extreme poverty. Other tribes were also forced onto reservations on land that was not particularly productive. In the late nineteenth century, the U.S. government also removed Indian boys and girls from their homes and educated them in military-style boarding schools in an effort to break their connections to their tribes and reeducate them to an "American" way of life.

By the early twentieth century, many of the problems of the previous century continued to plague impoverished boys and their families, but the welfare system changed somewhat in ways that probably advantaged some boys and their parents. Overcrowded housing and poor sanitation still took their toll on young lives. Needy mothers had little access to medical care, and so their sons and daughters were often born physically and mentally impaired. Childhood diseases spread rapidly in the neighborhoods of the poor, and when their high fevers went untreated, some boys suffered blindness and brain

damage. In 1921, the passage of the Sheppard-Towner Maternity and Infancy Protection Act helped to improve children's health somewhat. The legislation provided matching grants to the states to extend prenatal and postnatal care to any mother who sought it. Clinics staffed by nurses appeared throughout the country to provide medical advice and assistance to mothers and their children. The law was quite effective, but it ended in 1929 thanks to opposition from legislators who feared the spread of socialism and doctors who feared the loss of business as mothers turned to public clinics for medical aid. Eventually, provisions of the Social Security Act of 1935 resurrected many of the features of the Sheppard-Towner Act.

Mothers of impoverished boys gained some help in providing them medical care in the early twentieth century, and they also gained some aid from states and localities to provide their sons with the basic necessities of life. As before, boys were most likely to be poor if their mothers were divorced or deserted. Such women still had a difficult time finding well-paying jobs and, when they became desperate, still relied on orphanages and foster care programs to take in their sons and daughters. Beginning in 1911 in Illinois, states began to pass "mothers' pension" laws that gave impoverished single mothers money to help them support their families. Before the Depression, all states but two had passed such laws, although the money they provided mothers was minimal, and very little of it went to African American mothers, among the poorest in the nation. In 1935, with the passage of the Social Security Act, mothers' pensions (funded by states) were taken over by the federal government program called Aid to Dependent Children (later renamed Aid to Families with Dependent Children). ADC provided needy mothers with money to help them buy the food, clothing, and housing that they and their sons and daughters needed. Although ADC was not overly generous, it did provide more aid than mothers' pensions had, and that aid went to more mothers (including African Americans).

The Great Depression of the 1930s was a particularly traumatic time for impoverished boys. The number of youngsters who lived in poverty grew as the unemployment rate skyrocketed. Parents found it hard to feed and clothe their children, and those who could not pay their rent were evicted and often ended up living in shanties they constructed by hand. Boys who were old enough to find work often quit school, hopped on railroad freight cars, and crisscrossed the country searching for employment. They camped out with other young and old tramps in vacant lots. During the 1930s, there was also a massive drought that produced soil erosion and drove thousands of southwestern farmers off their land. Many fled the Dust Bowl lands for California, where families with sons and daughters found it easier to find work picking fruit and vegetables than did single men. Wages were extraordinarily low for such families, many lived in shanties, and their children were very likely to become sick and quite unlikely to attend school regularly.

During World War II, economic conditions improved, and the country almost achieved full employment. In the years after the war, both sanitary conditions and medical care improved, helping all children, including impoverished boys and girls. Even so, certain groups of boys continued to suffer from the consequences of poverty, including poor housing and ill health. Rural children (many of whom were African American) who lived far from medical facilities were especially at risk; they often did not receive vaccinations for diphtheria, whooping cough, tetanus, and smallpox. Native American boys and girls living on reservations where medical facilities were minimal were especially likely to suffer from pneumonia, influenza, typhoid, and dysentery.

As economic conditions improved in the 1950s and 1960s, the remaining poverty in the country seemed an anomaly. To end that poverty, President Lyndon Johnson launched a War on Poverty in the 1960s. The goal of the program was to prevent poverty, and so, many of its programs were directed at young people. Head Start offered free preschool care to boys and girls, Upward Bound helped boys and girls prepare for college, and the Job Corps sought to train boys for jobs that paid a decent wage. Johnson lost interest in the War on Poverty as the war in Vietnam heated up, and his successor, President Richard Nixon, dismantled much of the program. Nonetheless, Head Start and Upward Bound continued, and Medicaid and food stamps (created in 1963 and 1964, respectively, and not officially parts of the War on Poverty) also continued. Medicaid paid the doctor and hospital bills of poor children and adults, and food stamps made possible a healthier diet for impoverished families.

Despite improved welfare programs, in the late twentieth century poverty among boys and girls remained a serious social problem. In the late 1970s and 1980s the distribution of wealth in the country became more inequitable. The wealthiest Americans gained a greater share of the national income (the top 20 percent controlled 46.9 percent of the wealth in 1992), and poorer Americans lost ground (in 1992 the poorest 20 percent of the population had just 3.8 percent of the nation's wealth) (Jones and Weinberg 2000, 4). In 1992, about one child in five lived below the poverty line. The majority of them were white, and most of their parents had jobs. They lived scattered throughout the country in communities large and small, although poverty of children in urban areas was most obvious. As in the past, boys living in families headed by a single mother were most likely to experience poverty. Jobs for such mothers still paid little, child care was expensive, and welfare payments were not adequate to lift these families out of poverty (Sherman 1994, 4–8).

As in the past, impoverished boys of today face serious health risks. They are more likely than nonpoor children to be small for their age and to suffer from deafness, blindness, or physical or mental disabilities. They are also more likely than their nonpoor contemporaries to score lower on intelligence quotient (IQ) tests, have learning disabilities, fall behind grade level in school, and drop out of high school. Impoverished boys living in inner cities, especially those who are African American, have few decent-paying job opportunities available to them. Most urban factories have closed down, and jobs in the growing service economy are located mainly in suburbs. The ubiquitous advertising industry continues to create wants among youth, including those who are poor. Needy boys and girls also watch television and want the same clothes, shoes, and music that more well-off children seek. One way poor boys obtain these objects is through the underground economy of drug dealing. Violence and the sale of drugs appear to be inseparable. Boys who live in impoverished urban areas where drug dealing is common are very

likely to be victims of violent assault or to witness violence and murder in their communities.

Priscilla Ferguson Clement

See also Foster Care; Gangs; Guns; Illegal Substances; Juvenile Courts; Juvenile Delinquency; Orphanages; Placing Out; Reformatories, Nineteenth-Century; Reformatories, Twentieth-Century; Runaway Boys

References and further reading
Ashby, Leroy. 1997. *Endangered Children: Dependency, Neglect, and Abuse in American History.* New York: Twayne Publishers.
Jones, Arthur F., Jr., and Daniel H. Weinberg. 2000. *Current Population Reports: The Changing Shape of the Nation's Income Distribution, 1947–1998.* Washington, DC: U.S. Census Bureau.
Nightingale, Carl Husemoller. 1993. *On the Edge: A History of Poor Black Children and Their American Dreams.* New York: Basic Books.
Riley, Patricia, ed. 1993. *Growing Up Native American.* New York: Avon Books.
Sherman, Arloc. 1994. *Wasting America's Future: The Children's Defense Fund Report on the Costs of Child Poverty.* Boston: Beacon Press.
West, Elliott. 1996. *Growing Up in Twentieth Century America: A History and Reference Guide.* Westport, CT: Greenwood Press.

Preachers in the Early Republic

Around the year 1800 at a Kentucky camp meeting, a ten-year-old boy began to exhort a crowd of the pious and the curious. Held aloft by two men so that he could be seen by all, he dropped a handkerchief and cried: "Thus, O sinner, will you drop into hell unless you forsake your sins and turn to God." This display of eloquence, self-possession, and piety in so young a lad is said to have stunned his audience and moved many to tears of repentance.

Such are the wonders on which the lore of early southern evangelicalism lingers, and there is no mystery about the reason. Young, single white men who embraced religion in their teens and early twenties comprised the ranks from which evangelicals in the South recruited their ministers for many decades after the American Revolution. Those promising male converts came to be called "young gifts," a term connoting the consensus that they possessed unique spiritual talents and had been bestowed upon the churches by an approving deity. In both senses, they embodied the glorious future of evangelicalism.

Presbyterians profited least from the young gifts raised up in their midst. Most church leaders insisted that all those called by God to preach required the weightier imprimatur of a classical education at Princeton or at least a few years in a backwoods academy dispensing rudimentary knowledge of Latin and Greek. That requirement discouraged many young men, who had neither the money nor, they feared, the ability to master the mysteries of ancient languages and academic life. Their reticence made it impossible for the Presbyterians to train and field a large number of ministers quickly and to fill pulpits as the U.S. population moved southward and westward. As a result, Presbyterians in the South generally confined their postwar evangelism to enclaves of receptive Scots-Irish settlers and fell far behind in the competition for new members.

By contrast, the Methodists and Baptists emerged in the decades after the American Revolution as the South's strongest evangelical churches, in part because both groups dispensed with a for-

mally educated clergy. They regarded inner claims to divine appointment as sufficient authorization, the truth of which would be tested when young men apprenticed as itinerant preachers. No time was lost when a young gift rose up in their midst. Among the Baptists, that promising young man was first encouraged to open public religious meetings with a prayer or to close them by delivering an exhortation or leading the congregation in a hymn. He might also be urged to expound on passages from the Bible at household gatherings of family and neighbors. If he completed those exercises satisfactorily, he was then licensed to preach and, if he proved his mettle in the pulpit, could expect to be ordained as an "elder" (as Baptists styled their ministers) within a few years. The Methodists cultivated an eager recruit by licensing him to exhort or appointing him to serve as a class leader and then urging him to accompany an itinerant on his rounds for a few months. If a young man showed the makings of a minister, he was assigned to a circuit and received "on trial" into the "traveling connection" of itinerant preachers. If he proved his worth, after two years he was admitted to their itinerancy in "full connection."

Not only were the Baptists and Methodists able to marshal more preachers than the Presbyterians, but they were also prepared to use them more effectively. Most Presbyterian clergy were settled ministers serving a particular congregation (or two or three neighboring churches), whereas many young Methodists and Baptists began their ministerial careers as itinerants, traveling and preaching to both established congregations and gatherings of the unchurched. That mode of deploying their clergy enabled the Baptists and Methodists to reach an increasingly dispersed population—the tens of thousands of southern families who, during the decades after the American Revolution, filtered southward into the Georgia frontier and swarmed westward into Kentucky, Tennessee, and southern Ohio. Drawing mainly on young, single men as itinerants also ensured an inexhaustible supply of cheap and enthusiastic young evangelists, a group attuned to the concerns of the lay faithful, especially younger men and women, from whose ranks they had recently been plucked.

Fresh-faced youths also drew the merely curious to religious meetings. The spectacle of a "boy preacher" caused as much of a sensation at the turn of the century as it had in the 1740s, when George Whitefield first claimed that title. Popular acclaim for John Crane, who from the age of nine attracted audiences in middle Tennessee, won him his first circuit at sixteen, and Jacob Young, at the comparatively ripe age of twenty-six, swelled with pride when another Methodist minister rode away after hearing his sermon, shouting: "Young Whitefield! Young Whitefield!" At the same age, Jeremiah Norman noted that his sermons brought out "perhaps more than would have been if they had not the expectation of hearing the young performer." Prodigies bowled over the Baptists, too. After twenty-one-year-old Wilson Thompson wowed a Kentucky congregation in 1810, a senior minister dubbed him "the beardless boy," a name by which, as Thompson said, "I was spoken of for some years." In later life Jeremiah Jeter recalled that when he was traveling with another young Baptist preacher in western Virginia in the 1820s, "it was represented that two Bedford plowboys had suddenly entered the ministry and were turning the world up-

side down, exciting almost as much interest as a dancing bear" (Heyrman 1997).

In itself, the process of culling novice preachers from the ranks of young male converts stirred local excitement. William Watters, who joined the Methodists in 1771 and soon thereafter entered the itinerancy, reported that in his Maryland neighborhood, "my conversion was . . . much talked of, as also my praying in a short time after without a book, which, to some, appeared a proof that there was a notable miracle wrought on me indeed." Decades later, the appearance of likely prospects still aroused the laity's interest: in 1810, Martha Bonner Pelham in southern Ohio gossiped in a letter to her sister-in-law in Virginia that a "smart revival" among the Methodists had yielded one young male convert "who is expected to make a preacher." When novices proved their powers to evoke strong emotions, congregations rejoiced, like the Methodists of one Kentucky society who came away from Jacob Young's first sermon "bathed in tears," so gratified that "they clustered round me, shook my hand." And when his contemporary Thomas Cleland showed talent as an exhorter at a local religious gathering, "it was noised abroad that 'little Tommy Cleland' . . . had commenced *preaching*," and his neighbors early sought him out to speak and pray in private homes and to offer spiritual counsel to troubled souls (Heyrman 1997).

Most men singled out as young gifts at first professed their unworthiness. Undeniably sincere in his humility was the fledgling Methodist itinerant who, as he confided his fears to Francis Asbury after retiring for the night, trembled so much that "the bed shook under him." Among the Baptists, Wilson Thompson hesitated even to enter the pulpit, fearing that "it was too sacred a place for me," and quailed at "the very thought of attempting to preach before the old and wise men of the Church, and before preachers." Such worries prompted the young Methodist Philip Gatch to test his preaching skills in Pennsylvania rather than his native Maryland neighborhood, feeling that "it would be less embarrassing to me." But after displaying due modesty about assuming so great a calling, most novices threw themselves into the Lord's work with the untiring energy and unflagging zeal of all youthful aspirants. Often within a matter of months, the same young men who had agonized over entering the clergy were casting themselves as latter-day apostles, boasting of their heroic sufferings for the faith and their skill in winning new converts (Heyrman 1997).

However well they may have succeeded, southern Baptists and Methodists did not set out to create a cult of youth. Even though congregations prayed for young gifts to be raised up from their ranks, even though multitudes thronged to the sermons of "boy preachers," evangelicals never took the position that religious virtuosity resided exclusively or even mainly in the young. But their clergy and pious laypeople did create a climate within the churches that celebrated youthful adepts. The working of wonders among the young at once attested to divine approval of evangelical aims while also advertising their affinities with the primitive Christian church. And in practical terms, postwar Baptists and Methodists had set themselves an ambitious agenda of proselytizing a predominantly youthful population spread over a vast territory. Such a goal dictated their reliance on a traveling clergy, which meant that much of the energy fueling the engines of evangelism would come from men who had spiritual conviction, physical stamina, and, in some cases, financial support from their families. In practice, then, young preachers were endowed with extraordinary authority as spiritual models and religious leaders.

Christine Leigh Heyrman

See also Early Republic

References and further reading
Andrews, Dee E. 2000. *The Methodists and Revolutionary America.* Princeton, NJ: Princeton University Press.
Boles, John B. 1972. *The Great Revival, 1787–1805: The Origins of the Southern Evangelical Mind.* Lexington: University of Kentucky Press.
Cartwright, Peter. 1856. *The Autobiography of Peter Cartwright, the Backwoods Preacher.* Edited by W. P. Strickland. Cincinnati: L. Swormstedt and A. Poe.
Hatch, Nathan. 1989. *The Democratization of American Christianity.* New Haven, CT: Yale University Press.
Heyrman, Christine Leigh. 1997. *Southern Cross: The Beginnings of the Bible Belt.* New York: Alfred A. Knopf.
Young, Jacob. 1857. *Autobiography of a Pioneer.* Cincinnati: Jennings and Pye; New York: Eaton and Mains.

Prostitution

Prostitution is the exchange of sex for money or one or more of the necessities of life and is also commonly referred to as "sex work," "commercial sex," "sex trading," "survival sex," and "hustling." Alternate terms for prostitution have evolved to deflect stigma from the individual and to emphasize various nonstigmatizing aspects of the sex-for-necessities exchange. For example, "hustling" is also used as a more general term to describe an assortment of illegal or quasilegal activities in which a young man participates to earn income. "Sex work" is another more general term that technically includes a range of activities in the sex industry, such as pornography and stripping. This particular term evolved in part to associate the activity with work, career, and entrepreneurship (Browne and Minichiello 1996). For the most part, these terms are used interchangeably to refer to prostitution.

The growth of commercial sex in the United States occurred in the early nineteenth century in the context of capitalism and urbanization. Poor boys lived in urban neighborhoods where prostitution of females proliferated. By the 1850s, girls as young as eleven or twelve years old were apprehended by local authorities for prostituting themselves in cellars and doorways. There is some evidence that boys engaged in this kind of activity as well, especially in such neighborhoods as the notorious Five Points district of New York City. The city's courts issued indictments for sodomy only in cases in which force was used or there was considerable disparity in age, and some arrests involved sodomy with boys as young as eleven. In the 1860s the poet Walt Whitman wrote of bringing home young men he met in the streets of New York City, Brooklyn, or Washington, D.C. The author Horatio Alger, who was dismissed from his Massachusetts pulpit in 1866 for the "revolting crime of unnatural familiarity with boys," could avoid censure in New York, where he wrote about the street boys he so admired. There also is some evidence that on the western frontier, cowboys hired younger males to spend the night with them, and that soldiers in the army also sought and probably paid for young male company (D'Emilio and Freedman 1988, 123, 124).

Although male sex work is not a new occurrence, it only recently has been the subject of systematic investigation, in part because it is covert and highly stigmatized. Although there are no precise estimates, there are believed to be at least 100,000 and as many as 300,000 young men involved in prostitution in the United States (Cohen 1987; Deisher, Robinson, and Boyer 1982). Male sex workers are typically in their teens and are hired by older men (Coleman 1989). Heterosexual prostitution among youth is rare. Adolescent sex workers typically do not have pimps, partly because as men they do not feel as vulnerable as women and perhaps because as males they have been socialized to seek and expect independence. Although most sex workers in the United States are white, ethnic minority youth are overrepresented in the population (Fisher, Weisberg, and Marotta 1982).

There are two main categories of male sex workers. One subgroup, called "street sex workers," solicits services in bars and clubs, on the streets, and in bus and train stations. By and large, these young men come from lower-class backgrounds and are more likely to use hard drugs, to have no other occupation, and to have more clients but fewer steady ones (de Graaf et al. 1994; Waldorf 1994). A second subgroup includes young men who solicit through escort agencies, phone chat lines, and the Internet. These young men, called "call boys," tend to come from middle-class backgrounds, have more education, and have stable living arrangements. With very few exceptions, research studies have focused on "street" sex workers. Thus information about adolescent male prostitutes reviewed below provides a description of a segment of the sex working population—those at highest risk.

A boy's first hustling experience typically occurs at age fourteen, with more active sex work involvement starting around age fifteen or sixteen (El-Bassel et al. 2000). However, the average age of initiation appears to be dropping, and it is becoming increasingly common to see boys as young as twelve engaging in sex work (Deisher, Robinson, and Boyer 1982). Some young men stay involved in prostitution for extended periods, whereas others move on to other means of supporting themselves, both legal and illegal. Because younger men are favored by clients and because the lifestyle is dangerous and taxing, few youth stay involved in sex work well past adolescence. Unlike female prostitutes, who may continue on far into adulthood, boys tend to age out of prostitution earlier, usually in their mid-teens and early twenties (Sponsler 1993).

Although there is variability, the pathways leading to male sex work are inextricably linked to family stress, parental alcohol or drug problems, and abuse and neglect, quite frequently compounded by poverty. Abuse is a major precipitant of running away from home. Other young men are "thrown away," that is, forced to leave, commonly because of their sexual orientation. Homeless youth who cannot or do not return home must learn strategies for survival. Although some obtain jobs in the formal economy, most lack the skills and resources to do so and must quickly turn to illegal or quasilegal means of financial support. Indeed, homelessness is the single greatest risk factor leading to involvement in sex work. Although estimates vary widely, it appears that most young men involved in street-based prostitution are or have been homeless (Weisberg 1985). Young men are typically unaware of male prostitution before leaving home. In contrast to females who are introduced to sex work by pimps, young men usually learn about it from

other youth, who may themselves be involved in it.

Boys support themselves through prostitution when they experience insurmountable barriers to work in the legal economy. For example, some are too young to get a work permit, and others do not have and cannot get the proper identification necessary for the job application. Others are concerned that working in the formal economy would allow them to be traced to their parents, from whom they have run away. And on average, sex workers have no more than a tenth grade education (Fisher, Weisberg, and Marotta 1982), further limiting their occupational prospects. Nor are they aware of services or programs that might prepare them for the workplace. A substantial minority have children (El-Bassel et al. 2000), which creates additional financial pressures. Some young men turn to prostitution because they believe it is superior to other criminal survival acts such as selling drugs. In fact, young men are less likely to be arrested for prostitution than for other illegal activities (Coleman 1989). Sex workers also experience psychological and social barriers to working in the formal economy. Early negative family experiences, including physical and sexual abuse, and leaving home at a young age contribute to developmental and skill deficits as well as mental health problems that interfere with traditional work. Sex work may be a way, and in many cases the only way, for a young man to have power and control over his life.

Boys report that they gain various benefits from sex work. These include freedom, entertainment, excitement, sex, time to socialize, peer group support, and a favorable amount of income for nominal effort. In addition, a need for adult male attention and affection or a desire to control adult males may be underlying motivations for some young men.

Substance use is a critical factor in the lives of many young men involved in sex work. Although boys may use drugs prior to becoming involved in sex work, typically substance use increases drastically after they begin hustling (Coleman 1989). Alcohol and marijuana are the substances most commonly used, followed by crack cocaine (El-Bassel et al. 2000). For some, substance use is a means of self-medicating for experiences of psychological distress and depression. Injection drug use is a serious concern for many and is linked to the transmission of HIV and hepatitis B and C. In a series of two studies done on the West Coast, as many as 50–70 percent of adult street hustlers and almost 40–50 percent of nonstreet hustlers had injected a substance (Waldorf 1994). Rates of injection among adolescent sex workers are believed to be lower on the East Coast. The most commonly injected substance is heroin, with cocaine, amphetamine, crack cocaine, and ketamine also reported. Youth heavily involved in drug use are compelled to get income to support their habits; thus serious drug use is often tied to heavy involvement in sex work. Sex workers have great difficulties accessing drug treatment programs and often have trouble completing them, sometimes because they find them restrictive or that staff are insensitive and intolerant.

Contrary to the stereotype, males involved in sex work do not necessarily view themselves as gay or bisexual. Indeed, as many as 25–40 percent view themselves as heterosexual and have female partners in addition to their male clients (El-Bassel et al. 2000; Pleak and Meyer-Bahlburg 1990). Although sex work may not be their preferred means of supporting themselves compared to other illegal activities (e.g., robbery, burglary, selling drugs, and pimping young females), they turn to it when other avenues are closed to them. For many who identify as straight, having sex with men can trigger confusion, shame, and distress. Straight-identified sex workers are difficult for service providers to contact and assist.

Gay and bisexually identified youth involved in sex work experience multiple sources of stress and isolation, often as a result of their stigmatized sexual identity as well as their involvement in prostitution. They are significantly more likely to run away from or be thrown out of their homes than their straight peers. And homelessness, as has been discussed, is a major risk factor for involvement in sex work. These boys are frequently marginalized and shunned by families and traditional services and systems.

A substantial minority of boys involved in sex work are "transgendered": that is, they experience their gender as female and dress and behave accordingly. They work in both female and transgendered "stroll" areas (sex work venues) and, less frequently, in male venues. Transgendered youth face special risks and are frequently the target of harassment and violence, both by clients and by other men. Anecdotal reports even suggest that they are murdered at higher rates.

Sex workers are infected with HIV, syphilis, hepatitis B and C viruses, and other sexually transmitted infections at high rates. Although there are few studies that focus exclusively on hustling youth, existing data indicate that 25–50 percent of young men involved in sex work are HIV-positive (Elifson, Boles, and Sweat 1993; Waldorf 1994), and even more are infected with syphilis and hepatitis B and

C viruses. Young men who inject drugs in addition to engaging in sex work are even more likely to be HIV-positive, although sexual risk is primary. More gay-identified youth are infected than their bisexual and heterosexual counterparts.

However, most of the time young men contract infections through their romantic or unpaid partners, not through their sex work clients. Contrary to the stereotype, sex workers do not customarily have unprotected sex with their paying partners. In fact, sex workers use condoms during anal intercourse, a potentially risky activity associated with the transmission of pathogens, the majority of the time (Pleak and Meyer-Bahlburg 1990; Waldorf 1994). In addition to condom use, sex workers have a range of other strategies they use to reduce their risk of exposure to disease and of exposing their clients, including the activities they agree to engage in (Browne and Minichiello 1995). It is typical for a youth to receive only oral sex, a lower-risk activity, and many will even use a condom while doing so. However, sex work does have its threats to sexual safety. Sex workers, regardless of sexual identity, are more likely to engage in risky behavior with steady clients, with those to whom they are sexually attracted, or when they are in dire need of drugs (de Graaf et al. 1994). Furthermore, congruent with their sexual orientation and desires, gay youth are more likely than straight or bisexually identified young men to receive anal intercourse, an activity associated with higher risk for exposure to sexually transmitted infections. (This does not mean, however, that straight-identified boys do not engage in the act, only that they do so less frequently. Sexual identity is a thorny issue, particularly for young people, and identity is, at best, an imperfect

prediction of behavior.) Based on these well-established behavior patterns and other epidemiological data, there is no good evidence that prostitutes are vectors of HIV transmission to their clients.

Indeed, as noted above, boys are much more likely to be infected with a sexually transmitted infection, including HIV, by a romantic or nonpaying partner than a paid client. Sex workers rarely use condoms with their male romantic or unpaid partners or with female partners. Because working life is associated with negative social judgments, it is important for young men to create a separate "sphere" in personal relationships, where condoms are not used (Joffe and Dockrell 1995).

However, sex work still has significant hazards. Violence is endemic. Young men are often victimized. The mortality rate for male sex workers is high; they overdose on drugs, contract fatal illnesses, and die from violence at high rates (Sponsler 1993). Sex workers, particularly transgendered youth, are targeted by police. Incarceration related to sex work, drugs, or other survival strategies is very common. The majority of adolescent male prostitutes have been arrested at least once (Weisberg 1985).

Prostitution can be psychologically and socially destructive. A young sex worker is at a critical stage of development, yet typically is not in school, lacks legitimate employment, and lacks access to positive and nonexploitative role models. As a result, he risks missing out on developing the personal, social, occupational, and educational skills necessary for success in the adult world. The stigma of prostitution is often internalized, and sex workers experience low self-esteem. Working at night and sleeping during the day further break down contact between the youth and the rest of the world. Heavy involvement in sex work can have a negative impact on relationships. Sex workers report that they have trouble forming stable relationships; intimacy is thwarted by fears of closeness or affection, the partner's reaction to his past, and a dislike for control or restriction in relationships (Fisher, Weisberg, and Marotta 1982).

Their need for services is great, including health care, mental health care, and drug treatments, as well as HIV prevention intervention. Yet there are numerous serious barriers to their receiving services. First, it is difficult for service providers to identify and reach the youth, given their unpredictable lifestyles. Outreach efforts in which the staff of community-based organizations go to the areas where youth are working are key and effective. However, not surprisingly given their difficult backgrounds, sex workers are generally disinclined to get involved with traditional systems, and many do not use services at all or are hesitant to do so. There also may be mismatches between sex workers' needs and service structures and insufficient funding for appropriate services. Most traditional facilities are ill-equipped to meet their needs.

The process of leaving sex work can be difficult and protracted. Sex workers get their social support on the street and experience stigma and ostracism from their old communities. Their financial needs and limited educational and occupational experiences do not dissipate over time. The longer they are involved in sex work, the more pronounced the mismatches become between their developmental competencies and what is expected of them by society, and the harder it is to join the "straight" world. Yet numerous young men do leave prostitution by choice or circumstance. Physicians and social service organizations play an important role in this transition. Many take a harm-reduction approach, helping youth to stay safe if and when they engage in sex work and decreasing their reliance on sex work for survival, often by helping them obtain housing, addressing mental health concerns, and helping them develop skills for work in the formal economy. Others exit sex work on their own because of circumstances related to failing health, drug treatment, or incarceration.

Marya Viorst Gwadz

See also Same-Sex Relationships; Sexuality; Sexually Transmitted Diseases

References and further readings
Browne, J., and V. Minichiello. 1996. "The Social Meanings behind Male Sex Work: Implications for Sexual Interactions." *British Journal of Sociology* 46, no. 4: 598–622.
———. 1996. "The Social and Work Context of Commercial Sex between Men: A Research Note." *Australian and New Zealand Journal of Sociology* 32, no. 1: 86–92.
Cohen, M. 1987. *Juvenile Prostitution.* Washington, DC: National Association of Counties Research.
Coleman, E. 1989. "The Development of Male Prostitution Activity among Gay and Bisexual Adolescents." *Journal of Homosexuality* 17, no. 2: 131–149.
de Graaf, R., et al. 1994. "Male Prostitutes and Safe Sex: Different Settings, Different Risks." *AIDS Care* 6, no. 3: 277–288.
Deisher, R., G. Robinson, and D. Boyer. 1982. "The Adolescent Female and Male Prostitute." *Pediatric Annals* 11, no. 10: 819–825.
D'Emilio, John, and Estelle Freedman. 1988. *Intimate Matters: A History of Sexuality in America.* New York: Harper and Row.
El-Bassel, N., R. F. Schilling, L. Gilbert, S. Faruque, K. L. Irwin, and B. R. Edlin. 2000. "Sex Trading and Psychological

Distress in a Street-based Sample of Low Income Urban Men." *Journal of Psychoactive Drugs* 32, no. 2: 259–267.

Elifson, K. W., J. Boles, and M. Sweat. 1993. "Risk Factors Associated with HIV Infection among Male Prostitutes." *American Journal of Public Health* 83, no. 1: 79–83.

Fisher, B., D. K. Weisberg, and T. Marotta. 1982. *Report on Adolescent Male Prostitution.* San Francisco: Urban and Rural Systems Associates.

Joffe, H., and J. E. Dockrell. 1995. "Safer Sex: Lessons from the Male Sex Industry." *Journal of Community and Applied Social Psychology* 5, no. 5: 333–346.

Maloney, P. 1980. "Street Hustling: Growing Up Gay." Unpublished manuscript.

Pleak, R. R., and H. F. Meyer-Bahlburg. 1990. "Sexual Behavior and AIDS Knowledge of Young Male Prostitutes in Manhattan." *Journal of Sex Research* 27, no. 4: 557–587.

Sponsler, C. 1993. "Juvenile Prostitution Prevention Project." *WHISPER* 13, no. 2: 3–4.

Waldorf, D. 1994. "Drug Use and HIV Risk among Male Sex Workers: Results of Two Samples in San Francisco." Pp. 114–131 in *The Context of HIV Risk among Drug Users and Their Sexual Partners.* Edited by R. J. Battjes, Z. Sloboda, and W. C. Grace. NIDA Research Monograph. Rockville, MD: National Institute on Drug Abuse.

Weisberg, D. K. 1985. *Children of the Night: A Study of Adolescent Prostitution.* Lexington: D. C. Heath.

R

Radio
See Great Depression; Toys; World War II

Rap
See African American Boys

Reading
See Books and Reading, 1600s and 1700s; Books and Reading, 1800s; Books and Reading, 1900–1960; Books since 1960

Reformatories, Nineteenth-Century

Reformatories were institutions created to punish and reform youthful boys who were poor and homeless or who had committed crimes. Constructed first in northeastern cities and named "houses of refuge," reformatories for juveniles spread to other cities as the nation expanded westward. Most served only white boys, although some admitted black youths as well but kept them segregated from whites. Both the courts and parents of misbehaving boys committed youngsters to reformatories. These asylums closely resembled prisons, although they did provide boys with basic language, math, and vocational skills. Upon release boys either went to work for artisans, shopkeepers, and farmers or they returned to live with their natural families.

Prosperous, reform-minded New York City men founded the nation's first reformatory for boys in 1825. Concerned about the growth of youthful crime in the city and about the failure of adult prisons to reform young criminals, well-off New Yorkers formed the Society for the Reformation of Juvenile Delinquents in 1823 and completed construction of the New York House of Refuge two years later. Bostonians established a similar institution in 1826, as did Philadelphians in 1828.

All three cities were in the earliest stages of industrialization, and their new factories attracted teenage farm boys seeking employment and excitement in the city. Such boys usually came to the city alone and unsupervised by parents. When not working, boys hung out on street corners, gambled, drank, and sometimes yelled obscenities at passersby. Immigrants from Ireland and Germany also migrated to northeastern cities. Weakened by the long sea voyage, some died and left their children to manage on their own. Others made it to the United States, but fathers had to work long hours for low pay, and mothers had to labor so long and hard to provide basic food and housing for themselves and their families that children of immigrants often went unsupervised. They wandered the city streets, played pranks on one another, swam naked

Inmates march to their dorms at the Approved School, Jeffersonville, Indiana, 1938. (Bettmann/Corbis)

off the wharves in the summer, built huge bonfires for warmth and entertainment in the winter, stole apples from the stalls of peddlers, and in general made older, more established city residents uneasy.

Before the construction of reformatories, boys arrested for committing crimes entered city jails and, if convicted, adult prisons. By 1816, jails and prisons in New York, Boston, and Philadelphia were so overcrowded that boys were not always separated from adult criminals. Reformers feared both the rise of the juvenile crime rate and the probability of boys learning to commit ever more serious crimes in prison. As cities appeared in the Midwest and Far West, they copied the institutions, like juvenile reformatories, already established in eastern cities. In both parts of the country, founders of reformatories were chiefly concerned with saving white males from lives of poverty and crime. Although the vast majority of children in reformatories were white boys, officials also admitted some black youths and some girls of both races as well. When reformatories admitted blacks, they usually kept them segregated from whites. Girls were also housed separately from boys. In the nineteenth century, there were few reformatories built in the South, where most black boys and girls lived, perhaps because it was such an agrarian area and reformatories were chiefly an urban phenomenon.

By and large, Protestant men founded reformatories. They expected to teach the boys in their charge Protestant religious and moral values. Reformers were distrustful of immigrants, many of whom were Catholic, and quite willing to convert Catholic boys in their charge. Alarmed by the Protestantism preached in reformatories, Catholic parents and religious leaders in some cities eventually formed their own reformatories to preserve the faith and values of Catholic boys.

When a house of refuge or reformatory first opened its doors, the boys who entered came directly from prisons and jails. Courts soon committed others. Nonetheless, throughout the nineteenth century, most boys in reformatories had not committed crimes but were simply poor, homeless, or vagrant. The state had the right to intervene in the lives of poor youngsters thanks to the doctrine of *parens patriae*. Articulated first by a Pennsylvania court in 1838, the doctrine allows state governments to provide for a boy or girl when their natural parents do not properly care for them.

Eventually, not only courts but also impoverished parents placed boys in reformatories. Working-class parents expected their sons to find jobs as soon as they were physically able and to contribute a good part of their earnings to the family. Throughout the nineteenth century, when most men could not earn enough at unskilled jobs in factories to support their families, the labor of children, especially boys, was essential to the well-being of many families. When boys kept their earnings for themselves or refused to work or even to attend school, they angered their parents. Needy families were rarely willing or able to support a boy who neither earned his own keep nor helped his family financially. Parents sometimes committed such boys to reformatories for disciplinary purposes.

The first reformatories constructed were large, walled institutions. Boys were housed in cells furnished only with a small cot, table, and chair. Windows had bars on them. Boys wore uniforms and marched from their cells to the washroom, the dining hall, the schoolroom, and back. Often officials expected boys to remain silent except during occasional periods of recreation. In the second half of the nineteenth century, some cottage-style reformatories were constructed in which boys of the same age lived in more homelike buildings, often supervised by a couple who served as parental figures.

In all reformatories boys spent most of their time at school and at work. Officials believed that if boys were to be saved from lives of poverty and crime, they had to acquire basic literacy skills as well as learn proper habits of work. Reformatories contained classrooms where boys spent about four hours a day learning reading, writing, and arithmetic from male and female teachers. Since most boys in these asylums were thirteen to fourteen years old and illiterate, they were a difficult bunch to teach. Many were foreign-born, had found English-speaking public schools unwelcoming, and so had attended them rarely. Others faced no language barrier but often had to stay out of school to help their parents and so fell behind in school and dropped out. Still others may have wanted to go to school, but until the 1880s in many cities there were not enough public schools to accommodate all who wanted to attend. Since most boys remained in reformatories for just one to three years, often in that time they could not catch up on all the education they had missed when younger. Nonetheless, teachers in reformatories estimated that by the time they were released, most boys could read the Bible, and many could also write a letter to their friends.

Just as important as formal education was vocational training. Reformatory officials believed boys had to be prepared for employment if they were going to be properly reformed. At first, reformatories made connections with contractors who paid asylum officials for the labor of boys in asylum workshops. There boys learned to bind books, cane seats in chairs, and make baskets and umbrellas. Most boys disliked the boring, repetitive labor in contract shops and rebelled against it, usually by not working very hard but occasionally by burning down asylum workshops. During economic depressions, contractors sometimes closed the shops entirely, leaving the boys with no work. By 1884, free adult laborers objected so strongly to contract labor in institutions that many states banned it. Thereafter, reformatory officials established their own workshops in which they tried to teach boys how to use tools and to make and maintain objects needed in the institution.

Boys did not always accept reformatory values and discipline passively. They created their own subculture within institutions. Older boys sometimes sexually exploited younger boys. Many boys made fun of youths who cooperated with officials and tried to follow the rules and reform. At the Western House of Refuge in Pennsylvania, boys who reported violators of the rules to officials were ridiculed by fellow inmates as "softies" or as "lungers" because they would "lunge" forward willingly to gain favor with officials. Catholic boys who resented Protestant efforts to convert them would sing out of turn and yell obscenities during Sunday religious services in asylums. The ultimate rebellion against reformatories was running away, and a minority of boys were always willing to do just that, even

at the risk of physically injuring themselves. Boys stole ladders and scaled the walls of reformatories, only to fall and break arms or legs in the process.

Officials did not treat such infractions of the rules lightly. Punishments of boys in reformatories were often quite harsh. At the very least, a boy would be whipped. He might also be placed in a solitary, darkened cell, sometimes without clothes, and forced to eat bread and water for days at a time. At the Westborough Reform School in Massachusetts in the 1870s, officials locked disobedient boys into a "sweatbox" that was 10 inches deep by 14 inches wide, with three 1-inch slits for air holes. Boys who spent a week crammed in such a box often found it difficult to stand up and walk after being released (Pisciotta 1982, 415).

Officials expected that with proper discipline, education, and vocational training, boys would be reformed within one to three years after entering a reformatory. At that point officials preferred to indenture the boys out to local artisans or farmers, who would agree to feed and clothe the boys until they were eighteen years of age in return for their labor. In this fashion boys could be separated from their parents, whom asylum officials disliked and distrusted, and their reformation completed by hardworking citizens. Until the Civil War, most boys left reformatories to be indentured. However, during the war, when there was an upsurge of boys incarcerated in reformatories probably because their fathers were at war and their mothers were working outside the home and unable to keep them under control, reformatory officials found it difficult to find enough persons willing to indenture boys. Many potential employers of boys were themselves preparing to fight in the war and unable to take on and train boy laborers. After the war, as mechanization of farming proceeded rapidly, many farmers, always the most likely to indenture boys, replaced boy labor with machine labor.

When indenturing became less popular, reformatory officials, unwilling to expend more dollars to retain boys until they were eighteen and old enough to live and work on their own, returned most boys to their families. Asylum officials never liked having to return boys to mothers and fathers who had presumably not cared for them adequately in the first place, but both boys and their parents probably preferred this arrangement. Boys did not have to live with strangers often far away from their families, friends, and their city homes. Parents did not lose their children permanently but regained their company and their labor fairly promptly.

Priscilla Ferguson Clement

See also Apprenticeship; Foster Care; Indentured Servants; Orphanages

References and further reading
Hawes, Joseph M. 1971. *Children in Urban Society: Juvenile Delinquency in Nineteenth-Century America.* New York: Oxford University Press.
Hess, Albert G., and Priscilla F. Clement, eds. 1993. *History of Juvenile Delinquency: A Collection of Essays on Crime Committed by Young Offenders, in History and in Selected Countries.* Vol. 2. Aalen, Germany: Scientia Verlag.
Mennel, Robert M. 1973. *Thorns and Thistles: Juvenile Delinquency in the United States, 1825–1940.* Hanover, NH: University Press of New England.
Pisciotta, Alexander W. 1982. "Saving the Children: The Promise and Practice of Parens Patriae, 1838–1898." *Crime and Delinquency* 28, no. 3 (July): 410–425.
Schneider, Eric C. 1992. *In the Web of Class: Delinquents and Reformers in Boston, 1810s–1930s.* New York: New York University Press.

Reformatories, Twentieth-Century

In 1900, the United States had fewer than 100 reformatories, almost all of them in the Northeast or the upper midwestern states. The average age of boys committed to them was fourteen, although some took boys as young as ten. The average stay lasted slightly less than two years. Most of the boys had immigrant parents, but approximately 15 percent of them were African Americans (Schlossman 1995, 375).

Over the course of the twentieth century, the administrators of the juvenile justice system became increasingly disenchanted with reformatories as a method for the rehabilitation of youth. Early in the century, reformers attempted to transform these institutions into surrogate homes and schools for poor boys and young criminal offenders. When this process failed, subsequent generations worked to remove most boys from institutional settings and place them into alternative programs for rehabilitation and training. Although these efforts did result in the removal of most noncriminal boys from reformatories, the implementation of these proposals never matched the rhetoric. Widespread social fears about increasing crime consistently forced the courts to make the removal of young criminal offenders from society their first priority.

A late-nineteenth-century movement to substitute family care for institutional care sparked some of the earliest outcries against reformatories. Armed with studies performed by experts in the newly emerging sciences of psychology and sociology, Progressive reformers protested the monotony and lack of individual attention for children in institutional care. Convinced that delinquency resulted from environmental factors rather than from the immorality of the individual child, child welfare advocates argued that the efforts of reformatories to break down the will of a boy and compel his blind obedience to authority only increased the likelihood of his becoming a repeat offender. Instead, psychiatrists argued that children needed advisers to assist them in developing confidence in their own abilities.

These reformers envisioned the newly created juvenile court system, first implemented in Chicago in 1899, as the type of system that could remain flexible and focus on the individual child (Rothman 1980, 215; Mennel 1973, 131–132). Juvenile court judges retained broad discretionary powers in determining placements for the youths who came into their courts. They examined the totality of the juvenile's environment rather than simply the individual offense. Although their discretionary authority resulted in differing philosophies among these courts, most judges viewed reformatories as a last resort utilized only for serious or repeat offenders. In most juvenile courts, probation became the first option because it allowed children to remain with their families while receiving guidance and discipline from probation officers. If they deemed the home environment inappropriate for children (as they often did, especially in immigrant families), judges sought foster care options. Like Homer Folks, a leading reformer and champion of probation, many judges viewed incarceration of children as "opiates for the community" that "turn its mind away from its own serious problems" (Rothman 1980, 219–220).

Yet in certain cases, even the reformers acknowledged the necessity of institutionalization. As a result, many judges and reformers advocated the creation of new state schools for boys that emphasized not only basic educational skills but also vocational training. Judges generally committed older boys to these institutions (the average age of commitment rose slowly until by the 1930s it was sixteen), and they shortened their stays in these schools from an average of almost two years to approximately one (Schlossman 1995, 373).

Existing reformatories had to change both their methods and their public images in order to compete with these new schools. They changed their names from "houses of refuge" and "reformatories to "training schools," "industrial schools," or simply "boys' schools." They attempted to shift from a military model to a campus one, utilizing the latest scientific techniques to train their boys to survive in an industrial society. Administrators extended school hours and moved away from cell-block or dormitory living arrangements and toward the cottage design, with a small number of children supervised by an adult with the highest educational and moral background. Ideally, children would have their own rooms and feel they lived in a normal, familial community.

One prominent example of this model was the George Junior Republic, opened in Freeville, New York, in 1895. At this school children voted, held political office, and had jobs as bankers, judges, police officers, and store owners, among others. The children made money and were allowed to retain it in a savings account. Those citizens who broke the rules went to jail, where they wore striped suits and worked on rock piles. By 1920 a combination of politics and internal dissension caused the disintegration of this school, but other schools, most famously Father Edward Flanagan's Boys Town outside Omaha, Nebraska, followed its model in a modified form.

The Whittier State Reform School in California also implemented a radically different approach to juvenile rehabilitation. In 1912, its new director, Fred Nelles, emphasized the need for individual treatment programs based on psychological testing and counseling of inmates. With the assistance of the psychology departments at Stanford and the University of California at Los Angeles, Nelles recommended specific placements in cottages, classes, work assignments, and even recreational programs. He attempted to control the population of his school, focusing on younger, noncriminal boys who scored well on intelligence tests. He kept the boys in school for five and a half hours a day (an extraordinary amount of time for reform schools during this period), and beyond academics he emphasized character development through intramural sports and an active Boy Scouts program.

As a reform school system grew in the southern states, another new model arose in 1897 with the founding of Virginia Manual Labor School for black youths. Most southern institutions admitted whites only, although a few had admitted both races while retaining strictly separate housing and curricula for whites and blacks. The Virginia Manual Labor School, however, hoped to provide agricultural and vocational training for blacks based on Booker T. Washington's philosophy of racial uplift through labor.

Even though the ideology of reformers and the juvenile court judges promoted dramatic change within the reformatory system, in reality the lasting changes did not match their ideals. Most historians agree that the number of incarcerated children did not decrease as a consequence of the strategies of the juvenile courts. A lack of funding by state legislatures meant an inability to garner equip-

ment for vocational training, to pay enough teachers to educate the inmates, and to hire psychiatrists to attend to therapeutic needs. Overcrowding destroyed the ideal of the cottage system. The undesirability of jobs at juvenile institutions meant that few employees had the required skills to assist the boys intellectually or emotionally. Military rules and language began to slowly return. Discipline and institutional maintenance, rather than rehabilitation, became the administrators' chief priorities. Training schools typically isolated their students from the outside world, allowing them to write one letter and receive one visitor a month. Corporal punishment remained standard, and students often attacked each other. A national survey of boys discharged from training schools indicated that only 55 of the 751 boys had records free of disciplinary action (Mennel 1973, 277). Sexual assaults among inmates regularly appeared as one of the leading causes of such actions.

The rise of scientific approaches to treatment also had disturbing consequences for juvenile offenders. Although many scientists believed criminal behavior derived from the child's environment, another group argued that such activities resulted from genetic abnormalities. These scientists attempted to identify physical traits that suggested a propensity toward criminal behavior in youths. They measured heads and the strength of children's grasps, among other physical characteristics, in an effort to identify children they labeled "moral imbeciles" or "defective delinquents." Subsequently, they attempted to establish separate institutions for these children and occasionally even sterilized them.

In the post–World War II period, the number of reform schools and inmates increased substantially. Between 1950 and 1970, the inmate population increased over 75 percent, from 35,000 to 62,000. The number of publicly operated reform schools grew to almost 200, not including several hundred camps, group homes, and private institutions. Yet crime rates continued to increase, and the length of stay in these schools continued to decline to an average of less than one year by 1970 (Schlossman 1995, 383–384).

Sensitized by the civil rights movement and a growing distrust of law enforcement, critics began to question the methods of social control employed by both the juvenile court systems and reformatories. Lawyers, who had effectively been removed from the juvenile court process, argued that the system failed to protect the constitutional rights of the children to due process of law. Social scientists pointed to increasing crime rates as evidence that the juvenile justice system did not work. They viewed the expectations that the system could simultaneously prevent delinquency and solve nearly every youth problem as unrealistic. Furthermore, they theorized that entry into the juvenile justice system, and in particular periods of incarceration, stigmatized children and isolated them even further from the rest of society. Both groups emphasized the injustice of entrapping noncriminal youths in the system because of their poverty or unstable homes.

A final effort to achieve juvenile rehabilitation through reformatories resulted in the creation of youth authority agencies that centralized control over placement and treatment of delinquent youths. Its advocates believed that rehabilitation problems would lessen once experts controlled the entire process. As in earlier efforts, a lack of funding and qualified personnel undermined these attempts. Ironically, however, this process led to the emergence of the deinstitutionalization and community treatment movements, which sought to promote nonresidential (or at least noninstitutional) methods of juvenile rehabilitation.

The most powerful youth authority developed in California, where in 1961 it led the movement to revise the state juvenile code. The new code distinguished more clearly between criminal and noncriminal juveniles within the system and increased the due process rights of youths. It also launched the Community Treatment Project in parts of Stockton and Sacramento. This social experiment grouped children according to their maturity level and assigned them randomly to either a reformatory or community treatment program. A select group of youth authority agents, given both small caseloads and additional resources, supervised these youths. The results from this program allegedly demonstrated the superiority of community programs, in terms of both rehabilitation and financial savings to the state. Despite arguments that the scientific justification for the experiment was shallow and misleading, these results caused momentum in favor of community programs to grow during the 1960s and 1970s. Most dramatically, the commissioner of the Massachusetts Department of Youth Services, after determining that he could not keep them "caring and decent," decided to close all reform schools in the state in 1972 and replace them with a network of small, generally nonsecure group homes. In 1974, Congress further encouraged this approach by passing the Juvenile Justice and Delinquency Prevention Act, which provided grant funds for the development of state and local delinquency prevention programs emphasizing diversion and de-institutionalization.

Once again, however, these reforms did not effect widespread change. Incarceration rates dropped during the 1970s, but juveniles who would have gone to public institutions may instead have been sent to group homes and private custodial centers. By the 1980s, the rate of juvenile incarceration reached an all-time high of more than 200 juveniles per 100,000. More than 50 percent of this population was African American. Ironically, more recent developments in juvenile justice seem to advocate the sentencing of young offenders to penitentiaries rather than reformatories; the number of youths under age eighteen held in adult prisons rose from 3,400 in 1985 to 7,400 in 1997 (Talbot 2000).

Paul Ringel

See also Boys Town; Foster Care; Juvenile Courts

References and further reading
Mennel, Robert M. 1973. *Thorns and Thistles: Juvenile Delinquency in the United States, 1825–1940.* Hanover, NH: University Press of New England.
Miller, Jerome G. 1991. *Last One over the Wall: The Massachusetts Experiment in Closing Reform Schools.* Columbus: Ohio State University Press.
Rothman, David J. 1980. *Conscience and Convenience: The Asylum and Its Alternatives in Progressive America.* Boston: Little, Brown.
Schlossman, Steven. 1995. "Delinquent Children: The Juvenile Reform School." In *The Oxford History of the Prison.* Edited by Norval Morris and David J. Rothman. New York: Oxford University Press.
Talbot, Margaret. 2000. "The Maximum Security Adolescent." *New York Times Magazine,* September 10.

Religion
See Bar Mitzvah; Muscular Christianity; Parachurch Ministry; Preachers in the Early Republic; Sunday Schools

Revolutionary War
Boys, some as young as ten or twelve years old, played an important part in the American Revolution. In creating the Continental Army with George Washington as its commander in chief, the new Congress of the United States suggested a minimum age limit of sixteen for its servicemen. However, many recruiters did not ask too many questions about the age of volunteers when they had trouble finding enough men to meet their quotas. Most boys served the Patriot cause by enlisting in their state militia or by joining the Continental Army. Almost all served as ordinary soldiers, but a few became officers even though they were still teenagers. The youngest served as drummer boys. Some worked as spies behind enemy lines. Others joined the Continental Navy or served on privateers—pirate ships that preyed on enemy shipping. Those who served for the duration of the war usually had a combination of these experiences because they were moved between different kinds of activities as the war dragged on.

Complete statistics on the service of boys in the Revolution, like data for all other servicemen, are patchy. Complete records survive for only a few regiments and then only for short periods of time. One such record for a four-year period from New Jersey shows that approximately 10 percent of soldiers were under eighteen. Another from Maryland for the year 1782 shows 25 percent between fourteen and nineteen, and if calculated only on native-born rather than foreign-born soldiers, the number becomes 37 percent. A Virginia study shows that about 5 percent of that state's troops were fourteen or fifteen years old. The preponderance of boys and young men in the army was a constant, but it seems likely that the number of younger soldiers increased as the war progressed and the army became more desperate for manpower.

Boys had a variety of reasons for enlisting. Some joined because they supported the cause of independence from Britain, out of a desire to be part of a big adventure, from peer pressure, or from a combination of these. A few had less conventional reasons. One young man, Eli Jacobs, served in the Massachusetts Continentals and the state militia for a variety of short terms from the age of fourteen but only signed on for a longer term following an argument with his stepmother (Dann 1980, 59).

Others were drawn into service by financial need. All during the war, states offered a variety of bounties, usually cash or clothing, to attract poor boys or men into the service. This was a particularly good way for boys to contribute to their families' welfare. Research indicates that for many poor boys, the bounty money was probably a significant inducement. In Maryland, the bounty was equal to one-quarter of the taxable property owned by the family of the average recruit. Enlistment brought in some needed ready cash to a family. Also, if the recruit was a dependent rather than a contributing family member, signing up meant he would now be fed and clothed by the army and no longer be an expense to his family.

Other boys helped their families by serving as substitutes for older family members. As the war progressed, states had introduced a draft for eligible men.

However, the man drafted did not need to go if he could pay someone to go in his place or find a relative to swap places with him. For some poor families who could not afford to lose the labor or wages of a father or older brother, a younger son might be sent instead to meet the obligation. However, if his father did go off to serve, a son's labor became even more essential to the family. It meant young boys had to assume greater responsibilities to their families at an earlier age.

One fifteen-year-old who wanted to be part of the big adventure was Joseph Plumb Martin of Massachusetts. He was living and working on his grandfather's farm when war broke out in 1775, and even though he did not really understand the Patriot cause, he very much wanted to be called "a defender of my country," and he was sure the Americans were "invincible." He was unsure of his ability to endure the hardships of a soldier's life, but finally he let his friends talk him into signing on. They bantered with him, saying, "If you will enlist I will." And so young Martin, at sixteen, found himself a soldier signing up for six months. He reenlisted when his term was up and continued to serve until the end of the war in 1783, during which time he endured much hardship (Martin 1993, 11–13).

Service offered some boys the opportunity for social advancement. Jeremiah Greenman was seventeen and not yet trained in any skill when he enlisted in the army in 1775. No information is available about his political knowledge at the time, although his diary indicates that he acquired some as the war progressed. His diary also shows us that he went from having basic literacy skills to being a sophisticated writer and a thoughtful reader. By the war's end, he had embarked on a program of self-education, choosing his books carefully from the recommendations of others or popular advice books. The war also tested his resolve. In the first year, on the Quebec campaign he had endured hunger, cold, and a nine-month period as a British prisoner of war—all before his eighteenth birthday. After a time at home following that experience, the young Rhode Islander, now age nineteen, signed up again, this time serving as a sergeant. He seems to have thrived under his new responsibilities and by age twenty-one was an ensign in the Second Rhode Island Regiment (Greenman 1978).

Although many boys who served ended the war as poor as they began, that was not true for all of them. Some boys signed on to go to sea on American privateers in the hope of making their fortunes. A privateer was a privately owned vessel that operated by special commission granted by Congress and was essentially engaged in piracy. Its mandate was to run down and seize enemy merchant ships. The goods seized in the attack were later sold and the proceeds split among the owners, officers, and crew. The potential rewards attracted men of all ages despite the considerable risks of life at sea and the danger of being seized by the British and either held as a prisoner or impressed to serve in the British Navy.

Joshua Davis and Ebenezer Fox were two boys who decided to try their luck on the high seas, but neither had the opportunity to make their fortunes. Davis had served with the Massachusetts militia since he was fifteen but at nineteen decided go to sea. Unfortunately, his ship was captured by a British frigate, and he was forced to serve in the British Navy for nine months, then was held in a prison at Plymouth, England, before again having to serve at sea for the British. The young man was twenty-seven before he was able to escape and return to Boston, a free man, in 1787, four years after the war's end.

Fox was no more fortunate. He had run away to sea at the age of twelve in 1775 and worked as a cabin boy on an American merchant ship traveling to the West Indies. After war was declared, he narrowly avoided capture by the British and decided to go home to Rhode Island to pursue a barber's trade. Boredom prompted him to try his luck at sea again in 1779, and at sixteen he signed on to join the navy. Now he experienced battle against the British. He was part of a gun crew, responsible for swabbing out the cannon after firing and then ramming in the next shot of powder and ball. A few months later, the British captured the ship, and Fox was taken prisoner. The unfortunate seaman was held on the notorious prison ship the *Jersey*, moored off Long Island. In order to leave that awful prison, he agreed to join the British Army and soon found himself with a British regiment in Jamaica. From there, after a few months, he made his escape by fleeing to Cuba where, since Spain was an American ally, he hoped to find a ship bound for America. He was not disappointed. He signed on the American frigate *Flora*, but before it sailed, he was impressed onto a French naval vessel. The military alliance between France and the United States did not prevent the French captain from seizing any potential crew members he might need, no matter what their country of birth. Making his escape from the French warship, Fox fled to the *Flora* again and eventually returned home after the war's end, glad to be back to the quiet trade of barbering at the old age of twenty (Fox 1838).

Boys like Greenman, Fox, and Davis were lucky to survive their prison experiences. Prisons were notorious for the diseases and the consequent high mortality rates among the prisoners. When Fox was held on the *Jersey*, 1,000 other prisoners were already there, short of food, held in poorly ventilated space, with disease spreading rapidly among them. Of the three, Greenman had a somewhat better experience. Taken prisoner at Quebec in 1776, he and his fellow prisoners received adequate food. In winter, smallpox had been rampant among the prisoners, but he had not caught it. In the spring, Greenman noted that he and his fellows were able to keep themselves healthy and strong by playing ball in the yard. They were fortunate in that they were exchanged and released nine months after their capture. Although barefoot on his release, he was otherwise well.

The adventure of serving often led boys to use a wide variety of skills. Thomas Marble of Connecticut, for example, unintentionally served on land and sea. Enlisted in Connecticut regiments from the age of sixteen onward, Marble was with a detachment assigned to capture a British schooner and three sloops. To do this, he and his fellows were required to man whaleboats and sail them behind enemy lines to carry out the attack, which they did successfully. Before they could bring back their prisoners, they had to repair one of the sloops, which required all hands to turn their skills to ship repair too (Dann 1980, 327–330).

Younger boys usually saw less direct action in the war. Many of them were serving with their fathers in some capacity. Despite their young age, they usually received separate enlistment papers. They carried out a variety of duties, sometimes working as their fathers' servants, as messengers, or as drummers to the regiment. Israel Trask was ten years old when he went with his father, a lieu-

tenant in the Massachusetts line of the Continental Army, to camp in 1775. The young Trask served as a cook and messenger, though he noted that his father collected his pay and rations. The son of Major Putnam, a boy about thirteen, was also serving with this regiment as a drummer boy. That boy had the task, as many drummers did, of applying the lash as punishment to another soldier. The drummer was hoping he could use his father's influence to get out of the unpleasant duty, but he was required to do it (Dann 1980, 406–414).

Sometimes boys could move more inconspicuously than men behind enemy lines and so were occasionally used as spies. One such was William Johnson, who at the age of sixteen was serving in the New Jersey state militia. At twenty he became a spy for George Washington, entering the city of New York as a black-market merchant. His task was to make careful observations of military activity in the city and report it back to Washington. In addition, the commander in chief used Johnson to spread untrue reports in New York of American military plans in order to mislead the British (Dann 1980, 353–357).

Caroline Cox

References and further reading
Coggins, Jack. 1967. *Boys in the Revolution: Young Americans Tell Their Part in the War for Independence.* Harrisburg, PA: Stackpole Books.
Dann, John, ed. 1980. *The Revolution Remembered: Eyewitness Accounts of the War for Independence.* Chicago: University of Chicago Press.
Davis, Joshua. 1819. *Joshua Davis' Report.* Collections of the New England Historical and Genealogical Society.
Fox, Ebenezer. 1838. *The Revolutionary Adventures of Ebenezer Fox.* Boston: Monroe and Francis.

Greenman, Jeremiah. 1978. *Diary of a Common Soldier in the American Revolution, 1775–1783: An Annotated Edition of the Military Journal of Jeremiah Greenman.* Edited by Robert C. Bray and Paul E. Bushnell. Dekalb: Northern Illinois University Press.

Lender, Mark Edward. 1980. "The Social Structure of the New Jersey Brigade." In *The Military in America from the Colonial Era to the Present.* Edited by Peter Karsten. New York: Free Press.

Martin, Joseph Plumb. 1993. *Ordinary Courage: The Revolutionary War Adventures of Joseph Plumb Martin.* New York: Brandywine Press.

Papenfuse, Edward C., and Gregory A. Stiverson. 1973. "General Smallwood's Recruits: The Peacetime Career of the Revolutionary War Private." *William and Mary Quarterly* 30: 117–132.

Sellers, John R. 1974. "The Common Soldier in the American Revolution." In *Military History of the American Revolution.* Edited by Betsy C. Kysley. Washington, DC: USAF Academy.

Rock Bands

Rock bands have played a significant role in the identity formation of adolescent and preadolescent boys since the early 1960s. Whether as fans or as participants in their own bands, boys have formed strong group identities around the existence of rock bands and the cultural messages they present, especially those messages concerned with authority figures, sexuality, and self-worth.

By the early 1960s, the rock band had become the significant unit of popular music, replacing the traditional format of a bandleader, single musician, or vocal group working with an orchestra or session musicians. Following the formula of guitar, bass, and drums established by the blues bands of the early 1950s and taking their inspiration from early rock and roll musicians such as Chuck Berry and Buddy Holly, rock bands also changed the sound of popular music by making the guitar the central instrument. Beginning with the California surf bands of the early 1960s, such as the Champs, the Ventures, the Surfaris, and, most important, the Beach Boys, these four- or five-piece bands began to work together as self-contained units. In many cases, they made their own arrangements and composed their own material, jobs that traditionally had been performed in the music world by individuals separate from the musicians themselves.

The small size and singleness of purpose of rock bands led to their becoming close-knit entities, a feature enhanced by their homogenous makeup. For at the same time that rock bands were developing, rock music began to split from its rhythm and blues roots; as it did so, followers of popular music generally split along race lines, with rock becoming a medium dominated mostly by white men. With a few notable exceptions— Jimi Hendrix, Janis Joplin, and more recently the Bangles, Los Lobos, Living Color, and the riot grrrl bands—participation in rock bands, too, became almost exclusively white and male.

The great catalyst for most American boys' interest in rock bands was the arrival of the Beatles in the United States in February 1964. Their impact on popular music was instant and dramatic and paved the way for many other British groups as well as scores of imitators. Not only did they provide a blueprint for all rock bands that followed, but like the various forms of popular music that preceded them, they inspired fashions and sensibilities that were immediately adopted by teenage boys and girls. Their collar-length pageboy cuts and Cuban-heeled boots replaced the popular look of the 1950s—the leather motorcycle jacket and slicked-back haircut. This was the first change in a cycle of fashions inspired by subsequent bands and musical genres. The Beatles look, in turn, gave way to the bell-bottom jeans, T-shirts, and long hair of the late 1960s hippies; this look dominated the 1970s until the spiked hair and thin black ties of the new wave/punk movement became prevalent at the end of the decade. During the 1980s, jeans and black T-shirts with band logos worn by fans of the heavy metal "hair" bands became the fashion. In the 1990s, the baggy clothing and unkempt appearance of the alternative and grunge scene and the black clothing, makeup, body piercing, and tattoos of the Goth movement supplemented these rock fashion styles. Although each trend sought to replace a previous one, many looked back to and coexisted with other trends. Both boys and girls identified with a specific look; the look and the music that accompanied it became a significant part of their evolving identity.

But rock fashions alone have not been the only force to shape adolescent male identities. For some fans, identities have been forged through the hobby of collecting the recorded music and memorabilia generated by a given band or musical genre. For others, a fascination with the lifestyles of the bands begun in the early teenage years manifests itself in later life in the desire to follow the band on tours, as demonstrated by the Deadheads, followers of the Grateful Dead, and fans of the band Phish. For these fans, the experience of seeing a particular band live, often on numerous occasions, creates a powerful group identity.

An equally powerful shared experience for a teenage boy comes from joining a rock band, and many boys have been inspired to participate in a "garage band,"

named after the traditional rehearsal space, where they would attempt to master a repertoire of easy-to-play songs. Again, the Beatles and the so-called British invasion bands that followed them proved to be an early catalyst for garage bands. The success of the Beatles led to a widespread demand for inexpensive instruments, and manufacturers of cheap equipment enjoyed an unprecedented demand for their goods following the Beatles' arrival in the United States. By the mid-1960s, one manufacturer of cheap guitars, Kay, was producing 1,500 guitars a day (Wheeler 1990, 240). Demand, however, was so great that the domestic market could not keep pace, and more than 500,000 guitars were imported into the United States in 1966 (Wheeler 1990, 234). Although some boys were formally trained, the majority were self-taught. The rough and unschooled music produced by many of these bands in their attempts to imitate the style of rock music currently in fashion inspired several genres of rock music, including punk in the 1970s and grunge and alternative in the 1990s.

No one can say how many bands played only in the garage in which they practiced. Such is the volatile nature of teenage relationships that many probably played only a few rehearsals and others played only one or two performances at private parties or teen dances in front of their friends. Even so, participating in a band gave and continues to give adolescent boys a sense of belonging to a small clique, with its accompanying status in the larger peer group. As such, membership in a band closely resembles membership in a gang, with shifting allegiances, fighting, bonding, and shared identity all a part of the collective experience. But the lure of playing in a band is so great for those who experience it that many who participate in rock bands as adolescents often continue well into adulthood.

Rock music's traditional messages—sex, rebellion, hedonism, and adolescent identity—both influence and are influenced by teenagers as they journey through puberty. Musician John Mellencamp's story, for example, reflects the situation of many; for him, the decision to become involved with music was clearly a rebellion against the family and community values of his childhood in Indiana. Like many rock icons such as Jim Morrison of the Doors and Kurt Cobain of Nirvana, Mellencamp recalled a problematic childhood associated with domestic violence. For him, rock music was a rejection of his domestic life; it "was something my friends and I calculated the right people would hate" (White 1990, 602).

Such rebellion also finds voice in the lyrics of many rock songs exhorting listeners to party and indulge in drugs and alcohol, for many teens an ultimate rejection of family and community values. For others, such as singer Jon Bon Jovi, involvement with music was more about sex and self-esteem. In an interview, he recalled that at the age of fourteen when his first guitar teacher asked him why he wanted to play, he replied, "To get chicks, what else?" and added, "I was never very good at picking up girls, and I'm still not. . . . I had no lines, so music was my method" (White 1990, 763). Fellow New Jersey musician Bruce Springsteen also recalled the powerful effect the discovery of rock music had on the formation of his identity when he said, "I was dead until I was thirteen. I didn't have any way of getting my feelings out. . . . So I bought a guitar. The first day I can remember looking in a mirror and being able to stand what I was seeing was the day I had a guitar in my hand" (Marsh 1996, 15–16).

Although many critics have heralded the death of rock music ever since its inception in the 1950s, the recent popularity of hard rock bands such as Korn and Limp Bizkit has shown that guitar-centered rock music still holds sway over a significant number of young white boys. It is a powerful tool in forming their identity at a crucial point in their development. Fashions in music, clothing, and appearance will undoubtedly change, but rock music in some form or another will probably exist for much longer, providing boys with a focal point for coming to terms with their personal and social identities.

Bruce Pegg

See also Music

References and further reading
Marsh, Dave. 1996. *The Bruce Springsteen Story*. Vol. 1, *Born to Run*. New York: Thunder's Mouth Press.
Wheeler, Tom. 1990. *American Guitars: An Illustrated History*. New York: Harper.
White, Timothy. 1990. *Rock Lives: Profiles and Interviews*. New York: Holt.

Roosevelt, Theodore

The statesman, environmentalist, and domestic reformer who served from 1901 to 1909 as the twenty-sixth president of the United States, Theodore Roosevelt also distinguished himself as a naturalist, outdoorsman, historian, soldier, explorer, commentator on contemporary affairs, and husband and father of six children. Roosevelt was born into wealth and comfort in New York City on October 27, 1858, the second of four children and the older of two sons of Theodore Roosevelt, Sr., and Martha Bulloch Roosevelt. His privileged boyhood was sheltered in certain respects but expansive and stimulating in others. It was also heavily burdened by the very severe asthmatic condition that plagued him until his college years. One can locate in Theodore's boyhood many roots of his adult character and of the morally upright, energetic, high-achieving man he was to become. The influence of his father was to prove especially profound.

Known as "Teedie" among his intimates, young Theodore lived for his first fourteen years in a five-story brownstone located at 28 East 20th Street, which was a wedding gift to his parents from his millionaire paternal grandfather, Cornelius Van Schaak Roosevelt, a plate-glass importer and real estate investor. Theodore's mother Martha ("Mittie"), born in 1835, had grown up in a relatively prosperous but sometimes struggling slaveholding plantation family in Roswell, Georgia, from where she moved to New York upon her marriage in 1853. Theodore's father, Theodore, Sr., born in 1831, worked, along with an older brother, in grandfather Cornelius's firm. Theodore's three siblings were Anna ("Bamie"), born in 1855; Elliott ("Ellie"), born in 1860; and Corinne ("Conie"), born in 1861. The two other members of the household (aside from servants) were Martha's mother "Grandmamma" (until her death in 1864) and, as governess, Martha's older sister Anna (until her marriage in 1866). This core group of eight was frequently augmented by visiting relatives and family friends; Edith Carow ("Edie"), Corinne's favorite playmate and Theodore's childhood pal and future wife, was prominent among the latter.

For the young people who lived there, the Roosevelt home was a happy and protective place. Both Martha and Theodore,

Sr., were warm and loving and extremely attentive to the needs of their children. Of the two, Martha was the more vivacious, eccentric, and literary, traits that apparently were transmitted in abundance to her older son. The father, however, was the more dominant presence and the more influential figure. Decades later, in an autobiography written after his presidency, Theodore worshipfully remembered his father as

> the best man I ever knew. He combined strength and courage with gentleness, tenderness, and great unselfishness. He would not tolerate in us children selfishness or cruelty, idleness, cowardice, or untruthfulness. As we grew older he made us understand that the same standard of clean living was demanded for the boys as for the girls. . . . With great love and patience, . . . he combined insistence on discipline. . . . He was entirely just, and we children adored him. (Roosevelt 1985, 7–8).

The sheltered upper-class life of the Roosevelt children extended to their education, which was entrusted to private tutors, the first of whom was their aunt Anna. With the exception of a very brief and unsuccessful trial enrollment at a small private school near his home, Theodore's first experience as a student in an educational institution came at Harvard University in 1876.

Actually, because his parents clearly recognized his academic aptitude and interests, Theodore probably would have been sent to a top-flight boarding school prior to beginning his higher education. They were deterred from taking this path by the persistence of their older son's struggle with bronchial asthma, which had begun around the age of three. Theodore's asthma attacks were recurrent and extremely debilitating, at times bringing him to the verge of suffocation. Theodore, Sr., the boy's principal source of comfort and rescue when an asthma attack struck, spared no effort or expense as he and the young victim jointly battled the terrifying disease. All sorts of remedies were attempted, ranging from such dubious ones as consuming black coffee, swallowing ipecac, and smoking cigars to such potentially more constructive approaches as carriage rides for fresh air, summers in the countryside, and a regimen of rigorous physical exercise. Nevertheless, the condition was not finally conquered until Theodore was in college.

Between the ages of two and six, Theodore lived in a home in which the Civil War was an ever-present reality, particularly in light of his sectionally mixed parentage. Young Theodore came to side wholeheartedly with his fervently Unionist father, whereas the sympathies of his mother, aunt, and grandmother were solidly with the Confederacy. In deference to the sensibilities of his wife, whose brothers and other relatives were fighting for the South, Theodore, Sr., did not take up arms for the Union, although he hired a substitute for $1,000 after the draft was instituted in 1863. But he did work tirelessly, meeting with President Abraham Lincoln in Washington, D.C., to win legislation for and then to help to organize the voluntary allotment to their families of a portion of the soldiers' pay. On East 20th Street, his son Theodore was increasingly demonstrative about his pro-Union position. But whether at home or away, Theodore, Sr., was never sparing in expressions of his great love for his wife, and the marriage and the family's

unity survived the emotional strain of the war in remarkably good shape.

Between 1865 and 1871 Theodore, although asthmatic and quite frail, lived a mostly happy life among his parents and siblings and their small, elite social circle. He was an avid young reader who was particularly attracted to stories of adventure and heroism, and he was full of curiosity about the world. When he was seven or eight, his chance viewing of a dead seal laid out on a Broadway sidewalk generated tremendous excitement and appears to have sparked his lifelong passion for natural science. Between May 1869 and May 1870, the Roosevelts experienced an extensive transatlantic tour through Great Britain, Belgium, the Netherlands, Germany, Switzerland, Italy, Austria, and France. During the trip Theodore, who genuinely enjoyed seeing so many new places in the company of his family, kept a detailed diary marked by language that was rather precocious for a ten- to eleven-year-old. Moreover, the endurance displayed by Theodore as he hiked in the Alps with his father and the apparent benefit of these hikes to the boy's health led the father to advise the son soon after the journey: "Theodore, you have the mind, but you have not the body, and without the help of the body the mind cannot go as far as it should. You must *make* your body. It is hard drudgery . . . , but I know you will do it" (quoted in McCullough 1981, 112). The youth vowed to heed his father's summons, and so began an enduring commitment to strenuous physical activity.

The period 1872–1873 constituted a turning point for Theodore. After a humiliating encounter with two stronger boys during the summer of 1872, he began taking boxing lessons. Around the same time he received his first gun and learned to shoot, and he learned taxidermy. Perhaps most important, he realized that his vision was severely impaired and acquired his first spectacles, which, he said, "literally opened an entirely new world to me" (Roosevelt 1985, 19). In October 1872 the Roosevelts embarked on a second overseas odyssey, this one significantly more dramatic and rewarding for Theodore than the first. The family again visited England and continental Europe but in addition followed a greatly expanded itinerary that included Egypt, Palestine, Syria, Turkey, and Greece. For Theodore the leading highlight was the winter of 1872–1873, which was spent living on a well-staffed *dahabeah* (houseboat) that carried the group about 1,200 miles up and down the Nile River. Theodore's preoccupation during these months was collecting bird specimens, an activity abetted by the breech-loading shotgun presented to him by his father as a Christmas present and by his family's generous tolerance of foul-smelling taxidermal operations on deck. He was also fascinated by Egypt's ancient treasures. During most of the period from May 1873, when their father returned to the United States, until their own departure several months later, Theodore, Elliott, and Corinne lived as guests of the Minkwitz family in Dresden, Germany, where Theodore applied himself assiduously to the study of German and other subjects.

When Martha and her children arrived back in New York in November 1873, they took up residence in an "infinitely more luxurious" new uptown house complete with a well-equipped gymnasium on the top floor at 6 West 57th Street, near Central Park (McCullough 1981, 135). Theodore's grandfather Cornelius had passed away in 1871, leaving

each of his offspring a veritable fortune, and Theodore, Sr., put the best of everything into the family's new house, even as he increasingly devoted time and resources to his many and varied philanthropic pursuits.

In 1874 Arthur Cutler, a young Harvard graduate, was hired as Theodore's tutor and immediately began to prepare him for the Harvard entrance examination. Theodore's education up to that point had been uneven; he was very advanced in natural science, history, geography, German, and French but lagged in mathematics and classical languages. He and Cutler focused on the deficient areas, and the pupil's diligence bore fruit. He passed the exam during the summer of 1875, after which he continued to study with Cutler in anticipation of his impending enrollment at Harvard.

During his precollege years, Theodore blossomed physically and emotionally as well as intellectually. From 1874 on, the Roosevelts spent long summers on the northern shore of Long Island in Oyster Bay, New York, where as an adult Theodore would build Sagamore Hill, his and Edith's permanent home and the summer White House during his presidency. These youthful summers were a time of rapid personal growth and immense happiness for Theodore, with the wild and beautiful natural environment, the presence of teenage girls, and an abundance of time for reading. During the summer of 1876, Theodore's sister Anna, who often served as a third parent for the other three children, went up to Cambridge, Massachusetts, and secured a second-floor room in a boardinghouse at 16 Winthrop Street, which would serve as Theodore's primary residence until his graduation from Harvard in 1880. On his own for the first time, he threw himself into his studies and his recreational and social activities while maintaining a regular correspondence with his parents and siblings in New York. In one letter to his father, he wrote: "I do not think there is a fellow in college who has a family that love him as much as you all do me, and I am *sure* that there is no one who has a father who is also his best and most intimate friend, as you are mine" (quoted in McCullough 1981, 165). At Harvard Theodore neither smoked nor gambled, drank only in moderation, and was determined to (and did) remain sexually "pure" until marriage. (He would marry Alice Lee shortly after his graduation, tragically lose her to Bright's disease in 1884, and marry Edith Carow in 1886.) Even though the orientation of his churchgoing Presbyterian family had always been far more worldly than spiritual, Theodore also taught a Sunday school class in Cambridge. His intelligence, stamina, and diligence enabled him to achieve academic success as a freshman and to begin to excel as a sophomore in German, natural science, history, and rhetoric. His health was unexpectedly good; apparently, his asthma had finally been beaten. And his first published work, "The Summer Birds of the Adirondacks in Franklin County, N.Y.," a pamphlet coauthored with Harvard classmate Henry Minot, was produced in 1877.

For most people, it is nearly impossible to pinpoint the moment of transition from childhood to adulthood. For Theodore Roosevelt, however, it is easy: February 9, 1878, the day his forty-six-year-old father succumbed to stomach cancer after a brief, futile struggle. It was "the blackest day of my life" the young man soon afterward recorded in his diary. Theodore, Sr., had "shared all my

joys, . . . and soothed all the few sorrows I ever had. . . . The days of unalloyed happiness are now over forever" (quoted in Brands 1997, 85). Notwithstanding his grief, Theodore was fortified by images of his literary heroes and "discerned his duty. He must bear up under this trial and conduct himself as his father would have wished" (Brands 1997, 85). In the wake of his exceedingly painful loss, he matured rapidly, willingly assuming new responsibilities for his siblings and his mother. Having inherited from his father $125,000, a huge sum in 1878, he had the advantage of financial independence as he made the sudden transition from boyhood to manhood.

The father would never cease to be the son's compass; any contemplated course of action could always be evaluated in relation to the father's exacting moral standards. The father's devotion to and nurturing love for his wife and children became the model for the son's similar devotion and nurturing. The father's aversion to idleness would be honored by the son's advocacy of and enthusiastic engagement in "the strenuous life" and by his uncommonly diverse and astonishingly productive career. And the father's patriotism, hostility to corruption, and extensive philanthropic endeavors undoubtedly guided the son toward military service, public service, concern for the downtrodden, and an ambitious agenda of domestic reform. From 1878 until his own death in 1919, the adult Theodore Roosevelt would live a life he deemed worthy of his idealized father and in the process leave an enormous imprint on his country and the world.

William N. Tilchin

See also Muscular Christianity

References and further reading
Brands, H. W. 1997. *T. R.: The Last Romantic.* New York: Basic Books.
McCullough, David. 1981. *Mornings on Horseback.* New York: Simon and Schuster.
Morris, Edmund. 1979. *The Rise of Theodore Roosevelt.* New York: Coward, McCann, and Geoghegan.
Roosevelt, Theodore. 1985. *Theodore Roosevelt: An Autobiography.* 1913. Reprint, New York: Da Capo Press.

Runaway Boys

Family life has never been uniform or stable in America, and the family evolved as the nation changed from rural and agrarian to urban and industrial and then to the contemporary suburban postindustrial society. Over time, boys have left their homes in response to a variety of personal and social problems.

As early as the colonial era, some minors left home without permission, and many were confined with adult paupers and the indigent in municipal workhouses or almshouses until their relatives claimed them or were placed out as indentured servants or apprentices. Colonial-era selectmen found the runaway apprentice, like the bastard child or juvenile delinquent, a chronic problem. Benjamin Franklin (1706–1790) began his career as a Philadelphia printer in 1723 as a runaway Boston apprentice, and Benedict Arnold (1741–1801) was a Connecticut druggist's apprentice in 1755 when he ran away to join the army.

To some degree, eighteenth-century vagrants were discouraged by local laws against wandering strangers, but by the 1840s the railroad made working-class tramps more mobile. In addition, industrial America needed seasonal workers on farms, in orchards, on ranches, in mines, in lumber camps, and in canneries. Boys who left home, voluntarily or not, often became tramps or hoboes, the migratory workers who hiked or hopped freight trains in search of work. In 1886, Harry Houdini (1874–1926), the magician and escape artist, ran away from home at age twelve to begin his theatrical career. The novelist Jack London (1876–1916) was a teenage hobo in the 1890s, as in more recent times were Supreme Court justice William O. Douglas; attorney Melvin Belli; and songwriters Merle Haggard, Roger Miller, and Bruce "Utah" Phillips.

By the 1870s the "tramp menace" had begun to alarm civic leaders, who feared hordes of runaway boys and men descending on towns and cities. Charles Loring Brace, who founded the New York Children's Aid Society, described this social problem in *The Dangerous Classes of New York and Twenty Years Work among Them* (1872), as did the detective Allan Pinkerton in *Strikers, Communists, Tramps, and Detectives* (1878). Partly to deal with homeless youths, Massachusetts founded the nation's first state reform school in 1846, and antebellum Boston courts held juvenile sessions to separate young lawbreakers (runaways, truants, shoplifters, and petty thieves) from adult offenders. This reform led to the establishment of more formal juvenile courts in Boston, Chicago, and Denver by 1906.

The most famous (fictional) runaway American boy was Huckleberry Finn, Aunt Sally's orphaned foster child, who planned "to light out for the Territory" in the 1850s. The best-selling novelist Horatio Alger, Jr. (1832–1899), centered 100 melodramatic rags-to-riches novels on plucky boys who left home to seek fame and fortune in cities as newsboys, "street Arabs" (*Mark the Match Boy*, 1869), boot-

The director of a private charity that operates a shelter for runaways comforts a child in the dormitory. (Steve Raymer/Corbis)

blacks (*Ragged Dick*, 1867), or street musicians (*Phil the Fiddler*, 1872). Alger found inspiration on his visits to the ragamuffins and guttersnipes at Charles Loring Brace's Newsboys' Lodging House, who provided vivid material for his fiction.

In the era between the Civil War and World War II, many American teenage boys dreamed of becoming hoboes, an exciting rambling life hopping freight trains or riding the rails beneath Pullman cars. The poet Robert Service celebrated the "race of men who won't fit in . . . for theirs is the curse of gypsy blood" who created their own hobo slang, songs, sign language, and codes. Running away to go to sea; to join the army, navy, or the circus; or to become a cowboy has long been an American tradition, and the star-

struck girls who left home since the 1920s hoping to become Hollywood starlets have male counterparts too. For every rebellious flapper in the Roaring Twenties, there was a young sheikh who rejected puritanical values and lived for the present.

The growing problem of juvenile delinquents living on the Omaha streets attracted the attention of an Irish Catholic priest, Father Edward J. Flanagan (1886–1948). In 1917 he founded what would later be called Boys Town to provide a rural home for runaway boys, winning public support for the project and becoming a recognized expert on homeless juveniles. During the Depression an estimated 4 million Americans rode the rails, and at least 250,000 of these transients were runaway boys. Many large construction projects, and later the Tennessee Valley Authority and the Hoover Dam in the 1930s, attracted young tramps to remote work sites. Boys who rode trains illegally (without paying) were the subject of socially conscious Hollywood movies like *Wild Boys of the Road* (1933) and *Boys Town* (1938), as well as a more recent PBS documentary, *Riding the Rails* (1999).

The Depression and World War II disrupted millions of lives, and the postwar era of conformity did not embrace all Americans. Although historical data are not specific, the incidence of runaway boys in the twentieth-century United States may be related to the increased rate of divorce and the fragility of the nuclear family in industrial and postindustrial society.

In 1957 the novel *On the Road* by Jack Kerouac (1922–1969) inspired a new generation of boys to leave home for adventures exploring the country, from New York City's bohemian Greenwich Village to San Francisco's North Beach. The Beat generation hitchhiked across the country, indulging in sex, drugs, and alcohol and rejecting mainstream social values. These young people dropped out of society, detaching from family connections and finding freedom in perpetual movement. In the 1960s the Beats influenced the counterculture hippies, attracting many runaway flower children to the Haight Ashbury district in San Francisco.

Runaway boys in all eras have faced serious problems. Many who entered the hobo ranks were victimized by predatory homosexual men called "jockers," who recruited and exploited these boys as their "punks." A more recent form of this exploitation in big cities concerns men called "chickenhawks" recruiting run-

away boys or girls as prostitutes, often seeking inexperienced youths at urban bus and train stations. These are only some of the dangers runaways have faced. The brutal reality of life on the road was often overlooked or unknown, and even the most popular American illustrator, Norman Rockwell, depicted a runaway boy as a humorous innocent long after the dangers were understood. Most runaways found only loneliness, poverty, hunger, and exploitation in life on the road, quite unlike the romantic myths of the carefree hobo existence.

Nonetheless, there is some evidence that boys who run away from home benefit from both positive and negative experiences by learning to be more self-confident and independent. Some boys return home more willing to accept parental guidance and to communicate more with parents. Anger with one parent is frequently cited by runaways as the reason for leaving home, and puberty is a confusing time for parents and their children as sexual maturity and insecurity become important issues. The act of running away may be an impetus to develop new strengths. A boy may run away from home to reaffirm his faith in his own independence and then return home to follow normal routes to socially acceptable goals.

Still, for every boy who runs away from home to establish his independence, there are many more who leave home because of poverty. The number of American children living in poverty increased from 3.2 million in 1978 to 5.2 million in 1998, meaning that 22 percent of young children in the United States lived in poverty. Although most of these millions of children are African American (40 percent) or Latino (38 percent), the incidence of poverty among young white suburban children (16 percent) grew rapidly since 1975. These families include boys most at risk for running away due to poverty, family conflict, child abuse, or school problems. By 1971 runaways were recognized as such a serious problem that the National Runaway Switchboard was established in Chicago for crisis intervention with young people in danger of leaving home or attempting to return home. In cooperation with social service organizations and the Greyhound Bus Company, hotline staff encouraged runaways to phone their parents and offered a free bus ticket to their hometown.

The number of runaways to San Francisco in the 1950s and 1960s prompted the creation of Huckleberry House in 1967, which may be the oldest of the modern shelters for runaways who distrust established social service agencies. Covenant House opened in New York City in 1968 as a free shelter for street children. Founded by a Franciscan priest at Fordham University, it has become a well-known resource for street children. In its first twenty years, Covenant House served 100,000 runaways and inspired similar shelters in dozens of other cities. Today there is hardly a city in the United States that does not have a runaway population and nonprofit shelters to provide temporary care. Ironically, as runaways became more common in so many cities, they seemed less noticeable as a social problem. The temporary shelters and services became a permanent feature of modern social services. Rising juvenile delinquency rates in the period 1950–1960 led to an overhaul of the juvenile justice system, culminating in the Juvenile Justice and Delinquency Prevention Act of 1974, a watershed law deinstitutionalizing status

offenders. This law altered state responses to the runaway problem and diverted boys from jails and adult correctional facilities to community-based treatment and rehabilitative shelters. However, the trend toward decriminalization provided federal and state funds for nonsecure shelters, inadvertently increasing the number of runaways on the streets.

By 1999 National Runaway Switchboard data demonstrated that 1.3 million of the 63 million children in the United States were homeless or runaway youths or both. About 35 percent of those who seek help from social service agencies are boys fourteen to seventeen years old (86 percent) on the road for one week or less (61 percent). About seven out of ten runaway boys return home, but those who do not go home frequently find disease and violence on the streets. They often succumb to drug and alcohol abuse, malnutrition, and high-risk behavior leading to a desperate life of panhandling, prostitution, and short-term, poorly paid jobs.

Peter C. Holloran

See also Alger, Horatio; Boys Town; Franklin, Benjamin; Great Depression; Indentured Servants; Juvenile Delinquency; Orphanages; Poverty; Prostitution

References and further reading
Anderson, Nels, and Raffaele Rauty. 1998. *On Hobos and Homelessness.* Chicago: University of Chicago Press.
Bock, Richard, and Abigail English. 1973. *Got Me on the Run: A Study of Runaways.* Boston: Beacon Press.
Brevada, William. 1986. *Harry Kemp, the Last Bohemian.* Lewisburg, PA: Bucknell University Press.
Flynt, Josiah. 1972. *Tramping with Tramps.* Montclair, NJ: Patterson Smith.
Holloran, Peter C. 1994. *Boston's Wayward Children: Social Services for*

Homeless Children, 1830–1930. Boston: Northeastern University Press.

Minehan, Thomas. 1934. *Boy and Girl Tramps of America*. New York: Farrar and Rinehart.

Nackenoff, Carol. 1994. *The Fictional Republic: Horatio Alger and American Political Discourse*. New York: Oxford University Press.

Raphael, Maryanne, and Jenifer Wolf. 1974. *Runaway: America's Lost Youth*. New York: Drake Publishers.

Schaffner, Laurie. 1999. *Teenage Runaways: Broken Hearts and Bad Attitudes*. New York: Haworth Press.

Uys, Errol Lincoln. 1999. *Riding the Rails: Teenagers on the Move during the Great Depression*. New York: TV Books.

Whitbeck, Les B., and Dan R. Hoyt. 1999. *Nowhere to Grow: Homeless and Runaway Adolescents and Their Families*. New York: Aldine de Gruyter.

S

Same-Sex Relationships

Throughout history and across cultures, some boys within a society have been sexually attracted to other boys. In turn, some cultures at particular historic moments have encouraged, or even required through ritualistic means, boys to engage in same-sex behavior and emotional intimacies. Within these historical and cultural contexts, it is clear that some boys have shown greater interest in these intimacies, preferring over their life course to be primarily involved with other males. This pattern reflects a same-sex *sexual orientation*, which must be distinguished from same-sex *behavior*, which in turn must be distinguished from a same-sex *identity* (a label that is culturally available that one chooses for oneself). Although boys in most cultures and throughout recorded time have engaged in sexual behavior with other boys, some of these youths might very well have had a same-sex sexual orientation; however, only recently has this pattern of same-sex attractions, erotic desires, and behavior been given a name—gay or bisexual.

Three distinctions are necessary to understand modern concepts of same-sex relations among prepubescent and adolescent males.

- Boys engage in same-sex behavior for a variety of reasons and for vari-

ous lengths of time (homosexual *behavior*).
- Boys can be preferentially attracted to other males for an extended (perhaps lifetime) period (homosexual or bisexual *sexual orientation*).
- Boys are increasingly accepting this designation and coming to acknowledge to themselves and others their membership in a class of individuals (homosexual *sexual identity*).

These three may be consistent (a gay-identified young man who is exclusively attracted to and engages in sexual behavior with other males) or inconsistent (a heterosexually identified young man who is attracted to both males and females and exclusively engages in sexual behavior with other males).

These definitions are compounded when cultural context is considered. For example, a Brazilian young man is permitted by his culture to engage in same-sex behavior as long as he embraces machismo, or masculinity, by assuming traditionally dominant male roles, such as being the top, or inserter, during anal intercourse. Under these circumstances, he would not be considered gay, bisexual, or inappropriate. It is his receptive male partner who is considered to have had homosexual behavior and thus is labeled gay. Such cultural variations in the structure and meaning of juvenile male same-sex attractions and behaviors have been observed and recorded by social scientists for decades. Transgenerational same-sex behavior, historically the most common, involves culturally sanctioned or ritualized sexual relations among boys and older male "mentors." The boy may be as young as seven years, and the mentor may be a late adolescent, a young adult, or an elder in the community. Sexual relations occur once or continue for several years until the boy reaches physical or social maturity. This relationship may be culturally prescribed if deemed necessary for the boy to develop physically and spiritually into a man. Such behavior has been observed in ancient Greece and Rome, pre–Middle Ages Europe, Africa, various Islamic societies, early modern Japan and China, some Native American societies, and Polynesia. For example, in some Melanesian societies the homoerotic is indelibly coupled with the sacred, such as boy-inseminating rites performed in the belief that a prepubescent boy must receive semen through oral or anal sex donated by postpubertal males if he is to grow, masculinize, and become a social (warrior personality) and reproductive member of his society. Institutionalized marriages between boys and adolescent males have been documented in other cultures.

Thus, modern attempts to demonize, criminalize, or pathologize male-male sexual relationships are inconsistent with the vast sweep of the historical and cross-cultural record. In nearly two-thirds of nonindustrialized societies, select male-male sexual interactions are both normative and socially acceptable. Although cultures may ritualize same-sex relations among its juvenile males,

they seldom encourage *exclusive* same-sex relations as a lifetime pattern. The Greeks considered same-sex relationships (in which sexual relations were an essential component) between a youth and a male somewhat his senior to be the highest form of love; however, eventual heterosexual marriage and reproduction were expected of all.

The historical record also indicates that even in cultures that disapproved of or condemned male same-sex sexual conduct, more latitude was given to *juvenile* male-male sexual interactions, perhaps because the behavior was perceived to be less meaningful and less indicative of a lifelong pattern. As one 1900 guide for raising healthy children suggested, the sexual appetite is at its highest level during the most selfish period—adolescence. If girls are not available, then better that boys "experiment" with each other than deflower young girls. This perceived "homosexual phase" is believed to disappear once more "mature" (that is, heterosexual) sexual relations are culturally feasible.

Despite these cultural variations, one universal appears: regardless of cultural or historical context or judgment, some boys will be driven by their sexual orientation to preferentially desire, seek, and enact sexual relations with other males. Their proportion within any given population is difficult to determine but is likely to be under 10 percent. Among the Sambians of New Guinea, although all young boys begin their sexual careers at age seven exclusively with other males, ingesting their semen through oral sex, all marry at age sixteen and rarely have sexual relations with other males after age eighteen. However, around 5 percent of males continue to seek same-sex relations throughout their lives. Thus, 100 percent of Sambian boys *behave* homosexually, but 5 percent *appear to be* homosexual (Herdt 1987).

Social science research has seldom focused on same-sex behavior or orientation but rather on youths who *identify* as gay or bisexual. Little is known about the meaning and context of same-sex behavior among boys or the prevalence and lifestyles of those who have a gay or bisexual sexual orientation but who do not identify as such. Whether these individuals are typical of other male adolescents who are gay by orientation or behavior but do not identify as gay is unknown.

Professional journal articles about gay and bisexual boys began to appear in the 1970s and increased dramatically in the 1990s. The first empirical study on homosexual/bisexual youths was published thirty years ago in a leading medical journal. The protocol focused on sexual experiences, the disclosure of sexual identity to others, participation in the gay subculture, and counseling experiences. Many of these youths were Seattle hustlers; the number of sexual encounters with men ranged from 1 to 3,000, with a median of 50. Suicidal gestures, emotional turmoil, and problematic behavior were common among the sixteen- to twenty-two-year-olds, the result of their self-identification as gay or bisexual at an early age and subsequent marginalization or rejection by parents and others.

This study stood as the sole empirical investigation for fifteen years before several medical and clinical investigations, based on interviews or questionnaires given to small samples of troubled teenage boys who sought the services of mental or social support agencies, examined the stressors that placed boys at high risk for physical, mental, and social ill health. Most such youths reported school problems, substance abuse, and emotional

difficulties and had a history of sexually transmitted diseases, running away from home, and criminal behavior. Several had been hospitalized for mental health issues. Among these samples, at least one in three had attempted suicide, and others who had not, said they would consider it in the future. The researchers concluded that the stigma attached to homosexuality in American society made it highly unlikely that a boy could avoid personal and spiritual problems as the net outcome of acquiring a gay or bisexual identity.

Many health care professionals were so pleased to have *any* information on this heretofore invisible population that few raised methodological objections about the population sampled or the instruments used in these studies or protested the conclusions drawn about gay youth from these findings. Advocates cited this research to argue for the inclusion of gay youths in the deliberations of physicians, therapists, and educators and to help youths adapt to their stigmatized identity, which was believed to be inherently problematic. The goals were to alleviate the distress of gay youths, who often faced violence, discrimination, disdain, and ignorance, and to promote interventions and programs for them. Indeed, the most frequent topics in health-related articles on gay youth published since 1970 include suicide, acquired immunodeficiency syndrome (AIDS), victimization, violence, pregnancy, and sexual abuse.

Absent from this list are articles on resiliency, coping, and good mental health or articles describing youths with same-sex attractions who live productive, happy lives—or even articles describing normative development for gay youths. Based on the limited social science research to date, it is apparent that gay/bisexual boys:

- Are in many respects similar to all boys, regardless of sexual orientation. They too struggle with age-appropriate developmental tasks, such as negotiating attachment and separation from parents, linking their sexual desires with emotional intimacy, and assessing their standing among peers. Research has demonstrated that many variables, such as self-esteem, age of puberty, age of first sexual experience, and the negative impact of peer teasing do not vary by sexual orientation.
- Are also unique from heterosexual boys because of both biological and social factors. Research has shown that sexual orientation is the result to some degree of genetic or early biological origins. Thus it is to be expected that in some domains same-sex attracted boys diverge from heterosexual youths. One common example is the hormonally induced demasculinization and feminization of gay youths. In addition, given the inevitable heterocentric and homonegative culture in which most adolescents live, it is to be expected that individuals with same-sex desires, even those who do not claim a gay or bisexual identity, are affected. Although all boys are susceptible to being called "faggot" and "gay," gay youth are ridiculed more frequently, and the name-calling is likely to have more of an impact on their sense of self and safety.
- Vary among themselves, perhaps even to the extent of being more similar in some regards to heterosexual youths than to each other. Although stereotypes emphasize a "gay lifestyle," it is clear that gay

youths do not come in one package. Some are football players, whereas others are dancers; some are insensitive, selfish clods, whereas others are empathic, giving angels; some have had a thousand sex partners, whereas others are virgins. Young gay and bisexual boys as a group are more similar to heterosexual boys than to same-sex-attracted girls in preferring visual sexual stimuli and casual sexual encounters.

- Represent a minority of those with same-sex attractions. High school surveys reveal that 1 percent of young men report that they are gay or bisexual, but five to ten times that number report that they have same-sex desires, attractions, or behavior. Should only the former be the centerpiece of our research and attention? Too often information on gay/bisexual boys is derived from sexual identity categories rather than from their underlying sexual desires and behaviors.

The new generation of same-sex-attracted boys is clearly not as troubled as research would seem to indicate. More often than not, they reject sexual identity labels as a meaningful barometer of their lives. Indeed, such designations have become so plentiful and blurred that they are in danger of becoming irrelevant as predictors of behavior. The focus needs to shift from their troubled lives to their resiliency and abilities. The vast majority cope quite nicely with their sexuality and negotiate a healthy life. As a result of the 1990s visibility revolution, same-sex-attracted youth face the prospects of a far better life than that experienced by any previous generation. American culture has changed and continues to change in their favor.

Ritch C. Savin-Williams

See also Prostitution; Sexuality; Sexually Transmitted Diseases

References and further reading
Bass, Ellen, and Kate Kaufman. 1996. *Free Your Mind: The Book for Gay, Lesbian, and Bisexual Youth—and Their Allies.* New York: HarperCollins.
Ford, Clellan S., and Frank A. Beach. 1951. *Patterns of Sexual Behavior.* New York: Harper and Brothers.
Herdt, Gilbert. 1987. *The Sambia: Ritual and Gender in New Guinea.* New York: Holt, Rinehart, and Winston.
Herdt, Gilbert, and Andrew Boxer. 1993. *Children of Horizons: How Gay and Lesbian Teens Are Leading a New Way out of the Closet.* Boston: Beacon.
Nycum, Benjie. 2000. *XY Survival Guide: Everything You Need to Know about Being Young and Gay.* San Francisco: XY Publishing.
Ryan, Caitlin, and Donna Futterman. 1998. *Lesbian and Gay Youth: Care and Counseling.* New York: Columbia University Press.
Savin-Williams, Ritch C. 1990. *Gay, Lesbian, and Bisexual Youth: Expressions of Identity.* Washington, DC: Hemisphere.
———. 1998. *". . . And Then I Became Gay": Young Men's Stories.* New York: Routledge.
Savin-Williams, Ritch C., and Kenneth M. Cohen. 1996. *The Lives of Lesbians, Gays, and Bisexuals: Children to Adults.* Fort Worth, TX: Harcourt Brace College Publishing.

Schoolbooks

Schoolbooks define not only the content of the school curriculum but also values, interpretations, and beliefs that adults want children to acquire from schooling. The content is called the "manifest curriculum," and it derives from a curricular chain that originates with a needed curriculum, which is translated by professional organizations and state and local educational agencies into a desired curriculum. Textbook publishers then create from the desired curriculum the prescribed curriculum. The second component of schoolbooks, values and beliefs, is the hidden or latent curriculum and appears in the specific roles assigned to different sexes and family members within stories; the characterizations given of different ethnic, racial, and religious groups within geographies and histories; the settings selected for word problems in mathematics; and other treatments that portray or imply what is acceptable, desirable, and valuable in American society. On top of these components but less obvious to the student is a pedagogical apparatus that consists of questions, suggested projects, review, assessment, and even aids to learning and recall.

Although the majority of a child's reading in the elementary school is from school textbooks as just defined, more and more often since 1990, schools have assigned trade books and original stories written for boys as well as girls. These are distinguished from textbooks primarily by their more focused content and lack of a pedagogical apparatus. Over the entire history of schooling in the United States, different textbooks for boys and girls were not produced; nevertheless, the treatments of boys and of girls in these books has varied. For example, in stories in reading textbooks written prior to the 1960s, boys would most often succeed at their endeavors by themselves, whereas girls, if they did succeed, did so usually with the assistance of an adult.

Boys attending school in the seventeenth and eighteenth centuries started reading from a hornbook, which was a small board covered with a single, small sheet of paper imprinted with the alphabet

Learning to read—an illustration in McGuffey's second reader, *ca. 1840 (Library of Congress)*

in upper- and lowercase; syllables such as *ib, ab,* and *ob;* and the Lord's Prayer. Next in progression came the *New England Primer,* perhaps a speller such as Thomas Dilworth's *A New Guide to the English Tongue,* and later the Bible and a Psalter. Noah Webster's Blue-Back Speller, originally published in 1783 with the ponderous title *A Grammatical Institute of the English Language, Part I,* became a school favorite by 1790 and remained so for at least fifty years. The first major geography book published in the United States, Jedidiah Morse's *Geography Made Easy,* appeared in 1784 and, like several other geographies published in the United States in the late eighteenth and early nineteenth

centuries, displayed little tolerance for religions other than Protestantism.

What drove both the manifest and the latent curriculum in the early colonial period was religious training. No separation was made then between church and state, and textbooks similarly reflected the importance of Christianity in everyday life. The *New England Primer,* for example, which remained in use until almost the middle of the nineteenth century, begins with the alphabet, a syllabarium, and graded word lists but moves quickly to alphabet rhymes, "A— In Adam's Fall, We sinned All," and so on (Ford 1899, 69). These introductory exercises are followed by a catechism, Lord's

Prayer, and Apostle's Creed, all reflecting the Calvinist concern with the child falling into the clutches of the devil. Just after the middle of the eighteenth century, however, more secular versions were imported from England, and after the American Revolution, morality and character building replaced the outright presentation of religion, particularly in reading textbooks. Nevertheless, the Bible continued to appear in the school curriculum in some parts of the country until at least the Civil War.

Through the nineteenth century, a schoolboy would have encountered stories that more and more exalted individual achievement and material gain, reflecting changes in Protestant doctrine that occurred through that century. Nationalism was also a central feature of the latent curriculum, especially during the first half of the nineteenth century. With the common school (i.e., free public school) movement, beginning in the period 1830–1850 and with a continuing flood of immigrants entering the United States, the market for schoolbooks grew rapidly. Simultaneously, transportation, particularly by water, improved so that textbook publishers could reach a national market. The first to exploit this opportunity was the Cincinnati-based publishing house Truman and Smith, which developed a series of arithmetics written by a former schoolteacher, Joseph Ray, and a series of readers edited by William McGuffey and his brother Alexander Hamilton McGuffey. Ray's arithmetics, consisting of four basic texts plus variations on them, sold more than 120 million copies from their first publication in 1834 until well into the beginning of the twentieth century.

The McGuffey readers were equally successful, selling slightly more than 122 million copies and making millionaires of a number of their publishers. McGuffey himself received $1,000 in royalties for his efforts; in addition, he and his brother were paid a smaller amount for writing the fifth and sixth readers but were not given any royalties on these volumes. The McGuffey readers were revised frequently through the nineteenth century, the last major revision occurring in 1878–1879, after which about 60 million copies were sold. A boy who read the first editions, beginning in 1836, would have encountered a Calvinist world of sin and damnation with considerable praise for the western frontier, that pristine, uncluttered territory reaching through Ohio to the territories approaching the Mississippi River. A boy reading any of the series after the 1878–1879 revision would have encountered a far more secular world where regional interests were replaced by national ones. Even Abraham Lincoln's Gettysburg Address was ignored to avoid offending potential markets in the South.

After the period 1880–1890, achievement imagery began to decline in U.S. schoolbooks and was replaced by a social ethic. This change reflects a shift in American society from an agrarian life in which individual inventiveness was required to an urban existence in which cooperation within groups or communities was more important than individual action. The Protestant ethic that stressed hard work, competition, and individual thrift was replaced by a social ethic that derived its creativity and self-realization through group membership. The frontier was closed, both physically and mentally. For boys looking toward adulthood, expansion could no longer occur along horizontal dimensions but only along a vertical one, advancing within society rather

A teenage student with a pile of schoolbooks (Skjold Photographs)

than away from it. At the same time, educational psychology and the child development movements began to influence both the form and the content of schoolbooks. Type size was enlarged further, especially at the primary levels, vocabulary and sentence length were regulated, and illustrations became more common. A linear sequencing from simple and concrete to complex and abstract was adopted for most school subjects, leading to more child-centered schoolbooks at the lower grades, with an emphasis on self and family in social studies, nature stories in reading, and simple word problems based on everyday objects in arithmetic.

Whereas the schoolbooks found in most schools prior to the end of the nine-teenth century were selected by the school or school district, between 1890 and 1920 twenty-two states, mostly in the South and Southwest, instituted statewide adoption practices. Although the number of textbooks selected for each subject varied across these states, state adoption began as a means for controlling undesirable or illegal marketing practices by the publishers. In time, statewide adoption also became a mechanism for controlling the content of textbooks, particularly in the South where religious resistance to the teaching of evolution was strong. In 1925 Tennessee passed its famous monkey law, the Butler Bill, making it unlawful to teach any theory that denied the story of the divine creation of man as described in the Bible. Mississippi, Arkansas, and Oklahoma also passed similar laws, although Oklahoma's was quickly repealed.

From the Scopes Trial in 1925 to the 1982 U.S. District Court ruling against the required teaching of creationism to the 1999 decision by the Kansas Board of Education to remove questions on evolution from the statewide science test (reversed on February 14, 2001), the battle over the teaching of evolution has flamed intensely or smoldered but never totally burned out. With regard to schoolbooks, the main effect until recently has been a refusal by publishers to include discussions of evolution in science textbooks for the schools. Since 1990, however, major adoption states such as Texas and California have demanded adequate teaching of evolution, and the major publishers have reversed their earlier positions.

Schooling and especially schoolbooks of the nineteenth century have often been attacked for their overemphasis on rote learning. However, many of the nine-teenth-century schoolbooks that a boy would have encountered also encouraged logical reasoning and problem solving. *Stoddard's American Intellectual Arithmetic* (Stoddard 1866, iv) stressed the need "to invigorate and develop the reasoning faculties of the mind." Asa Gray's *Botany for Young People, Part II* claimed that it was written "to stimulate both observation and thought" (Gray 1875, vii). Similarly, a textbook on English grammar required written analyses of sentence structure that included what today would be called transformational analysis: for example, changing phrases such as "heavy gold" into sentences ("Gold is heavy"), changing declarative sentences to interrogative ones, and combining multiple short sentences into a single long one.

Prior to the Civil War, only a small number of textbook titles were published in the United States in languages other than English. The most common of these were the German-language ones, such as the *Hoch-Deutsches Lutherisches ABC und Namen Büchlein für Kinder* (1819). Afterward, however, non-English-speaking boys might have encountered bilingual readers in two types of schools. In the large cities of the Midwest that had substantial German-speaking populations (e.g., Milwaukee, Cincinnati, Chicago), German-English readers were often available. In some of these schools, the classroom language for certain days of the week was German and for the other days was English. (A small number of bilingual texts were also published in other languages, such as Spanish.) The other place where bilingual textbooks were encountered was on the Indian reservations, where missionary schools sometimes used bilingual readers. In most such schools, however, only English was allowed.

In the last decades of the nineteenth century, several states, including Wisconsin, passed laws requiring that core academic subjects—reading, writing, arithmetic, and American history—be taught only in English. (The Wisconsin law, called the Bennett Law and passed in 1889, was repealed in 1890, but in several states the laws remained.) With the outbreak of World War I, more states banned the teaching of school subjects in languages other than English (e.g., Nebraska). Nevertheless, after World War I, the Department of the Interior developed educational programs for immigrants and used materials in several languages developed by Francis Kellor, director of the New York League for the Protection of Immigrants.

As mentioned earlier, racial, religious, and ethnic slurs occurred in U.S. schoolbooks from at least the end of the eighteenth century. This practice continued into the twentieth century until after World War II. The 1902 edition of Alexis E. Frye's *Grammar School Geography*, in speaking of the *"black* or *Negro race"* (Frye's emphasis) south of the Sahara desert, asserted: "Such natives are very ignorant. They know nothing of books; in fact, they know little, except how to catch and cook their food" (Frye 1902, 33). *Appleton's Elementary Geography* defines Jews almost solely as people who "reject Christ as the Messiah" (1908, 15). The only fact of interest presented about Jerusalem is "Here our Saviour was buried..." (89). Some history textbooks from the 1920s and 1930s claimed that immigrants to the United States from eastern and southern Europe were ignorant, lacked respect for law and government, and might even want to see the U.S. government destroyed. Similar bias was expressed into the 1940s and 1950s against blacks and Chinese, with more subtle bias saved for Jews and occasionally

Catholics. Bias appeared both directly and indirectly, through language, stereotypical descriptions, and illustrations. In addition, it appeared negatively through the failure of textbook authors, particularly of history texts, to take a moral stand on issues such as segregation and racial quotas.

For fear of offending any particular market segment, textbooks became more and more bland and morally blind during the twentieth century. One researcher, in an extensive analysis of history textbooks, defined the perspective taken by the majority of the authors as the "natural disaster" theory of history (FitzGerald 1979). Events such as poverty, discrimination, and Watergate just *happened*; no individuals were ever named as responsible. Earlier in the twentieth century, analyses of history texts found a strong tendency toward extreme nationalism, what Arthur Walworth (1938, viii) called the "drum and trumpet" school of history. In 1986, People for the American Way, an organization that has periodically reviewed school textbooks, found the majority of the major U.S. history textbooks to be free of bias and to encourage critical and creative thinking. They also found a reversal of the dumbing down of the texts reported by an earlier review committee (Davis et al. 1986). Civics textbooks, however, were criticized by another review committee for their failure "to encourage young people to uphold their rights and carry out their obligations as citizens" (Carroll et al. 1987, i). On the style of writing, the committee reported, "They are good reference materials, but they read like the Federal Register" (Carroll et al. 1987, i).

Those who espouse a revisionist view of schooling in the United States view textbooks as an integral part of a hegemonic system, with those at the top carefully co-ordinating their actions to ensure that those below them remain in their places. Through manipulation of the latent curriculum, morality, docility, respect for authority, and the other trappings of a compliant, faithful worker are instilled in boys. Even if people and organizations with divergent goals, resources, and morals could coordinate their efforts and somehow gain uncontested control of the latent curriculum, there is little evidence to show that the aspirations, beliefs, and behaviors of boys are much affected by what they see in schoolbooks.

Richard L. Venezky

See also Schools for Boys; Schools, Public

References and further reading
Appleton's Elementary Geography. 1908. New York: American Book Company.
Carroll, James D., et al. 1987. *We the People: A Review of U.S. Government and Civics Textbooks.* Washington, DC: People for the American Way.
Davis, O. L., Jr., et al. 1986. *Looking at History: A Review of Major U.S. History Textbooks.* Washington, DC: People for the American Way.
De Charms, Richard, and Gerald H. Moeller. 1962. "Values Expressed in American Children's Readers: 1800–1950." *Journal of Abnormal and Social Psychology* 64: 136–142.
Elliott, David L., and Arthur Woodward, eds. 1990. *Textbooks and Schooling in the United States: Eighty-Ninth Yearbook of the National Society for the Study of Education, Pt. 1.* Chicago: National Society for the Study of Education.
Elson, Ruth. M. 1964. *Guardians of Tradition: American Schoolbooks of the Nineteenth Century.* Lincoln: University of Nebraska Press.
FitzGerald, Francis. 1979. *America Revised: History Schoolbooks in the Twentieth Century.* Boston: Little, Brown.
Ford, Paul L., ed. 1899. *The New England Primer.* New York: Dodd, Mead.
Frye, Alexis E. 1902. *Grammar School Geography.* Boston: Ginn.

Gray, Asa. 1875. *Botany for Young People, Part II: How Plants Behave.* New York: Ivison, Blakeman, and Taylor.

Hoch-Deutsches Lutherisches ABC und Namen Büchlein für Kinder. 1819. Germantown, PA: W. Billmeyer.

Monaghan, E. Jennifer. 1983. *A Common Heritage: Noah Webster's Blue-back Speller.* Hamden, CT: Archon Books.

Stoddard, John F. 1866. *The American Intellectual Arithmetic.* New York: Sheldon.

Venezky, Richard L. 1992. "Textbooks in School and Society." Pp. 436–461 in *Handbook of Research on Curriculum.* Edited by Philip W. Jackson. New York: Macmillan.

Walworth, Arthur. 1938. *School Histories at War.* Cambridge: Harvard University Press.

Schools for Boys

More than two centuries before Horace Mann's common school movement gave rise to coeducational, state-supported public schools in the 1840s, a lively complex of religious and independent boys' academies was thriving along the eastern seaboard. New York City's Collegiate School, which today enrolls 650 boys between kindergarten and grade twelve, was founded in 1628 in conjunction with the Dutch Reform Church. Because the school was forced to suspend operations during the American Revolution when the British occupied the city, Boston's Roxbury Latin School, founded in 1645 by the Reverend John Eliot, "Apostle to the Indians" (1604–1690), is able to claim that it is the oldest American school in continuous operation. Today Roxbury Latin enrolls just under 300 boys in grades seven through twelve and boasts one of the highest scholastic profiles in the United States.

In the colonial era, young children were schooled in "dame" or "petty" schools in which lessons in reading and writing were conducted by women and in which both boys and girls might be enrolled. However, more advanced education in early colonial academies was typically available only to boys. These academies were called "Latin" or "free" schools because they culminated in the study of Latin grammar and literature. The schools were open to all boys within a designated township, often without charge. The practice of limiting enrollment in Latin schools to boys in the seventeenth and eighteenth centuries derived from the prevailing assumption that only boys needed an advanced education because universities and learned professions were then open only to men. After the colonial period, as the new nation expanded westward, the "academy" model accommodated boys and girls in school together, although teachers often positioned boys and girls on opposite sides of the classroom and sometimes set them to different tasks.

Since their colonial beginnings, there has been a substantial connection between American boys' schools and their British forerunners. Before the American Revolution, suitably placed colonial boys of means would often be sent to school abroad, a practice greatly reduced but by no means curtailed after the war. Educated colonials who did not send their children abroad for their schooling were likely to send them to nearby Latin or grammar schools, such as Roxbury Latin, modeled directly on classics-oriented English grammar schools. A boy might enter such a school at age twelve or when he had demonstrated sufficient literacy. He would matriculate to university or other training when he was fourteen to seventeen years of age, depending on his facility in Latin. If a boy was unable to master the requirements of the higher

Boys walking down the hallway at Georgetown Preparatory School, ca. 1940 (Library of Congress)

Latin courses, he would depart, as Benjamin Franklin departed the Boston Latin school, and seek employment in farming or in the trades.

In the mid-nineteenth century a burst of reform in the English schools had a decisive effect on the shape of American education. Thomas Arnold's Rugby School, which had so transformed Tom Brown in Thomas Hughes's classic school saga, *Tom Brown's School Days* (1857), was also transforming England's other great private schools (called "public" in Britain) and grammar schools. These schools were organized into relatively small, relatively autonomous "houses," each overseen by a master and matrons but governed largely by older boys who were empowered to deal out physical punishment and to command menial labor. Up through this often elaborate hierarchy small, disestablished "fags" (temporary servants to older boys) like Tom Brown might emerge into "bloods" or "swells" (school heroes) with governing responsibilities themselves. This organizational scheme was grounded in a new wave of evangelistic piety and, combined with a phenomenal new emphasis on competitive "house" and school sports, came to be known as "muscular Christianity." This Victorian notion of school, extolled with such enthusiasm by Hughes in *Tom Brown's School Days*, Horace Vachell in *The Hill* (1905), set at Harrow School, and in thousands of stories in *Boys' Own Paper* and other publications for youth, would by the turn of the century embed itself firmly in the English national consciousness. This development occurred despite the fact that the schools and the milieu extolled were the exclusive preserve of the middle and upper classes.

Although overshadowed nationally by Mann's common school movement, the impact of Arnold's Rugby School in the United States was felt in the reform of a number of private academies and in the founding or revitalizing, mainly in New England and the mid-Atlantic states, of college preparatory schools—for example, St. Paul's in New Hampshire, Groton and St. Mark's in Massachusetts, and Lawrenceville in New Jersey. These new schools characteristically instituted a house system with prefects, stratified students by "forms" instead of classes, and established traditions of dress, custom, and privilege; but not all schools created a cricket program, as did St. Paul's. Typically, these new schools, like Arnold's Rugby, had strong religious foundations. Many of the founding headmasters saw their school mission primarily as a Christian commitment; such was the Reverend Endicott Peabody's orientation to Groton, the Reverend Henry Augustus Coit's to St. Paul's, and Father Frederick Sill's to Kent. Each of these men was personally acquainted with the English school model, as were hundreds of other American schoolmen of remarkably similar vocations. Even Sill, who established Kent School and vowed *not* to make it resemble an English country house or to train Kent School boys to be squires, had the English model firmly in mind, incorporated substantial parts of it, and used the rest as a point of departure. Without question the American private schools have looked to England, not only for structure but for a sense of continuity with their classical inheritance.

Toward the end of the nineteenth century, the ranks of leading American boys' schools were swollen by the founding of dozens of new "country day" schools, many of them west of the Appalachians. Cleveland's University School (1890), Baltimore's Gilman School (1897), Washington, D.C.'s St. Albans School (1909), and Dallas's St. Mark's School (1933) were heavily subscribed from the outset and soon demonstrated their capacity to prepare boys from those cities for leading universities.

Although independent boys' schools thrived throughout most of the twentieth century, they never—even when combined with hundreds of strong parochial boys' schools—enrolled as much as 5 percent of the American school population. As the post–World War II baby boom generation began reaching school age, many of the defining features of American private schools and of boys' schools in particular were energetically challenged. In a wave of what some cultural commentators have called the "adolescentization" of the United States, a number of traditional schools were substantially transformed between 1968 and 1975. An affluent generation called into question restrictive dress codes, limited opportunities for unsupervised socializing, required religious observances, and Saturday classes. Market research at the time revealed that the well-to-do were finding private schools, especially boarding schools, resistible. Some prospective students and their families felt single-sex schools to be especially astringent, and in consequence there was a significant movement toward coeducation led by such premier boys' boarding schools as the Phillips academies at Exeter and Andover, St. Paul's, Hotchkiss, and Groton.

When the coeducational conversion of former single-sex schools tapered off in the mid-1970s, the gender composition of independent schools had changed significantly. After the relatively late conversion to coeducation of strong boarding schools like Deerfield (1989) and Lawrenceville (1987), only a few boys' boarding schools remain in New England. However, south of the Mason-Dixon line, a number of exemplary boys' boarding schools, such as Virginia's Woodberry Forest School and Tennessee's McCallie School, continue to thrive. Throughout the wave of conversion to coeducation, most established day schools for boys were able to retain their founding mission.

The movement to coeducation challenged many boys' schools to articulate their mission and educational assumptions more forcefully. Former headmaster (St. Mark's in Dallas and St. Paul's in Concord, New Hampshire) and education historian David Hicks published an essay in *The American Scholar* (1996, 524–525) in which he argued that the modern coeducational boarding school had forgotten its founding purpose, which was not to enhance the opportunities and creature comforts of the privileged but rather to purge such children of unearned entitlements and "softness." The astringency of independent school life, including its temporary separation of the genders, was intentional, Hicks argued, a part of an overall program of "salutary deprivation."

As boys' schools reaffirmed their distinctive mission, they began articulating developmental and learning differences in boys and girls. Gender-based varia-

tions in tempo and learning style have been identified from the preschool through the high school years. Primary school girls generally demonstrate reading and writing proficiency earlier than boys do; middle school and high school boys' mathematical-logical capacities accelerate more rapidly than those of girls. Females reach the peak of their pubertal growth spurt a year or two sooner than boys. Each gender-based physiological difference is accompanied by distinctive psychological and social adjustments.

J. M. Tanner (1971) has demonstrated that girls' skeletons and nervous systems are at birth more fully developed than those of boys and that the maturational gap increases somewhat through early childhood. From their preschool years through their late teens, boys reveal a number of other gender-specific contours in their skeletal, motor, and neurological development. Boys develop language skills, the capacity for quantitative analysis, and large- and small-muscle proficiencies at a developmentally different tempo from girls.

The observed differences in boys' and girls' learning patterns have encouraged boys' schools to avoid inappropriately hastening the arrival of fine motor and language skills while seeking more opportunities to incorporate large-muscle motor activities in learning. Boys' schools from the early grades through high school are increasingly emphasizing physical application of learned principles. An all-boys learning environment may also bear positively on affective learning. Diane Hulse's 1997 study contrasting the values and attitudes of boys at coeducational and single-sex middle schools found, perhaps counterintuitively, that boys at single-sex schools felt less defensive, were less susceptible to peer pressures, felt safer in school, reported more comfort in their boy-girl relationships, revealed more egalitarian attitudes about gender roles, and viewed masculinity as inclusive of a wider range of behaviors than did similar boys in a coeducational setting.

Proponents of American boys' schools also began to articulate the educational consequences of cross-gender distraction, which had been a long-standing concern among American educators. The century's leading scholar of public schooling, James Coleman, complained in a 1961 book for and about state coeducational schools, *The Adolescent Society*, that the social agenda of American schools was threatening the learning agenda. Whether expressed or suppressed, sexual distraction has been seen as an impediment to focused activity and learning. Coleman saw cross-gender distraction most significantly at work in early adolescence through high school. In addition to the obvious distraction that results from heightened attention to grooming, posturing, and flirting, the suppression of erotic interest in the presence of attractive members of the opposite sex also diminishes the energy required to focus effectively on scholastic tasks. Alexander Astin (1977) has attributed the positive effects of single-sex colleges in the 1970s (when there still were single-sex colleges, including most of the leading colleges in the land) to "restricted heterosexual activity." Corroborating this view at the high school level, Tony Bryk and Valerie Lee's 1986 study comparing single-sex and coeducational parochial schools concluded with an invitation to reconsider schools in which adolescent boys' and girls' "social and learning environments are separated." This study found only positive outcomes for boys and girls in single-sex schools, as compared to their equivalents in coeducational schools.

At the outset of the new millennium, widespread concern about the health, well-being, and scholastic achievement of boys has been expressed in both learned journals and the popular media. Dramatic incidents of schoolyard violence and mayhem at the hands of schoolboys and worrying gaps between boys' and girls' tested abilities have been chronicled in the United States, Great Britain, and Australia. The perceived decline in boys' performance has notably not been the case for boys enrolled in boys' schools, a development that has stimulated a renewed interest in boys' schooling and in separate instruction of boys and girls within coeducational schools.

School initiatives targeting boys at risk, such as the Nativity Mission schools in Boston and New York, have favored an all-boys structure with encouraging early results. Presently, American independent boys' schools and parochial boys' schools are enjoying healthy enrollments and renewed vigor. In 1995 an International Boys' Schools Coalition was formally incorporated, including 108 North American schools as well as 53 schools from Canada, Australia, New Zealand, South Africa, Great Britain, and Japan. The mission of the coalition is to identify and to share best practices for schooling boys.

Richard Hawley

See also Military Schools; Schools, Public

References and further reading

Astin, W. A. 1977. *Four Critical Years: Effects of College on Beliefs, Attitudes, and Knowledge*. San Francisco: Jossey-Bass.

Bryk, Anthony, and Valerie Lee. 1986. "Effects of Single Sex Secondary Schools on Student Achievement and

Attitudes." *Journal of Educational Psychology* 78.

Coleman, James S. 1961. *The Adolescent Society.* New York: Free Press.

Hawley, Richard. 1991. "About Boys' Schools: A Progressive Case for an Ancient Form." *Teachers College Board* 92, no. 3.

Hicks, David. 1996. "The Strange Fate of the American Boarding School." *The American Scholar* 65, no. 4 (Autumn).

Hulse, Diane. 1997. *Brad and Cory: A Study of Middle School Boys.* Cleveland: Cleveland's University School Press.

Jarvis, F. W. 1995. *Schola Illustris: The Roxbury Latin School.* Boston: David Godine.

Newberger, Eli H. 1999. *The Men They Will Become.* New York: Perseus Books.

Riordan, Cornelius. 1990. *Girls and Boys in School: Together or Separate.* New York: Teachers College Press.

Tanner, J. M. 1971. "Sequence, Tempo, and Individual Variations in Growth and Development of Boys and Girls Aged Twelve to Sixteen." In *Twelve to Sixteen.* Edited by Jerome Kagan. New York: Norton.

Schools, Public

Public schools are educational institutions, usually coeducational, that evolved from small, private or home-based programs in the colonial era to large, publicly funded schools in the twentieth and twenty-first centuries. Tax-supported education developed slowly in the eighteenth and early nineteenth centuries. Rural and urban schools evolved in quite different directions in the nineteenth century. Schools in the South were the slowest to develop and the most discriminatory against African American boys and girls until well into the twentieth century. Regardless of where they studied, boys typically learned their lessons from female teachers in an environment that stressed independent learning and competition. By the end of the nine-teenth century, public schools prepared boys for work in agriculture and industry and girls for homemaking and childrearing. By the late twentieth century, schools sought to prepare boys and girls for specialized technological work roles.

In the seventeenth and eighteenth centuries, education took place in family or workplace settings as boys learned tasks, manners, and values in preparation for their adult lives. Children learned to read at home from their parents or perhaps in a dame school kept by a neighbor. Boys from well-to-do families were taught the classical languages—Latin and Greek—from a tutor who boarded in their home, or they were sent to live in the household of a minister or schoolmaster. Those from Virginia or South Carolina were often sent to English schools, leaving home as young as the age of seven or eight and not returning to America until their early twenties. Letters reveal their loneliness and the concern of distant parents, but many such boys had been sent to English relatives who kept in contact with them. In the northern colonies, boys as young as thirteen matriculated in American colleges, such as Harvard, founded in 1636; Yale, established in 1701; and the College of Philadelphia (later the University of Pennsylvania), set up by subscription of citizens in 1755. After 1693, boys in Virginia could receive higher education at the College of William and Mary in Williamsburg. The religious revivals of the Great Awakening in the 1740s injected new vigor into education as churches founded colleges to educate youth and train ministers in their version of Christian faith. New Light Presbyterians established the College of New Jersey (later named Princeton) in 1746, New York Anglicans founded King's College (later named Columbia) in

1754, Baptists started the College of Rhode Island (later named Brown) in 1764, and the Dutch Reformed Church in New Jersey subsidized Queen's (later named Rutgers) in 1766.

The American Revolution stimulated great interest in tax-supported education in order to inculcate republican principles and instill the moral restraint essential for citizenship. Early plans for the establishment of public schools, however, were rejected by state legislatures, largely because the United States was still a rural society, and a uniform system did not mesh with the existing social structure. Farmers and rural craftspeople, who depended on family labor, expected their children to work. Schooling could only be intermittent, fitted into the hours of the day or seasons of the year that the rhythms of an agricultural society allowed. In 1789, Massachusetts required towns of fifty or more families to provide district schools for at least six months of the year and towns of 200 or more families to provide a grammar school. Congressional ordinances governing the Northwest Territory in 1785 and 1787 stipulated that one of thirty-six sections of land in each township be set aside to support schools, although the policy had little effect. The more common pattern was that parents initiated schooling by hiring a teacher and providing a building for a "district" school in states where districts had been established or a "subscription" school where such districts did not exist. Throughout the nineteenth century, publicly supported rural schools became more common, although their growth was slower in the South.

Rural schools were in session about six months out of the year at times when children's labor was not in high demand on farms. Although some children at rural schools were very young, most boys and girls attended school between the ages of ten and fourteen; however, some boys whose labor was required in the fields nine months out of the year found time to go to school only during the three-month winter session. Such boys continued in school until late adolescence, unlike most farm girls, who completed their education by attending six months out of the year until they were fourteen.

In rural schools, children as young as two or three mingled with older scholars. The youngest boys and girls sat in the front, nearest to the teacher, and older children sat in the back of the classroom. Henry Ward Beecher, born in 1813, went to Widow Kilbourne's school in Litchfield, Connecticut, when he was three, bringing along sewing and knitting to keep him occupied. By age eight, he combined schooling with helping his father plant and hoe the garden, caring for the horse and cow, carrying wood, and drawing water from the well on winter mornings. Horace Greeley, born into a New Hampshire farming family in 1811, learned to read at age three from his mother. At age four, he boarded with his grandfather and attended district school with sixty other scholars, several of whom were almost grown. By the age of five, he rose at dawn to ride the horse while his father plowed, rushing to school when the lesson was almost over. When he was eight and nine, he skipped the summer session entirely to help his father clear land.

Daniel Drake grew up in Kentucky in the 1790s and started school at the age of five in a log cabin with paper windows and a puncheon floor. He later reported that students of all ages recited the same lesson aloud, gathering energy as they spoke. In rural schools, the teacher typically set the children's lessons and then examined them individually or in small groups for ten-minute periods. While one group of children was being examined, the rest listened or studied and prepared their own lessons. In later life, Daniel Drake found he could concentrate in almost any situation and thought it an advantage that he had learned to study in the midst of noise. He also appreciated the natural mingling of boys and girls, who—while they sometimes sat in different sections of the schoolroom—studied the same subjects and joined in running races and playing games. But Drake's father also depended on the labor of his son, and at the age of nine, Daniel had to leave lessons to help clear land. When he was fifteen years old, an injury to his father ended his intermittent schooling altogether, and Daniel worked the family farm alone. Such would have been his fate, had his illiterate father not been determined to have at least one educated child, sending him at age sixteen to Cincinnati to study medicine.

Education of boys in the rural South developed somewhat differently than it did in the rural Northeast, Midwest, and Far West. Before the Civil War, powerful southern white planters found little value in public education. They educated their own children in private schools, found little advantage in providing schooling for poor white children, and found no advantage in educating slave youngsters. During Reconstruction, the federal government and various private philanthropic groups joined with freedpersons to form public schools, which provided education to both white and black children in segregated facilities. Black boys and girls enthusiastically took advantage of these schools, since education had become a sign of freedom for blacks.

When Reconstruction ended and whites resumed control of local and state governments in the South, they kept the segregated public schools that were created during Reconstruction. However, southern whites spent less on their public schools than did rural folk elsewhere in the country, and southerners kept their schools open just three months out of the year. Prosperous southern whites had little investment in public schools since they continued to send their own children to private academies. Other rural southern whites were poorer than farmers elsewhere in the country, and because they required the labor of their sons and daughters virtually year-round, they sent them to school for short terms. African Americans in the South continued to enroll their children in school, but they became discouraged with the quality of the schools, which deteriorated once whites resumed control after Reconstruction. Whites allotted less money to black than to white schools, and black schools became overcrowded. Black parents were particularly likely to withdraw their sons from school once they reached the age of eleven. Boys' labor was required on black tenant and sharecropping farms, whereas girls could be spared to go to school longer to prepare for the one good profession open to them—teaching.

Boys who lived in cities, most of which were in the Northeast, experienced schooling somewhat differently than boys who attended rural schools. Innovation that led to systems of tax-supported education occurred in northeastern cities as commercial relationships eroded apprenticeship and manufacturing concentrated in larger units. In postrevolutionary decades, only Boston supported a system of public education. Responding to the Massachusetts law of 1789, Boston established an annually elected School Committee that supervised grammar schools for boys and girls aged seven to fourteen and a Latin school for boys over the age of ten. Only children who could already read were admitted to the grammar schools, and girls attended them fewer hours per day than boys and for shorter terms. Only about 12 percent of the city's children attended these public schools, but other well-to-do boys attended academies, and some children of the poor attended charity schools (Schultz 1973, 8–25). In Philadelphia and New York, efforts to develop systems of tax-supported schools occurred through charity schools designed for the urban poor. Reformers in both cities were attracted to the plan devised by Joseph Lancaster, an English Quaker, through which one teacher could instruct large numbers of children with the aid of student monitors. During the urban depression that followed the War of 1812, prominent citizens worried about the prevalence of vice and crime in poor neighborhoods and began to investigate how discipline could be instilled in children of paupers at minimum public expense. In 1817, the Pennsylvania legislature designated the city of Philadelphia the first school district in the state, and children of indigent parents began to attend tax-supported Lancasterian schools. The method also flourished in New York, and in 1825 the eleven free schools and monitorial high school became the basis of that city's public school system. In the 1820s New York teachers were called "operatives," and the machinelike replicability of the Lancasterian method was extolled as a means of expanding educational opportunity throughout the nation. Children—aided by older boys acting as monitors—learned to read, march in drill, and earn tickets to buy prizes in more than 150 Lancasterian schools in locations as distant as Cincinnati, Detroit, and New Orleans.

Although Lancaster's system seemed an educational panacea in the 1820s, it was too mechanical to mesh with the emerging domestic ideology of the new middle class. By the 1830s, school reformers admired the ideas of Johann Heinrich Pestalozzi, who urged creation of an atmosphere of security and affection to allow the unfolding of a child's nature. As capitalism transformed the northeastern economy, middle-class families relied less on the labor of their children, giving them more time to spend in school. In this new economic context, middle-class reformers advocated state-supported and supervised systems of education, with standardized, full-time schools taught by professional teachers. In 1837, Horace Mann, secretary of the new Massachusetts State Board of Education, lobbied the legislature for graded public schools, ten-month terms, and a uniform curriculum. Age grading dovetailed with a standardized curriculum, permitting children of the same age to learn the same subjects from different teachers and hence be properly prepared for the next grade. As public schools expanded in the 1840s, Mann rejected the efforts of the American Sunday School Union to include in the curriculum its line of evangelical children's literature. The message of the schools would be Protestant yet nonsectarian, designed to form character and teach values of republicanism and capitalism. As immigration increased, however, and Irish neighborhoods burgeoned in Boston, Philadelphia, and New York City, Catholic clergymen objected to this Protestant thrust of public schools and responded by forming their own educational institutions.

Neither did urban public schools recognize racial diversity. African Americans were often denied public schooling in northern cities until the 1840s and 1850s, when abolitionists demanded that they receive equal educational opportunities with whites (nonsegregated). After the Civil War, all northern cities opened schools to blacks; however, some cities accommodated them in schools separate from whites. Black parents, many of whom had moved to the North to make it possible for their children to attend school, made huge sacrifices to keep their sons and daughters in school. Mothers and fathers both worked outside the home, usually at low-wage jobs, so that black boys and girls could attend school. Between 1890 and 1940, "older black children were more likely to be in school than foreign-born children" (Walters and O'Connell 1988, 1145).

By the 1850s, public schools meshed neatly with domestic ideology. As middle-class mothers assumed responsibility for character formation in early childhood, children under the age of six were excluded from graded public schools. As school systems consolidated, administrators sought to save money by hiring female teachers, and boys spent more of their lives directed by women. In the lower grades of urban public coeducational schools, female teachers drilled all youngsters simultaneously in reading, writing, and arithmetic. Urban high schools, which in some cities were segregated by gender, continued throughout the nineteenth century to be staffed by more male than female teachers. Of course, few youngsters stayed in school long enough to enroll in a high school. Working-class boys were particularly likely to leave school by their early teens to find jobs to help support their families. Middle-class boys typically stayed in school longer to acquire the writing and numerical skills necessary for white-collar jobs, but middle-class girls stayed in school the longest because their labor was least needed by their parents, and school prepared them for the most popular professional job for women—teaching.

In the nineteenth century, white native-born and African American children were more likely to attend urban public schools than were foreign-born children. However, boys from certain ethnic groups were especially likely to be enrolled in city schools. Children of Scottish parentage, who shared the language and Protestant faith of common school founders, attended school in large numbers. So, too, did the sons and daughters of eastern European Jews who migrated to the United States after 1880 and settled largely in cities. Jewish parents valued education and learning and pushed their sons to succeed in public schools in order to prepare them for the commercial occupations that most Jewish men favored.

Although the opportunities for schooling for boys in the nineteenth century differed based on where they lived, their social class, race, ethnicity, and—if they enrolled in school—their educational experience was remarkably similar. Of course, the presence or absence of age-grading and the length of the school year differed for farm and city boys, but nearly all of them studied under the direction of female teachers who emphasized rote learning. In the four to five years most attended school, boys learned spelling, reading, writing, and math, along with some geography, literature, and history. Boys and girls learned writing by using a pen and copying words. Rarely did teachers assign compositions. Teachers taught math by drill.

Regardless of locale, nineteenth-century teachers also conveyed similar values to boys and girls in their classrooms.

They assigned students to sit at individual desks and to speak only to the teacher. Thus they made clear to boys that they should act as individuals and become self-reliant. Boys should not count on friends to help them with their lessons. Boys also competed constantly in schools: to correctly spell words, to appropriately read passages, and to pass a high school entrance exam. Teachers punished boys severely for stealing or defacing books or desks in order to convey to them the importance of respect for private property. Teachers and parents also expected boys to obey the teacher without question. Such behavior was seen as a way to prepare boys to obey appropriate authorities later in life.

In the twentieth century, extended public schooling became more widely accepted and more common for boys of all social classes, races, and ethnicities. However, early in the century during the Progressive era, the boys and girls most likely to take advantage of public education were white and middle-class. Yet by 1918, all states had enacted compulsory attendance laws. Parents in all social classes expected that boys would become breadwinners and therefore needed to learn various skills and attributes to equip them for whatever section of the labor market was their destiny. Conversely, girls needed to acquire knowledge to enable them to be good wives and mothers. The Smith-Hughes Act, passed by the federal government in 1917, provided funding to local schools to reinforce this gendered notion of the appropriate forms of vocational education for boys and girls. This legislation helped dictate separate and distinct programs for boys and girls in public schools for many decades.

The basic core curriculum in schools had remained the same since the nineteenth century. Reformers in the 1920s believed that schools should provide youth with more than the ability to read, write, and do math. Youngsters also needed to develop common social skills and to improve their physical health. In 1918, the National Educational Association outlined seven cardinal principles for both secondary and elementary schools, which included developing good health in youngsters, improving their command of basic skills, encouraging them to be responsible family members, enhancing vocational efficiency, promoting good citizenship, teaching worthy use of leisure time, and demonstrating ethical character. The end result of the 1920s reform movement was the expansion of extracurricular activities in schools, which reformers expected would cultivate appropriate social attitudes in youth. Organized school sport became a means of promoting a positive sense of self-worth for boys. The introduction of athletics had a fourfold effect: it became a solution that would reduce the dropout rate, it would create a masculine environment, it would give unruly males an outlet for their energy, and it would enhance the image of schools. Public school officials assumed control of school athletics, and the programs they administered raised new issues for boys—popularity, intensity, and exclusiveness.

In the twentieth century, as in the nineteenth, most public school teachers were female. Reformers complained that an all-female teaching force deprived boys of needed male role models. Growing divorce rates and increasing percentages of single-mother families increased concern about the lack of masculine influence available to boys in schools. However, local school boards continued to hire women in large part because they

A teacher assists one boy while the rest work on their assignments, 1938. (Bettmann/Corbis)

were less expensive to employ than were men.

In the post–World War II era, the baby boom increased the number of children who entered public schools and necessitated school expansion. Just as important, the launch of Sputnik in 1957 by the Soviet Union created a feeling of self-doubt in the United States and a concern that American education was behind Russian education. Congress enacted the National Defense Education Act, and science societies worked to invigorate American education. Within ten years, the "space race" led to an expanded science and math curriculum, not only in kindergarten through twelfth grade but also in higher education. Building a

strong education for a strong defense included problem-solving and learner-centered curricula. Reformers realized that American students were accustomed to memorizing facts but often unable to apply those facts. Hence in the new school curriculum, teachers encouraged students to solve problems. Textbook companies developed illustrated science texts with specific scope and sequenced outlines for each grade level. Although presumably all boys and girls were the target of evolved educational emphases, new textbooks in science and literature lacked any minority representation.

The emphasis on increasing student achievement highlighted another issue that Americans had long ignored—the poor quality of education available to most African American children. After the Supreme Court endorsed separate-but-equal facilities for black and white children in 1896, segregated schooling became the norm throughout the South. It was separate but hardly equal since southern states systematically spent less on black than on white schools. In 1954, the Supreme Court reversed itself and declared in favor of desegregated schools in *Brown v. Board of Education of Topeka, Kansas.* Schools in the South gradually desegregated, but in some cases, states bused black children to white schools and vice versa in order to implement desegregation quickly. In response, some white parents withdrew their children from public schools and enrolled them in all-white private and parochial schools instead.

Not only were there disparities between the educational opportunities of black and white children, there were also disparities between the educational achievement of white boys and girls. When math and science issues became preeminent, researchers soon discovered that girls fell behind boys in achievement in both subjects. Boys also lagged behind girls in reading and writing. Boys were more likely to be held back a grade in school, to be enrolled in special education classes, and to drop out of school. Technology was advancing rapidly, yet there seemed to be growing inequities in technological knowledge between boys and girls and between the youth of different social classes. International markets made it necessary to increase understanding of diversity, yet teachers claimed to be inexperienced in how to teach about diversity and how to handle students from diverse backgrounds in the classroom. Congress passed the Gender Equity in Education Act to help promote programs that emphasized diversity and to train teachers in nonsexist behavior. School reformers demanded that students learn teamwork and problem solving and achieve technological literacy.

To enhance equal educational opportunities for all children, Congress passed legislation creating America Goals 2000. President William J. Clinton signed this legislation on March 31, 1994. It acknowledged the rights of all children to an opportunity to learn, to well-trained teachers, and to a solid curriculum.

In response to the dramatic technological innovations in the early and mid-1990s, U.S. Secretary of Education Richard Riley released the nation's first educational technology plan in 1996, entitled *Getting America's Students Ready for the 21st Century: Meeting the Technological Literacy Challenges.* The program called for technology to become a part of elementary and secondary school education instruction in order to help the next generation of schoolchildren to be better educated and better prepared for new demands in the American economy. The plan was quite successful and was revised in 1999 to expand teacher training. Given the fact that boys have traditionally been more encouraged than girls to take advantage of training in technology, the new emphasis on technology in education is bound to enhance their opportunities. However, those boys from minority and less-affluent homes who do not have ready access to home computers and who attend schools that are poorly equipped may find access to technological training more problematic than do more affluent white boys.

There has been a major change in education at the end of the twentieth and beginning of the twenty-first centuries as the federal government has identified major problems in U.S. education and

A teacher assists three boys with their schoolwork, 1999. (Skjold Photographs)

poured money into emergency remedies. States have worked more closely than ever with the federal government to achieve national educational goals. Americans have worked hard, although not altogether successfully, to provide opportunities to all students regardless of gender or socioeconomic status. Some reformers see expanding access to technology as the answer to all educational problems, whereas others believe that education should focus more on teaching basic skills.

Jacqueline Reinier
Priscilla Ferguson Clement
Mabel T. Himel
Lisa Jett

See also Computers; Learning Disabilities; Military Schools; Schoolbooks; Schools for Boys; Sunday Schools; Vocational Education

References and further reading
Anderson, James D. 1988. *The Education of Blacks in the South, 1860–1935.* Chapel Hill: University of North Carolina Press.
Clement, Priscilla Ferguson. 1997. *Growing Pains: Children in the Industrial Age, 1850–1890.* New York: Twayne Publishers.
Education Commission of the States Task Force on Education for Economic Growth. 1983. *Action for Excellence: A Comprehensive Plan to Improve Our Nation's Schools.* Denver: Education Commission of the States.
Faludi, Susan. 1999. "The Betrayal of the American Man." *Newsweek* (September 13): 49–58.

Finkelstein, Barbara. 1989. *Governing the Young: Teacher Behavior in Popular Primary Schools in Nineteenth-Century United States.* London: Falmer Press.

Fuller, Wayne E. 1982. *The Old Country School: The Story of Rural Education in the Midwest.* Chicago: University of Chicago Press.

Kaestle, Carl F. 1973a. *The Evolution of an Urban School System: New York City, 1750–1850.* Cambridge, MA: Harvard University Press.

———. 1973b. *Joseph Lancaster and the Monitorial School Movement.* New York: Teachers College Press.

———. 1983. *Pillars of the Republic: Common Schools and American Society, 1780–1860.* New York: Hill and Wang.

Kalb, Claudia. 2000. "What Boys Really Want." *Newsweek* (July 10): 52.

Lewis, Theodore. 1997. "Toward a Liberal Vocational Education." *Journal of Philosophy of Education* 31, no. 3: 477–489.

Link, William A. 1986. *A Hard Country and a Lonely Place: Schooling, Society and Reform in Rural Virginia, 1870–1920.* Chapel Hill: University of North Carolina Press.

National Commission on Excellence in Education. 1983. *A Nation at Risk: The Imperative for Educational Reform.* ED 226 006. Washington, DC: Government Printing Office.

National Science Board Commission on Pre-College Education in Mathematics, Science and Technology. 1983. *Educating Americans for the 21st Century. A Report to the American People and the National Science Board.* ED 223 913. Washington, DC: U.S. Government Printing Office.

Perlman, Joel. 1988. *Ethnic Differences: Schooling and Social Structure among the Irish, Italians, Jews, and Blacks in an American City, 1880–1935.* New York: Cambridge University Press.

Reinier, Jacqueline S. 1996. *From Virtue to Character: American Childhood, 1775–1850.* New York: Twayne Publishers.

Sadker, Myra, and David Sadker. 1994. *Failing at Fairness: How Our Schools Cheat Girls.* New York: Touchstone.

Schultz, Stanley K. 1973. *The Culture Factory: Boston Public Schools, 1789–1860.* New York: Oxford University Press.

U.S. Department of Education. 2000. "The Federal Role in Education," http://www.ed.gov/offices/OUS/fedrole.html (accessed March 28).

Walters, Pamela Barnhouse, and Phillip J. O'Connell. 1988. "The Family Economy, Work, and Educational Participation in the United States 1890–1940." *American Journal of Sociology* 93: 1116–1152.

Scientific Reasoning

There are two broad views of science and scientists used to discuss boys' and girls' ability to reason like scientists. One view suggests that even young boys have the conceptual skills and other qualities of mind, such as curiosity and imagination, to explain phenomena and revise those explanations in just the same manner as scientists do. Albert Einstein (1950) claimed that the thinking of children and scientists differs only in the degree of precision, systematicness, and economy of their ideas. Many developmental psychologists agree with this characterization and liken children to little scientists who revise their false theories of the world (Carey 1985; Meltzoff and Gropnik 1996). The second view is that the scientific thinking of young boys and girls is intuitive and illogical, which is nothing like the formal and logical process of reasoning of scientists when they practice science. In this view, the ability to reason scientifically can be acquired by children as they grow up and go to school. The view that scientific reasoning is an ability that is learned over an extended period of time and schooling is consistent with more than a century of philosophical, educational, and social science research, notably by the Swiss psychologist Jean Piaget, remains an

Two boys look through a telescope while others look at a globe suspended from the ceiling. (Archive Photos)

important perspective in developmental psychology.

Support for each of these views exists, suggesting that young boys and girls have some but perhaps not all of the individual skills necessary to propose and evaluate explanations of the world in a manner like that of scientists. To do so, boys as well as girls must use four component scientific reasoning skills, including the ability to think theoretically, hypothetically, logically, and empirically. These are component scientific reasoning skills in the sense that they are implicated in every characterization of science.

Theoretical thinking is the process of forming theories by which to explain and predict a range of related phenomena. Even young children have been found to use theories to predict and explain how the mind works (psychology), how the body works (biology), and how things work in the physical world (physics) (Wellman and Gelman 1992). Children's intuitive theories are similar in structure to formal theories of scientists in that they are composed of both an integrated conceptual network of explanatory concepts and assumptions about causal mechanisms. For example, boys and girls, like adults and scientists, will appeal to forces (causal mechanisms) such as "gravity" (explanatory concept) to explain or predict the motion of falling objects. Although similar in structure, the causal mechanisms and explanatory concepts in children's theories are vague or inadequate compared to scientists' theories. Again from the domain of physics, boys and girls incorrectly predict the rate and trajectory of falling objects, a rather curious mistake they make about phenomena with which they are very familiar. Ironically, rather than making predictions about how objects fall on the basis of their memory of seeing them fall, they appeal to their (incorrect) theories. Thus, although children may be theoretical, their theories are often wrong, placing them in much the same boat as scientists of long-ago eras who also appealed to incorrect theories to predict and explain phenomena.

Hypothetical thinking is the ability to reason about possibilities, which often informs the human view of reality, and is used in science in a variety of ways. *Combinatorial possibilities* involve judgments enumerating all possible combinations of conditions or factors related to a target outcome, as in determining all combinations of chemicals that may have produced a particular reaction. Young boys and girls tend to be poor at such reasoning (Inhelder and Piaget 1958), although they perform better with more accessible and simplified versions of the task (Klahr 2000). The term *multiple sufficient possibilities* refers to recognition of situations in which there are no definite answers to questions about conditions or factors related to a target outcome. For example, any one of four chemicals mixed together might have caused a reaction to occur, resulting in each of the four chemicals being possible causes, even though one chemical is eventually identified as the actual cause. Boys and girls have difficulty remaining indeterminate about the status of each of multiple sufficient possibilities in a situation, often judging each to play a unique role in the outcome (Kuhn, Amsel, and O'Loughlin 1988). *Counterfactual possibilities* have to do with the construction of alternative accounts of reality that could have occurred but did not. Considered central in science, counterfactual possibilities are often used to express predictions and hypotheses (e.g., if X had been done, Y would have occurred). Young children appear to be quite capable of generating counterfactual possibilities regarding alternatives to well-understood causal event sequences. For example, children told about a little boy who tore his pants when playing outside will generate the counterfactual possibility that if he had not played outside, he would not have torn his pants. However, there remain questions regarding young children's ability to reason about counterfactual possibilities in other ways and in other domains (Amsel and Smalley 1999).

Logical thinking is the ability to draw conclusions from premises, irrespective of one's beliefs about the premises being asserted or the conclusions being drawn.

Such reasoning occurs in science when a prediction or hypothesis is derived from a theory (although reasoning about such hypotheses involves hypothetical thinking). In the past, philosophers have argued that logical deductions are the backbone of science because they provide the only basis for rationally justifying the activity (Braithewaite 1953; but see Lauden 1977). Young boys and girls perform well on simple logical reasoning tasks ("All bicycles have two wheels. The object in the box is a bicycle. Does it have two wheels?" Answer: yes). The difficulty for children arises when the nature of the logical deduction changes (e.g., "All bicycles have two wheels. The object in the box does not have two wheels. Is it a bicycle?" Answer: no), or when they do not believe that the premise or conclusion is true ("All bicycles have three wheels. The object in the box is a bicycle. Does it have three wheels?" Answer: yes) (Braine and O'Brien 1997). Fully appreciating the difference between an argument that is logically valid (wherein the conclusions can be drawn from the premise) but not true and one that is true but not logically valid does not appear to be possible until adolescence (Moshman 1999).

The term *empirical reasoning* refers to the processes involved in the evaluation of evidence and revision of theories. Accounts of such processes in science have ranged from strictly formal analysis of the confirmation or falsification of theories (e.g., Popper 1959) to psychological or historical analysis of the plausibility and coherence of explanations of phenomena (Lauden 1977). Children readily evaluate the plausibility and coherence of their explanations of phenomena and act like scientists in their reactions to explanatory failures. For example, young children will slowly but surely revise their theory that all blocks balance at their geometric center to account for the behavior of a block that has a weight hidden inside and thus balances off-center (Karmiloff-Smith and Inhelder 1974). But when children are asked to formally evaluate theories, they appear to reason less competently than scientists. Not only do children lack scientists' evidence-evaluation strategies to validly assess even simple patterns of evidence in formally appropriate ways, but they also fail to evaluate new evidence bearing on theories independent of their prior theoretical beliefs regarding the theory. More generally, when confronted with new information, young children tend to treat it as an explanatory opportunity (i.e., to provide an account for the new information in terms of their prior theoretical beliefs) instead of as a confirmatory or disconfirmatory opportunity (i.e., to assess the new information as evidence bearing on a theory in a systematic and unbiased manner).

These components of scientific reasoning work together to produce coordinated efforts at scientific reasoning. By three years of age, boys and girls are able to coordinate the scientific reasoning skills they have available to form, apply, and revise theories about a broad range of phenomena. These theories may be incorrect in terms of modern scientific knowledge, but they have a sophisticated conceptual structure. Moreover, such theories serve as a basis for the children's thoughts about counterfactual possibilities. Finally, the explanatory concepts and causal processes associated with the theory may be updated in light of repeated failure to successfully explain phenomena by reference to the theory. This form of scientific reasoning, sometimes called "inductive" or "abductive" reasoning, is effective for children to learn through trial and error. But when a situation calls for a formal analysis of specific theories, children have much difficulty. This form of scientific reasoning, sometimes called "hypothetico-deductive" reasoning, involves logically inferring hypotheses from theories, systematically collecting and analyzing evidence bearing on those hypotheses, and then confirming or disconfirming the theory. Children do not spontaneously reason according to the scientific method because they lack the skills to logically make predictions, particularly regarding theories they may disbelieve; to entertain theoretical possibilities regarding alternative hypotheses to ones they may believe to be true; and to evaluate evidence bearing on theories they prefer or dislike in a systematic and unbiased manner. Nonetheless, these skills emerge with age and education and can be promoted by science education programs that target the promotion of children's scientific reasoning skills in addition to their scientific knowledge.

Eric Amsel

References and further reading
Amsel, Eric, and J. David Smalley. 1999. "Beyond Really and Truly: Children's Counterfactual Thinking about Pretend and Possible Worlds." Pp. 99–134 in *Children's Reasoning and the Mind.* Edited by K. Riggs and P. Mitchell. Brighton, UK: Psychology Press.
Braine, Marty, and David O'Brien. 1997. *Mental Logic.* Mahwah, NJ: Lawrence Erlbaum.
Braithewaite, Richard Bevan. 1953. *Scientific Explanation: A Study of the Function of Theory, Probability and Law in Science.* Cambridge, UK: Cambridge University Press.
Carey, Susan. 1985. *Conceptual Change in Childhood.* Cambridge, MA: MIT Press.
Einstein, Albert. 1950. *Out of My Later Years.* New York: Philosophical Library.
Inhelder, Barbel, and Jean Piaget. 1958. *The Growth of Logical Thinking from*

Childhood to Adolescence. New York: Basic Books.

Karmiloff-Smith, Annette, and Barbel Inhelder. 1974. "If You Want to Get Ahead, Get a Theory." *Cognition* 3: 195–212.

Klahr, David. 2000. *Exploring Science: The Cognition and Development of Discovery Processes.* Cambridge, MA: MIT Press.

Kuhn, Deanna, Eric Amsel, and Michael O'Loughlin. 1988. *The Development of Scientific Thinking Skills.* Orlando, FL: Academic Press.

Kuhn, Thomas S. 1962. *The Structure of Scientific Reasoning.* Chicago: University of Chicago Press.

Lauden, Larry. 1977. *Progress and Its Problems.* Berkeley: University of California Press.

Meltzoff, Andrew, and Allison Gropnik. 1996. *Words, Thoughts, and Theories.* Cambridge, MA: MIT Press.

Moshman, David. 1999. *Adolescent Psychological Development: Rationality, Morality, and Identity.* Mahwah, NJ: Lawrence Erlbaum.

Popper, Karl Raimund. 1959. *The Logic of Scientific Discovery.* London, UK: Hutchinson.

Wellman, Henry, and Susan Gelman. 1992. "Cognitive Development: Foundational Theories of Core Domains." *Annual Review of Psychology* 43: 337–376.

Sexual Abuse

See Abuse

Sexuality

All human beings are inherently sexual. Infants, children, adolescents, and adults at different stages experience their sexuality in distinct ways. Sexuality evolves during childhood and adolescence, laying the foundation for adult sexual health and intimacy. Adolescent sexual health is defined by a broad range of knowledge, attitudes, and behaviors and cannot be defined solely on the basis of abstinence or preventive behaviors.

In colonial America, boys who grew up in large families in a mostly rural society were surrounded by sexuality. Children who shared beds with their parents witnessed the sexual act, and procreation by farmyard animals was a natural part of life. Yet societal and religious values linked sexuality to reproduction contained within marriage, and individual behavior was closely regulated by government. Nevertheless, there is plenty of historical evidence that boys experimented with sex. Parents and masters found it difficult to control the youthful behavior of children and servants, teenage college students engaged in wild behavior with young women of the town, and adolescents on southern plantations initiated sexual relationships with female slaves. In Puritan New England, buggery with an animal was a capital crime, and the perpetrator was forced to witness the killing of the animal prior to his own execution. Although such executions were rare, several Massachusetts and Connecticut teenage boys lost their lives for performing sexual acts with a cow, goat, or sheep.

By the end of the eighteenth century, individualistic values permeated post-Revolutionary America, and sexuality for pleasure began to be separated from procreation. Boys, who were viewed as inherently sexual, were encouraged to develop internalized restraint. In the increasingly capitalist economy of the nineteenth century, young apprentices and clerks who moved to urban centers were taught that control of appetite would contribute to success. Sexual intercourse should be delayed until marriage, and masturbation loomed as a significant danger. Learning to control his sexual urges was a way that a boy could build character. Gender roles became solidified in the nineteenth century, and boys and girls of the middle class who were raised separately found it difficult to establish easy relationships prior to marriage. Young males were more likely to find intimacy in rough physical play with other boys or in close same-sex friendships with other young men, some of which had romantic overtones.

The commercial economy and urban growth of the nineteenth century increased the availability of commercial sex, and boys and young men joined the clientele of urban prostitutes. Poor boys who lived in neighborhoods where vice prevailed earned extra money pimping for brothels. Teenage working-class boys and girls spent leisure time strolling together and attending dance halls. For treating a girl with his hard-won wages, a young man expected a return of sexual favors, resulting in a form of casual prostitution. Through organizations such as the New York Female Moral Reform Society, middle-class women of the 1830s attacked commercial sex, and mothers took on the responsibility of imploring their sons to be pure. But the influence of white women was less effective in the South, where the freedom of white boys on plantations continued to condone sexual initiation with slaves. Black boys also engaged in sexual experimentation with black girls, although any overture to a white woman or girl was certain to bring harsh consequences, which only increased in severity after emancipation.

Throughout American history, fear of social chaos has often focused on controlling the behavior of boys. By the late nineteenth century, advocates of competitive sports, a new muscular version of Christianity, and organizations such as the Young Men's Christian Association (YMCA) urged manly purity and attempted to elevate boys to the same sex-

ual standard as girls and women. Opponents of obscenity exhorted parents to monitor children's reading and to protect boys from the popular dime novels that often contained sexually explicit material. As a free market of sex increasingly permeated society, the ability to control one's sexuality came to define the boundaries of middle-class respectability.

The early twentieth century, however, initiated a new sexual era as an economy of advanced capitalism began to promote an ethic of indulgence. As work became more routine, individuals sought self-expression in their private lives. More boys and girls attended high school and began to live in a youth-centered world in which the sexes mingled. By the 1920s middle-class adolescents participated in a new youth subculture and engaged in the rituals of dating, necking, and then petting in the private space of the car. In white and black working-class communities, young men and women exchanged sexual favors. Homosexuals developed a distinct identity in a new sexual subculture.

Although families returned to more traditional behavior during hard times in the 1930s, these trends were accelerated in the period of social change that accompanied World War II. By the 1950s, petting was the most common teenage sexual experience. As the age of marriage dropped, however, sexual intercourse continued to be contained within marriage. Patterns of sexual behavior differed widely among young men and young women, as well as among youth from different backgrounds.

By the 1960s sexual liberalism was widespread as the singles life, the student movement, and the hippie counterculture all extolled sex as a source of personal freedom no longer linked to marriage. The business of sex churned out consumer products, and changing demographics of household size and structure condoned nonmarital sex. In this context, by the twenty-first century, sexual experience began at younger and younger ages, and the behavior of males and females has become more alike.

In the mid-1950s, just over a quarter of young women under age eighteen were sexually experienced (comparable information for young men is not available for that time period). Data from 1968 to 1970 indicate that 55 percent of young men and 35 percent of young women had intercourse by their eighteenth birthday; by 1977–1979, 64 percent of young men and 47 percent of young women had intercourse by their eighteenth birthday. These percentages continued to increase as the twentieth century progressed: 1986–1988 data show that 73 percent of young men and 56 percent of young women had intercourse by their eighteenth birthday (Alan Guttmacher Institute 1994).

Today's teenagers reach physical maturity earlier and marry later, and almost all of them experiment with some type of sexual behavior. Patterns of sexual activity are now fairly similar among young men and women from different socioeconomic, ethnic, and religious groups. According to 1995 research, 68 percent of young men and 65 percent of young women have had intercourse before their eighteenth birthday (Alan Guttmacher Institute 1999).

Historically, much of the research on adolescent sexuality has focused on pregnancy, contraceptive use, and sexually transmitted disease infection, and much of the available data are on adolescent females. However, two recent surveys measure sexual behavior among adolescent males. The Youth Risk Behavior Surveys (YRBS), conducted by the Centers for Disease Control and Prevention, assess the behaviors deemed most responsible for influencing health among the nation's high school students. The 1995 National Survey of Adolescent Males (NSAM) was designed primarily to examine the sexual and reproductive behaviors of a nationally representative sample of boys ages fifteen through nineteen.

In these studies, the majority of teen males reported having had sexual intercourse by age seventeen (59 percent, Sonenstein et al. 1997) or twelfth grade (64 percent, Kann et al. 2000). The older the teen, the more likely he was to report having had sexual intercourse: 27 percent of fifteen-year-old males had lost their virginity, compared with 85 percent of nineteen-year-old males (Sonenstein et al. 1997); and 45 percent of ninth grade males had had intercourse, compared with 64 percent of twelfth grade males (Kann et al. 2000). Overall, 12 percent of male students in grades nine to twelve reported having initiated sexual intercourse before thirteen years of age. Black male students (30 percent) were significantly more likely than Hispanic and white male students (14 percent and 8 percent, respectively) to have had sexual intercourse before thirteen years of age (Kann et al. 2000). In addition, black teen males initiated intercourse earlier than Hispanic or white males. Half of black teen males reported having had sexual intercourse by age sixteen; half of Hispanic teen males reported having had sexual intercourse by age seventeen; and half of white teen males reported having had sexual intercourse by age eighteen (Sonenstein et al. 1997).

According to data from the 1995 National Survey of Adolescent Males, teenage males' frequency of sexual intercourse was low. In the twelve months preceding the survey, more than one-half of sexually experienced teen males had intercourse fewer than ten times or not at all. Although young males' sexual activity tended to be episodic and punctuated by months-long periods of sexual inactivity, teen males had sexual intercourse more frequently as they got older (Sonenstein et al. 1997). In the 1999 Youth Risk Behavior Survey, 30 percent of ninth grade male students, 34 percent of tenth grade male students, 35 percent of eleventh grade male students, and 48 percent of twelfth grade male students reported engaging in sexual intercourse during the three months preceding the survey (Kann et al. 2000).

Overall, most teenage males' sexual relationships were monogamous. Among sexually experienced teen males, 54 percent had one partner or none in one year; 26 percent had two partners in one year; 14 percent had three or four partners in one year; and 6 percent had five or more partners in one year (Sonenstein et al. 1997). Nineteen percent of male students reported having had sexual intercourse with four or more partners during their lifetime; black male students (48 percent) were significantly more likely than Hispanic (23 percent) or white (12 percent) male students to have had sexual intercourse with four or more partners during their lifetime (Kann et al. 2000).

Data from the 1995 National Survey of Adolescent Males showed that most sexually experienced teenage boys and men had sexual partners who were close to their own age. The average age difference between sexually experienced males ages fifteen through nineteen and their most recent female partner was less than six months. However, 25 percent of sexually active sixteen-year-old males reported having a female partner who was fourteen

years old or younger, and 11 percent of sexually active nineteen-year-old males reported having a female partner who was fifteen years old or younger (Sonenstein et al. 1997).

According to recent data, the number of adolescents using condoms has increased since the early 1980s, but such use was still inconsistent. Sixty-six percent of male students who said they were currently sexually active reported using a condom during their last intercourse (Kann et al. 2000). Ninety percent of teen males ages fifteen through nineteen who reported having sexual intercourse reported having used condoms at some point in the year preceding the survey. However, only 44 percent reported using condoms every time they had intercourse. Forty-seven percent of sexually active black teen males reported consistent condom use, as compared to 46 percent of white and 29 percent of Hispanic sexually active teen males (Sonenstein et al. 1997).

Twelve percent of ninth to twelfth grade male students who were currently sexually active reported that their partner used birth control pills before their last incidence of intercourse (Kann et al. 2000). One-third of sexually active males ages fifteen through nineteen who reported using condoms 100 percent of the time also reported that their partners used the pill (Sonenstein et al. 1997). Although teen males were equally likely to have used an effective method of contraception regardless of age, condom use tended to decline with age (Sonenstein et al. 1997).

Among sexually experienced males ages fifteen through nineteen, 14 percent said that they had made a partner pregnant. Twenty-two percent of black, 19 percent of Hispanic, and 10 percent of white sexually experienced males ages fifteen through nineteen reported having made a partner pregnant. Six percent of all sexually experienced males ages fifteen through nineteen reported having fathered a child. Broken down by race, 10 percent of black, 8 percent of Hispanic, and 5 percent of white sexually experienced males ages fifteen through nineteen reported having fathered a child (Sonenstein et al. 1997). Overall, 5 percent of the ninth through twelfth grade male students in the 1999 Youth Risk Behavior Survey sample reported that they had gotten someone pregnant. Older male students were more likely than younger male students to have gotten someone pregnant, and black male students (13 percent) were more likely than Hispanic (7 percent) or white (3 percent) male students to have gotten someone pregnant (Kann et al. 2000).

Among currently sexually active students in grades nine through twelve, 31 percent of males had used alcohol or drugs at the time of their most recent sexual intercourse. Eight percent of males reported being hit, slapped, or physically hurt on purpose by their boyfriend or girlfriend, and 5 percent reported being forced to have sexual intercourse (Kann et al. 2000).

Approximately 20 percent of all high school students are enrolled in alternative high schools that serve students who are at risk for failing or dropping out of regular high school or are students who have been removed from their regular high school because of drug use, violence, or other illegal activity or behavioral problems. According to a recent study of youth in alternative high schools, the vast majority of males who attended such schools reported having had sexual intercourse (84 percent in grade nine and 88 percent in grade twelve). Sixty-six percent of males reported having had sexual intercourse in the three months preceding the survey. Thirty percent of male students enrolled in alternative high schools reported having initiated sexual intercourse before age thirteen. Fifty-seven percent reported having had four or more sexual partners in their lifetime. Fifty-five percent said that they had used a condom when they last had intercourse, compared with 13 percent who indicated that their partner used birth control pills before their most recent intercourse. Ninth grade male students enrolled in alternative high schools were significantly more likely (66 percent) to have reported condom use at last intercourse than males in twelfth grade (49 percent) (Grunbaum et al. 1999).

There is a public and professional consensus about what is sexually unhealthy for teenagers. Professionals, politicians, and parents across the political spectrum share a deep concern about unplanned adolescent pregnancy; out-of-wedlock childbearing; sexually transmitted diseases, including human immunodeficiency virus (HIV) and its ultimate result, acquired immunodeficiency syndrome (AIDS); sexual abuse; date rape; and the potential negative emotional consequences of premature sexual behaviors. However, there is little public, professional, or political consensus about what is sexually healthy for teenagers. The public debate about adolescent sexuality has often focused on which sexual behaviors are appropriate for adolescents and ignored the complex dimensions of sexuality.

Becoming a sexually healthy adult is a key developmental task of adolescence. Achieving sexual health requires the integration of psychological, physical, societal, cultural, educational, economic, and spiritual factors. Sexual health encompasses sexual development and reproductive health and such characteristics as the ability to develop and maintain meaningful interpersonal relationships; appreciate one's own body; interact with both genders in respectful and appropriate ways; and express affection, love, and intimacy in ways consistent with one's own values.

Adults can encourage adolescent sexual health by providing accurate information and education about sexuality, fostering responsible decisionmaking skills, offering young people support and guidance to explore and affirm their own values, and modeling healthy sexual attitudes and behaviors. Society can enhance adolescent sexual health by providing access to comprehensive sexuality education; affordable, sensitive, and confidential reproductive health care services; and education and employment opportunities. Adolescents should be encouraged to delay sexual behaviors until they are physically, cognitively, and emotionally ready for mature sexual relationships and their consequences. This support should include education about intimacy; sexual limit setting; social, media, peer, and partner pressure; the benefits of abstinence from intercourse; and the prevention of pregnancy and sexually transmitted diseases. Because many adolescents are or will be sexually active, they should receive support and assistance in developing their skills to evaluate their readiness for mature sexual relationships. Responsible adolescent intimate relationships, like those of adults, if any type of intercourse occurs, should be based on shared personal values and should be consensual, nonexploitive, honest, pleasurable, and protected against unintended pregnancies and sexually transmitted diseases (National Commission on Adolescent Sexual Health 1995).

Monica Rodriguez

See also Fathers, Adolescent; Pornography; Prostitution; Same-Sex Relationships; Sexually Transmitted Diseases

References and further reading
Alan Guttmacher Institute. 1994. *Sex and America's Teenagers.* New York: Alan Guttmacher Institute.
———. 1999. *Facts in Brief: Teen Sex and Pregnancy.* New York: Alan Guttmacher Institute.
D'Emilio, John, and Estelle Freedman. 1988. *Intimate Matters: A History of Sexuality in America.* New York: Harper and Row.
Grunbaum, Jo Anne, Laura Kann, Steven A. Kinchen, James G. Ross, Vani R. Gowda, Janet L. Collins, and Lloyd J. Kolbe. 1999. "Youth Risk Behavior Surveillance—National Alternative High School Youth Risk Behavior Survey, United States, 1988." *Centers for Disease Control and Prevention: MMWR Surveillance Summaries* 48, no. SS-7 (October 29).
Kann, Laura, Steven A. Kinchen, Barbara I. Williams, James G. Ross, Richard Lowry, Jo Anne Grunbaum, Lloyd J. Kolbe, and State and Local YRBSS Coordinators. 2000. "Youth Risk Behavior Surveillance—United States, 1999." *Centers for Disease Control and Prevention: MMWR Surveillance Summaries* 49, no. SS-5 (June 9).
National Commission on Adolescent Sexual Health. 1995. *Facing Facts: Sexual Health for America's Adolescents.* New York: Sexuality Information and Education Council of the United States.
Sexuality Information and Education Council of the United States (SIECUS). 1995. *SIECUS Position Statements on Sexuality Issues 1995.* New York: SIECUS.
Sonenstein, Freya L., Kellie Stewart, Laura Duberstein Lindberg, Marta Pernas, and Sean Williams. 1997. *Involving Males in Preventing Teen Pregnancy: A Guide for Program Planners.* Washington, DC: Urban Institute.

Sexually Transmitted Diseases

Sexually transmitted diseases (STDs) are infectious diseases transmitted primarily through sexual contact, although some may also be acquired through contaminated blood products and from mother to fetus. Physicians coined the term *sexually transmitted diseases* in the 1970s to eliminate the judgmental overtones of the older term *venereal diseases,* which was frequently equated with illicit sexual activity. The major STDs are syphilis, gonorrhea, genital herpes, genital warts, chlamydia, and human immunodeficiency virus (HIV), which causes acquired immunodeficiency syndrome (AIDS). Other diseases that may be sexually transmitted include trichomoniasis, bacterial vaginitis, cytomegalovirus infections, scabies, and pubic lice. STDs are the most common infectious diseases in the world and are most prevalent in teenagers and young adults. Despite advances in the treatment of infectious diseases during the twentieth century, control of STDs has been thwarted by views that depict these diseases as moral retribution for socially unacceptable behavior (Brandt 1985).

Until the late nineteenth century, physicians who studied STDs tended to focus on adult sufferers. Sexual activity outside marriage was tightly regulated, first by the church and later by the state, and STDs were seen as just punishment for those who violated moral standards (D'Emilio and Freedman 1988). More important, children and adolescents of both sexes were supposed to be asexual. Medical advice literature of the period warned that signs of sexual feelings in the young were an aberration and that parents should actively discourage such feelings by preventing their children from masturbating or reading romantic novels. Adolescent chastity was particularly important to native-born whites of the emerging middle class, who used sexual restraint, along with temperance and other forms of self-control, to distinguish themselves from laborers, immigrants, and African Americans (Moran 2000).

Medical advice literature also responded to what many saw as a disturbing trend in American family structure: growing numbers of adolescent boys were living away from home. The expansion of urban commerce led boys to leave family farms to take jobs as clerks in the nation's growing urban centers, all of which contained flourishing sex trades. Physicians and social reformers worried that adolescent boys living alone in the city would be enticed into lives of sexual depravity and wrote advice manuals warning that solicitation of prostitutes led to disease and premature death (Cohen 1999). Concerns about the "victimization" of young men by prostitutes prompted the formation of purity leagues, like the New York Magdalen Society, aimed at eliminating the blight of prostitution on the nation's cities. Reformers also promoted the creation of organizations such as the Young Men's Christian Association, which attempted to provide wholesome substitutes for prostitution and other urban vices but also inadvertently caused some young men to develop same-sex relationships (Gustav-Wrathall 1998).

During the late nineteenth and early twentieth centuries, medical discoveries shifted the focus of disease prevention efforts. The discovery of the microorganisms that caused many STDs enabled scientists to develop diagnostic tests that detected disease in women, who were less likely than men to show external physical symptoms until the disease was well advanced. These new diagnostic procedures disclosed that STDs were much more prevalent than originally assumed and were often the underlying cause of other medical problems such as impotence, sterility, and insanity. Medical advances also drew increasing attention to so-called innocent victims of these diseases, namely the wives and children of men who frequented prostitutes. Some physicians even made a distinction between "venereal" disease contracted through illicit sexual conduct and "innocent" forms caused by passage of the disease from husband to wife or through casual forms of contact with sufferers who had open sores on the mouth or skin. The New York City dermatologist L. Duncan Bulkley (1894) warned that nonvenereal transmission of syphilis was common and that the disease could be contracted through kissing, shaking hands, breastfeeding, circumcision, sharing utensils and bed linens with infected persons, and smoking cigarettes and cigars made by syphilitic operatives.

Today, medical experts recognize that nonsexual forms of transmission are extremely rare and that fears about "innocent" forms of contagion were shaped largely by class, race, and ethnic prejudice of the period. Rates of immigration were increasing during this time, and the birthrates among the white, native-born middle classes were declining, leading to fears that the latter were committing "race suicide" by failing to reproduce in adequate numbers. Detection of STDs in members of the "respectable" white, native-born middle classes exacerbated these fears of race suicide, since physicians recognized that these diseases could lead to sterility, miscarriage, stillbirths, and birth defects in surviving infants. Control of STDs therefore became linked with the eugenics movement of the early twentieth century, which hoped to improve the quality of human racial stock through selective breeding and reforms in public health (Pernick 1996). Eager to explain infection in "respectable" persons, physicians argued

that immigrant workers, particularly food service workers, domestic servants, and cigar and cigarette makers, should be tested for venereal diseases and, if infected, should be forbidden from working in these occupations (Tomes 1998). Physicians also advised against the practice, common in the South, of using black female servants as wet nurses for white infants, since physicians alleged that syphilis was endemic in the black population (Jones 1993). At times, anti-Semitism is also apparent in warnings about venereal disease: physicians alleged that the practice of ritual circumcision caused higher rates of syphilis in Jews than in gentiles.

Yet physicians recognized that sexual contact remained the primary form of transmission and used this fact to advocate the creation of sex education programs in public schools. At the same time, developments in child psychology, most notably the work of G. Stanley Hall and Sigmund Freud, postulated that awakening sexuality was a normal part of child and adolescent development but warned that youth's sexual impulses had to be channeled away from premature sexual activity. Controlling adolescent sexuality became more problematic during and after World War I, when standards of sexual morality among young people changed dramatically. Although not as drastic as the events of the 1960s, the "sexual revolution" of the 1920s directly challenged Victorian standards of sexual chastity. Changes in the sexual behavior of young people created new challenges for sex educators, as the goals of educating the young about sex and protecting them from premarital sex frequently came in conflict with each other. Opponents of sex education argued that these programs actually encouraged sexual activity. Proponents countered that scientific information transmitted by qualified educators was better than the myths and folk beliefs that young people acquired from their peers. Sex education advocates warned that boys were especially likely to acquire misinformation about sex, and these advocates were particularly concerned about the common belief among young men that sexual experience was vital to masculine identity. Yet public opposition to sex education in schools led schools to water down their programs or eliminate them entirely.

For this reason, young men received conflicting messages about sexuality. In private, many males shared a sexual double standard that linked sexual activity with masculinity and sexual chastity with virtuous womanhood. Since "respectable" women were forbidden to engage in premarital sexual activity, the only way a young man could gain sexual experience before marriage was to visit a prostitute, thereby exposing himself to infection. Psychologists warned that males who did not exhibit interest in heterosexual sexual activity were at risk of becoming homosexuals. At the same time, social conservatives continued to condemn premarital sexuality and view STDs as punishment for violation of social norms.

The prevalence of premarital sexual activity among young people continued to climb during the years following World War II. In addition, the discovery of antibiotics dramatically reduced the incidence of STDs. For example, the number of cases of primary and secondary syphilis fell from 66.4 per 100,000 in 1947 to 3.9 per 100,000 in 1957 (Brandt 1985, 171). Yet pockets of infection remained, particularly among populations who lacked access to adequate health care because of

racism, poverty, or geographic isolation. During the late 1960s, rates of STDs among white middle-class youth started to increase as young people from this group dropped out of mainstream society and embraced an alternative, hippie subculture that rejected middle-class norms of sexual behavior. These youths also tended to avoid "establishment" institutions such as hospitals and clinics, where they frequently encountered adults who disapproved of their lifestyle. Those who were under age twenty-one also feared that health care personnel would inform their parents should they seek medical treatment for STDs and would frequently avoid obtaining care until the disease was far advanced. In order to stem the spread of these diseases, specialists in adolescent medicine pushed for laws that would allow minors to obtain medical treatment without parental consent. Physicians at this time also coined the term *sexually transmitted disease* to eliminate the social stigma associated with the older term *venereal disease* (Prescott 1998).

The appearance of AIDS in the 1980s added new urgency to STD prevention efforts but also reaffirmed older prejudices about this category of disease. Because AIDs was first identified in gay men and intravenous drug users, public response to the disease was initially apathetic and reflected earlier sentiments that those who suffered from this category of disease somehow deserved their fate. Even those who acquired AIDs through nonsexual means were stigmatized. When Ryan White, a thirteen-year-old hemophiliac, contracted AIDs from tainted blood products in 1984, he and his parents were shunned by neighbors in their hometown of Kokomo, Indiana. Ryan's classmates called him a "fag," and school officials barred him from attending the town's high school. When ostracism turned to violence, the Whites moved to another town where public school officials took a more rational approach to his disease and were able to calm the fears of town residents. Ryan became a national celebrity and helped raise awareness about those living with AIDs, particularly other children and adolescents (White 1991). Yet White's story also reinforced distinctions between "innocent" victims of AIDs like himself and those who obtained the disease from less socially acceptable means. This double standard has meant that attempts to control the spread of AIDs and other STDs through safe sex and needle exchange programs continue to be problematic because many individuals still believe that these diseases are divine retribution for bad behavior.

Heather Munro Prescott

See also Disease and Death; Prostitution; Same-Sex Relationships; Sexuality

References and further reading
Brandt, Allan M. 1985. *No Magic Bullet: A Social History of Venereal Disease in the United States since 1880.* New York: Oxford University Press.
Bristow, Nancy K. 1996. *Making Men Moral: Social Engineering during the Great War.* New York: New York University Press.
Bulkley, L. Duncan. 1894. *Syphilis in the Innocent (Syphilis Insontium) Clinically and Historically Considered with a Plan for the Legal Control of the Disease.* New York: Bailey and Fairchild.
Cohen, Patricia Cline. 1999. *The Murder of Helen Jewitt.* New York: Vintage.
D'Emilio, John D., and Estelle B. Freedman. 1988. *Intimate Matters: A History of Sexuality in America.* New York: Harper and Row.
Gustav-Wrathall, John Donald. 1998. *Take the Young Stranger by the Hand: Same-Sex Relations and the YMCA.* Chicago: University of Chicago Press.
Jones, James. 1993. *Bad Blood: The Tuskegee Syphilis Experiment.* Rev. ed. New York: Free Press.
Moran, Jeffrey P. 2000. *Teaching Sex: The Shaping of Adolescence in the 20th Century.* Cambridge, MA: Harvard University Press.
Pernick, Martin S. 1996. *The Black Stork: Eugenics and the Death of "Defective" Babies in American Medicine and Motion Pictures since 1915.* New York: Oxford University Press.
Prescott, Heather Munro. 1998. *"A Doctor of Their Own": The History of Adolescent Medicine.* Cambridge, MA: Harvard University Press.
Tomes, Nancy. 1998. *The Gospel of Germs: Men, Women, and the Microbe in American Life.* Cambridge, MA: Harvard University Press.
White, Ryan, and Ann Marie Cunningham. 1991. *Ryan White: My Own Story.* New York: Dial Press.

Siblings

Western civilization has long used the concept of brotherhood to symbolize any relationship in which a strong bond is or should be present (Handel 1985). Brotherhood and, more recently, sisterhood have come to represent relationships built on a deeper commitment to one another, even in difficult times. These terms have come to symbolize both the great strength that can exist in relationships, such as the brotherhood identified among African American males, and the grievous betrayals that can similarly result, as evidenced in the biblical story of Cain and Abel, John Steinbeck's novel *East of Eden*, and William Shakespeare's play *Hamlet*.

Historically, the relationships between siblings, perhaps the most intense many human beings will experience, have come to represent both the best and the worst in how people treat one another. Although children and adolescents may avoid conflict with friends in order to preserve those relationships, sibling relationships, which do not operate under the same threat of termination, are likely to experience a heightened level of both warmth and conflict. The significance of the sibling bond during the growing years is becoming ever more evident.

Early theories of children's socioemotional development viewed the importance of sibling relationships as limited to the rivalry thought to define the relationships between siblings and their competition for parents' attention and other resources. Initial research focused on the structural makeup of children's sibling relationships, reasoning that it was the child's position in the family relative to his or her brothers and sisters that defined the importance of the sibling experience. Over time, greater consideration has been given to the quality of the relationship between siblings (Furman and Burhmester 1985) and the family characteristics that promote or hinder that quality (Brody, Stoneman, and McCoy 1992; Dunn and Kendrick 1981). More recently, research about siblings has moved to the examination of specific sibling unions. For example, research is currently under way that focuses on the importance of children's sibling relationships when one of the siblings is mentally or physically disabled (Mandleco et al. 1998), when one of the siblings is perpetrating incestuous or other abnormal behaviors (Adler and Schutz 1996), and when children are attempting to cope with the death or long-term illness of a sibling (Gallo and Knafl 1993). As a result, many unique qualities of this shared relationship are now being recognized, including the importance of children's sibling configurations, the ways in which sibling relationships change across childhood and adolescence, parents' impor-

Two brothers playing piggyback (Photodisc)

tance to the quality of siblings' relationships, and the significance of siblings as role models or as protectors against many of the stressful events occurring both within and without the family. Finally, sibling relationships are becoming increasingly recognized for their potential importance to other areas of children's and adolescents' lives.

In general, four characteristics of siblings' relationships have received particular attention: birth order, age spacing between siblings, number of siblings in a family, and the gender of siblings. Numerous studies have examined siblings' birth order as a predictor of children's successful development. Many have argued that being the oldest sibling is generally advantageous because it provides increased opportunities to function as a teacher and model for younger siblings. In contrast, others have speculated that being born later is advantageous because older siblings can serve as "pacemakers" of desirable behavior, allowing the younger siblings to better judge what they should realistically be able to achieve. In adulthood, firstborn siblings do appear to take on positions of responsibility and authority more often (Wagner, Schubert, and Schubert 1979, 88), but they also have greater anxiety and self-absorption compared to later-born siblings (Cloninger 2000, 120). Siblings provide children with many of the same reciprocal functions found in friendships, including rough-and-tumble and make-believe play, but the age differences typically found between older and younger siblings allow them to also provide complementary functions for one another. The complementary nature of their relationships is particularly evident in the teaching, modeling, helping, and caregiving often provided to later-born siblings by their older brothers or sisters (Dunn 1983, 805). These interactions provide later-born siblings with opportunities to observe and interact with older children while providing the older siblings with the opportunity to develop greater responsibility and skills in teaching and caregiving. It should be pointed out that these attempts at helping, managing, or teaching are not always well given by older siblings or well received by their later-born counterparts.

The importance of birth order appears to vary as a function of the age spacing between siblings (Teti, in press, 13). Children who are close in age to their siblings will likely have more intense relationships, exhibiting greater conflict as well as more shared interests and activities. In contrast, when greater age spacing exists, there are increased benefits regarding their respective roles as teachers and learners, helpers and those being helped.

An issue that has received a great deal of attention in conjunction with birth order is the number of siblings in children's families, particularly as it relates to children's level of intelligence. A number of studies have concluded that later-born siblings are likely to have lower intelligence than their older brothers and sisters. The logic behind these studies was that larger families produced children with lower intelligent quotients (IQ); thus, having more siblings present in a home when a child was born was thought to result in children growing up in a family context that was increasingly diluted intellectually. However, Joseph Rodgers and his colleagues (2000, 607) recently concluded that it was not the act of being in a large family that lowered children's IQs; rather, large families appear to be born to parents with lower IQs.

A final characteristic important to children's sibling experience is their gender. Children's gender indicates how and how much they are likely to interact with their siblings (Teti, in press, 17). In general, relationships among brothers as compared to sisters appear to be largely the same until late childhood and early adolescence, when brothers begin to perceive their relationships as less supportive, warm, and intimate than those with their sisters (Dunn 1996, 40; Furman and Buhrmester 1992, 110–111). Of greatest importance is not brothers versus sisters but whether the gender makeup of sibling pairs is similar or different. Even in the earliest stages of development, same-sex siblings begin to demonstrate more social and less agonistic behavior toward one another when compared to mixed-sex sibling pairs (Dunn and Kendrick 1981, 1271). In addition, later-born children in mixed-sex sibling pairs are progressively less likely to imitate the older siblings' behavior, compared to those in same-sex sibling pairs (Pepler, Abramovitch, and Corter 1981, 1346). Gender is also important to the socializing behavior of siblings born earlier; older sisters are more likely than their male counterparts to take on the role of teacher and manager for younger siblings, irrespective of the later-born siblings' gender (Stoneman, Brody, and MacKinnon 1986, 508). These gender differences appear to have become increasingly important as the average number of children within families has decreased (Mizell and Steelman 2000); in smaller families the importance of characteristics such as gender becomes increasingly pronounced.

Whether families are made up largely of boys or girls also appears to have implications for other aspects of family life. Several studies have found that the presence of sons rather than daughters is related to a lower probability of divorce occurring and lower consideration of divorce as an alternative by mothers (see Mizell and Steelman 2000), a difference thought to result from fathers' increased participation in the family when sons are present. Conversely, mothers of daughters were found to have higher marital satisfaction compared to mothers of sons (Abbott and Brody 1985, 81), which is thought to result from the greater number of household responsibilities girls generally take on relative to boys.

Siblings can have an impact on other children in the family from the moment they come into the world. The initial importance of later-born siblings to their older siblings is largely due to the impact they have on the siblings' previous interaction patterns with parents. When children first become siblings through the birth of a younger brother or sister, many are initially excited and intrigued by the novelty of having a new baby in the home, but it can also be a time of anxiousness and despair as the older child must learn the realities of sharing the parents' love and attention with the new infant. Parents can do much to ensure that older children feel secure and to prepare the older children for the changes that will likely occur when the infant finally arrives. As younger siblings move from infancy to early childhood, older siblings' interactions with their younger brothers or sisters change as the younger children become better able to move about, communicate, and eventually engage in reciprocal play (Dunn and McGuire 1992).

As siblings move into middle and late childhood, several interesting characteristics emerge. First, the warmth and conflict present between siblings are not very strongly linked to one another, indicating that the presence of one is not necessarily indicative of the others' absence (Furman and Buhrmester 1985, 457). Many sibling relationships appear to evidence high levels of both warmth and conflict. During this period of development, sibling relationships persist in demonstrating asymmetry in both positive qualities such as nurturance and admiration and negative qualities such as power and dominance. Also during this period, same-sex sibling relationships have been found to have more warmth and closeness but less conflict compared to opposite-sex sibling pairs of similar age spacing.

As siblings move from late childhood to adolescence, there is increasing egalitarianism between them but also a corresponding decline in the level of intensity in the relationship. Duane Buhrmester and Wyndol Furman (1985, 1396) found that siblings spend less time together during this period of development but otherwise experience little change in intimacy and affection. Others have found a general reduction in both the positive and negative characteristics of siblings' relationships (Brody, Stoneman, and McCoy 1994, 278). One explanation for these changes accompanying the onset of adolescence may be siblings' greater need for individualism and autonomy and their expanded opportunities for establishing new friendships, both of which are likely to reduce the intensity of siblings' relationships with one another.

Parents have an enormous effect on children's sibling relationships. In particular, they are important to siblings' relationships through their own relationships with each of their children, their approach to parenting the siblings, and the extent to which they treat each sibling differently. Several studies have found that mothers' and fathers' relationships with and behavior toward their children are important to the quality of their children's sibling relationships. Mothers' and fathers' parenting behavior is also important to siblings' interactions with each other, but in different ways. In general, mothers' greatest impact on children's sibling relationships results from their use of discipline. When mothers use more intrusive and controlling (Volling and Belsky 1992, 1219) or more punitive disciplinary techniques (Brody, Stoneman, and MacKinnon 1986, 233), siblings appear to be more aggressive toward one another. In contrast, fathers' importance to siblings' relationships is based more on the emotional dimensions of their relationships with their children. When fathers exhibit more positive affection and facilitative behavior in their interactions with their children, children evidence

more positive and less conflicted behavior toward their brothers and sisters (Brody, Stoneman, and McCoy 1994, 283; Volling and Belsky 1992, 1219). Other evidence of the importance of parents' relationships with their children to the children's sibling relationships has to do with children's attachments to their parents. Young children and their infant siblings had more positive and less negative sibling interactions when they were identified as being more securely attached to their mothers, a status that is likely to be found when mothers are responsive to their children's needs (Teti, in press, 28).

Parents can also affect the quality of siblings' relationships when they treat their children differently. However, parents cannot help but respond to their children somewhat differently. Because siblings generally differ in their age and development and often either are born with different temperaments or develop different personalities, parents must adjust their interactions with their children in order to appropriately respond to children's individual needs and actions. These differences in parental behavior toward siblings are often accepted and even expected by siblings. For example, older brothers and sisters expect their younger siblings to receive more attention from their parents as a result of their lower ability to function independently and their resulting increased dependence on parents. When parents and siblings have been examined together, parents generally directed greater amounts of both positive and negative behavior toward later-born children than their older siblings (Brody, Stoneman, and McCoy 1992, 649; Stocker, Dunn, and Plomin 1989, 725). In general, when parents' behavior toward their children moves away from this normative level of differential treatment, more negative emotionality is evidenced between siblings. When parents treat siblings differently, it is likely to significantly affect how children come to view themselves.

What is difficult to determine is whether excessive differential treatment of siblings by parents is a cause of siblings' negativity toward one another or a response to excessive negativity already present between siblings. An important component in understanding parents' differential treatment of their children is the siblings' temperaments. When children have been identified as being more temperamentally difficult than their siblings, differences are likely to exist in their relationships with their parents and how their parents manage their behavior. In their attempt to understand the importance of temperament for children's sibling relationships, Gene Brody, Zo Stoneman, and Kelly McCoy (1992, 649) contend that both individual temperaments and the relative differences between siblings' temperaments must be considered. Parents' treatment of their children appears to have more to do with relative differences in siblings' temperaments than with the difficulty of older or younger siblings' temperaments considered individually.

Because of their frequent exposure to one another, siblings can influence one another for both good and ill. This is particularly true for older siblings, who are more likely to function as models, teachers, and helpers for their later-born siblings. Within sibling relationships, children and adolescents are likely to learn the art of compromise and negotiation. If a boy gets mad at a friend, he can go home or even stop being that person's friend. However, sibling relationships necessitate that children work through problems and come to some type of resolution. In addition, because of the caregiving opportunities that naturally arise within the sibling relationship, many children are also likely to develop an early sense of empathy, responsibility, and respect for others through interactions with their siblings (Dunn 1983). Siblings do not always set good examples for one another, however: older siblings' involvement with illicit drugs, alcohol use, deviant behavior, and sexual activity have all been found to predict younger siblings' engagement in similar behavior (Conger and Reuter 1996; Rowe and Gulley 1992; Rogers and Rowe 1988). In assessing implications of sibling relationships, one challenge is to distinguish siblings' effects on one another from what are merely results of being reared in the same family environment.

Siblings can also act as buffers against many of the challenges faced by children and adolescents growing up. For example, Tracey Kempton and her colleagues (1991, 437) found that having a sibling was helpful to adolescents' efforts to adjust to their parents' divorce. In a similar manner, Patricia East and Karen Rook (1992, 170) found that many children with low levels of support from school friends had relatively high levels of support within their favorite sibling relationships. They concluded that children who became isolated at school appear to develop greater dependency on their brothers and sisters.

Finally, because relationships with siblings are generally permanent, they may provide children and adolescents with a unique socializing context that may serve to enhance their nonfamilial relationships, particularly with peers. For many children and adolescents, friendships may be difficult to maintain. Sibling relationships provide an opportunity for children and adolescents to learn appropriate relationship behavior. How this learning process occurs, however, is still not completely clear. Clare Stocker and Judy Dunn (1991, 239) contend that greater positive behavior in friendships appears to result from lessons learned in negative sibling experiences. In contrast, McCoy, Brody, and Stoneman (in press, 406) propose that having a difficult temperament may be a major hindrance to establishing positive friendships. They contend that learning how to establish a positive sibling relationship may negate the negative challenges with friends that may result from having a more difficult temperament.

The relationships boys experience with brothers and sisters have historically been viewed as significant, but until recently little consideration was given to the quality of the relationship itself. Most research focused only on children's different experiences as a result of their different positions (i.e., first, middle, or last born) within the family. As researchers have begun to study the implications of the relationships between siblings, they have discovered a number of new factors important to children's individual development and to the sibling relationship itself. They have also come to better understand the benefits sibling relationships can provide children during difficult times. Because of their often intense nature, some of the strongest sibling relationships are not those devoid of conflict but often those in which both warmth and conflict are present (Stormshak, Bellanti, and Bierman 1996). As a result, sibling relationships provide an environment in which boys can explore important social skills such as caregiving, compromise, and negotiation but can also be a context in which to learn about competition, dominance, and aggression. Understanding the strengths and challenges inherent in sib-

ling relationships can provide families with a more harmonious home environment as well as better prepare children and adolescents for their relationships outside the home.

J. Kelly McCoy

References and further reading
Abbott, Douglas A., and Gene H. Brody. 1985. "The Relation of Child Age, Gender, and Number of Children to the Marital Adjustment of Wives." *Journal of Marriage and the Family* 47: 77–84.
Adler, Naomi A., and Joseph Schutz. 1996. "Sibling Incest Offenders." *Child Abuse and Neglect* 19: 811–819.
Brody, C. J., and L. C. Steelman. 1985. "Sibling Structure and Parental Sex-Typing of Children's Household Tasks." *Journal of Marriage and the Family* 47: 265–273.
Brody, Gene H., Zolinda Stoneman, and Carol MacKinnon. 1986 "Contributions of Maternal Child-rearing Practices and Interactional Contexts to Sibling Interactions." *Journal of Applied Developmental Psychology* 7: 225–236.
Brody, Gene H., Zolinda Stoneman, and J. Kelly McCoy. 1992. "Parental Differential Treatment of Siblings and Sibling Differences in Negative Emotionality." *Journal of Marriage and the Family* 54: 643–651.
———. 1994. "Contributions of Family Relationships and Child Temperaments to Longitudinal Variations in Sibling Relationship Quality and Sibling Relationship Styles." *Journal of Family Psychology* 8: 274–286.
Buhrmester, Duane, and Wyndol Furman. 1990. "Perceptions of Sibling Relationships during Middle Childhood and Adolescence." *Child Development* 61: 1387–1398.
Cloninger, Susan C. 2000. *Theories of Personality: Understanding Persons.* 3d ed. Upper Saddle River, NJ: Prentice-Hall.
Conger, Rand D., and Martha A. Reuter. 1996. "Siblings, Parents and Peers: A Longitudinal Study of Social Influences in Adolescent Risks for Alcohol Use and Abuse." Pp. 1–30 in *Sibling Relationships: Their Causes and*

Consequences. Edited by G. H. Brody. Norwood, NJ: Ablex.

Dunn, Judy. 1983. "Sibling Relationships in Early Childhood." *Child Development* 54: 787–811.

———. 1996. "Brothers and Sisters in Middle Childhood and Early Adolescence: Continuity and Change in Individual Differences." Pp. 31–46 in *Sibling Relationships: Their Causes and Consequences.* Edited by Gene H. Brody. Norwood, NJ: Ablex.

Dunn, Judy, and C. Kendrick. 1981. "Social Behavior of Young Siblings in the Family Context: Differences between Same-Sex and Different-Sex Dyads." *Child Development* 52: 1265–1273.

Dunn, Judy, and Shirley McGuire. 1992. "Sibling and Peer Relationships in Childhood." *Journal of Child Psychology and Psychiatry* 33: 67–105.

East, Patricia L., and Karen S. Rook. 1992. "Compensatory Patterns of Support among Children's Peer Relationships: A Test Using School Friends, Nonschool Friends, and Siblings." *Developmental Psychology* 28: 163–172.

Furman, Wyndol, and Duane Buhrmester. 1985. "Children's Perceptions of the Qualities of Sibling Relationships." *Child Development* 56: 448–461.

———. 1992. "Age and Sex Differences in Perceptions of Networks of Personal Relationships." *Child Development* 63: 103–115.

Gallo, Agatha M., and Kathleen A. Knafl. 1993. "The Effects of Mental Retardation, Disability, and Illness on Sibling Relationships: Research Issues and Challenges." Pp. 215–234 in *Siblings of Children with Chronic Illnesses: A Categorical and Noncategorical Look at Selected Literature.* Edited by Zolinda Stoneman and Phyllis Waldman Burman. Baltimore: Paul H. Brookes Publishing.

Handel, Gerald. 1985. "Central Issues in the Construction of Sibling Relationships." Pp. 493–523 in *The Psychosocial Interior of the Family.* Edited by Gerald Handel. New York: Aldine de Gruyter.

Kempton, Tracey, Lisa Armistead, Michelle Wierson, and Rex Forehand. 1991. "Presence of a Sibling as a Potential Buffer Following Parental Divorce: An Examination of Young Adolescents." *Journal of Clinical Child Psychology* 20: 434–438.

Mandleco, Barbara L., Susanne F. Olsen, Clyde C. Robinson, Elaine S. Marshall, and Mary K. McNeilly-Choque. 1998. "Social Skills and Peer Relationships of Siblings of Children with Disabilities." Pp. 106–120 in *Children's Peer Relations.* Edited by P. T. Slee and K. Rigby. New York: Routledge.

McCoy, J. Kelly, Gene H. Brody, and Zolinda Stoneman. In press. "Temperament and the Quality of Youths' Best Friendships: Do Sibling and Parent-Child Relationships Make a Difference?"

Mizell, C. Andre, and Lala C. Steelman. 2000. "All My Children: The Consequences of Sibling Group Characteristics on the Marital Happiness of Young Mothers." *Journal of Family Issues* 21: 858–887.

Pepler, Deborah J., Rona Abramovitch, and Carl Corter. 1981. "Sibling Interaction in the Home: A Longitudinal Study." *Child Development* 52: 1344–1347.

Rodgers, Joseph L., H. Harrington Cleveland, Edwin van den Oord, and David C. Rowe. 2000. "Resolving the Debate over Birth Order, Family Size, and Intelligence." *American Psychologist* 55: 599–612.

Rogers, Joseph L., and David C. Rowe. 1988. "Influence of Siblings on Adolescent Sexual Behavior." *Developmental Psychology* 24: 722–728.

Rowe, David C., and Bill L. Gulley. 1992. "Sibling Effects on Substance Use and Delinquency." *Criminology* 30: 217–233.

Stocker, Clare, and Judy Dunn. 1991. "Sibling Relationships in Childhood: Links with Friendships and Peer Relationships." *British Journal of Developmental Psychology* 8: 227–244.

Stocker, Clare, Judy Dunn, and Robert Plomin. 1989. "Sibling Relationships: Links with Child Temperament, Maternal Behavior, and Family Structure." *Child Development* 60: 715–727.

Stoneman, Zolinda, Gene H. Brody, and Carol MacKinnon. 1986. "Same-sex and Cross-sex Siblings: Activity Choices, Roles, Behavior, and Gender Stereotypes." *Sex Roles* 15: 495–511.

Stormshak, Elizabeth A., Christina J. Bellanti, and Karen L. Bierman. 1996.

"The Quality of Sibling Relationships and the Development of Social Competence and Behavioral Control in Aggressive Children." *Developmental Psychology* 32: 79–89.

Teti, Douglas M. In press. "Sibling Relationships." In *Interiors: Retrospect and Prospect in the Psychological Study of Families.* Edited by J. McHale and W. Grolnick. Mahwah, NJ: Erlbaum.

Volling, B. L., and Jay Belsky. 1992. "The Contribution of Mother-Child and Father-Child Relationships to the Quality of Sibling Interaction: A Longitudinal Study." *Child Development* 63: 1209–1222.

Wagner, Mazie E., Herman J. P. Schubert, and Daniel S. P. Schubert. 1979. "Sibship-Constellation Effects on Psychological Development, Creativity, and Health." *Advances in Child Development and Behavior* 14: 57–148.

Skateboarding

Skateboarding is not just a sport; it is a mind-set, an attitude, an industry, and a cultural phenomenon. Many believe that the skateboard was invented by people in the surfing business approximately forty years ago. Naturally, surfers want to surf, even when weather conditions are poor. Until the 1950s, surfing was exclusively a male sport, and many boys wanted to find an alternative to surfing waves when the ocean was flat. Some give credit to Bill Richards, who opened a California surf shop in 1962. Bill and his son Mark made a deal with the Chicago Roller Skate Company to produce sets of skate wheels. These were mounted to square wooden boards, and the new craze of "sidewalk surfing" was born. When clay wheels entered the picture, this new boys' sport really started to roll. In 1965, the first National Skateboard Championships aired on ABC's *Wide World of Sports,* and skateboarding was even featured on the cover of *Life* magazine that same year. These days,

skateboarding is all about boys performing urban acrobatics and radical moves like "riding the rails," "pulling ollies," and "50-50 grinds." Skateboarders have created their own subculture that includes a unique style of dress, a "thrasher" mind-set, and a unique vocabulary. According to the latest statistics, skateboarding is the sixth largest participatory sport in the United States, with more than 6 million "terra surfers" in the country. And true to its birthplace, almost half of them live in California.

Skateboarding has a rich history filled with innovation and creativity. The first types of skateboards were actually more like scooters, which date back to the early 1900s. Some say the very first skateboard was simply a scooter with the push bar broken off. Over the next fifty years, boys changed the look of the scooter and took off the milk crate; they dismantled roller skates and nailed them onto two-by-four planks of wood. By the late 1950s, surfing was becoming increasingly popular, and boys began to think of cruising on these pieces of plywood as "sidewalk surfing." The first commercially made skateboards hit the marketplace in 1959.

The birth of the commercial skateboard industry brought new and exciting advancements in both the board and in the wheels used. Clay wheels made the ride much smoother and provided improved traction over steel wheels, so new tricks became possible. In the early 1960s companies such as Makaha and Hobie sold more than 50 million boards within a three-year period. Skateboarding had become a wildly popular sport for boys almost overnight. In 1962, the first retail skateboard shop opened its doors on October 6 in North Hollywood, California. The shop was called Val Surf and was primarily a surf shop, but owner Bill Richards and his two sons, Mark, age fifteen, and Kurt, age eighteen, began to realize that there might be a real market for the skateboard. Val Surf joined up with surfboard maker Hobie Alter, whose name was synonymous with surf culture, and together they designed a line of skateboards. Hobie was the first to come out with a pressure-molded fiberglass skateboard. These boards became popular with boys very quickly.

Then, suddenly, skateboarding entered its first slump when the fad almost completely died out in the fall of 1965. ABC's Wide World of Sports covered the first national skateboarding championships, held at La Palma Stadium in Anaheim, California, in 1965. They were also covered by CBS and NBC. Skateboarding was then featured on the cover of *Life* magazine on May 14, 1965, and inside, the skateboard was described as an exhilarating and dangerous joyriding device similar to a hot-rod car. The backlash from all the hyped-up media coverage was immediate. The American Medical Association declared that skateboards were the newest medical menace. A group of safety experts announced that skateboarding was unsafe, urged stores not to sell skateboards, and advised parents not to buy them for their sons. Skateboarding would experience a series of peaks and valleys over the next forty years, with a major slump about every ten years. That first slump was due in part to the reckless riding of skateboarders themselves, but it was also caused by an inferior product. Skateboard manufacturers were in a hurry to get their first boards out on the market, so they had done very little research, and only minimal effort was put into designing a safe skateboard. Manufacturers simply replaced the squeaky steel roller-skate

Teenager skateboarding on a ramp, 1996 (Duomo/Corbis)

wheels with a quieter, smoother clay wheel and made a few refinements to the devices that held the wheels onto the board (called "trucks"). However, clay wheels still did not grip concrete roads very well, and boys of all ages across the nation were taking some very nasty falls. Cities started to ban skateboards in response to safety and health concerns, especially after a few boys were fatally injured. Skateboarding virtually disappeared from public view.

The first generation of skateboarders had established the foundation of techniques, tricks, and style, even though these boys and young men were severely limited by poor equipment. In 1969,

Richard Stevenson of Los Angeles, California, received a patent for a skateboard with a tail. He designed this "kicktail" for technical reasons. He added an upward curve at the back of the skateboard in order to make the board more maneuverable, more like a real surfboard. This innovation earned him the title of "father of the skateboard." Two years later a man named Frank Nasworthy reinvented the wheel—he actually designed a new polyurethane wheel for roller skates, but it worked beautifully on skateboards as well.

By 1973 skateboarding was fully revived, and sidewalk surfers were riding the "second wave" on a board with a new shape and urethane wheels. The urethane wheel would completely revolutionize the sport; it provided much better traction and speed and allowed skateboard enthusiasts to develop new tricks and much more difficult maneuvers. Skateboards increased in width from 6–7 inches to more than 9 inches, which improved stability on vertical surfaces. Dozens of board manufacturers were now putting graphics on the undersides of their boards. Skateboarding stickers were also wildly popular with boys.

Vertical skating in empty swimming pools would soon become a mainstay of the sport, along with acrobatics in cylindrical pipes. *SkateBoarder* magazine was back on the rack, and the sport was on a roll once again. In 1976, the first modern outdoor skateboard parks were built in Florida and in California, followed by hundreds of other parks all over the United States. The "tamer" horizontal and slalom styles of skateboarding were replaced with the more popular vertical, aerial, and acrobatic maneuvers.

Although a number of key skateboard tricks have been developed over the years, the "ollie" has dominated skateboarding for the past twenty years. Alan Gelfand, nicknamed "Ollie," developed the maneuver in Florida in the late 1970s. A year after he started skateboarding at the age of twelve, he decided to experiment with lip slides. He realized he could achieve a small amount of "air" if he popped his board while doing the lip slide maneuver. The Ollie "pop" finally became the "ollie" aerial that is now infamous. This move involves tapping the tail of the board down while jumping in the air and kicking the front foot forward. Proper execution results in the board jumping in the air with the skater; the board should stay directly under the skater's feet for a proper landing. This trick allowed a completely new type of skateboarding to evolve called "street skating." When street skating, boys perform tricks on, over, or against obstacles in and near streets. The ollie became the fundamental trick of modern-day skateboarding and allowed boys to fly over stairs, benches, rails, low walls, and other objects. Many believe that the ollie is the single greatest maneuver ever invented. Some estimate that the ollie became the foundation or "building block" for 80 percent of the street tricks and about 60 percent of the vertical tricks performed by boys.

In just two years during the late 1970s, more than 40 million skateboards were purchased in the United States. More than 300 parks designed exclusively for skateboarding opened across the country, and boys also skated in empty swimming pools, on sloping concrete surfaces, or any place they could find. However, skating's old enemy—safety—was once again a major concern. Insurance became so expensive that many skateboard park owners were forced to shut down, and most parks were bulldozed. By the end of 1980 skateboarding had died its second death, and many boys abandoned the sport altogether.

By 1983, legal issues were being dealt with in a serious and innovative manner, and skate parks were being revived. In October 1984, the Bones Brigade video premiered. Produced by the Powell Peralta skateboard corporation, it would become one of the main factors in revitalizing skateboarding. The video featured Lance Mountain as the official host traveling to different skate locations to check out the action. Members of the Bones Brigade included such key skaters as Ray "Bones" Rodriguez, Steve Caballero, Alan "Ollie," Gelfand, and Mike McGill. These young men had a unique combination of talent, skill, style, grace, and charisma. They were featured riding in backyard ramps, pools, skate parks, and down steep hills at exhilarating speeds. The video would go on to sell some 30,000 copies, and skateboarding was soon riding its "third wave." Vertical (or "vert") riding took off in 1984, and launch ramps became popular. Toward the end of the 1980s, street skating was in vogue. With a focus on technical tricks and "pulling ollies," skateboarding took on a whole new attitude. During this era, such magazines as *Thrasher* and *Poweredge* began publication. Powell Peralta went on to produce two other videos and was a dominant influence in lifting skateboarding to even higher altitudes as a tremendously popular boys' sport. By 1991, a worldwide recession hit, and the skateboard industry was not spared. Manufacturers experienced huge financial losses. But as before, dedicated boys and young men would help the sport to survive and would reinvent skateboarding once again.

Skateboarding is currently riding its "fourth wave." Skateboarders wear XX-large shirts, and shorts fall well below the knee. The street sport of skateboarding has become a subculture for boys, complete with cult heroes and legends. The growth of cable and satellite television and computers and the Internet has led to a greater worldwide awareness of skateboarding. A number of competitive skateboarding events in the 1990s provided exposure for the sport. In 1991, the National Skateboarding Association, which had been founded ten years earlier in 1981, held competitions in France, Germany, Spain, and the United States. In 1995 the World Cup Skateboarding organization became the leading organizer of skateboarding contests. The same year, ESPN 2 "Extreme Games" brought skateboarding into living rooms across the country, and it was selected as a featured sport in the 1996 Olympics opening ceremonies. It became quite common to see boys participating in skateboarding competitions on television, although the sport had to share the limelight with roller blading and snowboarding events. Apparently, the popularity of skateboarding was further enhanced by the development of snowboards, which were closely associated with skateboards; many boys participated in both sports. At the end of the 1990s, the focus of many skateboarders was still street style, and the industry included numerous manufacturers, marketers, and sponsors. Professional skaters often went on to develop their own product lines and manage their own companies.

It appears that skateboarding may be riding a "permanent wave" because of the enthusiasm of dedicated skaters who keep the sport alive. Because of the efforts of the International Association of Skateboard Companies, more parks are scheduled for construction in other states in the first few years of the next millennium. It is even possible to visit one of three skateboard museums: Skatopia, located in Rutland, Ohio; the Huntington Beach International Skate and Surf Museum, located in Huntington Beach, California; and the Skatelab Museum, located in Simi Valley, California (www.skatelab.com). The museum boasts a very large collection of skateboards, skateboard products, and memorabilia. The display also includes scooters from the 1930s, the precursor to the modern skateboard.

Skateboarding is a sport worthy of serious attention, and it has brought countless hours of fun and exhilaration to the boys who skate and to spectators, as well. Pure and simple, skateboarding is the positive release of explosive energy; it is pure fun, excitement, and exhilaration, sometimes scary, sometimes mellow, and sometimes gnarly. It is spontaneous art, it is choreographed discipline. It is freedom, it is self-expression. It is here to stay.

Robin D. Mittelstaedt

References and further reading
Brooke, Michael. 1999. *The Concrete Wave: The History of Skateboarding.* Toronto, Ont.: Warwick.
Cassorla, Albert. 1976. *The Skateboarder's Bible.* Philadelphia: Running Press.
Davidson, Ben. 1976. *The Skateboard Book.* New York: Grosset and Dunlap.
Dixon, Pahl, and Peter Dixon. 1977. *Hot Skateboarding.* New York: Warner Books.
Weir, La Vada. 1977. *Skateboards and Skateboarding.* New York: Pocket Books.

Skiing

Immigrants from the Scandinavian countries and Finland brought skiing to the United States in the mid-nineteenth century, but boys' skiing should be seen in the wider context of winter recreation, including sledding and snowshoeing. Until the 1940s, boys who skied lived chiefly in New England, the upper Midwest, the Rocky Mountains, or Sierra Nevada. From the 1850s to the early 1900s, skiing was primarily utilitarian, a way of getting to school or work when the snow was deep. A few skiing clubs in California sponsored downhill races in the 1850s, and skiers in the Midwest specialized in ski jumping. The renown of the Norwegian explorer Fridtjof Nansen, who crossed Greenland on skis in 1888 and wrote a popular book about it, is credited with inspiring ski clubs throughout northern Europe, Canada, and the United States that promoted good health, fellowship, and amateur competition. At about the same time, English sportsmen were discovering the challenge of downhill skiing in the Alps and introducing it to Americans in New England. By 1905 when the National Ski Association (NSA) was founded to regulate and promote the sport in the United States, the stage was set for the mass marketing of what had been an immigrant pastime.

Skiing grew slowly but steadily in the years between 1900 and 1945. Two distinct types of skiing emerged, Nordic (cross-country) and Alpine (downhill and slalom), but in the years before mechanical lifts, all skiing involved climbing uphill. Ski clubs sprang up around the country, and many colleges followed Dartmouth College's lead in holding winter carnivals and sponsoring ski races. When the first Olympic winter games were held in Chamonix, France, in 1924, the U.S. team was sponsored by the Minneapolis Ski Club and the NSA, and all but one member was a Scandinavian immigrant. The only competitions were

Nordic style, jumping, and cross-country, but that was about to change. British sportsman Arnold Lunn had organized the first slalom race in 1922, and in 1925 a slalom race was held as part of the Dartmouth winter carnival. It was won by Charlie Proctor, the first native-born American to become a skiing superstar.

Proctor was born in 1906 and grew up in Hanover, New Hampshire, where his father taught physics at Dartmouth College. He got his first pair of skis at the age of four, and by age eleven he was winning the boys' ski jump competitions. He also competed in cross-country races, representing the United States in both events in the 1928 Olympics at St. Moritz, Switzerland. He later developed ski resorts and ski runs from New England to Sun Valley, Idaho, established ski schools, and designed and manufactured ski equipment. Proctor was hardly alone. All across the country boys were taking up skiing, competing in races, and soon finding ways to make money as ski instructors or ski resort developers. Wayne Poulsen, who helped popularize Squaw Valley, site of the 1960 Winter Olympics, made his first pair of skis at age eleven in 1926. In 1932 he took third place in the junior division of the National Ski Jumping Championships in Tahoe City, California. Proctor and Poulsen were part of the new generation that was helping to create the basis for the post–World War II boom in recreational skiing. Their enthusiasm and the glamour associated with winning ski jumps and races were reflected in illustrated articles in magazines for boys such as *The Youth's Companion* and *Boys' Companion: The Magazine for Boy Building*. In January 1913, Frank Merriwell, the athletic hero of Gilbert Patten's (Burt L. Standish's) popular novels for boys, appeared in a ski-

A little boy skiing in Colorado, 2000 (Bob Winsett/Corbis)

ing adventure published in *New Tip Top Weekly*.

The mechanization of skiing was also important to its increase in popularity. In the early 1930s, railroads in New England began to run special trains for skiers from Boston and other cities to Maine, Vermont, and New Hampshire ski hotels. In 1936 the first European-style luxury ski resort opened in Sun Valley, Idaho, its clientele arriving exclusively on the Union Pacific Railroad. Moreover, Sun Valley had the world's first chairlift to take skiers to the top of a mountain. The first rope tows had been built in Switzerland, Canada, and the United States a few years earlier. By the late 1930s, the number of American skiers was increasing rapidly, but the entry of the United States into World War II in 1941 put restrictions on recreational travel and slowed the expansion of skiing for a few years. By the 1950s, however, skiing had emerged as one of the most popular leisure activities, and families began making regular winter trips to new or expanded ski resorts such as Aspen, Colorado; Sugarloaf, Maine; and Taos, New Mexico. Since the 1950s, skiing became a recognizable lifestyle with an emphasis on luxurious living, high-tech gear, and designer clothing, a far cry from a boy's homemade hickory or pine boards with leather straps.

Why and how skiing became the symbol and substance of late-twentieth-century opulence is a complex and often disheartening story, partially told in Annie Gilbert Coleman's insightful essay, "The Unbearable Whiteness of Skiing." Through their Alpine-style architecture and advertising, many American ski resorts promote a myth of European aristocratic living and racial purity. As ski areas have become increasingly dependent on technology, from mechanical lifts rising through deforested mountainsides, to machine-made snow, to mechanical snow grooming, to chemical treatments to preserve snow on trails and remove it from parking lots, some skiers have returned to simpler, more environmentally friendly styles of skiing. Others, as Coleman points out, have made efforts to introduce racial and ethnic minority children to the fun of skiing. Although few boys today experience the pleasure of setting off from their family's farm on homemade skis, many boys still complete the cycle of boyhood from child to youth by progressing from one winter sport to another. Considering skiing in the context of other winter activities helps place it in boy culture.

Although the ski industry claims that a child who can walk can ski, most boys experience snow first on sleds, and sledding preceded skiing as a boy's winter activity in the nineteenth century. The appeal of sledding, or "coasting" as it was once called, is the risk involved in lying prone, face forward in the style called "belly-bump" as the sled careens down a steep hill. An added thrill comes from endangering passersby. Most of the paintings of boys sledding in the 1840s and 1850s show sledders terrifying pedestrians and tumbling into snow. Emily Dickinson captured such moments perfectly:

> Glass was the Street—in tinsel Peril
> Tree and Traveller stood—
> Filled was the Air with merry venture
> Hearty with Boys the Road—
> Shot the lithe Sleds like shod vibrations
> Emphasized and gone
> It is the Past's supreme italic
> Makes this Present mean—
> (Johnson 1970, 630)

Homemade sleds were often little more than boards the width of a child with barrel-stave runners nailed to each side, yet when the first manufactured sleds appeared in the 1840s they were frequently considered inferior. One reason is the eternal struggle between boys and adults over safety. In an 1859 patent application for a sled, B. P. Crandall claimed that medical authorities condemned the practice of lying on the stomach while sledding, so he designed a sled that prevented it. However, the design was not popular. Toboggans were favored in some regions, especially after the success of toboggan rides at the Montreal Winter Carnival in 1883, but the invention of the "Flexible Flyer" sled by Samuel Allen in 1889 made the model synonymous with sledding and became the favorite of boys throughout the country. Allen's sled could be steered using either feet or hands, facilitating both the style approved by adults and the boys' own choice. Moreover, the Flexible Flyer was painted with an American eagle holding arrows in both talons, continuing the martial spirit of mid-nineteenth-century boys who named their sleds "General Grant," "Flying Cloud," and "Young America" and painted them with pictures of Indians, horses, and flags.

The 1950s saw the introduction of metal and plastic saucers, popular with some *because* they were difficult to steer. Many different styles of plastic sleds have been on the market since the 1970s, most of them designed for small children sledding in soft snow. For speed on packed, icy slopes, the Flexible Flyer still rules. Regional variations in over-the-snow transport may still be found. In Minnesota, boys made "bumpers" from apple barrel staves cleated together at both ends with a rope attached to the front cleat. The rider stood sidewise with a boot braced against each cleat, holding the rope in one hand and a pole for pushing, balancing, and steering in the other. In French Canada, boys made and rode *pite* or *tapeculs*, a kind of one-ski scooter.

Canadian boys in general preferred snowshoeing, and boys in the United States used snowshoes more than skis until the early twentieth century. Skis were called "Norwegian snowshoes" for many years after their introduction. In his 1882 handicraft guide *The American Boy's Handy Book*, Daniel Beard instructed boys on how to build a toboggan and skis, and *The Young Folks' Cyclopedia of Games and Sports* (1890) devoted a separate entry to snowshoes but placed skis in a paragraph in skating. Rivalries between boys on snowshoes and boys on skis continued well into the twentieth century. Henry Ives Baldwin, later chief forester of New Hampshire, began skiing in 1908 and used his single pole with a hook on one end to catch rides behind delivery wagons. He was especially proud of being able to defeat boys on snowshoes in cross-country races. In his boys' adventure novel, *Ski Patrol*, the avalanche expert Montgomery Atwater describes a thrilling 40-mile chase and capture of a game poacher on snowshoes by a boy on skis.

Sleds, skis, and snowshoes appear together in the pages of toy and sporting goods catalogs from the 1920s on. Shoppers at FAO Schwarz in 1952 had a choice of pine or maple ski sets in four lengths from 4 to 6 feet, with toe clamp or cable binding. Seven years later, parents could buy "sidewalk" skis in even shorter lengths for children as young as two. According to ski industry statistics, there was a significant increase in the number of skiers under eighteen years of age in the 1960s. Boys' skiing had expanded beyond the northern states as winter vacations allowed families to visit ski areas regularly. As skiing developed among boys, new styles emerged. Freestyle skiing, involving aerial acrobatics off small jumps, began attracting boys in the 1950s, and by 1988 it was an event in the Winter Olympics. By that time, however, boys had been lured away from skiing by snowboarding. Invented in 1965, the snowboard attracted boys already familiar with surfboards and skateboards. The broad single plank allowed the skillful to perform astonishing maneuvers and acrobatics on ski slopes. National competitions began in 1980, and snowboarding made its Olympic debut at Nagano, Japan, in 1998. Snowboarders increasingly annoy skiers at resorts with their apparent recklessness, disregard of fashion, and colorful slang. Snowboarding seems to have restored boy culture to the ski slopes.

Bernard Mergen

References and further reading
Allen, E. John B. 1993. *From Skisport to Skiing: One Hundred Years of American Sport, 1849–1940.* Amherst: University of Massachusetts Press.
Atwater, Montgomery M. 1943. *Ski Patrol.* New York: Random House.
Baldwin, Henry Ives. 1989. *The Skiing Life.* Concord, NH: Evans Printing.
Coleman, Annie Gilbert. 1996. "The Unbearable Whiteness of Skiing." *Pacific Historical Review* 65 (November): 583–614.
Johnson, Thomas H., ed. 1970. *The Complete Poems of Emily Dickinson.* London: Faber and Faber.
Mergen, Bernard. 1997. *Snow in America.* Washington, DC: Smithsonian Institution Press.
Skiing Heritage: Journal of the International Skiing History Association. 1989– . Quarterly. 499 Town Hill Road, New Hartford, CT 06057.

Slave Trade

In the nineteenth-century United States, the domestic slave trade was a constant presence in nearly every enslaved boy's life. Millions of young men found themselves being torn from their families and friends against their will or having their parents or siblings taken from them by this process. The trauma of such sales could be devastating, and many boys vividly remembered decades later the effect that it had upon their lives. The majority of enslaved boys probably never stood upon an auction block, nor were they marched overland to the deep South in a manacled slave coffle. Still, the threat of sale was pervasive, and even those who did not become personally involved in the slave trade never knew for sure whether or not they would be sold one day and forcibly taken away from the ones they loved.

Although the buying and selling of human beings had always been a part of American society, the nature of this traffic changed over time. In the colonial period, most slaves sold in British North America were individuals imported from Africa or the West Indies. Following the American Revolution, however, this changed, especially after the closing of the African trade in 1808. After that date, all Americans who wanted to purchase slaves would have to buy them from among the existing slave population within the United States. The invention of the cotton gin in the 1790s also led to an increased demand for slaves as white southerners began expanding into the old Southwest to grow that lucrative crop. The result was the emergence of an indigenous, or domestic, slave trade by the early nineteenth century that transported thousands of enslaved men and women from the upper South (which had a supposed surplus of slaves) to the lower South (where slaves were in great demand) each year. It has been estimated that between 1790 and 1860, Americans transported more than 1 million African American slaves from the upper South to the lower South; approximately two-thirds of these slaves arrived there as a result of sale. Moreover, twice as many individuals were sold locally (Deyle 1995). Therefore, by the nineteenth century, this domestic slave trade had certainly become a most common form of commerce in the Old South.

Enslaved boys made up a large part of this domestic slave trade. For one thing, a large percentage of the nineteenth-cen-

Slave families lived with the threat of separation through sale. South Carolina plantation, nineteenth century. (Library of Congress)

tury American slave population were children. More than two-fifths of antebellum slaves were younger than age fifteen, and one-third were younger than age ten (Schwartz 2000). Also, even though enslaved girls were often sold at an earlier age than boys because girls tended to mature sooner, boys sold at somewhat higher prices and were frequently in greater demand because of their labor potential. It is impossible to know exactly how many enslaved boys were actually sold, but one recent study (Tadman 1989, 45) claims that between 1820 and 1860 at least 10 percent of all teenagers in the upper South became commodities in the interregional trade, and more than twice that many were sold locally. It is quite likely that similar rates

of sale, if not even higher, occurred throughout the South.

Most males sold into the interregional slave trade were between the ages of fifteen and twenty-five, but boys much younger could always be found. This proved especially true during times of economic prosperity when demand for slaves was greater. In general, though, extremely young children were usually sold with their mothers. They were easier to sell that way, and most buyers did not want to raise a very young child for several years before getting a positive return on their investment. Still, it was not unusual for boys eight years old or even younger to find themselves sold into the slave trade. In part to counter complaints against such practices from northerners, a few southern states passed laws prohibiting the sale of children under the age of ten without their mothers. Unfortunately, these laws were easily skirted and often not enforced. Moreover, they did nothing to stop the even greater number of sales to owners within the same state.

Therefore, some very young enslaved boys found themselves being sold frequently and for a variety of reasons. Louis Hughes was born in 1832 and encountered his first sale at the age of six. Within the next six years he would be sold three more times to different owners within his native state of Virginia before being placed on an auction block in Richmond and sold to a planter from Mississippi at the age of twelve. Unlike many adult slaves who were sometimes sold as punishment for a supposed infraction, most enslaved boys were usually sold because their owner needed cash. Ironically, in some cases enslaved black children were sold to help finance the education of their owner's privileged white children or help in other ways to support their owner's lavish lifestyle. In Georgia, the enslaved boy John Brown was sold at the age of ten to help finance the construction costs of a new plantation house for his owner (Davis 1993).

Another frequent reason for the sale of enslaved boys was legal action to settle the debts of their owners. One recent study in South Carolina found that roughly half of all the slave sales in that state between 1820 and 1860 were the result of some form of court action. One of the most common types of sale based upon legal action was those to settle estates. Nothing worried enslaved Americans more than the death of their owners, since that often meant that sales would occur to divide up and settle their estates. As the former slave Frederick Doug

lass noted, the death of an owner was a time of "high excitement and distressing anxiety" for most American slaves. Sometimes the slaves were split up among their former owner's descendants, but it was also common to sell the slaves individually at public auction to bring the biggest return for the estate. Therefore, at such times it was not unusual for boys as young as four or five to be sold away from their family and friends for the rest of their lives.

Naturally, most enslaved boys and their families tried to resist such sales as best they could. In order to protect her children from being sold, Moses Grandy's mother used to hide him and his brothers and sisters in the woods in North Carolina until she got a promise from her owner that he would not sell them. The former slave Henry Watson also remembered how whenever a strange white man arrived on his plantation in Virginia, he and the other slave children would run and "hide ourselves until the man had gone" (Webber 1978, 187). Parents also frequently put up a fight and protested vehemently when owners attempted to take their children away from them through sale. In fact, such scenes were so common that many owners resorted to deceptive tactics when selling children, such as carrying out the transaction when the parents were absent or claiming they were just hiring out the boy for a short time period when they were actually selling him for life.

For their part, enslaved boys also often tried to resist a sale. One former Virginia slave remembered how "young'uns fout and kick lak crazy folks" when they were placed on the auction block, while others used other ploys to negotiate a sale. At the age of nine, Ambrose Headen was forced to leave his family in North Carolina, walk 14 miles to a slave market, and place himself upon an auction block. After three hours of physical inspection and intense bidding, he was sold to a local planter who was known for his cruelty. Headen began crying uncontrollably until the planter, at the urging of others, resold the young boy to another buyer, just as he had hoped (Schwartz 2000, 171; Davis 1993, 673).

Although some individuals, such as Headen, were able to alter a sale to their liking or even negate an undesirable one by running away or causing a scene, for most, there was little that could be done to prevent this ever-present reality of life for enslaved Americans. After the humiliation of the auction block, those boys sold in the interregional trade were usually manacled to other slaves in a long coffle and forced to march overland to their destination in the deep South. For most slaves from the upper South, such a fate was often considered worse than death because of the region's frontier conditions, subtropical climate, rampant diseases, and extreme working conditions. And, of course, for young boys it meant being thrown into a totally alien environment and forced to survive without the comforts and resources of their family and friends.

Naturally, such an event had a tremendous impact upon the boys who found themselves caught up in it, and it was something that most of them remembered for the rest of their lives. In fact, for many, it was the moment when they first came to realize that they were slaves and that they and their families could be treated differently from the white people around them. After being sold at the age of four, the Maryland slave Charles Ball had to watch as his new owner whipped his mother when she tried to plead with

the man not to take her young child away. More than fifty years later Ball admitted that "the terrors of the scene return with painful vividness upon my memory" (Ball 1969, 18). For most enslaved boys, especially those sold into the interregional trade, sale meant that they would almost certainly never see their families or friends again, and in many respects, it brought the same type of finality as death. Yet most continued to remember their families and homes, if only in their dreams. After being sold from his family in Virginia, Lewis Clarke noted how his "thoughts continually by day and my dreams by night were of mother and home." And the former South Carolina slave Caleb Craig later in life acknowledged that he still had "visions and dreams" of his mother "in my sleep, sometime yet" (Webber 1978, 113; Jones 1990, 43).

Although the majority of enslaved boys never experienced the trauma of sale personally, the slave trade still had a constant effect upon their lives. For one thing, even if they were never sold themselves, it is quite likely that most enslaved boys would have had other family members or friends sold away from them, and it is hard to overemphasize the impact that having a parent sold away could have upon a young boy's life.

In addition, most enslaved boys at one time or another witnessed the slave trade and heard stories about its operations and effects. For those living in southern cities or near county courthouses, slave auctions were common, and both black and white southerners were present at their proceedings. Other boys lived near country roads and frequently observed the many slave coffles as they trudged their victims, including many children, toward the slave markets of the deep

South. One former slave from Texas, Calvin Moye, was constantly in fear of the many slave traders who passed by his place: "Dey was lots of dem speculators coming by de road in front of de plantation, and ever' time I see dem coming, cold chills run over me till I see dem go on by our lane" (Reinier 1996, 173).

Finally, the slave quarters were always full of tales of child snatching and kidnappers enticing little children into their wagons with trinkets and food. Although such stories were often based more on suspicion than on reality, cases of slave kidnapping were common enough to give credence to these fears. These stories exacerbated the feelings of fear already present within many enslaved families and also helped to keep numerous young boys from wandering too far away from home. Therefore, although it is true that most small children were probably not sold away from their parents, fears of such an event still influenced most young boys, and the slave trade had other ways of playing a powerful role in their lives.

Steven Deyle

See also African American Boys; Slavery

References and further reading
Ball, Charles. 1969. *Slavery in the United States.* 1837. Reprint, New York: Negro Universities Press.
Davis, Jack E. 1993. "Changing Places: Slave Movement in the South." *The Historian* 55 (Summer): 657–676.
Deyle, Steven. 1995. "The Domestic Slave Trade in America." Ph.D. diss., Columbia University.
Johnson, Walter. 1999. *Soul by Soul: Life inside the Antebellum Slave Market.* Cambridge, MA: Harvard University Press.
Jones, Norrece T., Jr. 1990. *Born a Child of Freedom, Yet a Slave: Mechanisms of Control and Strategies of Resistance in Antebellum South Carolina.* Hanover, NH: University Press of New England.
King, Wilma. 1995. *Stolen Childhood: Slave Youth in Nineteenth-Century America.* Bloomington: Indiana University Press.
Reinier, Jacqueline S. 1996. *From Virtue to Character: American Childhood, 1775–1850.* New York: Twayne Publishers.
Schwartz, Marie Jenkins. 2000. *Born in Bondage: Growing Up Enslaved in the Antebellum South.* Cambridge, MA: Harvard University Press.
Tadman, Michael. 1989. *Speculators and Slaves: Masters, Traders, and Slaves in the Old South.* Madison: University of Wisconsin Press.
Webber, Thomas L. 1978. *Deep Like the Rivers: Education in the Slave Quarter Community, 1831–1865.* New York: W. W. Norton.

Slavery

Among slaves in the American colonies, boys outnumbered girls. Although only a small number of Africans were brought to the mainland colonies in the early seventeenth century, the Atlantic slave trade increased slightly in the 1680s and greatly after 1700. Planters preferred to buy young male slaves with a lifetime of labor ahead of them. Although 15 to 20 percent of imported slaves were under the age of twelve, slave cargoes considered the most desirable were two-thirds "men-boys" (ages fourteen to eighteen) and one-third "women-girls" (ages thirteen to sixteen). As a result, when the slave trade was at its height, enslaved males in some localities numbered 180 for every 100 females. After being sold to planters at the port of Charleston, South Carolina, or at riverside wharves or county courthouses in Maryland and Virginia, as many as one-fourth of the imported slaves died during the first year, mostly from respiratory diseases. Yet these unhealthy conditions improved, and the skewed sex ratio balanced out by

A slave family on Smith's Plantation, Beaufort, South Carolina, mid-nineteenth century (Library of Congress)

the 1730s, when a native-born population came of age. By the mid-eighteenth century, the enslaved population was growing through natural increase, an unprecedented event for new world slavery. As population growth continued in the nineteenth century throughout the southern states, an increasingly large proportion of the enslaved were children. By 1860, when the U.S. census counted almost 4 million slaves, 56 percent were under the age of twenty (King 1995, xvii).

On plantations in the Tidewater area of the Chesapeake Bay and the Low Coun-

try of the Carolinas, children grew up in relatively stable slave communities. In the Chesapeake area, where tobacco plantations were smaller and men were forced to venture afield to find wives, only about half of the young children lived with both parents. Those whose fathers lived nearby remained with their mothers and other relatives. On large Carolina rice plantations, which required a large labor force, children were more likely to live with both parents. Slave boys received English names from their masters but often African ones from their parents, who recognized kinship ties by naming sons for absent fathers or their grandfathers or uncles. These ties were reinforced by shared daily life. Families and relatives lived together in "quarters" of double rows of one- or two-room log or clapboard cabins, where boys slept with siblings in lofts, on pallets, or in trundle beds. Sharing a common yard, slaves cooked and ate communally, and children were served from a single skillet or a wooden trough.

Chesapeake boys were put to work between the ages of five and ten. Working with kinship groups, they began with simple tasks in which they were instructed by parents or other relatives. Boys began fieldwork by chasing crows, helping stack wheat, or picking worms off tobacco plants. As they grew older, they picked tobacco and cradled wheat. They minded cows or chickens, cared for horses, toted drinking water to the fields, used mud or sticks to mend fences, and guided oxen when fields were plowed. Carolina slaves were given a task to be performed each day, and after it was finished, their time was their own. Boys of twelve or thirteen became three-quarter task hands, which could mean helping to plant and harvest rice or hoeing twelve rows or picking 30 pounds of cotton. In both areas, some boys were designated to be house servants for wealthy white families. As young as the age of five or six, they learned to fetch wood, build fires, carry food from the kitchen, fan flies from the table, and wash the dishes. Other boys were selected to learn skills and became carpenters, brick makers or layers, leatherworkers, or blacksmiths. Some were apprenticed to a white craftsman for three or four years, but most learned from skilled slaves or their fathers. In some families such skills were proudly passed from father to son. A slave boy with skills earned money for his master, who hired him out to other plantations or to urban artisans and collected his wages.

Enslaved and white Chesapeake boys grew up playing together. They wrestled, rode sticks they pretended were horses, and got into mischief. White children played school by teaching slave children their letters, sometimes whipping them when they forgot their lessons. But whites playing with black boys could be deliberately cruel, encouraging them to dangerous physical feats, enticing dogs to bite their toes, and purposely frightening them with actions and tales. In Carolina coastal parishes, where slaves greatly outnumbered whites, anxious parents drew a firmer line between their own children and their slaves. In both areas enslaved boys played by themselves in the quarters or woods, digging for worms, fishing, or hunting for opossum. In the yard they played ring games of their own devising, based on songs they improvised much as their parents and kinfolk did.

Interaction with white culture could create psychological conflicts for enslaved boys. When six-year-old Frederick Douglass left his grandmother's cabin in 1824 and found himself on Colonel Edward Lloyd's plantation on Maryland's Eastern Shore, he entered a self-sufficient community embracing thirteen farms and more than 500 slaves. Yet he gravitated toward the Great House, occupied by Colonel Lloyd and his family. Fred was hungry much of the time and associated the Great House with an abundance of food. He learned to finagle bread and butter by singing beneath the window of the daughter of his master (the manager of Lloyd's farms), who may have been his father. He also sat in on lessons with

Lloyd's son Daniel, five years his senior, whose Massachusetts tutor struggled to cure the white boy of speaking like a slave. Forming words along with Daniel, Fred learned the power of literacy and cultured English speech. Sent to Baltimore at age eight, he bribed white boys with bread to teach him his letters. By age eleven, he was able to match letters on boards in the shipyard with those in a Webster's speller he carried around in his pocket, and, in stolen moments, he taught himself to write. Frederick Douglass would flee slavery and become a distinguished speaker and writer for the abolitionist cause. Yet even while he emulated the genteel values of the Great House, he also regarded it with mixed anxiety and deep resentment (Reinier 1996).

Although slave owners of the eighteenth century considered small children a nuisance and of little market value, by the early nineteenth century, southeastern planters began to recognize the value of their surplus slaves. As seaboard lands declined in productivity, planters or their sons migrated west, transporting a labor force that often consisted of boys as young as ten to fourteen years of age. When Congress ended the Atlantic slave trade in 1808, the need of the expanding cotton frontier for labor accelerated the domestic trade. Southeastern planters, who recognized the commodity value of enslaved children, sold their surplus slaves to professional traders. These sales of adolescent and even much younger boys caused painful separations from their families. As early as 1789, four-year-old Charles Ball of Maryland was sold away from his mother and siblings. Sixty years later he vividly remembered how his mother walked beside the horse of his master, beseeching him not to sep-arate her family. In the 1840s eight-year-old Amos Abner Cotton of Virginia was sold to a trader when his master died and the estate was divided. His father, who was a craftsman and had made money by hiring himself out, attempted to buy back his son. But the trader refused, admonishing the anguished father, he "must think himself white." Separated from his family and sold to Kentucky, Amos was put to work cradling and binding wheat (Reinier 1996, 159–160).

Such separations brought disorder and despair to the new labor forces assembled in the Old Southwest. One-third of slaves brought to some Louisiana cotton parishes were "solitaires," mostly boys separated from family members or kin. Two-thirds of solitaires engaged in heavy labor on a sugar plantation were male. On these new sugar or cotton plantations, the rapidly assembled labor force was young; almost half the individuals could be under the age of seventeen. Families and communities similar to those in the southeastern states did not take shape until the 1840s and 1850s, when kinship groups worked the fields together. Boys as young as age five learned to work with the hoe and went to the fields with their parents during the cotton harvest. If they failed to keep up, they could feel the whip administered by overseer or driver. These boys also were profoundly aware of punishments of other slaves they heard about or witnessed. William Colbert recalled that when his older brother received a whipping for visiting a girl on another plantation, he sat on his parents' steps and cried. When William Moore saw his mother whipped, he ran around in circles and threw a rock at his master. Yet, throughout the South, enslaved boys themselves were more likely to be punished by a cruel or exasperated planter's wife, who shook them, pummeled their bare backs, or whipped them with a wooden paddle or a leather strap (Reinier 1996, 175).

After the Civil War, freed parents searched for the children from whom they had been separated. Many individuals walked long distances, dictated newspaper advertisements, or sought help from the only federally funded agency in the South, the Freedmen's Bureau. These families located some but not all of their scattered offspring. Orphaned boys stayed with other kinship groups until they could provide for themselves. Yet dangers remained for the newly freed boys as former slave owners sought to bind them in various forms of apprenticeship. Even after their emancipation, these formerly enslaved boys continued to be valued highly for their labor.

Jacqueline S. Reinier

See also African American Boys; Civil War; Douglass, Frederick; Plantations; Slave Trade; Washington, Booker T., and W. E. B. Du Bois

References and further reading
Federal Writers Project, Interviews with Former Slaves. 1930s. Chapel Hill: Southern Historical Collection, University of North Carolina.
Joyner, Charles. 1984. *Down by the Riverside: A South Carolina Slave Community.* Urbana: University of Illinois Press.
King, Wilma. 1995. *Stolen Childhood: Slave Youth in Nineteenth-Century America.* Bloomington: Indiana University Press.
Kulikoff, Allan. 1986. *Tobacco and Slaves: The Development of Southern Cultures in the Chesapeake, 1680–1800.* Chapel Hill: University of North Carolina Press.
Malone, Ann Patton. 1992. *Sweet Chariot: Slave Family and Household Structure in Nineteenth-Century Louisiana.* Chapel Hill: University of North Carolina Press.
McFeely, William S. 1991. *Frederick Douglass.* New York: Simon and Schuster.
Morgan, Phillip D. 1998. *Slave Counterpoint: Black Culture in the Eighteenth-Century Chesapeake and Low Country.* Chapel Hill: University of North Carolina Press.
Reinier, Jacqueline S. 1996. *From Virtue to Character: American Childhood, 1775–1850.* New York: Twayne Publishers.

Smoking and Drinking

Tobacco and alcohol are considered "gateway" drugs whose use by adolescent boys and children increases the likelihood of experimentation with illegal drugs. Tobacco use and alcohol consumption usually coincide with a number of other "problem behaviors" that account for more than 75 percent of deaths among adolescent males (CDC 1999). For these reasons, health professionals and educators are increasingly concerned about substance use among children and adolescents.

Tobacco, which contains the drug nicotine, is the chief ingredient in cigarettes, cigars, pipe tobacco, chewing tobacco (chew), and snuff. Nicotine is a toxic, addictive stimulant that produces a sense of alertness and well-being in smokers. It increases adrenaline production, quickens the heart rate, and depresses the appetite. Tars found in tobacco are carcinogenic, contributing to cancer of the lips, mouth, throat, lungs, and other organs. Heart disease among smokers results from other chemicals (including carbon monoxide) in tobacco. In addition, the Environmental Protection Agency (EPA) estimates that 3,000 lung cancer deaths per year result solely from secondhand smoke. Secondhand smoke has also been linked to cardiovascular disease, asthma, and pneumonia. Tobacco use is the chief preventable cause of death in the United States.

Although the word *cigarette* is the feminine form of *cigar*, cigarette smoking in America has historically been a male activity associated with poverty and low social class. By the late 1800s, immigrants from countries where smoking was common among the lower classes contributed to the increased sale of cigarettes in the United States. As early as 1879, the *New York Times* was warning about health concerns in stories with headlines like "Cigarettes Killed Him" and "Cigarette Fiend Dies." The public concurred: cigarettes were referred to as coffin nails, dope sticks, and the devil's toothpicks. Early promotions helped men and boys associate cigarettes with sex. Advertisements quoted doctors who talked of the "secret sexual practices" of smokers. Cigarette packs often came with picture cards of "actresses and beauties" bundled inside. Prior to World War I, however, women who smoked were thought to be chorus girls, actresses, prostitutes, or girls of poor reputation.

During the war, millions of American men smoked cigarettes provided for them by the government and civic groups. Obviously, not everyone agreed that cigarettes were health risks. Although popular evangelist the Reverend William Sunday told men that "there is nothing manly about smoking cigarettes. For God's sake, if you must smoke, get a pipe," smoking continued to be a male privilege after the war (Koven 1996, 5). Women began smoking in great numbers in the 1920s, specifically because tobacco was one of the markers that differentiated between the roles and conduct of the sexes. In a now-infamous public relations campaign called the "torches of liberty," debutantes paraded in the streets of New York City carrying cigarettes to symbolize female empowerment. Similar patterns emerged at the end of the twentieth century among youth, with boys first adopting the habit to show their masculinity, only to be overshadowed by girls smoking to show their equality to boys. Virginia Slims ad campaigns capture the sentiment well ("You've come a long way, baby"). One of the fastest-growing tobacco markets today is women in college.

According to the Centers for Disease Control and Prevention (CDC), nearly one-quarter of all male deaths can be attributed to two causes: cardiovascular disease and cancer. The CDC offers four alarming statistics from a 1999 nationwide survey of high school students: 76.1 percent of high school students eat less than the recommended daily servings of fruits and vegetables daily, 70.9 percent do not attend physical education classes daily, 34.8 percent currently smoke cigarettes, and 16 percent are overweight or at risk for obesity. All of these behaviors have been found to contribute to the risk of dying from cardiovascular disease and cancer. Clearly, habits initiated in the adolescent years contribute to adult mortality. Unfortunately, convincing a teenage boy to consider long-term health effects is a hard sell.

Cigarette smoking seems to be as typical among school-age boys as textbooks and recess. In the eleven states with the highest percentage of youthful smokers (Alabama, Arkansas, Kentucky, Louisiana, New Mexico, North Dakota, Ohio, South Carolina, South Dakota, Tennessee, and West Virginia), more than 75 percent of boys have tried smoking cigarettes. Only one state (Utah) falls under 50 percent.

Not surprisingly, Utah is one of the few states to consistently request identification of young people seeking to purchase cigarettes in stores and gas stations (CDC 1999).

Although ethnicity does not seem to affect experimentation with cigarettes (more than 80 percent of students have tried smoking by the end of high school), there are differences in habitual smoking and frequency of smoking. Euro-American boys are the most likely to smoke daily (29.3 percent), and they smoke more frequently (ten or more cigarettes a day). Euro-American boys are followed closely by Latin American boys, 21.1 percent of whom smoke daily. African American boys are the least likely to have a daily smoking habit (14.6 percent) and the least likely group to smoke ten or more cigarettes per day. The CDC does not report smoking data for other ethnic or racial groups. All these figures rise when smokeless tobacco (chew), pipe tobacco, and cigars are added. The increase in cigar smoking in adult males is paralleled in the adolescent population. Among high school–age Euro-American boys, 28.3 percent smoke cigars, and 18.8 percent use smokeless tobacco. When combined with cigarette use, approximately 50 percent of Euro-American boys use some form of tobacco. The figure drops to 37.8 percent for Latin American boys and 28.6 percent for African American boys (CDC 1999).

Experimentation with cigarettes, habitual smoking, and frequency of smoking all increase with age. By the twelfth grade, more than 80 percent of boys have tried smoking, more than 30 percent smoke on a daily basis, and more than 10 percent smoke more than ten cigarettes per day. Although over 60 percent have tried smoking by the time they enter high school, less than 20 percent had daily habits, and less than 5 percent were heavy smokers (CDC 1999). Although smoking cigarettes has actually decreased slightly among high school students since 1990, recent surveys indicate that the average age boys begin experimenting with smoking is twelve, with some starting much earlier (Chapin 2000).

As for alcohol, even Puritan forefathers drank. "The good creature of God," or whiskey to the Puritans, was used in the colonies as a universal medication. Alcohol was prescribed for colds, fevers, frosted toes, and snakebites. Parents gave it to children to bolster their good health and to cure their illnesses. People drank more alcohol in colonial days than they do today: three to seven times more per person per year. In the mid-1800s, temperance advocates who were concerned about the health and moral risks of alcohol use began a campaign to ban it. In 1919 they succeeded when the Eighteenth Amendment, which banned alcohol production and consumption in the United States, was added to the Constitution. Once alcohol consumption was illegal, it became part of the male domain. The association of alcohol with "undesirables," including poor Americans, African Americans, and immigrants, made drinking and drunkenness an ideal way for men to rebel against "the system." In addition to its association with rebellion, alcohol consumption has historically been (and continues to be) a form of male solidarity. Men's and boys' drinking in groups creates a sense of identity and group membership. It has been a social occasion, a purpose for socializing, and a rite of passage all in one.

Alcohol is a drug that acts as a sedative and an anesthetic, depressing mental and motor functions. The active chemical ingredient in beer, wine, and other alcoholic beverages is ethyl alcohol, a potentially addictive depressant of the central nervous system and the most widely used recreational drug in the world. Vital functions such as pulse rate, respiration, and blood pressure are all affected by alcohol use. Permanent damage to the brain, heart, liver, stomach, and reproductive organs (including male impotence) may result from alcohol abuse. In contrast to these long-term effects, auto accidents are a frequent short-term risk of alcohol abuse, contributing one of the main causes of death in men under the age of twenty-five. Alcohol abuse is also a major contributor to violence, sexual abuse, criminal behavior, and family dysfunction.

In the 1970s and 1980s, the formation of groups like Mothers Against Drunk Driving (MADD) and Students Against Drunk Driving (SADD) demonstrated increased public recognition of the dangers of alcohol. In 1985, President Ronald Reagan signed into law a uniform minimum drinking age of twenty-one. Stiffer penalties for drinking and driving have also become law. Despite increased public awareness of the issue, alcohol use has increased since 1990 and is more prevalent among boys than girls. Like tobacco use, alcohol use is reported as early as elementary school years, with the average boy first experimenting with alcohol at the age of twelve (CDC 1999).

According to the CDC, more than 80 percent of Euro-American and Latin American boys currently in high school have tried alcohol. Consistent with the patterns of tobacco use, African American boys (73.8 percent) are less likely than their white and Latino peers to have tried alcohol, but the overall percentage is high. Latin American boys (56.3 percent) are more likely than Euro-American boys (54.9 percent) and African American boys (39.1 percent) to drink on a regular basis; however, Euro-Americans (39.1) are more likely than Latin Americans (37.5 percent) and African Americans (17.4 percent) to binge drink (CDC 1999). Binge drinking is usually defined as drinking to the point of intoxication, which is frequently equated to five alcoholic beverages in one sitting for men (and three for women).

Experimentation with alcohol, regular drinking, and binge drinking all increase with age. By the twelfth grade, nearly 90 percent of boys have tried alcohol, more than 60 percent drink on a monthly basis, and nearly 50 percent binge drink. Although more than 70 percent have tried alcohol by the time they enter high school, less than 25 percent were early binge drinkers (CDC 1999).

The health consequences of tobacco and alcohol use and abuse and their contribution to adolescent mortality are just part of the current problem. Commonly referred to as "gateway drugs," alcohol and tobacco use frequently predicts experimentation with illegal drugs and later substance abuse. In a recent survey of middle school students, 30.9 percent of boys smoked, 54.5 percent drank, and 9.1 percent had already experimented with illegal drugs. Of the drug users, all reported also smoking and drinking. Of the students who never smoked cigarettes or consumed alcohol, none had experimented with illegal drugs (Chapin 2000).

In addition to serving as gateways to more serious substance abuse, alcohol and tobacco use coincide with other risky behaviors among young boys. Researchers in the 1970s first identified the trend, calling it "problem behaviors." Boys who smoke and drink also tend to take a variety of other risks like driving too fast, doing stunts, engaging in early sexual activity as well as risky sexual activity, carrying weapons, and participating in delinquent behaviors. A review of decades of research suggests the following:

1. Early initiation into smoking and drinking predicts heavier involvement in them later and more negative consequences.
2. Doing poorly in school or expecting to do poorly predicts substance abuse.
3. Impulsive behavior, truancy, and antisocial behavior are related to all other problem behaviors.
4. Low resistance to peer influences and having friends who engage in substance abuse are common to young boys who smoke and drink.
5. Substance abuse behaviors are associated with insufficient bonding to parents, inadequate supervision and communication from parents, and parents who are either too authoritative or too permissive.
6. Living in a poverty area or a high-density urban area is linked with smoking and drinking as well as other problem behaviors.
7. Rare church attendance is associated with most problem behaviors. (Hamburg 1992; 196)

Smoking and drinking behaviors often begin in the adolescent years for a number of reasons. The first is the nature of adolescence itself. Some of the most complex transitions of life occur during adolescence, as the body changes from a child's to an adult's, relationships with others take on new meanings and levels of intricacy, and individuals become increasingly independent. It is a time of expanding horizons and self-discovery. The

effects can be observed in children, but the processes begin to show serious consequences in adolescence that will affect individuals for the remainder of their adult lives.

A review of a decade of articles published in *Adolescence* revealed that the three most prevalent research issues (representing nearly half of all articles published) are problem behaviors (including smoking and drinking), sexuality, and values. One of the major conclusions of these studies was that adolescent boys were ill-equipped to face the increasing numbers of opportunities for substance use and abuse because they lacked sufficient decision making skills and sources of information. In general, boys' attitudes and experiences seem to be changing faster than their knowledge and coping skills.

A second explanation for why boys smoke and drink is a developmental one. All developing boys are saddled with "life tasks," which must be accomplished within developmental spans. Normative developmental stresses and responses to them play a major role in adolescence. According to John Hill (1983), there are five life tasks that take on special importance during adolescence: identity, or discovering and understanding the self as an individual; intimacy, or forming close relationships with others; autonomy, or establishing a healthy sense of independence; sexuality, or coming to terms with puberty and expressing sexual feelings; and achievement, or becoming a successful and competent member of society. Although these tasks are not unique to adolescents, the massive biological, psychological, and social changes occurring in adolescence cause these tasks to take on special significance.

Because a major task of adolescence is autonomy and parental controls tend to fall away rapidly during the period, it is not surprising that teens search out other sources of information. Peers and the mass media provide attractive alternative sources of information. Despite the amount of funding expended on antismoking and antidrinking campaigns targeted at adolescent boys, health campaigns often fail because they do not understand that adolescent risk behaviors are functional, purposive, instrumental, and goal-directed and that the goals involved are often central in normal adolescent development (establishing autonomy, gaining peer acceptance, making the transition to adulthood, etc.). The mass media offers an array of attractive celebrity role models for adolescents, and emulation of these role models is common. The tobacco and alcohol industries are quick to take advantage of this phenomenon. Consider the following example: shortly after Brad Pitt was named the "sexiest man alive" in *People* magazine, his character in the upcoming film *Seven* became a smoker as part of a million-dollar deal with the production company. Paid product placement in films is a common technique for advertisers to connect with target audiences. The number of films targeted to adolescent boys makes movies ideal marketing tools. Images in the mass media may suggest to boys that cigarettes and alcohol are "cool" and "sexy," but the day-to-day influences of peers also greatly contribute to experimentation and habit formation. Smoking and drinking both play a role in identity formation among peer groups. Peers that smoke and drink create perceived norms that encourage similar behaviors.

A third method of explaining boys' use of tobacco and alcohol is rooted in biology. Pubertal development has been associated with changes in family interactions, parental feelings, peer relationships, patterns of intimacy, heterosexual interests and behavior, and educational achievements. Psychological adjustment to such sweeping changes affects how boys view themselves as men and as individuals, how and when they begin dating, how well they adjust to school, and how they perceive the family environment. Discussion of boys' experiences of spermarche (first orgasm) are generally a family taboo, sending early adolescents searching for information elsewhere. Boys who develop adult male physiques early receive instant admiration from peers; boys who develop later are subject to teasing (often starting in the locker room), which can lead to a sense of shame. The timing of biological maturation affects cognitive scope, self-perceptions, perceptions of the social environment, and personal values. These four variables are hypothesized to predict adolescent risk-taking behavior. Initial results from ongoing research suggest that compared with less mature boys, physiologically mature boys (defined by puberty) perceived less risk associated with driving and drinking, engaging in sex, smoking cigarettes, drinking beer and wine or hard liquor, and using drugs.

Testosterone levels in boys are directly related to thrill seeking or "sensation seeking." Boys with higher than average testosterone levels become sensation seekers; they exhibit a greater number of reckless or problem adolescent behaviors, such as unsafe sex, alcohol consumption, cigarette smoking, and drug use. In order to suppress such risky behaviors, high-sensation-seeking males require viable alternatives like amusement parks, skydiving, and extreme sports.

Still a fourth way of explaining why boys use tobacco and alcohol is cognitive.

Boys believe they are less likely than peers to be in alcohol-related accidents, become addicted to alcohol, or develop lung cancer later in life. This "optimistic bias" has been confirmed in hundreds of published studies. Adolescents in general believe they are invulnerable to harm. Although cardiovascular disease and cancer figure prominently in deaths among adolescents, young boys fail to perceive the link between their substance use habits and negative health outcomes. Because people act on their perceptions (rather than reality), understanding how boys think about smoking and drinking is a vital first step in efforts to reduce or extinguish the behaviors.

The fifth and last method of explaining boys' smoking and drinking habits is a social one. At no time is the tension between family members greater than when children first enter adolescence. This is when the focus of young people's lives shifts out of the family. Despite this, adolescents spend roughly 40 percent of their time at home with family members. Three of the major tasks of adolescence, identity clarification (Who am I?), sexuality (Am I attractive to girls? How do I approach girls? Is it wrong to masturbate? Could I be gay?), and separation (How can I be a man if my parents are still telling me what to do? Do my parents still love me?), are highly influenced by the ways families construe and connote them. Boys' experimentation with their appearance and behaviors can be disturbing to parents. However, family interactions emphasizing warmth, acceptance, and understanding tend to support higher levels of ego development and identity clarification in adolescents.

The environment provided by the family for these adolescent developmental tasks is vital. For instance, substance abuse often begins in adolescence; it is tied to a normal process of experimenting with new behaviors, becoming assertive, developing relationships outside the family, and leaving home. Substance abuse is often contingent on the quality of parent-adolescent relationships. As the influence of families diminishes, boys turn to peers and the media.

Not only a boys' family environment but his relationship with his peers can also influence whether or not he smokes and drinks. Forming and maintaining peer relationships are central to adolescent development. Adolescents who are accepted by peers have been shown to be high in self-esteem, social skills, and academic success. Those lacking in such relationships show poor psychological, social, and academic adjustment. Perceived peer norms are often the best predictor of adolescent substance abuse: if a young boy believes his friends think he should drink, he will likely drink.

Considering the multiple contributors to adolescent substance use, no single solution is possible. For instance, developmental and biological explanations suggest that substance use meets bona fide needs of adolescent boys, and thus the best solutions are those that offer healthy alternatives to meet developmental needs and sensation seeking. Cognitive explanations, on the other hand, suggest educational programs that emphasize personal risks associated with such behaviors.

Programs emphasizing the long-term effects of substance use have been largely unsuccessful, but those emphasizing the immediate physical and social effects have been more successful. The most promising results have occurred in prevention programs. Once youth begin using tobacco and alcohol, helping them quit becomes increasingly difficult. The

earlier boys begin using alcohol and tobacco, the less likely they will ever quit
the habits. Given the increasingly early
ages of experimentation with substance
use, efforts by parents, schools, and
health professionals must begin in preschool and elementary school.

John Chapin

See also Disease and Death; Illegal
Substances

References and further reading
Babbit, Nicki. 2000. *Adolescent Drug and
Alcohol Abuse: How to Spot It, Stop It,
and Get Help for Your Family.*
Sebastopol, CA: O'Reilly.
Behr, Edward. 1996. *Prohibition.* New
York: Arcade.
Burnham, John. 1993. *Bad Habits:
Drinking, Smoking, Taking Drugs,
Gambling, Sexual Misbehavior, and
Swearing in American History.* New
York: New York University Press.
CDC (Centers for Disease Control and
Prevention). 1999. "Division of
Adolescent and School Health's
Information Service Report." Silver
Springs, MD: Government Printing
Office.
Chapin, John. 2000. "Third-Person
Perception and Optimistic Bias among
Urban-Minority 'At-Risk' Youth."
Communication Research 27, no. 1:
51–81.
Feldman, Shirley, and Glen Elliot, eds.
1990. *At the Threshold: The Developing
Adolescent.* Cambridge, MA: Harvard
University Press.
Gall, Timothy, and Daniel Lucas, eds.
1996. *Statistics on Alcohol, Drug and
Tobacco Use.* Detroit: Thompson.
Hamburg, David. 1992. *Today's Children:
Creating a Future for a Generation in
Crisis.* New York: Times Books,
Random House.
Hill, John. 1983. "Early Adolescence: A
Research Agenda." *Journal of Early
Adolescence* 3: 1–21.
Jessor, Richard, and Shirley Jessor. 1977.
*Problem Behavior and Psychosocial
Development: A Longitudinal Study of
Youth.* New York: Cambridge
University Press.

Klier, Barbara, Jacquelyn Quiram, and
Mark Siegel, eds. 1999. *Alcohol and
Tobacco: America's Drugs of Choice.*
Wylie, TX: Information Plus.
Koven, Edward. 1996. *Smoking: The Story
behind the Haze.* Commack, NY: Nova
Science.
Lock, Stephen, and Lois Reynolds, eds.
1998. *Ashes to Ashes: The History of
Smoking and Health.* Atlanta, GA:
Rodopi.
Mooney, Cynthia, ed. 1999. *Drugs,
Alcohol and Tobacco: Macmillan
Health Encyclopedia.* New York:
Macmillan Library Reference.
Pacula, Rosalie. 1998. *Adolescent Alcohol
and Marijuana Consumption: Is There
Really a Gateway Effect?* Cambridge,
MA: National Bureau of Economic
Research.
Segerstrom, Suzanne, William McCarthy,
and Nicholas Caskey. 1993. "Optimistic
Bias among Cigarette Smokers." *Journal
of Applied Social Psychology* 23:
1606–1618.
Siegel, Mark, Alison Landes, and Nancy
Jacobs. 1995. *Illegal Drugs and Alcohol:
America's Anguish.* Wylie, TX:
Information Plus.
Stefanko, Michael. 1984. "Trends in
Adolescent Research: A Review of
Articles Published in *Adolescence."
Adolescence* 19, no. 73: 1–13.
Strasburger, Victor, and Don Greydanus,
eds. 1990. *Adolescent Medicine: The
At-Risk Adolescent.* Philadelphia:
Hanley and Belfus.
Tate, Cassandra. 1999. *Cigarette Wars.*
New York: Oxford University Press.
Torr, James, ed. 2000. *Alcoholism.* San
Diego, CA: Greenhaven Press.
Weinstein, Neil. 1987. *Taking Care:
Understanding and Encouraging Self-
Protective Behavior.* New York:
Cambridge University Press.
Winters, Paul, ed. 1997. *Teen Addiction.*
San Diego, CA: Greenhaven Press.

Sports, Colonial Era to 1920
During the colonial period, just as Native
American boys prepared themselves to be
physically tough as adults by practicing
archery, playing lacrosse, and running
foot races, Anglo boys engaged in sports

Skating outdoors. Lithograph, ca. 1885. (Library of Congress)

with utilitarian value, such as swimming, boating, hunting, fishing, and horseback riding. Their leisure lives were restricted by religious views and Sabbatarian issues about use of time for prayer: both Puritans in New England and Quakers in Pennsylvania frowned upon idleness, frivolity, and gambling. Catholic settlers in Maryland and elsewhere held a more relaxed view of acceptable activities based on their established European recreational patterns, which included the sports, games, and dancing that accompanied communal festivals and the celebration of saints' days. Although banned by the Puritan authorities in the Massachusetts colony in the early 1600s, the maypole dance on May Day attracted youth. Males throughout the colonies participated in games of skill and chance and at times joined in physical contests, particularly on established muster days when local militias gathered for drill.

As Europeans moved westward, taverns served as sites for food, drink, lodging, and entertainment in these frontier areas. There men and boys engaged in contests of physical skills and strength to measure their prowess. They bowled, wrestled, shot at targets, ran footraces, and played billiards, often for stakes or prizes. The prize for gander pulling was the goose itself, which hung suspended from a tree as riders attempted to pull its greased head and neck from its body. Gander pulling proved especially popular in the Dutch colony of New York, as did a game called "kolven," which resembled golf or hockey. Throughout the northern states, boys enjoyed winter activities like ice skating and sleighing whenever the weather permitted.

Young boys played with toys and marbles and enjoyed chase games such as tag. As they grew older, bowling games like skittles, quoits, or ninepins became popular, as did the various ball and bat games known as "rounders," "town ball," and "stool ball" that preceded organized baseball clubs. By the 1760s the colonists played cricket and racquet sports, and by 1802 a specialized site for such practice, the Allen Street Courts, had been established in New York. The Racquet Club of New York included minors among its membership in 1845.

In the southern colonies, white boys enjoyed similar forms of leisure. Slaves, however, were expected to participate in boxing matches for the entertainment of their masters, and black jockeys raced horses for the gentry who bet on the horse races. Southern black boxers Tom Molyneux and Bill Richmond proved so skillful that they traveled to England to compete in the boxing championship, winning their freedom in the process.

Along the southern frontier, the largely Scotch-Irish males practiced a particularly brutal form of "rough and tumble" wrestling that eschewed rules. Eye gouging, biting, scratching, hair pulling, and even emasculation determined one's hardiness, resolve, and social status among peers, who cheered their favorite fighter to punish his opponent. In the early 1800s, in other rural areas boys competed in contests at agricultural fairs by demonstrating their physical skills in farming. The first agricultural fair was held in 1810 in Pittsfield, Massachusetts, and other agricultural fairs soon followed.

Thanks to the antebellum urban health reform movement, sporting practices became more acceptable forms of leisure. Known as "muscular Christianity," the health reform campaign for males gained ascendance at midcentury. This program, spearheaded by white, middle-class reformers, stressed physical vigor, moral courage, and religion and provided advice to male youth on the healthfulness of sports as an antidote to urban temptations and sedentary ways. Reformers like Thomas Higginson believed that sports for boys promoted physical strength and training for their roles as men.

More organized forms of sport began to appear in urban areas as men formed athletic clubs during the antebellum period, and younger boys joined as junior members or formed their own contingents in imitation. One such club, the Knickerbockers of New York City, codified the rules of baseball in 1845, and its version, which differed from those of clubs in Massachusetts and elsewhere, eventually won widespread acceptance. The Potomac Boat Club, founded in 1859 along the Potomac River in the District of Columbia, helped to spread the enthusiasm for competitive rowing in the mid- and late nineteenth century. At the time, rowing enjoyed widespread popularity and drew huge crowds of spectators. Professional rowers stimulated young males and amateurs to form rowing clubs in locales with good waterways. The Potomac Boat Club competed against other rowing clubs and hosted athletic and social events for the middle- and upper-rank men and women coming to the club; the clubhouse hosted other sports, too, such as swimming and canoe races.

Like baseball, cricket enjoyed a great measure of popularity. It is estimated that

10,000 men and boys in 500 urban cricket clubs played the game throughout the United States by 1860. Baseball games between rival clubs often drew crowds of spectators that became commercialized events held in special enclosed sites. Professionalization soon followed, as nineteen-year-old James Creighton became the first acknowledged baseball player to accept payment for his athletic abilities. A fully professional baseball team, the Cincinnati Red Stockings, appeared in 1869. A year later, Chicago, a midwestern commercial rival, fielded its professional baseball team, the White Stockings (now known as the Chicago Cubs).

In 1852 boys participated in the first intercollegiate sport. That year a railroad company offered a vacation and prizes to the crews at Yale and Harvard Universities for a competition on Lake Winnipesaukee, the location of the railroad's New Hampshire resort. Both the regatta and its accompanying festivities drew public attention and paying customers to the sponsor.

Ethnic athletic clubs also organized leisure activities to promote their own language, values, and cultural traditions among youth. Some of these became commercialized spectacles that also drew the attention of American-born athletes and spectators. By the 1850s the Scots' Caledonian Club garnered 20,000 spectators at its Highland Games, which featured running, jumping, and weight-throwing contests that were eventually incorporated as modern track and field events.

Other ethnic clubs, such as the German Turners, Polish Falcons, and Czech Sokols, offered a broad range of activities to members, including study of ethnic literature, dance, gymnastics, soccer, bowling, rifling, and singing, all to encourage the retention of European practices. Jewish settlement houses and Young Men's Hebrew Associations, more intent on assimilation with the American mainstream culture, sponsored baseball, football, basketball, track, wrestling, and boxing teams for adolescents, teenagers, and young men within Jewish communities. Boxing and wrestling in particular helped Jews dispel the stereotypical notion that they were cerebral, physically weak, and feeble.

An 1866 book entitled *Athletic Sports for Boys* listed fishing, boxing, sailing, rowing, fencing, gymnastics, horsemanship, skating, swimming, and the driving of horse-drawn coaches as popular pastimes. As boys became teenagers and began courting girls, other social sports gained prominence. In the generation that followed the Civil War, croquet, roller skating, archery, tennis, and bicycling allowed young couples to engage in public leisure practices that enabled them to eschew the previously required chaperone.

During the late nineteenth century, baseball superseded cricket in popularity, and boys formed sandlot teams to challenge their urban rivals. Teams divided along neighborhood, ethnic, and racial lines, but integrated contests also occurred in northern cities. At the high school level, students organized into competitive leagues in imitation of the professional associations. Country clubs offered more elite sports such as golf and tennis for white youth during the 1880s–1890s. Prominent social and business leaders in cities like Boston, Philadelphia, and the suburbs of New York founded country clubs as places for their families and elite friends to engage in athletic and social activities. These country clubs provided an outdoor, rural setting for sports separate from the urban lower class and immigrants flooding into many cities in the United States in the 1880s. The Germantown Cricket Club in Philadelphia was founded in 1890–1891, and the club played a large role in the success of cricket. In addition, the Germantown Cricket Club promoted tennis for its members by building tennis courts for their use. By the 1920s, tennis surpassed cricket as the major sport for all members, including boys. In fact, the famous American tennis champion, Big Bill Tilden, was a member of the Germantown Cricket Club and learned to play tennis on the courts there. The Seabright Lawn Tennis and Cricket Club in Rumson, New Jersey, featured a cricket crease and three tennis courts when it was built in 1886. Seabright's members included competitive tennis champions. These country clubs provided the athletic facilities and training for upper-rank boys to participate in tennis.

Soccer, which was played in Boston high schools during the 1860s, evolved into American football on college campuses by the 1880s. Boys initiated their own games, organized leagues, and established rules. The game experienced explosive growth in the schools until the turn of the twentieth century, but as in baseball, that rapid growth was accompanied by lack of regulation, abuses, and public concern over the use of ineligible players and the wholesome uses of boys' leisure time. At the collegiate level, gambling and the emphasis on winning fostered professionalism, cheating, and the use of nonstudents in the quest for victories and bragging rights. Throughout the Progressive era (1890–1920), civic reformers and faculty members in the schools moved to exert greater adult control over boys' sports. The largest interscholastic leagues, such as the Public Schools Athletic League in New York City and the Cook County Athletic League in Chicago, came

Boys playing baseball, ca. 1900 (Library of Congress)

under adult supervision because of widespread allegations of cheating by boys.

The Young Men's Christian Association (YMCA), founded in the United Kingdom in 1844 and brought to the United States in 1851, offered sports and games to attract adherents to its cause, and civic groups established sandlots and playgrounds as safe havens for younger children, who had previously played in the streets. Urban settlement houses sponsored boys' athletic teams as well as a host of activities designed to assimilate the children of southern and eastern European immigrants who arrived in droves after 1880. In the schools, faculty and administrators assumed control of athletic teams, and trained physical educators served as coaches to provide guidance and instructions. In public parks, supervisors and playground attendants promoted Americanization through competition, teamwork, self-sacrifice, discipline, and sportsmanship. The Playground Association of America, founded by such urban reformers as Luther Gulick, Jane Addams, and Joseph Lee, sought to provide healthful boys' sports under the direction of adults in cities like Chicago, Boston, and New York. By the turn of the century, the playground movement assumed national proportions.

With the invention of basketball and volleyball by YMCA physical educators in the 1890s and the construction of field houses in urban parks after the turn of the century, adults maintained a year-round vigilance on boys' activities. The new indoor games allowed for winter pastimes conducted in publicly supervised facilities. Still, some youth escaped such watchful diligence. Middle-class and wealthier youth took up tennis and golf in country clubs outside city boundaries. Some working-class youths found employment as pin spotters in the urban bowling alleys often attached to saloons, and others formed town or neighborhood teams independent of the schools and parks. Some of the latter evolved into semipro and even professional units that engendered community pride and created social mobility for some young men who played baseball and football.

Baseball and boxing proved particularly attractive to working-class youth as a means to ready advancement both in their neighborhoods and in the American economy. Urban life and ethnic rivalries necessitated the toughness required to fight, and both sports promoted the aggressiveness of the American capitalist system and the physical prowess esteemed by

both the working class and the larger culture. Both sports produced a succession of ethnic heroes, such as John L. Sullivan and Mike "King" Kelly, Irish Americans, who symbolized a measure of acceptance and assimilation into American society for the Irish. By 1920 competitive sports and games exercised a powerful influence over American boys of diverse racial, ethnic, and religious backgrounds.

Gerald R. Gems
Linda J. Borish

See also Baseball; Boxing; Muscular Christianity; Tennis

References and further reading
Adelman, Melvin L. 1986. *A Sporting Time: New York City and the Rise of Modern Athletics, 1820–1870.* Urbana: University of Illinois Press.
Athletic Sports for Boys: A Repository of Graceful Recreations for Youth. 1866. New York: Dick and Fitzgerald.
Borish, Linda J. 1987. "The Robust Woman and the Muscular Christian: Catharine Beecher, Thomas Higginson and Their Vision of American Society, Health, and Physical Activities." *International Journal of the History of Sport:* 139–154.
———. Forthcoming. *Landmarks of American Sports.* American Landmarks Series. Edited by James O. Horton. New York: Oxford University Press.
Gems, Gerald. 1997. *Windy City Wars: Labor, Leisure, and Sport in the Making of Chicago.* Lanham, MD: Scarecrow Press.
———, ed. 1995. *Sports in North America: A Documentary History.* Vol. 5, *Sports Organized, 1880–1900.* Gulf Breeze, FL: Academic International Press.
Green, Harvey. 1988. *Fit for America: Health, Fitness, Sport, and American Society.* Baltimore: Johns Hopkins University Press.
Hardy, Stephen. 1982. *How Boston Played: Sport, Recreation, and Community, 1865–1915.* Boston: Northeastern University Press.
Kirsch, George B., ed. 1992. *Sports in North America: A Documentary History.* Vol. 3, *The Rise of Modern*

Sports, 1840–1860. Gulf Breeze, FL: Academic International Press.

Rader, Benjamin G. 1983. *American Sports: From the Age of Folk Games to the Age of Spectators.* Englewood Cliffs, NJ: Prentice-Hall.

Riess, Steven A. 1989. *City Games: The Evolution of American Urban Society and the Rise of Sports.* Urbana: University of Illinois Press.

Rotundo, Anthony. 1994. *American Manhood: Transformations in Masculinity from the Revolution to the Modern Era.* New York: Basic Books.

Smith, Ronald A. 1990. *Sports and Freedom: The Rise of Big-Time College Athletics.* New York: Oxford University Press.

Sports, 1921 to the Present

By the end of the nineteenth century organized sports for boys, such as baseball, football, and basketball leagues sponsored by ethnic clubs, schools, settlement houses, religious, and civic agencies, existed throughout the United States. Such groups expanded their efforts and influences throughout the twentieth century as adults increasingly managed and controlled boys' play in an effort to curb perceived abuses and prevent juvenile delinquency, especially of lower-class urban male youth.

By 1920 many large cities had joined the Playground Association of America in providing play spaces for urban children. Small children enjoyed neighborhood sandlots, and older ones frequented playgrounds, which were often located adjacent to the public schools. In such spaces male and female supervisors sought to train children to play in a particular manner; they wanted to teach American values of discipline, teamwork, and loyalty through supervised sporting activities. Although playgrounds had slides, swings, and gymnastic apparatus for free play, playground supervisors emphasized the American team sports of baseball, football, and basketball. Athletic supervisors expected boys to become better citizens by learning teamwork, self-sacrifice, a strong work ethic, and deference to authority. Track and field contests and fitness tests also instilled competitiveness, the basis for the capitalist economic system. Children received prizes and badges for goals reached as they vied for neighborhood and city championships.

Park districts and playgrounds often served as battlegrounds when competing ethnic or racial groups resided in neighborhoods close to the park and play areas. Progressive reformers encouraged boys of different races and ethnic groups to play sports together, and boys played relatively harmoniously until African Americans moved to northern cities in large numbers during World War I. Subsequently, officials segregated play areas, and violations of segregated spaces could lead to race riots. In 1919 such a case ensued in Chicago when a black youth wandered across the line marking a racially divided beach. White youths stoned and killed him, an incident that resulted in a citywide race riot that cost more than thirty lives. Similar though less violent confrontations took place between other members of ethnic groups, particularly traditional European rivals such as Poles and Jews.

In the larger park districts, teams, often composed of rival ethnic factions, vied for supremacy and bragging rights. By the 1920s boys had formed social-athletic clubs and basement clubs, where they gathered to play cards or other games, entertain friends, and sometimes engage in illicit activities. Dances and other fundraising activities provided these clubs with operating expenses or capital to gamble on athletic contests. Larger groups

High school football game, Georgia, 1941 (Library of Congress)

often enjoyed the financial support of local politicians, who provided clubhouse space, team uniforms, and sports equipment in return for political support and muscle during elections. Business owners, too, often supplied similar amenities for advertising and community pride.

Not only politicians and businesspeople but also newspapers used the public sporting spaces to promote their own entrepreneurial ventures. During the winter, newspapers promoted ice-skating races, known as the "Silver Skates," that produced local and urban champions. In the park field houses and in urban gyms, boxers trained for the Golden Gloves fights, sponsored by the *New York Daily News* and the *Chicago Tribune*. The pugilistic competition pitted champions from the urban rivals against one another as early as 1923. By the following decade, the newspapers organized in a national ef-

fort to promote boxing and their own circulation figures. By 1938 the Golden Gloves tournament drew 23,000 entries from twenty-six states, with winners forming an American team for competition with international foes. Newspapers also sponsored swimming races and bowling tournaments in various cities. The latter provided working-class boys with employment as pin spotters, and the sport enjoyed great popularity throughout the 1930s and 1940s. Bowling alleys became a traditional leisure setting for teenagers thereafter for both sport and socializing.

Many of the boxers in the Golden Gloves competitions represented the Catholic Youth Organization (CYO), founded in Chicago in 1930. The CYO offered a comprehensive sports program aimed at combating juvenile delinquency and urban gangs and promoting racial harmony. It featured its own international boxing team and the world's largest basketball league, with 130 teams in its Chicago-area parishes. Those two sports in particular offered greater opportunities for interracial competition. CYO boxing tournaments featured a wide variety of racial and ethnic competitors by the late 1930s.

Interscholastic competition in football, basketball, and baseball drew great media and popular attention, particularly for intercity matches, which had been popular since the turn of the century. Urban rivalries were played out among high school baseball teams, with city champions meeting in major league stadiums to determine preeminence. Even mediocre football teams traveled across the country to claim regional and national honors when their local seasons concluded. The Chicago Prep Bowl, an annual city championship played between the Catholic and public school leagues, drew 120,000 fans to Soldier Field in 1937, the largest crowd to ever witness a football game. Starting in 1928, the University of Chicago sponsored a national high school basketball championship tournament. Five years later, Catholics initiated their own national basketball championship at Loyola University in Chicago to accommodate parochial schools. The B'nai B'rith organized similar sporting opportunities for Jewish youth.

Ethnic athletic clubs, which had tried to retain European languages and values, emphasized gymnastics and soccer. By the 1920s, however, they began sponsoring baseball, football, and basketball teams in order to retain the support of their American-born offspring. For example, Young Men's Hebrew Associations (YMHAs) participated in interleague competitions with other ethnic groups, and they also played other non-Jewish youth teams.

Other organizations fostered the growth of American team sports as well. The American Legion, a military veterans' group, sponsored baseball teams for fifteen- to eighteen-year-old boys starting in 1925. Their first national championship followed a year later and gained television coverage in 1988. Nearly 95,000 players on 5,000 teams participated in the program in 1999. Little League Baseball offered competition for younger boys starting in 1939. By the end of the century, it had expanded to an international operation in over ninety countries with an annual televised championship game. The Pony League, founded in 1950, provided baseball for the remaining segment of the eight to eighteen age group. The Pop Warner football program fulfills a similar function. Started in 1929, the association organizes local leagues, consisting of flag football for boys ages five to eight and tackle football for boys ages seven to sixteen. By 1999 more than 300,000 participants vied for the national championship. In addition to the Pop Warner program, numerous smaller organizations and public park districts offer similar activities in football, basketball, and soccer. The American Youth Soccer Organization originated in California in 1964 and has since grown into a national operation with more than 600,000 players. A multitude of local, unaffiliated soccer programs swell that number considerably throughout the United States.

Two Young Men's Christian Association (YMCA) instructors, James Naismith and William G. Morgan, respectively, invented the games of basketball and volleyball in the 1890s. The physical educators of the YMCA have been instrumental in the international growth of both sports since the early twentieth century. The United States Volleyball Association was established in 1928. In addition to widespread interscholastic play of both sports at the high school level, boys' basketball has enjoyed phenomenal growth in local parks, churches, and community centers as well as neighborhood playgrounds and rural sites.

Numerous organizations have fostered a wide variety of individual sports. As early as 1880, cyclists organized as the League of American Wheelmen. Like other sports associations of the time, the League of American Wheelmen mandated segregation by prohibiting young black athletes from joining. Though most boys engage in cycling in an unorganized manner, recently motocross racing and mountain biking events have become more organized. Competitive national and international cycling championships attract many boys in the late twentieth century.

The United States Figure Skating Association, founded in 1921, provided national competition in the sport, and local skating clubs provided training facilities and coaching for boy skaters. Speed skating remains centered in particular northern climates such as Wisconsin and Minnesota. Roller skating, which was popular in the late nineteenth century, enjoyed a resurgence in the twentieth but gave way to other boys' sports as technology improved. Skateboarding began in California as an adaptation of surfing in the 1950s and spread across the United States, symbolic of a rebellious youth culture with its own particular dress, language, and physical style. The National Skateboarding Association formed in 1981, and the sport gradually moved toward mainstream incorporation thanks to organized, televised, national competitions thereafter. Roller blading also assumed national attention as part of the physical fitness movement in the last two decades of the twentieth century. By

1999 inline skating claimed 27 million practitioners, with another 3 million boys, most from thirteen to twenty years of age, who played street or roller hockey.

Boys took up winter sports in increasing numbers as well. Ice hockey, previously relegated to the tier of northern states, gained numerous adherents nationwide as indoor rinks sprouted around the country and boys joined peewee hockey leagues. Ice hockey teams and clubs for boys of various ages continue to be popular with male youth in many parts of the country. Ice hockey has grown in popularity among boys since the 1960s, with outstanding hockey players participating in intercollegiate competition when they get older. Other boys engaged in skiing, snowmobiling, or snowboarding, the youth culture winter counterpart to skateboarding that emerged in the 1960s. Now snowboarding competitions enable boys to display their physical skills and athleticism in organized events.

Even before skateboarding and snowboarding, surfing served as the sport of youthful dissent. Anglo-Hawaiian boys learned to ride the waves as native Hawaiians did in the early 1900s, and the activity spread to California beaches by midcentury. By the 1960s surfing had spawned a lifestyle that included particular dress, hairstyles, music, and consumerism and was often featured in movies. The American Surfing Association, established in 1976, fostered organized competitive events. Technology brought new sports to the beach in the form of parasailing and windsurfing in the latter half of the century. At public and private water facilities, both swimming and waterskiing maintained a longer history of competition and recreation than did surfing. Motorboats appeared by the 1920s, and they were soon towing skiers. The American Water Ski Association originated in 1939 and continued to gain increasing stature after World War II. Swimming, a timeless recreational and utilitarian activity, had a centuries-long competitive history but gained even greater participation with its inclusion in high school, park district, YMCA, and YMHA programs. Age-group teams and competitions abound throughout the United States today for various swimming and diving categories.

Boys have played golf since at least the 1890s, but the American Junior Golf Association was not established until 1977. The association showcases the talents of both boys and girls ages thirteen to eighteen in tournaments designed to attract college scholarships. Millions more play the game for purely recreational purposes. Country club links and public courses regularly draw boys to test their golf skills.

Like golf, racket sports experienced substantial growth during the twentieth century. Wealthier middle-class and upper-class boys began playing tennis in the 1880s. The game drew greater numbers of participants as it moved from country clubs to schools, inner-city parks, and independent programs. The National Junior Tennis League organized in 1968, and tennis academies tutor elite players. Tennis tournaments for boys of diverse ages take place at local, state, and national levels. The United States Tennis Association sponsors the national sixteen- and eighteen-year-old championships for outstanding junior tennis players. Most youth who play the game continue to do so on public and neighborhood courts. Although racquetball and badminton are less popular than tennis, these games' players pursue their pastimes in similar fashion, and the badminton players enjoy the status of interscholastic competition in some state high schools.

Both gymnastics and track and field, which are among the oldest sports, have experienced declining participation figures as fewer high schools field teams and programs and the public parks have shifted their focus to other team sports. Road races, however, continue to enjoy great popularity as part of the fitness movement, and running clubs offer youth exposure to the sport and training for races of varying distances. Private gymnastic clubs offer training for boys, mostly in urban areas.

Boys have taken to newer outdoor adventure sports in increasing numbers in recent decades. Rock climbing no longer requires an excursion to remote places. Climbing walls are more readily accessible in health clubs, school gymnasiums, and commercial facilities. New technology has made kayaking more affordable, and its practice requires only some nearby waterway. Even mountain biking, which previously required proximity to particular geographic areas, has been adapted in heartland communities with the construction of simulated courses, often built by boys themselves. In the late twentieth century, the commercial production of equipment for boys' sports promoted their participation in sports, whether in the water, in the gymnasium, or on the playing field.

Gerald R. Gems
Linda J. Borish

See also Basketball; Boxing; Football; Ice Hockey; Skateboarding; Skiing; Tennis

References and further reading
Berryman, Jack W. 1975. "From the Cradle to the Playing Field: America's Emphasis on Highly Organized

Competitive Sports for Preadolescent Boys." *Journal of Sport History* (Fall): 112–131.

Borish, Linda J. Forthcoming. *Landmarks of American Sports.* American Landmarks Series. Edited by James O. Horton. New York: Oxford University Press.

Erickson, Judith B. 1983. *Directory of American Youth Organizations.* Omaha, NE: Boys Town.

Gems, Gerald R. 1996. "The Prep Bowl: Sport, Religion and Americanization in Chicago." *Journal of Sport History* 23, no. 3: 284–302.

Goodman, Cary. 1979. *Choosing Sides: Playground and Street Life on the Lower East Side.* New York: Schocken Books.

Kirsch, George, Othello Harris, and Claire E. Nolte, eds. 2000. *Encyclopedia of Ethnic Sports in the United States.* Westport, CT: Greenwood Press.

Mormino, Gary Ross. 1982. "The Playing Fields of St. Louis: Italian Immigrants and Sport, 1925–1941." *Journal of Sport History* 9 (Summer): 5–16.

Rader, Benjamin G. 1983. *American Sports: From the Age of Folk Games to the Age of Spectators.* Englewood Cliffs, NJ: Prentice-Hall.

Riess, Steven. 1989. *City Games: The Evolution of American Urban Society and the Rise of Sports.* Urbana: University of Illinois Press.

Substance Abuse
See Illegal Substances

Suicide
The term *suicidal* refers to behavior intended to bring about one's death or the behavior of one who engages in life-threatening action and is indifferent to surviving it. The outcome of a suicidal action may be fatal (i.e., suicide) or nonfatal. *Suicidal ideation* refers to thinking or talking about killing oneself. Historically, in Western thought, suicide has been considered a male behavior. In the nineteenth century, numerous European and U.S. commentators argued that killing oneself required a degree of energy, courage, and intelligence that was incompatible with the nature of women. At the time, it was also assumed that suicide was a "disease" of "civilized people" and urban communities. "Simple" and "primitive" people, which at the time meant women, the less educated, and all non–western European people, were thought to be immune to suicide (Canetto 1997b; Kushner 1993).

Over the years it has become clear that suicide is not limited to males or to industrialized societies. Recent epidemiological studies show that in some countries (e.g., China), suicide is more common among females, particularly in certain age groups. In the United States, however, suicide is primarily a male death. In fact, it is a growing cause of death among young males. Suicide is the third leading cause of death for males ages fifteen to nineteen in the United States. Most of these suicides are by firearms, more specifically handguns (Canetto 1997b; Canetto and Lester 1995; Johnson, Krug, and Potter 2000).

Suicide rates are highest among Native American males, although there is significant variability across tribes. Historically, Euro-American youths have had much higher rates of suicide than African American youths. In recent decades, however, rates for African American male adolescents have increased more rapidly than rates for Euro-American male adolescents, such that the gap between the rates for these two groups is narrower. The increase in African American male youth suicide has been particularly substantial in the South (CDC 1998).

Suicide rates in boys exceed those in girls by a ratio of 5:1 (Canetto and Lester 1995). The gender difference in mortality holds across ethnic groups, although suicide rates vary greatly from group to group. Native American boys have higher rates of suicide than Native American girls, although the latter have higher rates of suicide than Euro-American boys. The paradox is that boys are two to three times less likely than girls to report suicidal ideation or to engage in nonfatal acts of suicidal behavior (Canetto 1997a; Lewinsohn, Rohde, and Seeley 1996). Gender differences in nonfatal suicidal behavior are not found in all ethnic groups in the United States. For example, among native Hawaiians and some Native Americans (i.e., among Pueblo Indians but not Zuni Indians), adolescent males report similar rates of nonfatal suicidal behavior as adolescent females (Canetto 1997a; Howard-Pitney et al. 1992). Gay males have unusually high rates of nonfatal suicidal behavior relative to heterosexual males. No definitive information is available on rates of death by suicide among gay males (Remafedi 1999).

In the United States, suicidal behavior of all kinds is uncommon in boys and girls before puberty. The incidence of suicide increases more rapidly among males than among females during adolescence and young adulthood. In recent decades, the gender gap in suicide mortality has been widening, especially among some U.S. ethnic minority groups. Rates of suicide mortality for U.S. ethnic minority boys have increased markedly, leading to a growing gender gap. Suicide rates among girls of all U.S. ethnic groups have remained stable (Canetto 1997a; CDC 1998).

Male rates of suicide mortality exceed those of females in most countries where suicidality is recorded. The male predominance in suicide mortality among adolescents, however, is not universal. For example, in several South American, Caribbean, and Asian countries, including Brazil, Cuba, the Dominican Republic, Ecuador, Paraguay, the Philippines, Singapore, and Thailand, young females' suicide mortality exceeds that of young males. In Mauritius, young males and females have the same rates of suicide mortality (Canetto and Lester 1995; Johnson, Krug, and Potter 2000).

Why are boys less likely than girls to report depression, suicidal thoughts, and nonfatal suicidal behavior and, at the same time, more likely to die of suicide? Why do the gender differences in nonfatal suicidal behavior occur in some U.S. ethnic groups and not in others? Why are gay males at higher risk of nonfatal suicidal behavior than heterosexual males? The contrasting trends in nonfatal and fatal suicidal behavior in males and females have been called the "gender paradox" of suicidal behavior (Canetto and Sakinofsky 1998). Many theories have been proposed to explain this paradox. However, most fail to account for the variations in the gender paradox by ethnicity and sexual orientation. In other words, since the gender paradox of suicidal behavior is not universal, it needs to be understood in light of cultural factors.

A theory of gender and suicidal behavior that addresses cultural variability is the theory of cultural scripts (Canetto 1997b). This theory is grounded in the observation of a correspondence between social norms and actual behavior in different cultures. Persons tend to engage in the behaviors (including suicidal behaviors) that are meaningful and permissible in their community. Different communities have unique scripts of suicidal behavior, that is, specific conditions under which suicidal behavior is expected and by whom. The scenario of the suicidal act (including the actor, method, precipitants, and themes) and the consequences of the suicidal behavior are part of this script. Even though each suicide is in some way unique, it also shares some characteristics with other suicides from the same community. In other words, there are common and scripted elements in suicidal acts within cultures. One would expect cultural scripts of gender and suicidal behavior to be particularly influential among adolescents, who are in the process of defining their identity and may take messages about gender-appropriate behavior more seriously than adults.

In the United States, boys' low rates of suicidal ideation and behavior and their high rates of suicide mortality are consistent with dominant beliefs about masculinity and suicidal behavior. Studies indicate that it is considered unmasculine to talk about suicidal behavior and to survive a suicidal act. Adolescent males have a greater fear of disapproval over having suicidal thoughts than adolescent females. Nonfatal suicidal behavior in males receives more criticism than the same behavior in females. Males are particularly critical of other males who survive a suicidal act. Nonfatal suicidal behavior appears to be associated with some identification with or adoption of behaviors considered feminine across sexual orientations. In one study, boys who acted in ways perceived as feminine were more likely to engage in nonfatal suicidal behavior during adulthood than conventionally masculine boys or masculine girls. In another study, gay boys with a history of suicidal behavior were more likely to describe themselves as feminine than gay boys without a history of suicidal behavior. No studies so far have explored gender meanings of nonfatal suicidal behavior among ethnic minority adolescents. One could expect less gender-specific beliefs about nonfatal suicidal behavior in ethnic groups with similar gender rates of nonfatal suicidal behavior.

In the United States, killing oneself is viewed as masculine behavior. Male suicide is judged as less wrong and less foolish than female suicide, and males who kill themselves are considered more rational than females who kill themselves. In terms of precipitants, impersonal failures are viewed as more masculine than personal difficulties. For example, males who kill themselves following a relationship problem are considered more maladjusted than males who commit suicide after an achievement problem. Adolescent males say that they are less fearful of death and injury than same-age females. No studies so far have explored gender meanings of suicide among ethnic minority adolescents in the United States. The fact that male rates are higher than female rates within each ethnic group suggests that killing oneself is associated with masculinity across ethnic groups. Moreover, the growing disparity among male and female rates among African American adolescents may be an indication of the increasing influence of dominant beliefs about gender and suicide.

Gender differences in method probably account in part for males' higher rates of mortality from suicidal behavior. In the United States, boys are more likely than girls to use firearms and hanging as a method of suicide. The percentage of youth suicide in which a firearm is involved is highest in the United States as compared with countries of similar economic background. Firearms carry a high risk for immediate lethality. They do not allow much room for survival or rescue, even when the suicidal behavior occurs in public places (Canetto and Sakinofsky 1998). In the United States, firearms are assumed to be a masculine, "hard" suicide method, but poisoning is considered a feminine, "soft" method. At the same time, it is important to remember that gender meanings and the lethality of different methods are, to some degree, culture-specific. For example, in the United States, poisoning is a method that is more common in females than in males and is assumed to be feminine. It is also a method that in the United States has low lethality because it typically involves overdosing on medications, for which intervention is generally available and effective. In developing countries such as Sri Lanka, however, poisoning is not a method that is primarily used by females or a method that is considered feminine. Poisoning in developing countries typically involves household or farming poisons. Effective medical care for poisoning is not routinely accessible; hence poisoning is highly lethal. In Sri Lanka, males, like females, use poisoning as a primary method of suicide (Canetto 1997b).

It is unclear whether U.S. boys' suicide method preferences reflect their high intent to die because adolescents' knowledge of method lethality is often inaccurate. It is likely, however, that more male suicidal acts are intended as fatal. Most suicidal acts involve some planning. There is also a correlation between intent and lethality. At the same time, it is important to acknowledge that, in the United States, boys' choice of suicide method takes place against a cultural script that treats surviving a suicidal act as unmasculine. Consider the dominant language of suicidal behavior in the United States. The term *suicide attempt*, which used to refer to

nonfatal suicidal behavior, suggests that a person tried and failed at suicide. The terms *completed suicide* and *successful suicide* convey that dying of suicide represents a form of success. Given prevailing ideologies of masculinity, males may feel they cannot allow themselves to fail at suicide, even though success in this case means death.

The search for causes of adolescent suicidal behavior, fatal and nonfatal, spans many fields of research. A sampling of proposed risk factors includes genetic markers, national unemployment rates, parental education and income, childhood adversities, mental disorders, physical and sexual abuse, parental divorce, a family history of depression, suicidal behavior and substance abuse, cognitive style, coping skills, and exposure to suicide models. Information on risk factors and dynamics unique to suicidal males, however, is limited because most researchers do not focus on questions of gender and do not separately examine male data. Also, information on risk factors has not advanced enough to help predict individual suicidal behavior. Many young persons experience some or many of the risk factors, and yet never become suicidal.

In the United States, death by suicide is associated with a similar set of antecedents as nonfatal suicidal behavior. Among mental disorders, alcohol and substance abuse, conduct disorders, and depression have been most commonly associated with suicidal ideation and behavior, both fatal and nonfatal, among adolescents. Alcohol and substance abuse and conduct disorders appear to be stronger correlates of suicidal behavior for boys than for girls. Psychiatric co-morbidity increases the risk for all suicidal behaviors. Although psychopathology is considered by some the single most influential predictor of suicidal behavior, only a small proportion of adolescents with mental disorders engage in suicidal behavior; most do not. Physical illness and functional impairment may also play a role in nonfatal suicidal behavior. Low self-esteem, low academic achievement, peer difficulties, and social isolation have been identified as additional factors in nonfatal suicidal behavior. In addition, exposure to suicidal behavior (including a family history of suicidal behavior, recent suicidal behavior by a friend, and a person's own past suicidal episodes) has been found to increase the risk of all suicidal behaviors. Stressful life events, including turmoil and instability in key relationships and failures at school or work, can be precipitants of suicidal behavior in adolescents. Sexual abuse has emerged as a factor in gay male nonfatal suicidal behavior. In general, the more difficulties individuals have or have had, the more likely they are to engage in suicidal behavior. Although adversities increase the risk for suicidality, they are particularly potent in those adolescents with dysfunctional cognitive and coping styles. Finally, the availability of firearms is more of a risk factor for suicide in boys than for girls. Boys are more likely to use firearms in suicide. It is possible that, in the United States, guns may be perceived as a more masculine method.

A key issue in adolescent suicidal behavior is that risk factors affect boys and girls differently. Similar risk factors are associated with fatal suicidal behavior in boys and nonfatal suicidal behavior in girls. Relative to girls, boys seem protected from suicidal ideation and nonfatal suicidal behavior. At the same time, they have much higher rates of suicide mortality. One possibility is that boys have similar rates of suicidal ideation as girls but are less likely to admit it because of the stigma, for males, of talking about feeling suicidal. For the same reason, males may hide their nonfatal suicidal acts more often than females. It is also possible that professional caregivers are less willing to recognize and label as suicidal a variety of life-threatening behaviors in males. Many questions about boys and suicidal behavior remain unanswered. For example, it would be helpful to learn more directly what prevents boys from allowing themselves to survive a suicidal act and how beliefs of gender-appropriate suicidal behavior may influence boys' choice of suicide method and outcome.

The gender differences in suicidal behaviors and the variations in boys' suicidal behavior depending on ethnicity, nationality, and sexual orientation point to new directions in primary prevention. In the United States, suicide prevention programs should consistently address questions of gender, sexual orientation, and ethnicity. One possibility would be to include a didactic component on the epidemiology of gender and suicidal behavior across ethnicities and sexual orientations. Suicide prevention educational programs should also assess adolescents' beliefs about gender and suicidal behavior. If such an assessment revealed an endorsement of the notion that killing oneself is powerful and masculine, the program leaders should be prepared to engage adolescents in examining and challenging this dysfunctional belief. Finally, suicide prevention programs should also consider the implications of boys' critical attitudes toward persons who reveal suicidal thoughts or acts. Although these attitudes probably protect boys from nonfatal suicidal behavior, they also have negative consequences. In nonsuicidal boys, they are likely to signal an unwillingness to reach out to suicidal peers. In boys who are suicidal, negative attitudes toward nonfatal suicidal behavior may increase shame and interfere with help-seeking behavior. Ultimately, these attitudes may make it difficult for boys to allow themselves to survive a suicidal act.

Silvia Sara Canetto

References and further reading
Canetto, Silvia Sara. 1997a. "Meanings of Gender and Suicidal Behavior among Adolescents." *Suicide and Life-Threatening Behaviors* 27: 339–351.
———. 1997b. "Gender and Suicidal Behavior: Theories and Evidence." Pp. 138–167 in *Review of Suicidology*. Edited by R. W. Maris, M. M. Silverman, and Canetto. New York: Guilford.
Canetto, Silvia Sara, and David Lester. 1995. "Gender and the Primary Prevention of Suicide Mortality." *Suicide and Life-Threatening Behavior* 25: 58–69.
Canetto, Silvia Sara, and Isaac Sakinofsky. 1998. "The Gender Paradox in Suicide." *Suicide and Life-Threatening Behavior* 28: 1–23.
CDC (Centers for Disease Control and Prevention). 1998. "Suicide among Black Youths—United States, 1980–1995." *Journal of the American Medical Association* 279, no. 18: 1431.
Howard-Pitney, Beth, Teresa D. LaFromboise, Mike Basil, Benedette September, and Mike Johnson. 1992. "Psychological and Social Indicators of Suicide Ideation and Suicide Attempts in Zuni Adolescents." *Journal of Consulting and Clinical Psychology* 60: 473–476.
Johnson, Gregory R., Etienne G. Krug, and Lloyd B. Potter. 2000. "Suicide among Adolescents and Young Adults: A Cross-National Comparison of 34 Countries." *Suicide and Life-Threatening Behavior* 30: 74–82.
Kushner, Howard I. 1993. "Suicide, Gender, and the Fear of Modernity in Nineteenth-Century Medical and Social Thought." *Journal of Social History* 26, no. 3: 461–490.
Lewinsohn, Peter M., Paul Rohde, and John R. Seeley. 1996. "Adolescent Suicidal Ideation and Attempts: Prevalence, Risk Factors, and Clinical Implications." *Clinical Psychology: Science and Practice* 3, no. 1: 25–46.
Remafedi, Gary. 1999. "Suicide and Sexual Orientation." *Archives of General Psychiatry* 56: 885–886.

Sunday Schools

The first American Sunday schools were enlightened and philanthropic efforts founded in the 1790s to instill virtue in children, particularly unruly urban boys, in order to prepare them for citizenship. By the 1810s, however, evangelical educational methods worked out in England were introduced in the United States, with the purpose of eliciting religious conversion experiences in children. Taught by lay teachers representing various Protestant denominations, these Sunday schools were so popular in the early nineteenth century that a national association, the American Sunday School Union, was organized in 1824 to spread schools and their materials across the nation. Before public schools became widespread in the 1840s, many boys and girls learned disciplined behavior and how to read in Sunday schools. By midcentury, however, the ecumenical ideal was eclipsed by decentralized denominational schools designed to supplement public school education. At the same time, the emphasis on religious conversion was replaced by notions of Christian nurture, advocating the gradual religious development of children. Teaching methods were borrowed from public schools, and materials were designed to develop manly piety in boys. Yet, as Americans continued to focus their fears of social chaos on the behavior of male youth, the Sunday school remained an important

Sunday school in an agricultural workers' camp, Bridgeton, New Jersey, 1942 (Library of Congress)

institution for teaching not only religion but also self-discipline and correct social relations to boys.

During the seventeenth and early eighteenth centuries, Anglican, Congregational, and Lutheran ministers expected conversion or entry to communion to occur in the late teenage years or early twenties and did not attempt to elicit conversion experiences in children. In the late eighteenth century, the first American Sunday schools were based on those founded in England to ameliorate living conditions among the urban poor. Motivated by Pennsylvania's ratification of the federal Constitution in 1787 and passage of the First Amendment separating church and state in 1791, Benjamin Rush and other Philadelphia gentlemen turned

to the voluntary association, founding the First Day Society to conduct similar schools for children of their city. "Who can witness," Rush wrote, "the practices of swimming, sliding, and skating which prevail so universally on Sundays in most cities of the United States, and not wish for similar institutions to rescue our poor children from destruction?" (quoted in Reinier 1996, 79). Members of the First Day Society hoped to discipline children of the city's turbulent lower class, yet they also sought to provide elementary education for boys who would become apprentices and eventually urban citizens. And they hoped that their schools would become a model for tax-supported education throughout the state. The schools they supported from 1791 until 1820 taught orderly habits, literacy, and skills yet were grounded in Christianity. Boys and girls were expected to attend public worship at their respective churches, and the Bible was used as a textbook. Annual public examinations rewarded scholarly progress and good behavior with the society's approval and a "premium," usually a little book, whereas misbehavior was punished by shame and, if repeated, exclusion from school. By 1810 members of the society considered their experiment a success; their annual report concluded: "A recurrence to the early minutes has given in Evidence that some of the Lads then steadily attended the School and received Premiums for good Behavior and Improvement in their studies . . . [and] have since become opulent and respectable Members of the community" (quoted in Reinier 1996, 80).

Shortly after, however, evangelical educational methods imported from England were introduced in the United States when the Reverend Robert May conducted an interdenominational Sunday school also directed at Philadelphia working-class children. May deliberately attempted to evoke an emotional response by preaching on themes of death and judgment. He clearly sought to elicit a conversion experience in the children, his volunteer assistant teachers offered religious instruction rather than secular elementary education, and his system of rewards taught children the values and procedures of a cash economy. A child who recited correctly a lesson memorized from Scripture or catechism earned a black ticket. A number of black tickets bought a red one; and a number of red tickets purchased a premium, usually a hymnbook or catechism. Riding the crest of religious enthusiasm generated by revivals of the Second Great Awakening, these evangelical

methods were immensely popular. As Sunday schools proliferated in the city, in 1817 young men and their merchant supporters formed the Philadelphia Sunday and Adult School Union. Within a year they were conducting 43 interdenominational Sunday schools that instructed 5,658 children and 312 adults. The schools initially had been intended for children from poor and working-class families, but by 1820 they were also attracting children of the affluent. That same year, members of the First Day Society realized that their more secular effort had been superseded, and, ceasing to operate their schools, they voted to donate their remaining funds to the Philadelphia Sunday and Adult School Union (Reinier 1996, 89).

In 1818 managers of the interdenominational union drew up "Internal Regulations for the Sunday Schools." Their first goal was the spread of literacy. The union printed alphabet cards and a spelling book in order that children could be instructed in reading until they mastered the difficult Bible. Equally important was formation of orderly habits; regulations stressed industry, punctuality, and cleanliness. "Order is delightful," the managers wrote, "and although it imposes restraint upon the scholars it will be found to be pleasing to them in practice" (quoted in Reinier 1996, 89). But the primary purpose of the Sunday school was to save souls. As adults began to focus on what they called "early piety," they sought to elicit conversion experiences in boys and girls as young as seven or eight years of age. According to the internal regulations, Sunday school teaching required three methods. The "expounding" method was lecture, and the "catechetical" method was question and answer. Neither could be effective, however, without "exhortation," through which the emotions of the child were "awakened" to be receptive to religious instruction. By 1820 the Philadelphia Sunday and Adult School Union was reproducing religious tracts in order to elicit the desired response. Many of these tracts were originally from England, and the managers were never fully satisfied with them, objecting that they reflected British rather than American "civil government, manners, and customs." For example, they rejected a British theme of contented poverty as unsuitable for aspiring Americans. But they did retain descriptions of the deaths of pious children as an appropriate method of awakening.

In 1824 the Philadelphia Sunday and Adult School Union conducted more than 700 Sunday schools in 17 states, in which more than 7,000 teachers instructed 48,000 students. In that year alone the union republished 133,000 imported tracts, which it distributed not only in the mid-Atlantic states but north to New England, south to the Carolinas and Mississippi, and west throughout Kentucky, Tennessee, Ohio, Indiana, and Missouri (American Sunday School Union 1825, 32–33). Seeking to continue the spread of its influence, it reorganized as a national association, the American Sunday School Union, and began to produce materials for a national market. Its new lay Committee of Publications rejected British tracts that focused on child death. Instead, the committee designed a new evangelical children's literature that wove its religious message into such topics as natural science. Viewing boys as untamed animals, the new Sunday school books taught internalized restraint, reminding children that God watched them all the time. Potential citizens were instructed in self-discipline by books such as *Election Day*, which featured examples of worthy and unworthy voters (American Sunday School Union 1827). And a male role model was provided in *Life of George Washington*, in which the exemplary character of the first president had been formed and his animal nature tamed by the influence of his pious mother (Reed 1829).

Some nineteenth-century boys did turn to evangelical religion when faced with their own illness or the death of a sibling or parent. Twelve-year-old James Riker, Jr., of New York City, born in 1822, was embarrassed when his father's clerk, a Methodist who shared his bedroom, encouraged him to kneel in prayer, and was ashamed to tell his family about the incident. When stricken with typhus fever the following summer, however, he was soothed when his sister sang hymns she had learned at a Methodist meeting. Shortly after, his mother died suddenly from cholera. A few months later, James experienced religious conversion at a revival the family attended at the New York Seventh Presbyterian Church (Reinier 1996, 92). Other boys, such as the Methodist John H. Vincent of Illinois, born in 1830, found efforts to elicit conversion in children "gloomy" and "morbid." As an adult, he felt that the religion of his childhood encouraged excessive emotionalism and that it had deprived him of a spontaneous "boy life." He preferred an approach more like the new literature of the American Sunday School Union and "the stability of the Sunday school to the upheavals of a revival" (quoted in Boylan 1988, 91).

Although by 1830 the American Sunday School Union was a genuine nationalizing force, its evangelical message was rejected by freethinkers, Roman Catholics, Quakers, Unitarians, and Jews. Denominations such as the Methodists were skeptical of its ecumenical appeal and began to organize their own Sunday schools. Middle-class reformers began to advocate tax-supported and state-supervised systems of education, with full-time schools taught by professional teachers. When managers of the American Sunday School Union urged adoption of the new evangelical children's literature in the Massachusetts public schools in 1838, Horace Mann, a Unitarian and secretary of the state board of education, strenuously objected. The new common schools would offer a Protestant republican curriculum but avoid sectarian instruction. By the 1840s, as public schools became widespread, Sunday schools were increasingly decentralized and supported by religious denominations to instruct children in particular doctrines. A new generation rejected the earlier emphasis on a cataclysmic conversion experience and urged concepts of Christian nurture, or the gradual development of religious sensibility in children. Teachers adopted new educational methods such as those of Johann Heinrich Pestalozzi, and the Sunday school, which no longer taught reading, became a supplement to the public school.

Yet especially in times of social chaos, Sunday schools continued to teach self-discipline to boys. During and after Reconstruction in the South, freed children and adults learned to read in Sunday schools taught by white or black teachers. Mission schools in northern cities and on the western frontier brought in the unchurched and taught values of public order and decorum, separating the rough from the respectable. Many urban missions became neighborhood institutions that offered social services and founded industrial schools. As the nineteenth century progressed, ministers and lay teachers feared that boys were being socialized largely by mothers and female teachers and advocated a more muscular Christianity. They urged that Sunday school literature reflect the behavior of real boys and that the curriculum include opportunity for spontaneity and robust play.

In the early twentieth century, leaders in a variety of fields attacked the faith in moral absolutes that previously had permeated American society. Pragmatic educators such as John Dewey advocated an open world of change rather than fixity, and the use of science to achieve human goals. Public schools became increasingly secularized, a trend reinforced by Supreme Court interpretation of the First Amendment in decisions that barred religious instruction in public schools (*McCullum v. Board of Education*, 1948) and outlawed school prayer (*Engel v. Vitale*, 1962) and compulsory Bible reading in the classroom (*Abington School District v. Shempp*, 1963). In this context, religious instruction was confined to the denominational Sunday school, supplemented by a variety of parachurch organizations. Yet the evangelical thrust of the earlier American Sunday School Union and later versions of Protestant fundamentalism was never fully extinguished. The revival of evangelical Protestantism in the 1980s made religious education in public schools once more a political issue. Fears of social and cultural chaos still focused on the behavior of male youth. In the diverse, pluralistic American society of the twenty-first century, the use of religious instruction and faith-based organizations to instill self-discipline in boys is still a matter of public concern and often of contentious debate.

Jacqueline S. Reinier

See also Books and Reading, 1800s; Muscular Christianity; Parachurch Ministry; Preachers in the Early Republic

References and further reading
American Sunday School Union.
   1825–1830. *Annual Reports.*
   Philadelphia: American Sunday School
   Union.
———. Committee of Publications. 1827.
   Election Day. Philadelphia: American
   Sunday School Union.
Boylan, Anne M. 1988. *Sunday School:*
   The Foundation of an American
   Institution, 1790–1880. New Haven:
   Yale University Press.
Marsden, George M. 1990. *Religion and*
   American Culture. New York: Harcourt
   Brace Jovanovich.
Reed, Anna. 1829. *Life of George*
   Washington. Philadelphia: American
   Sunday School Union.
Reinier, Jacqueline S. 1996. *From Virtue to*
   Character: American Childhood,
   1775–1850. New York: Twayne
   Publishers.

Superheroes

In 1938, Detective Comics (later DC Comics) introduced Superman, the first and best-known superhero, described in the first issue as "Champion of the oppressed, the physical marvel who has sworn to devote his existence to those in need!" Thus was born the prototype for subsequent superheroes who would appeal so powerfully to young boys—flashy costumes, secret identities, technical gadgetry, and tests of superhuman strength in which moral virtue prevails. Superman was followed the next year by another DC creation, Batman, a more humanized superhero. As the United States was about to enter World War II in 1941, Marvel Comics developed the Human Torch and its first huge star, Captain America, who regularly used his powers against the Nazis. After the comic book slump of the 1950s, Marvel went on to create in rapid succession a new generation of superheroes: the Fantastic Four (1961), the Incredible Hulk (1962), Thor (1962), Spiderman (1962), the X-men (1963), and Conan the Barbarian (1970). In fact, these well-known characters represent only a small fraction of the superheroes Marvel created, many of whom lasted only a few issues. The oddest was the 1941 creation the Whizzer, who gained superstrength by injecting himself with mongoose blood, a stunt unconvincing even by comic book standards.

Although the birth of comic book superheroes can be traced to the late 1930s, this genre combined the visual techniques of earlier comic strips with the storytelling that existed in dime novels and pulp fiction, which began to appear in the 1840s. Comic books are part of a long tradition of popular fiction that emphasized fast-moving (and often quickly written) stories of adventure, horror, violence, and the supernatural. *The Adventures of Tom Sawyer* opens with Tom immersed in the imagined world of pirates that he derived from Ned Buntline's dime novel *The Black Avenger of the Spanish Main: Or, The Fiend of Blood.* The world of pulp fiction was often violent, with many of the western adventures featuring killing, scalping, and drinking blood. The adventures of Davy Crockett, who became a mythic figure in dime novels after his death at the Alamo, contain descriptions that even by today's standards seem graphic. In one brawl Crockett describes the damage he did to his opponent: "His eye stood out about half an inch, and I felt the bottom of the socket with the end of my thumb" (quoted in Schechter 1996, 32). And unlike the heavily moralized stories such as those that would appear in the McGuffey readers, the dime novels existed for pure pleasure and escape.

Batman and Robin (Adam West and Ward Burt) from the television series (Kobol Collection)

Not surprisingly, boys often had to escape the surveillance of parents to read dime novels. Novelist Booth Tarkington would sneak away to the stables, or he would hide his books behind acceptable ones like *Pilgrim's Progress* by John Bunyan (1678). In the late nineteenth century, antivice groups led by Anthony Comstock began to target publishers of dime novels, whom they saw as endangering children too innocent and vulnerable to protect themselves. Comstock compared these novels to "literary poison, cast into the foundations of our social life . . . infecting the pure life and heart of our youth" (quoted in Beisel

1997, 70). This anxiety about popular culture and boyhood would resurface in the 1950s, when comic books—including the superheroes—would come under attack. It would again become a major political issue at the turn of the millennium as parents expressed concern about violence in video games, movies, and the hugely popular extension of superheroes—professional wrestling.

Beginning in the late 1940s, psychologist Frederic Wertham waged a one-man crusade against comic books. His claims that they contributed to juvenile delinquency led to congressional hearings and the "voluntary" decision to create a

Comics Code Authority to censor comic books. Wertham noted that by the time he is eighteen, the typical boy comic book reader would have absorbed a minimum of 18,000 pictorial beatings, shootings, stranglings, blood puddles, and torturings to death. Although Wertham's primary target was crime comics, he found Superman objectionable because he operated outside the law and because he belonged to a "superrace" that looked down at its inferiors; readers who identified with superheroes were presumably seduced into a form of racism. Wertham was especially concerned about Batman and his homoerotic attraction to Robin. Wonder Woman was, in Wertham's view, a man-hating lesbian.

As odd as Wertham's views seem today, his fight against comic books relies on three assumptions that would persist in subsequent challenges to films, television, and video games. First, childhood is a time of innocence, a term that connotes both ethical purity and defenselessness. The child is not equipped to mediate in any way the messages of popular culture, and boys in particular are seen as predisposed to imitative action. Second, researchers examining the effects of violence in the media effectively bypassed children, rarely interviewing them or exploring their perceptions—preferring to view them as helpless victims involved in a stimulus-response situation (Tobin 2000). And third, violence in the media is a single construct that includes both the Kennedy assassination and Superman hitting Lex Luther. In other words, "violence" is conflated into a single definable stimulus. This reduction is justified by the often repeated but dubious claim that children cannot distinguish between fantasy and reality—a failure that is the byproduct of their innocence.

From the standpoint of the censors, institutions like the home and school must be bastions that protect children from the poisonous influences of popular culture. Protecting childhood innocence requires vigilance on the part of parents and other adult authorities. As Comstock urged, "Let fathers, mothers, and teachers watch closely over the pockets, desks, and rooms of their children. Be sure that the seeds of moral death are not in your homes and schools" (quoted in Beisel 1997, 71). Yet advocates of dime novels and comic books turn this argument on its head. The surveillance that characterizes home and school creates the need for a subversive, aggressive literature that allows escape from (and mockery of) legitimate authority. Reading becomes a form of "underlife," a term used by Erving Goffman (1961) to explain a healthy form of resistance to being defined by institutional roles. So according to critics of popular culture, the home and school are protective bastions; according to supporters that very protectiveness pushes young boys to seek out subversive literature.

Some of the appeals of superhero comics are obvious—and hardly pathological. Unlike the elite literature of the schools, the plots move quickly to epic confrontation. In fact, one of the consistent complaints boys have about the literature they read in schools is that it moves too slowly (Millard 1997). The superhero landscape is cleared of legitimate authority: the Gotham City police are always so inadequate to the task that Superman's heroic action is necessary. The characters are dramatically illustrated; the idealized bodies of the male heroes are skillfully rendered, and those of female heroes like Wonder Woman have unmistakable sex appeal. The plotlines touch on readers' interest in transforming technological change, for example, the concern about nuclear radiation (the Incredible Hulk) and biological mutation (the Fantastic Four).

Although comic books are often dismissed as lacking three-dimensional characters, the writers at Marvel saw characterization as central to their work. Stan Lee, creator of Spiderman and other enduring superheroes at Marvel, conceived of the character as realistically human even while establishing Spiderman's ability to walk on buildings like an insect and shoot webs that allowed him to swing freely: "we do our best to treat ol' Spidey as if he could be your next door neighbor. Despite his superpowers, he still had money problems, dandruff, domestic problems, allergy attacks, self-doubts and unexpected defeats. In other words we try to think of him as real and to depict him accordingly" (Daniel 1993, 9).

For all the fantasy that surrounds superheroes, their stories touch on real anxieties of young adolescent boys who feel themselves to be awkward misfits like Peter Parker, the imaginative, alienated, "real-life" character who transforms into Spiderman. The superhero stories suggest self-transformative possibilities—even the timid and hesitant are capable of virtuous heroism. In the words of Marvel historian Les Daniel, Spiderman "remains Everyman, the super hero who could be you" (1993, 96). Even the Charles Atlas bodybuilding advertisements on the backs of many issues in the 1950s and 1960s reinforced this promise of physical and social self-transformation for boys.

The superheroes also became the subjects of satire and parody, particularly in the pages of *Mad Magazine*. Superman became Superduperman; Flash Gordon became Flesh Garden. In the 1960s the TV version of Batman was played as self-parody, particularly in the fight scenes when the action was punctuated by exclamations ("POW," "BOP," "CRUNCH") written comic book–style within the action. Dave Gilkey provided young readers with such epic titles as *Captain Underpants and the Perilous Plot of Professor Poopypants* and *Captain Underpants and the Invasion of the Incredibly Naughty Cafeteria Ladies from Outer Space*. But the most popular incarnation of self-parodying superheroes was undoubtedly professional wrestling as it began to aim for an audience of adolescent and preadolescent boys in the 1980s.

Professional wrestling has been televised since the late 1950s, and many of the basic techniques were developed early on: the colorful names (Gorgeous George, Bobo Brazil, Argentina Roco, Haystack Calhoun) and special finishing tactics, often particular to a wrestler, like the Coco Bop, the Stomach Claw, the Piledriver, and the Sleeper Hold. Unlike superhero stories in which virtue prevails, victory was regularly achieved by deceit, often the use of an illegal substance hidden in the wrestlers' trunks and employed when the feckless referee was invariably knocked senseless during critical moments in the bout. In the 1980s, bodybuilding techniques helped wrestlers sculpt their muscles to resemble the dimensions of comic book heroes. Their outfits were colorful spandex, and their props became more elaborate: Jake the Snake would enter the ring with a python around his neck; Ravishing Ricky Rude would spray his opponents with an atomizer containing perfume; and the Undertaker would carefully place his beaten opponent in a coffin at the end of each match.

In the 1990s the World Wrestling Federation, presided over by Vincent McMahon, became so popular that Monday Night

Raw, the most popular show on cable television, began to threaten a staple of male sports viewing, Monday Night Football. At one point in early 2000, two of the top three nonfiction best-sellers were "written" by professional wrestlers—Mankind (Mick Foley) and the Rock (Dwayne Johnson). Wrestlers also gained political prominence with Jesse "The Body" Ventura winning the governorship of Minnesota and the Rock speaking in prime time to the Republican National Convention.

To the standard features of professional wrestling, McMahon added soap opera, a constantly shifting story of sexual and professional intrigue in which he and his family played a part. Much of this story is played out in elaborate monologues between matches in which wrestlers would air their grievances, issue challenges, and express their feelings in a parody of New Age manhood. The announcers, the straight men in the drama, take this intrigue absolutely seriously, commenting on a spat between Stephanie McMahon and Triple H with the same seriousness ("Look at her eyes. Is she mad or what?") as they do the matches themselves. For boys who are expected to conform to the rules at home, in school, and when they play sports, these wrestling productions are particularly attractive because they self-consciously challenge codes of appropriate behavior and speech and flaunt traditional athletic fairness.

Over time, various versions of superhero genres have consistently created anxiety about the socialization of boys. Plato banished the poets from his imagined republic because their stories of the Trojan War would create unhealthy and uncritical emulation. Stendhal's classic novel, The Red and the Black (1830), is a cautionary tale about the idolization of heroes in the Napoleonic wars. Psychologists in the United States have consistently warned that extensive exposure to violent materials can increase aggressiveness, prompting periodic campaigns to restrict access for children. But the enduring popularity of superhero stories is evidence of the developmental function of the genre. They provide a way for boys to escape, even to mock and subvert adult authority that seems so confining. Mark Twain caught this appeal when he described the conclusion of Tom Sawyer's pirate adventures: "The boys dressed themselves, hid their accouterments, and went off grieving that there were no outlaws anymore and wondering what modern civilization could claim to have done to compensate for their loss. They said they would rather be outlaws a year in Sherwood Forest than President of the United States forever" (1946, 88)

Thomas Newkirk

See also Books and Reading, 1900–1960; Comic Books

References and further reading
Beisel, Nicola. 1997. *Imperiled Innocents: Anthony Comstock and Family Reproduction in Victorian America.* Princeton: Princeton University Press.
Daniel, Les. 1993. *Marvel: Five Fabulous Decades of the World's Greatest Comics.* Introduction by Stan Lee. New York: Abrams.
Goffman, Erving. 1961. *Asylums: Essays on the Social Situation of Mental Patients and Other Inmates.* Garden City, NY: Anchor/Doubleday.
Leland, John. 2000. "Why America Is Hooked on Professional Wrestling." *Newsweek* 135, no. 6 (February 7): 46.
Millard, Elaine. 1997. *Differently Literate: Boys, Girls and the Schooling of Literacy.* London: Falmer Press.
Sabin, Roger. 1996. *Comics, Comix and Graphic Novels: A History of Comic Art.* London: Phaidon.

Schechter, Harold. 1996. "A Short Corrective History of Violence in Popular Culture." *New York Times Magazine* (July 7): 32–33.

Tobin, Joseph. 2000. *"Good Guys Don't Wear Hats": Children Talk about the Media.* New York: Teachers College Press.

Twain, Mark (Samuel Clemens). 1946. *The Adventures of Tom Sawyer.* New York: Grosset and Dunlap.

Wertham, Frederic. 1953. *Seduction of the Innocent.* New York: Rinehart.

———. 1996. "The Psychopathology of Comic Books." *American Journal of Psychotherapy* 50, no. 4 (Fall): 472–490.

T

Teams

Athletic teams have played a central role in the lives of American boys. Playing on teams has been one of their favorite pastimes. Teams have provided one of the most important sites for organizing social structures and cultural patterns among boys. Adults have endorsed team sports as critical educational and political tools, and sports have also been battlegrounds between children and adults over control of the leisure time of American boys.

Teams of North American boys played sports before the United States came into existence. Native American boys engaged in a variety of traditional games. Boys from North America's eastern woodland tribes staged youthful contests called the "little war," a highly competitive stick-and-ball game with important political, military, and religious meanings. When Europeans arrived in North America, they labeled the little war "lacrosse." During the conquest and colonization of North America, European settlers brought a variety of traditional team sports to their new homes, including premodern forms of football and English bat-and-ball games. Colonial boys often organized games of "cat," "nines," "stool ball," and football or played in village games with adult men. After the English colonies in North America won their political independence from Great Britain in the Amer-

ican Revolution, boys in the new United States continued to play traditional European team sports, especially bat-and-ball games. These bat-and-ball games provided the foundation for the creation of baseball—one of the most popular games for American boys in the nineteenth and twentieth centuries.

The creation of baseball in 1845 in New York City by Alexander Cartwright and the Knickerbocker Base Ball Club marked the beginning of a major shift in the importance of team sports in the lives of American boys. Baseball began as a city game, played first by young middle-class and working-class men, but was quickly adopted by boys in urban areas. From cities in the industrializing northeastern United States, the new game with its "official" written and standardized rules began to spread throughout the United States and supplant the traditional boys' bat-and-ball games in towns, villages, and rural hamlets.

During the 1840s and 1850s, in the same era in which baseball was created, the United States began to be transformed from a traditional, rural-agricultural nation into a modern, urban-industrial nation. These changes had an enormous impact on the lives of American boys and on their sports. The Industrial Revolution would increase the amount of leisure time available to upper-class and middle-class boys and, after many decades, working-class boys. At the same time, changes in work, home, and family life created by the new industrial economy also limited the amount of adult control over the boys' expanded leisure time. Many adults grew increasingly concerned about these changes and sought mechanisms to adjust the lives of American boys to the new social order. Team sports became a very popular tool in the efforts to adapt boys' lives to modern social conditions.

In earlier American society, team sports had been one of a multitude of recreational activities for boys, no more important than many of the other forms of physical activity that shaped their lives. In the new, rapidly modernizing American society, team sports would take on novel and important roles. They would replace the physical challenges of farm labor, hunting, and logging that had faced earlier generations of American boys. While boys were learning the skills necessary to succeed in the corporate bureaucracies of the industrial system by participating in team sports, they were also avoiding dangerous vices such as crime, gangs, violence, alcohol, and drugs. Team sports would be endorsed as the key to preparing American boys for the duties of citizenship in a democratic republic and to teaching them honor, courage, integrity, cooperation, and perseverance. Team sports would be advertised as one of the best ways to build a strong and vital American nation.

American promoters of team sports for boys as a nation-building device were greatly influenced by British ideas linking athletics for youth to the construction of a strong, modern nation. The English writer Thomas Hughes's immensely popular 1857 novel, *Tom Brown's School Days*, captured the imaginations of generations of American schoolboys and adult athletic boosters. The book declared that team sports (especially cricket and the original form of rugby football) were the most important character-building activity for boys. Hughes advocated "muscular Christianity" for young boys, arguing that sound bodies trained through team sports produced not only sound minds but sound spirits.

Many Americans wholeheartedly accepted Hughes's assertions. *Tom Brown's School Days* inspired American authors. The most popular imitations of Hughes's sporting formula began to appear by the 1890s, led by the 208 volumes in Gilbert Patten's (Burt L. Standish's) Merriwell series and the numerous books in Edward Stratemeyer's Rover Boy series. Books about sports teams proved enormously popular among young American readers. The American fascination with sports has produced a vast body of didactic literature, and sports books for boys continue to comprise an important genre in American literature.

Tom Brown's School Days also sparked a team sports boom in American schools. In the period from the 1850s through the 1890s, team sporting clubs based on British models sprouted at elite schools and colleges in the United States. Originally, these teams were organized and supervised by the boys themselves, as were the sports of the fictional Tom Brown and his chums. Sports teams in American high schools in the 1870s and 1880s were generally run without adult oversight and sometimes in spite of adult resistance. Interscholastic leagues organized by boys began to appear in American cities. Boston's Interscholastic Football Association, formed in 1888, was a student-run organization that created a flourishing league in that city.

By the 1890s adults had decided that team sports were far too important a tool for social organization to be left in the hands of boys. A new group of professional "boy workers," as they were called at that time, took control of youth athletics. They used another British institution that flowered in the United States, the Young Men's Christian Association (YMCA), to spread the doctrine of "muscular Christianity" through team sports among American boys. The YMCA had been founded in 1844 in England by evangelical Protestants, including Tom Brown's creator, Thomas Hughes, and George Williams. The YMCA quickly spread to the United States in the 1850s. After the American Civil War (1861–1865), as the United States rapidly modernized and urbanized, the YMCA began to institute adult-directed sports programs to attract American boys to wholesome recreations. By the 1890s the YMCA had more than 250,000 members and had built more than 300 gymnasiums throughout the United States.

Under the leadership of athletic evangelist Luther Halsey Gulick (1865–1918), the YMCA promoted competitive team sports as mechanisms for turning American boys into vital citizens of the republic. The YMCA sponsored teams in baseball and football, two popular sports among boys that had been Americanized from earlier British forms. The YMCA also organized team sports that were more common throughout the Anglo-American world: track and field, lacrosse, ice hockey, soccer football, and rugby football. Americans so loved these competitive team games that in the 1890s Gulick challenged the faculty at the YMCA training college in Springfield, Massachusetts, to invent a team game that could be played indoors during cold North American winters when weather conditions made it impossible to play baseball, football, or other sports in large parts of the United States. A Canadian instructor at the YMCA school, James Naismith, responded in 1891 by inventing basketball. In 1895 a graduate of the Springfield training academy, William G. Morgan, created volleyball for the YMCA's arsenal of team sports.

Both of these new team sports, especially basketball, became enormously popular games for American boys. The YMCA spread the new sports first around the United States and then around the world. Basketball, which required only modest amounts of equipment and space, and was characterized by relatively simple rules, adapted well to urban environments. In rapidly expanding U.S. cities, basketball quickly became a playground staple.

Other institutions to ensure adult supervision of boys' leisure time also sprang up in American cities. By the mid-1890s, adults had taken control of sports teams at American elementary and secondary schools. YMCA leader Gulick was the key figure in the creation of the first interscholastic sports organization in the United States. Gulick and his colleagues in New York City founded the Public Schools Athletic League (PSAL) in 1903. The PSAL sponsored competitions in baseball, basketball, crew, cross-country, lacrosse, soccer, and track and field and became the model for the creation of interscholastic team sports leagues in Baltimore, Chicago, and many other American cities.

"Boy workers" also used settlement houses (reform organizations in turn-of-the-century American inner cities designed to Americanize immigrants and improve the lot of the urban poor by teaching them middle-class values) to take control of team sports. Settlement houses, such as Jane Addams's nationally renowned Hull House in Chicago, created team sports competitions. In 1902, New York City organized the Inter-Settlement Athletic Association to promote team sports among immigrant boys. In 1906, settlement house leaders and other progressive reformers founded the Playground Association of America. Luther Gulick served as the first president of this new organization, and Jane Addams was the first vice president. By 1917 the playground and parks movement had managed to create recreational sports programs in 504 American cities. A park and playground building frenzy had altered the nation's urban landscape and created a host of new sites for teams of American boys to play their games.

By the 1920s team sports were firmly embedded in the lives of American boys. They had been planted in schools, in municipal recreation departments, and in the new parks and playgrounds. In addition, the ideas of "muscular Christianity" that had originally animated the American quest to inspire boys to play team sports had been supplanted by new scientific theories that argued that team sports were crucial instruments in the development of boys from childhood through adolescence into adulthood. The new scientific theories, added to the older religious endorsement of competitive sports, made athletic teams a permanent feature of American society. The new scientific ideas also confirmed the common belief that team sports for American boys needed adult supervision. Throughout the twentieth century, self-organized "sandlot" baseball and "pickup" basketball games declined, while adult-controlled games grew. By the last three decades of

the twentieth century, self-organized team games had become a rarity. Adult-managed sport had come to dominate the recreational lives of American boys.

Beginning in the 1920s, a decade labeled by contemporaries as "the golden age of sport," comprehensive programs of interscholastic sports spread throughout the American school system. Elementary and secondary schools developed strong athletic programs for boys centered on team sports—especially baseball, basketball, football, and track and field. Sociologists Robert and Helen Lynd, in their landmark 1929 study of an "average" American town, were amazed by the importance of high school basketball in American society. The Lynds' "Middletown" was actually Muncie, Indiana, and they reported that basketball had become the dominant pastime in middle America. Other regions of the United States also developed intense passions for high school sports. High school football preoccupied many communities, especially in Texas and Pennsylvania. High school baseball became very popular in the growing sunbelt regions of the American South and Southwest. High school sports teams became central to community life and shaped the identities of villages, towns, and urban neighborhoods.

Younger boys were trained for future roles on high school teams by elementary school athletic programs and by a growing number of extrascholastic sports leagues. The Pop Warner football league for young boys, named after the famous early-twentieth-century football coach Glenn "Pop" Warner, began in 1929. In 1939 Little League Baseball was created by lumber company employee Carl Stotz in Williamsport, Pennsylvania. Both leagues modeled themselves after professional sporting practices, employing uniforms, marked playing fields, player drafts, and other features derived from the pros. Dominated by adult coaches and officials, Little League and Pop Warner football imitated professional sports by focusing on winning and elite competition rather than recreation and sport for all.

Both leagues struggled until after World War II, when they took off rapidly. By 1970 more than a million players annually played Pop Warner football. Pop Warner "bowl games" appeared in several American cities, including a "Junior Orange Bowl" in Miami. By the late 1950s nearly a million American boys in 47 states and 22 foreign nations were playing on 19,500 Little League teams. In 1963 the Little League World Series appeared for the first time on television. It soon became a summer staple. By 1990 Little League baseball had 2.5 million players in 16,000 different leagues that spread across all 50 U.S. states and 40 foreign countries.

The success of Little League baseball and Pop Warner football inspired the creation of many other team sports leagues in a wide variety of sports. Basketball leagues drew huge numbers of players. Beginning in the 1970s, youth soccer took off, eventually drawing more participants than the baseball, football, or basketball programs. The National Alliance for Youth Sports, founded in 1981, sought to regulate youth sports for the more than 20 million participants that it estimated participated annually in out-of-school sports programs. Millions of more boys participated in school-based sports.

The rise of elite teams of young athletes raised concerns in American society. Since the late 1800s, critics of competitive interscholastic and extrascholastic sports have raised questions about the

benefits of these programs for American boys. They worried that these programs neglected the vast majority of boys and nurtured only the best athletes. The focus on elite competition left too many boys off teams. Many professional physical educators promoted sports programs focused on recreation and enjoyment that catered to all boys to replace the professionalized models that were limited to only the very best players. Critics also noted that the win-at-any-cost mentality spawned by elite teams undercut the values that participation in team sports was supposed to teach American boys. In their estimation, fair play, honor, honesty, and other virtues were trampled by blind devotion to victory.

From the late 1800s to the present, many observers have also condemned the behavior of adults in youth sports programs. They point to the unsettling and recurrent history of uncivil and even violent outbursts by coaches and parents during games. Assaults and even murders of adult officials, coaches, and fans by other adults have plagued youth sports. Incidents of physical, emotional, and sexual abuse of children by adult coaches have tarnished leagues. Critics note that school sports have become so important that teachers are sometimes pressured to give academic favors to athletes. They observe that youth sports have become so significant in the lives of many American communities that boys who do not "make the team" feel excluded from society, whereas boys who do "make the team" face enormous pressures to perform at extraordinary levels. Exposés of abuses in youth sports have appeared regularly in the media since the 1920s. A variety of reform groups and local, state, and national governments have sought to curb abuses. Some reformers have even suggested returning control of team sports from adults back to children.

As the twenty-first century begins, the chorus of criticism continues. The debate over the structure and function of modern team sports for boys has not yet retarded the growth of youth leagues and school sports in the United States. As they have for more than a century, most American adults continue to believe that team sports are one of the most important parts of boys' lives. Although they feel uneasy with some of the recurring abuses appearing in sports programs, they are still committed to the idea that team sports make boys fit for modern society. Boys continue to flock to team games for their own reasons. Team sports remain a central feature of American boyhood.

Mark Dyreson

See also Baseball; Basketball; Football; Games; Muscular Christianity; Native American Boys; Young Men's Christian Association

References and further reading
Bissinger, H. G. 1990. *Friday Night Lights: A Town, a Team, a Dream.* Reading, MA: Addison-Wesley.
Boyer, Paul. 1978. *Urban Masses and Moral Order in America, 1820–1920.* Cambridge: Harvard University Press.
Cavallo, Dominick. 1981. *Muscles and Morals: Organized Playgrounds and Urban Reform, 1880–1920.* Philadelphia: University of Pennsylvania Press.
Dyreson, Mark. 1998. *Making the American Team: Sport, Culture, and the Olympic Experience.* Urbana: University of Illinois Press.
Fine, Gary Alan. 1987. *With the Boys: Little League Baseball and Preadolescent Culture.* Chicago: University of Chicago Press.
Goodman, Cary. 1979. *Choosing Sides: Playground and Street Life on the Lower East Side.* New York: Schocken Books.
Hardy, Stephen. 1983. *How Boston Played: Sport, Recreation and Community, 1865–1915.* Boston: Northeastern University Press.
Kett, Joseph F. 1977. *Rites of Passage: Adolescence in America: 1790 to the Present.* New York: Basic Books.
Lynd, Robert S., and Helen Merrell Lynd. 1929. *Middletown: A Study in Contemporary American Culture.* New York: Harcourt Brace.
Macleod, David I. 1983. *Building Character in the America Boy: The Boy Scouts, YMCA, and Their Forerunners, 1870–1920.* Madison: University of Wisconsin Press.
———. 1998. *The Age of the Child: Children in America, 1890–1920.* New York: Twayne.
Nasaw, David. 1985. *Children of the City: At Work and at Play.* New York: Doubleday.
Oriard, Michael. 1982. *Dreaming of Heroes: American Sports Fiction, 1860–1980.* Chicago: Nelson-Hall.
Rader, Benjamin. 1999. *American Sports: From the Age of Folk Games to the Age of Televised Sports.* 4th ed. Upper Saddle River, NJ: Prentice-Hall.
Riess, Steven A. 1989. *City Games: The Evolution of American Urban Society and the Rise of Sports.* Urbana: University of Illinois Press.
———. 1995. *Sport in Industrial America, 1850–1920.* Wheeling, IL: Harlan Davidson.
Yablonsky, Lewis, and Jonathan Brower. 1979. *The Little League Game: How Kids, Coaches, and Parents Really Play It.* New York: New York Times Books.

Teasing
See Bullying

Television: Cartoons
Animation, which is traditionally associated with child audiences, has played an important role in communicating implicit gender messages to American boys and girls in the twentieth century—particularly when broadcast via "the electronic babysitter," television. Although

Rocky, Bullwinkle, and friends, 1960 (Photofest)

animated films were assumed to hold appeal for both adults and children in the first half of the century, by the end of World War II, younger audiences were conceived as the main consumers of cartoons. Coinciding with the advent of daily broadcast programming across the United States, animation on television quickly became targeted exclusively at children. As the "science" of target market research developed throughout the latter half of the century, specific cartoons increasingly narrowed their sought-for audience. Consequently, television cartoons have often divided child viewers according to gender, helping to exemplify and regulate social concepts of

masculinity and femininity to boys and girls. Over the years, animation (and "children's programming" in general) has had to deal with changing social ideas of what was appropriate for children to watch. Often, though not always, these changes included gender concepts that would affect how animation spoke to and about boys.

Quite early in television's history, animation became a programming staple. Stations quickly began broadcasting shorts originally produced for the theatrical screen by major studios like Warner Brothers or Disney. Yet original animation (made directly for television) began as early as 1948 with the premiere of

Crusader Rabbit (1948–1951). Animation has always attracted viewers from all age groups, but producers, network executives, and (most important) advertisers consistently conceptualized animation as appealing primarily to children. Consequently, much of television animation has been aimed at younger audiences in choices of characters, plotlines, types of humor, and visual design. The development of a "limited animation" style for made-for-TV cartoons, necessitated by the quick turnaround times for these programs as well as the low returns expected from them, was considered allowable because television executives thought that children would not mind the lack of production detail common to theatrical animation.

Most early original TV animation aimed at children ostensibly tried to attract both boys and girls indiscriminately. Cartoons produced by Jay Ward (*Crusader Rabbit; Rocky and Bullwinkle*, 1959–1961) and the production house of Hanna-Barbera (*Huckleberry Hound*, 1958–1962; *Yogi Bear*, 1961–1963) did not overtly play up gender roles. Yet all the heads of the animation studios and most of the animators themselves were male, and whether by design or not, practically all of the major cartoon protagonists were male. This predominance subtly establishes the "natural" dominance of men in American society by representing "maleness" as a sort of default category. Although being male is considered ordinary and unexceptional in these cartoons, the few female characters appearing in individual episodes conspicuously display difference and exception from the norm. This is similar to the creation of a "woman's film" genre in Hollywood, which ghettoizes one circle of films and silently assumes that all other "normal" films are "men's films." This concept continually reappears in animated programs to the present day. *The Smurfs* (1981–1990), for example, differentiates its large cast of characters by giving them easy-to-recognize personality traits: Brainy, Grouchy, and so on. Smurfette's recognizable personality trait is that she's the only female, thus marking being female as different, but the male gender of the other Smurfs goes unnoticed.

In 1961, Newton Minow, the newly appointed chairman of the Federal Communications Commission (FCC), famously announced to the annual meeting of the National Association of Broadcasters (NAB) that he considered commercial broadcast television to be a "vast wasteland." Minow included cartoons in his list of what he considered mind-numbing and unseemly programming, particularly in their relation to "screaming, cajoling and offending" commercials (Barnouw 1990, 300). By the 1960s, all three networks had begun programming Saturday mornings with animation and other shows aimed at children. This change was precipitated by advertisers (including toy manufacturers such as Mattel) using new methods in target research to isolate specific consumer groups, even though children had been acknowledged as a separate consumer group as early as the mid-1950s. Animated programs were consequently conceived as a vehicle to deliver young consumers to those advertisers hawking products aimed at children (particularly toys and breakfast cereals).

In ensuing years, target marketing would break down populations into increasingly smaller chunks. Children themselves would be segmented into three different age groups—as well as by gender. As a result, animated programs began to reach out to more specified target groups, the better for sponsors to advertise their products. In the late 1960s, the first sustained wave of cartoons with female protagonists appeared (*Penelope Pitstop*, 1969–1971; *Josie and the Pussycats*, 1970–1974), and other cartoons increasingly seemed aimed solely at male children. Dramatic cartoons like *Johnny Quest* (1964–1965) simultaneously assumed that boys would be fascinated with violent action, adventure, and technological or mechanical gadgetry and taught them that such interests would mark them as successfully masculine.

At the same time, various media watchdogs raised concerns that television was imparting messages about sex and violence to young minds. Social scientists began experiments to test how much children's behavior was influenced by watching violent or sexually explicit programs. Even though the 1970 Presidential Commission's Report on Obscenity and Pornography announced no definite proof that media's images of sex and violence affected children's behavior, discussion about television's detrimental effect on children continued apace. The rise of race activism and women's liberation fueled further critiques. As a consequence, a number of animated series attempted to become more socially responsible, often by including a moral lesson at the end of each episode about the value of hard work, fair play, and getting along with others. Animated series during this time like *Fat Albert and the Cosby Kids* (1972–1984), *Sesame Street* (1969–present), *Super Friends* (1973–1985), and *Schoolhouse Rock* (1973–1979) saw an increase in representation of racial and ethnic minorities and some discussion of environmental concerns. Yet discussions of how gender roles were presented basically went unaddressed. Representations of race and ethnicity in these cartoons predominantly meant representations of males, silently assuming that racial uplift meant asserting male power in these communities. Similarly, although many of these new cartoons included both male and female characters, the male characters were often associated with mechanics, sports, and outdoor activity (i.e., traditional masculine activities), and the female characters were usually associated with nurturing and trying to look pretty (i.e., traditional feminine activities).

When the Reagan administration relaxed federal regulations over the television industry in the 1980s, advertisers took advantage of the situation to flood syndicated children's programming with series that were themselves half-hour advertisements for various toy lines. More than ever before, these shows drew clear boundaries between "boys' play" and "girls' play." *My Little Pony* (1986–1990) and *Strawberry Shortcake* (1982–1984) plainly aimed at indoctrinating girls into conventional femininity, and *He-Man* (1983–1985) and *GI Joe* (1985–1987) just as plainly aimed at indoctrinating boys into consuming images of hypermasculinity. The outcry by critics eventually saw the waning of this style of programming. Although these critics often pointed out the blatantly gendered messages in these cartoons, their outcry focused more specifically on the overt attempts to commercialize children's television.

Simply because certain cartoons were envisioned to appeal to a certain gender does not mean that actual boys and girls watched or reacted in the ways that animators, advertisers, or network programmers had predicted. Although most boys would have eschewed "girly" cartoons (or felt peer pressure to avoid watching them), claiming that all boys reacted this way is too monolithic. Similarly, the appeal of such programs as *GI Joe* and *He-Man* seems to have differed from individual to individual. Predominantly, boys seemed to enjoy these cartoons as enactments of masculine power and aggression and desired to emulate these animated heroes. Yet, many homosexual men recall enjoying these shows as boys from a vastly different perspective, allowing them a secret space to begin desiring (rather than identifying with) these male figures.

Television animation since the 1980s has seen a huge shift in industry structure. The rise of cable stations such as Nickelodeon and the Cartoon Network has increased the number of outlets available for viewing cartoons on television (and simultaneously eroded the perceived need for the commercial networks to keep Saturday mornings as exclusively for children). Also, partly in response to the criticisms of 1980s television animation, certain programs such as *Where in the World Is Carmen Sandiego?* (1994–present) attempt to appeal to both boys and girls. Further, the rise in popularity of adult-oriented animation in prime-time programming (*The Simpsons*, 1989–present; *South Park*, 1997–present) often satirizes the clichéd gender messages presented in older TV animation. Intriguingly, the debut of such series helped spur calls for a ratings system for American television and the development of "V-chip" technology to block children's access to "unsafe" programs.

The need of advertisers to sell "girls' toys" and "boys' toys" still facilitates divisions in animation programming. The increasing popularity of importing Japanese animated series to American television often maintains this gender separation. *Anime* such as *Sailor Moon* (first aired in Japan in 1990–1995) and *Robotech* (first aired in Japan in 1984–1989) often adopted the conventions from Japanese comic books (*manga*) that are divided into *shonen* (male) and *shojo* (female) genres. From the TV series adaptation of Disney's *The Little Mermaid* (1992–1994) to the *New Adventures of Batman and Superman* (1997–), much of American broadcast animation continues to instill in male and female children notions of what role models they are supposed to value and how to successfully enter into adult gendered behavior.

Sean Griffin

See also Video Games

References and further reading
Barnouw, Erik. 1990. *Tube of Plenty: The Evolution of American Television*. 2d rev. ed. Oxford: Oxford University Press.

Englehardt, Tom. 1987. "Children's Television: The Strawberry Shortcake Strategy." In *Watching Television: A Pantheon Guide to Popular Culture*. Edited by Todd Gitlin. New York: Pantheon.

Kinder, Marsha. 1991. *Playing with Power in Movies, Television, and Video Games*. Berkeley: University of California Press.

———, ed. 1999. *Kids' Media Culture*. Durham, NC: Duke University Press.

Kline, Stephen. 1993. *Out of the Garden: Toys and Children's Culture in the Age of TV Marketing*. London: Verso.

Levi, Antonia. 1996. *Samurai from Outer Space: Understanding Japanese Animation*. Chicago: Caris Publishing.

Palmer, Patricia. 1986. *The Lively Audience: A Study of Children around the TV Set*. Sidney: Allen and Unwin.

Schramm, Wilbur, Jack Lyle, and Edwin Parker. 1961. *Television in the Lives of Our Children*. Palo Alto: Stanford University Press.

Seiter, Ellen. 1995. *Sold Separately: Parents and Children in Consumer Culture*. New Brunswick, NJ: Rutgers University Press.

Woolery, George. 1983. *Children's Television: The First Twenty-Five Years.* Metuchen, NJ: Scarecrow.

Young, Brian M. 1990. *Television Advertising and Children.* Oxford: Oxford University Press.

Television: Domestic Comedy and Family Drama

The family has long been the focus of contradictory impulses in American social life. On the one hand, it is imagined as a haven from the daily tensions of social, political, and economic life. On the other, it is considered a primary location for correcting current social ills through the proper upbringing of children—the adults of the future. From their beginnings, television networks have struggled with this contradiction, attempting to appear modern and socially relevant without alienating the family audiences so important to their advertisers, and social critics have alternately praised the medium as a means for bringing families together or blamed it for the decline of the institution (cf. Murray 1990). Boys have loomed large in this delicate negotiation, representing the fragile innocence of childhood, the main force of modernization in the home, and the nation's social future. Prime-time television's representations of boys in family life, then, have not so much reflected the reality of any given moment as they have the hopes, fears, and ideals associated with boyhood and the family.

Because the early producers of live television dramas often tackled difficult issues of the day, the 1950s are often called the golden age of television. In live dramas such as *Marty* (1956) and *The Days of Wine and Roses* (1958) and in long-running series such as *Mama* (1949–1957), families struggled to find their place in the rapidly changing postwar American landscape. These dramas offered narratives of upward mobility and assimilation into a greatly expanded middle class and depicted families as struggling to negotiate intergenerational conflicts between the traditional extended family and the new suburban nuclear family. Grown sons faced the difficult task of leaving behind strong ethnic and neighborhood affiliations, and aging parents struggled to adjust to a modern world in which they represented a past being left behind (Lipsitz 1990). In these dramas of assimilation, the transition from immigrant roots to mainstream American culture was often refigured as an Oedipal struggle in which a grown son had to overcome his desire to care for his mother or had to demonstrate the superiority of his new life to his hidebound father. Even though chronologically an adult, the son did not become a man until he had severed his connections to his parents and the old world.

Because their embrace of controversy made them unpopular with networks eager to attract advertisers, by the end of the 1950s these live dramas were gradually overshadowed by situation comedies, which also dealt with issues of upward mobility and modernization but through laughter rather than pathos (Boddy 1990). In sitcoms such as *The Life of Riley* (1949–1950, 1953–1958) and *The Honeymooners* (1955–1956), buffoonish, working-class husbands desperately tried to maintain their failing authority over wives and children (Spigel 1992). On *The Life of Riley*, father Chester was head of the family in name only, with son Junior often correcting him on matters of domestic technology and current language

A scene from a 1953 episode of The Life of Riley *(Photofest)*

and mores. In the more upscale world of *The Adventures of Ozzie and Harriet* (1952–1966), sons Ricky and Dave also regularly corrected father Ozzie's misperception of himself as "with it." In the extremely popular show *I Love Lucy* (1951–1957), Lucy Ricardo constantly schemed to break out of her role as housewife and into a career in entertainment, whereas her bandleader husband Ricky fought a losing battle to maintain a patriarchal authority based in his Cuban roots, and the program provided a fascinating intersection of issues of ethnicity and gender (Desjardins 1999). Following Lucille Ball's on-air pregnancy and the birth of Desi Arnaz, Jr., "Little Ricky" grew up on television as a miniature version of his father, often joining Ricky on the bandstand from which Lucy was repeatedly barred and presenting the image

of an unbroken line of patriarchal succession from father to son.

As the 1950s progressed, the networks played on the popularity of these television families by offering progressively blander, more suburban versions of boyhood and family life such as *Leave It to Beaver* (1957–1963) and *The Dick Van Dyke Show* (1961). In these situation comedies, fathers, though quirky, were more competent than their predecessors, wives and children were docile and pleasant, and their homes were models of suburban decorum. Fathers and sons shared an uneasy intimacy in which Dad attempted to pass on wisdom from his youth, while his son patiently sorted out the archaic advice from the useful. When fathers attempted to apply outmoded standards of discipline, TV sons turned to their mothers to bring Dad up-to-date. Throughout the decade, African Americans were relegated to roles as servants or appeared as entertainers in evening variety programming. With the exception of Desi Arnaz, Latinos were largely absent from prime time, as were Asian Americans. In an era in which men of color were still often referred to as "boys," for children of color the father-son relationship was not a representational reality, and television offered a social landscape from which they and their families were largely absent. Generally speaking, the television family grew whiter and more affluent as the 1950s progressed, moving from environments marked by class and ethnicity to more homogeneous suburban surroundings.

By the middle of the 1960s, the bland family of late 1950s prime time was infiltrated by unruly members whose differences had to be contained or disguised. On *Bewitched* (1964–1972), advertising executive husband Darren made futile demands on his wife, Samantha, not to practice witchcraft. When both daughter Tabitha and son Adam developed supernatural powers, Darren became even more disempowered. On *The Munsters* (1964–1966), a family of ghouls tried unsuccessfully to adjust to their suburban surroundings, and Frankenstein-father Herman was often at a loss as to how to counsel his werewolf son, Eddie, on how to fit in. The characters on *The Addams Family* (1964–1966), however, lived to confound their straight-laced neighbors, and parents Morticia and Gomez reveled in their overweight and sadistic son Pugsly's habit of tormenting his peers. Although the fathers in these programs continued to be bumbling and ineffectual, situation comedies such as these simultaneously depicted the family as a primary location for society's repression of a boy's individuality and as the place where boys might effectively mount an assault on those constraints (Spigel 1991).

Other 1960s popular prime-time depictions of family life tended to mix genres, as in *Bonanza* (1959–1973), a western centered on the family of widower Ben Cartwright, and *My Three Sons* (1960–1972), which blended comedy and drama in a family also lacking a mother figure. *Family Affair* (1966–1971), which featured an advertising executive raising his orphaned niece and nephew, and the short-lived *Courtship of Eddie's Father* (1969–1972) also blended comedy and drama around men as single parents. These programs offered a corrective to popular 1950s fears of the father emasculated by his wife's power as manager of the domestic economy and primary parental authority in the life of their children. As such, they played upon calls by childrearing professionals for fathers to take a more active role in their sons' lives and upon popular concerns that a father's increased domestic presence might feminize him and, by extension, his son. The plots of these programs often revolved around efforts by the father to occupy the unfamiliar role of primary caregiver and to understand how he could negotiate that traditionally feminine role from a masculine perspective. The grown or growing sons of these single fathers, in turn, performed a more sensitive version of masculinity, offering the emotional support that their absent mothers would have provided. These relationships depicted both fathers and sons as empowered by their efforts to understand and support each other rather than estranged by that familiarity as they often had been in the 1950s.

By the end of the 1960s and the rise of the women's movement, single mothers became more visible on prime-time television. In 1968, Diahann Cannon starred in the first dramatic lead for a black woman, as *Julia* (1968–1971), a single mother and nurse raising a son. A year later, Shirley Jones played a stage mother and performer in the persistently popular *The Partridge Family* (1970–1974), a situation comedy about a traveling family of pop singers in which the responsibility of raising three sons and two daughters was shared by the mother and the band's bachelor manager. On *Alice* (1976–1985), a single mother replaced her dreams of becoming a country singing star with a job as a truck-stop waitress in order to raise her son. Each of these programs reversed the problem of single-father comedies and dramas, placing the focus on the needs of the female lead to maintain a strong relationship with her child(ren) while providing for them. The sons of these single mothers often attempted to provide the emotional support of an absent husband or lover, and these plot points were usually resolved by the mother acknowledging her son's effort while restoring his right to be a child. Both types of single-parent programs, however, raised concerns about a boy's ability to develop a stable gender identity when faced with the absence of one parent and addressed them through a mix of comedy and drama.

Prime-time representations of the family in the 1960s questioned straightlaced late-1950s domestic configurations in order to tap into tensions created by the increasing economic and social power of women and children. Television in the 1970s, however, seemed to reprise the early 1950s model in which the family became the site of intergenerational struggles over ethnicity, race, class, and gender. Particularly in the live situation comedies of Norman Lear, the American family appeared as a battleground over identity. On *The Jeffersons* (1975–1985), a bigoted black man, George Jefferson, constantly bridled at his son's marriage to the daughter of a mixed-race couple and at his wife's refusal to join him in a blanket condemnation of all white people. *Sanford and Son* (1972–1977) offered intergenerational conflict in the form of an elderly black junk dealer whose stereotypical ghetto masculinity was undermined by his educated adult son's demands that he conform to more acceptable middle-class norms of behavior. *Good Times* (1974–1979) portrayed a working-class, two-income, black family's struggles to stay together and get ahead. On *Good Times*, the teenage son, J.J., was an aspiring painter who celebrated ghetto smarts and street language, often to the frustration of his hardworking parents. Esther Rolle and John Amos,

who portrayed the parents, objected to the show's increasing emphasis on J.J., arguing that his character encouraged negative stereotyping of young black men; both quit the show at different points over this concern (MacDonald 1983). Although these programs were of extremely high quality and critically acclaimed, their white writers, directors, and producers often condescended to their subjects, suggesting that working-class and poor whites and blacks offered object lessons in outdated behavior and thinking or examples of noble humanity to an implicitly white and middle-class audience (cf. Barker 2000). In particular, they offered few examples of stable and positive family life in which sons gained from meaningful and mutually respectful relationships with their parents.

At the same time as some prime-time families struggled to resolve larger social tensions around integration, identity, and the reconfiguration of the nuclear family, other programs sought to remedy this dissolution via nostalgic representations of childhood innocence and stable and separate gender identities. *The Brady Bunch* (1969–1974) presented a blended family in which three boys and three girls faced the problems of suburban adolescence with minimal guidance from their loving parents. The program's recurring narrative theme revolved around petty hostilities between the boys and the girls, keeping the two genders in clearly defined camps. *Happy Days* (1974–1984) returned to a mythic 1950s in which the weightier issues of the 1960s and 1970s had not yet happened. The Great Depression formed the backdrop for *The Waltons* (1972–1981), a tale of a poor rural family whose intimacy and love allowed them to face hardship as a unit. The ongoing story in both *Happy Days* and *The Waltons* fo-

The dysfunctional Bundy family, from Married . . . with Children *(Photofest)*

cused on the eldest son, replacing models of Oedipal conflict with warm, sentimental cooperation and depicting the male passage into adulthood as a gradual attainment of increased rights and responsibility and the willing support of parental authority. Reflecting the demographic power of late baby-boom adolescents, each of these series emphasized sibling relationships and represented parents as competent and available but not central to family life.

In the 1980s, savvy audiences inured to these two versions of the family found ironic pleasure in the absurdity of prime-time family melodramas, beginning with the openly satirical *Soap* (1977–1981) and continuing with *Dallas* (1978–1991), *Dynasty* (1981–1989), and *Falcon Crest* (1981–1990). Like daytime soaps, these programs inverted the idea of the family as a location for social stability and safety, treating it instead as a convenient

vehicle for petty vengeance and self-aggrandizement, the vulnerable point in an individual's social and personal armor. The sons of these imaginary American aristocrats connived with equal enthusiasm against parents and siblings as the programs converted hostility against the upper class and unease with the family as an economic unit into a cynical inversion of the ideal American family.

By the end of the decade this representational trend spawned situation comedies—such as *Married . . . with Children* (1987), *The Simpsons* (1989–present), and *Roseanne* (1988–1997)—that treated the family as a parodic nightmare growing out of the American dream (cf. Kerwin 1994). Each of these programs featured playful gender antagonism as a central narrative feature, with sons and fathers mounting a mutual and usually feeble defense against the aggressive and often more sensible feminism of female family members.

These shows featured working-class families indifferent or hostile to the middle-class values inherent in that dream, living in a world far more ideologically and socially complex than the depictions of stable suburban family that continued in programs such as *Family Ties* (1982–1989), *Growing Pains* (1985–1992), and *The Wonder Years* (1988–1993). Drawing on popular discourses of the dysfunctional family—in which ideals of proper family life were mobilized to repress the needs of individual family members—these programs reveled in their impropriety and in the human frailty of their characters. In many ways, these domestic parodies represented a rebellion against the enormous social and ideological burden that television families had been made to carry—particularly in their tacit acceptance of sons and fathers as more significantly connected to the larger world of public social life. By the early 1990s, leaders of the Christian right declared these extremely popular dysfunctional prime-time families a threat to "family values," with the resulting brouhaha culminating in candidate Dan Quayle's famous denunciation of fictional character Murphy Brown's choice to have a child out of wedlock.

During the 1980s and 1990s, *The Cosby Show* (1984–1992) provided a counterexample to the stereotype of black family life in general and father-son relationships in particular as fragmented and economically and socially impoverished. The Huxtable family featured two professional, middle-class parents, respectful children, and an emotionally rich home life. Taking his cue from his parents, the Huxtables' teenage son, Theo, treated his sisters with warmth and respect (within the bounds of adolescence) and received the same in kind. Simultaneously praised for offering positive role models and criticized as unrealistic, the program bore the weight of the lack of widespread representations of black family life on television. (Asian American and Latino families continue to be conspicuously absent in prime time.) By the early 1990s and the birth of alternative networks such as United Paramount Network (UPN) and Warner Brothers (WB), programs such as *Sister, Sister* (1994–present) and *Moesha* (1996–present) also offered models of stable black family life. Unlike *The Cosby Show*, however, these programs targeted the profitable teen market, with plots centered on female adolescent characters, and parents appeared on the sidelines to offer moral guidance and provide narrative frames for their children's experience.

Through the 1990s and into the twenty-first century, prime-time representations of boyhood and family life have continued to emphasize relationships between adolescents and children while marginalizing parents. On popular programs such as *Beverly Hills 90210* (1990–2000), *Dawson's Creek* (1998–present), and *Buffy the Vampire Slayer* (1997–present), parents, although loving and supportive, either rarely appear or do not fully understand what their children are doing or feeling. Although the gender relations in these programs are relatively traditional, in each the boys and young men must attempt to deal with the girls and young women in their lives as equals. In the logic of consumer demographics, however, these programs are aimed primarily at teenage girls, with plots that balance action with emotional relationships and personal development. Teenage boys are considered to prefer the violence and sexism of action programming. Yet these programs enjoy significant demographic crossover in terms of both age and gender, indicating, perhaps, that although the nuclear family of prime-time television, either as an ideal or as a problem, no longer resonates with boys and young men, nontraditional "families" of friends do.

Generally, television has always struggled to negotiate tensions between the ideal and the real, and the television family has been a prime location for those negotiations. From television's earliest days, a widespread popular belief that the medium affects the behaviors and life choices of children, particularly of boys, has endured. (Consider the outcry after the 1999–2000 spate of schoolyard assaults, most of which were committed by teenage boys.) There is no solid evidence to support this belief, but its persistence points to the incredible expectations we hold for the medium and its representations. Although we can always hope that television will play a role in helping boys (and girls) become the adults we would wish them to be, it is more reasonable to expect that television can show us how we have imagined boyhood and family life at any given historical moment, offering us a richer understanding of the place of boys in our social life.

Nicholas Sammond

References and further reading
Ang, Ien, and Joke Hermes. 1991. "Gender and/in Media Consumption." In *Mass Media and Society*. Edited by James Curran and Michael Gurevitch. New York: Routledge.

Barker, David. 2000. "Television Production Techniques as Communication." In *Television: The Critical View*. 6th ed. Edited by Horace Newcomb. New York: Oxford University Press.

Barnouw, Erik. 1978. *The Sponsor: Notes on a Modern Potentate*. New York: Oxford University Press.

Boddy, William. 1990. *Fifties Television: The Industry and Its Critics*. Chicago: University of Illinois Press.

Desjardins, Mary. 1999. "Lucy and Desi: Sexuality, Ethnicity, and TV's First Family." In *Television, History, and American Culture: Feminist Critical Essays*. Edited by Mary Best Haralovich and Lauren Rabinovitz. Durham, NC: Duke University Press.

Haralovich, Mary Best, and Lauren Rabinovitz, eds. 1999. *Television, History, and American Culture: Feminist Critical Essays*. Durham, NC: Duke University Press.

Kerwin, Denise. 1994. "Ambivalent Pleasure from *Married . . . with Children*." In *Television: The Critical View*. 5th ed. Edited by Horace Newcomb. New York: Oxford University Press.

Lipsitz, George. 1990. *Time Passages: Collective Memory and American Popular Culture*. Minneapolis: University of Minnesota Press.

MacDonald, J. Fred. 1983. *Blacks and White TV: African Americans in Television since 1948*. Chicago: Nelson Hall.

Murray, Michael D. 1990. "A Real Life Family in Prime Time." In *Television and the American Family*. Edited by Jennings Bryant. Hillsdale, NJ: Lawrence Erlbaum Associates.

Newcomb, Horace, ed. 2000. *Television: The Critical View*. 6th ed. New York: Oxford University Press.

Spigel, Lynn. 1991. "From Domestic Space to Outer Space: The 1960s Fantastic Family Sitcom." In *Close Encounters: Film, Feminism, and Science Fiction*. Edited by Constance Penley, Elisabeth Lyon, Lynn Spigel, and Janet Bergstrom. Minneapolis: University of Minnesota Press.

———. 1992. *Make Room for TV: Television and the Family Ideal in Postwar America*. Chicago: University of Chicago Press.

Television: Race and Ethnicity

To discuss race and ethnicity in television in terms of boyhood requires dealing with two central issues, representation and identification. The question of racial

A scene from Good Times, 1976: J.J. (Jimmie Walker, left) talks to his younger brother Michael (Ralph Carter, right) (Photofest)

and ethnic representation on television is of ongoing concern in American society. As recently as 1999, complaints were filed against the industry, and boycotts were organized by the National Association for the Advancement of Colored People (NAACP) in an attempt to address the lack of, or the quality of, representations of racial and ethnic groups on television as a whole and on network television in particular. Since the advent of and widespread popularity of network television in the late 1940s and 1950s, the impact of the medium on the American family has been explored by sociologists, psychologists, media scholars, and politicians. It is indisputable that television is one of the most influential and widespread media formats. Acknowledging

television's ability to participate in the shaping of identity as well as its role in providing information on the world around us, the medium's ability to address the needs and concerns of racial and ethnic groups has been called into question. Throughout the history of television, white American boys had televisual representations with which they could identify, from Timmy in Lassie (CBS, 1954–1971) to Beaver Cleaver of Leave It to Beaver (CBS/ABC, 1957–1963) to even Bart of The Simpsons (Fox, 1989–). In contrast, the possibilities for racial representation of, or racial identification for, boys of other groups were limited by the medium's choice of representation and America's troubled racial past and contentious present.

At its inception, television was perceived by many in the black community as a possible impartial space for African American representation in the media. African American magazines such as Ebony reported such beliefs in the pages of their magazines. As early as 1951, network television shows also espoused a treatise of tolerance. The Texaco Star Theater presented a musical revue called "The United Nations of Show Business," hosted by Danny Thomas and Milton Berle. The show suggested that prejudice could not exist on television and that there was room for anyone regardless of race or ethnicity.

Although network television executives openly promised that television productions would not be biased, their rhetoric contrasted with the reality, in which minority participation was minimal at best and was limited to very specified roles, such as that of musical entertainer. The major network series that included black casts, Beulah (1950–1953) and Amos 'n' Andy (1951–1953), created controversy because they were based on stereotypes of African Americans. Although oral histories reveal that the shows were enjoyed by segments of the black community, there was also significant criticism of them. This type of atmosphere within the industry determined the viewing position of young boys of minority backgrounds. Ensconced in a televisual white world, minority boys would have watched and enjoyed mainstream entertainment programming. However, many oral histories have reported the excitement that existed within black households when an African American appeared on television in a guest appearance or actually had a show created for him or her, such as the short-lived *Nat King Cole Show* (1956–1957). In terms of television, as in many other aspects of life, members of many minority communities within the United States identified first with issues of race and ethnicity before turning to those of age. A brief look at some aspects of American television in terms of racial programming will clarify this assertion.

African Americans exploded onto the television screen in the late 1950s and 1960s in the realm of news, news specials, and documentaries. The United States was involved in more than a decade of social unrest, the culmination of generations of racial oppression. The harsh reactions to the civil rights movement's tactics of nonviolent protest were covered by the media. Urban uprisings were at a high point in the late 1960s and early 1970s. In the 1960s, all three major networks addressed the country's racial upheaval. For example, in 1968, American Broadcasting Companies (ABC) television produced *Time for Americans*, National Broadcasting Company (NBC) produced *What's Happening to America*,

and Columbia Broadcasting System (CBS) brought out *Of Black America*, all in-depth series on racial issues. However, television still remained more accepting of moderate leaders such as Martin Luther King, Jr., and Ralph Abernathy while producing such documentaries as Mike Wallace's five-part series for CBS, *The Hate That Hate Produced*, which discussed the so-called Negro racism of the Nation of Islam, or the "black Muslims," whose concepts of separatism, revolution, black control, and self-defense had begun to resonate with large segments of the African American population. Television shows such as *Black Journal* (1968–1976) produced news by and for the black community and often provided a viewpoint opposite to those of mainstream news networks. Here, African American boys could truly find images of themselves and news topics of interest to them. *Black Journal* gave voice to the young black male leaders disparaged by mainstream media, such as Huey P. Newton and Bobby Seale, and featured figures and organizations that appealed to black youth. The program also often interviewed youth working within the community and overtly encouraged youth participation in political struggles.

Outside news programming, race would not come to the forefront of television until the 1970s, and the show that catapulted black youth culture onto U.S. television screens was *Soul Train* (1970–). The music, performances, and dancers of Soul Train have been a part of African American culture and the American television landscape since 1970. Don Cornelius invested his own money to create a pilot for *Soul Train*, which he then took to the merchandising manager for the five Sears Roebuck stores located in Chicago's inner-city community. With

Sears as a sponsor and an agreement from WCIU-TV, *Soul Train* premiered in Chicago on August 17, 1970. In October 1971, *Soul Train* made its debut in eight new urban markets and was very successful. The show caught on quickly and became the benchmark for style and hipness in 1970s American society. As the show's tag line suggested, it was "the hippest trip in America." The young dancers in the *Soul Train* line were the stars of the show. All high school and college students, they sported naturals and other contemporary hairstyles, and were dressed in the hip accouterments of the day: bell bottoms, broad-collared shirts, and wide belts. They set the clothing and dance styles for the American public. The *Soul Train* dancers primarily performed to the music of contemporary black artists. The list of guest appearances on *Soul Train* reads like a Who's Who of black artists of the 1970s, many of whom have cultural currency today: James Brown, Curtis Mayfield, B. B. King, the Temptations, Stevie Wonder, Aretha Franklin, the Jackson Five, and Marvin Gaye. *Soul Train* remains the longest-running syndicated show on television.

In the 1970s in general, images of African Americans and members of some other racial and ethnic groups increased in entertainment network television, particularly in situation comedies, as shows such as *Sanford and Son* (NBC, 1972–1977), *The Jeffersons* (CBS, 1975–1985), and *Chico and the Man* (NBC, 1974–1978) premiered on network television. However, it was *Good Times* (CBS, 1974–1979), *Welcome Back, Kotter* (ABC, 1975–1979), and *What's Happening!!* (ABC, 1976–1979) that specifically targeted the young racial and ethnic male. *Good Times*, for instance, was the first

sitcom to have a black nuclear family. The story focused on the father, James (John Amos), who worked long hours for little pay or was out of work and looking for a job; Florida (Esther Rolle), the mother who was struggling to make ends meet and keep her family together; and Thelma (BernNadette Stanis), the intelligent daughter who was determined to succeed. The young male characters in the show, J.J., or James Junior (Jimmie Walker), the eldest son, and Michael (Ralph Carter), the youngest son, represented different sides of urban black life. J.J. was the artist, a self-proclaimed ladies' man, and the stereotypical comic relief for the show. Michael was the voice of militancy who spoke the rhetoric of the revolution and was often called the "militant midget" by other characters. Most of the story lines surrounding Michael's character dealt with situations that many urban and minority youth faced. For example, in "IQ Test" (1974), Michael deliberately fails the intelligence quotient (IQ) test because he believes that such tests are biased. "Michael the Warlord" (1976) addressed the youngest son's involvement with a street gang.

ABC created the popular multiethnic youth sitcom *Welcome Back, Kotter*, with such characters as John Travolta's Vinnie Barbarino, Lawrence Hilton-Jacobs's Freddie Boom-Boom Washington, Robert Hegyes's Juan Epstein, and Ron Palillo's Arnold Horshack as the Sweathogs, a classroom of students at James Buchanan High School in Brooklyn. ABC concurrently developed *What's Happening!!*, which used the West Coast as its setting and a group of Los Angeles high school students. The show was based on the 1975 film *Cooley High* and featured actors Ernest Thomas as Roger Thomas, and

Haywood Nelson, Jr., and Fred Berry as his best friends, Dwayne and Rerun.

Black life also broke into Saturday morning animation in the 1970s with such shows as *The Jackson Five* (ABC, 1971–1973), based on the famous Motown all-boy singing group of the same name; *I Am the Greatest* (NBC, 1977–1978), based on the adventures of Muhammad Ali; and the show that perhaps had the largest impact, *Fat Albert and the Cosby Kids* (CBS, 1972–1984). *Fat Albert* was hosted by comedian Bill Cosby and featured the characters Fat Albert, Mush Mouth, Weird Harold, and Donald. Based on Cosby's boyhood friends, each episode usually incorporated a moral lesson.

The 1970s proved to be a high point for ethnic and racial television programming, particularly as it addressed boyhood. In the 1980s a backlash began that led to an almost complete disappearance of racial and ethnic characters from network television. Young minority male characters, in particular, were seemingly removed from their typical environments and, when featured on television, were placed within the care of the all-white world. Examples of this include *Diff'rent Strokes* (NBC/ABC, 1978–1985) and *Webster* (ABC, 1983–1987). Each of these shows featured young black boys who were adopted into all-white middle- and upper-class families after the death of their parents. One of the only shows with a black cast to gain and sustain popularity during the 1980s was another production of Bill Cosby, *The Cosby Show* (NBC, 1984–1992). Again using his own life as a basis for his comedy, Cosby took Americans through the growth and development of his televisual family, which included his son Theo, portrayed by Malcolm Jamal-Warner, who aged from preadolescence to young adulthood during the run of the program. Theo would deal with life issues ranging from growing up in a family of girl siblings to coping with dyslexia, attending college, living away from home, and choosing a job. Because of the longevity of the show, it was one of the most complete examples of the development of the young black male in the realm of television.

With the advent of cable and growth in the number of available channels, the opportunities for niche marketing increased, and new cable channels such as Black Entertainment Television (BET) were the result. Stations such as Nickelodeon and the Disney Channel, which targeted youth audiences, also created shows that were inclusive of the ethnic and racial population increasingly visible in American society. However, in the late 1980s and 1990s, the televisual forum that produced the greatest impact on youth in general, with a particular impression on young boys of racial and ethnic backgrounds, had a musical format. Music Television (MTV) created a space that specifically addressed youth culture and the role of both boys and girls as producers and consumers of contemporary rhythm and blues, pop, rap, and hip-hop. MTV did not specifically carry rap music until the premiere of *YO! MTV Raps* in 1988, when it realized that it could no longer ignore this widespread art form. Since then, because of the popularity of rap music and hip-hop as a whole, the music videos of so-called minority artists, who are in the majority on MTV, have flooded the station in regular rotation and in the new programs that incorporate their music, such as *The Lyricist's Lounge* and *Total Request Live* (TRL). The impact of hip-hop as visualized

The family of The Cosby Show *(Photofest)*

through MTV can be seen not only on young boys of diverse races but also on American culture as a whole, through the music as well as clothing, language, and style.

Christine Acham

See also African American Boys; Asian American Boys

References and further reading
Gray, Herman. 1995. *Watching Race: Television and the Struggle for Blackness*. Minneapolis: University of Minnesota Press.
Jhally, Sut, and Justin Lewis. 1992. *Enlightened Racism: The Cosby Show, Audiences and the Myth of the American Dream*. Boulder, CO: Westview Press.
MacDonald, J. Fred. 1992. *Blacks and White TV: Afro Americans in Television since 1948*. Chicago: Nelson-Hall Publishers.
McNeil, Alex. 1996. *Total Television*. New York: Penguin.

Television: Westerns

For many years, Westerns were one of the most popular genres of television shows, appealing to both children and adults and frequently sparking merchandising crazes and inspiring childhood play. The Western owes much of its popularity to hordes of male youth idolizing cowboy and outlaw heroes and fantasizing about a life of adventure and freedom on the frontier. Although Westerns were not produced only for a young male audience, writers and producers quickly recognized the importance of these fans and often took them into consideration. Consequently, the Western genre can be read as a prime example of how mass media taught American boys concepts of national identity and pride while merging those concepts with specific models of masculinity. Girls may also have been attracted to the Western genre (the early 1950s TV series *Annie Oakley* serves as an example of the genre that attempted to speak to young female fans), but the prevalence of male protagonists whose main emotional attachment was either to their comic sidekick or their horse heavily gendered the genre as male. During the period of their highest popularity, the late 1950s to the early 1960s, a consistent majority of the ten top-rated (most watched) TV shows in the United States were Westerns. The popularity of the form declined in the 1960s, and by most accounts the format was dead by the 1980s.

Hollywood film Westerns had been a staple of American film production since the early 1900s, when they evolved out of other Western media entertainment such as the dime novel and the Wild West show. The Western usually was set during the period of the Indian wars on the Great Plains (roughly 1850–1900) and told a story about a "good bad man"—a cowboy hero who was often a loner and a rebel but who came to aid the of settlers when needed. The "forces of nature" that the white settlers often battled against frequently included Native Americans, or as they were known within the genre, "Redskins" or "Injuns." Many critics of the Western understand the genre as a system of mediated texts that in some way attempts to "justify" the genocide of Native American people by depicting them as a cultureless hostile menace in need of eradication so that "civilization" (i.e., white Christian patriarchy) could prevail. This concept of Manifest Destiny (the alleged God-given right of white people to colonize the globe) was a dominant belief in the nineteenth century, and it lingered well into the twentieth century in some areas of the United States, especially within the thematic meaning of the Western film genre. The filmic Western went through many periods of change and evolution before being critiqued and parodied in the 1960s and 1970s. It is no longer a very popular Hollywood genre (perhaps because of its inherent racism), but according to some sources, one-fifth of all Hollywood films produced before 1960 could be considered Westerns.

The TV Western drew its main inspiration from Hollywood B-Westerns (cheaply produced and quickly made films that did not feature major stars or high budgets) as well as radio Westerns. Radio Westerns such as *The Lone Ranger,* which had been on the air since 1933, could be easily adapted to television with the simple addition of visual images to preexisting scripts and situations. *The Lone Ranger* ran on the American Broadcasting Companies (ABC) network from 1949 to 1957 and made its titular star (Clayton Moore) and sidekick buddy Tonto (Jay Silverheels) into American icons; their catch phrases "Kemo Sabe" and "Hi-Yo, Silver, away!" are still recognized in the twenty-first century. A more usual method of producing TV Westerns was the adaptation of B-Western filmmaking units into television producing units. For example, B-Western film stars Gene Autry and Roy Rogers moved from the movies to TV with ease. *The Roy Rogers Show* aired on NBC from 1951 to 1957, and *The Gene Autry Show* ran on CBS from 1950 to 1956. Autry's Flying A Productions also produced many other Westerns during this period, including *The Range Rider* (in syndication, 1951–1953), *Death Valley Days* (in syndication, 1952–1970), *Annie Oakley* (in syndication, 1952–1956), *Buffalo Bill Jr.* (in syndication, 1955), and *The Adventures of Champion* (CBS, 1955–1956). Roy Rogers and Gene Autry were

actually singing cowboy stars who had become popular in the 1930s and 1940s via radio and the movies. Their western heroes were gentlemen cowboys, and they wooed audiences with song as well as "clean living" heroics.

The vast majority of these Western TV shows were shot on film (unlike much of early live television) and could thus exploit outdoor settings and action-filled narratives. As the B-Westerns they evolved from were assumed to attract mainly "kiddie matinee" audiences, their transfer to television predicated an emphasis on younger viewers during the first years of commercial television in the United States (roughly the late 1940s and early 1950s). The television resurgence of the career of William Boyd as *Hopalong Cassidy* (NBC, 1949–1951; in syndication, 1952–1954), who specifically appealed to his young fans in ads and public appearances, stands as an overt example. Many parents of the era considered TV Western heroes to be good role models for young boys. Many, like Gene Autry, publicized their own "Ten Cowboy Commandments" of proper behavior. The earliest TV cowboys were also merchandising phenomena. When Walt Disney aired a three-part telling of the legend of *Davy Crockett* on ABC in 1954–1955, the resultant avalanche of toy merchandising (coonskin caps, rifles, moccasins, tents, etc.) further indicated the genre's appeal to young (predominantly male) children. Yet underneath this simple schoolyard Western playacting lay more disturbing ideological meanings: the common sentence, "The only good Injun is a dead Injun," usually part of the game of cowboys and Indians, is equally well known as "Hi-Yo, Silver, away!"

By the mid-1950s, the kiddie matinee cowboy shows were being transformed

The Lone Ranger and Tonto hunt down the bad guys, 1955. (Kobol Collection)

into the so-called adult Western, with shows such as *Gunsmoke* (CBS, 1955–1975), *Cheyenne* (ABC, 1955–1963), and *Bonanza* (NBC, 1959–1973) going on the air for the first time. The adult Western on TV coincided with the arrival of adult Westerns on movie screens. In place of simplified cowboy action heroes, now arose more psychologically complex (and in some cases outright neurotic) Western characters. The genre's racism was challenged in movies such as *Broken Arrow* (1950), which attempted to depict Native American cultures in more accurate ways; *Broken Arrow* also became an ABC TV show from 1956 to 1958. Generally, the TV Westerns differed from their filmic counterparts in several ways. TV Westerns tended to be less violent and not as potentially controversial as were filmic Westerns. This characteristic had as much to do with the demands of series narrative as it did with television censorship codes: the need for recurring characters made it very difficult to kill them off as easily as in the movies. Many TV Westerns eventually became more like domestic or community melodramas than filmic Westerns. *Gunsmoke*, for example, reconstitutes a family unit with a mother-figure (Miss Kitty), a father-figure (Marshall Matt Dillon), a brother-figure (Doc), and various son-figures. *Bonanza* was directly structured around an all-male family and sought to be everything to all audiences: a situation comedy, an action adventure series, and a family melodrama set in the West. Allegedly, the show's creator, Dave Dotort, had designed the show to combat "Momism," the 1950s idea that women were having an effeminizing (and therefore negative) effect on American masculinity. As such, the show became an effective voice of patriarchal

moralizing and national identity building during the Cold War era.

By the late 1950s, there were so many Western series on the air that the public became overly familiar with their styles and narrative patterns. (In 1959 alone there were forty-eight Western series on the air.) TV satirist Ernie Kovacs could include Western parodies in his famous comedy specials, and entire Western TV shows that parodied the genre began to appear. Perhaps the most famous of these was *Maverick* (ABC, 1957–1962), which starred James Garner as a card shark and comic grafter. Although that characterization alone was enough to critique the idea of the heroic westerner, the show would also frequently spoof other popular TV shows, such as *Gunsmoke* and *Bonanza*, and even cop and crime shows, such as *The Untouchables* and *Dragnet*. By the mid-1960s, ABC was airing *F Troop* (1965–1967), a situation comedy that presented its cavalrymen as con men, idiots, and buffoons.

Perhaps most interesting were generic hybrids such as *The Wild Wild West* (CBS, 1965–1969). As the 1960s progressed and James Bond fever swept the globe, TV shows about spies, such as *The Man from UNCLE* (NBC, 1964–1968), became very popular. *The Wild Wild West* might be considered a combination of TV Western and TV superspy spoof, focusing on the adventures of Jim West (Robert Conrad) and Artemus Gordon (Ross Martin), two secret service agents in the nineteenth-century Wild West. They routinely rode horses, engaged in fisticuffs and gunplay, but also battled mad geniuses with high-tech spy gadgetry. Although most young boys probably responded to *The Wild Wild West* as an example of a rousing male-dominated buddy action show, others may have responded more to the show's latent homoeroticism, especially surrounding its star Robert Conrad's tight pants and proclivity for bare-chested heroics. Still, even as the TV Western was mutating into parodies, hybrids, and potential deconstructions, another family Western, *The Big Valley* (ABC, 1965–1969), made its debut and lasted for several years. In it, Barbara Stanwyck played the matriarch of a western family; like *Bonanza*, the show was perhaps more of a family melodrama set in the West than a Western per se.

By 1970, the major networks (NBC, CBS, and ABC) realized that their Westerns and rural comedies (shows such as *The Andy Griffith Show, The Beverly Hillbillies, Petticoat Junction*, and *Gomer Pyle USMC*) were enormously popular, but with the "wrong" audiences. In other words, these shows were watched by children and adults in rural and lower socioeconomic classes, and thus even though such audiences gave the shows very high ratings, they did not give the television advertisers high sales profits. Decisions were made at all networks (but especially at CBS) to jettison rural programming in favor of urban crime dramas and sitcoms (*All in the Family, The Mary Tyler Moore Show*) in order to capture a more upscale consumer audience. Many Westerns fell under the ax. Perennial favorites such as *Gunsmoke* and *Bonanza* would hold on for a few more years, but new Western hybrids such as *Kung Fu* (ABC, 1972–1975), which might be thought of an "Eastern," and urban detective shows with Western heroes, such as *McCloud* (NBC, 1970–1977), became the newest incarnation of the TV Western.

Later manifestations of the TV Western include *Little House on the Prairie* (NBC, 1974–1982), a series created by and starring Michael Landon of *Bonanza* fame, but it too was actually more of a family melodrama set in the past than a Western with cowboy heroes, Indians, and gunplay. More recent shows like *Dr. Quinn, Medicine Woman* have exploited a certain Western flavor but little of the thematic mythology of the classical Western genre. In the 1990s, more "faithful" Western fare such as *The Magnificent Seven* (based on the movie of the same name) has failed to find a television audience. Whether one points to growing audience sophistication, changing national demographics, or the genre's inherent racism and sexism, the Western in its classical incarnation is for the most part dead in both contemporary American film and television.

Harry M. Benshoff
Sean Griffin

See also Films

References and further reading
Barson, Michael. 1985. "The TV Western." Pp. 57–72 in *TV Genres: A Handbook and Reference Guide*. Edited by Brian G. Rose. Westport, CT: Greenwood Press.
Brauer, Ralph. 1975. *The Horse, the Gun, and the Piece of Property: Changing Images of the TV Western*. Bowling Green: Popular Press.
Buscombe, Edward. 1988. *The BFI Companion to the Western*. New York: Da Capo Press.
Buscombe, Edward, and Roberta E. Pearson. 1998. *Back in the Saddle Again: New Essays on the Western*. London: BFI Press.
Cameron, Ian, and Douglas Pye. 1996. *The Book of Westerns*. New York: Continuum.
Cawelti, John G. 1985. *The Six-Gun Mystique*. Rev. ed. Bowling Green: Bowling Green University Popular Press.

Coyne, Michael. 1997. *The Crowded Prairie: American National Identity in the Hollywood Western.* New York: St. Martin's Press.

Jackson, Ronald. 1994. *Classic TV Westerns: A Pictorial History.* New Jersey: Carol Publishing Group.

Parks, Rita. 1982. *The Western Hero in Film and Television.* Ann Arbor: UMI Research Press.

Schatz, Thomas. 1981. *Hollywood Genres: Formulas, Filmmaking, and the Studio System.* New York: Random House.

Slotkin, Richard. 1992. *Gunfighter Nation: The Myth of the Frontier in Twentieth-Century America.* New York: Atheneum.

West, Richard. 1987. *Television Westerns: Major and Minor Series, 1946–1978.* North Carolina: McFarland.

Tennis

Although Americans played forms of tennis as early as the eighteenth century, not until 1873 did an Englishman, Major Walter Wingfield, invent lawn tennis, a game played on a rectangular court by two players or two pairs of players who use rackets to hit the ball back and forth over a low net that divides the court. Socialite Mary Outerbridge, after observing British officers at play, brought this version of the racket game from Bermuda to the New York area in 1874. It gained popularity among the society set and took root in New England. By 1875 a tournament was held near Boston. The famed English tourney at Wimbledon began in 1877. Californians returning from a trip to England established the sport in the Santa Monica area by 1879. The United States Lawn Tennis Association (USLTA) was organized in 1881, representing thirty-four clubs. That August its first championship matches were held at the casino in Newport, Rhode Island. The "L" was dropped from the USLTA in 1975 because the organization's tournaments were held on a variety of surfaces, chiefly hard court and clay.

In 1883, Ivy League boys won the first intercollegiate tourney, and they continued to dominate the sport until 1921, when Stanford's Philip Neer broke the string. From 1883 to 1921, all the champions hailed from all-male colleges: fifteen from Harvard, eight from Yale, and five from Princeton. The Olympic Games included tennis competition from 1896 (Athens) through 1924 (Paris). Boys in the United States had new game skills to learn and sports heroes to emulate.

Opportunities to master tennis fundamentals and to play the sport improved. The playground movement, begun in the 1870s with a social service purpose, led to ten cities building such recreational facilities between 1890 and 1900. As early as 1878, John H. Vincent introduced lawn tennis in the summer to the western New York Chautauqua, a religious, recreational, educational, and cultural program begun at Chautauqua Lake in 1874 and a movement that became popular in the United States and Canada by the early twentieth century. The Young Men's Christian Association (YMCA) and private boys' camps for the well-to-do provided diverse activities. A major leap forward was the formation by Luther Gulick of the Public Schools Athletic League (PSAL) in New York City in 1903. Open to all boys, and especially those of average skills, the innovative program offered a dozen sports, including tennis, by 1907. (A girls' branch of PSAL was formed in 1905.) President Theodore Roosevelt wholeheartedly backed the sports-for-all-boys concept, which was designed to improve discipline, sportsmanship, loyalty, and athletic ideals in competitions leading to city championships.

Young tennis players practice their strokes. (Courtesy of Harold Ray)

By the mid-1890s, boys' sports were finally accepted as a legitimate part of school programs. Michigan and Wisconsin led the way by regulating track and field, football, baseball, and tennis. The PSAL played a significant role in popularizing interscholastic sport. By 1910 athletic leagues modeled after the PSAL had been formed in seventeen cities. Although lawn tennis was not as popular among boys as were football, baseball, and basketball, tennis was one of the top ten fastest-growing sports. By the early 1920s a National Federation of High School Athletic Associations (NFHSAA) had been established, winning prompt endorsement by the National Association of Secondary School Principals. By 1928 scholastic tennis championships existed in twenty states. When all-weather courts were introduced in the early 1920s, tennis's popularity grew steadily. Companies such as Kellogg in Battle Creek, Michigan, and Hawthorne in Chicago, Illinois, offered recreational tennis programs for their employees and their families. At the end of the 1930s, there were thousands of courts across the country, ranging from clay to newer compositions of many kinds. Although tennis had become a major spectator sport, boys and girls could enjoy tennis via intramural, extramural, interscholastic, club, and after-school recreational programs. One offshoot was platform paddle tennis, originally called "paddle tennis," devised in New York City in 1921. Played on half-size tennis courts, this game was an exciting urban recreational activity. By 1936, with development of 12-foot-high wire walls, it became a popular off-season game for tennis buffs.

Under the aegis of the USTA, a wide variety of tennis tournaments evolved in which boys could test their skills. The Interscholastic Boys' 18 singles tournament began in 1891 in Cambridge, Massachusetts, with Robert Wrenn of Cambridge Latin winning the event. Disrupted by World War I and again from 1925 to 1935, it has been hosted since 1970 on college campuses. A doubles tournament was added in 1936. Boys' 15 singles were added in 1916. Vincent (Vinnie) Richards won in 1917, added three 18-and-under titles, and then earned a gold medal in the 1924 Olympics in Paris. Richards later became an outstanding performer on the international circuit and enjoyed a stint as a broadcaster. (Because of a dispute over amateur versus professional status, tennis disappeared as an Olympic sport between 1924 and 1988.)

Other age-group tournaments for boys included the National Jaycees Championships, which ran until 1966, and the National Public Parks Championships. In the late twentieth century and into the twenty-first century, USTA tournaments for youths proliferated. As of the year 2000, the adjective *super* was thrown into the mix, with the USTA Super National Boys 18–16 Hard Court Championships, held each August in Kalamazoo, Michigan. Other tournaments include a series of other USTA Super Nationals (Winter, Spring, and Clay Court events).

The rite of passage among young male tennis players in the United States is the USTA Boys' 18–16 Championships. The tournament was initially hosted by the West Hills Tennis Club in Forest Hills, New York, in 1916. The first Boys' 18 singles winner was Harold Throckmorton. With the exception of the inaugural tournament, the event has always been held in late summer, normally in August. After the beginning in Forest Hills, it was moved back and forth from the East Coast to the Midwest before finding a permanent home at Kalamazoo College in southwestern Michigan in 1943. This venerable liberal arts institution, founded in 1833, proved to be an excellent site blessed with enthusiastic community support. In the twenty-first century, the USTA Super National Boys' 18–16 Hard Court Championships still utilize this hospitable home.

Winners in eighteen-and-under singles and doubles competition in the USTA Super National Hard Court Championships receive automatic berths, as wild card entries, in the U.S. Open in Flushing Meadows, New York, an obvious example of a rite of passage. Finals in the eighteen competition are the best of five sets, as at the U.S. Open, a true test for the emerging young male tennis players. All other matches in the tournament are best of three sets. Robert Falkenburg took the 1943 singles title. A repeat winner in 1944, he won Wimbledon four years later. Dr. A. B. Stowe directed the tournaments until he was killed in an automobile accident in 1957. A new site, fittingly named Stowe Stadium, was constructed in 1946. Today, its eleven lighted courts boast the all-weather Deco Turf II, which is also used in the U.S. Open. Typically, more than 3,000 spectators view the talented boys in the 18–16 singles finals each August. More than 100,000 have attended the tourney since its move to Kalamazoo—locally dubbed "the 'Zoo." Sportsmanship trophies are a cherished part of the Nationals' tradition. In 1958 the Allen B. Stowe Sportsmanship Award was introduced to honor players in eighteen-and-under singles;

Paul Palmer of Phoenix, Arizona, was the first recipient. The respect the tennis community had for the distinguished African American tennis player Arthur Ashe was evident when Kalamazoo College bestowed an honorary doctorate of humane letters on the popular athlete in 1992.

Youngsters dream of earning international acclaim by winning the U.S. Open, established in 1881; the French Open (1891); the Australian Open (1905); or the prestigious Wimbledon tournament (1877); to win singles crowns in all of them in one season equals a Grand Slam. Most of the United States' future Grand Slam champions competed as boys at Stowe Stadium. Some famous Wimbledon winners are Bob Falkenburg, Tony Trabert, Rod Laver, Chuck McKinley, Stan Smith, Jimmy Connors, Arthur Ashe, John McEnroe, Andre Agassi, and Pete Sampras. Aussie Laver, who won at "the 'Zoo" in 1956, was the first to take the Grand Slam championships twice. Top-ten rankings often include former Nationals players such as Sampras, Agassi, Michael Chang, and Jim Courier. Curiously, Sampras, Agassi, and Courier never won in singles at Kalamazoo. Just before his thirteenth birthday in 1984, Sampras played the longest three-set match (five hours, twenty-three minutes) in the history of the Nationals, losing to Texan T. J. Middleton. He also lost in 1987 to Courier who, in turn, was defeated by Chang in the Boys' 18 finals.

African American boys are making an impact on the sport once dominated by white males. Timon Corwin, director of the USTA Super National Hard Court 18–16 Championships and a former NCAA Division III singles champion at Kalamazoo College, believes that "sport kind of transcends race and classes."

Young tennis player in California, 2000 (Joe McBride/Corbis)

Nonetheless, tennis, like golf, is an individual sport, and both favor boys from prosperous families because to succeed at national and international levels boys require costly private instruction, and there is no immediate guarantee of financial success. Corwin emphasizes the importance of role models for blacks in tennis and golf: "Mali Vai Washington, when he reached the singles finals at Wimbledon, thanked Arthur Ashe. And in golf, Tiger Woods thanked Lee Elder. The Williams sisters (Venus and Serena) really have made an impact in tennis for African-American girls, and they have thanked Althea Gibson" (personal interview with Bob Wagner, fall 2000).

The first African Americans who played tennis had to form the American Tennis Association (1916) because racial barriers then prevented them from competing in all other tournaments, which were for whites only. When Arthur Ashe was moving into the junior tennis ranks, segregation still prevailed in the South. "The difficulty was that I never qualified for Kalamazoo from my home section [in the South]," Ashe reveals. "I had to qualify through the Eastern section. I could also play in Middle Atlantic events, but I could not play in my home state. For all of us black kids we had to arrange any attempt to get to Kalamazoo outside the South." But Ashe opened the door for other black players like Martin Blackman, a player from the Bronx who became the first African American in either age group to win a singles championship when he defeated Michael Chang in the sixteen-and-under final in 1986. Blackman also won the doubles with Chang that year, but he lost in the eighteen-and-under singles final two years later to Tommy Ho from Winter Haven, Florida. In 1991, J. J. Jackson from Henderson, North Carolina, became the second black to win the sixteen-and-under singles. Mali Vai, Mashiska Washington, and Lex Carrington also figured prominently in the tournament in Kalamazoo. This change in the rite of passage in tennis could be called the "Arthur Ashe legacy."

Certainly, tennis is no longer a sport exclusively for well-off white boys. Boys of various races and social backgrounds learn to play tennis in diverse ways. Julian, who grew up in a barrio in East Los Angeles, recalls learning the fundamentals of the game at age fourteen in the alleys and streets. He played without a net. Charles, who grew up in Kalamazoo, changed from baseball to tennis at age fourteen; he developed into a university-level champion and a ranked senior competitor. Harold, a product of a rural New York community where baseball and basketball were the most popular sports, learned to play tennis in college. Today's facilities and programs provide multiple options for boys, and many start by elementary school (personal interview with H. L. Ray, fall 2000).

Harold Ray
Robert Wagner

References and further reading
Ashe, Arthur, and Arnold Rampersad. 1993. *Days of Grace*. New York: Alfred A. Knopf.
Ashe, Arthur, with Alexander McNabb. 1995. *Arthur Ashe on Tennis*. New York: Alfred A. Knopf.
Betts, John R. 1974. *America's Sporting Heritage: 1850–1950*. Reading, MA: Addison-Wesley.
Collins, Bud. 1989. *My Life with the Pros*. Pp. 1–15. New York: Dutton.
Feinstein, John. 1991. *Hard Courts*. New York: Villard Books.
Galenson, David W. 1993. "The Impact of Economic and Technological Change on the Careers of American Men Tennis Players, 1960–1991." *Journal of Sport History* 20, no. 2 (Summer): 127–150.
Grimsley, Will. 1971. *Tennis: Its History, People and Events*. Englewood Cliffs, NJ: Prentice-Hall.
Ladd, Wayne M., and Angela Lumpkin, eds. 1979. *Sport in American Education: History and Perspective*. Reston, VA: NASPE-AAHPERD.
Lumpkin, Angela. 1985. *A Guide to the Literature of Tennis*. Westport, CT: Greenwood Press. (An excellent tool for researchers and aficionados.)
Nelson, Rebecca, and Marie J. MacNee, eds. 1996. *The Olympics Factbook*. Detroit: Visible Ink Press.
Phillips, Dennis J. 1989. *Teaching, Coaching and Learning Tennis: An Annotated Bibliography*. Metuchen, NJ: Scarecrow Press.
Stowe, Catherine, M. 1978. "The National Junior and Boys Tennis Championships

(June)." Unpublished history project, Kalamazoo, MI.

U.S. Lawn Tennis Association. 1931. *Fifty Years of Lawn Tennis in the United States.* New York: USLTA.

————. 1972. *Official Encyclopedia of Tennis.* New York: Harper and Row.

U.S. Tennis Association. 1995– . *Tennis Yearbook.* Lynn, MA: H. O. Zimman.

Wagner, Bob. 1992. *The Nationals and How They Grew in Kalamazoo.* Kalamazoo, MI: J-B Printing. (Oral histories.)

Theatre

Mimesis, or playacting, has been an ingredient of boyhood in America since the country's earliest settlements, just as theatre has been part of an American experience of childhood, albeit a marginalized component of cultural activity. The study of theatre for young audiences, particularly in gender-specific terms, remains relatively unexplored. Theatre as an art form and a profession has struggled for acceptance in the United States in part because many early settlers' evangelical beliefs focused on the denial of enjoyment in exchange for spiritual reward and in part because a frontier mentality eschewed any activity that smacked of aristocratic pretension. Theatre targeted toward an audience of boys and girls was considered a frivolous endeavor until the twentieth century and emerged in the contexts of education and social work rather than artistic enterprise. The goals of the earliest children's theatres were to educate immigrant children and assist them in learning the language and to provide decent and respectable entertainment for children and families. Most pioneers of the children's theatre movement were women, which further served to exclude the field from serious theatre scholarship.

Children's theatre consists of two distinct fields of endeavor: children's theatre (or theatre for young audiences, as it is now called), defined as theatre performed by adults and targeted toward an audience of children; and creative dramatics, theatrical activity for boy and girl performers that focuses on the process and experience of creating rather than on the finished production. From its inception, formal children's theatre relied to a great extent on the adaptation of traditional folk and fairy tales for its content, but with the advent of postmodern critical readings of these stories, contemporary artists have begun writing and performing original plays in lieu of these adaptations. Although criticism of fairy tales based on gender issues has become popular and feminist critiques of adult theatre have generated controversy, little scholarship has been directed toward gender and performance in children's theatre. Contemporary children's theatre productions occur in every state in professional, community, or educational theatres, and although these theatres face different issues from those of the early twentieth century, the stated goals of education and entertainment remain components of nearly every group performing for or with children.

The history of children's theatre in America is not easily traced. Nellie McCaslin's groundbreaking work provides a thorough and accepted compilation of information; other sources of information are dissertations written for graduate degrees and records from individual children's theatre companies. Prior to the twentieth century, boys and girls mainly attended theatrical performances targeted toward adult or family audiences. Although there were isolated incidents of theatrical productions geared specifically toward children, such as puppet plays that were given on the plantations owned by both George Washington and Thomas Jefferson, traveling troupes were common, such as the Shakespearean actors encountered by the fictional Huck Finn in Mark Twain's novel. These troupes targeted their plays toward family attendance. In addition to formal theatrical productions, informal entertainments encouraged family attendance, and the Wild West shows performed by Kit Carson and William Cody drew groups of rowdy gallery boys who came to applaud their heroes.

The first well-documented theatre specifically for boys and girls, the Children's Educational Theatre (CET), was founded in 1903 at the Educational Alliance in New York City. Its founder, Alice Minnie Herts, was a social worker who held strong commitments to the education of underprivileged children and to the performing arts. The first production offered by CET was Shakespeare's *The Tempest*, a play that incorporated a large and colorful vocabulary with the excitement of an entertaining and magical plot. This production was followed by performances of adaptations of classic fairy tales. The success of CET encouraged the establishment of similar children's theatre companies in major cities across the country. Samuel Clemens (pseudonym Mark Twain) was a strong supporter of children's theatre and became a member of CET's board.

Although the concept of theatre targeted toward children caught on at the community level, few professional productions were mounted, and none survived for long. This lack of financial success increased professional disinterest in the field, but the Association of Junior Leagues of America, a women's service organization, took up the cause. Young women who recently graduated from colleges or preparatory schools often volunteered for dramatic activities with and for children. Another association that helped the children's theatre movement to flourish was the Drama League of America, founded in 1910 to promote the establishment of community theatres across the country. Although the Drama League focused primarily on theatre for adults with the mission of ensuring that all citizens, not just those in major cities, had the opportunity to see theatrical performances, they provided guidance and stimulated grassroots activity that included children's theatre. The Depression saw the establishment of the Federal Theatre Project (FTP) as a temporary relief measure for unemployed performers and technicians. These performers were mandated to provide entertainment linked with education, and FTP companies produced children's theatre in several states across the country.

The first institution of higher education to organize a children's theatre was Emerson College in Boston in 1920. Soon educational theatre became an established field of study at several colleges and universities, and in 1936 a group of professors met to form the American Educational Theatre Association. In an attempt to identify themselves as professional theatre artists more than as educators, the group became the American Theatre Association. Rising costs and budget cuts brought about the association's demise in 1986, but by that time it had succeeded in making educational theatre an accepted component in an arts curriculum.

Early attempts to introduce dramatization into the schools, particularly as accompaniment to the study of literature, became part of the Progressive education movement of the early twentieth century. The first person to differentiate between children's theatre and creative dramatics was Winifred Ward, who taught at Northwestern University and worked in the public schools in Evanston, Illinois. The publication in 1930 of her suggested guidelines for creative dramatics directed attention to the possibilities for the use of theatre in the education of the whole child, and by the 1950s there was a movement to include training in creative dramatics in the curricula of several colleges and universities.

The field of creative dramatics consists of informal drama, often improvisational in nature, undertaken for the benefit of the players rather than for an audience. It is difficult to measure the benefits of participation other than by observation. Participation in creative dramatics hopes to inspire and foster qualities such as creativity, social cooperation, sensitivity, physical poise and flexibility, communications skills and fluency in language, emotional stability, a sense of morality, and an appreciation of drama. Every leader of creative dramatics teaches boys and girls her or his individually developed or chosen games and exercises to address these goals. Studies have been conducted only recently in the public elementary schools to assess the impact of creative dramatics on children's scores on standardized tests, with promising results. Although the field of creative dramatics is often associated with preschool and primary education, these activities also occur in community centers, religious institutions, correctional facilities, and recreational programs.

Early children's theatre performances were plays that targeted adults and families as well as children. Many of William Shakespeare's plays, particularly those that dealt with magic, were deemed suitable for children's audiences. Another adult play that encouraged the attendance of children was the adaptation of Harriet Beecher Stowe's *Uncle Tom's Cabin* (1851–1852). As children's theatre gained acceptance, adaptations of fairy tales provided much of the content. Since children's theatre continued to be considered education or social work rather than serious theatre, the field remained ignored by most serious writers. One notable exception was J. M. Barrie, whose 1904 play *Peter Pan*, the story of a boy who refuses to grow up, continues to be performed frequently. One of the first noteworthy writers of children's plays was Charlotte Chorpening, director at the Goodman Theatre in Chicago and faculty member at Northwestern University during the 1930s. Many of Chorpening's plays are adaptations of classic fairy tales, as are those of another noted early writer of children's plays, Aurand Harris.

During the latter decades of the twentieth century, the fairy tales that formed the basis of many children's theatre plays came under scrutiny by psychologists and literary critics, particularly those interested in feminist theory. Bruno Bettelheim's 1976 book *The Uses of Enchantment*, despite later criticism, continues to be the seminal text in the Freudian interpretation of fairy tales. These interpretations focus on gender relationships, and many fairy tales have undergone fierce examination in consideration of archetypes and gender roles. Although much study has been devoted to fairy tales from feminist perspectives, few have explored fairy tales and folk stories in relation to masculinity and gender identity. Many of the more popular adaptations of fairy and folk tales, such as *Cinderella, Alice in*

Wonderland, The Wizard of Oz, Snow White, and *Sleeping Beauty,* focus on central female figures. Jack Zipes, scholar and author of numerous books on fairy tales, devotes some attention to the presentation of role models for boys in *Fairy Tales and the Art of Subversion* (1983). Fairy tales that have been adapted for the stage that feature boys as central characters (for example, the Grimm brothers' "Adventures of Tom Thumb" and "Jack and the Beanstalk") encourage boys to explore, take risks, go out into the world and face challenges, outwit their opponents, and take responsibility for ensuring the security of home and family. However, despite the emergence of the field of gender studies in academia, little examination of children's theatre, performance, and gender has surfaced.

The strongest factor that has influenced the choice of stories for performance has been the link between education and entertainment in children's theatre. In the final decades of the twentieth century, fairy tales that were designed to socialize children and teach them proper behavior came under fire as gender roles came to be questioned. Fairy tales teach girls to be passive and compliant, become good homemakers and housekeepers, and wait for the handsome prince to fulfill their dreams. In contrast, boys learn to be aggressive, adventuresome, clever, and courageous from fairy tales. In conjunction with gender differences, concerns about violence and its effects on children also surfaced. Fairy tales teach children to deal with conflict, and boy characters confront ogres, witches, thieves, and robbers whose threats are physical. From these tales, boys learn to fight bravely as well as to use their intellectual abilities to overcome their foes. They also learn to be competitive, aggressive, and acquisitive in order to gain money and power. This aggression often is directed toward an antagonist who is a fantastic, less-than-human being (ogres, giants) or toward someone who has been cast in the role of Other due to racial, ethnic, or gender differences. In a society that has come to embrace diversity and gender equality, this aggression toward other humans based on difference is no longer deemed appropriate or desirable social behavior, and reason, often portrayed in fairy tales as wit and cunning, rather than violence, has become the socially acceptable way of dealing with interpersonal conflicts. Competition, aggression, and the acquisition of money and power remain desirable characteristics and goals for young males, but in a society fearful of physical aggression, fairy tales that valorize violence as a means of conflict resolution face strong criticism.

At the dawn of the twenty-first century, children's theatres face many of the same problems encountered by the field's founders a century ago. Chief among these is the qualified respect offered children's theatre and its practitioners from professionals in theatre. For many serious theater artists, children's theater continues to belong to the realm of education rather than art. However, these attitudes are beginning to shift as original plays by respected professional playwrights are commissioned and performed and as children's theatres focus on artistic quality in lieu of or in addition to educational messages. Those theatres that continue to focus on education as a primary goal are faced with new issues to explore artistically, such as the use of tobacco and drugs, child abuse, racial and ethnic discrimination, and the effects of divorce on children.

Carol Schafer

See also Melodrama; Performers and Actors; Vaudeville

References and further reading
Bedard, Roger L., ed. 1984. *Dramatic Literature for Children: A Century in Review*. New Orleans, LA: Anchorage Press.
Bedard, Roger L., and C. John Tolch, eds. 1989. *Spotlight on the Child: Studies in the History of American Children's Theatre*. Westport, CT: Greenwood Press.
Bettelheim, Bruno. 1976. *The Uses of Enchantment: The Meaning and Importance of Fairy Tales*. New York: Alfred A. Knopf.
Croteau, Jan Helling. 2000. *Perform It! A Complete Guide to Young People's Theatre*. Portsmouth, NH: Heinemann.
McCaslin, Nellie. 1971. *Theatre for Children in the United States: A History*. Norman: University of Oklahoma Press.
———. 1987. *Historical Guide to Children's Theatre in America*. Westport, CT: Greenwood Press.
Siks, Geraldine Brain, and Hazel Brain Dunnington, eds. 1967. *Children's Theatre and Creative Dramatics*. Seattle: University of Washington Press.
Ward, Winifred. 1958. *Theatre for Children*. Anchorage, KY: Children's Theatre Press.
Youth Theatre Journal. 1986– . American Association of Theatre for Youth (formerly *Children's Theatre Review*).
Zipes, Jack. 1983. *Fairy Tales and the Art of Subversion: The Classical Genre for Children and the Process of Civilization*. New York: Wildman Press.

Toys

Little has changed as much in the history of American boys as have the number and kinds of their toys. From colonization until the Civil War era, male children had relatively few playthings, especially after the toddler years. The pressures of work on farms and in trades limited the time of play. In those times of settlement and relative scarcity, parents seldom thought of toys as tools of learning or character building. The young learned their sex roles and job skills by assisting in their father's or a master's daily work. And religious strictures against idleness, especially in Puritan New England, made games suspect. In many families, adults brought out toys only on special holidays. A common toy dating back to sixteenth-century Germany was Noah's ark, a play set complete with animal figures, but parents allowed children to play with it only on Sundays, presumably to teach a Bible story. Most important, however, was simply the relative paucity of manufactured luxury goods of any kind. Many manufactured toys were expensive and until the end of the nineteenth century were often imported from Germany.

This scarcity, of course, did not mean that early American boys had no toys. At least in more wealthy, free, and settled families, infants and toddlers received teething toys, rattles, hobbyhorses, jumping jacks, and building blocks. These playthings grew more elaborate in the nineteenth century, with the availability of mechanical push toys that rang bells or toy instruments (horns, drums, and pianos). These "child quieters" were used to divert those too young to work.

Even if older boys were given few toys, they found time to play and often made their own toys. They improvised, creating fantasy worlds with whittled sticks, castaway bits of cloth, stones, gourds, wheel rims, and mother's clothespins. More often, however, they played their own, often rough, games in unsupervised groups. Particularly in rural and small-town America where the press of parents' work and the availability of open space gave boys ample opportunity to form into small gangs, they tested each other's courage and displayed loyalty at play without necessarily requiring toys. Finally,

Nineteenth-century boys played with miniatures of adult life, like this 1895 cast-iron horse and fire wagon made by Wilkens. (Courtesy, The Strong Museum, Rochester, NY)

toys were probably more available for boys than for girls. In American portraits taken between 1830 and 1870, 66 percent of boys are shown with toys, whereas only 20 percent of girls were depicted with any plaything, mostly dolls.

Only after 1865 did American manufacturers produce toys in large numbers, and then often as a sideline. Manufacturers of wood, metal, mechanical, and print and paper goods often produced miniatures of their "adult" products or used waste materials to make modest batches of cheap children's playthings for Christmas sales. Pennsylvania upholsters made toy drums from scrap. Samuel Leeds Allen manufactured farm equipment but diversified with the famous Flexible Flyer sled in 1889, and the immigrant Al-

bert Schoenhut of Philadelphia imported German toys until he had the resources to manufacture his own line of toys in 1872. Toys remained secondary retail items, often sold by peddlers of housewares or from hardware catalogs. They were almost afterthoughts because they were relatively unimportant to parents.

When cast-iron toys began replacing tin-plated toys in the 1860s, cheap, easily varied molds became possible. Improved and cheaper brass clockwork mechanisms also stimulated the production of a plethora of mechanical toys. For example, in 1868, a son of watchmakers named Edward R. Ives of Plymouth, Connecticut, began manufacturing a vast array of windup toys, often on topical themes: fiddle players, performing bears, black preachers, and General

Grant smoking. Other manufacturers copied English parlor science devices from the 1820s and 1830s (like the flashcard "moving picture" and the more sophisticated zoetrope, in which a paper strip of pictures appears to be animated when viewed through turning slits on a drum) and moralizing games of chance (like the "Mansion of Happiness"). More innovative toys from the 1860s included sand molds and cap and air guns. Roller skating also became a popular family activity in 1875, and children's pedal toys began to appear shortly after the introduction of velocipedes and bicycles made for adults in the 1870s. The mechanical savings bank (featuring a figure that shot a bear or danced when a coin was deposited) taught the parent-approved lesson of thrift even as it amused all. Charles Crandall (1833–1905) introduced interlocking building blocks for construction play. Most of these toys were still too expensive for any but the affluent (a clockwork figure cost from $1 to about $3 when daily wages were scarcely that high). But even the poor could afford cheap "penny toys" (wooden tops, tiny toy swords, and crude animal figures, for example).

Most late-nineteenth-century toys were essentially miniatures of adult tools and invited boys to anticipate adult male sex roles. Toy catalogs featured toy hammers, saws, and even garden tool sets for boys and dolls and miniature houseware sets for girls. With notable exceptions, these toys were not designed to encourage fantasy (there were no masks or cowboy hats, no figures made in the image of boy heroes). Gradually toys were becoming substitutes for training in work. They also served as tools for more solitary play encouraged by parents desiring to isolate their sons from the influence of unsupervised gangs.

A series of changes clustering around 1900 created new toys for young boys. Manufacturers began to address boys' imaginations rather than just parents' concerns. Although children had little pocket money, boys' magazines from the 1870s onward offered young readers rather expensive toy steam engines for selling subscriptions to their magazines. In the 1900s, parents also began to give children allowances, in part to teach them shopping skills. Toy makers responded by advertising heavily in boys' magazines. This publicity was the secret of the success of such "staple" toys as Flexible Flyer sleds and Albert C. Gilbert's erector sets.

Increasingly, manufacturers featured toys for older boys. The percentage of American males between the ages of fourteen and nineteen years old who worked had decreased from 61 percent in 1890 to 40 percent around 1930 (Bureau of the Census 1965, 70). Middle-class boys of ten to even sixteen years of age could look to sophisticated construction sets as fun but practical training for modern careers in engineering and science. Such toys appealed as well to parents who wanted their older sons to spend their playtime "wisely."

Toys became even more sex-stereotyped as boys' toys increasingly idealized technology, constant innovation, and the values of competition and teamwork. By contrast, a new generation of playthings for females featured companion and baby dolls, encouraging emotional attachments and nurturing. Of course, male children also played with dolls; part of the reason for the 1906 craze for the teddy bear was that it was a masculine image that attracted little boys. Still, the gender divide shaped the vision of the future: to boys it promised an exciting public world of mechanical progress and to girls a personal life of warm relationships and fashion.

Many boys' toys from 1900 to 1950 closely reflected dramatic changes in transportation, science, communications, and construction. The introduction of toy cars and airplanes closely followed the real things. Chemistry and other science sets introduced boys to the secret processes of nature. Boys' playthings also gloried in media and communications technology, including working cameras, slide projectors, phonographs, and radios. All these toys attempted to minimize the barrier between the plaything and the real thing. They taught boys to admire the technologies of the future and allowed youths to imagine themselves in control of modern power.

From the 1910s to the 1960s, model electric trains were the capstone toy for many middle-class American boys. Facilitated by Joshua Lionel Cowen's 1906 introduction of the electric current transformer, the electric locomotive made boys feel powerful. Central to the appeal were the carefully designed replicas of coal and refrigerated cars, colorful boxcars, and cabooses that gave boys a sense of being part of a real world of commerce and success; and the miniatures of roundhouses, railroad crossing signals, and other accessories completed the romance.

In this period the media and educators were beginning to encourage fathers to spend more time with their sons. The pressures of work may have prevented many fathers from following this advice, and surveys showed that boys still preferred their mothers. But men did embrace the idea of fathering through play with their sons. Electric train manufacturers encouraged boys to make "the lad the pal to dad" by getting the father involved with their train play.

Another favorite toy was the construction set. The best-known examples were Tinkertoys, Lincoln logs, and especially Albert C. Gilbert's erector sets (1913). Boys were supposed to bolt together Gilbert's metal strips to make models of modern railroad and industrial equipment. But he provided more. Gilbert gave boys a dream of play, accomplishment, and preparation for future success. In his ads and catalogs, Gilbert touted his own fun-filled but also successful life and promised in his various promotions that lads who played with his construction and science toys were bound to become engineers and business titans. Boys responded by building models of specialized machines of the rail era: jib cranes, swing bridges, pile drivers, inclined delivery shoots, and coal tip cranes.

One element of contemporary boys' toys was, however, relatively rare in early-twentieth-century toys—war play. Toy weapons were, of course, sold. Cap guns appeared as early as 1859, pop guns had their debut in the early 1870s, and the Daisy Air Rifle (BB gun) began its long success in 1888. A few cowboy suits with holsters and revolvers appeared shortly before World War I. Battleships and even machine guns arrived during that conflict. But all these items were designed to promote bonding with older brothers and fathers at war. Daisy advertised its toy rifles as essential tools in making boys into men and never glorified violence or destruction. Toy gun sales dropped off sharply after World War I. The excitement of trains, cars, commercial flight, and construction prevailed over war toys in boys' play in the thirty years after 1900.

A major shift in boys' playthings began in the 1930s during the Great Depression. In response to reduced sales, toy makers offered cheaper toys, often sold by the piece. Ironically, this tended to make it possible for children to purchase their own toys. Thus ten-year-old boys, using their earnings from running errands, could buy single miniature cars or rubber toy soldiers rather than have to wait for an adult to purchase a complete set of metal soldiers. Boys had long collected objects that surrounded them. In the 1930s, the collecting habit began to shift from amassing shells or bottle caps to collecting the constantly expanding number of military figures sold in dime stores.

Toy companies also began to license images of popular media personalities to increase sales. Talking movies, especially color cartoons, greatly increased the appeal of film to boys, and during the Depression theaters offered Saturday matinees that featured children's fare. Westerns and space heroes like Buck Rogers, but also Mickey Mouse and other Disney cartoon personalities, attracted boys. Network radio introduced widely popular after-school adventure programs designed especially for boys. They shaped boys' play by introducing stories and images designed specifically for children that required toys to serve as props for the reenactment of their dramatic narratives. Radio serials gave voices and sound effects to the images in the daily comic strips. For example, Chester Gould's "Dick Tracy" (a comic strip introduced in 1931 that shortly afterward also became a radio program) featured strong images and colors, manly personalities, and striking situations that could be easily converted into boys' toys like the Dick Tracy Jr. Click Pistol. When boys listening to the radio heard Tracy's police car screech down the street and his gun fire as he chased crooks, they wanted

"official" Dick Tracy police cars and pistols. Buck Rogers, an American accidentally sent to the twenty-fifth century, became the hero of a long-lasting science fiction adventure program. The makers of the Daisy Air Rifle offered a Buck Rogers Space Pistol at 25 cents in 1934 to supplement stagnant sales of their $5 BB gun.

In the 1930s, the hero began to replace the machine as the central prop of play. Although the construction sets of the 1910s and 1920s called the boy to imitate practical men and to imagine his future role in an orderly world of economic and technological progress, the new male fantasy toy beckoned the youth to a faraway realm where conflict dominated. No longer did technology seem to offer a future of progress and prosperity. Rather than inviting the boy to identify with the father (often unemployed in the Depression), the new toys evoked an image of strong men free from the bonds of family. The cowboy star, tough detective, boxer, spaceman, and superhero became father substitutes. In the 1930s, Tom Mix, Dick Tracy, Popeye, Buck Rogers, and Superman offered boys a wide variety of toys (both guns and windup figures). They all shared a common penchant for fighting and subduing enemies rather than constructing things or achieving goals. And they all lived in a world where a boy could forget he was a child and the fact that he may have had an unheroic father without a steady job.

The 1930s saw an extraordinary growth in toy weaponry in fantasies of the Wild West, G-men against criminals, and intergalactic war. The combination of more aggressive marketing of toy guns and general anxiety about crime in the gangster-ridden 1930s produced a negative public reaction. In 1934 and 1935, Rose Simone,

GI Joe underwent many transformations, thus revealing a changing world of boys' play. The large GI Joe is a doll that boys in the 1960s dressed and play=acted the duties of real U.S. Navy frogmen. Underneath is the 1995 version, GI Joe Extreme, a pair of fantastic figures designed merely for combat. (Courtesy, Alexander Cross, State College, PA)

of its cost), but it was an extravagant example of the toy as promoter of progress. Chemcraft claimed that its new science sets drew on wartime discoveries in plastics, wonder drugs, and atomic energy to inspire a new generation of children to be inventors. The new technology of jet propulsion was mirrored in the model airplanes offered by plastics manufacturers like Revell. Science fiction films and comics inspired a curious run of space toys in the early 1950s. These included plastic green "men from Mars," space helmets, battery-operated robots, and even a Space Scout Spud Gun that shot "harmless little plugs of raw potato up to 50 feet." More realistic were the toy miniatures that celebrated the space program and missile development in the late 1950s. The appeal was less to war than to science and its industrial applications in the future. Only in the mid-1950s did many toys appear celebrating World War II combat and then only as a historical event commemorated along with other past heroics. Most of this celebration of men's deeds and technology in boys' toys was more peaceful and prosaic—model bulldozers, trucks, and service stations offered by companies like Tonka.

The postwar period also produced a craze for cowboy toys that went well beyond the well-established traditions of cowboy suits, holster sets, and Lincoln logs. Cheaply made miniature frontier towns, ranches, and especially forts let boys reenact cowboy-and-Indian dramas seen at the movies. Radio and movie cowboys, including Hopalong Cassidy, Roy Rogers, Cisco Kid, Davy Crockett, and the Lone Ranger, graced the toy shelves of the late 1940s and early 1950s. But in the five years after 1955, the prime-time westerns that were designed for the whole family and that attracted fathers as

a militant opponent of weapons toys, organized a bonfire in Chicago into which guns gathered from children in sixty area schools were thrown.

In certain ways, toys popular during the post-1945 baby-boom generation harked back to the toys of pre-1930 generations. In a period of new scientific advances and perhaps closer bonds between fathers and sons, many new playthings were miniatures of contemporary technology. Gilbert's Atomic Energy Set may have been a commercial failure (because much as sons made western toys ever more popular. Both romantic settings—space travel in the future and western heroes in the past—were imaginative worlds that fathers and sons could share.

Although the 1950s seemed to be a throwback, the decade did mark the beginning of mass advertising of toys on television programs directly to children, a change that eventually revolutionized boys' play. Although the *Mickey Mouse Club* was not the first children's show to promote toys when it first appeared on television in 1955, its advertising was aggressively designed to appeal to the child's imagination rather than to the parents' values. Mattel toys proved that year-round advertising featuring child actors could create mass rushes to buy "burp guns" and "Fanner 50 smoking cap guns" even outside the Christmas gift season. Increasingly, boys pressured their parents into buying "must-have" toys after seeing them on television. Playthings began to represent the world of boys' fantasy as presented in the contemporary media. Instead of toys being sold to parents (and thus designed to please them), playthings increasingly were sold that appealed to boys' imagination.

The 1960s and 1970s witnessed a transition to another phase in the history of toys, dominated by the action figure and video game in which playthings became props or electronic means for reenacting fantasy stories. For the most part, these toys were divorced from the memories and expectations of parents. Not only did parents find these toys increasingly alien from their recollections of their own childhoods, but these playthings increasingly had no connection to the boys' future.

The most revealing example of this change is found in the history of Hasbro's GI Joe. When this figure first appeared in

1964, it was a boy's dress-up doll, realistically representing the average soldier. Unlike those cheap and impersonal plastic soldiers of the 1950s, GI Joe had movable limbs and was 1 foot tall; thus, he could be posed and equipped with the latest military clothing and weaponry. Boys could play war the way their fathers might have fought in Europe in World War II or in Korea. And they could dress their Joes in battle gear similar to that worn by conscripted uncles or older brothers serving their two-year stints in the army of the mid-1960s. GI Joe still connected fathers with sons.

In the late 1960s, however, GI Joe suffered major changes. By 1967, as the Vietnam War heated up and adults (like pediatrician Benjamin Spock) attacked war toys, sales decreased. Beginning in 1970, Hasbro responded to a growing hostility to war toys among adults by transforming the "fighting" Joes into an "Adventure Team" in which the hero searched for sunken treasure and captured wild animals. As the Vietnam War wound down to its bitter end in 1975, it was awkward to sell military toys glorifying contemporary jungle warfare. In 1976, with the Vietnam War in the past, GI Joe once again became a fighter. Although the new "Super Joe" had shrunk to 8 inches (because of higher costs for plastic) and no longer could be dressed, he was even more exciting to boys as a high-tech warrior. GI Joe did not rejoin the ranks of enlisted men and was no longer part of a world that fathers, uncles, or older brothers had ever experienced. Instead, his laser beams and rocket command vehicles helped him fight off aliens. The object of play was to pit good guys against bad guys, not to imitate real military life. Play no longer had anything to do with the experience of fathers and their hopes for their sons' future.

These action figures set the stage for the craze stimulated by the movie trilogy *Star Wars* from 1977 to 1983. During these years and beyond, American boys were inundated with toy figures, vehicles, and play sets built around the play of reenacting the onscreen rivalry of Darth Vader and Luke Skywalker. The theme of violence was very pronounced in these action figures and their many imitators. Still, because the violence was so unrealistic, it was easy for boys not to take it seriously. Action figures used wildly imaginary weapons, and conflict was reduced to the scale of the play sets. Parents no longer dressed their sons like soldiers or even gunslinging cowboys. Instead of turning their backyards into play battlefields or dueling with cap gun and holster in family dens, boys were allowed to collect tiny warriors that reminded no adult of any war they had ever known. The conflicting feelings of adults toward the military were avoided, allowing most parents to ignore the war play of their young. At the same time, war play became detached from whatever historical or moral purpose that military toys had earlier embodied.

Star Wars and GI Joe toys were just the beginning. Mattel's He-Man and Masters of the Universe, appearing in 1982, closely paralleled the Star Wars formula. The youthful, blond, and muscular He-Man and his team of good guys fought the aged, bony, and evil Skeletor and his horde. A major feature of the Mattels line was Castle Grayskull, which was shaped like a mountain. The figures in effect played "king of the mountain" at Grayskull, the center of the fray in a "fantastic universe beyond all time." There were many imitations in the 1980s and 1990s: the Transformers, Dino-Riders, Teenage Mutant Ninja Turtles,

Power Rangers, and Pokémon, for example. These action figures and their accompanying play sets were all linked to fantastic stories. Many were products of television cartoon series shown on Saturday mornings and in after-school hours that featured action-figure images. Indeed, following the liberalization of rules on children's television in 1982, many of these cartoons were developed for the toy companies specifically to promote their product lines. Thus, they were called "program-length commercials."

Beginning in 1972, action figures competed with and often paralleled video games. Simple games like electronic Ping-Pong played in arcades were quickly supplemented with video action available on home game consoles for television and handheld electronic toys. These products introduced younger boys to electronic interactive play. Although this craze died in the early 1980s with the collapse of Atari and other manufacturers of video games, the much improved graphics and action of Nintendo and other video systems from 1988 onward brought the video game back. These interactive electronic adventures heavily emphasized fantasy violence and brought criticism for their increasing intensity, addictive attraction, and tendency to isolate boys from others.

While action figures, video games, and other toy fads sparked repeated concern among parents and educators, traditional toys like marbles, yo-yos, and even imaginative construction toys like Lego found it difficult to compete. By the end of the twentieth century, American boys' toys were drawn primarily from a never-ending and always changing world of media fantasy.

Gary Cross

See also Comic Books; Films; Superheroes; Television: Cartoons; Video
Games

References and further reading
Bruegman, Bill. 1992. Toys of the Sixties.
Akron, OH: Cap'n Penny Productions.
Bureau of the Census. 1965. The
Statistical History of the United States.
Washington, DC: Government Printing
Office.
Calvert, Karin. 1992. Children in the
House: The Material Culture of Early
Childhood, 1600–1900. Boston:
Northeastern University Press.
Cross, Gary. 1997. Kids' Stuff: Toys and
the Changing World of American
Childhood. Cambridge, MA: Harvard
University Press.
Gilbert, Albert C., with Marshall
McClintock. 1953. The Man Who Lives
in Paradise. New York: Rinehart.
Greenfield, Laurence. 1991. "Toys,
Children, and the Toy Industry in a
Culture of Consumption, 1890–1991."
Ph.D. diss., Ohio State University.
Hewitt, Karen, and Louis Roomet. 1979.
Educational Toys in America: 1800 to
the Present. Burlington, VT: Robert Hull
Fleming Museum.
Kline, Stephen. 1993. Out of the Garden:
Toys and Children's Culture in the Age
of TV Marketing. New York: Verso.
O'Brien, Richard. 1990. The Story of
American Toys. London: New
Cavendish Books.
Payton, Crystal. 1982. Space Toys. Sedalia,
MO: Collectors Compass.
West, Elliott, and Paula Petrik, eds. 1992.
Small Worlds: Children and
Adolescents in America, 1850–1950.
Lawrence: University of Kansas Press.
Whitton, Blair. 1981. American
Clockwork Toys, 1862–1900. Exton, PA:
Schiffer Publishing.

Transitions (through Adolescence)

During adolescence, boys undergo many
transitions as they move from childhood
to adulthood. Although these transitions
are challenging for many, if not all, boys,
most will meet these challenges successfully. Entry into adolescence involves puberty, enrollment in a new type of school
(that is, middle or junior high school),
new cognitive skills, changing relationships with peers that will start to include
sexual experiences, and changing relationships with parents that often include
more frequent arguments as boys seek
greater independence. The exit from adolescence or entry into adulthood also involves many important transitions, including enrolling in advanced education,
entering military service, or beginning a
first full-time job; being able to support
oneself financially; and engaging in relationships with romantic partners that
may be longer lasting and more stable
than the relationships of adolescence. In
between these major transitions are other
important developmental landmarks as
boys grow from children to adults. Part of
becoming an adult is not just looking
more like an adult but also taking on the
roles of adults (Graber and Brooks-Gunn
1996). Exploration of the roles of adulthood, or figuring out what it means to be
an adult, is one of the challenges of adolescence, with new roles emerging at
each transition.

In nearly every culture or society, there
is a period between childhood and adulthood during which individuals are expected to learn the roles of an adult
(Schlegel and Barry 1991). The length of
the adolescent period may vary; some individuals will need to make transitions at
younger or older ages depending on their
opportunities and experiences. The second decade of a child's life in its entirety
is often defined as adolescence. In addition, adolescence is usually divided into
three main transitional periods: entry
into or early adolescence, middle adolescence, and late adolescence. There are no
exact ages for each period, but each one
usually matches a time when a boy
makes a school change, at least in the

United States. During the entire decade of adolescence, cognitive development increases boys' abilities to understand future outcomes, make plans and decisions, and think in abstract terms. These developmental advances interconnect with changes in feelings and behaviors as boys develop their identities and intimate relationships.

The entry into adolescence, or early adolescence, typically stretches from ages eleven to fourteen. During this period, most boys will experience the transition of puberty, the school transition from elementary to middle school, and relationship and role changes with parents and peers. Puberty is not a single event—boys do not go to bed one night with the body of a child and then wake up the next morning with the body of an adult. Instead, most boys will take four to five years from the beginning to the end of puberty. Boys may begin to show outward signs of puberty anywhere from age nine to thirteen and a half and still be in the range of normal development. Thus, some boys may go through puberty mainly during the middle school years, if they start in late elementary school and finish by age thirteen or fourteen, whereas others may experience most of puberty during high school, if they start in middle school and finish by age eighteen.

On average, boys' puberty usually begins with the appearance of pubic hair and changes in the genitals occurring between eleven and eleven and a half years of age (Marshall and Tanner 1970). These changes may be noticeable mainly to the boy himself. In contrast, many of the other changes of puberty are noticeable to boys and those around them. For example, vocal changes and the appearance of facial hair are noticed by others as well as by the boys themselves. The growth spurt in height begins around eleven and a half years of age. On average, the most rapid changes in height occur around age fourteen for boys. There is also a spurt in strength after the growth spurt, with boys adding a substantial amount of muscle (54 percent of body weight) by the end of puberty.

These changes in physical appearance have been associated with behavior and adjustment changes for boys. Typically, all boys are likely to have periods of time when they are uncomfortable with their changing bodies. Although growing in height and muscle may make an adolescent boy feel more like an adult, different parts of the body tend to grow at different times, leading to that "gangly" feeling; acne is common throughout puberty; and many boys may be self-conscious about their changing bodies, especially in the locker room. With increasing focus in the media—television, magazines—on a lean, muscular body type for men, more boys are starting to have problems with body image as they go through puberty. These types of experiences and external pressures make puberty a challenging transition for boys. In addition, some boys may be particularly sensitive about their developing bodies (Graber, Petersen, and Brooks-Gunn 1996). For example, boys who mature later than their peers may be sensitive to being shorter and less muscular when other boys have already grown. Boys who mature earlier than their peers seem to have an advantage in sports and physical activities, especially in the middle school years, as they are bigger and stronger than other boys.

By the end of the pubertal transition, boys will have gone from having the body of a child to one that looks (and functions) much more like an adult's body. Most boys in the United States will also make a school transition around this same time. This transition is not merely to a *new* school but usually to a very different type of school (Graber and Brooks-Gunn 1996). For example, most middle or junior high schools are much larger than the elementary schools that boys attended in childhood. Students frequently change classrooms and teachers every period, a situation that often prevents them from making personal connections with teachers. In addition, grading standards are often higher, workload usually increases, and students are expected to work independently more of the time. Taken together, these changes in school context can be a difficult transition for boys. Most boys will find these changes somewhat stressful but eventually get used to the new expectations and situation by the second semester or the next year. However, it is important to remember that boys in general more often have difficulties at school, as evidenced by their higher rates of learning and reading disabilities (Sommers 2000). Boys who have struggled with schoolwork in the elementary years are at increased risk for having increased problems at this time and throughout adolescence.

The entry into adolescence also includes transitions in the family environment. As most parents will confirm, arguing between young adolescents and parents is a common experience (Steinberg 1990). As adolescents mature, so does their capacity to think critically and make decisions on their own. As boys take on more responsibility at school and begin to look older, they often want to make more of their own decisions and question rules established by parents. In the big picture, arguments are over the struggle for independence or autonomy, but in the reality of day-to-day experi-

ence, arguments are usually over chores, curfew, and similar issues. The frequency of arguments seems to peak during mid-puberty (Steinberg 1990). Over time, the rate of arguing declines as parents begin to give their adolescent sons more control over or input into rules and regulations. For most families, maintaining warm and supportive relationships during this time helps the adolescent feel secure while testing the waters of independence. Some research has found that it is mothers rather than sons who seem to be most upset by the arguing (Steinberg 1990). Mothers and daughters seem to maintain more closeness during early adolescence, whereas mothers often feel that their sons are more rejecting of their concerns and affection.

Finally, boys' relationships with their peers also make a transition at this time. Perhaps in part because of the larger school context, young adolescent boys more often make friends based on shared interests rather than just hanging out with the kids who live in their neighborhoods. As boys begin to think about who they are and who they want to be as adults, they may seek out friends whom they perceive to have similar interests and goals. Friendships in early adolescence may seem transitory as individuals explore different groups with whom they want to identify. At the same time, boys begin to explore sexual and dating situations. Usually, young adolescents start going out in mixed-gender groups and may engage in kissing or exploration games at parties. Making the transition to intercourse is not common for young adolescent boys, but about one in five boys will have intercourse by age fourteen (Alan Guttmacher Institute 1994).

The transitions of early adolescence are not made quickly but set boys on the course of continuing adolescent challenges. Middle adolescence (ages fifteen to seventeen or eighteen) most often encompasses the high school years. The transitions of this period are more varied: some boys make them, but others may not. Most boys typically become licensed drivers during middle adolescence. Little is known about how this transition is experienced by boys, but it seems likely that most feel that they are one step closer to adulthood via this achievement. In particular, driving often allows more freedom and independence from parents to pursue social activities. At this time, dating is more common, and more and more boys make serious sexual transitions; by age seventeen, nearly 60 percent of boys have had intercourse (Alan Guttmacher Institute 1994).

During the course of high school, many boys will also become workers. Certainly, some boys will have had part-time jobs at earlier ages, but it is common for boys to engage in more formal part-time employment experiences in middle adolescence. Becoming a worker is a positive experience for many boys because a job brings them additional challenges (e.g., balancing school and work, making new friends, being responsible) while also giving them more money to spend on activities that they choose for themselves. However, boys who spend too much time working (more than twenty hours per week) during the school year often are more disengaged from school and may engage in more problem behaviors (e.g., drinking or smoking) (Steinberg and Avenevoli 1998).

By late adolescence, boys again face numerous simultaneous transitions as they begin to move closer to taking on adult roles. Although the entry into adolescence is defined by many transitions

that typically are experienced by nearly every boy (e.g., puberty, school transition), late adolescence (ages eighteen to twenty) and the transition to adulthood are perhaps more complicated because these transitions depend more on the opportunities available to young men as well as their own desires. Across adolescence, boys form their ideas about what they want to be as adults—workers, spouses, fathers, and so on. As such, they prepare to take on adult roles and define these roles based on what they would like to be, along with the opportunities that are available to them.

The transition to adulthood may be quite long or quite short and may occur quickly or slowly. For example, boys typically begin living away from home during late adolescence and the transition to adulthood. Initially, they may not be financially independent from parents and family but are often finishing high school, continuing their education (e.g., college or trade school), entering the military, or starting their first full-time job. Some young men will not finish the level of education or training that they want and may find themselves redefining the type of worker they will be. For adolescents who do not go on to college, some may struggle to find more regular, consistent work, making it difficult to become financially self-sufficient or to go on to support a family. Young men who go on to college frequently do not become financially self-sufficient or start a family until they have finished college and have started working. In addition, a few young men may never marry or have children, whereas others become parents while they are still adolescents. Information from the Census Bureau indicates that the median age of first marriage for men is currently just under twenty-seven years of age (Lugaila 1998). Thus the transitions to stable marital and family roles occur later for boys than they did in the 1960s and 1970s. It has been suggested that the entire period from ages eighteen to twenty-five is an extended transitional period (Arnett 2000).

In general, most boys navigate the transitions of adolescence successfully. That is not to say that they will not experience some stress and a lot of challenges. Rather, most adapt to the changes and develop the skills they need to manage the challenges of each transition. Certainly, boys who enter adolescence with better coping skills, supportive family relationships, positive friendships, and success in school usually fare well during this time period. However, even for these boys, a particular transition may upset the system. In order to keep boys on a healthy pathway to adulthood and to move boys from less healthy pathways to healthy ones, continued attention to the challenges of each transition are needed. Targeting programs, community resources, and family supports for the times when transitions are most common will help a greater number of boys successfully take on adult roles.

Julia A. Graber

See also Adolescence; Bodies; Fathers, Adolescent; Learning Disabilities; Mothers; Same-Sex Relationships; Sexuality; Smoking and Drinking

References and further reading
Alan Guttmacher Institute. 1994. *Sex and America's Teenagers*. New York: Alan Guttmacher Institute.

Arnett, Jeffrey J. 2000. "Emerging Adulthood: A Theory of Development from the Late Teens through the Twenties." *American Psychologist* 55: 469–480.

Graber, Julia A., and Jeanne Brooks-Gunn. 1996. "Transitions and Turning Points: Navigating the Passage from Childhood through Adolescence." *Developmental Psychology* 32: 768–776.

Graber, Julia A., Anne C. Petersen, and Jeanne Brooks-Gunn. 1996. "Pubertal Processes: Methods, Measures, and Models." Pp. 23–53 in *Transitions through Adolescence: Interpersonal Domains and Context*. Edited by Julia A. Graber, Jeanne Brooks-Gunn, and Anne C. Petersen. Mahwah, NJ: Erlbaum.

Lugaila, Terry A. 1998. "Marital Status and Living Arrangements: March 1998 (Update)." *Current Population Reports*. U.S. Bureau of the Census Publication no. P20-514. Washington, DC: U.S. Department of Commerce.

Marshall, William A., and James M. Tanner. 1970. "Variations in the Pattern of Pubertal Changes in Boys." *Archives of Disease in Childhood* 45: 13–23.

Schlegel, Alice, and Herbert Barry III. 1991. *Adolescence: An Anthropological Inquiry*. New York: Free Press.

Sommers, Christina H. 2000. "The War against Boys." *The Atlantic Monthly* (May): 59–74.

Steinberg, Laurence. 1990. "Autonomy, Conflict, and Harmony in the Family Relationship." Pp. 255–276 in *At the Threshold: The Developing Adolescent*. Edited by Shirley Feldman and Glen R. Elliott. Cambridge, MA: Harvard University Press.

Steinberg, Laurence, and Shelli Avenevoli. 1998. "Disengagement from School and Problem Behaviors in Adolescence: A Developmental-Contextual Analysis of the Influence of Family and Part-time Work." Pp. 392–424 in *New Perspectives on Adolescent Risk Behavior*. Edited by Richard Jessor. New York: Cambridge University Press.

V

Vaudeville

A form of live, popular entertainment in the United States from the late nineteenth century through the early twentieth century, vaudeville consisted of a variety of diverse short acts that included music, dance, trained animals, and eccentric feats and was designed to appeal to the entire family. In the mid-1800s, New York City theatrical managers such as P. T. Barnum (1810–1891) and Tony Pastor (1837–1908) sought to provide wholesome entertainment that would attract workingmen, their wives, and their children. In creating the variety format, Pastor drew from traditions such as the minstrel show, which used blackface song-and-dance numbers to grotesquely parody life on southern plantations; the concert saloon, where male comedians might be accompanied by scantily clad chorus girls; and the English music hall, which also interspersed comical sketches with musical numbers. These earlier forms were not appropriate for family viewing, since they contained sexually suggestive songs and jokes. Furthermore, these performances were presented in drinking houses, where the entertainment encouraged the purchase and consumption of liquor and patrons quickly became rowdy and even violent. In response to these conditions, Pastor and other vaudeville managers who followed him instituted strict regulations about the language, content, and costumes of the vaudeville acts in order to develop and maintain a theatrical experience appropriate for women and children.

Throughout the history of theatrical entertainment, societies around the world have wrestled with issues of propriety in public performances and the right of a government to censor artists. This struggle has been particularly fierce in the United States, a nation founded by religious refugees from Europe who lived by strict moral codes. Their deep sense of morality (periodically expressed by governmental prohibitions against acting) prevented professional theater from fully developing as a commercial venture until the industrialization of the East Coast in the 1820s. Even when permanent theaters and touring companies did develop, much of the public feared the corruption of audiences by the new ideas, behaviors, and costumes presented on stage.

By 1865, theaters that presented complete plays, whether written by Americans or imported from Europe, were known as "legitimate" theaters and appealed to the more highly educated, wealthier classes of society. The music, comedy sketches, animal acts, and dancing preferred by many working-class men were most prominent in the concert saloons notorious for drinking, brawling, and connections to prostitution. In particular, the presence of female performers in flesh-colored tights that displayed the shape of their legs, who performed high kicks while singing sexually suggestive lyrics, contributed to the reputation of moral corruption in the concert saloons. It was this environment that Tony Pastor sought to change by providing the songs, dance, and comedy of the variety format in a clean, well-furnished auditorium that evoked the glamour of the "legitimate" theaters. In appealing to working-men to bring their wives and children to this new type of "clean" theater, Pastor targeted a huge new audience—complete families. Pastor encouraged mothers to take charge of their families' leisure hours by providing a "wholesome" venue where all members of the family could feel safe and comfortable. His success soon inspired the proliferation of many variety theaters, not only in New York but across the country. The further efforts of producers B. F. Keith (1846–1914) and Edward F. Albee (1857–1930) resulted in a huge touring network: variety performers traveled by train from New York to San Francisco and back again, presenting the same acts to audiences everywhere. Although urban families were more likely to experience vaudeville than those in remote rural areas, this network was the beginning of a national popular culture. Nearly every class of people in every part of the country could laugh at the same jokes and learn the same songs. It was Keith who insisted on calling the form "vaudeville," a word that comes from the French vaux-de-Vire, a type of satirical song from the town of Vire in Normandy. He believed that the exotic French word lent sophistication to the variety show. Indeed, working- and middle-class audiences enjoyed paying mere pennies to visit the elegant vaudeville

palaces of Keith and Albee, which resembled the fancy legitimate theaters where drama and opera were presented.

Several aspects of the vaudeville format were particularly appealing to women and children. First of all, lyric sheets, sheet music, and whole booklets of music called "songsters" were available at performances for a few pennies. A child who purchased a lyric sheet on the way into the theater could sing along with the musical numbers. Families who owned a piano or guitar could then play the music at home and remember the acts they had seen at the theater. In the days before radio, this kind of public ownership of current music was a popular diversion.

Second, the vaudeville theaters generally presented several performances of all the acts on a bill in one afternoon. For the price of a ticket, a child could enter the theater in the middle of a bill and stay until he had seen everything. Although young girls were generally kept at home with their mothers during the workweek, afternoon shows were ideal for a boy who had time after school before dinner or who spent his days selling newspapers or slinging water buckets for the fire department. The boys generally sat in the cheapest seats up in the highest balcony, which was called the "gallery." They would buy bags of peanuts and their song sheets and settle in for a rowdy session of singing, cheering, and throwing peanut shells down upon the audience and stage below. Although this sounds like extremely unruly behavior today, the atmosphere of the vaudeville theater involved much more give-and-take between actors and spectators than today, and much of this behavior was expected, if not entirely condoned. Managers often gauged the success of particular acts according to the applause, foot stomping, cheers, and insults raining down from the gallery during a performance.

Third, there were quite a few young people to be seen on the stage, which must have been exciting for boys in the audience. Children performed as tap and ballet dancers; singers of both popular tunes and operatic arias; dramatic interpreters of Shakespearean monologues; high-flying acrobats and contortionists; snappy-patter comedians; and animal tamers, sharing the stage with dogs, cats, all manner of rodents, birds, goats, and the occasional horse. Irish comedians Edward Harrigan (1845–1911) and Tony Hart (1855–1891), who opened their own theater in 1876, began touring as young children. Harrigan played guitar and sang original compositions, and Hart dressed as a young girl and sang heart-wrenching melodramatic ballads. As adults, Harrigan and Hart used choruses of children—including Harrigan's own sons—in some of their most popular shows. Lotta Crabtree of San Francisco (1847–1924) gained fame by dancing jigs and polkas. She won such a devoted following that she erected a public drinking fountain to thank her audiences. James Cagney (1904–1986), later a successful film star, began his career as a tap dancer, or "hoofer," and learned many of his athletic moves from the other dancers and acrobats he met in vaudeville. Fred Astaire (1899–1987) began ballroom dancing on the vaudeville circuit, and Milton Berle (b. 1908) appeared with his young partner, Elizabeth Kennedy (b. 1909), in wisecracking comedy skits.

Many acrobatic and musical teams featured siblings or families, such as Ruth and Giles Budd, who performed in the 1910s. As the older of the two, Ruth carried and tossed her little brother both on the ground and while hanging from the trapeze. The Marx Brothers, Harpo (1893–1964), Gummo (1894–1977), Chico (1891–1961), and Groucho (1890–1977), slept all four in one bed as they toured the country throughout their adolescence—before hitting the big time as movie stars. Gummo, who joined the army in 1918, was replaced by his youngest brother Zeppo (1901–1979) but later returned to show business as a talent agent. Gummo managed his brothers' act for many years. Buster Keaton (1895–1966) began performing with his family at the age of five, in a type of comedy act known as "slap-bang." Slap-bang revolved around Three Stooges–type misunderstandings that would result in wild fights, including comical punches and eye gouges and the use of special props to hit, poke, and slap. Buster's name actually came from his ability to withstand an enormous amount of physical abuse by training himself to twist, roll, and fall away from the blows.

"Slap-bang" in particular attracted the attention of reformers who were concerned about the physical and moral health of children in vaudeville. Unfortunately, many of the youngest performers were exploited as cheap labor, educated poorly and improperly fed, and abandoned once their youthful appeal wore off. Such conditions mirrored the abuse of working children in industrial jobs and were not unique to the theater world. But one man, Elbridge T. Gerry, was particularly disturbed by the long hours, lack of schooling, and poor health of child actors. In 1874, he founded the Society for the Prevention of Cruelty to Children and wrote many articles publicizing and denouncing the working conditions in theaters. Many vaudevillians recall the disruptive practices of the "Gerry society," which worked to "save" the children by protesting at performances and bringing legal suits against parents, guardians, and theater managers. Sadly, these children sometimes provided the only livelihood for their families, and the interruption in their careers only worsened their situation.

Of course, such controversy did not prevent boys from attending the theater. The content of songs and comedy sketches seen in vaudeville usually reflected current concerns, including the trials and tribulations of the growing immigrant populations arriving in the coastal cities. Young spectators might recognize aspects of themselves or their friends during performances of Irish, German, Jewish, Italian, and Chinese impersonators. Although many of the performers were in fact immigrants, the characters they portrayed were so exaggerated—emphasizing differences of dress, speech, or mannerism—that they could all be called "impersonators." For instance, the "stage Jew" character had a grotesque face with blackened teeth and a hooked nose enhanced by makeup. He spoke strongly accented English peppered with ridiculous exclamations such as "Und I vish dot I vas dead!" ("And I wish that I was dead!"). The blackface character featured enormous pink lips and wide eyes in contrast to the burnt cork used to darken his face. He, too, spoke an exaggerated dialect intended to mock the inability of African Americans to speak English "correctly." He would either shuffle around the stage in rags or dart about in fancy, bright-colored clothing he wore to imitate wealthy white people. Such characters usually tried to better their position in life through some scheme, such as finding a tree that grows ham on it, only to be knocked back down by their own stupidity or the superiority of the white society they tried to join. Many historians believe

that vaudeville humor provided a release for ethnic tensions in crowded urban areas, where minorities could laugh at themselves and others as an alternative to violent confrontation. Others describe such ethnic performances as detrimental to the reputation and actual economic conditions of poor immigrants in this country. In either case, vaudeville attracted many ethnic groups as spectators. Therefore, a trip to the theater exposed young people to various cultures—and stereotypes of cultures—both on and off the stage. This may have provided boys with a sense of diverse community, but it also may have contributed to anxieties about life in the increasingly crowded and complicated city.

By the late 1920s, the emergence of moving pictures threatened vaudeville's popularity. Furthermore, the Great Depression closed most remaining theaters. People had lost the extra income to devote to entertainment. When the economy recovered, live performance continued in the forms of musical theater, which presented one long play with musical interludes, and legitimate drama. The song-and-dance girls and cruder comedians of vaudeville were absorbed into the disreputable genre of burlesque, which turned the "leg shows" of the early concert saloons into outright striptease acts. But many of the most successful, family-oriented entertainers, such as the Marx Brothers and George Burns (1896–1996), gave up live performance and went on to great acclaim in radio, film, and television.

Television became the vaudeville of the late twentieth century. Its format provides a wide variety of distractions, including music, dance, drama, and comedy. Like vaudeville, its schedule is flexible, and its ticket price is fairly low. Also like vaudeville, television continues to struggle with standards of propriety, issues of censorship, and the demands of a competitive marketplace. This is particularly true because of television's role as entertainment for families and children. Boys can now identify with the action heroes, rap stars, and young comedians of television as they once did with Buster Keaton or James Cagney. But this targeting of young audiences by television draws the attention of governmental agencies and parental "watchdog" groups who follow in the footsteps of Elbridge Gerry in trying to protect young people from morally corrupt images and ideas. Ultimately, morality is interpreted by each individual, and the relationship of entertainment to that interpretation is unclear. With the ascendancy of the personal computer, boys can make even more individualized choices about what entertainment to view and how to interpret it. Television may follow vaudeville into the darkness offstage, to be replaced by the enormous online variety show.

Leslie Pasternack

See also Melodrama; Performers and Actors; Theatre

References and further reading
Brockett, Oscar G., and Frank Hildy. 1999. *History of the Theatre.* 8th ed. Boston: Allyn and Bacon.
Erdman, Harley. 1997. *Staging the Jew: The Performance of an American Ethnicity, 1860–1920.* New Brunswick: Rutgers University Press.
Gilbert, Douglas. 1940. *American Vaudeville, Its Life and Times.* New York: McGraw-Hill.
Green, Abel, and Joe Laurie, Jr. 1951. *Show Biz: From Vaude to Video.* New York: Henry Holt.
Kibler, M. Alison. 1999. *Rank Ladies: Gender and Cultural Hierarchy in American Vaudeville.* Chapel Hill: University of North Carolina Press.
Levine, Lawrence W. 1997. *Highbrow/ Lowbrow: The Emergence of Cultural Hierarchy in America.* Cambridge, MA: Harvard University Press.
Moody, Richard. 1980. *Ned Harrigan: From Corlear's Hook to Herald Square.* Chicago: Nelson-Hall.
Slide, Anthony. 1994. *The Encyclopedia of Vaudeville.* Westport, CT: Greenwood Press.
Snyder, Robert W. 1989. *The Voice of the City: Vaudeville and Popular Culture in New York.* New York: Oxford University Press.
Stein, Charles W., ed. 1984. *American Vaudeville as Seen by Its Contemporaries.* New York: Alfred A. Knopf.
Toll, Robert. 1976. *On with the Show! The First Century of Show Business in America.* New York: Oxford University Press.

Video Games

Video games comprise an array of computer-based entertainment products whose form combines an animated graphical user interface and the real-time interpretation of user input, applied to a fictional, playful, or nonutilitarian goal. Evolving from an oscilloscope display of simple animation running on a room-sized computer at New York's Brookhaven National Laboratory in 1958 into the contemporary three-dimensional virtual-reality systems sold as consumer electronics for the home, in their approximately forty years of existence video games have grown from an experiment conceived to explore possibilities of representation and user interaction in cybernetic systems into a mass-market medium rivaling the film industry in terms of revenue. Current revenues for video games are estimated at $10 billion yearly for the domestic American market.

Within recent media culture, video games tend to be characterized in one of

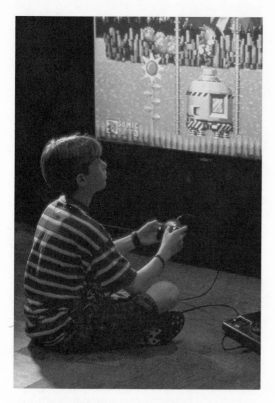

A boy playing "Sonic the Hedgehog," 1990s (Bill Varie/Corbis)

two ways. First, video game mastery is thought to constitute a masculine rite of passage of sorts, in which boys bond with each other and pass into adulthood with an upper hand over girls by having attained superior familiarity with the computer skills critical in an information society. Alternatively, video games have been characterized as an addictive, infantile form of fantasy activity through which males act out antisocial tendencies in the abstract world of "cyberspace." When the knowledge became public that the "school shooters" responsible for the 1999 deaths of fourteen teenagers (including themselves) and one teacher at Columbine High School in Littleton, Colorado, had been avid players of violent video games, whose competitive goals revolved around causing murder and mayhem to gain points, media hysteria about video games' contribution to youth violence reached fever pitch. Several themes can be discerned within this intersection of technology, violence, and masculinity.

Video games are a technology-intensive product. Although the success of a hit game may rival that of a hit movie, musical recording, or television show, video games literally are software in the functional sense. User interaction with a programmed computer is central to the ways consumers create meaningful experiences with these products. The popularity of video games and hardware has overturned a key paradigm in the technology sector. In the 1970s and 1980s, video games constituted a manufacturing sector that inherited technologies from more advanced sectors, such as graphics rendering for scientific visualization or military applications, once the technologies became affordable through increased economies of scale. Currently, however, research and development of a variety of technologies, such as three-dimensional graphics rendering, artificial intelligence, and physical modeling, is directed toward primary deployment in the consumer-oriented, mass-market, high-value sector of video games.

Consumers of video games have been primarily, but not exclusively, young males. In recent years, the average age range targeted by video game marketers has increased from the teenage male demographic to the eighteen- to thirty-five-year-old adult male, and increasing numbers of females have appeared as consumers. In the early years of home computing, the primary audience for video games was perceived to be teenage computer hobbyists oriented toward gaming and programming. The more recent, graphics-intensive 32- and 64-bit machines such as Sony Corporation's very successful PlayStation console have established a mainstay audience with an older demographic, targeting nightclub, dance, and other young adult cultures. In their evolution from hobbyist machine to mass-market entertainment, the demographics of video game consumers have trended upward.

Following the development of an adult market for video games and amid concern among adults and parents that children are being exposed to harmful and violent influences through the medium, a voluntary ratings system was adopted by a consortium of video game developers in 1994, modeled on the ratings system used by the motion picture industry. The ratings system adopted by the computer gaming industry indicates the broadly profitable sectors of the gaming industry; significantly, the ratings cover an even broader spectrum of specific age ranges than the ratings system for films. Video game ratings are EC, for "early childhood" gamers from three years old and-up; E, for "everyone," or general audiences older than six years; T, for "teen" audiences older than thirteen years; M, for "mature" audiences older than seventeen years; AO, for "adults only," meaning consumers older than eighteen years; and RP, "rating pending," meaning not yet rated by the Entertainment Software Ratings Board (ESRB). Content descriptions may also appear on packaging, indicating what one of these generic ratings might mean for specific products. They fall into categories such as "violent," which may range from cartoon violence to "realistic" bloody gore; "language," from mild to strong, including profani-

ties; "sexual themes," including "strong sexual content"; "comic mischief," including "gross vulgar humor"; and glorified "use of drugs or alcohol."

Since the establishment of the ratings system, more than 7,000 titles have been reviewed, with participation in the system comprising up to 85 percent of video game publishers, according to the ESRB in 2000 (Gudmundsen 2000). The ratings systems for video games have been paralleled by ratings systems for websites and software filtering devices for television and Internet content, indicating a broad expansion of concern by public-interest groups and lawmakers with regard to digital media content in direct proportion to the growing reach of the distribution of these products and the profitability of their markets. In addition, arcade operators such as GameWorks, a joint venture of DreamWorks SKG, Universal Studios, and Sega Corporation have responded to pressure from federal lawmakers by banning consumers younger than sixteen from playing video games considered violent in their arcades.

The film industry's involvement in the video game market reaches back to the first heady days of runaway profitability, when Warner Communications acquired Pong pioneer Atari Corporation in 1976. The television industry cemented a longer-standing interest in the possibility of delivering interactive television to consumers in 1972, with Magnavox offering the first home video game system, the Odyssey.

Even as industry response to public concerns of youth exposure to game violence has increased under pressure from lawmakers, the concerns themselves are not new. Protests were reportedly voiced with regard to the 1976 arcade game, Death Race, based on the exploitation movie *Death Race 2000.* In spite of the primitive graphics of early games, the gratuitous violence of Death Race, in which arcade game drivers scored points by running over fleeing pedestrians, was enough to spark an outcry. In the early and mid-1990s, advanced graphics techniques meant that games like Doom, a "first-person shooter" in which gamers raced down three-dimensional corridors and blasted all comers to gory bits in order to stay alive and win points, and Mortal Kombat, in which victorious characters were pictured graphically ripping out the bloody spines of their fallen opponents, appeared particularly threatening to impressionable youth playing in the privacy of their own homes—or worse yet, alone in their own rooms.

These debates on the negative values of video games have occurred in the midst of changing conditions in the video game market. The 1983 film *WarGames* dramatized the dangers of a young boy who was both hacker and gamer, but it also suggested that only computer-literate youth with a keen sense of the value of play over the value of conflict could avoid apocalyptic Cold War conflagration invited by the proposed Star Wars missile defense system. Hackers and gamers seem more to be separate camps today, largely because video games now are so complex that an amateur user able to program a game single-handedly would be extremely rare (early game machines like the beloved Atari did offer users the capability of programming their own games). With the sophistication of graphical user interfaces, real-time three-dimensional graphics, and complex gestural input sequences controlling onscreen action, gaming and programming have fallen into overlapping but distinct domains of reception and production, respectively.

Still, although the text-oriented adventures of early home gaming might be found now only in less profitable or noncommercial domains of networked multiuser dungeons (MUDs) or object-oriented MUDs (MOOs), the broad genres of video game play have largely remained static over the years, with hybrids between genres arising to take advantage of advances in computing power. Genres include computerized versions of traditional games, such as chess and solitaire; role-playing fantasies derived from games like Dungeons and Dragons; simulations of realistic action situations such as jet flight and drag racing; war games such as the classics Tank and Space Invaders; first-person shooters such as Doom; adventure explorations such as Myst; competition games such as Bust a Groove, in which players show off their best "dance moves"; simulations of science, history, or culture such as Sim City; cybernetic versions of earlier arcade games such as the shooting gallery; sports games based on major-league athletics such as football and basketball; and "edutainment" such as "Where in the World Is Carmen Sandiego?"

As graphics, sound, and interaction capabilities have increased, games have hybridized genres, with adventure taking place in three-dimensional worlds where action sequences lead to riddle-solving activities, rewarded by full-motion video playback that advances the narrative by revealing more details of character or background. In recent years, the perceived computer advantage held by boys by virtue of their being the primary marketing target for video games has led to research, development, and design of a new genre: girl games.

Girl games have been oriented toward attracting girls who, as a group, are observed to turn away from computers as they enter the teen years, becoming more interested in social activities oriented toward communication and sharing as opposed to activities dominated by boys such as competitive sports, and video games or technical activities such as computer programming. The genre of girl games has been forwarded as a way of bringing young girls closer to computers, enhancing girls' familiarity with common hardware and software platforms and paradigms, and broadening computer-based play to include less competitive, nonviolent activities. Approaches taken to achieve these goals have been controversial, even as the games produced toward these ends have been various. Games such as Barbie Fashion Designer have sold in massive quantities, qualifying as bona fide hits in the software marketplace and demonstrating that the market for girls can be as large and as profitable as that aimed at boys. However, critics have responded to such products in positive and negative ways.

Some girl games have been criticized for reducing female identity and pleasure to traditional norms of beauty and bodily appearance. In this sense, competition is not absent from girl games, which turn out not simply to emphasize communication and sharing but also restage an older problem of women competing against each other for men's attention. From this perspective, the video game industry is held to allow room for games for girls so long as the games perpetuate traditional roles for women. Feminist entrepreneurs in the field have characterized purportedly male-oriented video games as uninteresting and have attempted to design games that move beyond traditional girls' play activities. These entrepreneurs' goal is to engage and encourage the positive values of nurturing and communicating that girls are thought to be good at and interested in. Yet, some female gamers have responded by pointing out that there is nothing at all "boring" about exploring unknown planets, fighting off alien invaders, and building new worlds—traditionally male fantasies made accessible to girls and women through gaming.

The relationship between boyhood and computer play has shifted as consumer products and recreational environments have changed. Where once, in a less technological culture, boys might have formed their responses and engagements with masculinity in clubs and groups outside the home, out of sight of fathers, mothers, and sisters, today fewer open spaces outside the home exist to play in, and fewer noncommercial, safe settings are available to set play in, especially in large cities. Traditional American roles for boys are undergoing stress, and the environments in which these roles are established are increasingly urban and domestic. Even though the computer makes a virtual setting for play possible, if gaming is meant to transition boys into the workplace, the passage from boyhood to manhood may be less clear than previously, since the setting of the play approximates the setting of work. Yet although gaming seems certain to bring youth closer to computers in general, the specific value of commercial video game play for developing work skills seems less apparent than in earlier years, when gamers might program their own play activities. Amid these tensions, the violent video game might signify a certain loss: the "first-person shooter" might emblematize an increasing lack of meaningful play activities available to growing boys as cultural values shift.

James Tobias

See also Computers

References and further reading
AtariWorld.com. "The Atari Timeline," http://www.atariworld.com/AtariTimeline.html (accessed December 27, 2000).

Bennahum, David S. 1998. *Extra Life: Coming of Age in Cyberspace.* New York: Basic Books.

Buckingham, David. 1993. *Children Talking Television: The Making of Television Literacy.* London: Falmer Press.

Formanek-Brunell, Miriam. 1993. *Made to Play House: Dolls and the Commercialization of American Girlhood 1830–1930.* New Haven: Yale University Press.

GeekComix.com. "A Brief History of Home Video Games," http://www.geekcomix.com/vgh/main.shtml (accessed December 27, 2000).

Graetz, J. M. 1981. "The Origin of SpaceWar." *Creative Computing* (August).

Greenfield, Patricia Marks. 1984. *Mind and Media: The Effects of Television, Video Games, and Computers.* Cambridge: Harvard University Press.

Gudmundsen, Jinny. 2000. "Strategy for Parents: Use Ratings, Be Involved. Choosing Titles by the Letters." *Los Angeles Times,* October 26, T8.

Herz, J. C. 1997. *Joystick Nation: How Computer Games Ate Our Quarters, Won Our Hearts and Rewired Our Minds.* New York: Little, Brown.

Huffstutter, P. J., and Claudia Eller. 2000. "GameWorks to Restrict Youngsters at Arcades." *Los Angeles Times,* October 6, C1.

Hunter, William. 2000. "The Dot Eaters: Videogame History 101," http://www.emuunlim.com/doteaters/index.html (accessed December 27, 2000).

Jenkins, Henry. "'Complete Freedom of Movement': Video Games as Gendered Play Spaces." Pp. 262–297 in *From Barbie to Mortal Combat: Gender and Computer Games.* Edited by Henry Jenkins and Justine Cassell. Cambridge, MA: MIT Press.

Kafai, Yasmin B. 1998. "Video Game Designs by Girls and Boys: Variability and Consistency of Gender Differences." Pp 90–117 in *From Barbie to Mortal Kombat: Gender and Computer Games.* Edited by Henry Jenkins and Justine Cassell. Cambridge, MA: MIT Press.

Kinder, Marsha, ed. 1999. *Kids' Media Culture.* Durham: Duke University Press.

Kline, Stephen. 1993. *Out of the Garden: Toys, TV and Children's Culture in the Age of Marketing.* London: Verso.

Rushkoff, Douglas. 1996. *Playing the Future: How Kid's Culture Can Teach Us to Thrive in an Age of Chaos.* New York: HarperCollins.

Sheff, David. 1993. *Game Over: How Nintendo Zapped an American Industry, Captured Your Dollars, and Enslaved Your Children.* New York: Random House.

Videogames.com. "The History of Video Games," http://www.videogames.com/features/universal/hov/ (accessed December 27, 2000).

"Voices from the Combat Zone: Game Grrrlz Talk Back." Pp. 328–341 in *From Barbie to Mortal Combat: Gender and Computer Games.* Edited by Henry Jenkins and Justine Cassell. Cambridge, MA: MIT Press.

Violence, History of

American boys encounter violence in each of the three major settings of their lives—their homes, their schools, and their communities. Abusive parents and siblings, bullying students, teachers who inflict physical punishment, and threatening communities and gang members all impose violent and potentially harmful risks to young boys. It stands to reason that boys who fear victimization at the hands of others will develop their own violent tendencies as a means of defense and protection. In this way, a cycle of violence is initiated. This cycle is far from new; its roots can be traced through centuries of history. But in a modern world with modern weapons, aggression can result in much more serious consequences for both the victims and perpetrators of violence. In order to stop the cycle, violence in the lives of American boys must be understood as an ongoing tradition that has a long history and an undetermined future.

Violence against boys in their families is far from new. Colonial religious leaders taught parents that children were born tainted with sin and that a child's disobedience was the manifestation of this sin. Parents were told to stifle expressions of sin (e.g., resistance and willfulness) with stern and often harsh disciplinary practices. Fathers were the unchallenged rulers of children and the primary family disciplinarians until the late eighteenth and early nineteenth centuries. However, as the mode of production shifted from the family to the market, men left their primary role as day-to-day heads of families to work outside the home, and women became the primary keepers of children. It is thought that severe corporal punishment and child abuse decreased with this shift to maternal discipline.

Today, this pattern remains. Mothers are overwhelmingly the primary caregivers of American children, and by extension, mothers are their primary disciplinarians as well. National data indicate that women are more likely than men to physically abuse their children (Sedlak and Broadhurst 1996), but this finding could merely be a result of the fact that children spend much more time with their mothers than with their fathers. Even though most children spend more time with their mothers, 89 percent of children who are sexually abused by one of their birth parents are sexually abused by their fathers (Sedlak and Broadhurst 1996). In addition, 23 percent of physically abused children, 14 percent of emotionally abused children, and 46 percent of sexually abused children are abused by adoptive, step-, or foster parents (Sedlak and Broadhurst 1996). A significantly higher number of sexual abuse cases are perpetrated by stepfathers as compared to biological fathers, biological mothers, and nonbiological mothers.

In 1994, one-third of all child murders in the United States for which there was a known perpetrator involved a child being killed by a family member (Greenfeld 1996). By their second birthday, more than 90 percent of American children sustain at least one act of physical aggression at the hands of their parents (Straus and Gelles 1990). Physical abuse in childhood has been linked to many forms of maladjustment, including insecure primary attachments, posttraumatic stress disorder, academic difficulty, diminished self-esteem, delinquency, and violence (see Wekerle and Wolfe 1996 for a review). The Third National Incidence Study of Child Abuse and Neglect (NIS-3) estimated that boys from infancy to age seventeen sustain physical abuse at a rate of more than 9 per 1,000 (Sedlak and Broadhurst 1996). Although this rate does not differ significantly from the corresponding rate for girls, The NIS-3 data also indicate that, although boys are less likely than girls to be sexually abused, they are more likely to be emotionally neglected. Also, boys tend to be more seriously injured by physical abuse than girls. The U.S. Department of Health and Human Services reported in 1996 that child maltreatment appears to be on the rise.

Children are not only victimized directly in their families but also *indirectly* through exposure to violence between their parents. As with corporal punishment of children, wife beating has been common throughout history. Laws supported a husband's use of physical aggression as a means of getting his wife to conform to his demands. For example, the

English "Rule of Thumb Law" allowed husbands to beat their wives with objects as long as the objects were no thicker than the man's thumb. Historical reviews of colonial life portray men as the primary—if not *sole*—perpetrators of marital violence. This is no longer the case, as evidence suggests that men and women perpetrate marital violence at similar rates and frequencies. This changing trend can be explained largely by the fact that marital violence is less about physical aggression and more about inequality and the struggle for marital power. As women gained status and economic independence in American society, they became more resistant to their husbands' attempts to assert power over them. Surprisingly, national data reveal that women are as likely as men to *initiate* marital violence, refuting the notion that women only engage in marital violence defensively in response to attacks initiated by their husbands. However, marital violence perpetrated by men tends to result in more physical harm than does marital violence perpetrated by women (Stets and Straus 1990).

Today, millions of American children are exposed to marital violence each year. Specific estimates range from 3.3 million (Carlson 1984) to more than 10 million (Straus 1992). Research indicates that children exposed to marital violence exhibit less social competence and more aggression, anxiety, depression, and withdrawal than do their nonexposed counterparts (for reviews, see Edelson 1999; Fantuzzo and Lindquist 1989). Analyses of national data suggest that boys are more likely than girls to witness violence between their parents (Vorrasi, Eckenrode, and Izzo 2000).

Since the 1990s, violence perpetrated by children against their parents has received increased attention due, in part, to a series of highly publicized instances of parricide (the killing of one's parent or parents). For example, in Los Angeles in 1989, brothers Eric and Lyle Menendez, who complained of years of physical, psychological, and sexual abuse at the hands of their parents, shot and killed their mother and father. In 1997 in Pearl, Mississippi, sixteen-year-old Luke Woodham savagely killed his mother and hours later opened fire on his classmates, killing three. Woodham cited a desire for peer acceptance as his motive for killing his mother. In Springfield, Oregon, in 1998, fifteen-year-old Kip Kinkel, citing a desire to save his parents from the embarrassment they would have endured having to tell their friends that their son was charged with illegal possession of a stolen firearm, shot and killed his mother and father.

Despite recent interest, parricide remains an uncommon occurrence. National estimates indicate that parricides account for approximately 2 percent of all murders in this country (Dawson and Langan 1994). Several risk factors are common to most instances of parricide, including patterns of child abuse and neglect, alcohol abuse, social isolation, mental illness, suicidal ideation, and access to firearms. A study by Adam Weisman and Kaushal Sharma (1997) found that approximately 75 percent of parricide offenders have criminal records prior to killing their parent(s), but the best predictor of parricide remains the gender of the assailant. With only a handful of exceptions, parricide offenders are overwhelmingly male.

Not only in the home but also in schools, boys have been the victims and the perpetrators of violence. At the outset of colonization in the seventeenth century, American schools were set up by their Puritan founders to ensure that everyone could read the Bible. Acting in loco parentis, teachers, who were almost all male until the nineteenth century, used the same harsh punishments as parents. Children were required to submit to the will of the teacher just as they would with their own parents. Violence against children in the schools had the potential to be even harsher than that in the home because parents had fewer children to manage and a greater stake in youngsters' well-being than did teachers. Furthermore, the school setting was conducive to neither learning nor good behavior, especially for younger children. Pupils of all ages and abilities learned together. Lessons were dull and repetitive. Generally, the only reading material was the Bible, and teachers were poorly trained, often having little more education than their pupils and no formal training in teaching.

Although whipping and flogging were the most usual punishments, there were other more unusual forms of violence inflicted upon students. For example, children were forced to hold an inkstand or book at arm's length or made to bend over before a hot stove and remain in this position with one finger on a peg in the floor (Bybee and Gee 1982). Other reported punishments included wedging children's mouths open with a wooden block, tying them to a chair leg for an hour, and locking them in closets (Crews and Counts 1997). The Reverend Warren Burton explained that "such methods of correcting offenders have been in use time out of mind" (Bybee and Gee 1982).

In the middle of the eighteenth century, reports appeared depicting school discipline problems, student rebellions, and attacks on teachers. One schoolmaster, for example, was set upon by three large boys after he hit the younger brother of one of them, drawing blood. The boys wrested his weapon from him, dragged him out of the schoolhouse, and threw him down a steep incline (Bybee and Gee 1982).

As the population of the United States grew and diversified with the influx of immigrants, a need for universal education was perceived. The 1830s saw the rise of the common school movement, the main thrust of which was to instill a uniform set of social and moral values in the country's youth. At this time, the control of schools began shifting from the community to the state. Although one of the tenets of the common school movement was that harsh punishments be avoided, physical violence against children remained common in the schools. As state regulation of education spread, parents had less influence over how their children were treated in school. Several court rulings in the latter half of the nineteenth century overrode parental authority in favor of teacher authority, including the authority to use violent means to control student behavior (Rovetta and Rovetta 1968). Nevertheless, court records of this period show evidence of a growing concern from parents regarding the use of violence in maintaining school discipline.

Another shift in education at this time was the movement toward training and hiring women as teachers, especially of younger children. Women teachers were less likely than their male counterparts to use physical force to control children's behavior. This, along with the public outcry against corporal punishment, resulted in restrictions on its practice in many states beginning in the middle of the nineteenth century and continuing until recently (Rovetta and Rovetta 1968). Schools became more child-centered.

Curriculum became more relevant and interesting, and discipline became gentler. A period of relative calm reigned in the nation's schools in the first half of the twentieth century (Crews and Counts 1997). A 1949 survey revealed that school principals considered student lying and disrespect to be the biggest problems in their schools.

Though corporal punishment is no longer endorsed in most schools, teacher violence against children remained and has continued to the present time. By 1989, twenty-one states had abolished corporal punishment, but thirteen states still authorized its use by teachers or other school personnel (Hyman 1990). There is little evidence, however, that a return to more violent means of controlling student behavior would result in a reduction of student violence against peers or teachers. Children who are hit by teachers when they are too small to fight back may retaliate when they have grown (Welsh 1976). That schools in the past were described as battlegrounds between students and teachers suggests that corporal punishment was never very effective even when it was the normative form of discipline. Teachers who used it successfully appear to have done so because they were bigger and stronger than their pupils and could beat them in hand-to-hand combat. With the increased availability of handguns, however, even the smallest children have the potential to win a battle against the teacher.

Although interpersonal violence among students is mentioned before the middle of the twentieth century, it is difficult to determine its prevalence and severity. Where references to bullying or fighting are made, it is in the context of other discipline problems and not portrayed as any more severe than other rule violations. As severe forms of physical punishment were still sanctioned, however, it is possible that physical violence per se was not frowned upon, but only the disruption that fighting caused to classroom routine. However, by 1956, school violence, especially student attacks on teachers, became a general concern.

Desegregation brought a new form of violence to the schools—threats to the students by the general public. Early attempts at desegregation in the South required the National Guard to protect African American children not only from other students and teachers but from white parents and community members who were opposed to integrated schools (Crews and Counts 1997). Interracial violence is still a problem in many schools, but the phenomenon is usually associated with gang activity and therefore seen as part of the more general issue of gang violence in schools. It is often unclear when violence should be defined as "bullying," a phenomenon common to almost every school. However, when violence is defined as "gang activity," it generally implies a more serious problem than does "bullying." The use of weapons and symbols, and specific attacks against students of certain races or ethnic groups are usually indicators of gang-related violence.

The 1970s saw a tremendous increase in student-perpetrated violence against teachers and fellow students (Warner, Weist, and Krulak 1999). Moreover, students began carrying and using weapons more frequently, resulting in more severe consequences of this violence. In the last two decades of the twentieth century, many students felt that they needed to bring a weapon to school in order to protect themselves from bullies and gangs. A Harvard School of Public Health survey reported that 12 percent of children, kindergarten through twelfth grade, re-ported carrying weapons to school in 1995, with handguns accounting for one-third of these reports (Kopka 1997). A rash of "school shootings" in the 1980s and 1990s raised public alarm about guns in schools, especially because these shootings were not committed by gang members but rather by upper-middle-class white boys who had been victim-ized by bullies. These acts of "retaliatory violence" spurred many school adminis-trators to adopt a "no tolerance" position regarding guns, racism, and violence in their schools. Nevertheless, in 1993, 82 percent of school principals reported an increase in violence in their schools dur-ing the previous five years, 60 percent of schools had at least one weapons inci-dent, and 13 percent reported at least one knifing or shooting (Warner, Weist, and Krulak 1999). Some sources indicate a leveling-off of interstudent violence in the mid- to late 1990s, but others report an increase up to the present time (Warner, Weist, and Krulak 1999).

Not only do boys encounter violence in their homes and schools, but they also ex-perience it in their communities. Youth gangs have existed in America since the late eighteenth century. Gang members have typically been young urban males from poor neighborhoods. The gang phe-nomenon grew in size as massive waves of immigrants poured through cities such as New York, Chicago, Boston, and Philadelphia in the mid- to late 1800s. Anti-Catholic riots and immigrant lynch-ings in urban areas forced many Irish, Jew-ish, and Italian immigrants to form pro-tective gangs due to constant fear of harassment and brutality at the hands of prejudiced men and police officers who blamed the immigrants for all of society's ills (Klein 1995).

Slum neighborhoods such as New York City's Five Points and Hell's Kitchen were the breeding ground for many of the early youth gangs. These groups were generally set up along racial or ethnic lines. Some gangs, like the Irish Molly Maguires and the Sicilian Cosa Nostra, were formed as American branches of old world gangs. Other gangs such as the Irish Bowery Boys in New York City and the white southern Ku Klux Klan were formed as distinctly American organiza-tions (Klein 1996).

The members of the first American gangs were impoverished. Illicit econo-mies offered poor boys a way to make a lot of money very quickly. Gang crimes soon escalated from petty theft, fighting, and burglary to extortion, strikebreaking, and other organized rackets such as "numbers running," prostitution, and gambling. By the end of the nineteenth century, the template for American gangs was set. Gangs were groups of young men of the same race and ethnicity who engaged in criminal activities, used symbols in com-munications, controlled specific territo-ries, and ran illicit economies within those territories (Curry and Decker 1998). Since these gangs functioned outside the law, conflicts between gangs were settled by themselves—typically in a violent fashion.

The immigration boom in the early part of the twentieth century, coupled with the advent of Prohibition in 1920, changed the face of gang crime completely. Gangsters now had millions of potential customers who would pay top dollar for illegal alco-hol. The distilling, bottling, transporta-tion, distribution, and selling of illegal al-cohol became a billion-dollar industry. Organized crime became a profession run by adult men rather than teenage delin-quents, but when Prohibition ended, the mob had to branch out into other areas in order to remain profitable. Youth gang members became the primary salesmen of organized crime's new cash crop—illegal drugs.

In the latter half of the twentieth century, the face of urban youth gangs changed from primarily European groups to Hispanic and African American groups. The main source of income for these gangs was the sale and distribution of illegal drugs, such as marijuana, cocaine, amphetamines, and heroin. Hispanic gangs such as the Latin Kings and Latin Disciples and African American gangs such as the Vice Lords and Black Disciple Nation took control of the drug trade in large territories of major cities like New York and Chicago. In southern California, Mexican American gangs, or *cholos* dominated most drug trafficking between America and Mexico. In Los Angeles, the African American rival gangs, the Bloods and the Crips, became so large and prosperous that they crossed state lines and are now nationwide organizations with activity reported in forty-two states (Skolnick et al. 1988). The estimated number of gangs grew exponentially, from 2,000 gangs with 100,000 members in 1980 to over 31,000 gangs with 846,000 members in 1996 (Moore and Terrett 1998).

The use of intense stimulants, coupled with an increased access to high-powered rapid-fire weapons and a heightened demand for illegal drugs, resulted in a resurgence of gang violence (Klein and Maxson 1989). Deadly gunfights between rival gangs known as "gangbangs" and planned ambushes in the form of "drive-by" shootings became commonplace in many American cities. The aggressive defense of gang territories and the use of identifying "colors" such as blue for the Crips and red for the Bloods led to frequent street violence that often resulted in the death of innocent bystanders. The introduction of crack cocaine in the 1980s only increased the violence. Crack is a less expensive yet highly addictive form of cocaine that provides the user with an intense but quick high, resulting in a heightened demand for the drug. The "crack epidemic" led to an unprecedented government focus on gang violence and drug use during the Reagan era.

Currently, the typical gang member is a male between the ages of twelve and twenty-four; his average age is seventeen to eighteen. Traditional territorial gangs average about 180 members, but gangs that specialize in a certain area of drug trafficking average about 25 members. However, some large city gangs number in the thousands and the largest nationally affiliated gangs number in the tens of thousands (Howell 1998). According to a nationwide survey, about 90 percent of all gang members are either African American or Hispanic; the other 10 percent are either Asian or white (Curry and Decker 1998). Though other researchers have found slightly different percentages, the overrepresentation of African Americans and Hispanics in gangs is a stable finding across studies. Although gang violence among African Americans is typically related to the drug trade, Hispanic gang violence is more often the result of disputes over gang territory or "barrio" (Block, Christakos, and Przybylski 1996). Though they still comprised a very small minority of youths in America, gangs were more predominant in the 1990s than they were in the 1970s and 1980s (Klein 1995).

Recent trends in gang activity include elevated drug use and violence, increased female membership, and the migration of gang affiliations across city and state lines. Nevertheless, the reasons for joining a gang remain the same. These reasons include protection from other gangs, access to money from illicit economies, increased prestige, excitement, and a strengthened sense of identity and belonging. Some of the corresponding risk factors for gang membership are the presence of gangs in the neighborhood, poverty, lack of economic or social opportunity, high levels of crime, lack of adult male role models, academic failure, friends or family members in gangs, delinquency, aggression, victimization, and alcohol or drug use. Intervention and gang prevention programs have focused on these risk factors, but consistent positive results for any one type of program have not yet been found (Howell 1998).

Gang violence is usually directed at other gangs. A longitudinal study in Chicago found that 75 percent of gang-related homicides were intergang killings, 11 percent were intragang, and only 14 percent involved the killing of a nongang victim (Block, Christakos, and Przybylski 1996). Gang members are sixty times more likely to be killed than nongang members, and gang homicides are unique in that each killing creates an extremely high potential for deadly retaliation (Morales 1992). Though drug trafficking is common among inner-city gangs, it is not the prime cause of gang violence. Most gang homicides are the result of intergang conflict, territorial disputes, acts of retaliation, and defending gang "honor" or reputation (Block, Christakos, and Przybylski 1996). Major cities such as New York, Boston, Chicago, and Los Angeles are currently working to reduce gang violence by establishing community-based programs grounded in social prevention, vocational rehabilitation, and strict gun control (Howell 1998).

Violence has always been a significant part of American life throughout the nation's history. The country was founded by a bloody revolution, reconstructed after a brutal civil war, and defended through a succession of fierce military conflicts. It must be remembered that many of America's soldiers were young boys—barely eighteen years old or less—who were taken out of school or off the farm and expected to kill and die for their country. The violence demanded of these boys by their nation was not invented in army training camps. American boys learned to fight at home, in school, and in the streets of their community. Many of them learned how to take punches from abusive parents, teachers, schoolyard bullies, and street gangs. Many of them also learned how to throw punches from the same people. The double-edged dilemma of violence in the lives of American boys should be understood as a product of both the violence expected of them and the violence inflicted upon them by American society.

William Indick
Joseph A. Vorrasi
Faith Markle

See also Abuse; Bullying; Discipline; Gangs; Schools, Public; Violence, Theories of

References and further reading
Block, Carolyn Rebecca, Antigone Christakos, and R. Przybylski. 1996. "Street Gangs and Crime: Patterns and Trends in Chicago." *Research Bulletin.* Chicago: Criminal Justice Information Authority.
Bybee, Rodger W., and E. Gordon Gee. 1982. *Violence, Values, and Justice in the Schools.* Boston: Allyn and Bacon.

Carlson, Eve B. 1984. "Children's Observations of Interparental Violence." In *Battered Women and Their Families*. Edited by A. R. Roberts. New York: Springer Publishing.

Crews, Gordon A., and M. Reid Counts. 1997. *The Evolution of School Disturbance in America: Colonial Times to Modern Day*. Westport, CT: Praeger.

Curry, G. David, and Scott H. Decker. 1998. *Confronting Gangs: Crime and Community*. Los Angeles: Roxbury.

Dawson, John M., and Patrick A. Langan. 1994. *Murder in Families*. Washington, DC: U.S. Department of Justice, Bureau of Justice Statistics.

Edelson, Jeffery. L. 1999. "Children's Witnessing of Adult Domestic Violence." *Journal of Interpersonal Violence* 14, no. 8: 839–870.

Fantuzzo, John W., and Carrol U. Lindquist. 1989. "The Effects of Observing Conjugal Violence on Children: A Review and Analysis of Research Methodology." *Journal of Family Violence* 4, no. 1: 77–93.

Garbarino, James. 1998. *Lost Boys: Why Our Sons Turn Violent and How We Can Save Them*. New York: Free Press.

Greenfeld. Lawrence A. 1996. *Child Victimizers: Violent Offenders and Their Victims*. Washington, DC: Office of Juvenile Justice and Delinquency Prevention.

Howell, James C. 1998. "Youth Gangs: An Overview." *Juvenile Justice Bulletin*. Washington, DC: U.S. Department of Justice, Office of Juvenile Justice and Delinquency Prevention.

Hyman, Irwin A. 1990. *Reading, Writing and the Hickory Stick: The Appalling Story of Physical and Psychological Abuse in American Schools*. Lexington, MA: Lexington Books.

Hyman, Irwin A., and James H. Wise. 1979. *Corporal Punishment in American Education: Readings in History, Practice, and Alternatives*. Philadelphia, PA: Temple University Press.

Klein, Malcolm W. 1995. *The American Street Gang*. New York: Oxford University Press.

———. 1996. "Gangs in the United States and Europe." *European Journal on Criminal Policy and Research* (special issue): 63–80.

Klein, Malcolm W., and Cheryl Lee Maxson. 1989. "Street Gang Violence." Pp. 198–234 in *Violent Crime, Violent Criminals*. Edited by M. E. Wolfgang and M. A. Weiner. Newbury Park, CA: Sage.

Kopka, Deborah L. 1997. *School Violence: A Reference Handbook*. Santa Barbara, CA: ABC-CLIO.

Moore, John P., and Craig P. Terrett. 1998. *Highlights of the 1996 National Youth Gang Survey*. Washington, DC: U.S. Department of Justice, Office of Juvenile Justice and Delinquency Prevention.

Morales, Armando. 1992. "A Clinical Model for the Prevention of Gang Violence and Homicide." Pp. 105–118 in *Substance Abuse and Gang Violence*. Edited by R. C. Cervantes. Newbury Park, CA: Sage.

Rovetta, Catherine Humbargar, and Leon Rovetta. 1968. *Teacher Spanks Johnny: A Handbook for Teachers*. Stockton, CA: Willow House Publishers.

Sedlak Andrea J., and Debra D. Broadhurst. 1996. *Third National Incidence Study of Child Abuse and Neglect: Final Report*. Washington, DC: U.S. Department of Health and Human Services.

Skolnick, Jerome H., Theodore Correl, Elizabeth Navarro, and Roger Rabb. 1988. *The Social Structure of Street Drug Dealing*. Unpublished report to the Office of the Attorney General of the State of California. Berkeley: University of California at Berkeley.

Stets, Joan E., and Murray A. Straus. 1990. "Gender Differences in Reporting Marital Violence and Its Medical and Psychological Consequences." Pp. 151–165 in *Physical Violence in American Families: Risk Factors and Adaptations to Violence in 8,145 Families*. Edited by M. A. Straus and R. J. Gelles. New Brunswick, NJ: Transaction.

Straus, Murray A. 1992. *Children as Witnesses to Marital Violence: A Risk Factor for Lifelong Problems among a Nationally Representative Sample of American Men and Women*. Report of the 23rd Ross Roundtable. Columbus, OH: Ross Laboratories.

Straus, Murray A., and Richard J. Gelles, eds. 1990. *Physical Violence in American Families: Risk Factors and*

Adaptations to Violence in 8,145 Families. New Brunswick, NJ: Transaction.

U.S. Department of Education, National Center for Education Statistics. 1998. *Violence and Discipline Problems in U.S. Public Schools: 1996–1997.* NCES 98-030. Washington, DC: U.S. Government Printing Office.

U.S. Departments of Education and Justice. 2000. *Indicators of School Crime and Safety, 2000.* NCES2001-017/NCJ-184176. Washington, DC: U.S. Government Printing Office.

Vorrasi, Joseph A., John J. Eckenrode, and Charles V. Izzo. 2000. *Intergenerational Transmission of Marital Violence: A Gender-Similarity Hypothesis.* Paper presented at the Fifth International Conference on the Victimization of Children and Youth, Durham, NH.

Warner, Beth S., Mark D. Weist, and Amy Krulak. 1999. "Risk Factors for School Violence. *Urban Education* 34: 52–68.

Weisman, Adam M., and Kaushal K. Sharma. 1997. "Parricide and Attempted Parricide: Forensic Data and Psychological Results." In *The Nature of Homicide: Trends and Changes.* Washington, DC: U.S. Department of Justice, Office of Justice Programs, National Institute of Justice.

Wekerle, Christine, and David A. Wolfe. 1996. "Child Maltreatment." In *Child Psychopathology.* Edited by E. J. Mash and R. A. Barkley. New York: Guilford Press.

Welsh, Ralph S. 1976. "Severe Parental Punishment and Delinquency: A Developmental Theory." *Journal of Clinical Child Psychology* 5, no. 1: 17–21.

Violence, Theories of

Theories about the origin of violence can be classified on the basis of whether their authors locate the causes of violence in the organism itself, in its environment, or in both places. The biological purist spots the cause of violence in the organism itself. Sarnoff Mednick (1977) has provided an explanation of this type. According to him, punishment is both the most practi-

cal and efficient means for teaching children to behave as adults wish. He believes that children become violent because they inherited a dull central nervous system that prevents them from learning from punishment. His entire theory can be boiled down to three simple propositions: (1) children's genes determine the sensitivity of their central nervous systems; (2) the sensitivity of children's central nervous systems determines their level of fearfulness; and (3) children's fearfulness determines whether they can learn from punishment.

For example, a boy who inherits a dull central nervous system feels the urge to react violently when provoked. Because past punishment has failed to make him fearful of taking violent action, he acts on rather than inhibits this urge. No matter how repeatedly or severely these boys are punished, they are incapable of learning to inhibit their violent urges. A boy who inherits a sensitive central nervous system will also feel the urge to react violently when provoked, but because of past punishment, this boy will become fearful and inhibit his violent urge. The inhibition of this urge reduces this boy's fearfulness, which rewards him for his nonviolent reaction. According to this theory, boys more often than girls become violent because the genes that wire the central nervous system are sex-linked.

Unlike the biological purists, the environmental purist spots the cause of violence in boys' living habitats rather than in their bodies. Marvin Wolfgang and Franco Ferracuti (1967, 143) provide an environmental theory of violence. They equate the environment with a culture, the principal components of which are norms and values. However, the cultural environment is heterogeneous. The norms and values that prevail in one environmental niche may not prevail in another. Their basic underlying assumption is that children absorb the prevailing norms and values of their environmental niche like a dry sponge dropped into a large pool of water (Sutherland 1973, 43). According to them, boys become violent from living in a "subculture of violence," an environmental niche in which "pro-" rather than "antiviolent" norms and values prevail. The subculture of violence explanation is also based on three simple propositions: (1) children are exposed to different environmental niches or subcultures; (2) children who have been exposed more to violent rather than nonviolent subcultures absorb "pro-" rather than "antiviolent" norms and values; and (3) the absorption of proviolent norms and values creates a violence-prone personality.

Thus, it is the relative amount of exposure that children have had to violent and nonviolent subcultures that accounts for their violent behavior. For example, when someone provokes a boy who has had greater exposure to a violent subculture, his norms would dictate that he act violently rather than nonviolently, and his values would cast his taking violent action in a positive light and his taking nonviolent action in a negative one. In contrast, a boy who has had greater exposure to a nonviolent subculture would have the opposite reactions. According to this theory, boys more often than girls become violent, not because their central nervous systems are wired differently but because boys have more contact with violent subcultures.

Unlike the biological and environmental purists, eclectics spot the causes of violence in multiple factors located in the organism and the environment rather than in one or the other place alone.

Dorothy Lewis (1992, 1998) prefers an eclectic theory. According to her, at least five biological and environmental factors must come together for children to become violent. The first factor is the "XY syndrome," from which all males suffer, Lewis believes (1998, 287–288). Because, according to her, the XY syndrome is a genetically determined condition that has two defining characteristics, high androgen production and a "masculinized brain," she locates this syndrome wholly in the body. Like the XY syndrome, brain damage, the second factor, is also located in the body and therefore is an organic factor. If children suffer injuries that disrupt the pathways between their frontal lobes and the brain's reptilian base buried beneath it, then they cannot control their primitive urges. Lewis (1998, 288) describes this condition as analogous to driving a truck with worn-out brakes.

The third organic factor is an overly sensitive amygdala, the portion of the brain "hidden within each temporal lobe" that is primarily responsible for "our sense of fear." Regarding this brain disorder, Lewis (1998, 288) observes: "We cannot do without the amygdala. But fear is often the nidus for paranoia. A certain amount of fear is necessary for survival. On the other hand, too much can make us dangerous." The concentration level of neurotransmitters in the brain is the fourth organic factor. Lowered levels of neurotransmitters such as serotonin cause children to be irritable and prone to anger (1998, 289). Unlike the first four factors, the fifth and final factor, "violent abuse," is the only environmental factor. It can result from children being either the actual victim of a physical attack or an eyewitness to one. In either case, the violent abuser provides them with a role model for their own future violent behavior.

In short, the presence of two or three of these factors in a child's life is not enough to make him or her become violent. Instead, all five factors must coalesce for this to happen (1992, 387–389). Brain damage (factor two), amygdala disorder (factor three), and neurotransmitter depression (factor four) only make children susceptible to becoming violent. In order for them to succumb to this susceptibility, they must also be violently abused (factor five). More boys than girls become violent, not because girls suffer significantly less often from brain damage, amygdala disorders, depressed neurotransmitter levels, or violent abuse but because of their immunity to the XY syndrome (factor one).

The chief weakness of the violence theories of biological purists, environmental purists, and eclectics is that they do not take into account the essential character of "human experience." The term *human experience* refers to the outer physical reactions together with the inner thoughts and emotions that occur when human beings interact with their environment at a particular point in time (Dewey 1929). Both a higher organism—one with a mind—and an environment are needed for a human experience to occur. However, a human experience results from the interaction of the human organism *as a whole* and not some special organ of it, such as the brain alone, with its environmental niche. Moreover, human organisms, their environmental niche, and their ongoing experiences exist in an *interdependent* relationship to one another (Mead 1934, 129). The experience produced from the interaction between a human being and the environment changes, however slightly, not only the human organism but also the environmental niche, such as a neighborhood.

The newly changed organism and environmental niche, in turn, change all the human organism's subsequent experiences, which still in turn change both the human organism and its environmental niche even further. Thus, the relationship between human organisms and environmental niches are not only interdependent but also *developmental* (Lowontin, Rose, and Kamin 1984, 265–290; Montagu 1985; Lewontin 2000). Because of the interdependent and developmental nature of this relationship, children, like adults, always play an *active* rather than merely passive role in their own violent transformations (Athens 1997, 22–27; 115–120; Blumer 1997, 3–6).

Lonnie Athens (1992) develops another theory to explain violent behavior in boys and girls. The name of the theory is "violentization," which he formed from combining the words "violent" and "socialization." Although first published more than a decade ago (Athens 1989), this theory remained relatively unknown until Richard Rhodes (1999) popularized it. In this entry, he revises the theory in two ways. First, he renames two of the four stages to make more explicit the ubiquitous role dominance plays (Athens 1998). Second, he explains why more boys than girls become violent.

Violentization is composed of both unitary and composite experiences. A unitary experience is a distinct, elementary experience that cannot blend with other elemental experiences any more than oil can mix with water, whereas a composite experience is composed of distinct, elemental experiences that coalesce. Whether unitary or composite, the experiences comprising violentization do not occur all at once but occur over a process with four separate stages that build on each other like the layers of a cake.

The first stage is "brutalization," a composite experience made up of three distinct elemental experiences: violent subjugation, personal horrification, and violent coaching. During "violent subjugation," authentic or would-be subjugators, such as fathers, stepmothers, older siblings, neighbors, or schoolmates, use or threaten to use physical force to make a perceived subordinate accept their domination. Violent subjugation can be practiced in one of two ways. It is practiced coercively when a subjugator seeks to make a perceived subordinate comply with a specific command and uses only enough force to achieve this limited goal. In contrast, when a person seeks to teach perceived subordinates a lasting lesson about his or her dominance over them and uses more than enough force to achieve their promise of future submission, that person is practicing retaliative subjugation. Although both forms are brutal, coercive subjugation is relatively merciful. During coercive subjugation, subordinates can immediately stop getting battered by complying with their subjugator's present command, whereas during retaliatory subjugation, a subordinate is not afforded this precious luxury.

During "personal horrification," the second elemental experience that comprises brutalization, perceived subordinates do not undergo violent subjugation themselves, but they witness someone close to them, such as a mother, brother, close friend, neighbor, or schoolmate, undergoing it. Although not as physically traumatic as violent subjugation, this experience can be even more psychologically damaging. Moreover, after undergoing personal horrification, perceived subordinates can be effectively subjugated for a while, at least by physical intimidation alone.

"Violent coaching" is the final elemental experience that comprises brutalization. During this experience, a superordinate takes on the role of coach and assigns a perceived subordinate the role of novice. The coach instructs novices that they should not try to avoid, appease, ignore, or run from their would-be subjugators but instead physically attack them. Thus, the coach's goal is to prompt violent conduct on the part of the novice, which, ironically, the novice could later direct against the coach. In a West Baltimore neighborhood, violent coaching is known as "crimping 'em up," which the inhabitants define as "the process by which older kids toughen up younger ones" (Simon and Burns 1997, 205–206).

Coaches have a variety of techniques at their disposal for prompting novices to take violent action against would-be subjugators. One technique is "vain glorification." Here, coaches regale novices with personal anecdotes about their own or their cronies' violent actions in which they portray themselves as heroes, or at least antiheroes, and their would-be subjugators as villains. The pleasure that novices derive from hearing their coaches' stories makes them long for the day when they can finally have their own violent feats to brag about. "Ridicule" is a second technique that coaches use to provoke violence on the part of novices. The coach belittles the novice for his reluctance or refusal to physically attack people who try to subjugate him. The coach continuously mocks the novices until the realization sinks in that it is better for him to physically attack a potential subjugator than to suffer any more derision from the coach.

Coaches who prefer a less subtle technique than either vain glorification or ridicule can always use "coercion," a special case of violent subjugation (described earlier) in which superordinates either threaten or actually harm a novice for refusing to obey their instructions to physically attack some would-be subjugator. Novices quickly get the message that it would be smarter for them to physically attack some other subjugator than to get physically harmed by their coach. "Haranguing" is still another technique. Here, the coach relentlessly rants and raves about hurting would-be subjugators without ever belittling, physically threatening, or appealing to novices' vanity, as the other techniques do. Novices are repeatedly told the same thing in the hope that it will eventually sink into their heads.

A final technique that a coach can use for prompting novices to take violent action is "besiegement." If a single technique will not prompt a novice to take violent action against potential subjugators, then coaches can always resort to a combination of techniques. Because besiegement combines all the techniques described previously, except for haranguing, a coach can make novices endure the pain and anxiety of ridicule and coercion if they refuse to physically attack a would-be subjugator while assuring them of certain relief from this pain and anxiety, as well as the added enjoyment of vain glorification, if they do succeed in harming him or her physically.

Boys' and girls' passage through the brutalization stage may differ. Although girls may undergo violent subjugation and personal horrification as often as boys, boys undergo violent coaching more often than girls. Because violent coaches suffer from the same gender bias as many other members of society, usually they expect girls to follow the traditionally female subordinate role rather than the customarily male superordinate role. Coaches

less frequently encourage violent behavior in a girl than in a boy because they find it more acceptable for girls to rely on charm and guile rather than brute force to settle dominance disputes. Thus, girls may just as often as boys enter the brutalization stage, but boys much more often complete this stage.

The second stage in the violentization process is "defiance" (formerly labeled "belligerency"). Unlike brutalization, defiance is a unitary yet nuanced experience. During this experience, subordinates seek to resolve the crisis into which their brutalization has thrown them. While agonizing over their brutalization, they repeatedly ask themselves why they are being brutalized and what, if anything, they can do about it. In a desperate search for answers, they revisit episodes of their past violent subjugation, personal horrification, and violent coaching. Reliving these experiences, which consumes them with hostility toward themselves and other people, produces an epiphany. They realize belatedly that their violent coaches may have had a point after all: the only real way that they can put a stop to their brutalization is to become violent themselves. If, in the wake of this epiphany, subordinates decide finally to heed their violent coaches' instructions, then they make a "mitigated violent resolution"—they resolve from that moment on to kill or gravely harm anyone who attempts to violently subjugate them. The making of this resolution not only marks the graduation from the second stage but also the birth of a potential violent criminal.

In contrast to boys' and girls' pointedly different passages through the brutalization stage, they traverse the defiance stage in much the same way. Girls who enter this stage are no less apt than boys to complete it. Although more boys than girls probably experience violent coaching, those girls who have undergone the same violent coaching as boys are just as likely as their male counterparts to have an epiphany during this stage about the necessity for taking grievous violent action against future subjugators. Cases 14 and 6 provide examples of boys who had attained this plateau in their violence development:

Case 14: I wanted to stay away from everybody and wanted everybody to stay away from me. I didn't want to be fooled around with by people. I told myself that if anybody fools around with me bad anymore, I am going to go off on them. I was ready to kill people, who fooled and fooled around with me and wouldn't stop. (Athens 1992, 60)

Case 6: People had messed with me long enough. If anybody ever messed with me again, I was going to go up against them. I was going to stop them from messing bad with me. If I had to, I would use a gun, knife, or anything. I didn't mess with other people, and I wasn't letting them mess with me anymore. My days of being a chump who was too frightened and scared to hurt people for messing with him were over. (Athens 1992, 61)

"Dominance engagement" (formerly labeled "violent performance") is the third stage in the violentization process. Unlike brutalization but like defiance, dominance engagement is also a unitary yet nuanced experience. During this stage perceived subordinates test the mitigated violent resolution that they formed earlier during the defiance stage. Of course, the circumstances must be just right: some would-be superordinate must threaten or actually use violence in an attempt to subjugate the perceived subordinate, and the perceived subordinate must think that he has at least a fighting chance. The would-be superordinate must remain undeterred by the perceived subordinate's likely physical resistance to violent subjugation. Finally, no third party must intervene and prevent the perceived subordinate from putting his resolve to the full test.

As important as the circumstances surrounding a dominance engagement is its immediate outcome. There are several possible outcomes: a major or minor victory, a major or minor defeat, and a draw or no decision. In a major victory, the perceived subordinate scores a clear-cut win and in the process inflicts serious injuries upon the would-be superordinate. A major defeat is simply the reverse. A minor victory or defeat is the same as major ones, except that no one is seriously injured. A "no decision" occurs when the engagement never progressed to the point that a winner or loser could be declared: it ends before any of the combatants could inflict serious injuries upon the other. In contrast, a draw is an engagement that did progress beyond that point, but still no clear winner or loser could be determined. Here, the combatants inflicted equally grievous injuries upon one another. The most common outcomes of dominance engagements are minor victories and defeats as well as draws and no decisions, whereas the least common are major defeats and victories. Before putative subordinates can move on to the next stage, they must achieve at least one, and usually more, major victories.

Boys and girls differ dramatically in how they fare in dominance engagements.

Girls usually fare worse than boys for a variety of reasons. Because more boys than girls reach this stage of violence development, girls are more likely to confront boys than other girls during physical dominance engagements. The greater physical size of adolescent boys, their greater participation in physical contact sports and delinquent gangs, and their greater knowledge of and access to lethal weapons all give them a decided edge in winning dominance engagements against girls. In fact, girls can provide a ready source of "cheap" major or minor victories that budding violent males can use to advance their stalled violence development (Rhodes 1999, 286–312). Thus, girls who reach the dominance engagement stage are much less likely than boys to pass through it.

The fourth and final stage of violentization is "virulency." Unlike defiance and dominance engagement but like brutalization, virulency is a composite experience composed of three elemental experiences. "Violent notoriety," the first elemental experience, refers to the recognition that former subordinates suddenly acquire from their major victory over a would-be or former subjugator during a dominance engagement. Although previously spoken of as being incapable or only possibly capable of violence during dominance engagements, these former subordinates are now spoken about as if they are not only capable of violence but proficient in it.

The second elemental experience, "social trepidation," flows directly from the first. However, unlike violent notoriety, social trepidation does not refer to how people talk about a boy in his absence but how they act toward him in his presence. In contrast to the past, people now act more deferentially and cautiously toward the former subordinate. Moreover, they now take special pains not to challenge or slight him in any way, because they fear igniting a dominance engagement that they could lose.

If this newly ordained superordinate decides to embrace rather than reject his violent notoriety and the social trepidation that it generates, then he will undergo the final elemental experience, "malevolency." Overly impressed with his sudden rise from a lowly subordinate to a lofty superordinate, he becomes arrogant. He now resolves to gravely harm or even kill someone for any provocation, however slight. After making this new violent resolution, he is transformed from a person who would only resort to violence to resist his or an intimate's violent subjugation to a person who relishes any opportunity to violently subjugate others. Undergoing the malevolency experience marks the completion not only of the virulency stage but also of the entire violentization process. At the end of this stage, a "violent" criminal becomes an "ultraviolent" one (see, for example, Shakur 1993).

As is true of the dominance engagement stage, more boys than girls pass through the virulency stage. Because in American society, cold, ruthless acts of violence are more closely associated with males, Americans are much more apt to consider males more dangerous and to fear them more than females. That same gender bias makes it much easier for young men than women to gain violent notoriety, engender social trepidation, and accept a malevolent identity. Thus, at least in the case of creating barriers to violence development, sexism seems to work to the distinct disadvantage of boys and to the distinct advantage of girls (Kipnis 1999, ix–xi). Cases 9 and 33 below provide examples of boys who have finished the entire violentization process and become ultraviolent criminals:

Case 9: I became a go-getter. I would go after people's asses for pissing me off in any fucking way at all. I meant what I said to people and said what I meant to them. They better listen to what I said because I wasn't playing games any more, but for keeps. I was ready to kill anybody who walked the streets. (Athens 1992, 77)

Case 33: I was ready to throw down with everything that I had. If a motherfucker loses his teeth, then he lost some teeth. If he loses his eye, then he lost an eye, and he loses his life, then he lost a life. It didn't matter to me. The way I looked at it was that is just one less motherfucker this world will have to put up with. (Athens 1992, 79)

It is important to keep in mind that human beings, their environmental niches, and their experiences are interdependent and exist in a developmental relationship. As people progress through the stages of the violentization process, the role that they play in their environmental niches changes dramatically. During the brutalization stage, they merely play the role of convenient victims on which the other, more violent occupants of their niche can practice violent subjugation, personal horrification, and violent coaching. At this early point in people's violence development, their environmental niche molds them more than they mold it. Until they enter the defiance stage, form a mitigated violent resolution, and become violent themselves, they are not yet mentally prepared to reject playing the role of a victim of

brutalization and start playing the role of a physical resister against it. Moreover, they do not actually put their new role into action until after they enter the dominance engagement stage and score some major or minor victories or defeats against their would-be brutalizers. However, after they finally graduate to the virulency stage, form an unmitigated violent resolution, and become ultraviolent, they change from playing the role of physical resisters against their would-be brutalizers to that of ruthless brutalizers themselves. The irony is that complete progression through the violentization process makes the roles that people play in their environmental niches go full circle from those of hapless victims to vicious victimizers. With the addition of every new ultraviolent person to an environmental niche, it becomes that much more dangerous and hazardous to everyone who occupies it. Thus, by the end of the last stage of people's violence development, they mold their environmental niche more than it molds them.

Although the process of violentization usually takes several years to complete, it sometimes can be completed in only a few months. If the latter happens, then the process becomes a "cataclysmic experience." The completion of violentization is always contingent upon a person undergoing all the experiences of each stage and all the stages in the process. Thus, fortunately, only a few of the boys and girls who begin the process of violentization ever finish it. Nevertheless, a greater proportion of the boys who start the process complete it because, at this point in the evolution of American society, girls have a harder time completing all the stages, except for defiance. Boys and girls can start and finish the violentization process at almost any age, but boys usually start and finish it at a younger age than girls. Unfortunately, no matter how much younger males are when they finish violentization, the females who finally complete the process can be every bit as deadly as their male counterparts.

Once boys or girls start the violentization process, how can they be prevented from completing it and becoming ultraviolent adults? The key to prevention lies in stopping them from entering as many stages of the violentization process as possible. If children have not entered the brutalization stage, then they must be kept from ever starting it. Home and neighborhood monitoring programs might prevent children's violent subjugation, personal horrification, and violent coaching, but only if they could be vigorously implemented. Specially designed educational programs directed against the use of violence to achieve dominance could no doubt prove effective, if properly integrated into and administered across the entire adult and juvenile community.

Once children have entered the defiance stage, the goal of intervention must be to stop them from making a mitigated violent resolution and thereby completing this stage. Individual counseling aimed at helping children to draw an insight from their brutalization other than the need to act violently toward other people who seek to violently subjugate them could prove extremely helpful here. However, once children graduate from the defiance stage and enter into the dominance engagement stage, individual counseling alone usually proves to be ineffective, no matter how intense or prolonged. At this stage in their violence development, children need to undergo antiviolent, primary group resocialization. Drawing on many of the same techniques used during vio-

lent coaching but now directed at a new goal, new mentors who were once themselves violent individuals could teach these children nonviolent means of waging and winning dominance engagements and supervise them as they practice their newly learned techniques.

Unfortunately, after children have progressed to the virulency stage of their violence development, few effective countermeasures now exist to stop them from replacing their mitigated violent resolution with an unmitigated one and becoming ultraviolent adolescents. In fact, at this late stage in a child's violence development, most interventions will have the reverse effect of the one intended. Instead of diminishing the child's violent notoriety and the social trepidation that it engenders, belated attempts at intervention will only make it more rather than less inevitable that the child will undergo the culminating experience of malevolency. Thus, the earlier in the violentization process at which one intervenes with the appropriate measures, the more likely that the intervention will succeed at the least risk to the community.

Lonnie Athens

See also Gangs; Guns; Suicide
References and further reading
Athens, Lonnie. 1989. *The Creation of Dangerous Violent Criminals*. London: Routledge.
———. 1992. *The Creation of Dangerous Violent Criminals*. Urbana: University of Illinois Press.
———. 1997. *Violent Criminal Acts and Actors Revisited*. Urbana: University of Illinois Press.
———. 1998. "Dominance, Ghettoes, and Violent Crime." *The Sociological Quarterly* 39 (Fall): 673–691.
Blumer, Herbert. 1997. "Foreword." Pp. 3–6 in *Violent Criminal Acts and Actors Revisited* by Lonnie Athens. Urbana: University of Illinois Press.

Dewey, John. 1929. *Experience and Nature.* La Salle: Open Court.

Kipnis, Aaron. 1999. *Angry Young Men.* San Francisco: Jossey-Bass.

Lewis, Dorothy. 1992. "From Abuse to Violence: Psychophysiological Consequences of Maltreatment." *Journal of the American Academy of Child and Adolescent Psychiatry* 31 (May): 383–391.

———. 1998. *Guilty by Reason of Insanity.* New York: Fawcett-Columbine.

Lewontin, Richard. 2000. *The Triple Helix: Gene, Organism, and Environment.* Cambridge: Harvard University Press.

Lewontin, Richard, Steven Rose, and Leon Kamin. 1984. *Not in Our Genes: Biology, Ideology, and Human Nature.* New York: Pantheon.

Mead, George. 1934. *Mind, Self and Society.* Chicago: University of Chicago Press.

Mednick, Sarnoff. 1977. "A Biosocial Theory of Learning Law-abiding Behavior." Pp. 1–8 in *Biosocial Bases of Criminal Behavior.* Edited by S. Mednick and K. Christiansen. New York: Garner.

Mednick, Sarnoff, Vicki Pollock, Jan Volavka, and William Gabriella. 1982. "Biology and Violence." Pp. 21–80 in *Criminal Violence.* Edited by Marvin Wolfgang and Neil Weiner. Beverly Hills: Sage.

Montagu, Ashley. 1985. "The Sociobiology Debate: An Introduction." Pp. 24–33 in *Biology, Crime and Ethics: A Study of Biological Explanations for Criminal Behavior.* Edited by Frank Marsh and Janet Katz. Cincinnati: Anderson.

Rhodes, Richard. 1999. *Why They Kill: The Discoveries of a Maverick Criminologist.* New York: Alfred A. Knopf.

Shakur, Sanyika. 1993. *Monster: The Autobiography of an LA Gang Member.* New York: Penguin.

Simon, David, and Edward Burns. 1997. *The Corner: A Year in the Life of an Inner City Neighborhood.* New York: Broadway.

Sutherland, Edwin. 1973. "Susceptibility and Differential Association." Pp. 42–43 in *Edwin H. Sutherland on Analyzing Crime.* Edited by K. Schuessler. Chicago: University of Chicago Press.

Wolfgang, Marvin, and Franco Ferracuti. 1967. *The Subculture of Violence: Toward an Integrated Theory in Criminology.* London: Tavistock.

Vocational Education

Vocational education is formal schooling that prepares a young person for a job. It has perennially been the object of contentious debate, typically centered on issues of race and class (e.g., Oakes 1985). Gender equity is also an issue because over the years, vocational education for boys has prepared them better than it has girls for a wide range of comparatively high-paying jobs. In a 1994 report to the U.S. Congress on the status of vocational education, a blue-ribbon panel found that there were gender differences and evidence of sex stereotyping in the course-taking patterns of secondary school students. One important difference was that girls were significantly more likely than boys to earn their vocational credits in consumer and home economics. Boys were more likely than girls to take courses in agriculture and trade and industry. The statistics revealed that 91 percent of students who concentrated in trade and industry courses (e.g., welding, machine shop) were boys, whereas 87 percent of those who concentrated in health courses were girls (National Assessment of Vocational Education [NAVE] Independent Advisory Panel 1994).

These gender differences evidenced in the last decade of the twentieth century represented accumulated school practice that spanned several decades; its origins antedated the formalization of vocational education as a school subject. Perhaps more than any other subject in the American high school curriculum, vocational education has been the one most prone to

Young men receiving instruction in aviation mechanics, South Charleston, West Virginia, ca. 1935–1943 (Library of Congress)

gender stereotyping, with girls and boys being deliberately exposed to quite different forms of vocational and career knowledge. The peculiar sociology of the subject results from the fact that the school curriculum mirrors normative societal practice. Vocational education has traditionally taken its cue directly from labor markets, selecting as vocational subjects replicas of actual jobs in the economy. Historically, labor markets have been segmented by gender, with some types of work assigned to women and other types to men. These work patterns sometimes reflect deliberate choices by boys and girls, but more often than not they reflect societal expectations of each gender. Labor markets also evidence gender inequities in pay and in opportunities for advancement.

For most of the twentieth century, vocational education in the schools merely reproduced the gender stereotypes and inequities of labor markets. The vocational education and career guidance literature of the early decades of the twentieth century shows that it was commonplace to project careers in terms of gender. For example, in a book on career choice, Lewis Smith and Gideon L. Blough (1929) delineated careers for men and for women. Men's careers were in the realms of manufacturing, transportation and communication, the professions, public service, extraction of minerals, oil refining, and agriculture and animal husbandry. Women's careers were in the commercial field, homemaking, personal service, and a few professions. Similar distinctions are evident in a work titled "Vocations for

Girls," in which Mary Lingenfelter and Harry Kitson (1939) offered nursing, home economics, cosmetology, and office work as careers for girls while setting forth medicine, dentistry, engineering, and science as careers primarily for boys. These stereotypes were openly acknowledged by persons like college professor David Hill, who wrote: "In the vocational education of women the opportunities for work and for happiness in the home should be promoted at every step" (1920, 355).

Gender roles in the acquisition of occupational skill were present in colonial America, not just in the kinds of trades available to boys as opposed to girls but also in the terms of their respective contracts (Mays 1952). Boys could not complete their apprenticeships until they reached age twenty-one, whereas girls completed theirs when they reached age eighteen or were married. Society expected boys to become masters of small shops, but girls were expected to engage in housewifery.

In the nineteenth century, with the decline of the craft age and the rise of the machine age, apprenticeship became somewhat outmoded. Vocational education became the way to learn how to operate machines. Courses were offered initially in skill-oriented mechanic schools and later in after-work continuation schools that were attached to factories. Although manual training became an elementary school subject for both sexes, it ultimately made its way into later grades of schooling, solidifying as a subject essentially for boys. Over the decades, manual training evolved into industrial arts ("shop") and, more recently, into technology education.

A new pedagogy suited to the mass transmission of skills was needed, and manual training became that new pedagogy. At the 1876 Centennial Exposition held in Philadelphia, mathematics professor Calvin Woodward of Washington University of St. Louis saw the Russian exhibit, which featured a display of a formalized way of dissecting and teaching skills. This system simplified the way in which occupations could be taught. Woodward set the gender tone for the subject by establishing a manual training school for boys ages fourteen to eighteen in 1880 in St. Louis. The curriculum included theory and practice relating to hand and machine tool use on woods, metals, and plastics, along with mathematics, science, and literature.

Woodward reported (1889) that a follow-up of early graduates of the school showed that large numbers of the boys had opted for higher education; they chose professions such as medicine, dentistry, architecture, and engineering. He promoted the career possibilities of manual training, arguing that although it was essentially in the realm of general education, it was but a step to a trade. The results from his school showed the subject to be a precursor not just of trades but of professions. Manual training was the one subject in the curriculum that could respond directly to the changing economic landscape, that is, the shift from an agrarian economy to a machine economy. But the primary beneficiaries of this new dimension of knowledge were boys. They learned drafting, which was the language of industry, and the basis of communication across trades and professions such as architecture and engineering. They also learned to operate machines and use tools.

At the turn of the twentieth century, with pressure building to increase the pool of skilled workers in the country, industrial lobbyists made a strong push for the creation of separate and autonomously run vocational schools funded by federal dollars. One of the strongest opponents of this push was John Dewey, noted American philosopher and educator, whose argument was that promotion by schools of early career choice would be inherently undemocratic, since such a process would limit the future possibilities of children. In any case, he argued, vocations were not purely economic; they extended into the family and into community life (Dewey 1916). Vocationalist advocates led by David Snedden, then Massachusetts commissioner of education, won the day. Their lobbying culminated with the passage in 1917 of the Smith-Hughes Act, which established federal funding for vocational education on a gendered basis, that is, home economics for girls and agriculture and industrial programs for boys. This basic funding approach dictated the nature of programs for almost all of the twentieth century, and its effects are reflected in the findings of the NAVE report to Congress, as described at the beginning of this entry.

As the vocational education movement gathered energy late in the nineteenth century, some questioned whether such training applied to women, saying: "After all, they were not going to be the 'captains of industry' and they were not going to furnish labor for the industrial machines that would compete with Germany's growing industrial strength" (Powers 1992, 9). Jane Powers contended that male leaders of the vocational education movement were opposed to women's role in the workforce. She documented growth among the ranks of women in factories in the early decades of the twentieth century, not just in clerical jobs but in manufacturing and mechanical jobs. Opposition to women in these jobs grew among male workers, who felt women and children in the workforce were depressing men's wages and decreasing their bargaining power. Women indeed were an exploited class of labor, performing low-paying and low-skill jobs.

Unfortunately, whether through vocational education in the upper grades or through industrial arts in the middle grades, schools reproduced these gender stereotypes about which Powers wrote. The same gender strictures that confronted women in the factories of the 1890s through the 1910s applied in the offering of vocational subjects in the schools. The typical American adult male looking back on his school experience would have industrial arts as a memory and could possibly attribute his skill in operating hand and machine tools or in performing mechanical and electrical chores around the home to skill and knowledge acquired in such classes. That would not be the case for the typical American woman. The whole culture of tool and machine use and the three-dimensional world of making and building and constructing have been treated as the preserve of males.

In the last two decades of the twentieth century, important changes occurred that offered hope for meaningful reform of vocational subjects, not just in terms of content but in terms of access. Industrial arts has evolved into technology education. The old content of woodworking, metalworking, and drafting was discarded and replaced with broader themes such as power and energy, construction, communication, and bio-related technologies. Correspondingly, the pedagogic focus has shifted from acquiring skills with tools to learning design and problem solving. New modular laboratory designs have replaced the old tool shops, and machine interfaces with computers are now the norm. These new laboratories are a far cry from the old factory-type ones that excluded girls. With the hard industrial edge of vocational subjects removed, there is anecdotal evidence that girls are finding these classes much more to their liking. Standards for vocational subjects have been developed and published, thanks to grants from the National Aeronautic and Space Agency and the National Science Foundation. The new democratic goal for vocational education is "technology for all Americans" throughout grades K–12 (International Technology Education Association 2000).

Federal laws, especially the Carl D. Perkins Acts of 1984 and 1990, have also affected vocational education. Informed by contemporary concerns for fairness and equal opportunity, these pieces of legislation directed the states to establish gender equity as a guiding criterion for program funding. The acts also established integration of academic and vocational education as a fundamental curriculum principle. Thus, traditional vocational education has been unraveling, to be replaced by a "new vocationalism" (e.g., Grubb 1996; Lewis 1997). Advocates of the new vocationalism draw heavily on the democratic thought and vocationalist ideals of John Dewey, particularly his view that vocations could form the context for teaching children about work and not about narrow job preparation.

The reforms in technology education and vocationalism draw common inspiration from the new economy. New emphases on knowledge work and information mean that the nature of work has been fundamentally transformed. Technology has significantly transformed work and jobs, eliminating many traditional crafts (see especially Zuboff 1988). Skill itself is being redefined. Indeed, many now believe that so-called soft skills, such as solving problems, thinking critically, learning how to learn, communicating, and working as a team, are more critical now than technical skills (e.g., Secretary's Commission on Achieving Necessary Skills 1991; Gray and Herr 1995). The U.S. Department of Education has backed away from old categorizations such as trade and industrial education, agriculture, and home economics and instead proposed sixteen "career clusters," including information technology, manufacturing, health science, financial services, construction, business and administrative services, legal and protective services, human services, hospitality and tourism, audiovisual technology and communication services, public administration and government, retail-wholesale, scientific research, engineering and technical services, agricultural and natural resources, and transportation and distributive services (U.S. Department of Education 2000). In contrast to narrow job categories, clusters provide for exploration. Specific vocational choices can be postponed until the postsecondary years, and careers can then be pursued in two-year technical colleges and community colleges.

Some of those who support the new vocationalism offer a critical science perspective, meaning that they think schools should question inappropriate societal practice rather than accede passively. Accordingly, they want the new vocational curriculum to deal squarely with continuing workplace inequities, such as gender stereotyping, racism, sexual harassment, and the glass ceiling. Joe

Kincheloe (1999) speaks of a gendered workplace where patriarchy continues to be the predominant ideology and where women are kept in their place. Penny L. Burge and Steven M. Culver (1994) speak of a "gendered economy" that has the effect of expanding the career aspirations of boys and curtailing those of girls. These authors want vocational education deliberately to adopt strategies that would reject common workplace practice and teach more ideal practices, such as boys and girls working collaboratively rather than competitively. Such sentiments are shared by Patricia Carter (1994), who calls on vocational education to respond to the need for workplace equity—for an end to sexual harassment and gender segregation so that women and girls can step out of traditional roles into nontraditional ones.

The new changes in technology education and vocational education go in the direction of altering the sociology of these subjects. They have the potential for leveling the playing field for girls and boys, giving them both the same breadth of exposure in the school curriculum. Consequently, boys and girls both can get early glimpses of the whole world of work that can help them make important career and life decisions and by which they come closer to realizing their fullest potential.

Theodore Lewis

See also Apprenticeship; Computers

References and further reading

Burge, Penny L., and Steven M. Culver. 1994. "Gender Equity and Empowerment in Vocational Education." Pp. 51–63 in *Critical Education for Work: Multidisciplinary Approaches*. Edited by Richard D. Lakes. Norwood, NJ: Ablex.

Carter, Patricia A. 1994. "Women's Workplace Equity: A Feminist View." Pp. 67–81 in *Critical Education for Work: Multidisciplinary Approaches*. Edited by Richard D. Lakes. Norwood, NJ: Ablex.

Dewey, John. 1916. *Democracy and Education*. New York: Macmillan.

Gray, Kenneth C., and Edwin L. Herr. 1995. *Other Ways to Win: Creating Alternatives for High School Graduates*. Thousand Oaks, CA: Corwin Press.

Grubb, W. Norton. 1996. "The New Vocationalism: What It Is, What It Could Be." *Phi Delta Kappan* 77, no. 8: 533–546.

Hill, David S. 1920. *Introduction to Vocational Education: A Statement of Facts and Principles Related to the Vocational Aspects of Education below College Grade*. New York: Macmillan.

International Technology Education Association. 2000. *Standards for Technological Literacy: Content for the Study of Technology*. Reston, VA: ITEA.

Kincheloe, Joe L. 1999. *How Do We Tell the Worker? The Socioeconomic Foundations of Work and Vocational Education*. Boulder, CO: Westview Press.

Lewis, Theodore 1997. "Toward a Liberal Vocational Education." *Journal of Philosophy of Education* 31, no. 3: 477–489.

Lingenfelter, Mary R., and Harry D. Kitson. 1939. *Vocations for Girls*. New York: Harcourt Brace.

Mays, Arthur B. 1952. *Essentials of Industrial Education*. New York: McGraw-Hill.

National Assessment of Vocational Education, Independent Advisory Panel. 1994. *Interim Report to Congress*. Washington, DC: U.S. Department of Education.

Oakes, Jeannie. 1985. *Keeping Track: How Schools Structure Inequality*. New Haven, CT: Yale University Press.

Powers, Jane B. 1992. *The "Girl Question" in Education: Vocational Education for Young Women in the Progressive Era*. Washington, DC: Falmer Press.

Secretary's Commission on Achieving Necessary Skills (SCANS). 1991. *What Work Requires of Schools: A SCANS Report for America 2000*. Washington, DC: U.S. Department of Labor.

Smith, Lewis W., and Gideon L. Blough. 1929. *Planning a Career: A Vocational Civics.* New York: American Book Company.

U.S. Department of Education. 2000. *Career Clusters: Adding Relevancy to Education.* Pamphlet. Washington, DC: U.S. Department of Education.

Woodward, Calvin M. 1889. "The Results of the St. Louis Manual Training School." *Journal of Proceedings and Addresses.* Session of the year 1889, held in Nashville, TN, National Education Association.

Zuboff, Shoshana. 1988. *In the Age of the Smart Machine.* New York: Basic Books.

W

Washington, Booker T., and W. E. B. Du Bois

The childhoods of Booker T. Washington and W. E. B. Du Bois, the two most significant leaders of the African American community in the late nineteenth and early twentieth centuries, illustrate that although young African American men faced common problems, their childhoods could differ significantly. In spite of racism and other restrictions that limited their freedom in the second half of the nineteenth century, the range of experiences that African American males faced during childhood and youth was extensive. Booker T. Washington and W. E. B. Du Bois faced very different experiences as boys, but their childhoods also contained significant common elements. One was born and raised in the South, the other in New England; one was born into servitude, the other into a family that had been free for generations; and one made his own way with little family or community support, whereas the other found considerable community and some family support. Both, of course, encountered race and racism but did so in greatly different contexts and settings and consequently responded differently; both also confronted poverty and economic deprivation and grew up in families that were buffeted by social, cultural, economic, and racial stress. Out of these circumstances both turned to education as the way to overcome the limits they faced. Finally, both achieved remarkable success as educators and as leaders.

Booker Taliaferro Washington was born on a farm near Hale's Ford in the foothills of the Blue Ridge Mountains in Franklin County, Virginia. In his autobiographical writings, Washington gives his birth date as 1857, 1858, or 1859; it was more likely 1856. Washington's mother Jane was a slave who worked on James Burroughs's farm. His father, a white man, has never been identified. The Burroughs farm was midsized and in 1860 employed ten slaves—four adults and ten children. Among the ten were Jane, Booker's mother; Sophie, his aunt; Munroe, who may have been his uncle; and another adult male. The children included Booker himself; John, his older brother; and Amanda, his younger sister. The other three children may have been Sophie's. By 1860 Jane had married Washington, a slave belonging to the farmer who lived across the road from the Burroughs place. Slavery was not conducive to a comfortable family life. Jane lived with her children in a dirt-floor, one-room cabin, the distinguishing feature of which was a large hole in the floor, which Burroughs used in the winter to store sweet potatoes. Her chores as cook for Burroughs left little time for her own children. Booker recalled that during this period, he never sat at a table and shared a meal with his family. He also recalled that the rigors of slavery robbed his mother of her health and vitality.

William Edward Burghardt Du Bois was born on February 23, 1868, in Great Barrington, Massachusetts. His mother, Mary Burghardt Du Bois, was a member of the Burghardt clan that had lived in the Great Barrington region since the colonial period. By the end of the Civil War they were a fixture in the community, working as housemaids, waiters, farmers, and small shopkeepers. His father, Alfred Du Bois, was born in Haiti, the grandson of a prominent planter and physician who divided his time between the mainland and the islands. Alfred Du Bois arrived in Great Barrington as a drifter with no job and few prospects and likely a wife in New York. He married Mary Burghardt over the objections of her family in early February 1868, a few weeks before the birth of their son. Alfred Du Bois remained with Mary only about a year. After her husband left, Mary lived for a time on the farm of her parents and then moved into Great Barrington. She suffered from depression and then in 1875 or 1876 from a stroke, which left her partially crippled. Part-time work as a housemaid and frequent assistance from her sisters and brothers enabled her to maintain a life on the edge of poverty for herself and her sons. William and his older half-brother Adelbert Burghardt also took odd jobs and contributed to the support of the family. In spite of these hardships, Du Bois remembers that his mother made sure that his schooling proceeded without interruption.

The defining element in the early childhood of Booker T. Washington was slavery and its accompanying poverty and family stress. Simple issues such as food and clothing stood out in Washing-ton's memory. Although his mother's job as cook for the farm ensured that food of some sort would always be available, meals remained a hit-or-miss affair, "a piece of bread here and a scrap of meat there . . . a cup of milk at one time and some potatoes at another" (Washington 1901, 219). When this system left the children hungry, Washington recalled that his mother would awaken them late at night and provide them with eggs or a chicken that she had somehow secured. Clothing was also limited. His sole garment during early childhood was a coarse shirt made of rough flax, which when new was so painful to wear that he often went without clothing. His first shoes were a pair of wood-soled clogs that he received for Christmas when he was eight years old. As a slave he was expected to work, even as a young child. His job included operating the fans that kept the flies away from the Burroughs' dining table at mealtime, carrying water to workers, and performing other light chores around the farm. Even though slavery ended when he was nine years old, the young Washington recognized the barriers that race and slavery placed between blacks and whites. Although the Burroughs children were his playmates with stick horses, marbles, or games of tag or on fishing excursions, there was an invisible barrier at the schoolroom door. Education was for white children only. Work, too, was segregated, reserved for blacks. Finally, there was the incident that indelibly defined slavery in young Washington's mind. As he recalled, the vision of his uncle, stripped naked, tied to a tree, and whipped across his bare back with a cowhide strip as he cried for mercy "made an impression on my boyish heart that I shall carry with me to my grave" (Washington 1900, 12).

The Civil War and emancipation radically altered Washington's childhood. In 1864 his stepfather escaped from Lynchburg, where he had been hired out to a tobacco factory, and fled to Malden, West Virginia, where he found employment in the salt mines. In August 1865 he sent for his now-emancipated wife and stepchildren. Economically, life in Malden was not a great improvement over life on the Burroughs farm. They lived in a dilapidated cabin, in a crowded neighborhood of similar dwellings, amid garbage, raw sewage, throngs of poor blacks and even poorer whites, and violence and vice—an environment that shocked and offended the young Washington. Booker and his brother James were immediately put to work packing salt. Their stepfather confiscated all their wages, which soured any relationship that might have developed between stepfather and stepsons. The one advantage that Washington found in Malden was school. Over the objections of his stepfather but with the support of his mother, Washington began attending the school for blacks that opened in late 1865, first at night and then during the day between early-morning and late-afternoon stints in the salt mines. This first effort at education was frequently interrupted by the work demands that his stepfather imposed, first in the salt mines and then in the coal mines. In 1867 he escaped the control of his stepfather when he took a job as a domestic in the home of General Lewis Ruffner, one of the wealthiest citizens of Malden. There Washington served as houseboy, companion, and eventually protégé for Viola Ruffner, General Ruffner's New England wife. From Viola Ruffner, the young Washington not only found refuge from the salt mines and his stepfather's home, but he also was imbued with the values of hard work, honesty, cleanliness, books, and education, as well as the example of gentility that the Ruffners' home represented. Washington would later credit her for much of his early education and especially with preparing him for college.

Du Bois's childhood in Great Barrington was shielded from many of the problems of race and Reconstruction, but it was affected by his mother's declining health and economic condition. Following the departure of her husband in 1869, Mary Du Bois and her two sons lived with her parents, Othello and Sarah Burghardt, until her father's death in 1874 forced the sale of the family farm and a move into the city. Following her mother's death a year later, Mary Du Bois and her two sons relocated again to a dilapidated house they shared with an even poorer white family on Railroad Street in the heart of Great Barrington's saloon, gambling, and prostitution district. In this setting Mary soon suffered her debilitating stroke, further limiting her economic prospects. The family's income became increasingly dependent on the earnings of Adelbert and the part-time jobs of William.

As the family's prospects sank, Mary Du Bois put all of her energy into the development of her son William. She used the obvious social lessons of the world outside their door to teach him the dangers of alcohol, gambling, and loose women. More important, she emphasized education. The young Du Bois began regular education at age five or six, after the family moved back to Great Barrington. From the beginning he excelled as a student and attracted the attention of his teachers as well as some of the prominent members of the community. Du Bois's academic ability brought rapid promotion and also prompted local intervention into the family's economic situation. As Du Bois prepared to enter high school, local citizens arranged for the family to move to a more suitable home. Du Bois was the only African American student in the local high school. The principal, Frank Hosmer, arranged for Du Bois to take the college preparatory curriculum, made sure that he had the expensive books and other materials needed for that course of study, and started mother and child thinking about college.

Du Bois's social contacts during this period were not with Great Barrington's small African American community but almost exclusively with his white classmates and with the children of the families who employed his mother. He was conscious of the economic differences that separated him from his classmates but initially seemed to think that race was of no significance. As he grew older, this idealistic vision of American democracy was undermined by a series of events that marked the racial boundaries, even in the relatively liberal atmosphere of Great Barrington. The first, the refusal of a young girl in one of his classes to accept an exchange of greeting cards, which probably occurred early in his high school days, was followed by other small rejections that forced him to recognize the extent of racial feeling in the United States.

As their childhoods came to an end, both Booker T. Washington and W. E. B. Du Bois left the homes of their youth in pursuit of higher education. While working in the salt mines, Washington had learned from another worker that Hampton Institute in Hampton, Virginia, would allow impoverished blacks to work to pay the costs of their education. In 1872, with 50 cents in his pocket, collected in nickels and dimes from family and friends and with the blessing of his mother, the sixteen-year-old set out on the 500-mile trek to seek admission to Hampton. Three years later he graduated as one of its top students. Du Bois's plans for college developed more traditionally. By his senior year he had selected his college of choice, Harvard University. His plans hit a snag, though, when his mother died shortly after his March 1885 graduation. Once again, however, benefactors came to his rescue. The African American community took him in, made sure that he had food and shelter in the months following his mother's death, and provided him with a well-paying summer job. Principal Hosmer and three other white citizens collected funds from local churches to pay for Du Bois's college education, but they stipulated that he attend Fisk University, not Harvard. Du Bois did not object. In September 1885 the seventeen-year-old Du Bois arrived in Nashville, Tennessee, prepared to commence his studies. Three years later, with his Fisk B.A. in hand, Du Bois entered Harvard University.

Cary D. Wintz

See also African American Boys; Civil War; Jobs in the Nineteenth Century; Slavery

References and further reading
Aptheker, Herbert, ed. 1997. *The Correspondence of W. E. B. Du Bois.* Vol. 1, *Selections 1877–1934.* Amherst: University of Massachusetts Press.
Du Bois, W. E. B. 1920. *Darkwater: Voices from within the Veil.* New York: Harcourt, Brace, and Howe.
———. 1940. *Dusk of Dawn: An Essay toward an Autobiography of a Race Concept.* In *W. E. B. Du Bois: Writings.* Edited by Nathan Huggins. New York: Harcourt, Brace, and Company. Reprint, New York: Library of America, 1986.
———. 1968. *Autobiography of W. E. B. Dubois: A Soliloquy on Viewing My*

Life from the Last Decade of Its First Century. New York: International Publishers.

Harlan, Louis R. 1972. *Booker T. Washington: The Making of a Black Leader, 1856–1901.* New York: Oxford University Press.

Lewis, David Levering. 1993. *W. E. B. Du Bois: Biography of a Race.* New York: Henry Holt.

Marable, Manning. 1986. *W. E. B. Du Bois: Black Radical Democrat.* Boston: Twayne Publishers.

Rudwick, Elliott M. 1969. *W. E. B. Du Bois: Propagandist of the Negro Protest.* New York: Atheneum.

Washington, Booker T. 1900. *The Story of My Life and Work.* In *The Booker T. Washington Papers.* Vol. 1, *The Autobiographical Writings.* Edited by Louis R. Harlan. Chicago: J. L. Nichols. 1972. Reprint, Urbana: University of Illinois Press.

———. 1901. *Up from Slavery: An Autobiography.* In *The Booker T. Washington Papers.* Vol. 1, *The Autobiographical Writings.* Edited by Louis R. Harlan. New York: Doubleday, Page. 1972. Reprint, Urbana: University of Illinois Press.

Washington, George
See Manners and Gentility

Work
See Jobs in the Seventeenth and Eighteenth Centuries; Jobs in the Nineteenth Century; Jobs in the Twentieth Century

World War II

Just as World War II had an enormous impact on the lives of adults in the United States, so too did it profoundly shape the experiences of American boys. Like their adult counterparts, boys (and girls) were mobilized to help with the war effort, and they performed important services such as collecting scrap materials, planting victory gardens, and buying war bonds and stamps. The war also influenced the games and leisure activities of boys of all ages. Virtually all of the toys, comic books, magazines, radio programs, and movies boys encountered dealt with either combat or patriotic themes. Viewed as future soldiers, boys between the ages of fourteen and seventeen were considered to be of exceptional importance to the U.S. war effort, and schools and government programs created specialized courses to promote their physical fitness and premilitary training. Even as national propaganda campaigns, bond drives, advertising, and shared popular culture materials encouraged commonalities within American boys' wartime activities, differences in racial, class, and ethnic background often resulted in divergent experiences—especially for thousands of Japanese American boys, who spent much of the war behind the barbed-wire walls of internment camps.

With millions of adults entering the military and taking war industry jobs, government agencies increasingly called upon children to perform essential home-front tasks. While high school–age boys and girls served the war effort through part-time employment, children between the ages of six and thirteen completed their wartime jobs on a completely voluntary basis. Despite expanded roles for women in the workforce, the tasks boys and girls performed often conformed to traditional gender stereotypes. As historians William Tuttle (1993) and Robert Kirk (1994) have noted, girls were more likely to engage in "nurturing" activities such as caring for small children, knitting socks and blankets, canning produce, and rolling bandages, whereas boys took on more "masculine" duties like collecting salvage, building model airplanes for military and

A group of schoolboys gathering scrap metal during World War II (Archive Photos)

civilian training sessions, and serving as junior air raid wardens.

Of all the tasks young boys across the country performed, scrap collection was probably the most crucial to the war effort. With serious rubber, paper, and metal shortages during the war, the tin cans, old raincoats, newspapers, copper pans, and other materials boys collected in their wagons helped conserve valuable resources and saved countless hours of adult labor. Although boys could participate in a variety of school and community salvage campaigns, the Boy Scouts of America were especially effective in mobilizing boys as "scrap troopers." In the summer of 1941, for example, after learning of the nation's aluminum shortage, the Boy Scouts collected 11 out of the 12 million pounds of aluminum brought in during a nationwide pots and pans drive—

enough, the Army estimated, to make 1,700 planes. Throughout the war, the Boy Scouts continued to receive special recognition for their additional contributions to salvage drives. By the war's end, they had gathered more than 23 million pounds of tin, 109 million pounds of rubber, 370 million pounds of scrap metal, and 3 million books.

In addition to collecting scrap metals, paper, and rubber, boys in rural areas were called upon to fill other special roles. Young boys did extra chores around the farm and gathered milkweed pods for the stuffing in life preservers, and boys fourteen and older joined the Future Farmers of America. These young agricultural workers not only grew crops and raised livestock, but they also learned to repair farm machinery and increase food production. Children's agricultural work, however, was not confined to rural areas; boys and girls throughout the country planted and tended "victory gardens." Even in cities where open land was scarce, park officials set aside plots for elementary school children to plant vegetable gardens.

Another important way that boys contributed to the war on the home front was through purchasing war bonds and stamps. Boys and girls alike would bring their nickels, dimes, and quarters to school once a week to buy stamps for their war stamp books. Once a child filled his book with $18.75 in stamps, he could trade it in for a war bond at the post office. Many schools charted their students' fund-raising efforts with classroom posters that translated stamp and bond sales into military purchases. Children in smaller schools might watch their savings turn into equipment for a single soldier, but pupils in larger schools could count the number of bombs, tanks, planes, or ammunition rounds they helped build with their money. Although gender did not affect children's participation in the war stamp and bond drives, class differences often did. Poorer children were often ashamed of their inability to purchase as many defense stamps as their affluent peers. The embarrassment was so great for one ten-year-old boy in Kokomo, Indiana, that he "swallowed a worm on a dare in order to win 25 cents to buy a war stamp and be, as he said, 'like the rest of the kids'" (Tuttle 1993, 125).

The United States' full-scale mobilization for war not only fostered youth participation in home-front programs, but also it encouraged boys to think of themselves as potential servicemen. Boys as young as three could be found pretending to be "airplane men" shooting at Japanese Zeros with wooden boards as guns. As they got older, though, school-age boys required greater verisimilitude in their war games, and they often went to elaborate lengths to fashion uniforms, first-aid kits, guns, and other weapons that looked as real as possible. Although the combat scenarios that boys played out varied from neighborhood to neighborhood, two axioms generally held true: the Americans were ultimately always victorious, and no one wanted to be the enemy. Recruiting younger boys or, occasionally, girls solved the latter problem.

Once boys reached adolescence, their interest in combat and war games could be channeled into more formal outlets. The Young Men's Christian Association (YMCA), for example, created "Boymandos" programs throughout the nation to provide premilitary fitness classes and general athletic training. Teenage boys could also join the High School Victory Corps, a nationwide organization designed to prepare high school students for war service—military and civilian. Freshmen and sophomores could serve only as general members, but junior and senior boys could join the air, land, or sea branches, which provided their members with uniforms, insignia, specialized coursework, and military drill and calisthenics. Although membership in the corps was voluntary, participation in school physical education programs was not. Because the War Department estimated that more than 80 percent of sixteen- and seventeen-year-olds would enter military service during the war, most high school physical education programs tried to cultivate the types of skills and physiques boys would need in basic training and combat. Ultimately, millions of boys did serve in the military, often patriotically enlisting as soon as they turned seventeen.

A young boy with a helmet lies on the floor playing with a toy army, 1940s (Archive Photos)

If boys did not get their fill of the war by participating in school, YMCA, Boy Scout, or other programs, they could immerse themselves in war news and action through popular culture. Although they often contained fantastic story lines and superhuman heroes, comic books, radio programs, and movies were generally saturated with war topics and appeals for patriotism. The messages of these popular culture materials were so influential, in fact, that Robert Kirk dubbed them the "unofficial instruments of national policy" for children (1994, 36). Even before World War II began, boys were introduced to the "Horrors of War" via 1-cent bubble gum cards manufactured by Gum Inc. of Philadelphia. The

cards graphically depicted Japanese atrocities in China and offered explanatory captions in order to teach children "the importance of peace." When World War II started, Gum Inc. created a "War News Pictures" series of cards, which children could collect to learn about the war in Europe. Boys and girls could also keep abreast of war information and practice for civilian defense jobs by amassing Coca-Cola plane identification cards, Wonder Bread warship guides, and Junior Air Raid Warden games.

Reading comic books was a far more popular activity for boys and girls—especially during the later years of the war, when shortages curtailed chewing gum sales. Between the ages of six and twelve, boys and girls alike were avid comic book readers, buying roughly 12 million copies a month. Wartime studies revealed that boys were more likely to follow a greater number of serials and were generally drawn to more bellicose comics. Nevertheless, children of both sexes and of all ethnic backgrounds ran to comic book dealers each month to purchase the latest adventures of Batman, Captain Marvel, Superman, Blackhawk, and Wonder Woman.

Radio programs were also popular forms of entertainment for boys during the war, and on average they listened fourteen hours a week. Boys and girls tuned in after school primarily to adventure shows such as *Jack Armstrong—That All American Boy, Dick Tracy, Little Orphan Annie, The Shadow, Gangbusters, The Lone Ranger,* and *Superman.* Like comic books, these programs reinforced patriotic feelings and exhorted children to do their share in the home-front battle. Radio also provided young listeners with much of their war news. Some children in larger cities even had their own interactive news programs, in which stations provided listeners with maps, tiny flags, and pins so they could chart overseas campaigns at home. Other news and entertainment came from the Saturday matinee movie, an enduring 1940s ritual for children between the ages of seven and thirteen. Boys and girls spent most of Saturday afternoon at the movie theater, watching a double feature (which often included a battle or spy film), public-service cartoons, and sometimes a government-funded documentary.

Although movies, radio shows, and comics inspired patriotism and provided countless hours of entertainment for boys during the war, they also reinforced existing racial and ethnic prejudices. Popular representations of Japanese as bestial or subhuman, Italians as bumbling, and Germans as vicious regularly produced wartime hatred and cruelties among boys. In Detroit, for example, neighborhood boys frequently called seven-year-old Rick Caesar "Mussolini" and chased him because of his Italian heritage. German American boys often masked their ethnic identity, masquerading as Swiss or Polish to avoid jeers and physical abuse.

Ultimately, though, Japanese American boys experienced the most dramatic and long-term persecution. Although only a handful of Italian- and German-born children were temporarily excluded from "sensitive areas" of the United States, more than 30,000 Japanese American youths were imprisoned in internment camps under Executive Order 9066. Evacuated from their homes in March 1942, these children and their families first went to assembly camps and then to detention centers in remote parts of the country. At most centers, children lived with their families in one-room apartments, each measuring 8 by 20 feet or 12 by 20 feet in size. Orphans and foster children, however, were placed in the children's village at the Manzanar Relocation Center in southern California. Regardless of the location, children spent much of their time in class or after-school recreational programs. Nevertheless, Japanese American boys in the camps still found time to play sandlot baseball, marbles, and the same war games that other boys throughout the country were enjoying. Despite their loss of civil liberties, Japanese American boys were generally quite patriotic, and they actively participated in war bond and salvage collection drives.

Italian, German, and Japanese American boys, however, were not the only ones to experience ethnic prejudice and racial violence during the war. Despite public images of and appeals for national unity, existing racial tensions came to a head in many wartime communities. In the summer of 1943 alone, more than 242 race riots erupted in 47 different cities, involving thousands of men and teenage boys. African, Mexican, and Native American boys migrating with their families to new cities for war-related work often encountered tremendous hostility and suspicion from their white peers. When faced with the contradictions between national self-representations of American unity, equality, and democracy and the realities of segregation and discrimination, some youths of color had trouble determining who the real enemy was. After being prevented by whites from moving into his new home in Detroit, one African American boy declared, "I'm a Jap from now on" (quoted in Tuttle 1993, 165).

Another problem exacerbated by the war was juvenile delinquency. Teacher shortages, an insufficient number of day-care facilities, an increase in parents' out-of-home working hours, and expanded employment opportunities for youths all contributed to more juvenile crime. During the war, juvenile arrests as a whole rose by more than 20 percent, and in some cities like San Diego, boys' incarcerations increased by 55 percent or more. Although boys and girls under seventeen were both committing more crimes, the infractions that youths carried out generally varied by sex. Police arrested teenage girls for prostitution or being "V-girls" (juveniles who had sex with servicemen), whereas they apprehended boys for theft, vandalism, or fighting. In response to the rise in juvenile delinquency and the public outcry over the "decline in youth values," communities instituted ten o'clock curfews and constructed teen centers and canteens where youths could dance, play cards, shoot pool, and socialize. Programs such as these reinforced popular sentiment that boys and girls were important to the war effort and to America's future.

Christina S. Jarvis

See also Comic Books

References and further reading
Baruch, Dorothy W. 1942. *You, Your Children and War.* New York: D. Appleton-Century Company.
Kirk, Robert William. 1994. *Earning Their Stripes: The Mobilization of American Children in the Second World War.* New York: Peter Lang.
Lingeman, Richard R. 1976. *Don't You Know There's a War On? The American Home Front 1941–1945.* New York: Capricorn Books.
Skoloff, Gary, et al. 1995. *To Win the War: Home Front Memorabilia of World War II.* Missoula, MT: Pictorial Publishing.
Spencer, Lyle M., and Robert K. Burns. 1943. *Youth Goes to War.* Chicago: Science Research Associates.
Tuttle, William M. 1993. *"Daddy's Gone to War": The Second World War in the Lives of America's Children.* New York: Oxford University Press.
Werner, Emmy E. 2000. *Through the Eyes of Innocents: Children Witnesses of World War II.* Boulder, CO: Westview Press.

Wrestling
See Superheroes

Y

Young Life
See Parachurch Ministry

Young Men's Christian Association

The Young Men's Christian Association (YMCA) originated in the mid-nineteenth century as a voluntary association to bolster the faith and mold the character of Protestant men and boys and then evolved into a fee-based membership organization run by paid staff that provided varied services, including physical training, to both sexes and all ages. Early YMCAs accepted boys in their early teens as full members but began separate programs for those under age sixteen during the 1870s. The YMCA espoused balanced religious, intellectual, social, and physical development, but by the 1890s gymnasiums (later swimming pools as well) achieved lasting prominence as the most widely used YMCA facilities. YMCA boys' work grew rapidly in the early twentieth century, exceeding 200,000 American boys enrolled by 1920, as staff sought to make themselves specialists in adolescent boyhood. YMCA men supervised the start of Boy Scouting in the United States, but saw it outgrow YMCA boys' work. Starting around the 1920s, the focus of YMCA programming grew more diffuse as local associations enrolled non-Protestants, women and girls, and young boys in addition to the teenage boys and the men of all ages who formed the YMCA's more traditional constituency. Critics in the late twentieth century regretted the YMCA's loss of religious focus and its concentration on providing services, especially physical exercise, for fee payers. But YMCAs also furnished varied social services and enrolled millions of boys and girls under age eighteen.

George Williams formed the first Young Men's Christian Association in 1844 in London, England, banding his fellow clerks together to preserve their faith amid urban temptations. During the early 1850s similar associations sprang up in North American cities, offering prayer meetings, Bible classes, libraries, and literary societies. Although the associations federated at the state and international (U.S. and Canada) levels, each level raised its own budget and remained independent, permitting the wide diversity of local programming that has characterized YMCAs to this day. Since in the nineteenth century even youths in white-collar jobs commonly worked at ages when their twentieth-century counterparts would have been schoolboys, early YMCAs admitted boys in their early teens as full members. By the 1870s, however, as the original members grew older, many YMCAs required a minimum age, usually sixteen.

At first predominantly evangelistic in their approach, YMCA men soon compro-

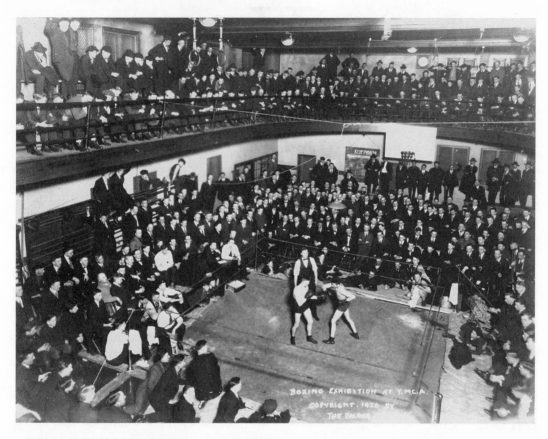

A boxing exhibition at the YMCA, ca. 1920 (Library of Congress)

mised between revivalist and antirevivalist Protestants, continuing to seek conversions but stressing the gradual growth in character preferred by antirevivalists. YMCAs of the 1860s and 1870s broadened their programs, erected buildings to house them, hired professional staff (known as "secretaries"), and defined their mission as "the improvement of the spiritual, mental, social and physical condition of young men" (Hopkins 1951, 107). As a cult of muscular Christianity took hold among white-collar workers who wanted to be good, respectable, and yet manly, by the 1890s gymnasiums became the main attraction. There young clerks could work off troubling energies

and strengthen a sense of masculinity diminished by sedentary work, submission to a boss's orders, and the advent of female coworkers. In search of group activities less regimented than calisthenics, YMCA men invented two gymnasium games, basketball in 1891 and volleyball in 1895. Basketball quickly took hold among the YMCA's younger members and by the early 1900s became a mainstay of public school and church athletics as well. YMCA swimming pools, though still uncommon before 1900, foreshadowed the prominence of aquatics in twentieth-century YMCAs. Luther Gulick, the international YMCA's first secretary for physical education, proposed an inverted triangle, symbolizing the physical, mental, and spiritual sides of human nature, to publicize YMCA determination to train the whole man. The red triangle became the YMCA's ubiquitous emblem in the 1890s.

Separate programs for boys, usually defined as ages ten to sixteen, got under way in the 1870s but grew slowly until the 1890s. Early YMCA workers held weekly religious meetings and Bible study, often judging success by the numbers of boys who accepted Christ. On the theory that character required control of all errant impulses, YMCA men put the boys through long gymnastic drills. In the 1890s, though, with the advent of team sports and swimming, recreation began to outweigh disciplinary training. Though both remained important into the 1920s, the balance shifted from conversion toward character building. This developmental approach gained strength around 1900 as boys' work specialists discovered adolescence. The new term, popularized by students of the psychologist G. Stanley Hall (among them Luther Gulick), gave concerns about youth a scientific-sounding rationale. Though a time of crisis when sexual and other new instincts flooded in upon teenagers, adolescence in Hall's view was also an era of great promise when religious conversion and idealistic enthusiasm were natural. But teenagers needed supervision and guidance at this vulnerable stage. Under Gulick's tutelage, Edgar M. Robinson (1867–1951), the international YMCA's first secretary for boys' work, sought to make the guidance of adolescents the raison d'être of YMCA boys' work and persuaded most junior departments to raise their age limits to twelve through seventeen.

Most YMCA junior members were sons of the middle class. They could afford fees to use the gymnasium and pool, and most were promising recruits for the parent association, since the YMCA's founding fathers had restricted full membership to members of evangelical churches, defined in 1869 to mean orthodox Protestant denominations. Except in smaller northern cities where African Americans were few, YMCAs were racially segregated, with separate branches operating under black leadership. Despite their anger at white racism, college-educated elites commonly supported black YMCAs as safe public spaces free of white control and devoted to advancement of the young.

Middle-class boys needed supervision and religious nurture, YMCA workers believed, since short school days left ample free time, and most boys quit Sunday school in their early teens. At the same time, YMCA men expressed extravagant fears that such boys were losing their masculinity—freed of physical labor, raised by mothers while fathers worked, and taught by female schoolteachers, they were going soft. Robinson denounced the boy who has been "kept so carefully wrapped up in the 'pink cotton wool' of an overindulgent home, [that] he is more effeminate than his sister, and his flabby muscles are less flabby than his character" (Macleod 1983, 48). Widespread suspicion that religiosity was unmanly exacerbated the panic. In response, the YMCA offered building-centered activities throughout the school year and summer camping, both focused on gymnastics, sports, swimming, and hobbies, with further religious commitments for a minority. In 1909–1910, 78 percent of YMCA juniors enrolled for gymnastics and sports, 37 percent joined Bible classes, and just under 5 percent took "decisions for Christian life" (Macleod 1983, 252, 265). Starting around 1910, YMCA boys' workers sought to embed these decisions in a sequence of conventional moral development by inviting boys to take a "Forward Step": deciding for Christ, joining the church, giving regularly, doing committee work, and especially giving up habits such as smoking and masturbation.

Since YMCA boys' work lacked a core program as tightly defined as scouting, junior members could decide which activities to join and which to avoid. Early in the century secretaries were already voicing what later became a persistent criticism of the YMCA, worrying that they were merely selling privileges for a fee. Efforts at community outreach beyond the building-centered, fee-based activities accentuated the diffuseness of YMCA boys' work, however. In 1910 Robinson supervised the transfer of Boy Scouting to the United States but had to let the Boy Scouts of America organize separately. After an enthusiastic start, YMCAs sponsored fewer and fewer Boy Scout troops. Led by David Porter, a Rhodes scholar who later headed the YMCA's college division, YMCA men took the Forward Step into high schools and organized Hi-Y clubs. By the 1920s these were the most successful religious clubs in many high schools, although they could not match the prestige of independent fraternities. During the 1920s, boys' workers also sought to reorient their programs around small-group methods centered on the boys' varied interests. Compared with scouting, the YMCA enjoyed considerable success among high school and other older boys; the median age of YMCA junior members from 1900 through the early 1920s was about fifteen. Yet the YMCA could not match the Boy Scouts of America's explosive growth, from none before 1910 to 377,000 boys in 1920. By comparison, YMCA junior departments enrolled 31,000 boys in 1900 and 219,000 by early 1921, plus 41,000 in Hi-Y.

Further diffusion followed as YMCAs recruited all ages and broke the gender barrier in their quest for members. The late 1920s saw the creation of a "Friendly Indian" (as opposed to hostile?) program for boys under age twelve. In 1930 city YMCA members included 83,000 boys under age twelve and 232,000 of ages twelve through seventeen. By 1963 there were at least 557,000 and 479,000, respectively, plus 181,000 girls under age twelve and 246,000 girls ages twelve through seventeen. Together, they comprised just over half the YMCA's total membership. As early as 1933, women gained full membership, though their numbers grew only gradually. By 1995 the YMCAs claimed 14 million members in the United States, of whom almost half were female and fully half were still under age eighteen.

Although the national YMCA (Canada had organized separately) declared against segregation in 1946, southern white YMCAs resisted fiercely; racists could not imagine sharing a pool with African Americans. By 1967, however, the national board voted to require pledges of nondiscrimination from all YMCAs.

Religious requirements relaxed in ways that alarmed YMCA traditionalists. In 1936 the National Council's program services committee commissioned a guiding statement that defined the YMCA as "a world-wide fellowship of men and boys, united by a common loyalty to Jesus, for the purpose of developing Christian personality and building a Christian society" (Hopkins 1951, 524). Already conversion and Protestant orthodoxy were losing ground to personal development and social values. Since by 1951 nearly two-fifths of members were Roman Catholic or Jewish, YMCAs had to accommodate religious diversity. Thus by 1969 at the YMCA's Camp Becket in Massachusetts, the old ritual "wherein boys had taken Jesus to be their personal chum had . . . vanished. In its place was an evening candlelight service, at the height of which boys rose to pledge their commitment to building a just society" (Putney 1997, 237).

The postwar YMCA followed the middle class to the suburbs; a building boom erected 338 family YMCAs by 1956, offering a wide variety of recreation to fee payers of all ages. Youth soccer and youth basketball for both sexes blossomed in the 1970s. Indicative of the YMCA's abandonment of dogmatic moral instruction was the claim that "values education was the central and pervasive theme" of the basketball program, "articulated in terms of participation, good sportsmanship, skills development, and competition" (Johnson 1979, 392). Troubled by the social turmoil of the late 1960s, some associations accepted government funds and developed fairly successful programs for inner-city youths. But secretaries and laypeople loyal to the suburban branches often resisted change, and social concern waned by 1975, though a residue of job counseling, tutoring, and other community uplift programs remained in center-city branches. Family-oriented activities and service to individuals through values clarification and personal fitness programs predominated. As fitness and athletics became the main attraction, YMCAs of the 1980s and 1990s invested heavily in upscale facilities to rival private health clubs.

Some critics see in YMCA history a story of declension, although their concerns differ. John Gustav-Wrathall laments the loss of the "intense friendship"

fused with religious conversion and devotion to the YMCA that inspired young men's "ardent loyalty" to the nineteenth-century YMCA (Gustav-Wrathall 1998, 46). Pioneer boys' workers likewise were often bachelors or as-yet-unmarried men devoted to the welfare of boys. But as early as the 1880s, Gustav-Wrathall believes, the addition of "physical culture and vigilance against sexual immorality" brought trouble (Gustav-Wrathall 1998, 46). The new emphasis on physical development and availability of public spaces potentially sexualized relationships. How much this involved boys is uncertain. Critics who exposed scandals in 1887 at the Chicago YMCA and in 1912 in Portland, Oregon, both mentioned "men and boys" (Gustav-Wrathall 1998, 164), but they were hostile observers, and the actual ages involved went unreported. Alerted by Hall's ideas to the power of sexual instincts in adolescence and the need for sublimation as well as by the evident anxieties of conscientious YMCA juniors, YMCA boys' workers of the early twentieth century put considerable energy into getting boys to pledge abstinence from masturbation. By the 1920s, expectations that secretaries would marry and increasing recruitment of women and girls undermined the remaining single-sex ethos of the YMCA. Denial of more acceptable emotional and religious outlets, Gustav-Wrathall suggests, may have helped to foster active gay cruising in downtown YMCAs of the post–World War II decades.

Some historians have made a habit of denouncing American culture for shifting from sturdy, inner-directed character in the Victorian era to therapeutic and narcissistic values during the twentieth century. Clifford Putney argues similarly that the post–World War II YMCA drifted, unsure of its mission, and then, after an interlude of social reform in the late 1960s and early 1970s, it turned to the gratification of individual needs through values clarification and physical fitness, making sure that members "felt good." Quoting Christopher Lasch, Putney describes "the contemporary climate [as] therapeutic, not religious" and criticizes the YMCA for abandoning its earlier religiously based character building (Putney 1997, 243, 244). As a membership organization heavily dependent on fees, however, the YMCA was weakly equipped to challenge American culture once the reformism of the Great Society era waned. And even in its heyday, despite the intense religious commitments it induced among a minority, YMCA character building for boys inculcated mainly a forceful conventionality. This was evident in the late 1910s when boys' workers tried to formalize the YMCA ideal of fourfold character development in a Christian Citizenship Training Program. Seeking symmetrical development, group leaders were to score each boy's physical, intellectual, religious, and social "efficiency," plotting the four resulting numbers on a chart with crossed axes: When the four points were joined, the lines formed a quadrilateral—more or less lopsided according to how badly, for instance, the boy's religious score fell short of his physical one. Thus the perfect boy was a big square (Macleod 1983, 125). In practice, many boys had to be pressured to enroll for more than sports and gymnastics.

David I. Macleod

See also Adolescence; Basketball; Boy Scouts; Camping; Muscular Christianity; Young Men's Hebrew Association

References and further reading
Gustav-Wrathall, John Donald. 1998. *Take the Young Stranger by the Hand: Same-Sex Relations and the YMCA.* Chicago: University of Chicago Press.
Hopkins, C. Howard. 1951. *History of the Y.M.C.A. in North America.* New York: Association Press.
Johnson, Elmer L. 1979. *The History of YMCA Physical Education.* Chicago: Association Press.
Macleod, David I. 1983. *Building Character in the American Boy: The Boy Scouts, YMCA, and Their Forerunners, 1870–1920.* Madison: University of Wisconsin Press.
Mjagkij, Nina. 1994. *Light in the Darkness: African Americans and the YMCA, 1852–1946.* Lexington: University Press of Kentucky.
Putney, Clifford. 1997. "From Character to Body Building: The YMCA and the Suburban Metropolis, 1950–1980." Pp. 231–249 in *Men and Women Adrift: The YMCA and YWCA in the City.* Edited by Nina Mjagkij and Margaret Spratt. New York: New York University Press.
Zald, Mayer N. 1970. *Organizational Change: The Political Economy of the YMCA.* Chicago: University of Chicago Press.

Young Men's Hebrew Association

In 1854 in Baltimore, Maryland, a group of upper-class German Jewish immigrants established the first Young Men's Hebrew Association (YMHA), marking the beginning of that organization's crusade to promote literary, social, moral, and athletic activities for Jewish youth in the United States. In other urban areas, prominent German Jews organized YMHAs (originally named Young Men's Hebrew Literary Associations) to provide social, literary, recreational, and religious activities for Jewish young men often excluded from Protestant social clubs because of anti-Semitism. The YMHAs patterned themselves after the Young Men's Christian Association, established in the

Sabbath blessing at the nursery school of the YMHA and YWHA (Shirley Zeiberg)

United States in 1851, offering facilities for reading and recreation and to promote spiritual values for Jewish youth. Following the Civil War, the YMHA movement expanded greatly. YMHAs in late-nineteenth-century cities offered educational classes, athletics, lectures, and social programs in an effort to assimilate numerous Jewish immigrant young men and boys into American life. As the number of YMHAs increased and a national governing association emerged, plans developed to merge Young Men's Hebrew Associations and Young Women's Hebrew Associations (YWHAs), serving as the forerunner of the Jewish Community Center movement in the twentieth century.

The influx of European Jewish immigrants in the last decades of the nineteenth century prompted Jewish civic and religious leaders to build YMHAs to aid new immigrants with Americanization programs of English classes, civics, and physical education and sports within a Jewish environment. By 1900 about 100 Jewish YMHAs were in the United States, serving German Jews and newer European immigrants and their children. The organization of the New York City YMHA in 1874—the 92nd Street YMHA still in existence—and the Philadelphia YMHA in 1875 initiated the growth of "Jewish Ys" and expanded programs for young men and boys. YMHAs in cities like New York, Philadelphia, Louisville, and New Orleans developed permanent facilities attracting new members and advancing athletics for young men. Many YMHAs expanded from rooms for libraries and social clubs to include gymnasiums, swimming pools, bowling alleys, billiard rooms, and other recreational facilities. The New York YMHA provided gymnasium equipment in 1875 and then opened a full gymnasium in 1877 to serve the athletic interests of young men and boys. By integrating physical fitness with spiritual values, YMHAs wanted to promote "muscular Judaism," like the "muscular Christianity" for Protestant male youth encouraged by the Young Men's Christian Association, and encouraged athletics and religion to counter stereotypes of Jews as weak. By 1910 more than 100 YMHAs existed with a membership of 20,000, and other YMHAs formed to serve Jewish communities.

At the Jewish Ys, however, the issue of participating in sports on the Sabbath required the attention of YMHA directors. The New York City YMHA faced the Sabbath issue by keeping the gymnasium open on the Sabbath only for "lighter exercises" and stipulating that "members were not allowed to practice on the trapeze and horizontal bars" (Rabinowitz 1948, 51). The YMHA of Louisville, organized primarily for the assistance of eastern European immigrants by well-established Jews like Isaac W. Bernheim, a Kentucky distiller and philanthropist, completed its gymnasium in 1890. Boys' and men's gymnasium classes were held on Monday, Wednesday, Friday, and Saturday; but the Saturday gymnasium schedule was in the evening from 8:00 to 9:30 P.M. to avoid religious conflicts on the Sabbath. YMHA administrators also emphasized the need to prohibit gambling and drinking by young men in the YMHA facilities.

As other YMHAs built athletic facilities, the sports programs for boys increased, and competitive teams and champions emerged from some of these Jewish Ys. Jewish young men and boys participated in basketball, boxing, swimming, wrestling, track and field, baseball, volleyball, bowling, handball, tennis, Ping-Pong, and other sports. In particular, YMHA basketball teams competed against other YMHA teams and Jewish settlements in leagues, as well as against YMCA teams, independent teams, and Amateur Athletic Union teams for various age groups; YMHA boys and young men's basketball players frequently competed in regional as well as national athletic competitions in the early to mid-1900s. The 92nd Street YMHA basketball teams gained national recognition under the guidance of their excellent physical education staff, led by outstanding basketball player and coach Nat Holman. Several YMHAs hosted competitive swimming meets sanctioned by the Amateur Athletic Union, drawing boys as both athletes and spectators.

YMHAs often sponsored outdoor summer camps for boys of various ages that focused on sporting activities and Jewish cultural life in rural settings. Some camps followed Jewish laws regarding kosher food and Sabbath observance, but others offered a Reform Judaism context as boys left urban areas for outdoor experiences. YMHA, affiliated boys' summer camps included Louisville's YMHA Camp, the 92nd Street YMHA's Surprise Lake Camp, Philadelphia YMHA's Camp Arthur, and St. Louis's "Y" Camp at the Lake of the Ozarks. Information about summer camps, as well as announcements about happenings in music, drama, debate, physical education, various clubs, and Jewish holiday celebrations for members, appeared in YMHA publications. House organs like the *Y.M.H.A. Bulletin* of the 92nd Street YMHA, the *Y Journal* of the St. Louis YMHA-YWHA, the *Chronicler* of the Louisville YMHA, and the *Criterion* of the Paterson, New Jersey, YMHA-YWHA publicized the boys' athletic results and physical education and social programs.

Jewish population centers changed in several cities in the first decades of the twentieth century, as Jews relocated from old ethnic centers to other parts of the same cities or to other cities, and YMHAs responded by reorganizing and relocating to reach Jewish youth. To facilitate cooperation and advice between YMHAs and YWHAs, in 1921 the National Jewish Welfare Board (JWB) was organized. The JWB became the national governing body for YMHAs and YWHAs and the National Council of Young Men's Hebrew and Kindred Associations founded in 1913. The JWB actively promoted the merger of YMHAs and YWHAs and sought to develop them into Jewish Community Centers (JCCs) by the mid-twentieth century, thus combining Jewish and American cultural interests. For example, the Baltimore YMHA-YWHA, built in 1930, brought together the city's Jewish community in a new facility for religious, educational, athletic, and social activities. A national campaign to improve Jewish community life for Americans of all social classes and religious backgrounds prompted staff of the JWB to work with local communities desiring to renovate YMHAs-YWHAs or build new JCCs. Throughout the United States today, JCCs offer an array of educational classes, lectures, concerts, Jewish holiday celebrations, sports, and recreational activities for Jewish youth.

Linda J. Borish

See also Basketball; Camping; Young Men's Christian Association

References and further reading
Borish, Linda J. 1996. "National Jewish Welfare Board Archives, Young Men's–Young Women's Hebrew Association Records: A Research Guide." Archives and Manuscript Collections, American Jewish Historical Society, Waltham, MA, and New York, NY, November, 1–16.

———. 1999. "'An Interest in Physical Well-Being among the Feminine Membership': Sporting Activities for Women at Young Men's and Young Women's Hebrew Associations." *American Jewish History* 87, no. 1 (March): 61–93.

Kirsch, George B. 2000. "Young Men's Hebrew Association." Pp. 501–502 in *Encyclopedia of Ethnicity and Sports in the United States.* Edited by George B. Kirsch, Othello Harris, and Claire E. Nolte. Westport, CT: Greenwood Press.

Kraft, Louis. 1941. "Center, The Jewish." In *The Universal Jewish Encyclopedia.* Edited by Isaac Landman.

Langfeld, William. 1928. *The Young Men's Hebrew Association of Philadelphia: A Fifty-Year Chronicle.* Philadelphia: Young Men's and Young Women's Hebrew Association of Philadelphia.

Levine, Peter. 1992. *Ellis Island to Ebbets Field: Sport and the American Jewish Experience.* New York: Oxford University Press.

Rabinowitz, Benjamin. 1948. *The Young Men's Hebrew Association (1854–1913).* New York: National Jewish Welfare Board.

Riess, Steven A., ed. 1998. *Sports and the American Jew.* Syracuse: Syracuse University Press.

BIBLIOGRAPHY

Abbott, Douglas A., and Gene H. Brody. 1985. "The Relation of Child Age, Gender, and Number of Children to the Marital Adjustment of Wives." *Journal of Marriage and the Family* 47: 77–84.

Abel, Ernest. 1977. *The Handwriting on the Wall: Toward a Sociology and Psychology of Graffiti.* Westport, CT: Greenwood Press.

Accessibility of Firearms and the Use of Firearms by or against Juveniles. 2000. Washington, DC: Office of Juvenile Justice and Delinquency Prevention, U.S. Department of Justice.

Achatz, Mary, and Crystal A. MacAllum. 1994. *Young Unwed Fathers: Report from the Field.* Philadelphia: Public/Private Ventures.

Acker, Joan. 1987. "Sex Bias in Job Evaluation: A Comparable Worth Issue." In *Ingredients for Women's Employment Policy.* Edited by C. Bose and G. Spitze. Albany: SUNY Press.

———. 1988. "Class, Gender and the Relations of Distribution." *Signs: Journal of Women in Culture and Society* 13.

———. 1989. *Doing Comparable Worth: Gender, Class and Pay Equity.* Philadelphia: Temple University Press.

———. 1990. "Hierarchies, Jobs, Bodies: A Theory of Gendered Organizations." *Gender and Society* 4, no. 2.

Acker, Joan, and Donald R. Van Houten. 1974. "Differential Recruitment and Control: The Sex Structuring of Organizations." *Administrative Science Quarterly* 19, no. 2.

Adams, Judith. 1991. *The American Amusement Park Industry. A History of Technology and Thrills.* Boston, MA: Twayne Publishers.

Adelman, Melvin L. 1986. *A Sporting Time: New York City and the Rise of Modern Athletics, 1820–1870.* Urbana: University of Illinois Press.

Adler, Naomi A., and Joseph Schutz. 1995. "Sibling Incest Offenders." *Child Abuse and Neglect* 19: 811–819.

Ahmed, Yvette, and Peter K. Smith. 1994. "Bullying in Schools and the Issue of Sex Differences." Pp. 70–83 in *Male Violence.* Edited by John Archer. New York: Routledge.

Ahrons, Constance, and Richard B. Miller. 1993. "The Effect of the Postdivorce Relationship on Parental Involvement: A Longitudinal Analysis." *American Journal of Orthopsychiatry* 63, no. 3: 441–450.

Alan Guttmacher Institute. 1994. *Sex and America's Teenagers*. New York: Alan Guttmacher Institute.

———. 1999. *Facts in Brief: Teen Sex and Pregnancy*. New York: Alan Guttmacher Institute.

Alexander, Lloyd. 1968. *The High King*. New York: Bantam Doubleday Dell.

Alger, Horatio. 1872. *Phil the Fiddler; or, the Story of a Young Street Musician*. New York: Federal Book Company.

———. 1973. *Silas Snobden's Office Boy*. 1889–1890. Reprint, Garden City, NY: Doubleday.

———. 1985. *Ragged Dick; or, Street Life in New York*. 1867. Reprinted in *Ragged Dick and Struggling Upward*. New York: Penguin.

Allen, E. John B. 1993. *From Skisport to Skiing: One Hundred Years of American Sport, 1849–1940*. Amherst: University of Massachusetts Press.

Allen, Gay Wilson. 1981. *Waldo Emerson: A Biography*. New York: Viking.

Allen, Sarah M., and Alan J. Hawkins. 1999. "Maternal Gatekeeping: Mothers' Beliefs and Behaviors That Inhibit Greater Father Involvement in Family Work." *Journal of Marriage and the Family* 61: 199–212.

American Association of Orthodontists. 2001. "Orthodontics Online," http://www.aaortho.org/ (accessed in March).

American Camping Association. 1998. *Accreditation Standards for Camp Programs and Services*. Martinsville, IN: ACA.

———. 1999. *Guide to ACA-Accredited Camps*. Martinsville, IN: ACA.

———. 2000. "ACA Fact Sheet," http://www.acacamps.org/media (accessed June 25).

American Sunday School Union. 1825–1830. *Annual Reports*. Philadelphia: American Sunday School Union.

———. Committee of Publications. 1827. *Election Day*. Philadelphia: American Sunday School Union.

Amsel, Eric, and J. David Smalley. 1999. "Beyond Really and Truly: Children's Counterfactual Thinking about Pretend and Possible Worlds." Pp. 99–134 in *Children's Reasoning and the Mind*. Edited by K. Riggs and P. Mitchell. Brighton, UK: Psychology Press.

Anderson, James D. 1988. *The Education of Blacks in the South, 1860–1935*. Chapel Hill: University of North Carolina Press.

Anderson, Kristen. 1997. "Gender Bias and Special Education Referrals." *Annals of Dyslexia* 47: 151–162.

Anderson, Nels, and Raffaele Rauty. 1998. *On Hobos and Homelessness*. Chicago: University of Chicago Press.

Andrews, Dee E. 2000. *The Methodists and Revolutionary America*. Princeton, NJ: Princeton University Press.

Ang, Ien, and Joke Hermes. 1991. "Gender and/in Media Consumption." In *Mass Media and Society*. Edited by James Curran and Michael Gurevitch. New York: Routledge.

Anonymous. 1724. *Onania; or the Heinous Sin of Pollution, and All Its Frightful Consequences, in Both Sexes, Considered*. 10th ed. Boston: John Phillips.

Anson, J. L., and Robert F. Marchesani, Jr., eds. 1991. *Baird's Manual of American College Fraternities*. 20th ed. Indianapolis: Baird's Manual Foundation.

Anthony, Michael J. 2000. *Foundations of Ministry: An Introduction to Christian Education for a New Generation*. Grand Rapids, MI: Baker Books.

Anti-Slavery Melodies: For the Friends of Freedom; Prepared by the Hingham Anti-Slavery Society. 1843. Hingham: Elijah B. Gill.

Appleby, Joyce. 2000. *Inheriting the Revolution.* Cambridge: Harvard University Press.

Appleton's Elementary Geography. 1908. New York: American Book Company.

Aptheker, Herbert, ed. 1997. *The Correspondence of W. E. B. Du Bois.* Vol. 1, *Selections 1877–1934.* Amherst: University of Massachusetts Press.

"Are Newspapers Taking Advantage of Child Labor?" 1988. *Stark Metropolitan Magazine* (April): 8–10.

Aries, Philippe. 1962. *Centuries of Childhood: A Social History of Family Life.* Translated by Robert Baldick. New York: Vintage.

Arnett, Jeffrey J. 2000. "Emerging Adulthood: A Theory of Development from the Late Teens through the Twenties." *American Psychologist* 55: 469–480.

Ascione, Frank, and Phil Arkow, eds. 1998. *Child Abuse, Domestic Violence and Animal Abuse.* West Lafayette, IA: Purdue University Press.

Ashby, LeRoy. 1973. *Silas Snobden's Office Boy.* 1889–1890. Reprint, Garden City, NY: Doubleday.

———. 1983. *Saving the Waifs: Reformers and Dependent Children, 1890–1917.* Philadelphia: Temple University Press.

———. 1997. *Endangered Children: Dependency, Neglect, and Abuse in American History.* New York: Twayne Publishers.

Ashe, Arthur, with Alexander McNabb. 1995. *Arthur Ashe on Tennis.* New York: Alfred A. Knopf.

Ashe, Arthur, and Arnold Rampersad. 1993. *Days of Grace.* New York: Alfred A. Knopf.

Astin, W. A. 1977. *Four Critical Years: Effects of College on Beliefs, Attitudes, and Knowledge.* San Francisco: Jossey-Bass.

AtariWorld.com. "The Atari Timeline," http://www.atariworld.com/AtariTimeline.html (accessed December 27, 2000).

Athens, Lonnie. 1989. *The Creation of Dangerous Violent Criminals.* London: Routledge.

———. 1992. *The Creation of Dangerous Violent Criminals.* Urbana: University of Illinois Press.

———. 1997. *Violent Criminal Acts and Actors Revisited.* Urbana: University of Illinois Press.

———. 1998. "Dominance, Ghettoes, and Violent Crime." *Sociological Quarterly* 39 (Fall): 673–691.

Athletic Sports for Boys: A Repository of Graceful Recreations for Youth. 1866. New York: Dick and Fitzgerald.

Atlas, Rona, and Debra Pepler. 1998. "Observations of Bullying in the Classroom." *Journal of Educational Research* 92: 1–86.

Atwater, Montgomery M. 1943. *Ski Patrol.* New York: Random House.

Austin, Joe. 2001. *Taking the Train: Youth, Urban Crisis, Graffiti.* New York: Columbia University Press.

Avery, Gillian. 1975. *Childhood's Pattern: A Study of Heroes and Heroines of Children's Fiction, 1750–1950.* London: Hodder and Stoughton.

———. 1994. *Behold the Child: American Children and Their Books 1621–1922.* Baltimore: Johns Hopkins University Press.

Avrich, Paul. 1980. *The Modern School Movement: Anarchism and Education in the United States.* Princeton: Princeton University Press.

Axtell, James, ed. 1981. *The Indian Peoples of Eastern America: A Documentary History of the Sexes.* New York: Oxford University Press.

Ayers, William. 1997. *A Kind and Just Parent: The Children of Juvenile Court.* Boston: Beacon Press.

Aykesworth, Thomas. 1987. *Hollywood Kids: Child Stars of the Silver Screen from 1903 to the Present.* New York: Dutton.

Babbit, Nicki. 2000. *Adolescent Drug and Alcohol Abuse: How to Spot It, Stop It, and Get Help for Your Family.* Sebastopol, CA: O'Reilly.

Badger, Anthony. 1989. *The New Deal: The Depression Years, 1933–1940.* New York: Noonday Press.

Bagnall, William. 1893. *The Textile Industries of the United States.* Cambridge: Riverside Press.

Bailey, Anthony. 1980. *America, Lost and Found.* New York: Random House.

Bailey, Beth L. 1988. *From Front Porch to Back Seat.* Baltimore: Johns Hopkins University Press.

Baird, Leonard L. 1977. *The Schools: A Profile of Prestigious Independent Schools.* Lexington, MA: D. C. Heath.

Baker, Karen (external relations, Boy Scouts of America). 2000. Telephone conversation, May 30.

Baldwin, Henry Ives. 1989. *The Skiing Life.* Concord, NH: Evans Printing.

Ball, Charles. 1969. *Slavery in the United States.* 1837. Reprint, New York: Negro Universities Press.

Bancroft, Hubert Howe. 1888. *California Inter Pocula.* San Francisco: History Company.

Bardaglio, Peter W. 1992. "The Children of Jubilee: African American Childhood in Wartime." Pp. 213–229 in *Divided Houses: Gender and the Civil War.* Edited by Catherine Clinton and Nina Silber. New York: Oxford University Press.

Barish, Evelyn. 1989. *Emerson: The Roots of Prophecy.* Princeton: Princeton University Press.

Barker, David. 2000. "Television Production Techniques as Communication." In *Television: The Critical View.* 6th ed. Edited by Horace Newcomb. New York: Oxford University Press.

Barnett, James. 1954. *The American Christmas: A Study in National Culture.* New York: Macmillan.

Barnouw, Erik. 1978. *The Sponsor: Notes on a Modern Potentate.* New York: Oxford University Press.

———. 1990. *Tube of Plenty: The Evolution of American Television.* 2d rev. ed. Oxford: Oxford University Press.

Barson, Michael. 1985. "The TV Western." Pp. 57–72 in *TV Genres: A Handbook and Reference Guide.* Edited by Brian G. Rose. Westport, CT: Greenwood Press.

Barth, Richard P., Mark Claycomb, and Amy Loomis. 1988. "Services to Adolescent Fathers." *Health and Social Work* 13: 277–287.

Barton, Bruce. 1925. *The Man Nobody Knows: A Discovery of the Real Jesus.* Indianapolis: Bobbs-Merrill.

Baruch, Dorothy W. 1942. *You, Your Children and War.* New York: D. Appleton-Century Company.

Bass, Ellen, and Kate Kaufman. 1996. *Free Your Mind: The Book for Gay, Lesbian, and Bisexual Youth—and Their Allies.* New York: HarperCollins.

Batchelor, Dean. 1995. *The American Hot Rod.* Osceola, WI: Motorbooks International.

Bateson, Gregory. 1972. "A Theory of Play and Fantasy." Pp. 177–193 in *Steps to an Ecology of Mind.* New York: Ballantine.

Baur, John E. 1978. *Growing Up with California: A History of California's Children.* Los Angeles: Will Kramer.

Beach, E. P. 1888. "A Day in the Life of a Newsboy." *Harper's Young People* 9 (January 17): 202.

Beal, C. R. 1994. *Boys and Girls: The Development of Gender Roles.* New York: McGraw-Hill.

Beckman, Frank J. 1962. "The Vanished Villains: An Exercise in Nostalgia." Unpublished manuscript, Billy Rose Theater Collection, New York Public Library at Lincoln Center.

Bedard, Roger L., ed. 1984. *Dramatic Literature for Children: A Century in Review.* New Orleans, LA: Anchorage Press.

Bedard, Roger L., and C. John Tolch, eds. 1989. *Spotlight on the Child: Studies in the History of American Children's Theatre.* Westport, CT: Greenwood Press.

Bederman, Gail. 1989. "'The Women Have Had Charge of the Church Work Long Enough': The Men and Religion Forward Movement of 1911–1912 and the Masculinization of Middle-Class Protestantism." *American Quarterly* 41, no. 3 (September): 432–465.

———. 1995. *Manliness and Civilization: A Cultural History of Gender and Race in the United States, 1880–1917.* Chicago: University of Chicago Press.

Behr, Edward. 1996. *Prohibition.* New York: Arcade.

Beisel, Nicola. 1997. *Imperiled Innocents: Anthony Comstock and Family Reproduction in Victorian America.* Princeton: Princeton University Press.

Beiswinger, George L. 1985. *One to One: The Story of the Big Brothers/Big Sisters Movement in America.* Philadelphia: Big Brothers/Big Sisters of America.

Belk, Russell. 1987. "A Child's Christmas in America: Santa Claus as Deity, Consumption as Religion." *Journal of American Culture* 10, no. 1: 87–100.

———. 1990. "Halloween: An Evolving American Consumption Ritual." In *Advances in Consumer Research.* Vol. 17. Edited by M. Goldberg, Gerald Gorn, and Richard Pollay. Chicago: University of Chicago Press.

Bellesiles, Michael A. 2000. *Arming America: The Origins of the National Gun Culture.* New York: Alfred A. Knopf.

Bellingham, Bruce. 1984. "'Little Wanderers': A Socio-Historical Study of the Nineteenth Century Origins of Child Fostering and Adoption Reform, Based on Early Records of the New York Children's Aid Society." Ph.D. diss., University of Pennsylvania.

Bendroth, Margaret Lamberts. 1997. "Men, Masculinity, and Urban Revivalism: J. Wilbur Chapman's Boston Crusade." *Journal of Presbyterian History* 75, no. 4 (Winter): 235–246.

Beneke, Timothy. 1997. *Proving Manhood: Reflections on Men and Sexism.* Berkeley: University of California Press.

Bennahum, David S. 1998. *Extra Life: Coming of Age in Cyberspace.* New York: Basic Books.

Bennett, Paula, and Vernon A. Rosario II, eds. 1995. *Solitary Pleasures: The Historical, Literary, and Artistic Discourses of Autoeroticism.* New York: Routledge.

Bennett, William, John DiIulio, and John Waters. 1996. *Body Count: Moral Poverty—and How to Win America's War against Crime and Drugs.* New York: Simon and Schuster.

Benshoff, Harry M. 1997. *Monsters in the Closet: Homosexuality and the Horror Film.* Manchester: Manchester University Press.

Benston, M. L. 1985. "The Myth of Computer Literacy." *Canadian Women's Studies* 5: 20–22.

Berch, B. 1984. "For Women the Chips Are Down." *Processed World* 11, no. 2: 42–46.

Bergman, Andrew. 1971. *We're in the Money: Depression America and Its Films.* New York: New York University Press.

Bernstein, Irving. 1985. *A Caring Society: The New Deal, the Worker, and the Great Depression.* Boston: Houghton Mifflin.

Bernstein, Rhona J. 1996. *Attack of the Leading Ladies: Gender, Sexuality and Spectatorship in Classic Horror Cinema.* New York: Columbia University Press.

Berrol, Selma C. 1995. *Growing Up American: Immigrant Children in America Then and Now.* New York: Twayne.

Berryman, Jack W. 1975. "From the Cradle to the Playing Field: America's Emphasis on Highly Organized Competitive Sports for Preadolescent Boys." *Journal of Sport History* (Fall): 112–131.

Best, Joel. 1985. "The Myth of the Halloween Sadist." *Psychology Today* 19: 14–19.

Best, Joel, and Gerald Horiuchi. 1985. "The Razor Blades in the Apple: The Social Construction of Urban Legends." *Social Problems* 32: 488–499.

Bettelheim, Bruno. 1976. *The Uses of Enchantment: The Meaning and Importance of Fairy Tales.* New York: Alfred A. Knopf.

Betts, John R. 1974. *America's Sporting Heritage: 1850–1950.* Reading, MA: Addison-Wesley.

Bezilla, Robert, ed. 1988. *America's Youth: 1977–1988.* Princeton, NJ: Gallup.

Bigelow, Jim. 1994. *The Joy of Uncircumcising! Exploring Circumcision: History, Myths, Psychology, Restoration, Sexual Pleasure and Human Rights.* 2d ed. Aptos, CA: Hourglass Books.

Biller, H. B. 1981. "Father Absence, Divorce, and Personality Development." In *The Role of the Father in Child Development.* 2d ed. Edited by M. E. Lamb. New York: John Wiley.

Bissinger, H. G. 1990. *Friday Night Lights: A Town, a Team, a Dream.* Reading, MA: Addison-Wesley.

Blacher, Jan. 1994. *When There's No Place Like Home: Options for Children Living Apart from Their Natural Families.* Baltimore: P. H. Brookes Publishers.

Blake, Peter. 1973. "The Lessons of the Parks." *Architectural Forum* (June): 28ff.

Blankenhorn, David. 1995. *Fatherless America: Confronting Our Most Urgent Social Problem.* New York: Basic Books.

Bliven, Bruce. 1968. "A Prairie Boyhood." *The Palimpsest* 49, no. 8: 308–352.

Block, Carolyn Rebecca, Antigone Christakos, and R. Przybylski. 1996. "Street Gangs and Crime: Patterns and Trends in Chicago." *Research Bulletin.*

Chicago: Criminal Justice Information Authority.

Block, Jeanne H., Jack Block, and Per F. Gjerde. 1986. "The Personality of Children Prior to Divorce: A Prospective Study." *Child Development* 57, no. 4: 827–840.

———. 1988. "Parental Functioning and the Home Environment in Families of Divorce: Prospective and Concurrent Analyses." *Journal of the American Academy of Child and Adolescent Psychiatry* 27: 207–213.

Bloom, John. 1997. *A House of Cards: Baseball Card Collecting and Popular Culture.* Minneapolis: University of Minnesota Press.

Blumer, Herbert. 1997. "Foreword." Pp. 3–6 in *Violent Criminal Acts and Actors Revisited* by Lonnie Athens. Urbana: University of Illinois Press.

Bock, Richard, and Abigail English. 1973. *Got Me on the Run: A Study of Runaways.* Boston: Beacon Press.

Boddy, William. 1990. *Fifties Television: The Industry and Its Critics.* Chicago: University of Illinois Press.

Boles, John B. 1972. *The Great Revival, 1787–1805: The Origins of the Southern Evangelical Mind.* Lexington: University of Kentucky Press.

Books, Sue, ed. 1998. *Invisible Children in the Society and Its Schools.* Mahwah, NJ: Erlbaum.

Borish, Linda J. 1987. "The Robust Woman and the Muscular Christian: Catharine Beecher, Thomas Higginson and Their Vision of American Society, Health, and Physical Activities." *International Journal of the History of Sport:* 139–154.

———. 1996. "National Jewish Welfare Board Archives, Young Men's–Young Women's Hebrew Association Records: A Research Guide." Archives and Manuscript Collections, American Jewish Historical Society, Waltham, MA, and New York, NY, November, 1–16.

———. 1999. "'An Interest in Physical Well-Being among the Feminine Membership': Sporting Activities for Women at Young Men's and Young Women's Hebrew Associations." *American Jewish History* 87, no. 1 (March): 61–93.

———. Forthcoming. *Landmarks of American Sports.* American Landmarks Series. Edited by James O. Horton. New York: Oxford University Press.

Bose, Michael. 1987. "Boys Town: New Ways but Respect for the Past." *U.S. News and World Report,* March 20: 38–39.

Boston Temperance Songster: A Collection of Songs and Hymns for Temperance Societies, Original and Selected. 1844. Boston: William White.

Bosworth, Kris, Dorothy L. Espelage, and Thomas R. Simon. 1999. "Factors Associated with Bullying Behavior in Middle School Students." *Journal of Early Adolescence* 19: 341–362.

Boy Scouts of America. 1998. "Annual Report," http://www.scouting.org/excomm/98annual/yir1998.html (accessed May 28, 2000).

———. 1999. "1999 Annual Report," http://bsa.scouting.org/nav/pub/news.html (accessed May 14, 2001).

Boyd, Billy Ray. 1998. *Circumcision Exposed: Rethinking a Medical and Cultural Tradition.* Freedom, CA: Crossing Press.

Boyd, Brendan, and Frederick Harris. 1973. *The Great American Baseball Card Flipping, Trading, and Bubble Gum Book.* New York: Warner Paperbacks.

Boyer, Paul. 1978. *Urban Masses and Moral Order in America, 1820–1920.* Cambridge: Harvard University Press.

Boylan, Anne M. 1988. *Sunday School: The Foundation of an American Institution, 1790–1880.* New Haven: Yale University Press.

Boys and Girls Clubs of America. 2000. "Who We Are: The Facts," http://www. bgca.org/whoweare/facts.asp (accessed May 14, 2001).

Brace, Charles Loring. 1872. *The Dangerous Classes of New York and Twenty Years' Work among Them.* New York: Wynkoop and Hallenbeck.

Bragg, George W. 1999. *The Big Book.* Privately published. Cf. http://216.147. 109.215/bragg.html (accessed March 11, 2001).

Braine, Marty, and David O'Brien. 1947. *Mental Logic.* Mahwah, NJ: Lawrence Erlbaum.

Braithewaite, Richard Bevan. 1953. *Scientific Explanation: A Study of the Function of Theory, Probability and Law in Science.* Cambridge, UK: Cambridge University Press.

Brands, H. W. 1997. *T. R.: The Last Romantic.* New York: Basic Books.

Brandt, Allan M. 1985. *No Magic Bullet: A Social History of Venereal Disease in the United States since 1880.* New York: Oxford University Press.

Brauer, Ralph. 1975. *The Horse, the Gun, and the Piece of Property: Changing Images of the TV Western.* Bowling Green: Popular Press.

Brave Boys: New England Traditions in Folk Music. 1995. New World Records.

Breen, T. H., and Stephen Innes. 1980. *"Myne Owne Ground": Race and Freedom on Virginia's Eastern Shore,* 1640–1676. New York: Oxford University Press.

Brevada, William. 1986. *Harry Kemp, the Last Bohemian.* Lewisburg, PA: Bucknell University Press.

Brewer, John. 1997. *The Pleasures of the Imagination: English Culture in the Eighteenth Century.* New York: Farrar, Straus and Giroux.

Bristow, Nancy K. 1996. *Making Men Moral: Social Engineering during the Great War.* New York: New York University Press.

Brockett, Oscar G., and Frank Hildy. 1999. *History of the Theatre.* 8th ed. Boston: Allyn and Bacon.

Brody, C. J., and L. C. Steelman. 1985. "Sibling Structure and Parental Sex-Typing of Children's Household Tasks." *Journal of Marriage and the Family* 47: 265–273.

Brody, Gene H., Zolinda Stoneman, and Carol MacKinnon. 1986. "Contributions of Maternal Child-rearing Practices and Interactional Contexts to Sibling Interactions." *Journal of Applied Developmental Psychology* 7: 225–236.

Brody, Gene H., Zolinda Stoneman, and J. Kelly McCoy. 1992. "Parental Differential Treatment of Siblings and Sibling Differences in Negative Emotionality." *Journal of Marriage and the Family* 54: 643–651.

Bronner, Simon J. 1988. *American Children's Folklore.* Little Rock, AR: August House.

Brooke, Michael. 1999. *The Concrete Wave: The History of Skateboarding.* Toronto, Ont.: Warwick.

Brooks, Tim, and Earle Marsh. 1979. *The Complete Directory to Prime Time Network TV Shows 1946–Present.* New York: Ballantine.

Brown, Sally. 1990. *If the Shoes Fit: Final Report and Program Implementation Guide of the Maine Young Fathers Project.* Portland: Human Services Development Institute, University of Southern Maine.

Browne, J., and V. Minichiello. 1995. "The Social Meanings behind Male Sex Work: Implications for Sexual Interactions." *British Journal of Sociology* 46, no. 4: 598–622.

———. 1996. "The Social and Work Context of Commercial Sex between Men: A Research Note." *Australian and New Zealand Journal of Sociology* 32, no. 1: 86–92.

Browne, Porter Emerson. 1909. "The Mellowdrammer." *Everybody's Magazine* (September): 347–354.

Browning, Don, ed. 1997. *From Culture Wars to Common Ground: Religion and the American Family Debate.* Louisville: Westminister/John Knox.

Bruegman, Bill. 1992. *Toys of the Sixties.* Akron, OH: Cap'n Penny Productions.

Brumberg, Joan J. 1997. *The Body Project: An Intimate History of American Girls.* New York: Random House.

Bryant, Brenda. 1990. "The Richness of the Child-Pet Relationship." *Anthrozoös* 3, no. 4: 253–261.

Bryant, Jennings. 1985. Testimony to the Attorney General's Commission on Pornography Hearings. Houston, Texas.

Bryk, Anthony, and Valerie Lee. 1986. "Effects of Single Sex Secondary Schools on Student Achievement and Attitudes." *Journal of Educational Psychology* 78.

Buckingham, David. 1993. *Children Talking Television: The Making of Television Literacy.* London: Falmer Press.

Buhle, Mari Jo, Paul Buhle, and Dan Georgakas, eds. "Contributions of Family Relationships and Child Temperaments to Longitudinal Variations in Sibling Relationship Quality and Sibling Relationship Styles." *Journal of Family Psychology* 8: 274–286.

———. 1994. 1998. *Encyclopedia of the American Left.* 2d ed. New York: Oxford University Press.

Buhrmester, Duane, and Wyndol Furman. 1990. "Perceptions of Sibling Relationships during Middle Childhood and Adolescence." *Child Development* 61: 1387–1398.

Bulkley, L. Duncan. 1894. *Syphilis in the Innocent (Syphilis Insontium) Clinically and Historically Considered with a Plan for the Legal Control of the Disease.* New York: Bailey and Fairchild.

Bullough, Vern L. 1976. *Sexual Variance in Society and History.* Chicago: University of Chicago Press.

Bureau of the Census. 1965. *The Statistical History of the United States.* Washington, DC: Government Printing Office.

Burge, Penny L., and Steven M. Culver. 1994. "Gender Equity and Empowerment in Vocational Education." Pp. 51–63 in *Critical Education for Work: Multidisciplinary Approaches.* Edited by Richard D. Lakes. Norwood, NJ: Ablex.

Burger, Jim. 1976. *In Service: A Documentary History of the Baltimore City Fire Department.* Baltimore: Paradigm Books.

Burnham, John. 1993. *Bad Habits: Drinking, Smoking, Taking Drugs, Gambling, Sexual Misbehavior, and Swearing in American History.* New York: New York University Press.

Burstyn, Varda. 1999. *The Rites of Men: Manhood, Politics, and the Culture of Sport.* Toronto: University of Toronto Press.

Burton, Linda M., Peggy Dilworth-Anderson, and Cynthia Merriwether–de Vries. 1995. "Context and Surrogate Parenting among Contemporary Grandparents." *Marriage and Family Review* 20: 349–366.

Buscombe, Edward. 1988. *The BFI Companion to the Western*. New York: Da Capo Press.

Buscombe, Edward, and Roberta E. Pearson. 1998. *Back in the Saddle Again: New Essays on the Western*. London: BFI Press.

Bushman, Richard. 1992. *The Refinement of America: Persons, Houses, Cities*. New York: Alfred A. Knopf.

Butterfield, Lyman H., ed. 1961. *The Adams Papers: Diary and Autobiography of John Adams*. Cambridge, MA: Belknap Press of Harvard University Press.

———. 1966. *The Earliest Diary of John Adams: June 1753–April 1754, September 1758–January 1759*. Cambridge, MA: Belknap Press of Harvard University Press.

Bybee, Rodger W., and E. Gordon Gee. 1982. *Violence, Values, and Justice in the Schools*. Boston: Allyn and Bacon.

Cabot, James Elliot. 1887. *A Memoir of Ralph Waldo Emerson*. 2 vols. Boston: Houghton Mifflin.

Caillois, Roger. 1979. *Man, Play, and Games*. Translated by Meyer Barash. New York: Schocken Books.

Calvert, Karin. 1992. *Children in the House: The Material Culture of Early Childhood, 1600–1900*. Boston: Northeastern University Press.

Camara, K., and G. Resnick. 1989. "Styles of Conflict Resolution and Cooperation between Divorced Parents: Effects on Child Behavior and Adjustment." *American Journal of Orthopsychiatry* 59, no. 4: 560–575.

Cameron, Ian, and Douglas Pye. 1996. *The Book of Westerns*. New York: Continuum.

"Camping Then and Now." 1999. *Camping Magazine* 72 (November–December): 18–31.

Canada, G. 1998. *Reaching Up for Manhood: Transforming the Lives of Boys in America*. Boston: Beacon Press.

Canetto, Silvia Sara. 1997a. "Meanings of Gender and Suicidal Behavior among Adolescents." *Suicide and Life-Threatening Behaviors* 27: 339–351.

———. 1997b. "Gender and Suicidal Behavior: Theories and Evidence." Pp. 138–167 in *Review of Suicidology*. Edited by R. W. Maris, M. M. Silverman, and Canetto. New York: Guilford.

Canetto, Silvia Sara, and David Lester. 1995. "Gender and the Primary Prevention of Suicide Mortality." *Suicide and Life-Threatening Behavior* 25: 58–69.

Canetto, Silvia Sara, and Isaac Sakinofsky. 1998. "The Gender Paradox in Suicide." *Suicide and Life-Threatening Behavior* 28: 1–23.

Cannon, Donald J. 1977. *Heritage of Flames*. New York: Doubleday.

Caplow, Theodore. 1984. "Rule Enforcement without Visible Means." *American Journal of Sociology* 89, no. 6: 1306–1323.

Caplow, Theodore, Howard Bahr, and Bruce Chadwick. 1983. *All Faithful People: Change and Continuity in Middletown's Religion*. Minneapolis: University of Minnesota Press.

Cappon, Lester J., ed. 1959. *The Adams-Jefferson Letters*. Chapel Hill: University of North Carolina Press.

Carey, Susan. 1985. *Conceptual Change in Childhood.* Cambridge, MA: MIT Press.

Carlson, Eve B. 1984. "Children's Observations of Interparental Violence." In *Battered Women and Their Families.* Edited by A. R. Roberts. New York: Springer Publishing.

Carnegie Council on Adolescent Development, Task Force on Youth Development and Community Programs. 1992. *A Matter of Time: Risk and Opportunity in the Nonschool Hours.* New York: Carnegie Corporation of New York.

Carp, E. Wayne. 1998. *Family Matters: Secrecy and Adoption in the History of Adoption.* Cambridge, MA: Harvard University Press.

Carp, E. Wayne, ed. 2001. *Historical Perspectives on American Adoption.* Ann Arbor: University of Michigan Press.

Carr, Lois Green, and Russell R. Menard. 1979. "Immigration and Opportunity: The Freedman in Early Colonial Maryland." Pp. 206–242 in *The Chesapeake in the Seventeenth Century.* Edited by Thad W. Tate and David L. Ammerman. New York: W. W. Norton.

Carr, Lois Green, and Lorena S. Walsh. 1979. "The Planter's Wife: The Experience of White Women in Seventeenth-Century Maryland." In *A Heritage of Her Own: Toward a New Social History of American Women.* Edited by Nancy F. Cott and Elizabeth H. Pleck. New York: Simon and Schuster.

Carr, Lois Green, Russell R. Menard, and Lorena S. Walsh. 1991. *Robert Cole's World: Agriculture and Society in Early Maryland.* Chapel Hill: University of North Carolina Press.

Carrier, James. 1986. *Learning Disability: Social Class and the Construction of Inequality in American Education.* Westport, CT: Greenwood Press.

Carroll, James D., et al. 1987. *We the People: A Review of U.S. Government and Civics Textbooks.* Washington, DC: People for the American Way.

Carson, Cary, Ronald Hoffman, and Peter J. Albert, eds. 1994. *Of Consuming Interests: The Style of Life in the Eighteenth Century.* Charlottesville: University Press of Virginia.

Carter, Patricia A. 1994. "Women's Workplace Equity: A Feminist View." Pp. 67–81 in *Critical Education for Work: Multidisciplinary Approaches.* Edited by Richard D. Lakes. Norwood, NJ: Ablex.

Cartmill, Matt. 1993. *A View to a Death in the Morning: Hunting and Nature through History.* Cambridge, MA: Harvard University Press.

Cartwright, Peter. 1856. *The Autobiography of Peter Cartwright, the Backwoods Preacher.* Edited by W. P. Strickland. Cincinnati: L. Swormstedt and A. Poe.

Cary, Diana Serra. 1979. *Hollywood's Children: An Inside Account of the Child Star Era.* Boston: Houghton Mifflin.

Case, Carl. 1906. *The Masculine in Religion.* Philadelphia: American Baptist Publishers Society.

Cashin, Joan E. 1991. *A Family Venture: Men and Women on the Southern Frontier.* New York: Oxford University Press.

Casper, Lynne, and Kenneth Bryson. 1998. *Co-resident Grandparents and Their Grandchildren: Grandparent Maintained Families.* Population Division Working Paper no. 26. Washington, DC: Population Division, U.S. Bureau of the Census.

Cassorla, Albert. 1976. *The Skateboarder's Bible.* Philadelphia: Running Press.

Cassuto, Leonard. 1997. *The Inhuman Race: The Racial Grotesque in American Literature and Culture.* New York: Columbia University Press.

Catalogue of American Portraits, National Portrait Gallery, Smithsonian Institution. http://www.npg.si.edu/inf/ceros.htm (accessed March 24, 2001).

Cavallo, Dominick. 1981. *Muscles and Morals: Organized Playgrounds and Urban Reform, 1880–1920.* Philadelphia: University of Pennsylvania Press.

Cawelti, John. 1965. *Apostles of the Self-Made Man: Changing Concepts of Success in America.* Chicago: University of Chicago Press.

———. 1985. *The Six-Gun Mystique.* Rev. ed. Bowling Green: Bowling Green University Popular Press.

Cayton, Andrew R. L. 1993. "The Early National Period." Vol. 1, p. 100 in *Encyclopedia of American Social History.* Edited by Mary Kupiec Cayton, Elliott J. Gorn, and Peter W. Williams. New York: Scribner's.

Cayton, Mary Kupiec. 1989. *Emerson's Emergence.* Chapel Hill: University of North Carolina Press.

CDC (Centers for Disease Control and Prevention). 1998. "Suicide among Black Youths—United States, 1980–1995." *Journal of the American Medical Association* 279, no. 18: 1431.

———. 1999. "Division of Adolescent and School Health's Information Service Report." Silver Springs, MD: Government Printing Office.

Censer, Jane Turner. 1984. *North Carolina Planters and Their Children, 1800–1860.* Baton Rouge: Louisiana State University Press.

Chafetz, Janet. 1980. "Toward a Macro-Level Theory of Sexual Stratification." *Current Perspectives in Social Theory* 1.

Champlin, John D., Jr., and Arthur E. Bostwick. 1890. *The Young Folks' Cyclopedia of Games and Sports.* New York: Henry Holt.

Chancer, Lynn. 1998. *Reconcilable Differences: Confronting Beauty, Pornography, and the Future of Feminism.* Berkeley: University of California Press.

Chapin, John. 2000. "Third-Person Perception and Optimistic Bias among Urban-Minority 'At-Risk' Youth." *Communication Research* 27, no. 1: 51–81.

Chapman, P. D. 1988. *Schools as Sorters: Lewis M. Terman, Applied Psychology and the Intelligence Testing Movement, 1890–1930.* New York: New York University Press.

Charry, Ellen T. 2001. "Will There Be a Protestant Center?" *Theology Today* (January): 453–458.

Check, James. 1995. "Teenage Training: The Effects of Pornography on Adolescent Males." Pp. 89–91 in *The Price We Pay: The Case against Racist Speech, Hate Propaganda, and Pornography.* Edited by Laura J. Lederer and Richard Delgado. New York: Hill and Wang.

Chenery, Mary Faeth. 1991. *I Am Somebody: The Messages and Methods of Organized Camping for Youth Development.* Martinsville, IN: ACA.

Chesney-Lind, Meda, and John Hagedorn, eds. 1999. *Female Gangs in America.* Chicago: Lake View Press.

Child Welfare League of America. 1994. *Kinship Care: A Natural Bridge.* Washington, DC: Child Welfare League of America.

Children's Defense Fund. 1988. *Adolescent and Young Adult Fathers: Problems and Solutions.* Washington, DC: Children's Defense Fund.

Children's Hospital of Philadelphia. *Annual Report.* 1895.

Chodorow, Nancy. 1979. *The Reproduction of Mothering.* Berkeley: University of California Press.

Chotner, Deborah. 1992. *American Naive Paintings.* Washington, DC: National Gallery of Art.

Christensen, Clark. 1995. "Prescribed Masturbation in Sex Therapy: A Critique." *Journal of Sex and Marital Therapy* 21 (Summer): 87–99.

Christie, A. A. 1997. "Using Email within a Classroom Based on Feminist Pedagogy." *Journal of Research on Computing in Education* 30, no. 2 (December).

———. 2000. "Gender Differences in Computer Use in Adolescent Boys and Girls." Unpublished raw data.

Church, Robert, and Michael W. Sedlack. 1976. *Education in the United States: An Interpretive History.* New York: Free Press.

Circumcision Information and Resource Pages. 2001. "United States Circumcision Incidence," http://www.cirp.org/library/statistics/USA (accessed March 9, 2001).

Clapp, David. 1822–1823. "Diary." Worcester, MA: American Antiquarian Society.

Clark, Cindy Dell. 1995. *Flights of Fancy, Leaps of Faith: Children's Myths in Contemporary America.* Chicago: University of Chicago Press.

Clark, Ronald W. 1983. *Benjamin Franklin: A Biography.* New York: Random House.

Clark-Hine, Darlene, and Earnestine Jenkins, eds. 1999. *A Question of Manhood: A Reader in U.S. Black Men's History and Masculinity.* Bloomington: Indiana University Press.

Cleaveland, Agnes Morley. 1977. *No Life for a Lady.* Lincoln: University of Nebraska Press.

Clement, Priscilla Ferguson. 1997. *Growing Pains: Children in the Industrial Age, 1850–1890.* New York: Twayne Publishers.

Clemmer, E. J., and E. W. Hayes. 1979. "Patient Cooperation in Wearing Orthodontic Headgear." *American Journal of Orthodontics* 75, no. 5: 517–524.

Clinton, Catherine. 1998. *Civil War Stories.* Athens: University of Georgia Press.

Cloninger, Susan C. 2000. *Theories of Personality: Understanding Persons.* 3d ed. Upper Saddle River, NJ: Prentice-Hall.

Clover, Carol J. 1992. *Men, Women, and Chainsaws: Gender in the Modern Horror Film.* Princeton: Princeton University Press.

Cockrell, Dale, ed. 1989. *Excelsior: Journals of the Hutchinson Family Singers, 1842–1846.* New York: Pendragon Press.

Coggins, Jack. 1967. *Boys in the Revolution: Young Americans Tell Their Part in the War for Independence.* Harrisburg, PA: Stackpole Books.

Cohen, M. 1987. *Juvenile Prostitution.* Washington, DC: National Association of Counties Research.

Cohen, Patricia Cline. 1999. *The Murder of Helen Jewitt.* New York: Vintage.

Cole, Phyllis. 1998. *Mary Moody Emerson and the Origins of Transcendentalism: A Family History.* New York: Oxford University Press.

Coleman, Annie Gilbert. 1996. "The Unbearable Whiteness of Skiing." *Pacific Historical Review* 65 (November): 583–614.

Coleman, E. 1989. "The Development of Male Prostitution Activity among Gay and Bisexual Adolescents." *Journal of Homosexuality* 17, no. 2: 131–149.

Coleman, James S. 1961. *The Adolescent Society: The Social Life of the Teenager and Its Impact on America.* New York: Free Press.

Collins, Bud. 1989. *My Life with the Pros.* New York: Dutton.

Collis, B. 1987. "Psycho-social Implications of Sex Differences in Attitudes towards Computers: Results of a Survey." *International Journal of Women's Studies* 8, no. 3: 207–213.

Comics Scene 2000. 2000. New York: Starlog Group.

Committee on Injury and Poison Prevention, American Academy of Pediatrics. 1997. *Injury Prevention and Control for Children and Youth.* Edited by Mark D. Widome. Elk Grove Village, IL: American Academy of Pediatrics.

"Concerning Black Bass." 1884. *American Angler* 5, April 19.

Conde, Yvonne M. 1999. *Operation Pedro Pan: The Untold Exodus of 14,048 Cuban Children.* New York: Routledge.

Conger, Rand D., and Martha A. Reuter. 1996. "Siblings, Parents and Peers: A Longitudinal Study of Social Influences in Adolescent Risks for Alcohol Use and Abuse." Pp. 1–30 in *Sibling Relationships: Their Causes and Consequences.* Edited by G. H. Brody. Norwood, NJ: Ablex.

Connell, R. W. 1987. *Gender and Power.* Stanford: Stanford University Press.

———. 1995. *Masculinities.* Berkeley: University of California Press.

Coontz, Stephanie. 1988. *The Social Origins of Private Life: A History of American Families, 1600–1900.* New York: Verso.

———. 1992. *The Way We Never Were: American Families and the Nostalgia Trap.* New York: Basic Books.

Cormier, Robert. 1974. *The Chocolate War.* New York: Laureleaf.

Cowan, Ruth Schwartz. 1979. "From Virginia Dare to Virginia Slims: Women and Technology in American Life." *Technology and Culture* 20: 51–63.

Cowart, M. F., R. W. Wilhelm, and R. E. Cowart. 1998. "Voices from Little Asia: 'Blue Dragon' Teens Reflect on Their Experience as Asian Americans." *Social Education* 62, no. 7: 401–404.

Coyne, Michael. 1997. *The Crowded Prairie: American National Identity in the Hollywood Western.* New York: St. Martin's Press.

Crews, Gordon A., and M. Reid Counts. 1997. *The Evolution of School Disturbance in America: Colonial Times to Modern Day.* Westport, CT: Praeger.

Crime in the United States 1999. 2000. Washington, DC: Federal Bureau of Investigation, U.S. Department of Justice.

Crimmins, Eileen. 1981. "The Changing Pattern of American Mortality Decline, 1940–1977." *Population Development Review* 7: 229–254.

Cross, Gary. 1997. *Kids' Stuff: Toys and the Changing World of American Childhood.* Cambridge, MA: Harvard University Press.

Croswell, T. R. 1898. "Amusements of Worcester Schoolchildren." *The Pedagogical Seminary* 6: 314–371.

Croteau, Jan Helling. 2000. *Perform It! A Complete Guide to Young People's Theatre.* Portsmouth, NH: Heinemann.

Cruise, David, and Alison Griffiths. 1992. *Net Worth: Exploding the Myths of Pro Hockey.* Toronto: Penguin Books.

Csikszentmihalyi, Mihaly, Kevin Rathunde, and Samuel Whalen. 1993. *Talented Teenagers: The Roots of Success and Failure.* New York: Cambridge University Press.

Culin, Stewart. 1891. "Street Games of Boys in Brooklyn, N.Y." *Journal of American Folklore* 4, no. 14: 221–237.

Cummings, E. Mark, and Patrick Davies. 1994. *Children and Marital Conflict: The Impact of Family Dispute and Resolution.* New York: Guilford Press.

Cummings, Scott, and Daniel Monti. 1993. *Gangs.* Albany: State University of New York Press.

Cunliffe, Marcus. 1968. *Soldiers and Civilians: The Martial Spirit in America, 1775–1865.* Boston: Little, Brown.

Cunningham, Hugh. 1991. *The Children of the Poor: Representations of Childhood since the Seventeenth Century.* Oxford: Basil Blackwell.

Curry, G. David, and Scott H. Decker. 1998. *Confronting Gangs: Crime and Community.* Los Angeles: Roxbury.

Dale, Edward Everett. 1959. *Frontier Ways: Sketches of Life in the Old West.* Austin: University of Texas Press.

Danbom, David B. 1974. "The Young America Movement." *Journal of the Illinois State Historical Society* 67: 294–306.

———. 1995. *Born in the Country: A History of Rural America.* Baltimore: Johns Hopkins University Press.

Daniel, Clifton, ed. 1987. *Chronicle of the 20th Century.* New York: Prentice Hall.

Daniel, Les. 1993. *Marvel: Five Fabulous Decades of the World's Greatest Comics.*

Introduction by Stan Lee. New York: Abrams.

Daniel, Thomas M., and Frederick C. Robins, eds. 1997. *Polio.* Rochester: University of Rochester Press.

Daniels, Elizabeth. 1989. "The Children of Gettysburg." *American Heritage* 40 (May–June): 97–107.

Dann, John, ed. 1980. *The Revolution Remembered: Eyewitness Accounts of the War for Independence.* Chicago: University of Chicago Press.

Davidson, Ben. 1976. *The Skateboard Book.* New York: Grosset and Dunlap.

Davies, Richard G. 1983. "Of Arms and the Boy: A History of Culver Military Academy, 1894–1945." Ph.D. diss., School of Education, Indiana University.

Davis, Jack E. 1993. "Changing Places: Slave Movement in the South." *The Historian* 55 (Summer): 657–676.

Davis, Joshua. 1819. *Joshua Davis' Report.* Collections of the New England Historical and Genealogical Society.

Davis, O. L., Jr., et al. 1986. *Looking at History: A Review of Major U.S. History Textbooks.* Washington, DC: People for the American Way.

Davis, Owen. 1914. "Why I Quit Writing Melodrama." *American Magazine* (September): 28–31.

———. 1931. *I'd Like to Do It Again.* New York: Farrar and Rinehart.

Dawson, John M., and Patrick A. Langan. 1994. *Murder in Families.* Washington, DC: U.S. Department of Justice, Bureau of Justice Statistics.

De Charms, Richard, and Gerald H. Moeller. 1962. "Values Expressed in American Children's Readers: 1800–1950." *Journal of Abnormal and Social Psychology* 64: 136–142.

de Graaf, R., et al. 1994. "Male Prostitutes and Safe Sex: Different Settings, Different Risks." *AIDS Care* 6, no. 3: 277–288.

Dean, John I. 1992. "Scouting in America, 1910–1990." Ed.D. diss., University of South Carolina.

Deisher, R., G. Robinson, and D. Boyer. 1982. "The Adolescent Female and Male Prostitute." *Pediatric Annals* 11, no. 10: 819–825.

D'Emilio, John D., and Estelle B. Freedman. 1988. *Intimate Matters: A History of Sexuality in America.* New York: Harper and Row.

Denning, Michael. 1987. *Mechanic Accents: Dime Novels and Working-Class Culture in America.* New York: Verso Press.

Denniston, George C. 1999. *Male and Female Circumcision: Medical, Legal and Ethical Considerations in Pediatric Practice.* Norwell, MA: Kluwer Academic.

Derevensky, Jeffrey L., Rina Gupta, and Giuseppe Della Cioppa. 1996. "A Developmental Perspective of Gambling Behavior in Children and Adolescents." *Journal of Gambling Studies* 12, no. 1: 49–66.

Desjardins, Mary. 1999. "Luci and Desi: Sexuality, Ethnicity, and TV's First Family." In *Television, History, and American Culture: Feminist Critical Essays.* Edited by Mary Best Haralovich and Lauren Rabinovitz. Durham, NC: Duke University Press.

Desrockers, Robert E., Jr. 1999. "Not Fade Away: The Narrative of Venture Smith, an African American in the Early Republic." In *A Question of Manhood: A Reader in U.S. Black Men's History and Masculinity.* Vol. 1. Edited by Darlene Clark-Hine and Earnestine Jenkins. Bloomington: Indiana University Press.

Destrehan, Nicholas A. 1850. "Memoirs" in "Letter Book." Historic New Orleans Collection, New Orleans, LA.

Dewey, John. 1916. *Democracy and Education.* New York: Macmillan.

———. 1929. *Experience and Nature.* La Salle: Open Court.

Dexter, Franklin Bowditch. 1919. *Ancient Town Records.* Vol. 2: *New Haven Town Records, 1662–1684.* New Haven: New Haven Colony Historical Society.

Deyle, Steven. 1995. "The Domestic Slave Trade in America." Ph.D. diss., Columbia University.

Dicey, Edward. 1863. *Six Months in the Federal States.* London: Macmillan. Reprint, Herbert Mitgang, ed., 1971. *Spectator of America.* Chicago: Quadrangle Books.

DiIulio, John J., Jr. 1995. "The Coming of the Super-Predators." *The Weekly Standard* (November 27): 23–27.

Dixon, Pahl, and Peter Dixon. 1977. *Hot Skateboarding.* New York: Warner Books.

Dobrin, Michael, and Philip E. Linhares. 1996. *Hot Rods and Customs: The Men and Machines of California's Car Culture.* Oakland: Oakland Museum of California.

Doherty, William J. 1998. *The Intentional Family.* Reading, MA: Addison-Wesley.

Donelson, Kenneth L., and Alleen Pace Nilsen. 1996. *Literature for Today's Young Adult.* 5th ed. Reading, MA: Addison-Wesley.

Don't Give the Name a Bad Place: Types and Stereotypes in American Musical Theater, 1870–1900. 1978. New World Records.

Douglas, Mary. 1975. "Jokes." Pp. 90–114 in *Implicit Meanings: Essays in Anthropology* by Mary Douglas. London: Routledge and Kegan Paul.

Douglas, Susan. 1999. *Listening In: Radio and the American Imagination.* New York: Times Books.

Douglass, Frederick. 1855. *My Bondage and My Freedom.* Reprint, New York: Dover Publications, 1969.

Drury, Clifford Merril. 1974. "Growing Up on an Iowa Farm, 1897–1915." *Annals of Iowa* 42, no. 3: 161–197.

———. 1998. *American Youth Violence.* New York: Oxford University Press.

Dryfoos, Joy G. 1990. *Adolescents at Risk: Prevalence and Prevention.* New York: Oxford University Press.

Du Bois, W. E. B. 1920. *Darkwater: Voices from within the Veil.* New York: Harcourt, Brace, and Howe.

———. 1940. *Dusk of Dawn: An Essay toward an Autobiography of a Race Concept.* In *W. E. B. Du Bois: Writings.* Edited by Nathan Huggins. New York: Harcourt, Brace, and Company. Reprint, New York: Library of America, 1986.

———. 1968. *Autobiography of W. E. B. Dubois: A Soliloquy on Viewing My Life from the Last Decade of Its First Century.* New York: International Publishers.

Dundes, Alan. 1987. "The Dead Baby Joke Cycle." Pp. 3–14 in *Cracking Jokes.* Berkeley, CA: Ten Speed Press.

Dunn, Judy. 1983. "Sibling Relationships in Early Childhood." *Child Development* 54: 787–811.

———. 1996. "Brothers and Sisters in Middle Childhood and Early Adolescence: Continuity and Change in Individual Differences." Pp. 31–46 in *Sibling Relationships: Their Causes and Consequences.* Edited by Gene H. Brody. Norwood, NJ: Ablex.

Dunn, Judy, and C. Kendrick. 1981. "Social Behavior of Young Siblings in the Family Context: Differences Between Same-Sex and Different-Sex Dyads." *Child Development* 52: 1265–1273.

Dunn, Judy, and Shirley McGuire. 1992. "Sibling and Peer Relationships in Childhood." *Journal of Child Psychology and Psychiatry* 33: 67–105.

Dyk, Walter. 1938. *Son of Old Man Hat: A Navaho Autobiography.* Lincoln: University of Nebraska Press.

Dyreson, Mark. 1998. *Making the American Team: Sport, Culture, and the Olympic Experience.* Urbana: University of Illinois Press.

"Early American Impressions." 1904. *The American Field: The Sportsman's Journal* 61, no. 17 (April 23).

Early Minstrel Show, The. 1998. New World Records.

East, Patricia L., and Karen S. Rook. 1992. "Compensatory Patterns of Support among Children's Peer Relationships: A Test Using School Friends, Nonschool Friends, and Siblings." *Developmental Psychology* 28: 163–172.

Eastman, Charles A. 1902. *Indian Boyhood.* 1902. Reprint, New York: Dover Publications, 1971.

Edelson, Jeffery. L. 1999. "Children's Witnessing of Adult Domestic Violence." *Journal of Interpersonal Violence* 14, no. 8: 839–870.

Eder, Donna. 1997. "Sexual Aggression within the School Culture." In *Gender, Equity, and Schooling: Policy and Practice.* Edited by Barbara J. Bank and Peter M. Hall. New York: Garland.

Eder, Donna, with Catherine Colleen Evans and Stephen Parker. 1995. *School Talk: Gender and Adolescent Culture.* New Brunswick, NJ: Rutgers University Press.

Education Commission of the States Task Force on Education for Economic Growth.

1983. *Action for Excellence: A Comprehensive Plan to Improve Our Nation's Schools.* Denver: Education Commission of the States.

Eells, Eleanor. 1986. *Eleanor Eells' History of Organized Camping: The First Hundred Years.* Martinsville, IN: ACA.

Einstein, Albert. 1950. *Out of My Later Years.* New York: Philosophical Library.

Eisenstadt, S. N. 1956. *From Generation to Generation: Age Groups and Social Structure.* New York: Free Press.

Ekrich, Arthur A. 1956. *The Civilian and the Military.* New York: Oxford University Press.

El-Bassel, N., R. F. Schilling, L. Gilbert, S. Faruque, K. L. Irwin, and B. R. Edlin. 2000. "Sex Trading and Psychological Distress in a Street-based Sample of Low Income Urban Men." *Journal of Psychoactive Drugs* 32, no. 2: 259–267.

Elder, Glen H., Jr. 1974. *Children of the Great Depression: Social Change in Life Experience.* Chicago: University of Chicago Press.

Elfenbein, Jessica Ivy. 1996. "To 'Fit Them for Their Fight with the World': The Baltimore YMCA and the Making of a Modern City, 1852–1932." Ph.D. diss., University of Delaware.

Elifson, K. W., J. Boles, and M. Sweat. 1993. "Risk Factors Associated with HIV Infection among Male Prostitutes." *American Journal of Public Health* 83, no. 1: 79–83.

Elliott, David L., and Arthur Woodward, eds. 1990. *Textbooks and Schooling in the United States: Eighty-Ninth Yearbook of the National Society for the Study of Education, Pt. 1.* Chicago: National Society for the Study of Education.

Ellis, Havelock. 1900. *The Evolution of Modesty; the Phenomena of Sexual Periodicity; Auto-Eroticism.* Philadelphia: E. A. Davis.

Ellis, Joseph J. 1993. *Passionate Sage: The Character and Legacy of John Adams.* New York: W. W. Norton.

Elson, Ruth Miller. 1964. *Guardians of Tradition: American Schoolbooks of the Nineteenth Century.* Lincoln: University of Nebraska Press.

Elster, Arthur B., and Michael E. Lamb, eds. *Adolescent Fatherhood.* Hillsdale, NJ: Erlbaum.

Emerson, Mary Moody. 1993. *The Selected Letters of Mary Moody Emerson.* Edited by Nancy Craig Simmons. Athens: University of Georgia Press.

Emerson, Ralph Waldo. 1844. "The Young American." *The Dial* (April).

———. 1903–1904. *The Complete Works.* 12 vols. Edited by Edward W. Emerson. Boston: Houghton Mifflin.

———. 1939. *Letters of Ralph Waldo Emerson.* 6 vols. Edited by Ralph L. Rusk. New York: Columbia University Press.

———. 1960–1978. *Journals and Miscellaneous Notebooks of Ralph Waldo Emerson.* Edited by William H. Gilman et al. Cambridge: Harvard University Press.

Emery, R. E. 1988. *Marriage, Divorce, and Children's Adjustment.* Newbury Park, CA: Sage.

Emery, R. E., E. M. Hetherington, and L. F. Dilalla. 1984. "Divorce, Children, and Social Policy." Pp. 189–266 in *Child Development Research and Social Policy.* Edited by H. W. Stevenson and A. E. Siegel. Chicago: University of Chicago Press.

Empey, LaMar T., and M. C. Stafford. 1991. *American Delinquency: Its Meaning and Construction.* 3d ed. Belmont, CA: Wadsworth.

Englehardt, Tom. 1987. "Children's Television: The Strawberry Shortcake Strategy." In *Watching Television: A Pantheon Guide to Popular Culture.* Edited by Todd Gitlin. New York: Pantheon.

English Country Dances: From Playford's Dancing Master, 1651–1703. 1991. Saydisc.

Erdman, Harley. 1997. *Staging the Jew: The Performance of an American Ethnicity, 1860–1920.* New Brunswick: Rutgers University Press.

Erickson, Judith B. 1983. *Directory of American Youth Organizations.* Omaha, NE: Boys Town.

Escobar, Edward J. 1999. *Race, Police, and the Making of a Political Identity: Relations between Chicanos and the Los Angeles Police Department, 1900–1945.* Berkeley: University of California Press.

Espelage, Dorothy, and Christine Asidao. In press. "Conversations with Middle School Students about Bullying and Victimization: Should We Be Concerned?" *Journal of Emotional Abuse.*

Espelage, Dorothy L., and Melissa K. Holt. In press. "Bullying and Victimization during Early Adolescence: Peer Influences and Psychosocial Correlates." *Journal of Emotional Abuse.*

Espelage, Dorothy L., Kris Bosworth, and Thomas R. Simon. 2000. "Examining the Social Environment of Middle School Students Who Bully." *Journal of Counseling and Development* 78: 326–333.

Evans, Walter. 1972. "The All-American Boys: A Study of Boys' Sports Fiction." *Journal of Popular Culture* 6: 104–121.

Ewbank, Douglas. 1987. "History of Black Mortality and Health before 1940." *Milbank Quarterly* 65, supp. 1: 100–128.

Ewing, Elizabeth. 1977. *History of Children's Costume.* New York: Charles Scribner's Sons.

Fagan, Jeffrey, and Franklin E. Zimring, eds. 2000. *The Changing Borders of Juvenile Justice: Transfer of Adolescents to the Criminal Court.* Chicago: University of Chicago Press.

Fagot, Beverly I., Katherine C. Pears, Deborah M. Capaldi, Lynn Crosby, and Craig S. Leve. 1998. "Becoming an Adolescent Father: Precursors and Parenting." *Developmental Psychology* 34: 1209–1219.

Faludi, Susan. 1999. "The Betrayal of the American Man." *Newsweek* (September 13): 49–58.

Fantuzzo, John W., and Carrol U. Lindquist. 1989. "The Effects of Observing Conjugal Violence on Children: A Review and Analysis of Research Methodology." *Journal of Family Violence* 4, no. 1: 77–93.

Faragher, John Mack. 1979. *Women and Men on the Overland Trail.* New Haven: Yale University Press.

Farish, Hunter Dickinson, ed. 1957. *Journal and Letters of Philip Vickers Fithian, 1773–1774: A Plantation Tutor of the Old Dominion.* Williamsburg, VA: Colonial Williamsburg.

Farmer, Silas. 1889. *The History of Detroit and Michigan.* Detroit: Silas Farmer.

Fass, Paula S. 1977. *The Damned and the Beautiful: American Youth in the 1920s.* New York: Oxford University Press.

Fass, Paula S., and Mary Ann Mason, eds. 2000. *Childhood in America.* New York: New York University Press.

Federal Writers Project, Interviews with Former Slaves. 1930s. Chapel Hill: Southern Historical Collection, University of North Carolina.

Feinstein, John. 1991. *Hard Courts*. New York: Villard Books.

Feld, Barry C. 1999. *Bad Kids: Race and the Transformation of the Juvenile Court*. New York: Oxford University Press.

Feldman, Shirley, and Glen Elliot, eds. 1990. *At the Threshold: The Developing Adolescent*. Cambridge, MA: Harvard University Press.

Feretti, Fred. 1975. *The Great American Book of Sidewalk, Stoop, Dirt, Curb, and Alley Games*. New York: Workman.

Ferling, John E. 1992. *John Adams: A Life*. Knoxville: University of Tennessee Press.

———. 1994. *John Adams: A Bibliography*. Westport, CT: Greenwood Press.

Fetto, John. 1999. "Happy Campers." *American Demographics* 21, no. 7 (July): 46–47.

Findlay, John M. 1992. *Magic Lands*. Seattle: University of Washington Press.

Fine, Gary Alan. 1987. *With the Boys: Little League Baseball and Preadolescent Culture*. Chicago: University of Chicago Press.

Fine, M. 1991. *Framing Dropouts: Notes on the Politics of an Urban Public High School*. Albany: State University of New York Press.

Fingerhut, Lois, and Joel Kleinman. 1989. *Trends and Current Status in Childhood Mortality*. Washington, DC: National Center for Health Statistics.

Finkelstein, Barbara. 1989. *Governing the Young: Teacher Behavior in Popular Primary Schools in Nineteenth-Century United States*. London: Falmer Press.

———. 2000. "A Crucible of Contradictions: Historical Roots of Violence against Children in the United States." *History of Education Quarterly* 40, no. 1: 1–22.

Finn, William J. 1939. *The Art of the Choral Conductor*. Evanston, IL: Summy-Birchard Publishing.

Firearm Injuries and Fatalities. 2000. Atlanta: National Center for Injury Prevention and Control, Centers for Disease Control and Prevention.

Fischer, David Hackett. 1989. *Albion's Seed: Four British Folkways in America*. New York: Oxford University Press.

Fisher, B., D. K. Weisberg, and T. Marotta. 1982. *Report on Adolescent Male Prostitution*. San Francisco: Urban and Rural Systems Associates.

Fiske, George W. 1912. *Boy Life and Self-Government*. New York: Association Press.

FitzGerald, Francis. 1979. *America Revised: History Schoolbooks in the Twentieth Century*. Boston: Little, Brown.

Flanagan, D. P., and J. L. Genshaft, eds. 1997. "Issues in the Use and Interpretation of Intelligence Testing in Schools." *School Psychology Review* 26: 2.

Flanagan, D. P., J. Genshaft, and P. L. Harrison, eds. 1997. *Contemporary Intellectual Assessment: Theories, Tests and Issues*. New York: Guilford.

Florey, Francesca A., and Avery M. Guest. 1988. "Coming of Age among U.S. Farm Boys in the Late 1800s: Occupational and Residential Choices." *Journal of Family History* 13, no. 2: 233–249.

Flynt, Josiah. 1972. *Tramping with Tramps*. Montclair, NJ: Patterson Smith.

For Youth by Youth. 2001. "About 4-H," http://www.4-H.org (accessed May 14, 2001).

Forbush, William B. 1907. *The Boy Problem.* 3d ed. Boston: Pilgrim Press.

Ford, Clellan S., and Frank A. Beach. 1951. *Patterns of Sexual Behavior.* New York: Harper and Brothers.

Ford, Larry. 2001. "Boychoir—Past, Present and Future," http://www.boychoirs.org (accessed March 11, 2001).

———. 2001. "Donald Collup Singing Alleluja by Wolfgang Amadeus Mozart," http://www.boychoirs.org/collup.html (accessed March 11, 2001).

Ford, Larry, Gene Bitner, and Lindsay Emery. 2001. "The World of Treble Voices," http://216.147.109.215/contents.html (accessed March 11, 2001).

Ford, Paul Leicester, ed. 1897. *The "New England Primer": A History of Its Origin and Development.* New York: Dodd, Mead.

Ford, Paul L., ed. 1899. *The New England Primer.* New York: Dodd, Mead.

Formanek-Brunell, Miriam. 1993. *Made to Play House: Dolls and the Commercialization of American Girlhood 1830–1930.* New Haven: Yale University Press.

Forrest, Suzanne. 1998. *The Preservation of the Village: New Mexico's Hispanics and the New Deal.* Albuquerque: University of New Mexico Press.

Foucault, Michel. 1980. *The History of Sexuality.* Vol. 1: *An Introduction.* New York: Vintage.

Fox, Ebenezer. 1838. *The Revolutionary Adventures of Ebenezer Fox.* Boston: Monroe and Francis.

Frank, Michael L., and Crystal Smith. 1989. "Illusion of Control and Gambling in Children." *Journal of Gambling Behavior* 5, no. 2: 127–136.

Franklin, Barry. 1987. *Learning Disabilities: Dissenting Essays.* New York: Falmer Press.

Franklin, Benjamin. 1959. *Autobiography and Selected Writings.* New York: Holt, Rinehart and Winston.

———. 1959. *Autobiography.* New York: Holt, Rinehart, and Winston.

Franklin Fire Company. 1856. "Minutes." Missouri Historical Society, St. Louis Volunteer Fireman Collection.

Frazer, Sir James. 1915. *The Golden Bough: A Study of Magic and Religion.* London: Macmillan.

Freeman, Evelyn B. 1985. "When Children Face Divorce: Issues and Implications of Research." *Childhood Education* 62, no. 2: 130–136.

Freeman, Norman. 1980. *Strategies of Representation in Young Children.* London: Academic Press.

Freeman, Norman, and Maureen V. Cox. 1985. *Visual Order.* Cambridge: Cambridge University Press.

Frye, Alexis E. 1902. *Grammar School Geography.* Boston: Ginn.

Fuller, Wayne E. 1982. *The Old Country School: The Story of Rural Education in the Midwest.* Chicago: University of Chicago Press.

Furman, Wyndol, and Duane Buhrmester. 1985. "Children's Perceptions of the Qualities of Sibling Relationships." *Child Development* 56: 448–461.

———. 1992. "Age and Sex Differences in Perceptions of Networks of Personal Relationships." *Child Development* 63: 103–115.

Gagne, Luc. 1995. *Moving Beauty.* Montreal, Quebec: Montreal Museum of Fine Art.

Gagner, Constance T., Teresa M. Cooney, and Kathleen Thiede Call. 1998. "The Effects of Family Characteristics and Time Use on Teenage Girls; and Boys'

Household Labor." Princeton University Center for Research on Child Well-being. Working Paper Series no. 98-1.

Gairdner, Douglas. 1949. "The Fate of the Foreskin." *British Medical Journal* 2 (1949): 1433–1437.

Galarza, Ernesto. 1971. *Barrio Boy.* Notre Dame: University of Notre Dame Press.

Galenson, David. 1981. *White Servitude in Colonial America: An Economic Analysis.* Cambridge: Cambridge University Press.

Galenson, David W. 1993. "The Impact of Economic and Technological Change on the Careers of American Men Tennis Players, 1960–1991." *Journal of Sport History* 20, no. 2 (Summer): 127–150.

Gall, Timothy, and Daniel Lucas, eds. 1996. *Statistics on Alcohol, Drug and Tobacco Use.* Detroit: Thompson.

Gallo, Agatha M., and Kathleen A. Knafl. 1993. "The Effects of Mental Retardation, Disability, and Illness on Sibling Relationships: Research Issues and Challenges." Pp. 215–234 in *Siblings of Children with Chronic Illnesses: A Categorical and Noncategorical Look at Selected Literature.* Edited by Zolinda Stoneman and Phyllis Waldman Burman. Baltimore: Paul H. Brookes Publishing.

Garbarino, James. 1999. *Lost Boys: Why Our Sons Turn Violent and How We Can Save Them.* New York: Free Press.

Gardella, Peter. 1985. *Innocent Ecstasy: How Christianity Gave America an Ethic of Sexual Pleasure.* New York: Oxford University Press.

Gardner, Howard. 1980. *Artful Scribbles: The Significance of Children's Drawings.* New York: Basic Books.

Garland, Hamlin. 1899. *Boy Life on the Prairie.* New York: Macmillan.

———. 1926. *Boy Life on the Prairie.* Boston: Allyn and Bacon.

Garlits, Don. 1990. *The Autobiography of "Big Daddy" Don Garlits.* Ocala, FL: Museum of Drag Racing.

Gault, Frank, and Claire Gault. 1977. *The Harlem Globetrotters.* New York: Walker.

GeekComix.com. 2000. "A Brief History of Home Video Games," http://www.geekcomix.com/vgh/main.shtml (accessed December 27, 2000).

Gems, Gerald R. 1996. "The Prep Bowl: Football and Religious Acculturation in Chicago, 1927–1963." *Journal of Sport History* 23, no. 3: 284–302.

———. 1997. *Windy City Wars: Labor, Leisure, and Sport in the Making of Chicago.* Lanham, MD: Scarecrow Press.

———. 2000. *For Pride, Patriarchy, and Profit: Football and the Incorporation of American Cultural Values.* Metuchen, NJ: Scarecrow Press.

Gems, Gerald, ed. 1995. *Sports in North America: A Documentary History.* Vol. 5, *Sports Organized, 1880–1900.* Gulf Breeze, FL: Academic International Press.

"General Social Survey." 1999. http://www.icpsr.umich.edu/GSS99/index.html.

Gerould, Daniel. 1983. *American Melodrama.* New York: Performing Arts Journal.

Giamatti, A. Bartlett. 1981. "Power, Politics, and a Sense of History." Pp. 166–179 in *The University and the Public Interest.* New York: Atheneum.

Gignilliat, Leigh R. 1916. *Arms and the Boy: Military Training in Schools.* Indianapolis: Bobbs-Merrill.

Gilbert, Albert C., with Marshall McClintock. 1953. *The Man Who Lives in Paradise.* New York: Rinehart.

Gilbert, Douglas. 1940. *American Vaudeville: Its Life and Times.* New York: McGraw-Hill.

Gilbert, James B. 1986. *A Cycle of Outrage: America's Reaction to the Juvenile Delinquent in the 1950s.* New York: Oxford University Press.

Gillham, Bill, and James A. Thomson, eds. 1996. *Child Safety: Problem and Prevention from Preschool to Adolescence: A Handbook for Professionals.* New York: Routledge.

Gillis, John R. 1974. *Youth and History: Tradition and Change in European Age Relations, 1770–Present.* New York: Academic Press.

Gilmore, D. 1990. *Manhood in the Making: Cultural Concepts of Masculinity.* New Haven: Yale University Press.

Gilmore, William J. 1989. *Reading Becomes a Necessity of Life: Material and Culture Life in Rural New England, 1780–1835.* Knoxville: University of Tennessee Press.

Girl Scouts. 2000. "About Us," http://www.girlscouts.org (accessed May 14, 2001).

Girls and Boys Town. 2000. "About Boys Town, History," http://www.boystown.org/home.htm (accessed September 5, 2000).

Giroux, Henry A. 1996. *Fugitive Cultures: Race, Violence and Youth.* New York: Routledge.

Gittens, Joan. 1994. *Poor Relations: The Children of the State in Illinois, 1818–1990.* Urbana: University of Illinois Press.

Glassner, Barry. 1995. "Men and Muscles." In *Men's Lives.* Edited by Michael Kimmel and Michael Messner. Boston: Allyn and Bacon.

Glenn, Myra C. 1984. *Campaigns against Corporal Punishment: Prisoners, Sailors, Women, and Children in Antebellum America.* Albany: State University of New York Press.

Goffman, Erving. 1961. *Asylums: Essays on the Social Situation of Mental Patients and Other Inmates.* Garden City, NY: Anchor/Doubleday.

———. 1961. *Encounters: Two Studies in the Sociology of Interaction.* Indianapolis: Bobbs-Merrill.

———. 1963. *Stigma.* Englewood Cliffs, NJ: Prentice-Hall.

———. 1967. *Interaction Ritual: Essays on Face-to-Face Behavior.* Garden City, NY: Anchor Books.

Goldstein, Arnold P. 1990. *Delinquents on Delinquency.* Champaign, IL: Research Press.

———. 1991. *Delinquent Gangs: A Psychological Perspective.* Champaign, IL: Research Press.

Goldstein, Ruth M., and Charlotte Zornow. 1980. *The Screen Image of Youth: Movies about Children and Adolescents.* Metuchen, NJ: Scarecrow Press.

Gollaher, David. 1994. "From Ritual to Science: The Medical Transformation of Circumcision in America." *Journal of Social History* 28, no. 1: 5–36.

Golomb, Claire. 1992. *The Creation of a Pictorial World.* Berkeley: University of California Press.

Gonzalez, Gilbert G. 1990. *Chicano Education in the Era of Segregation.* Philadelphia: Balch Institute Press.

Goodman, Cary. 1979. *Choosing Sides: Playground and Street Life on the Lower East Side.* New York: Schocken Books.

Goodman, Jules Eckert. 1908. "The Lure of Melodrama." *Bohemian Magazine* (February): 180–191.

Goodman, Nan. 1998. *Shifting the Blame: Literature, Law and the Theory of Accidents in Nineteenth-century America.* Princeton: Princeton University Press.

Gordon, Ian. 1998. *Comic Strips and Consumer Culture, 1890–1945.* Washington, DC: Smithsonian Institution Press.

Gordon, Linda. 1988. *Heroes of Their Own Lives: The Politics and History of Family Violence, Boston, 1880–1960.* New York. Viking.

Gorn, Elliott J. 1986. *The Manly Art: Bare-Knuckle Prize Fighting in America.* Ithaca: Cornell University Press.

Gorn, Elliott J., ed. 1998. *The McGuffey Readers: Selections from the 1879 Edition.* Bedford Series in History and Culture. Boston: Bedford/St. Martin's Press.

Goulart, Ron. 2000. *Comic Book Culture: An Illustrated History.* Portland, OR: Collectors Press.

Goulart, Ron, ed. 1990. *Encyclopedia of American Comics.* New York: Facts on File.

Gould, Steven J. 1981. *The Mismeasure of Man.* New York: Norton Press.

Graber, Julia A., and Jeanne Brooks-Gunn. 1996. "Transitions and Turning Points: Navigating the Passage from Childhood through Adolescence." *Developmental Psychology* 32: 768–776.

Graber, Julia A., Anne C. Petersen, and Jeanne Brooks-Gunn. 1996. "Pubertal Processes: Methods, Measures, and Models." Pp. 23–53 in *Transitions through Adolescence: Interpersonal Domains and Context.* Edited by Julia A. Graber, Jeanne Brooks-Gunn, and Anne C. Petersen. Mahwah, NJ: Erlbaum.

Grace, Catherine O'Neil. 1998. "Kids and Money: Valuable Lessons." *The Washington Post*, June 23, Z22.

Graebner, William. 1988. "Outlawing Teenage Populism: The Campaign against Secret Societies in the American High School, 1900–1960." *Journal of American History* 74: 411–435.

Graetz, J. M. 1981. "The Origin of SpaceWar." *Creative Computing* (August).

Grant, Barry Keith, ed. 1996. *The Dread of Difference.* Austin: University of Texas Press.

Grant, Julia. 1998. *Raising Baby by the Book: The Education of American Mothers.* New Haven: Yale University Press.

Gray, Asa. 1875. *Botany for Young People, Part II: How Plants Behave.* New York: Ivison, Blakeman, and Taylor.

Gray, Herman. 1995. *Watching Race: Television and the Struggle for Blackness.* Minneapolis: University of Minnesota Press.

Gray, Kenneth C., and Edwin L. Herr. 1995. *Other Ways to Win: Creating Alternatives for High School Graduates.* Thousand Oaks, CA: Corwin Press.

Greeley, Horace. 1868. *Recollections of a Busy Life.* New York and Boston: H. A. Brown and J. B. Ford.

Green, Abel, and Joe Laurie, Jr. 1951. *Show Biz: From Vaude to Video.* New York: Henry Holt.

Green, Harvey. 1988. *Fit for America: Health, Fitness, Sport, and American Society.* Baltimore: Johns Hopkins University Press.

Greenberg, Amy S. 1998. *Cause for Alarm: The Volunteer Fire Department in the Nineteenth-Century City.* Princeton: Princeton University Press.

Greenberg, Blu. 1985. *How to Run a Traditional Jewish Household.* New York: Simon and Schuster.

Greenberger, Ellen, and Lawrence Steinberg. 1986. *When Teenagers Work: The Psychological and Social Costs of Adolescent Employment.* New York: Basic Books.

Greenfeld. Lawrence A. 1996. *Child Victimizers: Violent Offenders and Their Victims.* Washington, DC: Office of Juvenile Justice and Delinquency Prevention.

Greenfield, Laurence. 1991. "Toys, Children, and the Toy Industry in a Culture of Consumption, 1890–1991." Ph.D. diss., Ohio State University.

Greenfield, Patricia Marks. 1984. *Mind and Media: The Effects of Television, Video Games, and Computers.* Cambridge: Harvard University Press.

Greenman, Jeremiah. 1978. *Diary of a Common Soldier in the American Revolution, 1775–1783: An Annotated Edition of the Military Journal of Jeremiah Greenman.* Edited by Robert C. Bray and Paul E. Bushnell. Dekalb: Northern Illinois University Press.

Greif, Richard S. 1997. *Big Impact: Big Brothers Making a Difference.* Boston: New Hat.

Greven, Philip J., Jr. 1977. *The Protestant Temperament: Patterns of Child-Rearing, Religious Experience, and Self in Early America.* New York: Alfred A. Knopf.

———. 1990. *Spare the Child: The Religious Roots of Punishment and the Psychological Impact of Physical Abuse.* New York: Vintage.

Grider, Sylvia Ann. 1996. "Conservation and Dynamism in the Contemporary Celebration of Halloween: Institutionalization, Commercialization, Gentrification." *Western Folklore* 53, no. 1: 3–15.

Grier, Katherine C. 1999. "Childhood Socialization and Companion Animals: United States, 1820–1870." *Society and Animals* 7, no. 2: 95–120.

Grimsley, Will. 1971. *Tennis: Its History, People and Events.* Englewood Cliffs, NJ: Prentice-Hall.

Griswold, Robert L. 1997. "Generative Fathering: A Historical Perspective." Pp. 71–86 in *Generative Fathering: Beyond Deficit Perspectives.* Edited by Alan J. Hawkins and David C. Dollahite. Thousand Oaks, CA: Sage.

Grossberg, Michael. 1985. *Governing the Hearth: Law and the Family in Nineteenth-Century America.* Chapel Hill: University of North Carolina Press.

Grove, Robert D., and Alice M. Hetzel. 1968. *Vital Statistic Rates in the United States, 1940–1960.* Washington, DC: National Center for Health Statistics.

Grubb, W. Norton. 1996. "The New Vocationalism: What It Is, What It Could Be." *Phi Delta Kappan* 77, no. 8: 533–546.

Grunbaum, Jo Anne, Laura Kann, Steven A. Kinchen, James G. Ross, Vani R. Gowda, Janet L. Collins, and Lloyd J. Kolbe. 1999. "Youth Risk Behavior Surveillance—National Alternative High School Youth Risk Behavior Survey, United States, 1988." Centers for Disease Control and Prevention: *MMWR Surveillance Summaries* 48, no. SS-7 (October 29).

Gruneau, Richard, and David Whitson. 1993. *Hockey Night in Canada: Sport, Identities, and Cultural Politics.* Toronto: Garamond Press.

Gudmundsen, Jinny. 2000. "Strategy for Parents: Use Ratings, Be Involved. Choosing Titles by the Letters." *Los Angeles Times,* October 26, T8.

Guimond, James. 1991. *American Photography and the American Dream.* Chapel Hill: University of North Carolina Press.

Gullotta, Thomas P., Gerald R. Adams, and Raymond Montemayor, eds. 1998. *Delinquent Violent Youth: Theory and Interventions.* Vol. 9, *Advances in Adolescent Development.* Thousand Oaks, CA: Sage.

Gustav-Wrathall, John Donald. 1998. *Take the Young Stranger by the Hand: Same-Sex Relations and the YMCA.* Chicago: University of Chicago Press.

Guthrie, J. 2000. "Not Geeks, Gangsters at Schools." *San Francisco Examiner,* May 14, C1, C5.

Gutman, Judith Mara. 1967. *Lewis W. Hine and the American Social Conscience.* New York: Walker.

———. 1974. *Lewis Hine 1874–1940: Two Perspectives.* New York: Grossman.

Haas, Lisbeth. 1995. *Conquests and Historical Identities in California, 1769–1936.* Berkeley: University of California Press.

Hacsi, Timothy A. 1997. *Second Home: Orphan Asylums and Poor Families in America.* Cambridge, MA: Harvard University Press.

Hahamovitch, Cindy. 1997. *The Fruits of Their Labor: Atlantic Coast Farmworkers and the Making of Migrant Poverty, 1870–1945.* Chapel Hill: University of North Carolina Press.

Hall, Donald E., ed. 1994. *Muscular Christianity: Embodying the Victorian Age.* Cambridge, UK: Cambridge University Press.

Hall, G. Stanley. 1904. *Adolescence: Its Psychology, and Its Relations to Physiology, Anthropology, Sociology, Sex, Crime, Religion, and Education.* 2 vols. New York: D. Appleton.

Hallock, Charles. 1873. *The Fishing Tourist: Angler's Guide and Reference Book.* New York: Harper and Bros.

Halsey, Rosalie V. 1911. *Forgotten Books of the American Nursery: A History of the Development of the American Story-Book.* Boston: Charles Goodspeed, 1969; Reprint, Detroit: Singing Tree Press.

Hamburg, David. 1992. *Today's Children: Creating a Future for a Generation in Crisis.* New York: Times Books, Random House.

Hamm, Charles. 1979. *Yesterdays: Popular Song in America.* New York: W. W. Norton.

Hammonds, Evelynn Maxine. 1999. *Childhood's Deadly Scourge: The Campaign to Control Diphtheria in New York City, 1880–1930.* Baltimore: Johns Hopkins University Press.

Hampsten, Elizabeth. 1991. *Settlers' Children: Growing Up on the Great Plains.* Norman: University of Oklahoma Press.

Handbook of Private Schools, The. 1926. 17th ed. Boston: Porter Sargent.

Handel, Gerald. 1985. "Central Issues in the Construction of Sibling Relationships." Pp. 493–523 in *The Psychosocial Interior of the Family.* Edited by Gerald Handel. New York: Aldine de Gruyter.

Hanson, Glen, and Peter Venturelli. 1995. *Drugs and Society.* 4th ed. Boston: Jones and Bartlett.

Haralovich, Mary Best, and Lauren Rabinovitz, eds. 1999. *Television, History, and American Culture: Feminist Critical Essays.* Durham, NC: Duke University Press.

Haraven, Tamara K. 1982. *Family Time and Industrial Time: The Relationship between the Family and Work in a New England Industrial Community.* Cambridge, UK: Cambridge University Press.

Hardy, Stephen. 1983. *How Boston Played: Sport, Recreation and Community, 1865–1915.* Boston: Northeastern University Press.

Hare, E. H. 1962. "Masturbatory Insanity: The History of an Idea." *The Journal of Mental Science* 108 (January): 2–25.

Harlan, Louis R. 1972. *Booker T. Washington: The Making of a Black Leader, 1856–1901.* New York: Oxford University Press.

Hatch, Nathan. 1989. *The Democratization of American Christianity.* New Haven, CT: Yale University Press.

Haven, Alice Bradley [Cousin Alice]. 1853. *"All's Not Gold That Glitters"; or, the Young Californian.* New York: Appleton and Company.

Hawes, Joseph M. 1971. *Children in Urban Society: Juvenile Delinquency in Nineteenth-Century America.* New York: Oxford University Press.

———. 1997. *Children between the Wars: American Childhood, 1920–1940.* New York: Twayne Publishers.

Hawes, Joseph, and N. Ray Hiner, eds. 1985. *American Childhood: A Research Guide and Historical Handbook.* Westport, CT: Greenwood Press.

Hawley, Frank, with Mark Smith. 1989. *Drag Racing: Drive to Win.* Osceola, WI: Motorbooks International.

Hawley, Richard. 1991. "About Boys' Schools: A Progressive Case for an Ancient Form." *Teachers College Board* 92, no. 3.

Haywood, C. Robert, and Sandra Jarvis. 1992. *A Funnie Place, No Fences: Teenagers' Views of Kansas, 1867–1900.* Lawrence: Division of Continuing Education, University of Kansas.

Hazen, Margaret Hindle, and Robert M. Hazen. 1992. *Keepers of the Flame: The Role of Fire in American Culture, 1775–1925.* Princeton: Princeton University Press.

Heimert, Alan, and Perry Miller. 1967. *The Great Awakening.* Indianapolis: Bobbs-Merrill.

Henderson, Robert W. 1947. *Ball, Bat and Bishop: The Origins of Ball Games.* New York: Rockport Press.

Hendler, Glenn. 1996. "Pandering in the Public Sphere: Masculinity and the Market in Horatio Alger." *American Quarterly* 48, no. 3 (September): 414–438.

Herdt, Gilbert. 1987. *The Sambia: Ritual and Gender in New Guinea.* New York: Holt, Rinehart, and Winston.

Herdt, Gilbert, and Andrew Boxer. 1993. *Children of Horizons: How Gay and Lesbian Teens Are Leading a New Way out of the Closet.* Boston: Beacon.

Herman, Daniel Justin. 2001. *Hunting and the American Imagination.* Washington, DC: Smithsonian Institution Press.

Herz, J. C. 1997. *Joystick Nation: How Computer Games Ate Our Quarters, Won Our Hearts and Rewired Our Minds.* New York: Little, Brown.

Herzog, E., and C. Sudia. 1973. "Children in Fatherless Families." In *Review of Child Development Research.* Vol. 3, *Child Development and Child Policy.* Edited by B. M. Caldwell and H. N. Riccuiti. Chicago: University of Chicago Press.

Hess, Albert G., and Priscilla F. Clement, eds. 1993. *History of Juvenile Delinquency: A Collection of Essays on Crime Committed by Young Offenders, in History and in Selected Countries.* Vol. 2. Aalen, Germany: Scientia Verlag.

Hess, R. D., and I. T. Miura. 1985. "Gender Differences in Enrollment in Computer Camps and Classes." *Sex Roles* 13: 193–203.

Hetherington, E. M. 1979. "Divorce: A Child's Perspective." *American Psychologist* 34: 851–858.

———. 1991. "Presidential Address: Families, Lies, and Videotapes." *Journal of Research on Adolescence* 1, no. 4: 323–348.

Hewes, Minna, and Gordon Hewes. 1952. "Indian Life and Customs at Mission San Luis Rey: A Record of California Indian Life Written by Pablo Tac, an Indian Neophyte." *The Americas* 9: 87–106.

Hewitt, Barnard. 1959. *Theatre U.S.A.: 1665–1957.* New York: McGraw-Hill.

Hewitt, Karen, and Louis Roomet. 1979. *Educational Toys in America: 1800 to the Present.* Burlington, VT: Robert Hull Fleming Museum.

Heyrman, Christine. 1997. *Southern Cross: The Beginnings of the Bible Belt.* Chapel Hill: University of North Carolina Press.

Hicks, David. 1996. "The Strange Fate of the American Boarding School." *The American Scholar* 65, no. 4 (Autumn).

Hilger, M. Inez. 1992. *Chippewa Child Life and Its Cultural Background.* 1951. Reprint, St. Paul: Minnesota Historical Society Press.

Hill, David S. 1920. *Introduction to Vocational Education: A Statement of Facts and Principles Related to the Vocational Aspects of Education below College Grade.* New York: Macmillan.

Hill, John. 1983. "Early Adolescence: A Research Agenda." *Journal of Early Adolescence* 3: 1–21.

Hine, Lewis. 1915. "The High Cost of Child Labor." Brochure. Washington, DC: Library of Congress.

Hiner, N. Ray, and Joseph M. Hawes, eds. 1985. *Growing Up in America: Children in Historical Perspective.* Urbana: University of Illinois Press.

Hinton, S. E. 1967. *The Outsiders.* Boston: G. K. Hall.

His Majestie's Clerks. 1996. *Goostly Psalmes: Anglo American Psalmody, 1550–1800.* Harmonia Mundi.

Hoben, Allan. 1913. *The Minister and the Boy: A Handbook for Churchmen Engaged in Boys' Work.* Chicago: University of Chicago Press.

Hoch-Deutsches Lutherisches ABC und Namen Büchlein für Kinder. 1819. Germantown, PA: W. Billmeyer.

Hochschild, Arlie R. 1997. *The Time Bind.* New York: Metropolitan Books.

Hodges, W. F., and B. L. Bloom. 1984. "Parent's Reports of Children's Adjustment to Marital Separation: A Longitudinal Study." *Journal of Divorce* 8, no. 1: 33–50.

Hodgson, Lynne. 1992. "Adult Grandchildren and Their Grandparents: The Enduring Bond." *International Journal of Aging and Human Development* 34: 209–225.

Hogan, Dennis, David Eggebeen, and Sean Snaith. 1996. "The Well-Being of Aging Americans with Very Old Parents." Pp. 327–346 in *Aging and Generational Relations over the Life Course.* Edited by Tamara Haraven. German: Aldine de Gruyter.

Hohman, Leslie B., and Bertram Schaffner. 1947. "The Sex Lives of Unmarried Men." *American Journal of Sociology* 52 (May): 501–507.

Holland, Kenneth, and Frank Ernest Hill. 1942. *Youth in the CCC.* Washington, DC: American Council on Education.

Hollander, Zander, ed. 1979. *The Modern Encyclopedia of Basketball.* New York: Doubleday.

Holliday, J. S. 1999. *Rush for Riches: Gold Fever and the Making of California.* Berkeley: University of California Press.

Hollinger, Joan H., et al., eds. 1989. *Adoption in Law and Practice.* New York: Mathew Bender.

Holloran, Peter. 1989. *Boston's Wayward Children: Social Services for Homeless Children, 1830–1930.* Rutherford, NJ: Fairleigh Dickinson University Press.

Holt, Marilyn. 1992. *The Orphan Trains: Placing Out in America.* Lincoln: University of Nebraska Press.

Holzman, Robert S. 1956. *The Romance of Firefighting.* New York: Bonanza Books.

Homicide Trends in the United States. 2001. Washington, DC: Bureau of Justice Statistics.

Hoobler, Dorothy, and Thomas Hoobler. 1994. *The Chinese American Family Album.* New York: Oxford University Press.

Hopkins, C. Howard. 1951. *History of the Y.M.C.A. in North America.* New York: Association Press.

Horatio Alger Association of Distinguished Americans, http://www.horatioalger.com.

Horn, James. 1979. "Servant Emigration to the Chesapeake in the Seventeenth Century." Pp. 51–95 in *The Chesapeake in the Seventeenth Century.* Edited by Thad W. Tate and David L. Ammerman. New York: W. W. Norton.

Horn, Maurice, ed. 1977. *The World Encyclopedia of Comics.* New York: Avon.

Horton, James, and Lois E. Horton, consulting eds. 1995. *A History of the African American People.* New York: Smithmark Publishers.

Howard-Pitney, Beth, Teresa D. LaFromboise, Mike Basil, Benedette September, and Mike Johnson. 1992. "Psychological and Social Indicators of Suicide Ideation and Suicide Attempts in Zuni Adolescents." *Journal of Consulting and Clinical Psychology* 60: 473–476.

Howell, James C. 1998. "Youth Gangs: An Overview." *Juvenile Justice Bulletin.* Washington, DC: U.S. Department of Justice, Office of Juvenile Justice and Delinquency Prevention.

Howell, Susan H., Pedro R. Portes, and Joseph H. Brown. 1997. "Gender and Age Differences in Child Adjustment to Parental Separation." *Journal of Divorce and Remarriage* 27, nos. 3–4: 141–158.

Huck, Charlotte. 1997. *Children's Literature in the Elementary School.* 6th ed. Boston: McGraw-Hill.

Huey, Wayne C. 1987. "Counseling Teenage Fathers: The 'Maximizing a Life Experience' (MALE) Group." *School Counselor* 35: 40–47.

Huff, C. Ronald, ed. 1990. *Gangs in America.* 1st ed. Newbury Park, CA: Sage.

Huffstutter, P. J., and Claudia Eller. 2000. "GameWorks to Restrict Youngsters at Arcades." *Los Angeles Times,* October 6, C1.

Hughes, Fergus P. 1999. *Children, Play, and Development.* Boston: Allyn and Bacon.

Huizinga, Johan. 1955. *Homo Ludens: A Study of the Play Element in Culture.* Boston: Beacon Press.

Hulse, Diane. 1997. *Brad and Cory: A Study of Middle School Boys.* Cleveland: Cleveland's University School Press.

Hunt, Alan. 1998. "The Great Masturbation Panic and the Discourses of Moral Regulation in Nineteenth- and Early Twentieth-Century Britain." *Journal of the History of Sexuality* 8 (April): 575–615.

Hunt, Lynn, ed. 1993. *The Invention of Pornography: Obscenity and the Origins of Modernity, 1500–1800.* New York: Zone Books.

Hunter, William. 2000. "The Dot Eaters: Videogame History 101," http://www.emuunlim.com/doteaters/index.htm (accessed December 27, 2000).

Hupp, Father Robert P. 1985. *The New Boys Town.* New York: Newcomen Society of the United States.

Hurtado, Alfred. 1988. *Indian Survival on the California Frontier.* New Haven: Yale University Press.

Hutchinson, Edward P. 1956. *Immigrants and Their Children, 1850–1950.* New York: Wiley.

Hutchinson Family's Book of Words. 1851. New York: Baker, Godwin and Co., Steam Printers.

Hyman, Irwin A. 1990. *Reading, Writing and the Hickory Stick: The Appalling Story of Physical and Psychological Abuse in American Schools.* Lexington, MA: Lexington Books.

Hyman, Irwin A., and James H. Wise. 1979. *Corporal Punishment in American Education: Readings in History, Practice, and Alternatives.* Philadelphia, PA: Temple University Press.

Hyman, Paula. 1990. "The Introduction of Bat Mitzvah in Conservative Judaism in Postwar America." *YIVO Annual* 19: 133–146.

Ide-Smith, Susan G., and Stephen E. Lea. 1988. "Gambling in Young Adolescents." *Journal of Gambling Behavior* 4, no. 2: 110–118.

IGTimes, in association with Stampa Alternativa. 1996. *Style: Writing from the Underground.* Terni, Italy: Umbriagraf.

Inge, M. Thomas. 1990. *Comics as Culture.* Jackson: University of Mississippi Press.

Inhelder, Barbel, and Jean Piaget. 1958. *The Growth of Logical Thinking from Childhood to Adolescence.* New York: Basic Books.

International Technology Education Association. 2000. *Standards for Technological Literacy: Content for the Study of Technology.* Reston, VA: ITEA.

Isenberg, Michael T. 1988. *John L. Sullivan and His America.* Urbana: University of Illinois Press.

Jackson, Donald, ed. 1978. *Letters of the Lewis and Clark Expedition.* Vol. 2. 1962. Reprint, Urbana: University of Illinois Press.

Jackson, Kathy Merlock. 1986. *Images of Children in American Film: A Sociocultural Analysis.* Metuchen, NJ: Scarecrow Press.

Jackson, Robert, and Edward Castillo. 1995. *Indians, Franciscans, and Spanish Colonization: The Impact of the Mission System on California Indians.* Albuquerque: University of New Mexico Press.

Jackson, Ronald. 1994. *Classic TV Westerns: A Pictorial History.* New Jersey: Carol Publishing Group.

Jacques, Brian. 1986. *Redwall.* New York: Putnam.

Jarvis, F. W. 1995. *Schola Illustris: The Roxbury Latin School.* Boston: David Godine.

Jeal, Tim. 1990. *The Boy-Man: The Life of Lord Baden-Powell.* New York: William Morrow.

Jefferson, Thomas. 1944. *Notes on Virginia.* First published in 1784. In *The Life and Selected Writings of Thomas Jefferson.* Edited by Adrienne Koch and William Peden. New York: Modern Library.

Jeffords, Susan. 1989. *The Remasculinization of America: Gender and the Vietnam War.* Bloomington: Indiana University Press.

Jeffrey, Linda, Demond Miller, and Margaret Linn. In press. "Middle School Bullying as a Context for the Development of Passive Observers to the Victimization of Others." *Journal of Emotional Abuse.*

Jendryka, Brian. 1994. "Flanagan's Island: Boys Town 1994." *Current* (November): 4–10.

Jenkins, Henry. "'Complete Freedom of Movement': Video Games as Gendered Play Spaces." Pp. 262–297 in *From Barbie to Mortal Combat: Gender and Computer Games.* Edited by Henry Jenkins and Justine Cassell. Cambridge, MA: MIT Press.

Jenkins, Philip. 1998. *Moral Panic: Changing Concepts of the Child Molester in Modern America.* New Haven, CT: Yale University Press.

Jessor, Richard, and Shirley Jessor. 1977. *Problem Behavior and Psychosocial Development: A Longitudinal Study of Youth.* New York: Cambridge University Press.

Jhally, Sut, and Justin Lewis. 1992. *Enlightened Racism: The Cosby Show, Audiences and the Myth of the American Dream.* Boulder, CO: Westview Press.

Joffe, H., and J. E. Dockrell. 1995. "Safer Sex: Lessons from the Male Sex Industry."

Journal of Community and Applied Social Psychology 5, no. 5: 333–346.

Johnson, Charles, and John McCluskey, Jr., eds. 1997. *Black Men Speaking.* Bloomington: Indiana University Press.

Johnson, Deidre. 1993. *Edward Stratemeyer and the Stratemeyer Syndicate.* Twayne United States Authors Series. New York: Twayne Publishers.

Johnson, Elmer L. 1979. *The History of YMCA Physical Education.* Chicago: Association Press.

Johnson, George E. 1916. *Education through Recreation.* Cleveland, OH: Survey Committee of the Cleveland Foundation.

Johnson, Gregory R., Etienne G. Krug, and Lloyd B. Potter. 2000. "Suicide among Adolescents and Young Adults: A Cross-National Comparison of 34 Countries." *Suicide and Life-Threatening Behavior* 30: 74–82.

Johnson, Susan Lee. 2000. *Roaring Camp: The Social World of the California Gold Rush.* New York: W. W. Norton.

Johnson, Thomas H., ed. 1970. *The Complete Poems of Emily Dickinson.* London: Faber and Faber.

Johnson, Walter. 1999. *Soul by Soul: Life inside the Antebellum Slave Market.* Cambridge, MA: Harvard University Press.

Jones, Arthur F., Jr., and Daniel H. Weinberg. 2000. *Current Population Reports: The Changing Shape of the Nation's Income Distribution, 1947–1998.* Washington, DC: U.S. Census Bureau.

Jones, James. 1993. *Bad Blood: The Tuskegee Syphilis Experiment.* Rev. ed. New York: Free Press.

Jones, Norrece T., Jr. 1990. *Born a Child of Freedom, Yet a Slave: Mechanisms of Control and Strategies of Resistance in*

Antebellum South Carolina. Hanover, NH: University Press of New England.

Jordan, Terry. 1993. *North American Cattle-Ranching Frontiers: Origins, Diffusion and Differentiation.* Albuquerque: University of New Mexico Press.

Joselit, Jenna Weissman. 1994. *The Wonders of America: Reinventing Jewish Culture, 1880–1950.* New York: Hill and Wang.

Joyner, Charles. 1984. *Down by the Riverside: A South Carolina Slave Community.* Urbana: University of Illinois Press.

Juvenile Offenders and Victims: 1999 National Report. 1999. Washington, DC: Office of Juvenile Justice and Delinquency Prevention, U.S. Department of Justice.

Juvenile Protective Department. 1935. "Street Traders of Buffalo, New York." Buffalo: Juvenile Protective Department, 13–14.

Kadushin, Alfred, and Judith A. Martin. 1998. *Child Welfare Services.* 4th ed. New York: Macmillan.

Kaestle, Carl F. 1973a. *The Evolution of an Urban School System: New York City, 1750–1850.* Cambridge, MA: Harvard University Press.

———. 1973b. *Joseph Lancaster and the Monitorial School Movement.* New York: Teachers College Press.

———. 1983. *Pillars of the Republic: Common Schools and American Society, 1780–1860.* New York: Hill and Wang.

Kafai, Yasmin B. 1998. "Video Game Designs by Girls and Boys: Variability and Consistency of Gender Differences." Pp 90–117 in *From Barbie to Mortal Kombat: Gender and Computer Games.* Edited by Henry Jenkins and Justine Cassell. Cambridge, MA: MIT Press.

Kalb, Claudia. 2000. "What Boys Really Want." *Newsweek* (July 10): 52.

Kalter, Neil, Amy Kloner, Shelly Schreier, and Katherine Okla. 1989. "Predictors of Children's Postdivorce Adjustment." *American Journal of Orthopsychiatry* 59, no. 4: 605–618.

Kann, Laura, Steven A. Kinchen, Barbara I. Williams, James G. Ross, Richard Lowry, Jo Anne Grunbaum, Lloyd J. Kolbe, and State and Local YRBSS Coordinators. 2000. "Youth Risk Behavior Surveillance—United States, 1999." Centers for Disease Control and Prevention: *MMWR Surveillance Summaries* 49, no. SS-5 (June 9).

Kanter, Rosabeth Moss. 1975. "Women and the Structure of Organizations: Explorations in Theory and Behavior." In *Another Voice: Feminist Perspectives on Social Life and Social Science.* Edited by M. Millman and R. M. Kanter. New York: Anchor Books.

———. 1977. *Men and Women of the Corporation.* New York: Basic Books.

Kaplan, Judy, and Linn Shapiro, eds. 1998. *Red Diapers: Growing Up in the Communist Left.* Urbana: University of Illinois Press.

Karmiloff-Smith, Annette, and Barbel Inhelder. 1974. "If You Want to Get Ahead, Get a Theory." *Cognition* 3: 195–212.

Keats, Ezra Jack. 1962. *The Snowy Day.* New York: Penguin.

Keise, Celestine. 1992. *Sugar and Spice! Bullying in Single-Sex Schools.* Stoke-on-Trent, Staffordshire, UK: Trentham Books.

Kelley, Florence, and Alzina P. Stevens. 1895. *Hull-House Maps and Papers.* New York: Crowell.

Kemp, John R., ed. 1986. *Lewis Hine Photographs of Child Labor in the New*

South. Jackson: University Press of Mississippi.

Kempton, Tracey, Lisa Armistead, Michelle Wierson, and Rex Forehand. 1991. "Presence of a Sibling as a Potential Buffer Following Parental Divorce: An Examination of Young Adolescents." *Journal of Clinical Child Psychology* 20: 434–438.

Kendrick, Walter. 1996. *The Secret Museum: Pornography in Modern Culture.* 2d ed. Los Angeles: University of California Press.

Kerber, Linda K. 1980. *Women of the Republic: Intellect and Ideology in Revolutionary America.* Chapel Hill: University of North Carolina Press.

Kerr, Leah M. 2000. *Driving Me Wild: Nitro-Powered Outlaw Culture.* New York: Juno Books.

Kerrigan, William Thomas. 1997. "'Young America!': Romantic Nationalism in Literature and Politics, 1843–1861." Ph.D. diss., University of Michigan.

Kerwin, Denise. 1994. "Ambivalent Pleasure from *Married . . . with Children.*" In *Television: The Critical View.* 5th ed. Edited by Horace Newcomb. New York: Oxford University Press.

Kessler, Christina. 2000. *No Condition Is Permanent.* New York: Philomel Books.

Kessler, Suzanne J. 1990. "The Medical Construction of Gender: Case Management of Intersexed Infants." *Signs* 16, no. 1.

Kett, Joseph. 1977. *Rites of Passage: Adolescence in America, 1790 to the Present.* New York: Basic Books.

Kibler, M. Alison. 1999. *Rank Ladies: Gender and Cultural Hierarchy in American Vaudeville.* Chapel Hill: University of North Carolina Press.

Kidd, A., and R. Kidd. 1990. "Social and Environmental Influences on Children's Attitudes toward Pets." *Psychological Reports* 67: 807–818.

Kidd, Bruce. 1996. *The Struggle for Canadian Sport.* Toronto: University of Toronto Press.

Kidd, Bruce, and John Macfarlane. 1972. *The Death of Hockey.* Toronto: New Press.

Kids and Guns. 2000. Washington, DC: Office of Juvenile Justice and Delinquency Prevention, U.S. Department of Justice.

Kiefer, Monica. 1948. *American Children through Their Books, 1700–1835.* Philadelphia: University of Pennsylvania Press.

Kimball, Marie. 1943. *Jefferson: The Road to Glory, 1743 to 1776.* New York: Coward-McCann.

Kimmel, Michael. 1996. *Manhood in America: A Cultural History.* New York: Free Press.

———. 2000. *The Gendered Society Reader.* New York: Oxford University Press.

Kincheloe, J. L., S. R. Steinberg, and A. D. Gresson III. 1997. *Measured Lies: The Bell Curve Examined.* New York: St. Martin's Press.

Kincheloe, Joe L. 1997. "*Home Alone* and 'Bad to the Bone': The Advent of a Postmodern Childhood." Pp. 31–52 in *Kinderculture: The Corporate Construction of Childhood.* Edited by Shirley R. Steinberg and Joe L. Kincheloe. Boulder, CO: Westview Press.

———. 1999. *How Do We Tell the Worker? The Socioeconomic Foundations of Work and Vocational Education.* Boulder, CO: Westview Press.

Kinder, Marsha. 1991. *Playing with Power in Movies, Television, and Video Games.* Berkeley: University of California Press.

Kinder, Marsha, ed. 1999. *Kids' Media Culture*. Durham, NC: Duke University Press.

Kindlon, Dan, and Michael Thompson. 1999. *Raising Cain: Protecting the Emotional Life of Boys*. New York: Ballantine.

King, Margaret J. 1981. "Disneyland and Walt Disney World: Traditional Values in Futuristic Form." *Journal of Popular Culture* (Summer): 114–140.

King, Stephen. 1981. *Danse Macabre*. New York: Everest House Publishers.

King, Wilma. 1995. *Stolen Childhood: Slave Youth in Nineteenth Century America*. Bloomington: Indiana University Press.

Kinsey, Alfred C., Wardell B. Pomeroy, and Clyde E. Martin. 1948. *Sexual Behavior in the Human Male*. Philadelphia: W. B. Saunders.

Kipnis, Aaron. 1999. *Angry Young Men*. San Francisco: Jossey-Bass.

Kirk, Robert William. 1994. *Earning Their Stripes: The Mobilization of American Children in the Second World War*. New York: Peter Lang.

Kirsch, George B. 2000. "Young Men's Hebrew Association." Pp. 501–502 in *Encyclopedia of Ethnicity and Sports in the United States*. Edited by George B. Kirsch, Othello Harris, and Claire E. Nolte. Westport, CT: Greenwood Press.

Kirsch, George B., ed. 1992. *Sports in North America: A Documentary History*. Vol. 3, *The Rise of Modern Sports, 1840–1860*. Gulf Breeze, FL: Academic International Press.

Kirsch, George, Othello Harris, and Claire E. Nolte, eds. 2000. *Encyclopedia of Ethnic Sports in the United States*. Westport, CT: Greenwood Press.

Kiselica, Mark S. 1995. *Multicultural Counseling with Teenage Fathers: A Practical Guide*. Thousand Oaks, CA: Sage.

———. 1999. "Counseling Teen Fathers." Pp. 179–198 in *Handbook of Counseling Boys and Adolescent Males*. Edited by A. M. Horne and M. S. Kiselica. Thousand Oaks, CA: Sage.

Klahr, David. 2000. *Exploring Science: The Cognition and Development of Discovery Processes*. Cambridge, MA: MIT Press.

Klein, Alan. 1993. *Little Big Man: Bodybuilding Subculture and Gender Construction*. Albany: State University of New York Press.

———. 1994. "The Cultural Anatomy of Competitive Women's Bodybuilding." In *Many Mirrors: Body Image and Social Relations*. Edited by Nicole Sault. New Brunswick, NJ: Rutgers University Press.

Klein, Malcolm W. 1995. *The American Street Gang*. New York: Oxford University Press.

———. 1996. "Gangs in the United States and Europe." *European Journal on Criminal Policy and Research* (special issue): 63–80.

Klein, Malcolm W., and Cheryl Lee Maxson. 1989. "Street Gang Violence." Pp. 198–234 in *Violent Crime, Violent Criminals*. Edited by M. E. Wolfgang and M. A. Weiner. Newbury Park, CA: Sage.

Klein, Malcolm W., Cheryl Maxson, and Jody Miller, eds. 1995. *The Modern Gang Reader*. Los Angeles: Roxbury.

Klepp, Susan, and Billy Smith, eds. 1992. *The Infortunate: The Voyage and Adventures of William Moraley, an Indentured Servant*. University Park: Pennsylvania State University Press.

Klier, Barbara, Jacquelyn Quiram, and Mark Siegel, eds. 1999. *Alcohol and Tobacco: America's Drugs of Choice.* Wylie, TX: Information Plus.

Klier, Barbara, Mark Siegel, and Jacquelyn Quiram, eds. 1999. *Illegal Drugs: America's Anguish.* Wylie, TX: Information Plus.

Kline, Stephen. 1993. *Out of the Garden: Toys and Children's Culture in the Age of TV Marketing.* London: Verso.

Klinman, Debra G., Joelle H. Sander, Jacqueline L. Rosen, Karen R. Longo, and Lorenzo P. Martinez. 1985. *The Teen Parent Collaboration: Reaching and Serving the Teenage Father.* New York: Bank Street College of Education.

Knox, Thomas W. 1881. *The Young Nimrods in North America: A Book for Boys.* New York: Harper and Brothers.

Kohler, Anna. 1897. "Children's Sense of Money." *Studies in Education* 1, no. 9: 323–331.

Kopka, Deborah L. 1997. *School Violence: A Reference Handbook.* Santa Barbara, CA: ABC-CLIO.

Kornhauser, Elizabeth Mankin. 1991. *Ralph Earl: The Face of the Young Republic.* Hartford, CT: Wadsworth Atheneum.

Koven, Edward. 1996. *Smoking: The Story behind the Haze.* Commack, NY: Nova Science.

Kowaleski, Michael., ed. 1997. *Gold Rush: A Literary Exploration.* Berkeley: Heyday Books and California Council for the Humanities.

Kraft, Louis. 1941. "Center, The Jewish." In *The Universal Jewish Encyclopedia.* Edited by Isaac Landman.

Kraushaar, Otto. 1972. *American Nonpublic Schools: Patterns of Diversity.* Baltimore: Johns Hopkins University.

Kuhn, Deanna, Eric Amsel, and Michael O'Loughlin. 1988. *The Development of Scientific Thinking Skills.* Orlando, FL: Academic Press.

Kuhn, Thomas S. 1962. *The Structure of Scientific Reasoning.* Chicago: University of Chicago Press.

Kulikoff, Allan. 1986. *Tobacco and Slaves: The Development of Southern Cultures in the Chesapeake, 1680–1800.* Chapel Hill: University of North Carolina Press.

Kurdek, L., and A. E. Siesky. 1980. "Children's Perceptions of Their Parents' Divorce." *Journal of Divorce* 3, no. 4: 339–378.

Kushner, Howard I. 1993. "Suicide, Gender, and the Fear of Modernity in Nineteenth-Century Medical and Social Thought." *Journal of Social History* 26, no. 3: 461–490.

———. 1998. *The Age of the Child: Children in America, 1890–1920.* New York: Twayne.

La Flesche, Francis. 1900. *The Middle Five: Indian Schoolboys of the Omaha Tribe.* 1900. Reprint, Madison: University of Wisconsin Press, 1963.

Ladd, Wayne M., and Angela Lumpkin, eds. 1979. *Sport in American Education: History and Perspective.* Reston, VA: NASPE-AAHPERD.

Ladd-Taylor, Molly, and Lauri Umanski, eds. 1998. *"Bad" Mothers: The Politics of Blame in Twentieth-Century America.* New York: New York University Press.

Lamb, Michael E. 1997. *The Role of the Father in Child Development.* 3d ed. New York: John Wiley and Sons.

Lambert, Barbara, ed. 1980. *Music in Colonial Massachusetts 1630–1820: Music in Public Places.* Boston: Colonial Society of Massachusetts.

Landale, Nancy S. 1989. "Opportunity, Movement, and Marriage: U.S. Farm Sons at the Turn of the Century." *Journal of Family History* 14, no. 4: 365–386.

Lane, Frederick S. III. 2000. *Obscene Profits: The Entrepreneurs of Pornography in the Cyber Age.* New York: Routledge.

Langfeld, William. 1928. *The Young Men's Hebrew Association of Philadelphia: A Fifty-Year Chronicle.* Philadelphia: Young Men's and Young Women's Hebrew Association of Philadelphia.

Lanzinger, I. 1990. "Toward Feminist Science Teaching." *Canadian Woman Studies* 13, no. 2.

LaRossa, Ralph. 1997. *The Modernization of Fatherhood: A Social and Political History.* Chicago: University of Chicago Press.

Latta, Alexander Bonner, and E. Latta. 1860. *The Origin and Introduction of the Steam Fire Engine Together with the Results of the Use of Them in Cincinnati, St. Louis and Louisville, for One Year, also, Showing the Effect on Insurance Companies, etc.* Cincinnati: Moore, Wilstach, Keys.

Lauden, Larry. 1977. *Progress and Its Problems.* Berkeley: University of California Press.

Lawes, Carolyn J. "Capitalizing on Mother: John S. C. Abbott and Self-Interested Motherhood." *Proceedings of the American Antiquarian Society* 108, pt. 2: 343–395.

Lawrence, Richard. 1998. *School Crime and Juvenile Justice.* New York: Oxford University Press.

Lears, T. J. Jackson. 1981. *No Place of Grace: Anti-Modernism and the Transformation of American Culture, 1880–1920.* New York: Pantheon Books.

Lee, Alfred McClung. 1937. *The Daily Newspaper in America: Evolution of a Social Instrument.* New York: Macmillan.

Lee, L., and G. Zhan. 1998. "Psychosocial Status of Children and Youth." Pp. 211–233 in *Handbook of Asian American Psychology.* Edited by L. Lee and N. Zane. Thousand Oaks, CA: Sage.

Lee, Sharon, and Marilyn Fernandez. 1998. "Trends in Asian American Racial/Ethnic Intermarriage: A Comparison of 1980 and 1990 Census Data." *Sociological Perspectives* 41, no. 2: 323–343.

Lee, Stacy. 1996. *Unraveling the "Model Minority" Stereotype: Listening to Asian American Youth.* New York: Columbia University Teachers College Press.

Leitenberg, Harold, Mark J. Detzer, and Debra Srebnik. 1993. "Gender Differences in Masturbation and the Relation of Masturbation Experience in Preadolescence and/or Early Adolescence to Sexual Behavior and Sexual Adjustment in Young Adulthood." *Archives of Sexual Behavior* 22 (April): 87–98.

Leland, John. 2000. "Why America Is Hooked on Professional Wrestling." *Newsweek* 135, no. 6 (February 7): 46.

Lemann, N. 2000. *The Big Test: The Secret History of the American Meritocracy.* New York: Farrar, Straus and Giroux.

Lemke, Bob. 1997. *Standard Catalog of Baseball Cards.* Iola, WI: Krause Publications.

Lender, Mark Edward. 1980. "The Social Structure of the New Jersey Brigade." In *The Military in America from the Colonial Era to the Present.* Edited by Peter Karsten. New York: Free Press.

L'Engle, Madeleine. 1962. *A Wrinkle in Time.* New York: Farrar, Straus and Giroux.

Leppek, Chris. 1995. "The Life and Times of Denver's Joe 'Awful' Coffee." *Western States Jewish History* 27, no. 1 (October): 43–61.

Lesko, Nancy, ed. 2000. *Masculinities at School.* Thousand Oaks, CA: Sage.

Leverenz, David. 1989. *Manhood and the American Renaissance.* Ithaca: Cornell University Press.

Levi, Antonia. 1996. *Samurai from Outer Space: Understanding Japanese Animation.* Chicago: Caris Publishing.

Levine, Lawrence W. 1997. *Highbrow/ Lowbrow: The Emergence of Cultural Hierarchy in America.* Cambridge, MA: Harvard University Press.

Levine, Peter. 1992. *Ellis Island to Ebbets Field: Sport and the American Jewish Experience.* New York: Oxford University Press.

Levinson, Stacey, Stacey Mack, Daniel Reinhardt, Helen Suarez, and Grace Yeh. 1991. "Halloween as a Consumption Experience." Undergraduate research thesis, Rutgers University School of Business.

Levy, Barry. 1988. *Quakers and the American Family: British Settlement in the Delaware Valley.* New York: Oxford University Press.

Levy, Jo Ann. 1992. *They Saw the Elephant: Women in the California Gold Rush.* Norman: University of Oklahoma Press.

Lewinsohn, Peter M., Paul Rohde, and John R. Seeley. 1996. "Adolescent Suicidal Ideation and Attempts: Prevalence, Risk Factors, and Clinical Implications." *Clinical Psychology: Science and Practice* 3, no. 1: 25–46.

Lewis, David Levering. 1993. *W. E. B. Du Bois: Biography of a Race.* New York: Henry Holt.

Lewis, Dorothy. 1992. "From Abuse to Violence: Psychophysiological Consequences of Maltreatment." *Journal of the American Academy of Child and Adolescent Psychiatry* 31 (May): 383–391.

———. 1998. *Guilty by Reason of Insanity.* New York: Fawcett-Columbine.

Lewis, Theodore 1997. "Toward a Liberal Vocational Education." *Journal of Philosophy of Education* 31, no. 3: 477–489.

Lewontin, Richard. 2000. *The Triple Helix: Gene, Organism, and Environment.* Cambridge: Harvard University Press.

Lewontin, Richard, Steven Rose, and Leon Kamin. 1984. *Not in Our Genes: Biology, Ideology, and Human Nature.* New York: Pantheon.

Ley, David, and Roman Cybriwsky. 1974. "Urban Graffiti as Territorial Markers." *Annals of the Association of American Geographers* 64: 491–505.

Lhamon, W. T., Jr. 1998. *Raising Cain: Blackface Performance from Jim Crow to Hip Hop.* Cambridge: Harvard University Press.

Licht, Walter. 1992. *Getting Work: Philadelphia, 1840–1950.* Cambridge, MA: Harvard University Press.

Limber, Susan P., P. Cunningham, V. Flerx, J. Ivey, M. National, S. Chai, and G. Melton. 1997. "Bullying among School Children: Preliminary Findings from a School-Based Intervention Program." Paper presented at the Fifth International Family Violence Research Conference, Durham, NH, June–July.

Linder, Marc. 1990. "From Street Urchins to Little Merchants: The Juridical Transvaluation of Child Newspaper Carriers." *Temple Law Review* (Winter): 829–864.

———. 1997. "What's Black and White and Red All Over? The Blood Tax on Newspapers." *Loyola Poverty Law Review* 3: 57–111.

Lingeman, Richard R. 1976. *Don't You Know There's a War On? The American Home Front 1941–1945.* New York: Capricorn Books.

Lingenfelter, Mary R., and Harry D. Kitson. 1939. *Vocations for Girls.* New York: Harcourt Brace.

Link, William A. 1986. *A Hard Country and a Lonely Place: Schooling, Society and Reform in Rural Virginia, 1870–1920.* Chapel Hill: University of North Carolina Press.

Lipsitz, George. 1990. *Time Passages: Collective Memory and American Popular Culture.* Minneapolis: University of Minnesota Press.

Lock, Stephen, and Lois Reynolds, eds. 1998. *Ashes to Ashes: The History of Smoking and Health.* Atlanta, GA: Rodopi.

Lomawaima, K. Tsianina. 1994. *They Called It Prairie Light: The Story of Chilocco Indian School.* Lincoln: University of Nebraska Press.

Lott, Eric. 1993. *Love and Theft: Blackface Minstrelsy and the American Working Class.* New York: Oxford University Press.

Lovejoy, Owen. 1910. "Newsboy Life: What Superintendents of Reformatories and Others Think about Its Effects." National Child Labor Committee, pamphlet no. 32 (June).

Lovell, Margaretta. 1988. "Reading Eighteenth-Century American Family Portraits: Social Images and Self Images." *Winterthur Portfolio* 22, no. 4 (Winter) 243–264.

Lowery, Carol R., and Shirley A. Settle. 1985. "Effects of Divorce on Children: Differential Impact of Custody and Visitation Patterns." *Family Relations: Journal of Applied Family and Child Studies* 34, no. 4: 455–463.

Lucas, Christopher J. 1994. *American Higher Education: A History.* New York: St. Martin's Press.

Lugaila, Terry A. 1998. "Marital Status and Living Arrangements: March 1998 (Update)." *Current Population Reports.* U.S. Bureau of the Census Publication no. P20-514. Washington, DC: U.S. Department of Commerce.

Lumpkin, Angela. 1985. *A Guide to the Literature of Tennis.* Westport, CT: Greenwood Press.

Lundstrom, Linden J. 1957. *The Choir School.* Minneapolis, MN: Augsburg Publishing House.

Lynch, Tom. 1878. "St. Louis: The Volunteer Fire Department, 1832–1858." *National Fireman's Journal* (August 3).

Lynd, Robert S., and Helen Merrell Lynd. 1929. *Middletown: A Study in Contemporary American Culture.* New York: Harcourt Brace.

MacCann, Donnarae, and Gloria Woodard, eds. 1989. *The Black American in Books for Children: Readings in Racism.* 2d ed. Metuchen, NJ: Scarecrow Press.

MacDonald, J. Fred. 1983. *Blacks and White TV: African Americans in Television since 1948.* Chicago: Nelson Hall.

MacDonald, Robert H. 1967. "The Frightful Consequences of Onanism: Notes on the History of a Delusion." *Journal of the History of Ideas* 28 (1967): 423–431.

MacLeod, Anne Scott. 1975. *A Moral Tale: Children's Fiction and American*

Culture, 1820–1860. Hamden, CT: Archon Books.

Macleod, David I. 1983. *Building Character in the American Boy: The Boy Scouts, YMCA, and Their Forerunners, 1870–1920.* Madison: University of Wisconsin Press.

———. 1998. *The Age of the Child: Children in America, 1890–1920.* New York: Twayne Publishers.

———. Forthcoming. *Landmarks of American Sports.* American Landmarks Series. Edited by James O. Horton. New York: Oxford University Press.

Malone, Ann Patton. 1992. *Sweet Chariot: Slave Family and Household Structure in Nineteenth-Century Louisiana.* Chapel Hill: University of North Carolina Press.

Malone, Dumas. 1948. *Jefferson the Virginian.* Boston: Little, Brown.

Maloney, P. 1980. "Street Hustling: Growing Up Gay." Unpublished manuscript.

Mandleco, Barbara L., Susanne F. Olsen, Clyde C. Robinson, Elaine S. Marshall, and Mary K. McNeilly-Choque. 1998. "Social Skills and Peer Relationships of Siblings of Children with Disabilities." Pp. 106–120 in *Children's Peer Relations.* Edited by P. T. Slee and K. Rigby. New York: Routledge.

Manfredi, Christopher P. 1998. *The Supreme Court and Juvenile Justice.* Lawrence: University of Kansas Press.

Mangan, J. A., and James Walvin, eds. 1987. *Manliness and Morality: Middle Class Masculinity in Britain and America, 1800–1940.* New York: St. Martin's Press.

Mangold, George B. 1936. *Problems of Child Welfare.* 3d ed. New York: Macmillan.

Marable, Manning. 1986. *W. E. B. Du Bois: Black Radical Democrat.* Boston: Twayne Publishers.

Marble, Scott. 189-. "Daughters of the Poor." Unpublished manuscript, Billy Rose Theater Collection, New York Public Library at Lincoln Center.

Mark, Diane Mei Lin, and Ginger Chih. 1993. *A Place Called Chinese America.* Dubuque, IA: Kendall/Hunt Publishing.

Marks, Stuart A. 1991. *Southern Hunting in Black and White: Nature, History, and Ritual in a Carolina Community.* Princeton, NJ: Princeton University Press.

Marling, Karal Ann, ed. 1997. *Designing Disney's Theme Parks: The Architecture of Reassurance.* New York: Flammarion.

Marsden, George M. 1990. *Religion and American Culture.* New York: Harcourt Brace Jovanovich.

Marsh, Dave. 1996. *The Bruce Springsteen Story.* Vol. 1, *Born to Run.* New York: Thunder's Mouth Press.

Marsh, Herbert W. 1991. "Employment during High School: Character Building or a Subversion of Academic Goals?" *Sociology of Education* 64: 172–189.

Marshall, William A., and James M. Tanner. 1970. "Variations in the Pattern of Pubertal Changes in Boys." *Archives of Disease in Childhood* 45: 13–23.

Marten, James. 1998. *The Children's Civil War.* Chapel Hill: University of North Carolina Press.

———. 1999. *Lessons of War: The Civil War in Children's Magazines.* Wilmington, DE: SR Books.

Martin, Chris. 1996. *The Top Fuel Handbook.* Wichita, KS: Beacon Publishing.

Martin, Joseph Plumb. 1993. *Ordinary Courage: The Revolutionary War*

Adventures of Joseph Plumb Martin. New York: Brandywine Press.

Marty, Martin E. 1984. *Pilgrims in Their Own Land: 500 Years of Religion in America*. New York: Penguin.

Mason, Daniel, and Barbara Schrodt. 1996. "Hockey's First Professional Team: The Portage Lakes Hockey Club of Houghton, Michigan." *Sport History Review* 27: 49–71.

Mather, Cotton. 1723. *The Pure Nazarite: Advice to a Young Man*. Boston: T. Fleet for John Phillips.

Mather, Fred. 1897. *Men I Have Fished With*. New York: Forest and Stream Publishing.

Mattingly, Paul H., and Edward W. Stevens, Jr. 1987. *"Schools and the Means of Education Shall Forever Be Encouraged": A History of Education in the Old Northwest, 1787–1880*. Athens: University of Georgia Press.

Maupin, Melissa. 1996. *The Ultimate Kids' Club Book: How to Organize, Find Members, Run Meetings, Raise Money, Handle Problems, and Much More!* Minneapolis: Free Spirit.

Maury, Ann. 1853. *Memoirs of a Huguenot Family*. New York: G. P. Putnam.

May, Elaine Tyler. 1980. *Great Expectations: Marriage and Divorce in Post-Victorian America*. Chicago: University of Chicago Press.

Mayes, Herbert R. 1928. *Alger: A Biography without a Hero*. New York: Macy-Masius.

Maynard, W. Barksdale. 1999. "'An Ideal Life in the Woods for Boys': Architecture and Culture in the Earliest Summer Camps." *Winterthur Portfolio* 34, no. 1 (Spring): 3–29.

Mays, Arthur B. 1952. *Essentials of Industrial Education*. New York: McGraw-Hill.

McAleer, John. 1984. *Ralph Waldo Emerson: Days of Encounter*. Boston: Little, Brown.

McCaslin, Nellie. 1971. *Theatre for Children in the United States: A History*. Norman: University of Oklahoma Press.

———. 1987. *Historical Guide to Children's Theatre in America*. Westport, CT: Greenwood Press.

McClellan, Keith. 1998. *The Sunday Game: At the Dawn of Professional Football*. Akron, OH: University of Akron Press.

McCloud, Scott. 1993. *Understanding Comics*. Princeton, WI: Kitchen Sink Press.

———. 2000. *Reinventing Comics*. New York: HarperPerennial.

McCoy, J. Kelly, Gene H. Brody, and Zolinda Stoneman. In press. "Temperament and the Quality of Youths' Best Friendships: Do Sibling and Parent-Child Relationships Make a Difference?"

McCullough, David. 1981. *Mornings on Horseback*. New York: Simon and Schuster.

McDaniel, Henry Bonner. 1941. *The American Newspaperboy: A Comparative Study of His Work and School Activities*. Los Angeles: Wetzel.

McFeely, William S. 1991. *Frederick Douglas*. New York: Simon and Schuster.

McGaw, Judith A. 1982. "Women and the History of American Technology." *Signs: Journal of Women in Culture and Society* 7: 798–828.

———. 1987. *Most Wonderful Machine: Mechanization and Social Change in*

Berkshire Paper Making, 1801–1885. Princeton, NJ: Princeton University Press.

McKelvey, Carole A., and JoEllen Stevens. 1994. *Adoption Crisis: The Truth Behind Adoption and Foster Care.* Golden, CO: Fulcrum Publishing.

McKenzie, Richard B., ed. 1998. *Rethinking Orphanages for the 21st Century.* Thousand Oaks, CA: Sage.

McKinney, C. F. N.d. "A Discussion of Leadership." Culver Military Academy, 7.

McLaughlin, Milbrey W., Merita A. Irby, and Juliet Langman. 1994. *Urban Sanctuaries: Neighborhood Organizations in the Lives and Futures of Inner-City Youth.* San Francisco: Jossey-Bass.

McNeal, James U. 1987. *Children as Consumers: Insights and Implications.* Lexington, MA: D.C. Heath.

———. 1992. *Kids as Customers: A Handbook of Marketing to Children.* New York: Lexington Books.

———. 1999. *The Kids Market: Myths and Realities.* Ithaca, NY: Paramount Market Publishing.

McNeil, Alex. 1996. *Total Television.* New York: Penguin.

Mead, George. 1934. *Mind, Self and Society.* Chicago: University of Chicago Press.

Mechling, Jay. 1986. "Children's Folklore." Pp. 91–120 in *Folk Groups and Folklore Genres.* Edited by Elliott Oring. Logan: Utah State University Press.

———. 2001. *On My Honor: The Boy Scouts and American Culture.* Chicago: University of Chicago Press.

Meckel, Richard A. 1990. *Save the Babies: American Public Health Reform and the Prevention of Infant Mortality 1850–1929.* Baltimore: Johns Hopkins University Press. 1998. Reprint, Ann Arbor: University of Michigan Press.

———. 1996. "Health and Disease." Pp. 757–786 in *Encyclopedia of the United States in the Twentieth Century,* vol. 2. Edited by Stanley I. Kutler et al. New York: Scribner's.

Mednick, Sarnoff. 1977. "A Biosocial Theory of Learning Law-abiding Behavior." Pp. 1–8 in *Biosocial Bases of Criminal Behavior.* Edited by S. Mednick and K. Christiansen. New York: Garner.

Mednick, Sarnoff, Vicki Pollock, Jan Volavka, and William Gabriella. 1982. "Biology and Violence." Pp. 21–80 in *Criminal Violence.* Edited by Marvin Wolfgang and Neil Weiner. Beverly Hills: Sage.

Meeks, Carol. 1998. "Factors Influencing Adolescents' Income and Expenditures." *Journal of Family and Economic Issues* 19, no. 2: 131–150.

Melson, G. 2001. *Why the Wild Things Are.* Cambridge, MA: Harvard University Press.

Meltzoff, Andrew, and Allison Gropnik. 1996. *Words, Thoughts, and Theories.* Cambridge, MA: MIT Press.

Mencken, H. L. 1982. *The American Language.* New York: Alfred A. Knopf.

Mennel, Robert M. 1973. *Thorns and Thistles: Juvenile Delinquency in the United States, 1825–1940.* Hanover, NH: University Press of New England.

Mergen, Bernard. 1982. *Play and Playthings: A Reference Guide.* Westport, CT: Greenwood Press.

———. 1997. *Snow in America.* Washington, DC: Smithsonian Institution Press.

Merrill, Liliburn. 1908. *Winning the Boy.* New York: Fleming H. Revell.

Metcalfe, Alan. 1987. *Canada Learns to Play: The Emergence of Organized Sport 1807–1904.* Toronto: McClelland and Stewart.

Milbrath, Constance. 1995. "Germinal Motifs in the Work of a Gifted Child Artist." Pp. 101–134 in *The Development of Artistically Gifted Children: Selected Case Studies.* Edited by Claire Golomb. Hillsdale, NJ: Erlbaum.

———. 1998. *Patterns of Artistic Development in Children: Comparative Studies of Talent.* New York: Cambridge University Press.

Milburn, William Henry. 1857. *The Rifle, Axe, and Saddle-Bags, and Other Lectures.* New York: Derby and Jackson.

Millard, Elaine. 1997. *Differently Literate: Boys, Girls and the Schooling of Literacy.* London: Falmer Press.

Miller, Jerome G. 1991. *Last One over the Wall: The Massachusetts Experiment in Closing Reform Schools.* Columbus: Ohio State University Press.

Miller, Joanne, and Susan Yung. 1990. "The Role of Allowances in Adolescent Socialization." *Youth and Society* 22, no. 2: 137–159.

Milliken, Randall. 1995. *A Time of Little Choice: The Disintegration of Tribal Culture in the San Francisco Bay Area, 1769–1810.* Menlo Park: Ballena Press.

Minehan, Thomas. 1934. *Boy and Girl Tramps of America.* New York: Farrar and Rinehart.

"Miseries of News-Girls." 1881. *New York Tribune,* February 20, 12.

Mishkind, Michael. 1987. "The Embodiment of Masculinity: Cultural, Psychological, and Behavioral Dimensions." In *Changing Men: New Directions in Research on Men and Masculinity.* Edited by Michael Kimmel. Newbury Park, CA: Sage.

Mishler, Paul C. 1999. *Raising Reds: The Young Pioneers, Radical Summer Camps, and Communist Political Culture in the United States.* New York: Columbia University Press.

Mizell, C. Andre, and Lala C. Steelman. 2000. "All My Children: The Consequences of Sibling Group Characteristics on the Marital Happiness of Young Mothers." *Journal of Family Issues* 21: 858–887.

Mjagkij, Nina. 1994. *Light in the Darkness: African Americans and the YMCA, 1852–1946.* Lexington: University Press of Kentucky.

Modell, John. 1989. *Into One's Own: From Youth to Adulthood in the United States, 1920–1985.* Berkeley: University of California Press.

Monaghan, E. Jennifer. 1983. *A Common Heritage: Noah Webster's Blue-back Speller.* Hamden, CT: Archon Books.

Monroy, Douglas. 1999. *Rebirth: Mexican Los Angeles from the Great Migration to the Great Depression.* Berkeley: University of California Press.

Montagu, Ashley. 1985. "The Sociobiology Debate: An Introduction." Pp. 24–33 in *Biology, Crime and Ethics: A Study of Biological Explanations for Criminal Behavior.* Edited by Frank Marsh and Janet Katz. Cincinnati: Anderson.

Moody, Richard. 1980. *Ned Harrigan: From Corlear's Hook to Herald Square.* Chicago: Nelson-Hall.

Moon, Michael. 1987. "'The Gentle Boy from the Dangerous Classes': Pederasty, Domesticity, and Capitalism in Horatio Alger." *Representations* 19 (Summer): 95–97.

Mooney, Cynthia, ed. 1999. *Drugs, Alcohol and Tobacco: Macmillan Health Encyclopedia.* New York: Macmillan.

Moore, Joan. 1991. *Going Down to the Barrio: Homeboys and Homegirls in Change.* Philadelphia: Temple University Press.

Moore, John Hammond. 1976. *Albemarle: Jefferson's County, 1727–1976.* Charlottesville: University Press of Virginia.

Moore, John P., and Craig P. Terrett. 1998. *Highlights of the 1996 National Youth Gang Survey.* Washington, DC: U.S. Department of Justice, Office of Juvenile Justice and Delinquency Prevention.

Moorhead, James. 1978. *American Apocalypse: Yankee Protestants and the Civil War: 1860–1869.* Louisville: Westminster/John Knox Press.

Moorhouse, H. F. 1991. *Driving Ambitions: A Social Analysis of the American Hot Rod Enthusiasm.* Manchester: Manchester University Press.

Morales, Armando. 1992. "A Clinical Model for the Prevention of Gang Violence and Homicide." Pp. 105–118 in *Substance Abuse and Gang Violence.* Edited by R. C. Cervantes. Newbury Park, CA: Sage.

Moran, Jeffrey P. 2000. *Teaching Sex: The Shaping of Adolescence in the 20th Century.* Cambridge, MA: Harvard University Press.

Morgan, Carol M., and Doran J. Levy. 1993. "Gifts to Grandchildren." *American Demographics* 9: 3–4.

Morgan, Edmund S. 1975. *American Slavery, American Freedom.* New York: W. W. Norton.

Morgan, Phillip D. 1998. *Slave Counterpoint: Black Culture in the Eighteenth-Century Chesapeake and Lowcountry.* Chapel Hill: University of North Carolina Press.

Morgan, Winona L. 1939. *The Family Meets the Depression.* Minneapolis: University of Minnesota Press.

Mormino, Gary Ross. 1982. "The Playing Fields of St. Louis: Italian Immigrants and Sport, 1925–1941." *Journal of Sport History* 9 (Summer): 5–16.

Morris, Brian. 1999. *In Favour of Circumcision.* Sydney, Australia: University of New South Wales Press.

Morris, Edmund. 1979. *The Rise of Theodore Roosevelt.* New York: Coward, McCann, and Geoghegan.

Morrison, Donna R., and Andrew J. Cherlin. 1995. "The Divorce Process and Young Children's Well-Being: A Prospective Analysis." *Journal of Marriage and the Family* 57, no. 3: 800–812.

Morrow, Johnny. 1860. *A Voice from the Newsboys.* New York: A. S. Barnes and Burr.

Mortimer, Jeylan T., and Michael D. Finch. 1996. "Work, Family, and Adolescent Development." Pp. 1–24 in *Adolescents, Work, and Family: An Intergenerational Developmental Analysis.* Edited by Mortimer and Finch. Thousand Oaks, CA: Sage.

Mortimer, Jeylan T., Michael D. Finch, Ryu Seongryeol, Michael J. Shanahan, and Kathleen Thiede Call. 1996. "The Effects of Work Intensity on Adolescent Mental Health, Achievement, and Behavioral Adjustment: New Evidence from a Prospective Study." *Child Development* 67: 1243–1261.

Moshman, David. 1999. *Adolescent Psychological Development: Rationality, Morality, and Identity.* Mahwah, NJ: Erlbaum.

Mountjoy, John J. 2000. "Shooting for Better Gun Control." *Spectrum* 73: 1–3.

Moynihan, Ruth Barnes. 1975. "Children and Young People on the Overland Trail." *Western Historical Quarterly* 6 (July): 279–294.

Munroe, Kirk. 1897. *The Ready Rangers: A Story of Boys, Boats, and Bicycles, Fire-Buckets and Fun.* Boston: Lothrop Publishing.

Murphy, Jim. 1990. *The Boys' War: Confederate and Union Soldiers Talk about the Civil War.* New York: Clarion Press.

Murray, Gail Schmunk. 1998. *American Children's Literature and the Construction of Childhood.* New York: Twayne Publishers.

Murray, Michael D. 1990. "A Real Life Family in Prime Time." In *Television and the American Family.* Edited by Jennings Bryant. Hillsdale, NJ: Erlbaum.

Music of the American Revolution: The Birth of Liberty. 1976. New World Records.

Musick, David. 1995. *An Introduction to the Sociology of Juvenile Delinquency.* Albany: State University of New York Press.

Myers, Gene. 1998. *Children and Animals.* Boulder, CO: Westview Press.

Myers, Robert. 1972. *Celebrations: The Complete Book of American Holidays.* New York: Doubleday.

Myers, Robert J., and Joyce Brodowski. 2000. "Rewriting the Hallams: Research in 18th Century British and American Theatre." *Theatre Survey* 41, no. 1: 1–22.

Myers, Walter Dean. 1988. *Scorpions.* New York: HarperCollins.

Nackenoff, Carol. 1994. *The Fictional Republic: Horatio Alger and American Political Discourse.* New York: Oxford University Press.

Nagle, Paul C. 1999. *Descent from Glory: Four Generations of the John Adams Family.* Cambridge, MA: Harvard University Press.

Napier, John Hawkins III, ed. 1989. "Military Schools." In *Encyclopedia of Southern Culture.* Vol. 1, *Agriculture— Environment.* New York: Anchor Press/Doubleday.

Nardinelli, Clark, and Curtis Simon. 1990. "Consumer Racial Discrimination in the Market for Memorabilia: The Case of Baseball." *Quarterly Journal of Economics* (August): 575–596.

Nasaw, David. 1985. *Children of the City at Work and at Play.* Garden City, NY: Anchor Books/Doubleday.

Nass, Robert. 1993. "Sex Differences in Learning Abilities and Disabilities." *Annals of Dyslexia* 43: 61–77.

"National Allowance Survey: How Do You Compare?" 1999. *Zillions* (January–February): 8–11.

National Assessment of Vocational Education, Independent Advisory Panel. 1994. *Interim Report to Congress.* Washington, DC: U.S. Department of Education.

"National Chores Survey." 1999. *Zillions* (March–April): 20–23.

National Commission on Adolescent Sexual Health. 1995. *Facing Facts: Sexual Health for America's Adolescents.* New York: Sexuality Information and Education Council of the United States.

National Commission on Excellence in Education. 1983. *A Nation at Risk: The Imperative for Educational Reform.* ED 226 006. Washington, DC: Government Printing Office.

National Science Board Commission on Pre-College Education in Mathematics, Science and Technology. 1983. *Educating Americans for the 21st Century. A Report to the American People and the National Science Board.* ED 223 913. Washington, DC: U.S. Government Printing Office.

National Youth Development Information Center. 2001. www.nydic.org (accessed May 14). Includes a directory of more than 500 national contemporary youth organizations with links to individual organization websites.

NCHS (National Center for Health Statistics). 2000. *Health, United States, 2000.* Hyattsville, MD: NCHS.

Nearing, Scott. 1907. "The Newsboys at Night in Philadelphia." *The Survey* 17 (February 2): 778–784.

Nee, Victor G., and Brett de Bary Nee. 1986. *Longtime Californ': A Documentary Study of an American Chinatown.* Stanford: Stanford University Press.

Neft, David, Richard Johnson, Richard Cohen, and Jordan Deutsch. 1976. *The Sports Encyclopedia: Basketball.* New York: Grosset and Dunlap.

Nelson, Murry. 1999. *The Originals: The New York Celtics Invent Modern Basketball.* Bowling Green, OH: Bowling Green University Popular Press.

Nelson, Rebecca, and Marie J. MacNee, eds. 1996. *The Olympics Factbook.* Detroit: Visible Ink Press.

Neslund, Douglas. 2001. "Voices of Angels" bookmarks, http://groups.yahoo. com/group/Voices_of_Angels/links (accessed March 11).

Neugarten, Bernice L., and Karol K. Weinstein. 1964. "The Changing American Grandparents." *Journal of Gerontology* 26: 199–204.

New England Primer Improved for the More Easy Attaining the True Reading of English, The. 1843. I. Webster, publisher.

"New York Newsboys, The." 1869. *The Leisure Hours* (November 1): 717.

New York SPCC (New York Society for the Prevention of Cruelty to Children). Scrapbook collections in the archives contain the following clippings: On Wallie Eddinger, Jr., see *New York Herald*, November 1, 1892; Peoria, Illinois, *Transcript*, February 10, 1892; and *Everybody's Magazine*, September 1, 1903. On Tommie Russell, see Tyrone, Pennsylvania, *Daily Herald*, January 25, 1892; *New York Recorder*, May 1, 1892; and *New York Herald*, December 29, 1897. On Elsie Leslie, see *Everybody's Magazine*, September 1, 1903; and *New York World*, April 10, 1910.

Newberger, Eli H. 1999. *The Men They Will Become.* New York: Perseus Books.

Newcomb, Horace, ed. 2000. *Television: The Critical View.* 6th ed. New York: Oxford University Press.

Newell, William Wells. 1883. *Games and Songs of American Children.* New York: Harper and Brothers.

"Newsboys and Newsgirls Constitute an Endangered Species." 2000. *Editor and Publisher* (January 31): 5.

"Newsboys of Old: How They Flourished in California Thirty Years Ago." 1882. *San Francisco Call*, January 29.

"Newsboys' Riot, A." 1877. *Detroit Evening News*, July 21, 4.

Nickerson, Craig. 1995. "Red Dawn in Lake Placid: The Semi-Final Hockey Game at the 1980 Winter Olympics as Cold War Battleground." *Canadian Journal of History of Sport* 26: 73–85.

Nightingale, Carl Husemoller. 1993. *On the Edge: A History of Poor Black*

Children and Their American Dreams. New York: Basic Books.

Noll, Mark. 1992. *A History of Christianity in the United States and Canada.* Grand Rapids, MI: Eerdmans.

Norris, Thaddeus. 1864. *The American Angler's Book.* Philadelphia: E. H. Butler.

Norton Family. *Norton Diaries, 1876–1895.* Copied and annotated by Helen Norton Starr. Manuscripts Division, Kansas State Historical Society, Topeka.

Nusbaum, Paul. 1994. "Crowded House: Fun and Gaming." *Philadelphia Inquirer,* May 29, 1994, 11ff.

Nycum, Benjie. 2000. *XY Survival Guide: Everything You Need to Know about Being Young and Gay.* San Francisco: XY Publishing.

Nye, F. Ivan, and Felix M. Berardo. 1973. *The Family: Its Structure and Interaction.* New York: Macmillan.

Nye, Russel. 1970. *The Unembarrassed Muse.* New York: Dial Press.

Oakes, Jeannie. 1985. *Keeping Track: How Schools Structure Inequality.* New Haven, CT: Yale University Press.

O'Brien, Richard. 1990. *The Story of American Toys.* London: New Cavendish Books.

O'Dell, Scott. 1967. *The Black Pearl.* New York: Bantam Doubleday Dell.

Ogletree, Shirley Matile, Larry Denton, and Sue Winkle Williams. 1993. "Age and Gender Differences in Children's Halloween Costumes." *Journal of Psychology* 127: 633–637.

Okami, Paul, and Laura Pendleton. 1994. "Theorizing Sexuality: Seeds of a Transdisciplinary Paradigm Shift." *Current Anthropology* 35 (February): 85–91.

Oliver, Ronald, Richard Hazler, and John Hoover. 1994. "The Perceived Role of Bullying in Small-Town Midwestern Schools." *Journal of Counseling and Development* 72, no. 4: 416–419.

Olweus, Dan. 1993. *Bullying at School: What We Know and What We Can Do.* Oxford, UK: Blackwell.

Oriard, Michael. 1982. *Dreaming of Heroes: American Sports Fiction, 1860–1980.* Chicago: Nelson-Hall.

Oring, Elliott. 1992. *Jokes and Their Relations.* University Press of Kentucky.

Osgood, Ernest Staples. 1929. *The Day of the Cattleman.* Minneapolis: University of Minnesota Press.

Otnes, Cele, Kyungseung Kim, and Young Cham Kim. 1994. "Yes Virginia, There Is a Gender Difference: Analyzing Children's Requests to Santa Claus." *Journal of Popular Culture* 28, no. 1: 17–29.

Pabilonia, Sabrina Wulff. 1999. "Evidence on Youth Employment, Earnings, and Parental Transfers in the National Longitudinal Survey of Youths 1997." Presented at the NLSY97 Early Results Conference at the Bureau of Labor Statistics, Washington, DC, November 18–19.

———. 2000. "Youth Earnings and Parental Allowances." University of Washington working paper.

Packard, Cynthia, and Ray B. Browne. 1978. "Pinball Machine: Marble Icon." Pp. 177–189 in *Icons of America.* Edited by Ray B. Browne and Marshall Fishwick. Bowling Green, OH: Bowling Green University Popular Press.

Pacula, Rosalie. 1998. *Adolescent Alcohol and Marijuana Consumption: Is There Really a Gateway Effect?* Cambridge, MA: National Bureau of Economic Research.

Pagani, Linda, Richard E. Tremblay, Frank Vitaro, Margaret Kerr, and Pierre McDuff.

1998. "The Impact of Family Transition on the Development of Delinquency in Adolescent Boys: A 9-Year Longitudinal Study." *Journal of Child Psychology and Psychiatry and Allied Disciplines* 39, no. 4: 489–499.

Palmer, Patricia. 1986. *The Lively Audience: A Study of Children around the TV Set.* Sidney: Allen and Unwin.

Papenfuse, Edward C., and Gregory A. Stiverson. 1973. "General Smallwood's Recruits: The Peacetime Career of the Revolutionary War Private." *William and Mary Quarterly* 30: 117–132.

Park, K. 1999. "'I Really Do Feel I'm 1.5!': The Construction of Self and Community by Young Korean Americans." *Amerasia Journal* 25, no. 1: 139–164.

Parke, Ross D. 1996. *Fatherhood.* Cambridge, MA: Harvard University.

Parks, Rita. 1982. *The Western Hero in Film and Television.* Ann Arbor: UMI Research Press.

Parks, Wally. 1966. *Drag Racing, Yesterday and Today.* New York: Trident Press.

Parsons, Michael J. 1987. *How We Understand Art: A Cognitive Developmental Account of Aesthetic Experience.* New York: Cambridge University Press.

Paulsen, Gary. 1993. *Harris and Me.* New York: Bantam Doubleday Dell.

Payton, Crystal. 1982. *Space Toys.* Sedalia, MO: Collectors Compass.

Peabody, James B., ed. 1973. *John Adams: A Biography in His Own Words.* New York: Newsweek, distributed by Harper and Row.

Peavy, Linda, and Ursula Smith. 1999. *Frontier Children.* Norman: University of Oklahoma Press.

Peiss, Kathy. 1986. *Cheap Amusements: Working Women and Leisure in Turn-of-the-Century New York.* Philadelphia: Temple University Press.

Pelligrini, Anthony D. In press. "The Roles of Dominance and Bullying in the Development of Early Heterosexual Relationships." *Journal of Emotional Abuse.*

Penney, David. 1993. "Indians and Children: A Critique of Educational Objectives." *Akwe:kon* [*Native Americas*] 10 (Winter): 12–18.

Penny Merriment: English Songs from the Time of the Pilgrims. 1986. Plimoth Plantation.

Pepler, Deborah J., Rona Abramovitch, and Carl Corter. 1981. "Sibling Interaction in the Home: A Longitudinal Study." *Child Development* 52: 1344–1347.

"Perch Fishing." 1873. *American Sportsman* 3 (December 13).

Perlman, Joel. 1988. *Ethnic Differences: Schooling and Social Structure among the Irish, Italians, Jews, and Blacks in an American City, 1880–1935.* New York: Cambridge University Press.

Pernick, Martin S. 1996. *The Black Stork: Eugenics and the Death of "Defective" Babies in American Medicine and Motion Pictures since 1915.* New York: Oxford University Press.

Petersen, David, ed. 1996. *A Hunter's Heart: Honest Essays on Blood Sport.* New York: Henry Holt.

Petersen, Paul. 2001. "A Minor Consideration." Gardena, CA: www.minorcon.org//history.html (accessed March 1, 2001).

Peterson, Merrill D. 1970. *Thomas Jefferson and the New Nation.* New York: Oxford University Press.

Peterson, Merrill, ed. 1984. *Thomas Jefferson: Writings*. New York: Library of America.

Peterson, Robert W. 1985. *The Boy Scouts: An American Adventure*. New York: American Heritage.

Peterson, Robert. 1990. *Cages to Jump Shots: Pro Basketball's Early Years*. New York: Oxford University Press.

Phillips, Dennis J. 1989. *Teaching, Coaching and Learning Tennis: An Annotated Bibliography*. Metuchen, NJ: Scarecrow Press.

Phinney, Jean S. 1989. "Stages of Ethnic Identity Development in Minority Group Adolescents." *Journal of Early Adolescence* 9, nos. 1–2: 34–49.

Phipps, William E. 1977. "Masturbation: Vice or Virtue?" *Journal of Religion and Health* 16: 183–195.

Pickering, Samuel F., Jr. 1993. *Moral Instruction and Fiction for Children, 1747–1820*. Athens: University of Georgia Press.

Pirog-Good, Maureen A. 1996. "The Education and Labor Market Outcomes of Adolescent Fathers." *Youth and Society* 28: 236–262.

Pisciotta, Alexander W. 1982. "Saving the Children: The Promise and Practice of *Parens Patriae*, 1838–1898." *Crime and Delinquency* 28, no. 3 (July): 410–425.

Platt, Anthony. 1977. *The Child Savers: The Invention of Delinquency*. 2d ed. Chicago: University of Chicago Press.

Pleak, R. R., and H. F. Meyer-Bahlburg. 1990. "Sexual Behavior and AIDS Knowledge of Young Male Prostitutes in Manhattan." *Journal of Sex Research* 27, no. 4: 557–587.

Pleck, Elizabeth H., and Joseph H. Pleck. 1997. "Fatherhood Ideals in the United States: Historical Dimensions." Pp. 33–48 in *The Role of the Father in Child Development*. 3d ed. Edited by Michael E. Lamb. New York: John Wiley and Sons.

Podbersek, A., Elizabeth Paul, and James Serpell, eds. 2000. *Companion Animals and Us*. Cambridge, UK: Cambridge University Press.

Polakow, Valerie, ed. 2000. *The Public Assault on America's Children*. New York: Teachers College Press.

Pollack, William. 1998. *Real Boys: Rescuing Our Sons from the Myths of Boyhood*. New York: Henry Holt.

Pond, Fred E. (Will Wildwood). 1919. *Life and Adventures of "Ned Buntline" with Ned Buntline's Anecdote of "Frank Forester" and Chapter of Angling Sketches*. New York: Cadmus Book Shop.

Popper, Karl Raimund. 1959. *The Logic of Scientific Discovery*. London, UK: Hutchinson.

Porter, Roy. 1995. "Forbidden Pleasures: Enlightenment Literature of Sexual Advice." Pp. 75–98 in *Solitary Pleasures: The Historical, Literary, and Artistic Discourses of Autoeroticism*. Edited by Paula Bennett and Vernon A. Rosario II. New York: Routledge.

Post, Robert C. 1998. "Hot Rods and Customs: The Men and Machines of California's Car Culture, at the Oakland Museum of California." *Technology and Culture* 39: 116–121.

———. 2001. *High Performance: The Culture and Technology of Drag Racing, 1950–2000*. Baltimore, MD: Johns Hopkins University Press.

Postol, Todd Alexander. 1997. "Creating the American Newspaper Boy: Middle-Class Route Service and Juvenile Salesmanship in the Great Depression." *Journal of Social History* (Winter): 327–345.

Powers, Jane B. 1992. *The "Girl Question" in Education: Vocational Education for Young Women in the Progressive Era.* Washington, DC: Falmer Press.

Powers, Stephen. 1999. *The Art of Getting Over: Graffiti at the Millennium.* New York: St. Martin's Press.

Prescott, Heather Munro. 1998. *"A Doctor of Their Own": The History of Adolescent Medicine.* Cambridge, MA: Harvard University Press.

Preston, Samuel H., and Michael R. Haines. 1991. *Fatal Years: Child Mortality in Late Nineteenth-Century America.* Princeton, NJ: Princeton University Press.

Pridmore, Jay. 1999. *Classic American Bicycles.* Osceola, WI: Motorbikes International.

Proctor, Nicholas Wolfe. 1988. "Bathed in Blood: Hunting in the Antebellum South." Ph.D. diss., Emory University.

Proffit, William R. 1993. *Contemporary Orthodontics.* 2d ed. St. Louis: Mosby Year Book.

Pruett, Kyle D. 2000. *Fatherneed.* New York: Free Press.

Public/Private Ventures. 2000. *Youth Development: Issues, Challenges, and Directions.* Philadelphia: Public/Private Ventures.

Pustz, Matthew. 1999. *Comic Book Culture: Fanboys and True Believers.* Jackson: University Press of Mississippi.

Putney, Clifford. 1997. "From Character to Body Building: The YMCA and the Suburban Metropolis, 1950–1980." Pp. 231–249 in *Men and Women Adrift: The YMCA and YWCA in the City.* Edited by Nina Mjagkij and Margaret Spratt. New York: New York University Press.

Putney, Clifford W. 1995. "Muscular Christianity: The Strenuous Mood in American Protestantism, 1880–1920." Ph.D. diss., Brandeis University.

Quay, H. C., ed. 1987. *Handbook of Juvenile Delinquency.* New York: Wiley.

Rabinowitz, Benjamin. 1948. *The Young Men's Hebrew Association (1854–1913).* New York: National Jewish Welfare Board.

Rader, Benjamin G. 1983. *American Sports: From the Age of Folk Games to the Age of Spectators.* Englewood Cliffs, NJ: Prentice-Hall.

———. 1999. *American Sports: From the Age of Folk Games to the Age of Televised Sports.* Upper Saddle River, NJ: Prentice-Hall.

Rand Youth Poll. 2000. *Teen-age Personal Spending Continues to Climb While Youths' Overall Impact on Economy Intensifies.* New York: Rand Youth Poll.

Randall, Henry S. 1858. *The Life of Thomas Jefferson.* New York: Derby and Jackson.

Randall, Willard Sterne. 1993. *Thomas Jefferson: A Life.* New York: Henry Holt.

Randolph, Sarah N. 1978. *The Domestic Life of Thomas Jefferson, Compiled from Family Letters and Reminiscences, by His Great-Granddaughter.* 1871. Reprint, Charlottesville: University Press of Virginia.

Raphael, Maryanne, and Jenifer Wolf. 1974. *Runaway: America's Lost Youth.* New York: Drake Publishers.

Rasmussen, Wayne D. 1989. *Taking the University to the People: Seventy-Five Years of Cooperative Extension.* Ames: Iowa State University Press.

Rayburn, Jim III. 1984. *Dance Children Dance: The Story of Jim Rayburn, Founder of Young Life.* Wheaton, IL: Tyndale.

Reagan, Daniel Ware. 1984. "The Making of an American Author: Melville and the Idea of a National Literature." Ph.D. diss., University of New Hampshire.

Rebora, Carrie, Paul Staiti, Erica E. Hirshler, Theodore E. Stebbins, Jr., and Carol Troyen. 1995. *John Singleton Copley in America.* New York: Metropolitan Museum of Art.

Reck, Franklin M. 1951. *The 4-H Story.* Ames: Iowa State College Press.

Reed, Anna. 1829. *Life of George Washington.* Philadelphia: American Sunday School Union.

Reinen, I. J., and T. Plomp. 1993. "Some Gender Issues in Educational Computer Use: Results of an International Comparative Survey." *Computers and Education: An International Journal* 20, no. 4: 353–365.

Reinier, Jacqueline S. 1996. *From Virtue to Character: American Childhood, 1775–1850.* New York: Twayne Publishers.

Reisner, Robert. 1971. *Graffiti: Two Thousand Years of Wall Writing.* New York: Cowles Book Company.

Remafedi, Gary. 1999. "Suicide and Sexual Orientation." *Archives of General Psychiatry* 56: 885–886.

Remondino, Peter C. 1891. *History of Circumcision.* Philadelphia: F. A. Davis.

Restad, Penne. 1995. *Christmas in America: A History.* New York: Oxford University Press.

Retherford, Robert D. 1975. *The Changing Sex Differential in Mortality.* Westport, CT: Greenwood.

Rhode, Deborah. 1997. *Speaking of Sex.* Cambridge: Harvard University Press.

Rhodes, Richard. 1999. *Why They Kill: The Discoveries of a Maverick Criminologist.* New York: Alfred A. Knopf.

Richards, Jeffrey H. 1995. *Mercy Otis Warren.* New York: Twayne Publishers.

Richardson, John, and Carl Simpson. 1982. "Children, Gender and Social Structure: An Analysis of the Contents of Letters to Santa Claus." *Child Development* 53: 429–436.

Riess, Steven A. 1989. *City Games: The Evolution of American Urban Society and the Rise of Sports.* Urbana: University of Illinois Press.

———. 1995. *Sport in Industrial America, 1850–1920.* Wheeling, IL: Harlan Davidson.

Riis, Jacob. 1890. *How the Other Half Lives.* 1997 Reprint, New York: Penguin.

Riley, Patricia, ed. 1993. *Growing Up Native American.* New York: Avon Books.

Riordan, Cornelius. 1990. *Girls and Boys in School: Together or Separate.* New York: Teachers College Press.

———. 1999. "The Silent Gender Gap: Reading, Writing and Other Problems for Boys." *Education Week* 19 (November): 46–49.

Risman, Barbara. 1999. *Gender Vertigo.* New Haven: Yale University Press.

Ritter, Thomas J., and George C. Denniston. 1996. *Say No to Circumcision: 40 Compelling Reasons.* Aptos, CA: Hourglass Books.

Ritvo, Harriet. 1987. *The Animal Estate.* Cambridge, MA: Harvard University Press.

Road and Track. New York: Hachette Fillipacci Magazines.

Roberts, Brian. 2000. *American Alchemy: The California Gold Rush and Middle Class Culture.* Chapel Hill: University of North Carolina Press.

Roberts, Randy. 1999. *But They Can't Beat Us: Oscar Robertson's Crispus Attucks Tigers.* Indianapolis: Indiana Historical Society.

Robinson, Bryan E. 1988. *Teenage Fathers.* Lexington, MA: Lexington Books.

Rod and Custom. Los Angeles: emap usa.

Rodder's Journal, The. Huntington Beach, CA: Rodder's Journal.

Rodgers, Joseph L., H. Harrington Cleveland, Edwin van den Oord, and David C. Rowe. 2000. "Resolving the Debate over Birth Order, Family Size, and Intelligence." *American Psychologist* 55: 599–612.

Rodkin, Philip C., Thomas W. Farmer, Ruth Pearl, and Richard Van Acker. 2000. "Heterogeneity of Popular Boys: Antisocial and Prosocial Configurations." *Developmental Psychology* 36, no. 1 (January): 14–24.

Roediger, David R. 1991. *The Wages of Whiteness: Race and the Making of the American Working Class.* New York: Verso.

Rogers, Joseph L., and David C. Rowe. 1988. "Influence of Siblings on Adolescent Sexual Behavior." *Developmental Psychology* 24: 722–728.

Rogers, Naomi. 1992. *Dirt and Disease: Polio before FDR.* New Brunswick, NJ: Rutgers University Press.

Rogers, Richard G. 1992. "Living and Dying in the U.S.A.: Sociodemographic Determinants among Blacks and Whites." *Demography* 29: 287–303.

Rogin, Michael. 1992. "Blackface, White Noise: The Jewish Jazz Singer Finds His Voice." *Critical Inquiry* 18 (Spring): 417–453.

Rohrbough, Malcolm. 1997. *Days of Gold: The California Gold Rush and the American Nation.* Berkeley: University of California Press.

Roosevelt, Theodore. 1913. *Theodore Roosevelt: An Autobiography.* 1985. Reprint, New York: Da Capo Press.

Rorabaugh, William J. 1986. *The Craft Apprentice: From Franklin to the Machine Age in America.* New York: Oxford University Press.

Roscoe, Will. 1991. *The Zuni Man-Woman.* Albuquerque: University of New Mexico Press.

Rosen, Ruth. 1982. *The Lost Sisterhood: Prostitution in America, 1900–1918.* Baltimore: Johns Hopkins University Press.

Rosenblum, Walter, Naomi Rosenblum, and Alan Trachtenberg. 1977. *America and Lewis Hine: Photographs 1904–1940.* Millerton, NY: Aperture.

Rosengarten, Theodore, ed. 1986. *Tombee: Portrait of a Cotton Planter.* New York: Quill Press.

Rosenheim, Margaret K., Franklin E. Zimring, David S. Tanenhaus, and Bernardine Dohrn, eds. 2001. *A Century of Juvenile Justice.* Chicago: University of Chicago Press.

Rosenthal, Michael. 1984. *The Character Factory: Baden-Powell and the Origins of the Boy Scout Movement.* New York: Pantheon Books.

Ross, Dorothy. 1972. *G. Stanley Hall: The Psychologist as Prophet.* Chicago: University of Chicago Press.

Rossi, Alice S., and Peter H. Rossi. 1990. *Of Human Bonding: Parent-Child Relations across the Life Course.* New York: Aldine de Gruyter.

Rothman, David J. 1980. *Conscience and Convenience: The Asylum and Its Alternatives in Progressive America.* Boston: Little, Brown.

Rotundo, Anthony. 1993. *American Manhood: Transformations in Masculinity from the Revolution to the Modern Era.* New York: Basic Books.

Rourke, Constance. 1928. *Troupers of the Gold Coast; or, The Rise of Lotta Crabtree.* New York: Harcourt Brace.

Rovetta, Catherine Humbargar, and Leon Rovetta. 1968. *Teacher Spanks Johnny: A Handbook for Teachers.* Stockton, CA: Willow House Publishers.

Rowe, David C., and Bill L. Gulley. 1992. "Sibling Effects on Substance Use and Delinquency." *Criminology* 30: 217–233.

Rowlings, J. K. 1997. *Harry Potter and the Sorcerer's Stone.* New York: Scholastic.

Royce, Josiah. 1886. *California: From the Conquest in 1846 to the Second Vigilance Committee in San Francisco.* Boston: Houghton Mifflin.

Rudgley, Richard. 1994. *Essential Substances: A Cultural History of Intoxicants in Society.* New York: Kodansha International.

Rudwick, Elliott M. 1969. *W. E. B. Du Bois: Propagandist of the Negro Protest.* New York: Atheneum.

Ruger, A. 1869. *Bird's Eye View of Young America: Warren County, Illinois.* Map, Warren County, IL. Library of Congress Map Division.

Rushkoff, Douglas. 1996. *Playing the Future: How Kid's Culture Can Teach Us to Thrive in an Age of Chaos.* New York: HarperCollins.

Rutland, Robert Allen. 1995. *A Boyhood in the Dust Bowl.* Boulder: University Press of Colorado.

Ryan, Caitlin, and Donna Futterman. 1998. *Lesbian and Gay Youth: Care and Counseling.* New York: Columbia University Press.

Ryan, Mary P. 1981. *Cradle of the Middle Class: The Family in Oneida County, New York, 1790–1865.* New York: Cambridge University Press.

———. 1982. *The Empire of the Mother: Americans Writing about Domesticity, 1830 to 1860.* New York: Institute for Research in History and Naworth Press.

Ryerson, Ellen. 1978. *The Best-Laid Plans: America's Juvenile Court Experiment.* New York: Hill and Wang.

Sabin, Roger. 1996. *Comics, Comix and Graphic Novels: A History of Comic Art.* London: Phaidon.

Sachar, Louis. 1998. *Holes.* New York: Farrar, Straus and Giroux.

Sadie, Stanley, ed. 1980. *The New Grove Dictionary of Music and Musicians.* London: Macmillan.

Sadker, Myra, and David Sadker. 1994. *Failing at Fairness: How Our Schools Cheat Girls.* New York: Touchstone.

Salinger, Sharon. 1987. *"To Serve Well and Faithfully": Labor and Indentured Servants in Pennsylvania 1682–1800.* Cambridge, UK: Cambridge University Press.

Saloutos, Theodore. 1964. *The Greeks in the United States.* Cambridge, MA: Harvard University Press.

Sammons, Jeffrey T. 1990. *Beyond the Ring: The Role of Boxing in American Society.* Urbana: University of Illinois Press.

Sanchez, Ellen, Trina Reed Robertson, Carol Marie Lewis, and Barri Rosenbluth. In press. "Preventing Bullying and Sexual Harassment in Elementary Schools: The Expect Respect Model." *Journal of Emotional Abuse.*

Sanchez, George I. 1940. *Forgotten People: A Study of New Mexicans.* Albuquerque: University of New Mexico Press.

Sanders, Jo. 1990. "Computer Equity for Girls: What Keeps It from Happening." Pp. 181–185 in *Fifth World Conference on Computers in Education in Sydney, Australia.* Amsterdam: Elsevier Science Publishing.

Sante, Luc. 1991. *Low Life: Lures and Snares of Old New York.* New York: Farrar, Straus and Giroux.

Santino, Jack. 1983. "Halloween in America: Contemporary Customs and Performances." *Western Folklore* 42, no. 1: 1–20.

———. 1994. *Halloween and Other Festivals of Life and Death.* Knoxville: University of Tennessee Press.

———. 1995. *All around the Year: Holidays and Celebrations in American Life.* Urbana: University of Illinois Press.

Saroyan, William. 1952. *The Bicycle Rider in Beverly Hills.* New York: Scribner's.

Sartain, William. 1864. "Young America Crushing Rebellion and Sedition." Engraving in Library of Congress Prints and Photographs Division.

Savin-Williams, Ritch C. 1990. *Gay, Lesbian, and Bisexual Youth: Expressions of Identity.* Washington, DC: Hemisphere.

———. 1998. "*. . . And Then I Became Gay": Young Men's Stories.* New York: Routledge.

Savin-Williams, Ritch C., and Kenneth M. Cohen. 1996. *The Lives of Lesbians, Gays, and Bisexuals: Children to Adults.* Fort Worth, TX: Harcourt Brace College Publishing.

Saxton, Alexander. 1990. *The Rise and Fall of the White Republic: Class Politics and Mass Culture in Nineteenth-Century America.* New York: Verso.

Schaffner, Laurie. 1999. *Teenage Runaways: Broken Hearts and Bad Attitudes.* New York: Haworth Press.

Scharff, Virginia. 1991. *Taking the Wheel: Women and the Coming of the Motor Age.* New York: Free Press.

Scharnhorst, Gary, and Jack Bales. 1981. *Horatio Alger, Jr.: An Annotated Bibliography of Comment and Criticism.* Metuchen, NJ: Scarecrow Press.

———. 1985. *The Lost Life of Horatio Alger., Jr.* Bloomington: Indiana University Press.

Schatz, Thomas. 1981. *Hollywood Genres: Formulas, Filmmaking, and the Studio System.* New York: Random House.

Schechter, Harold. 1996. "A Short Corrective History of Violence in Popular Culture." *New York Times Magazine* (July 7): 32–33.

Schlegel, Alice, and Herbert Barry III. 1991. *Adolescence: An Anthropological Inquiry.* New York: Free Press.

Schlossman, Steven L. 1977. *Love and the American Delinquent: The Theory and Practice of "Progressive" Juvenile Justice, 1825–1920.* Chicago: University of Chicago Press.

———. 1995. "Delinquent Children: The Juvenile Reform School." In *The Oxford History of the Prison.* Edited by Norval Morris and David J. Rothman. New York: Oxford University Press.

Schneider, Eric C. 1992. *In the Web of Class: Delinquents and Reformers in Boston, 1810s–1930s.* New York: New York University Press.

———. 1999. *Vampires, Dragons, and Egyptian Kings: Youth Gangs in Postwar New York.* Princeton: Princeton University Press.

Schob, David E. 1975. *Hired Hands and Plowboys: Farm Labor in the Midwest, 1815–1860.* Urbana: University of Illinois Press.

Schoenfeld, Stuart. 1988. "Folk Judaism, Elite Judaism and the Role of the Bar Mitzvah in the Development of the Synagogue and Jewish School in America." *Contemporary Jewry* 9, no. 1: 85.

"School Goals: Draft." 2000. Culver Academies, October 27.

Schramm, Wilbur, Jack Lyle, and Edwin Parker. 1961. *Television in the Lives of Our Children.* Palo Alto, CA: Stanford University Press.

Schrank, Robert. 1998. *Wasn't That a Time? Growing Up Radical and Red in America.* Cambridge: MIT Press.

Schultz, Stanley K. 1973. *The Culture Factory: Boston Public Schools, 1789–1860.* New York: Oxford University Press.

Schulz, John A., and Douglas Adair, eds. 1966. *The Spur of Fame: Dialogues of John Adams and Benjamin Rush, 1805–1813.* San Marino, CA: Huntington Library.

Schwartz, Marie Jenkins. 2000. *Born in Bondage: Growing Up Enslaved in the Antebellum South.* Cambridge, MA: Harvard University Press.

Schwarz, Ira M. 1989. *(In)Justice for Juveniles: Rethinking the Best Interest of the Child.* Lexington, MA: Lexington Books.

Schwarz, Ira M., ed. 1992. *Juvenile Justice and Public Policy.* Lexington, MA: Lexington Books.

Schwieder, Dorothy. 1993. *75 Years of Service: Cooperative Extension in Iowa.* Ames: Iowa State University Press.

Scieszka, Jon. 1992. *The Stinky Cheese Man and Other Fairly Stupid Tales.* New York: Penguin.

———. 1996. *The Time Warp Trio Series.* New York: Penguin.

Secretary's Commission on Achieving Necessary Skills (SCANS). 1991. *What Work Requires of Schools: A SCANS Report for America 2000.* Washington, DC: U.S. Department of Labor.

Sedlak Andrea J., and Debra D. Broadhurst. 1996. *Third National Incidence Study of Child Abuse and Neglect: Final Report.* Washington, DC: U.S. Department of Health and Human Services.

Segerstrom, Suzanne, William McCarthy, and Nicholas Caskey. 1993. "Optimistic Bias among Cigarette Smokers." *Journal of Applied Social Psychology* 23: 1606–1618.

Seiter, Ellen. 1995. *Sold Separately: Parents and Children in Consumer Culture.* New Brunswick, NJ: Rutgers University Press.

Sellers, Charles. 1991. *The Market Revolution: Jacksonian America, 1815–1846.* New York: Oxford University Press.

Sellers, John R. 1974. "The Common Soldier in the American Revolution." In *Military History of the American Revolution.* Edited by Betsy C. Kysley. Washington, DC: USAF Academy.

Sendak, Maurice. 1963. *Where the Wild Things Are.* New York: HarperCollins.

Serpell, James. 1986. *In the Company of Animals.* Oxford: Basil Blackwell.

Sexuality Information and Education Council of the United States (SIECUS). 1995. *SIECUS Position Statements on Sexuality Issues 1995.* New York: SIECUS.

Seymour, Harold. 1960. *Baseball: The Early Years.* New York: Oxford University Press.

———. 1990. *Baseball: The People's Game.* New York: Oxford University Press.

Shakeshaft, C. 1986. "A Gender at Risk." *Phi Delta Kappan* 67, no. 7: 499–503.

Shakur, Sanyika. 1993. *Monster: The Autobiography of an LA Gang Member.* New York: Penguin.

Shapiro, Jeremy, Rebekah L. Dorman, William H. Burkey, Carolyn J. Welker, and Joseph B. Clough. 1997. "Development and Factor Analysis of a Measure of Youth Attitudes toward Guns and Violence." *Journal of Clinical Child Psychology* 26: 311–320.

Shaw, Daniel S., Robert E. Emery, and Michele D. Tuer. 1993. "Parental Functioning and Children's Adjustment in Families of Divorce: A Prospective Study." *Journal of Abnormal Clinical Psychology* 21, no. 1 (February): 119–134.

Sheff, David. 1993. *Game Over: How Nintendo Zapped an American Industry, Captured Your Dollars, and Enslaved Your Children.* New York: Random House.

Shelden, Randall, Sharon Tracy, and William Brown. 1997. *Youth Gangs in American Society.* New York: Wadsworth.

Sheon, Aaron. 1976. "The Discovery of Graffiti." *Art Journal* 36, no. 1: 16–22.

Sherman, Arloc. 1994. *Wasting America's Future: The Children's Defense Fund Report on the Costs of Child Poverty.* Boston: Beacon Press.

Sherman, Miriam. 1986. "Children's Allowances." *Medical Aspects of Human Sexuality* 20, no. 4: 121–128.

Shilling, Chris. 1993. *The Body and Social Theory.* London: Sage.

Shoup, Laurence, and Randall Milliken. 1999. *Inigo of Rancho Posolmi: The Life and Times of a Mission Indian.* Menlo Park: Ballena Press.

Shulman, Harry M. 1932. "Newsboys of New York: A Study of the Legal and Illegal Work Activities during 1931." New York: Child Labor Committee, 13.

Siegel, Mark, Alison Landes, and Nancy Jacobs. 1995. *Illegal Drugs and Alcohol: America's Anguish.* Wylie, TX: Information Plus.

Siks, Geraldine Brain, and Hazel Brain Dunnington, eds. 1967. *Children's Theatre and Creative Dramatics.* Seattle: University of Washington Press.

Silverman, Kenneth. 1976. *A Cultural History of the American Revolution: Painting, Music, Literature, and the Theatre.* New York: Thomas Y. Crowell.

Simmons, Leo W. 1942. *Sun Chief: The Autobiography of a Hopi Indian.* New Haven, CT: Yale University Press.

Simmons, William S. 1986. *Spirit of the New England Tribes: Indian History and Folklore, 1620–1984.* Hanover: University Press of New England.

Simon, David, and Edward Burns. 1997. *The Corner: A Year in the Life of an Inner City Neighborhood.* New York: Broadway.

Simpson, Marc. 1994. *The Rockefeller Collection of American Art at the Fine Arts Museums of San Francisco.* San Francisco: Fine Arts Museums of San Francisco.

Simpson, Wayne. 1987. "Hockey." Pp. 169–229 in *A Concise History of Sport in Canada.* Edited by Don Morrow, Mary Keyes, Wayne Simpson, Frank Cosentino, and Ron Lappage. Toronto: Oxford University Press.

Singer, Ben. 1992. "A New and Urgent Need for Stimuli: Sensational Melodrama and Urban Modernity." Paper presented at the Melodrama Conference, British Film Institute, London.

Sinyard, Neil. 1992. *Children in the Movies.* New York: St. Martin's Press.

Sjostrom, Lisa, and Nan D. Stein. 1995. *Bullyproof: A Teacher's Guide on Teaching and Bullying for Use with Fourth and Fifth Grade Students.* Wellesley, MA: Wellesley College Center for Research on Women.

Sjovold, Carl-Petter. 1999. "An Angling People: Nature, Sport and Conservation in Nineteenth-Century America." Ph.D. diss., University of California at Davis.

Skal, David J. 1993. *The Monster Show: A Cultural History of Horror.* New York: Penguin.

——. 1998. *Screams of Reason: Mad Science and Modern Culture.* New York: W. W. Norton.

Skiing Heritage: Journal of the International Skiing History Association. 1989– . Quarterly. 499 Town Hill Road, New Hartford, CT.

Skolnick, Jerome H., Theodore Correl, Elizabeth Navarro, and Roger Rabb. 1988. *The Social Structure of Street Drug Dealing.* Unpublished report to the Office of the Attorney General of the State of California. Berkeley: University of California at Berkeley.

Skoloff, Gary, et al. 1995. *To Win the War: Home Front Memorabilia of World War II.* Missoula, MT: Pictorial Publishing.

Sleeter, Christine. 1986. "Learning Disabilities: The Social Construction of a Special Education Category." *Exceptional Children* 53: 46–54.

Slide, Anthony. 1994. *The Encyclopedia of Vaudeville.* Westport, CT: Greenwood Press.

Slotkin, Richard. 1992. *Gunfighter Nation: The Myth of the Frontier in Twentieth-Century America.* New York: Atheneum.

Smith, Abbott Emerson. 1947. *Colonists in Bondage: White Servitude and Convict Labor in America, 1607–1776.* New York: W. W. Norton.

Smith, Adam. 1776. *Wealth of Nations.* 1937. Reprint, New York: Modern Library.

Smith, I. Evelyn. 1947. "Adoption." Pp. 22–27 in *Social Work Year Book* 9. New York: Russell Sage Foundation.

Smith, John. 1907. *The Generall Historie of Virginia, New England and the Summer Isles Together with the True Travels, Adventures and Observations, and a Sea Grammar.* Vol. 1. Glasgow: J. Maclehose and Sons.

Smith, Kristin. 2000. *Who's Minding the Kids? Child Care Arrangements.* Washington, DC: U.S. Department of Commerce, Economic and Statistics Administration, U.S. Census Bureau.

Smith, Lewis W., and Gideon L. Blough. 1929. *Planning a Career: A Vocational Civics.* New York: American Book Company.

Smith, Page. 1962. *John Adams.* Vol. 1. Garden City, NY: Doubleday.

Smith, Peter K. 1991. "The Silent Nightmare: Bullying and Victimization in School Peer Groups." *The Psychologist: Bulletin of the British Psychological Society* 4: 243–248.

Smith, Robert A. 1972. *A Social History of the Bicycle: Its Early Life and Times in America.* New York: American Heritage Press.

Smith, Ronald A. 1990. *Sports and Freedom: The Rise of Big-Time College Athletics.* New York: Oxford University Press.

Snarey, John. 1993. *How Fathers Care for the Next Generation: A Four-Decade Study.* Cambridge, MA: Harvard University Press.

Snow, Richard. 1989. *Coney Island: A Postcard Journey to the City of Fire.* New York: Brightwater Press.

Snyder, H. N., et al. 1993. *Juvenile Court Statistics 1990.* Washington, DC: U.S. Department of Justice.

Snyder, Robert W. 1989. *The Voice of the City: Vaudeville and Popular Culture in New York.* New York: Oxford University Press.

Solomon, Robert C. 1974. "Sexual Paradigms." *The Journal of Philosophy* 71 (June): 336–345.

Sommers, Christina H. 2000. "The War against Boys." *The Atlantic Monthly* (May): 59–74.

Sonenstein, Freya L., Kellie Stewart, Laura Duberstein Lindberg, Marta Pernas, and Sean Williams. 1997. *Involving Males in Preventing Teen Pregnancy: A Guide for Program Planners.* Washington, DC: Urban Institute.

Southern, Eileen. 1971. *The Music of Black Americans.* New York: W. W. Norton.

Sowerby, Millicent E., comp. 1952–1959. *Catalogue of the Library of Thomas Jefferson.* Washington, DC: Library of Congress.

Spencer, Lyle M., and Robert K. Burns. 1943. *Youth Goes to War.* Chicago: Science Research Associates.

Spertus, Ellen. 1991. "Why Are There So Few Female Computer Scientists?" AI Lab Technical Report 1315. *Artificial MIT* (August).

Spigel, Lynn. 1991. "From Domestic Space to Outer Space: The 1960s Fantastic Family Sitcom." In *Close Encounters: Film, Feminism, and Science Fiction.* Edited by Constance Penley, Elisabeth Lyon, Lynn Spigel, and Janet Bergstrom. Minneapolis: University of Minnesota Press.

———. 1992. *Make Room For TV: Television and the Family Ideal in Postwar America.* Chicago: University of Chicago Press.

Spiller, Robert E. 1971. "Emerson's 'The Young American.'" *Clio* 1: 37–41.

Spinelli, Jerry. 1982. *Space Station Seventh Grade.* Toronto: Little, Brown.

Spitz, Rene A. 1952. "Authority and Masturbation: Some Remarks on a Bibliographical Investigation." *The Psychoanalytic Quarterly* 21 (October): 490–527.

Spitzer, Robert J. 1999. "The Gun Dispute." *American Educator* 23: 10–15.

Sponsler, C. 1993. "Juvenile Prostitution Prevention Project." *WHISPER* 13, no. 2: 3–4.

Sports Illustrated for Kids Omnibus Study. 1989. Cited on p. 29 in *Kids as Customers: A Handbook of Marketing to Children.* Edited by James U. McNeal. New York: Lexington Books, 1992.

Spring, Joel. 1974. "Mass Culture and School Sports." *History of Education Quarterly* 14 (Winter): 483–499.

Stack, Herbert J. 1946. "Greater Safety for Our Youth: An American Opportunity." *Journal of Educational Sociology* 20, no. 2: 114–123.

Standing Bear, Luther. 1933. *Land of the Spotted Eagle.* 1978. Reprint, Lincoln: University of Nebraska Press.

Statistics Research Group. 1997. *U.S. Pet Ownership and Demographics Sourcebook.* Schaumburg, IL: American Veterinary Medical Association.

Stefanko, Michael. 1984. "Trends in Adolescent Research: A Review of Articles Published in *Adolescence.*" *Adolescence* 19, no. 73: 1–13.

Steig, William. 1971. *Amos and Boris.* New York: Farrar, Straus and Giroux.

———. 1976. *Abel's Island.* Toronto: Collins Publishing.

Stein, Charles W., ed. 1984. *American Vaudeville as Seen by Its Contemporaries.* New York: Alfred A. Knopf.

Stein, Mark A. 1987. "Carriers—The Young Are Fading." *Los Angeles Times,* April 10, 1, 30–31.

Stein, Nan D. 1999. *Classrooms and Courtrooms: Facing Sexual Harassment in K–12 Schools.* New York: Teachers College Press.

———. In press. "What a Difference a Discipline Makes." *Journal of Emotional Abuse.*

Steinberg, Lawrence. 1982. "Jumping off the Work Experience Bandwagon." *Journal of Youth and Adolescence* 11, no. 3: 183–205.

———. 1990. "Autonomy, Conflict, and Harmony in the Family Relationship." Pp. 255–276 in *At the Threshold: The Developing Adolescent.* Edited by Shirley Feldman and Glen R. Elliott. Cambridge, MA: Harvard University Press.

Steinberg, Lawrence, Suzanne Fegley, and Sanford M. Dornbusch. 1993. "Negative Impact of Part-time Work on Adolescent Adjustment: Evidence from a Longitudinal Study." *Developmental Psychology* 29, no. 2: 171–180.

Steinberg, Laurence, and Shelli Avenevoli. 1998. "Disengagement from School and Problem Behaviors in Adolescence: A Developmental-Contextual Analysis of the Influence of Family and Part-time Work." Pp. 392–424 in *New Perspectives on Adolescent Risk Behavior.* Edited by Richard Jessor. New York: Cambridge University Press.

Stephan, Walter G., and Cookie W. Stephan. 1989. "Antecedents of Intergroup Anxiety in Asian-Americans and Hispanic-Americans." *International Journal of Intercultural Relations* 13: 203–219.

Stets, Joan E., and Murray A. Straus. 1990. "Gender Differences in Reporting Marital Violence and Its Medical and Psychological Consequences." Pp. 151–165 in *Physical Violence in American Families: Risk Factors and Adaptations to Violence in 8,145 Families.* Edited by M. A. Straus and R. J. Gelles. New Brunswick, NJ: Transaction.

Stevenson, Brenda E. 1996. *Life in Black and White: Family and Community in the Slave South.* New York: Oxford University Press.

Stewart, Jack. 1989. "Subway Graffiti: An Aesthetic Study of Graffiti on the Subway System of New York City, 1970–1978." Ph.D. diss., New York University.

Stine, R. L. 1995. *Goosebumps.* New York: Apple/Scholastic.

Stocker, Clare, and Judy Dunn. 1991. "Sibling Relationships in Childhood: Links with Friendships and Peer Relationships." *British Journal of Developmental Psychology* 8: 227–244.

Stocker, Clare, Judy Dunn, and Robert Plomin. 1989. "Sibling Relationships: Links with Child Temperament, Maternal Behavior, and Family Structure." *Child Development* 60: 715–727.

Stoddard, John F. 1866. *The American Intellectual Arithmetic.* New York: Sheldon.

Stoneman, Zolinda, Gene H. Brody, and Carol MacKinnon. 1986. "Same-sex and Cross-sex Siblings: Activity Choices, Roles, Behavior, and Gender Stereotypes." *Sex Roles* 15: 495–511.

Stormshak, Elizabeth A., Christina J. Bellanti, and Karen L. Bierman. 1996. "The Quality of Sibling Relationships and the Development of Social Competence and Behavioral Control in Aggressive Children." *Developmental Psychology* 32: 79–89.

Stouthamer-Loeber, Magda, and Evelyn H. Wei. 1998. "The Precursors of Young Fatherhood and Its Effect on Delinquency of Teenage Males." *Journal of Adolescent Health* 22: 56–65.

Stowe, Catherine M. 1978. "The National Junior and Boys Tennis Championships (June)." Unpublished history project, Kalamazoo, MI.

Strasburger, Victor, and Don Greydanus, eds. 1990. *Adolescent Medicine: The At-Risk Adolescent.* Philadelphia: Hanley and Belfus.

Straus, Murray A. 1992. *Children as Witnesses to Marital Violence: A Risk Factor for Lifelong Problems among a Nationally Representative Sample of American Men and Women.* Report of the 23d Ross Roundtable. Columbus, OH: Ross Laboratories.

Straus, Murray A., and Richard J. Gelles, eds. 1990. *Physical Violence in American Families: Risk Factors and Adaptations to Violence in 8,145 Families.* New Brunswick, NJ: Transaction.

Street Rodder. Anaheim, CA: McMullen Argus/PRIMEDIA Publishers.

Sung, Betty Lee. 1967. *Mountain of Gold: The Story of the Chinese in America.* New York: Macmillan.

Sutherland, Edwin. 1973. "Susceptibility and Differential Association." Pp. 42–43 in *Edwin H. Sutherland on Analyzing Crime.* Edited by K. Schuessler. Chicago: University of Chicago Press.

Sutton-Smith, Brian, Jay Mechling, Thomas W. Johnson, and Felicia R.

McMahon, eds. 1999. *Children's Folklore: A Source Book.* Logan: Utah State University Press.

Swearer, Susan, and Beth Doll. In press. "Bullying in Schools: An Ecological Framework." *Journal of Emotional Abuse.*

Szasz, Margaret Connell. 1985. "Native American Children." Pp. 311–332 in *American Childhood: A Research Guide and Historical Handbook.* Edited by Joseph M. Hawes and N. Ray Hiner. Westport, CT: Greenwood Press.

Tadman, Michael. 1989. *Speculators and Slaves: Masters, Traders, and Slaves in the Old South.* Madison: University of Wisconsin Press.

Talbot, Margaret. 2000. "The Maximum Security Adolescent." *New York Times Magazine,* September 10.

Tanenhaus, David S. 1998–1999. "Juvenile for the Child: The Beginning of the Juvenile Court in Chicago." *Chicago History* 27: 4–19.

Tanner, J. M. 1971. "Sequence, Tempo, and Individual Variations in Growth and Development of Boys and Girls Aged Twelve to Sixteen." In *Twelve to Sixteen.* Edited by Jerome Kagan. New York: Norton.

Tarratt, Margaret. 1970. "Monsters from the Id." Pp. 330–349 in *Film Genre Reader II.* Edited by Barry Keith Grant. Austin: University of Texas Press.

Tate, Cassandra. 1999. *Cigarette Wars.* New York: Oxford University Press.

Tattum, Delwyn P., ed. 1993. *Understanding and Managing Bullying.* Oxford: Heinemann.

Tattum, Delwyn P., and David A. Lane, eds. 1988. *Bullying in Schools.* Stoke-on-Trent, Staffordshire, UK: Trentham Books.

Tawa, Nicholas E. 2000. *High Minded and Low Down: Music in the Lives of*

Americans, 1800–1861. Northeastern University Press.

Taylor, Dwight. 1962. *Blood-and-Thunder.* New York: Atheneum.

Taylor, Henry C. 1970. *Tarpleywick: A Century of Iowa Farming.* Ames: Iowa State University Press.

Teenage Research Unlimited. 2000. *Teens Spend $153 Billion in 1999.* Northbrook, IL: Teenage Research Unlimited.

Teitelbaum, Kenneth. 1993. *Schooling for "Good Rebels": Socialist Education for Children in the United States, 1900–1920.* Philadelphia: Temple University Press.

Telander, Rick. 1976. *Heaven Is a Playground.* New York: St. Martin's Press.

Terkel, Studs. 1970. *Hard Times: An Oral History of the Great Depression.* New York: Pantheon.

Teti, Douglas M. In press. "Sibling Relationships." In *Interiors: Retrospect and Prospect in the Psychological Study of Families.* Edited by J. McHale and W. Grolnick. Mahwah, NJ: Erlbaum.

Thai, H. C. 1999. "'Splitting Things in Half Is So White!': Conceptions of Family Life and Friendship and the Formation of Ethnic Identity among Second Generation Vietnamese Americans." *Amerasia Journal* 25, no. 1: 53–88.

Theis, Sophie van Senden. 1937. "Adoption." Pp. 23–25 in *Social Work Year Book* 4. New York: Russell Sage Foundation.

"Then and Now: Newspaper Distributing in Detroit in the '50s." 1896. *Friend Palmer Scrapbook* (Detroit Public Library) 13 (May 26): 70.

Thomas, Glyn V., and A. M. Silk. 1990. *An Introduction to the Psychology of Children's Drawings.* New York: New York University Press.

Thomas, J. L. 1990. "The Grandparent Role: A Double Bind." *International Journal of Aging and Human Development* 31: 169–177.

Thomas, John C., ed. 1825. "Memoirs of Stephen Allen." New York: New York Historical Society.

Thomas, Keith. 1983. *Man and the Natural World: Changing Attitudes in England, 1500–1800.* London: Allen Lane.

Thompson, Warren S. 1949. "The Demographic Revolution in the United States." *Annals of the American Academy of Political and Social Sciences,* no. 262.

Thoreau, Henry David. 1962. *Walden, or, Life in the Woods.* New York: Time.

Thornberry, Terence P., Carolyn A. Smith, and Gregory J. Howard. 1997. "Risk Factors for Teenage Fatherhood." *Journal of Marriage and the Family* 59: 505–522.

Thorne, Barrie. 1983. *Gender Play.* New Brunswick, NJ: Rutgers University Press.

Thrasher, Frederic. 1963. *The Gang: A Study of 1,313 Gangs in Chicago.* Rev. ed. Chicago: University of Chicago Press.

Tobin, Joseph. 2000. *"Good Guys Don't Wear Hats": Children Talk about the Media.* New York: Teachers College Press.

Toll, Robert C. 1974. *Blacking Up: The Minstrel Show in Nineteenth-Century America.* New York: Oxford University Press.

———. 1976. *On with the Show! The First Century of Show Business in America.* New York: Oxford University Press.

Tomes, Nancy. 1998. *The Gospel of Germs: Men, Women, and the Microbe in American Life.* Cambridge, MA: Harvard University Press.

Torr, James, ed. 2000. *Alcoholism*. San Diego, CA: Greenhaven Press.

Townsend, John Rowe. 1971. *A Sense of Story: Essays on Contemporary Writers for Children*. Philadelphia: J. B. Lippincott.

Trattner, Walter I. 1970. *Crusade for the Children: A History of the National Child Labor Committee and Child Labor Reform in America*. Chicago: Quadrangle Books.

Triay, Victor Andres. 1998. *Fleeing Castro: Operation Pedro Pan and the Cuban Children's Program*. Gainesville: University Press of Florida.

"The Trout Brook." 1847. *Spirit of the Times* 17, June 19.

Tuan, Yi Fu. 1984. *Dominance and Affection: The Making of Pets*. New Haven: Yale University Press.

Tuhy, Carrie. 1981. "The Star Wars Generation Takes on Inflation." *Money* 11 (July): 88–96.

Turkle, S. 1984. *The Second Self: Computers and the Human Spirit*. New York: Simon and Schuster.

Tuttle, William M. 1993. *"Daddy's Gone to War": The Second World War in the Lives of America's Children*. New York: Oxford University Press.

Twain, Mark (Samuel Clemens). 1946. *The Adventures of Tom Sawyer*. New York: Grosset and Dunlap.

———. 1980. *Roughing It*. Reprint, New York: New American Library.

Ulrich, Laurel Thatcher. 1999. "Sheep in the Parlor, Wheels on the Common: Pastoralism and Poverty in Eighteenth Century Boston." Pp. 182–200 in *Inequality in Early America*. Edited by Carla Gardia Pestana and Sharon V. Salinger. Hanover: University Press of New England.

Uncle John. 1848. *Boys' Own Book of Sports, Birds, and Animals*. New York: Leavitt and Allen.

U.S. Census Bureau. 2000. *Statistical Abstract of the United States: 1999*. Washington, DC: Government Printing Office.

U.S. Census Bureau. "Marital Status and Living Arrangements," http://www.census.gov/population/www/socdemo/ms-la.html.

U.S. Congress. House of Representatives. Committee on Immigration and Naturalization. 1939. *Admission of German Refugee Children. Hearings before the Committee on Immigration and Naturalization, House of Representatives, 76th Congress, 1st Session on H.J. Res. 165 and H.J. Res. 168, Joint Resolutions to Authorize the Admission to the United States of a Limited Number of German Refugee Children. May 24–June 1, 1939*. Washington, DC: Government Printing Office.

U.S. Department of Education. 2000. *Career Clusters: Adding Relevancy to Education*. Pamphlet. Washington, DC: U.S. Department of Education.

———. 2000. "The Federal Role in Education," http://www.ed.gov/offices/OUS/fedrole.html (accessed March 28).

U.S. Department of Education, National Center for Education Statistics. 1998. *Violence and Discipline Problems in U.S. Public Schools: 1996–1997*. NCES 98-030. Washington, DC: U.S. Government Printing Office.

U.S. Departments of Education and Justice. 2000. *Indicators of School Crime and Safety, 2000*. NCES2001-017/NCJ-184176. Washington, DC: U.S. Government Printing Office

U.S. Immigration and Naturalization Service. 1999. *1997 Statistical Yearbook.* Washington, DC: Government Printing Office.

U.S. Immigration Commission. 1911. *Abstracts of Reports of the Immigration Commission.* Washington, DC: Government Printing Office.

U.S. Lawn Tennis Association. 1931. *Fifty Years of Lawn Tennis in the United States.* New York: USLTA.

———. 1972. *Official Encyclopedia of Tennis.* New York: Harper and Row.

U.S. Scouting Service Project. 2000. "BSA Declaration of Religious Principle," http://www.usscouts.org/aboutbsa/rp. html (accessed May 29, 2000).

U.S. Tennis Association. 1995– . *Tennis Yearbook.* Lynn, MA: H. O. Zimman.

Uys, Errol Lincoln. 1999. *Riding the Rails: Teenagers on the Move during the Great Depression.* New York: TV Books.

Venezky, Richard L. 1992. "Textbooks in School and Society." Pp. 436–461 in *Handbook of Research on Curriculum.* Edited by Philip W. Jackson. New York: Macmillan.

Vey, Shauna. 1998. "Protecting Childhood: The Campaign to Bar Children from Performing Professionally in New York City, 1874–1919." Ph.D. diss., City University of New York.

Vickers, Daniel. 1994. *Farmers and Fishermen: Two Centuries of Work in Essex County, Massachusetts, 1630–1850.* Chapel Hill: University of North Carolina Press.

Videogames.com. "The History of Video Games," http://www.videogames.com/ features/universal/hov/ (accessed December 27, 2000).

Viken, James P. 1978. "The Sport of Drag Racing and the Search for Satisfaction,

Meaning, and Self." Ph.D. diss., University of Minnesota.

"Voices from the Combat Zone: Game Grrrlz Talk Back." Pp. 328–341 in *From Barbie to Mortal Combat: Gender and Computer Games.* Edited by Henry Jenkins and Justine Cassell. Cambridge, MA: MIT Press.

Volling, B. L., and Jay Belsky. 1992. "The Contribution of Mother-Child and Father-Child Relationships to the Quality of Sibling Interaction: A Longitudinal Study." *Child Development* 63: 1209–1222.

Vorrasi, Joseph A., John J. Eckenrode, and Charles V. Izzo. 2000. *Intergenerational Transmission of Marital Violence: A Gender-Similarity Hypothesis.* Paper presented at the Fifth International Conference on the Victimization of Children and Youth, Durham, NH.

Voyer, Daniel, Susan Voyer, and M. P. Bryden. 1995. "Magnitude of Sex Differences in Spatial Abilities: A Meta-Analysis and Consideration of Critical Variables." *Psychological Bulletin* 117: 250–270.

Wager-Fisher, Mary. 1880. "The Philadelphia Newsboys." *Wide Awake* 11, no. 1 (July): 16, 18.

Wagner, Bob. 1992. *The Nationals and How They Grew in Kalamazoo.* Kalamazoo, MI: J-B Printing.

Wagner, Carolyn Ditte. 1979. "The Boy Scouts of America: A Model and a Mirror of American Society." Ph.D. diss., Johns Hopkins University.

Wagner, Mazie E., Herman J. P. Schubert, and Daniel S. P. Schubert. 1979. "Sibship-Constellation Effects on Psychological Development, Creativity, and Health." *Advances in Child Development and Behavior* 14: 57–148.

Waldorf, D. 1994. "Drug Use and HIV Risk among Male Sex Workers: Results of Two Samples in San Francisco." Pp. 114–131 in *The Context of HIV Risk among Drug Users and Their Sexual Partners.* Edited by R. J. Battjes, Z. Sloboda, and W. C. Grace. NIDA Research Monograph. Rockville, MD: National Institute on Drug Abuse.

Walett, Francis G., ed. 1974. *The Diary of Ebenezer Parkman, 1703–1782.* Worcester, MA: American Antiquarian Society.

Walker, Bonnie L., ed. 1996. *Injury Prevention for Young Children: A Research Guide.* Westport, CT: Greenwood Press.

Walker, Williston, Richard A. Norris, David W. Lotz, and Robert T. Handy. 1985. *A History of the Christian Church.* 4th ed. New York: Charles Scribner's Sons.

Wall, Helena. 1990. *Fierce Communion: Family and Community in Early America.* Cambridge, MA: Harvard University Press.

Wallace, Anthony. 1966. *Religion: An Anthropological View.* New York: Random House.

Wallerstein, J. S., and J. B. Kelly. 1980. *Surviving the Break-up: How Children and Parents Cope with Divorce.* New York: Basic Books.

Wallerstein, J. S., S. B. Corbin, and J. M. Lewis. 1988. "Children of Divorce: A 10-Year Study." In *Impact of Divorce, Single Parenting, and Stepparenting on Children.* Edited by E. M. Hetherington and Josephine D. Arasteh. Hillsdale, NJ: Erlbaum.

Walsh, Mark. 2000. "Hazing Is Widespread, Student Survey Shows." *Education Week* 20, no. 1 (September 6): 14.

Walters, Pamela Barnhouse, and Phillip J. O'Connell. 1988. "The Family Economy, Work, and Educational Participation in the United States 1890–1940." *American Journal of Sociology* 93: 1116–1152.

Walworth, Arthur. 1938. *School Histories at War.* Cambridge: Harvard University Press.

Ward Platt, M. P., and R. A. Little. 1998. *Injury in the Young.* Cambridge, UK: Cambridge University Press.

Ward, Paul. 1875. "Street Arabs: Bootblacks and Newsboys." *Oliver Optic's Magazine* 18 (December): 949.

Ward, Winifred. 1958. *Theatre for Children.* Anchorage, KY: Children's Theatre Press.

Warner, Beth S., Mark D. Weist, and Amy Krulak. 1999. "Risk Factors for School Violence." *Urban Education* 34: 52–68.

Washington, Booker T. 1900. *The Story of My Life and Work.* In *The Booker T. Washington Papers.* Vol. 1, *The Autobiographical Writings.* Edited by Louis R. Harlan. Chicago: J. L. Nichols. 1972. Reprint, Urbana: University of Illinois Press.

———. 1901. *Up from Slavery: An Autobiography.* In *The Booker T. Washington Papers.* Vol. 1, *The Autobiographical Writings.* Edited by Louis R. Harlan. New York: Doubleday, Page. 1972. Reprint, Urbana: University of Illinois Press.

Watkins, T. H. 1999. *The Hungry Years: A Narrative History of the Great Depression in America.* New York: Henry Holt.

Webb, Lester Austin. 1958. "The Origins of Military Schools in the United States Founded in the Nineteenth Century." Ph.D. diss., School of Education, University of North Carolina.

Webber, Thomas L. 1978. *Deep Like the Rivers: Education in the Slave Quarter Community, 1831–1865.* New York: W. W. Norton.

Weinstein, Neil. 1987. *Taking Care: Understanding and Encouraging Self-Protective Behavior.* New York: Cambridge University Press.

Weir, La Vada. 1977. *Skateboards and Skateboarding.* New York: Pocket Books.

Weisberg, D. K. 1985. *Children of the Night: A Study of Adolescent Prostitution.* Lexington: D.C. Heath.

Weisman, Adam M., and Kaushal K. Sharma. 1997. "Parricide and Attempted Parricide: Forensic Data and Psychological Results." In *The Nature of Homicide: Trends and Changes.* Washington, DC: U.S. Department of Justice, Office of Justice Programs, National Institute of Justice.

Weisman, Mary Lou. 1994. "When Parents Are Not in the Best Interests of the Child." *Atlantic Monthly* 274, no. 1 (July): 42–63.

Wekerle, Christine, and David A. Wolfe. 1996. "Child Maltreatment." In *Child Psychopathology.* Edited by E. J. Mash and R. A. Barkley. New York: Guilford Press.

Wellesley College Center for Research on Women. 1992. *The AAUW Report: How Schools Shortchange Girls—A Study of Major Findings on Girls and Education.* Washington, DC: AAUW Educational Foundation.

Wellman, Henry, and Susan Gelman. 1992. "Cognitive Development: Foundational Theories of Core Domains." *Annual Review of Psychology* 43: 337–376.

Welsh, Ralph S. 1976. "Severe Parental Punishment and Delinquency: A Developmental Theory." *Journal of Clinical Child Psychology* 5, no. 1: 17–21.

Werner, Emmy E. 1998. *Reluctant Witnesses: Children's Voices from the Civil War.* Boulder, CO: Westview Press.

———. 2000. *Through the Eyes of Innocents: Children Witnesses of World War II.* Boulder, CO: Westview Press.

Wertham, Frederick. 1953. *Seduction of the Innocent.* New York: Rinehart.

———. 1996. "The Psychopathology of Comic Books." *American Journal of Psychotherapy* 50, no. 4 (Fall): 472–490.

Wessel, Thomas, and Marilyn Wessel. 1982. *4-H: An American Idea 1900–1980.* Chevy Chase: National 4-H Council.

West, Candace, and Don Zimmerman. 1987. "Doing Gender." *Gender and Society* 1, no. 2.

West, Elliott. 1983. "Heathens and Angels: Childhood in the Rocky Mountain Mining Towns." *Western Historical Quarterly* (April): 145–164.

———. 1989. *Growing Up with the Country: Childhood on the Far-Western Frontier.* Albuquerque: University of New Mexico Press.

———. 1996. *Growing Up in Twentieth-Century America: A History and Reference Guide.* Westport, CT: Greenwood Press.

West, Elliott, and Paula Petrik, eds. 1992. *Small Worlds: Children and Adolescents in America, 1850–1950.* Lawrence: University of Kansas Press.

West, Richard. 1987. *Television Westerns: Major and Minor Series, 1946–1978.* City?: McFarland.

Westbrook, Robert. 1987. "Lewis Hine and the Two Faces of Progressive Photography." *Tikkun* 2 (April–May): 24–29. Reprinted in Leon Fink, ed. 2001. *Major Problems in the Gilded Age and Progressive Era.* 2d ed. Boston: Houghton Mifflin.

Wheeler, Raymond, and Francis Perkins. 1932. *Principles of Mental Development.* New York: Thomas Y. Crowell.

Wheeler, T. T., S. P. McGorray, L. Yorkiewicz, S. D. Keeling, and C. J. King. 1994. "Orthodontic Treatment Demand and Need in Third- and Fourth-Grade Schoolchildren." *American Journal of Orthodontics and Dentofacial Orthopedics* 106, no. 1: 22–33.

Wheeler, Tom. 1990. *American Guitars: An Illustrated History.* New York: Harper.

"Where Is Young Life?" 2001. http://www.younglife.org.

Whipple, Edward G., and Eileen G. Sullivan, eds. 1998. "New Challenges for Greek Letter Organizations: Transforming Fraternities and Sororities into Learning Communities." *New Directions for Student Services,* no. 81. San Francisco: Jossey-Bass.

Whisnant, David E. 1971. "Selling the Gospel News, or the Strange Career of Jimmy Brown the Newsboy." *Journal of Social History* 5, no. 3: 269–309.

Whitbeck, Les B., and Dan R. Hoyt. 1999. *Nowhere to Grow: Homeless and Runaway Adolescents and Their Families.* New York: Aldine de Gruyter.

White, Jerry. 1983. *The Church and the Parachurch: An Uneasy Marriage.* Portland: Multnomah Press.

White, Phillip, and James Gillett. 1994. "Reading the Muscular Body: A Critical Decoding of Advertisements in Flex Magazine." *Sociology of Sport Journal* 11: 18–39.

White, Ryan, and Ann Marie Cunningham. 1991. *Ryan White: My Own Story.* New York: Dial Press.

White, Shane, and Graham J. White. 1999. *Stylin: African American Expressive Culture, from Its Beginnings to the Zoot Suit.* Ithaca: Cornell University Press.

White, Timothy. 1990. *Rock Lives: Profiles and Interviews.* New York: Holt.

Whitfield, H. N., J. D. Frank, G. Williams, and J. A. Vale, eds. 1999. "Circumcision: BJU Supplement 1." *BJU International* 83, no. 1 (January).

Whitney, Irene, and Peter K. Smith. 1993. "A Survey of the Nature and Extent of Bullying in Junior/Middle and Secondary Schools." *Educational Research* 31, no. 1: 3–25. Nan Stein, 1999, *Classrooms and Courtrooms.*

Whitton, Blair. 1981. *American Clockwork Toys, 1862–1900.* Exton, PA: Schiffer Publishing.

Widmer, Edward L. 1998. *Young America: The Flowering of Democracy in New York City.* New York: Oxford University Press.

Wienke, Chris. 1998. "Negotiating the Male Body: Men, Masculinity, and Cultural Ideals." *The Journal of Men's Studies* 6, no. 2: 255–282.

Wilder, Laura Ingalls. 1961. *Farmer Boy.* New York: HarperCollins.

Wilentz, Sean. 1984. *Chants Democratic: New York City and the Rise of the American Working Class, 1788–1850.* New York: Oxford University Press.

Wilks, Corinne, and Catherine Melville. 1990. "Grandparents in Custody and Access Disputes." *Journal of Divorce and Remarriage* 13: 36–42.

Williams, Paul N. 1972. "Boys Town, America's Wealthiest City?" *Sun Newspapers of Omaha.* Special report, March 30.

Wilmeth, Don, with Tice L. Miller. 1996. *Cambridge Guide to American Theatre.* Cambridge: Cambridge University Press.

Wilson, Douglas L., ed. 1989. *Jefferson's Literary Commonplace Book.* Princeton: Princeton University Press. In Julian P. Boyd et al., eds. 1950– . *The Papers of Thomas Jefferson.* Princeton: Princeton University Press.

Wilson, Edward O. 1978. *On Human Nature.* Cambridge, MA: Harvard University Press.

Winkler, Karl Tilman. 1996. "Reformers United: The American and the German Juvenile Court, 1882–1923." Pp. 235–274 in *Institutions of Confinement: Hospitals, Asylums, and Prisons in Western Europe and North America 1550–1900.* Edited by Norbert Finzsch and Robert Juette. Cambridge: Cambridge University Press.

Winston, R. B., Jr., William R. Nettles III, and John H. Opper Jr., eds. 1987. "Fraternities and Sororities on the Contemporary College Campus." *New Directions for Student Services,* no. 40. San Francisco: Jossey-Bass.

Winters, Paul, ed. 1997. *Teen Addiction.* San Diego, CA: Greenhaven Press.

Wojciechowka, Maia. 1964. *Shadow of a Bull.* New York: Simon and Schuster.

Wolfenstein, Martha. 1954. *Children's Humor: A Psychological Analysis.* Bloomington: Indiana University Press.

Wolfgang, Marvin, and Franco Ferracuti. 1967. *The Subculture of Violence: Toward an Integrated Theory in Criminology.* London: Tavistock.

Wood, Robin. 1986. *Hollywood from Vietnam to Reagan.* New York: Columbia University Press.

Woodward, Calvin M. 1889. "The Results of the St. Louis Manual Training School." *Journal of Proceedings and Addresses.* Session of the year 1889, held in Nashville, TN, National Education Association.

Woolery, George. 1983. *Children's Television: The First Twenty-Five Years.* Metuchen, NJ: Scarecrow.

Worrell, Estelle Ansley. 1980. *Children's Costume in America 1607–1910.* New York: Charles Scribner's Sons.

Wright, Esmond, ed. 1989. *Benjamin Franklin: His Life as He Wrote It.* Cambridge, MA: Harvard University Press.

Wyatt-Brown, Bertram. 1982. *Southern Honor: Ethics and Behavior in the Old South.* New York: Oxford University Press.

Yablonsky, Lewis, and Jonathan Brower. 1979. *The Little League Game: How Kids, Coaches, and Parents Really Play It.* New York: New York Times Books.

Yep, Laurence. 1975. *Dragonwings.* New York: HarperCollins.

YMCA of the USA. 2001. "YMCA's at a Glance," http://www.ymca.net (accessed May 14, 2001).

"Yo, It's Time for Braces." 2001. http://tqjunior.thinkquest.org/5029/ (accessed in March, 2001).

Yoshimi, Jeff. 1997. "Hapas at a Los Angeles High School: Context and Phenomenology." *Amerasia Journal* 23, no. 1: 130–148.

Young America Admires the Ancients. 1783–1840. Library of Congress Prints and Photographs Division.

Young America!: The Organ of the National Reform Association. Formerly the *Workingman's Advocate.* 1844–1845. Library of Congress Newspapers and Periodical Division.

Young, Brian M. 1990. *Television Advertising and Children.* Oxford: Oxford University Press.

Young, Jacob. 1857. *Autobiography of a Pioneer*. Cincinnati: Jennings and Pye; New York: Eaton and Mains.

Youth Theatre Journal. 1986– . American Association of Theatre for Youth.

Zainaldin, Jamil S. 1979. "The Emergence of a Modern American Family Law: Child Custody, Adoption and the Courts." *Northwestern University School of Law* 73 (February): 1038–1089.

Zald, Mayer N. 1970. *Organizational Change: The Political Economy of the YMCA*. Chicago: University of Chicago Press.

Zaslow, Martha J. 1988. "Sex Differences in Children's Response to Parental Divorce: 1. Research Methodology and Postdivorce Family Forms." *American Journal of Orthopsychiatry* 58, no. 3: 355–378.

Zelizer, Viviana A. 1985. *Pricing the Priceless Child: The Changing Social Value of Children*. New York: Basic Books.

Zhou, M. 1999. "Coming of Age: The Current Situation of Asian American Children." *Amerasia Journal* 25, no. 1: 1–27.

Zimring, Franklin E. 1982. *The Changing Legal World of Adolescence*. New York: Free Press.

Zipes, Jack. 1983. *Fairy Tales and the Art of Subversion: The Classical Genre for Children and the Process of Civilization*. New York: Wildman Press.

Zopf, Paul E., Jr. 1992. *Mortality Patterns and Trends in the United States*. Westport, CT: Greenwood.

Zoske, J. 1998. "Male Circumcision: A Gender Perspective." *Journal of Men's Studies* 6, no. 2: 189–208.

Zuboff, Shoshana. 1988. *In the Age of the Smart Machine*. New York: Basic Books.

Zucci, John E. 1992. *The Little Slaves of the Harp: Italian Street Musicians in Nineteenth-Century Paris, London, and New York*. Montreal: McGill-Queen's University Press.

INDEX

About the Authors

Priscilla Ferguson Clement, professor of history at Pennsylvania State University, Delaware County, is the author of *Growing Pains: Children in the Industrial Age, 1850–1890.*

Jacqueline S. Reinier, professor emerita at California State University at Sacramento, is the author of *From Virtue to Character: American Childhood, 1775–1850.* Both scholars have published widely in children's history.